American Literature

Robert A. Bennett
Senior Author

GINN LITERATURE SERIES

READING LITERATURE

EXPLORING LITERATURE

UNDERSTANDING LITERATURE

TYPES OF LITERATURE

AMERICAN LITERATURE

ENGLISH LITERATURE

Spirit, that made those heroes dare . . .

American Literature

Andrew J. Porter, Jr.
Great Neck High School, N.Y.

Henry L. Terrie, Jr.
Dartmouth College

Robert A. Bennett
Brookline, Massachusetts

CONSULTANTS

Robert E. Beck, *English Consultant*
John Swett Unified School District
Crockett, California

Sharon L. Belshaw, *English Instructor*
Hopkins Junior High School
Fremont, California

Mary Gloyne Byler, *Consultant*
Association on American Indian Affairs
New York, New York

Kenneth L. Chambers, *Asst. Professor*
Black Studies Department
Wellesley College
Wellesley, Massachusetts

Barbara Z. Chasen
Instructional Support Team
Boston Public Schools
Boston, Massachusetts

Paula Grier, *Education Consultant*
Intercultural Development Research Association
San Antonio, Texas

Nicolás Kanellos, *Editor*
Revista Chicano-Riqueña
University of Houston
Houston, Texas

Ann Rayson, *Asst. Professor*
Department of English
University of Hawaii at Manoa
Honolulu, Hawaii

Ginn and Company

Acknowledgments

Grateful acknowledgment is made to the following publishers, authors, and agents for permission to use and adapt copyrighted materials:

Doubleday & Company, Inc., for the excerpt from "Foreword" and "Speech to the General Court" by John Winthrop from *The American Puritans: Their Prose and Poetry* by Perry Miller. Copyright © 1956 by Perry Miller. Reprinted by permission of Doubleday & Company, Inc. Also for "The Waking" copyright 1953 by Theodore Roethke from the book *The Collected Poems of Theodore Roethke* by Theodore Roethke. Reprinted by permission of Doubleday & Company, Inc. Also for the poems "I Hear America Singing," "A Noiseless Patient Spider," "One's Self I Sing," and "There Was a Child Went Forth" from *Leaves of Grass* by Walt Whitman.

Farrar, Straus & Giroux, Inc., for "The Prison" from *The Magic Barrel* by Bernard Malamud. Copyright © 1950 by Bernard Malamud. Copyright renewed © 1978 by Bernard Malamud. Also for "At the Fishhouses" from *Complete Poems* by Elizabeth Bishop. Copyright © 1947, 1969 by Elizabeth Bishop. Also for the poem "Musician" from *The Blue Estuaries* by Louise Bogan. Copyright © 1923, 1929, 1930, 1931, 1933, 1934, 1935, 1936, 1937, 1938, 1941, 1949, 1951, 1952, 1954, 1957, 1958, 1962, 1963, 1964, 1965, 1966, 1967, 1968 by Louise Bogan. Also for the poem "Water" from *For the Union Dead* by Robert Lowell. Copyright © 1962 by Robert Lowell. All reprinted by permission of Farrar, Straus & Giroux, Inc.

Harcourt Brace Jovanovich, Inc., for the excerpts from *A Walker in the City*, copyright 1951, 1979 by Alfred Kazin. Reprinted by permission of Harcourt Brace Jovanovich, Inc. Also for "The Life You Save May Be Your Own" by Flannery O'Connor. Copyright 1953 by Flannery O'Connor; renewed 1981 by Mrs. Regina O'Connor. Reprinted from *A Good Man Is Hard to Find and Other Stories* by Flannery O'Connor by permission of Harcourt Brace Jovanovich, Inc. Also for "The Jilting of Granny Weatherall" by Katherine Anne Porter. From *Flowering Judas and Other Stories*, copyright 1930, 1958 by Katherine Anne Porter. Reprinted by permission of Harcourt Brace Jovanovich, Inc. Also for "1(a" by E. E. Cummings. Copyright © 1958 by E. E. Cummings. Reprinted from his volume *Complete Poems 1913–1962* by permission of Harcourt Brace Jovanovich, Inc. Also for "maggie and milly and molly and may" by E. E. Cummings. Copyright © 1956 by E. E. Cummings. Reprinted from his volume *Complete Poems 1913–1962* by permission of Harcourt Brace Jovanovich, Inc. Also for "!" by E. E. Cummings. Copyright © 1950 by E. E. Cummings. Reprinted from his volume *Complete Poems 1913–1962* by permission of Harcourt Brace Jovanovich, Inc. Also for "Chicago" from *Chicago Poems* by Carl Sandburg, copyright 1916 by Holt, Rinehart and Winston, Inc.; renewed 1944 by Carl Sandburg. Reprinted by permission of Harcourt Brace Jovanovich, Inc. Also for the poem "The people will live on" from *The People, Yes* by Carl Sandburg, copyright 1936 by Harcourt Brace Jovanovich, Inc.; renewed 1964 by Carl Sandburg. Reprinted by permission of the publisher. Also for "New Face" by Alice Walker. From *Revolutionary Petunias and Other Poems*, copyright © 1973 by Alice Walker. Reprinted by permission of Harcourt Brace Jovanovich, Inc. Also for "The Beautiful Changes" by Richard Wilbur. From *The Beautiful Changes and Other Poems*, copyright 1947, 1975 by Richard Wilbur. Reprinted by permission of Harcourt Brace Jovanovich, Inc.

Harper & Row, Publishers, Inc., for the abridgment of "Seeing" from *Pilgrim at Tinker Creek* by Annie Dillard. Copyright © 1974 by Annie Dillard. Also for the excerpt abridged from pp. 11–40 in *Dust Tracks on a Road* by Zora Neale Hurston. (J. B. Lippincott) Copyright 1942 by Zora Neale Hurston; renewed 1970 by John C. Hurston. Also for "Night Chant/Blessing Way" from the Navaho, from pp. 146–147 in *House Made of Dawn* by N. Scott Momaday. Copyright © 1966, 1967, 1968 by N. Scott Momaday. Also for "Freedom"—July, 1940—in *One Man's Meat* by E. B. White. Copyright 1940, 1968 by E. B. White. Also for "The Man Who Saw the Flood" by Richard Wright. Copyright 1937 by Weekly Masses Co., Inc. from *Eight Men* by Richard Wright (1961) (World Publishing Co.). Also for "Our Town" from *Our Town: A Play in Three Acts* by Thornton Wilder. Copyright © 1938, 1957 by Thornton Wilder. Also for the poem "Life for my child is simple, and is good" from *The World of Gwendolyn Brooks* by Gwendolyn Brooks. Copyright 1949 by Gwendolyn Brooks Blakely. Also for the poem "truth" from *The World of Gwendolyn Brooks* (1971) by Gwendolyn Brooks. Copyright, 1945 by Gwendolyn Brooks Blakely. Also for the poem "From the Dark Tower" in *On These I Stand* by Countee Cullen. Copyright 1927 by Harper & Row, Publishers, Inc.; renewed 1955 by Ida M. Cullen. All reprinted by permission of Harper & Row, Publishers, Inc.

Holt, Rinehart and Winston for the excerpt from *The Bluest Eye* by Toni Morrison. Copyright © 1970 by Toni Morrison. Reprinted by permission of Holt, Rinehart and Winston, Publishers. Also for "Birches," "Departmental," "The Gift Outright," and "Stopping by Woods on a Snowy Evening," all from *The Poetry of Robert Frost* edited by Edward Connery Lathem. Copyright 1916, 1923, © 1969 by Holt, Rinehart and Winston. Copyright 1936, 1942, 1944, 1951 by Robert Frost. Copyright © 1964, 1970 by Lesley Frost Ballantine. Reprinted by permission of Holt, Rinehart and Winston, Publishers.

Houghton Mifflin Company for the poem "Patterns" from *The Complete Poetical Works of Amy Lowell* published by Houghton

Acknowledgments continue on page 766.

Table of Contents

2 A New Land: 1620–1750   126

3 A New Nation: 1750–1800   166

6 Twentieth Century: The Modern World   418

7 Twentieth Century: American Drama

8 Twentieth Century: Our Time

PROSE

American Literature

1

Major Themes
in American Literature

MAJOR THEMES IN AMERICAN LITERATURE

IN their reflections on America and Americans our writers have returned again and again to certain ideas or themes. In doing so they have frequently expressed our own half-realized thoughts about ourselves and about America. These themes have grown naturally out of our experience of living in this land. Indeed they are merely extensions of the effort to describe our environment and our manner of living in it and to express a vision of the future. One could give the themes a variety of names. In this book they are called "Sense of Place," "The Individual," and "The American Dream."

Sense of Place

All people, no matter where they reside, develop some "sense of place," some feeling of identification with home. This feeling operates at many levels—from the home and neighborhood to a region or the entire country. The time may even come when one will identify with earth as opposed to some other planet. The sense of place may involve a great complexity of feelings: loyalty at one level, for example, may well conflict with loyalty at another level. And sometimes the familiarity of home provokes a desire to leave and to try a new place.

There is an additional complication in the American sense of place, deriving from the way the country grew. The Europeans who came here in the seventeenth century had to transfer affections from their birthplaces to a strange and very different place. Such a change is not easily made; nor, when made, easily forgotten. For a long time, Americans from Europe lived with the problem of divided loyalty. While they looked westward to the American frontier and beyond, they also felt the strong cultural pull of Europe. This division of mind and heart has been repeated in all subsequent immigrant groups and was especially painful for those from Africa who were forced to come. As Robert Frost tells us in "The Gift Outright," we could own America simply by living in it. However, we could not be Americans until we had given ourselves to the land.

Concurrently with this acquisition of a sense of place by foreign settlers, Native Americans have been forced to struggle to maintain their sense of place. This has been difficult in the face of unrelenting pressure for more than three and a half centuries. Yet, Native American speakers and writers continue their effort to preserve for their people the memory of their original relationship to this land. For example, Leslie Silko's poem, "Where Mountain Lion Lay Down with Deer," reflects this effort.

Before We Were the Land's

When President John F. Kennedy was inaugurated in January, 1961, he invited Robert Frost (1874–1963) to read a poem during the ceremony. Frost chose "The Gift Outright," a poem written some years earlier. As Frost began to read, the slant of winter sunlight on the page made reading difficult and forced him to stop. Then, as the whole country shared an agony of suspense, the elderly poet put everyone at ease. He raised his head and calmly spoke "The Gift Outright" from memory. (Additional information on Frost is included in Unit 6 on page 499.)

The Gift Outright

ROBERT FROST

The land was ours before we were the land's.
She was our land more than a hundred years
Before we were her people. She was ours
In Massachusetts, in Virginia,
But we were England's, still colonials,   5
Possessing what we still were unpossessed by,
Possessed by what we now no more possessed.
Something we were withholding made us weak
Until we found out that it was ourselves
We were withholding from our land of living,   10
And forthwith found salvation in surrender.
Such as we were we gave ourselves outright
(The deed of gift was many deeds of war)
To the land vaguely realizing westward,
But still unstoried, artless, unenhanced,   15
Such as she was, such as she would become.

Study Questions

1. What do you think Frost means by the first five lines? What were we withholding? Why did this make us weak?

2. In lines 11–13 what did we have to do to find "salvation"?

3. How is this poem appropriate to The Sense of Place theme?

The Place as Retreat

In addition to teaching literature and creative writing, Leslie Silko (1948—) writes poetry and short stories. She has also published a novel, *Ceremony* (1977).

Leslie Silko was born on the Laguna Pueblo Reservation in Albuquerque, New Mexico. Much of her work is concerned with the traditional relationship of Native Americans with their environment. The poem included here, from her volume, *Laguna Woman* (1974), expresses that concern.

TAOS OVENS *Laura Gilpin*

Where Mountain Lion Lay Down with Deer

LESLIE MARMON SILKO

I climb the black rock mountain
   stepping from day to day
               silently.
I smell the wind for my ancestors
   pale blue leaves   5
   crushed wild mountain smell.
Returning
   up the gray stone cliff
   where I descended
       a thousand years ago.   10

Returning to faded black stone.
　where mountain lion lay down with deer.
It is better to stay up here
　　　　　watching wind's reflection
　　　　　in tall yellow flowers.　　　　　　　　15
The old ones who remember me are gone
　　the old songs are all forgotten
and the story of my birth.
How I danced in snow-frost moonlight
　　distant stars to the end of the Earth,　　　20
How I swam away
　　　　in freezing mountain water
　　　　narrow mossy canyon tumbling down
　　　　　　out of the mountain
　　　　　　　out of the deep canyon stone　　25
　　　　down
　　　　　the memory
　　　　　　　spilling out
　　　　　　　into the world.

Study Questions

1. The poem begins with a description of a journey. What is the nature of the journey? How do you know?

2. What is the speaker's destination? Why does the speaker feel it would be better to stay there? What does the journey's destination represent?

3. How does the speaker indicate that she has found her ancestors in lines 16–29? What are the implications of this "return"?

4. How does the form of lines 21–29 reflect the poet's meaning?

Landing in Virginia

Although ships from Norway, France, and Spain had been crossing the Atlantic for years, it was not until the beginning of the seventeenth century that two English colonies became permanent. In 1606 King James I of England granted charters to the London and Plymouth Companies to colonize America's Atlantic coast. The London Company immediately dispatched three ships.

Among the colonists from these ships who arrived at the capes of Chesapeake Bay in April 1607 was George Percy (1580–1632), son of the Earl of Northumberland. Young Percy kept a diary of his five years in Virginia. Only extracts from this record were preserved and eventually published in 1625. It was called *A Discourse of the Plantation of the Southern Colony in Virginia.* The following description of the landing in Virginia shows Percy's awareness of the primitive and bountiful new country. It is an early articulation of The Sense of Place theme.

from A Discourse of the Plantation of the Southern Colony in Virginia

GEORGE PERCY

THE TENTH DAY[1] we set sail and disembarked out of the West Indies, and bare our course northerly. The fourteenth day we passed the Tropic of Cancer. The one and twentieth day, about five o'clock at night there began a vehement tempest, which lasted all the night, with winds, rain, and thunders in a terrible manner. We were forced to lie at hull[2] that night, because we thought we had been nearer land than we were. The next morning, being the two and twentieth day we sounded;[3] and the three and twentieth and four and twentieth day, but we could find no ground. The five and twentieth day we sounded and had no ground at an hundred fathom. The six and twentieth day of April about four o'clock in the morning, we descried[4] the land of Virginia: the same day we entered into the Bay of Chesupioc[5] directly, without any let[6] or hindrance; there we landed and discovered a little way, but we could find nothing worth the speaking of, but fair meadows and goodly tall trees, with such fresh waters running through the woods, as I was almost ravished at the first sight thereof.

At night, when we were going aboard,

---

1 **tenth day:** April 10, 1607.
2 **lie at hull:** drift with the wind under very short sail.
3 **sounded:** measured depth of water.
4 **descried:** spied at a distance.
5 **Chesupioc:** Chesapeake Bay.
6 **let:** obstacle.

there came the savages[7] creeping upon all fours, from the hills like bears, with their bows in their mouths, charged us very desperately in the faces, hurt Captain Gabrill Archer in both his hands, and a sailor in two places of the body very dangerous. After they had spent their arrows, and felt the sharpness of our shot, they retired into the woods with a great noise, and so left us.

The seven and twentieth day we began to build up our shallop:[8] the gentlemen and soldiers marched eight miles up into the land; we could not see a savage in all that march; we came to a place where they had made a great fire, and had been newly aroasting oysters: when they perceived our coming, they fled away to the mountains, and left many of the oysters in the fire: we eat some of the oysters, which were very large and delicate in taste.

The [twenty-eighth] day we launched our shallop; the captain and some gentlemen went in her, and discovered up the Bay; we found a river on the south side running into the main; we entered it and found it very shoaled[9] water, not for any boats to swim. We went further into the Bay, and saw a plain plot of ground where we went on land, and found the place five mile in compass, without either bush or tree; we saw nothing there but a canoe, which was made out of the whole tree, which was five and forty foot long by the rule. Upon this plot of ground we got good store of mussels and oysters, which lay on the ground as thick as stones: we opened some and found in many of them pearls. We marched some three or four miles further into the woods, where we saw great smokes of fire. We marched to those smokes and found that the savages had been there burning down the grass, as we thought

either to make their plantation[10] there, or else to give signs to bring their forces together, and so to give us battle. We passed through excellent ground full of flowers of divers kinds and colors, and as goodly trees as I have seen, as cedar, cypress, and other kinds. Going a little further we came into a little plat of ground full of fine and beautiful strawberries, four times bigger and better than ours in England. All this march we could neither see savage nor town. When it grew to be towards night we stood back to our ships; we sounded and found it shallow water for a great way, which put us out of all hopes for getting any higher with our ships, which rode at the mouth of the river. We rowed over to a point of land, where we found a channel, and sounded six, eight, ten, or twelve fathom, which put us in good comfort. Therefore we named that point of land Cape Comfort.

The nine and twentieth day we set up a cross at Chesupioc Bay, and named that place Cape Henry. Thirtieth day, we came with our ships to Cape Comfort; where we saw five savages running on the shore; presently the captain caused the shallop to be manned, so rowing to the shore, the captain called to them in sign of friendship, but they were at first very timersome,[11] until they saw the captain lay his hand on his heart: upon that they laid down their bows and arrows, and came very boldly to us, making signs to come ashore to their town, which is called by the savages Kecoughtan. We coasted to their town, rowing over a river running into the main, where these savages swam over with their bows and arrows in their mouths.

When we came over to the other side, there was a many of other savages which directed us to their town, where we were entertained by them very kindly. When we came first aland they made a doleful noise, laying their faces to

---

7 **savages:** Europeans were unaccustomed to the lifestyle of the people residing in this country and sometimes called them savages.
8 **shallop:** small, light boat.
9 **shoaled:** too shallow or full of sand bars to permit easy navigation.

10 **plantation:** planting; cultivation.
11 **timersome:** timorous; fearful; timid.

the ground, scratching the earth with their nails. We did think that they had been at their idolatry. When they had ended their ceremonies, they went into their houses and brought out mats and laid upon the ground; the chiefest of them sat all in a rank; the meanest sort brought us such dainties as they had, and of their bread which they make of their maize or gennea wheat, they would not suffer us to eat unless we sat down, which we did on a mat right against them. After we were well satisfied they gave us of their tobacco, which they took in a pipe made artificially of earth as ours are, but far bigger, with the bowl fashioned together with a piece of fine copper. After they had feasted us, they showed us, in welcome, their manner of dancing, which was in this fashion: one of the savages standing in the midst singing, beating one hand against another, all the rest dancing about him, shouting, howling, and stamping against the ground, with many antic tricks and faces, making noise like so many wolves or devils. One thing of them I observed; when they were in their dance, they kept stroke with their feet just one with another, but with their hands, heads, faces, and bodies, every one of them had a several gesture; so they continued for the space of half an hour. When they had ended their dance, the captain gave them beads and other trifling jewels. They hang through their ears fowls' legs; they shave the right side of their heads with a shell, the left side they wear of an ell[12] long tied up with an artificial knot, with a many of fowls' feathers sticking in it. . . . Some paint their bodies black, some red, with artificial knots of sundry lively colors, very beautiful and pleasing to the eye, in a braver fashion than they in the West Indies. . . .

The twelfth day [of May] we went back to our ships, and discovered a point of land called Archer's Hope, which was sufficient with a little labor to defend ourselves against any enemy. The soil was good and fruitful, with excellent good timber. There are also great stores of vines in bigness of a man's thigh, running up to the tops of the trees in great abundance.

We also did see many squirrels, conies,[13] blackbirds with crimson wings, and divers other fowls and birds of divers and sundry colors of crimson, watchet,[14] yellow, green, murrey,[15] and of divers other hues naturally without any art using. We found store of turkey nests and many eggs. . . . If it had not been disliked, because the ship could not ride near the shore, we had settled there to all the colonies' contentment.

The thirteenth day, we came to our seating place in Paspihas country, some eight miles from the point of land which I made mention before; where our ships do lie so near the shore that they are moored to the trees in six fathom water. . . .

This river[16] which we have discovered is one of the most famousest rivers that ever was found by any Christian, it ebbs and flows a hundred and three-score miles where ships of great burden may harbor in safety. Wheresoever we landed upon this river, we saw the goodliest woods as beech, oak, cedar, cypress, walnuts, sassafras, and vines in great abundance, which hang in great clusters on many trees, and other trees unknown, and all the grounds bespread with strawberries, mulberries, raspberries, and fruits unknown; there are many branches of this river, which run flowing through the woods with great plenty of fish of all kinds; as for sturgeon all the world cannot be compared to it. In this country I have seen many great and large meadows having excellent good pasture for any cattle. There is also great store of deer both red and fallow.[17] There are bears, foxes, otters, beavers, muskrats, and wild beasts unknown. . . .

---

12 **ell**: The English ell is 45 inches or 114.5 cm.

13 **conies**: rabbits.
14 **watchet**: pale-blue.
15 **murrey**: dark-purplish, as mulberry.
16 **river**: James River.
17 **fallow**: a kind of deer smaller than the red.

The four and twentieth day [of May] we set up a cross at the head of this river, naming it King's River, where we proclaimed James King of England to have the most right unto it. When we had finished and set up our cross, we shipped our men and made for James Fort. By the way we came to Powhatan's Tower, where the captain went on shore, suffering none to go with him; he presented the commander[18] of this place with a hatchet which he took joyfully, and was well pleased.

But yet the savages murmured at our planting in the country, whereupon this Werowance made answer again very wisely of a savage, "Why should you be offended with them as long as they hurt you not, nor take anything away by force; they take but a little waste ground, which doth you nor any of us any good."

I saw bread made by their women which do all their drudgery. The men take their pleasure in hunting and their wars, which they are in continually, one kingdom against another. The manner of baking of bread is thus: after they pound their wheat into flour with hot water, they make it into paste, and work it into round balls and cakes. Then they put it into a pot of seething water; when it is sod[19] thoroughly, they lay it on a smooth stone. There they harden it as well as in an oven.

There is notice to be taken to know married women from maids, the maids you shall always see the fore part of their head and sides

18 **commander:** Powhatan, important Indian chief, father of Pocahontas.
19 **sod:** seethed, boiled.

shaven close, the hinder part very long, which they tie in a plait hanging down to their hips. The married women wear their hair all of a length and is tied of that fashion that the maids are. The womenkind in this country doth pounce and race their bodies, legs, thighs, arms, and faces with a sharp iron, which makes a stamp in curious knots, and draws the proportion of fowls, fish, or beasts, then with paintings of sundry lively colors, they rub it into the stamp which will never be taken away, because it is dried into the flesh where it is seared.

The savages bear their years well, for when we were at Pamonkies, we saw a savage by their report was above eight score years of age. His eyes were sunk into his head, having never a tooth in his mouth, his hair all gray with a reasonable big beard, which was as white as any snow. It is a miracle to see a savage have any hair on their faces; I never saw, read, nor heard, any have the like before. This savage was as lusty and went as fast as any of us, which was strange to behold. . . .

The fifteenth day of June, we had built and finished our fort which was trianglewise, having three bulwarks at every corner like a half moon, and four or five pieces of artillery mounted in them. We had made ourselves sufficiently strong for these savages. We had also sown most of our corn on two mountains; it sprang a man's height from the ground. This country is a fruitful soil, bearing many goodly and fruitful trees, as mulberries, cherries, walnuts, cedars, cypress, sassafras, and vines in great abundance.

Study Questions

1. Considering Percy's background, what might have caused him to write that he found "nothing worth the speaking of" in the New World? To what is he comparing Virginia?

2. On further inland expeditions, Percy finds much "worth the speaking of." What are these things? What seems to impress him most?

3. How would you describe Percy's awareness of place? Is he, for example, thoughtful and interpretive? humble or superior? Is he an awed tourist or a responsible reporter?

Vocabulary

Many English words have **multiple meanings.** A number of these words are found in Percy's "Discourse." For example, the selection contains the word *moor.* In some contexts, this word means "to secure (a ship) at a dock, using ropes or an anchor." In other contexts, the same word has this entirely different meaning: "an open, rolling wild tract of land, often having bogs and marshes."

A. Below are two lists. One is a list of definitions which relate to the sea, to navigation, or to a similar matter. Match these definitions with the words in List II.

LIST I

1. a small vessel propelled by oars, sails, or a motor, and used to move on water

2. a six-foot measurement of the depth of water

3. a protected place along a coastline; a shelter for boats or ships

4. a unit of nautical speed: 6080 feet, or 1.15 statute miles, per hour

5. to disembark, or go ashore, from a boat or ship

6. the open sea

7. to supply with sailors who will operate (a ship or boat)

8. the part of a river that empties into another body of water

9. to propel a boat by using oars

10. to measure the depth of (water) by dropping a calibrated line with a weight on its end

LIST II

1. knot		6. mouth	
2. land		7. water	
3. row		8. fathom	
4. boat		9. dock	
5. plumb		10. man	

B. Provide a second definition for each of the words in List II. If necessary, use a dictionary. The second definition should not relate to the sea or navigation.

The Western Frontier

The writers of the middle years of the nine-teenth century continued to record their amazement upon discovering additional natural wonders throughout the country. No writer appreciated the Western setting more than Samuel Langhorne Clemens, known and celebrated as Mark Twain (1835–1910).

The following selection, from *Roughing It* (1872), reveals Mark Twain's awareness of Lake Tahoe as one of the natural wonders of America. His description is enlivened by his broad humor, homely language, and exaggerated anecdotes. These features helped to establish Mark Twain as an entirely new voice in our literature. The selection also demonstrates another, less admirable, attitude—that of carelessness and irresponsibility—which Americans have shown toward their land. (For more on Clemens, see page 350.)

from Roughing It

SAMUEL LANGHORNE CLEMENS

IT WAS THE end of August, and the skies were cloudless and the weather superb. In two or three weeks I had grown wonderfully fascinated with the curious new country,[1] and concluded to put off my return to "the States"[2] awhile. I had grown well accustomed to wearing a damaged slouch hat, blue woolen shirt, and pants crammed into boot tops, and gloried in the absence of coat, vest, and braces. I felt rowdyish and "bully" (as the historian Josephus[3] phrases it, in his fine chapter upon the destruction of the Temple). It seemed to me that nothing could be so fine and so romantic. I had become an officer of the government, but that was for mere sublimity. The office was an unique sinecure. I had nothing to do and no salary. I was private Secretary[4] to his majesty the Secretary and there was not yet writing enough for two of us. So Johnny K— and I devoted our time to amusement. He was the young son of an Ohio nabob and was out there for recreation. He got it. We had heard a world of talk about the marvelous beauty of Lake Tahoe,[5] and finally curiosity drove us thither to see it. Three or four members of the Brigade[6] had been there and located some tim-

berlands on its shores and stored up a quantity of provisions in their camp. We strapped a couple of blankets on our shoulders and took an ax apiece and started—for we intended to take up a wood ranch or so ourselves and become wealthy. We were on foot. The reader will find it advantageous to go horseback. We were told that the distance was eleven miles. We tramped a long time on level ground, and then toiled laboriously up a mountain about a thousand miles high and looked over. No lake there. We descended on the other side, crossed the valley and toiled up another mountain three or four thousand miles high, apparently, and looked over again. No lake yet. We sat down tired and perspiring, and hired a couple of Chinamen to curse those people who had beguiled us. Thus refreshed, we presently resumed the march with renewed vigor and determination. We plodded on, two or three hours longer, and at last the Lake burst upon us—a noble sheet of blue water lifted six thousand three hundred feet above the level of the sea, and walled in by a rim of snow-clad mountain peaks that towered aloft full three thousand feet higher still! It was a vast oval, and one would have to use up eighty or a hundred good miles in traveling around it. As it lay there with the shadows of the mountains brilliantly photographed upon its still surface I thought it must surely be the fairest picture the whole earth affords.

We found the small skiff belonging to the Brigade boys, and without loss of time set out across a deep bend of the lake toward the landmarks that signified the locality of the camp. I got Johnny to row—not because I mind exer-

---

1 **country:** Nevada Territory.
2 **"the States":** Nevada was not admitted into the Union, as the thirty-sixth state, until 1864.
3 **Josephus:** Flavius Josephus (A.D. 37–95?), Jewish historian, author of *Antiquities of the Jews,* a history of the race from creation to the war with Rome in the 1st century A.D.
4 **private Secretary:** Samuel traveled as the unpaid secretary to his brother, who is humorously referred to here as "his majesty the Secretary."
5 **Lake Tahoe:** approximately twenty-one miles long and twelve miles wide, located on the California-Nevada line.
6 **Brigade:** U.S. soldiers stationed in the territory.

tion myself, but because it makes me sick to ride backwards when I am at work. But I steered. A three-mile pull brought us to the camp just as the night fell, and we stepped ashore very tired and wolfishly hungry. In a "cache" among the rocks we found the provisions and the cooking utensils, and then, all fatigued as I was, I sat down on a boulder and superintended while Johnny gathered wood and cooked supper. Many a man who had gone through what I had would have wanted to rest.

It was a delicious supper—hot bread, fried bacon, and black coffee. It was a delicious solitude we were in, too. Three miles away was a sawmill and some workmen, but there were not fifteen other human beings throughout the wide circumference of the lake. As the darkness closed down and the stars came out and spangled the great mirror with jewels, we smoked meditatively in the solemn hush and forgot our troubles and our pains. In due time we spread our blankets in the warm sand between two large boulders and soon fell asleep, careless of the procession of ants that passed in through rents in our clothing and explored our persons. Nothing could disturb the sleep that fettered us, for it had been fairly earned, and if our consciences had any sins on them they had to adjourn court for that night, anyway. The wind rose just as we were losing consciousness, and we were lulled to sleep by the beating of the surf upon the shore.

It is always very cold on that lake shore in the night, but we had plenty of blankets and were warm enough. We never moved a muscle all night, but waked at early dawn in the original positions, and got up at once, thoroughly refreshed, free from soreness, and brim full of friskiness. There is no end of wholesome medicine in such an experience. That morning we could have whipped ten such people as we were the day before—sick ones at any rate. But the world is slow, and people will go to "water cures" and "movement cures" and to foreign lands for health. Three months of camp life on

Lake Tahoe would restore an Egyptian mummy to his pristine vigor, and give him an appetite like an alligator. I do not mean the oldest and driest mummies, of course, but the fresher ones. The air up there in the clouds is very pure and fine, bracing and delicious. And why shouldn't it be?—it is the same the angels breathe. I think that hardly any amount of fatigue can be gathered together that a man cannot sleep off in one night on the sand by its side. Not under a roof, but under the sky; it seldom or never rains there in the summertime. I know a man who went there to die. But he made a failure of it. He was a skeleton when he came, and could barely stand. He had no appetite, and did nothing but read tracts and reflect on the future. Three months later he was sleeping out of doors regularly, eating all he could hold, three times a day, and chasing game over the mountains three thousand feet high for recreation. And he was a skeleton no longer, but weighed part of a ton. This is no fancy sketch, but the truth. His disease was consumption. I confidently commend his experience to other skeletons.

I superintended again, and as soon as we had eaten breakfast we got in the boat and skirted along the lake shore about three miles and disembarked. We liked the appearance of the place, and so we claimed some three hundred acres of it and stuck our "notices" on a tree. It was yellow pine timberland—a dense forest of trees a hundred feet high and from one to five feet through at the butt. It was necessary to fence our property or we could not hold it. That is to say, it was necessary to cut down trees here and there and make them fall in such a way as to form a sort of enclosure (with pretty wide gaps in it). We cut down three trees apiece, and found it such heartbreaking work that we decided to "rest our case" on those; if they held the property, well and good; if they didn't, let the property spill out through the gaps and go; it was no use to work ourselves to death merely to save a few acres of land. Next day we came back to build a

house—for a house was also necessary, in order to hold the property. We decided to build a substantial log house and excite the envy of the Brigade boys; but by the time we had cut and trimmed the first log it seemed unnecessary to be so elaborate, and so we concluded to build it of saplings. However, two saplings, duly cut and trimmed, compelled recognition of the fact that a still modester architecture would satisfy the law, and so we concluded to build a "brush" house. We devoted the next day to this work, but we did so much "sitting around" and discussing, that by the middle of the afternoon we had achieved only a halfway sort of affair which one of us had to watch while the other cut brush, lest if both turned our backs we might not be able to find it again, it had such a strong family resemblance to the surrounding vegetation. But we were satisfied with it.

We were landowners now, duly seized and possessed, and within the protection of the law. Therefore we decided to take up our residence on our own domain and enjoy that large sense of independence which only such an experience can bring. Late the next afternoon, after a good long rest, we sailed away from the Brigade camp with all the provisions and cooking utensils we could carry off—borrow is the more accurate word—and just as the night was falling we beached the boat at our own landing.

If there is any life that is happier than the life we led on our timber ranch for the next two or three weeks, it must be a sort of life which I have not read of in books or experienced in person. We did not see a human being but ourselves during the time, or hear any sounds but those that were made by the wind and the waves, the sighing of the pines, and now and then the far-off thunder of an avalanche. The forest about us was dense and cool, the sky above us was cloudless and brilliant with sunshine, the broad lake before us was glassy and clear, or rippled and breezy, or black and storm-tossed, according to Nature's mood; and its circling border of mountain domes, clothed with forests, scarred with landslides, cloven by canyons and valleys, and helmeted with glittering snow, fitly framed and finished the noble picture. The view was always fascinating, bewitching, entrancing. The eye was never tired of gazing, night or day, in calm or storm; it suffered but one grief, and that was that it could not look always, but must close sometimes in sleep.

We slept in the sand close to the water's edge, between two protecting boulders, which took care of the stormy night winds for us. We never took any paregoric to make us sleep. At the first break of dawn we were always up and running foot races to tone down excess of physical vigor and exuberance of spirits. That is, Johnny was—but I held his hat. While smoking the pipe of peace after breakfast we watched the sentinel peaks put on the glory of the sun, and followed the conquering light as it swept down among the shadows, and set the captive crags and forests free. We watched the tinted pictures grow and brighten upon the water till every little detail of forest, precipice and pinnacle was wrought in and finished, and the miracle of the enchanter complete. Then to "business."

That is, drifting around in the boat. We were on the north shore. There, the rocks on the bottom are sometimes gray, sometimes white. This gives the marvelous transparency of the water a fuller advantage than it has elsewhere on the lake. We usually pushed out a hundred yards or so from shore, and then lay down on the thwarts, in the sun, and let the boat drift by the hour whither it would. We seldom talked. It interrupted the Sabbath stillness, and marred the dreams the luxurious rest and indolence brought. The shore all along was indented with deep, curved bays and coves, bordered by narrow sand beaches; and where the sand ended, the steep mountainsides rose right up aloft into space—rose up like a vast wall a little out of the perpendicular, and thickly wooded with tall pines.

So singularly clear was the water, that where

it was only twenty or thirty feet deep the bottom was so perfectly distinct that the boat seemed floating in the air! Yes, where it was even *eighty* feet deep. Every little pebble was distinct, every speckled trout, every hand's-breadth of sand. Often, as we lay on our faces, a granite boulder, as large as a village church, would start out of the bottom apparently, and seem climbing up rapidly to the surface, till presently it threatened to touch our faces, and we could not resist the impulse to seize an oar and avert the danger. But the boat would float on, and the boulder descend again, and then we could see that when we had been exactly above it, it must still have been twenty or thirty feet below the surface. Down through the transparency of these great depths, the water was not *merely* transparent, but dazzlingly, brilliantly so. All objects seen through it had a bright, strong vividness, not only of outline, but of every minute detail, which they would not have had when seen simply through the same depth of atmosphere. So empty and airy did all spaces seem below us, and so strong was the sense of floating high aloft in mid-nothingness, that we called these boat excursions "balloon-voyages."

We fished a good deal, but we did not average one fish a week. We could see trout by the thousand winging about in the emptiness under us, or sleeping in shoals on the bottom, but they would not bite—they could see the line too plainly, perhaps. We frequently selected the trout we wanted, and rested the bait patiently and persistently on the end of his nose at a depth of eighty feet, but he would only shake it off with an annoyed manner, and shift his position.

We bathed occasionally, but the water was rather chilly, for all it looked so sunny. Sometimes we rowed out to the "blue water," a mile or two from shore. It was as dead blue as indigo there, because of the immense depth. By official measurement the lake in its center is one thousand five hundred and twenty-five feet deep!

Sometimes, on lazy afternoons, we lolled on the sand in camp, and smoked pipes and read some old well-worn novels. At night, by the campfire, we played euchre and seven-up to strengthen the mind—and played them with cards so greasy and defaced that only a whole summer's acquaintance with them could enable the student to tell the ace of clubs from the jack of diamonds.

We never slept in our "house." It never occurred to us, for one thing; and besides, it was built to hold the ground, and that was enough. We did not wish to strain it.

By and by our provisions began to run short, and we went back to the old camp and laid in a new supply. We were gone all day, and reached home again about nightfall, pretty tired and hungry. While Johnny was carrying the main bulk of the provisions up to our "house" for future use, I took the loaf of bread, some slices of bacon, and the coffeepot, ashore, set them down by a tree, lit a fire, and went back to the boat to get the frying pan. While I was at this, I heard a shout from Johnny, and looking up I saw that my fire was galloping all over the premises!

Johnny was on the other side of it. He had to run through the flames to get to the lake shore, and then we stood helpless and watched the devastation.

The ground was deeply carpeted with dry pine needles, and the fire touched them off as if they were gunpowder. It was wonderful to see with what fierce speed the tall sheet of flame traveled! My coffeepot was gone, and everything with it. In a minute and a half the fire seized upon a dense growth of dry manzanita chapparal[7] six or eight feet high, and then the roaring and popping and crackling was something terrific. We were driven to the boat by the intense heat, and there we remained, spellbound.

Within half an hour all before us was a tossing, blinding tempest of flame! It went surging up adjacent ridges—surmounted them and disappeared in the canyons beyond—burst into view upon higher and farther ridges, presently—shed a grander illumination abroad, and dove again—flamed out again, directly, higher and still higher up the mountainside—threw out skirmishing parties of fire here and there, and sent them trailing their crimson spirals away among remote ramparts and ribs and gorges, till as far as the eye could reach the lofty mountain fronts were webbed as it were with a tangled network of red lava streams. Away across the water the crags and domes were lit with a ruddy glare, and the firmament above was a reflected hell!

Every feature of the spectacle was repeated in the glowing mirror of the lake! Both pictures were sublime, both were beautiful; but that in the lake had a bewildering richness about it that enchanted the eye and held it with the stronger fascination.

We sat absorbed and motionless through four long hours. We never thought of supper, and never felt fatigue. But at eleven o'clock the conflagration had traveled beyond our range of vision, and then darkness stole down upon the landscape again.

---

7 **manzanita chapparal:** evergreen shrubs.

Study Questions

1. Which anecdotes are exaggerated? Why? Where else do you spot exaggerated expressions?

2. Point out other instances of the author's humor. Why can this humor be called broad rather than subtle?

3. At this time in American history many people were making money or dreaming of doing so—a recurring feature of The American Dream. Where is there indication here that Mark Twain had a similar dream?

4. It has been said that Mark Twain addressed his stories to the ear rather than to the eye. That is, he wrote as people speak, capturing the rhythms of ordinary speech. Find evidence to support this observation.

5. Explain how the concluding episode shows the campers' carelessness and irresponsibility toward the land. What is their reaction as they watch the fire? Yet how would you describe Mark Twain's attitude toward this place? Find examples of his attitude in his descriptions and anecdotes throughout the selection.

Leaving Home

Although he aspired to be a playwright, Thomas Wolfe (1900–1938) found his genius in prose fiction. Over the last ten years of his brief life he produced a massive fictional narrative of his own career. The principal volumes in the series are *Look Homeward, Angel* (1929), *Of Time and the River* (1935), *The Web and the Rock* (1939), and *You Can't Go Home Again* (published posthumously in 1940).

Much of his writing explored the complex feelings people often have towards home and family. The passage included here from *Of Time and the River* is one example of this interest. In it the town of Altamont is Wolfe's native Asheville, and Catawba is his home state, North Carolina.

from Of Time and the River

THOMAS WOLFE

THE JOURNEY from the mountain town of Altamont to the tower-masted island of Manhattan is not, as journeys are conceived in America, a long one. The distance is somewhat more than 700 miles, the time required to make the journey a little more than twenty hours. But so relative are the qualities of space and time, and so complex and multiple their shifting images, that in the brief passage of this journey one may live a life, share instantly in 10,000,000 other ones, and see pass before his eyes the infinite panorama of shifting images that make a nation's history.

First of all, the physical changes and transitions of the journey are strange and wonderful enough. In the afternoon one gets on the train and with a sense of disbelief and wonder sees the familiar faces, shapes, and structures of his native town recede out of the last fierce clasp of life and vision. Then, all through the waning afternoon, the train is toiling down around the mountain curves and passes. The great shapes of the hills, embrowned and glowing with the molten hues of autumn, are all about him: the towering summits, wild and lonely, full of joy and strangeness and their haunting premonitions of oncoming winter soar above him, the gulches, gorges, gaps, and wild ravines, fall sheer and suddenly away with a dizzy terrifying steepness, and all the time the great train toils slowly down from the mountain summits with the sinuous turnings of an enormous snake. And from the very toiling slowness of the train, together with the terrific stillness and nearness of the marvellous hills, a relation is established, an emotion evoked, which it is impossible to define, but which, in all its strange and poignant mingling of wild sorrow and joy, grief for the world that one is losing, swelling triumph at the thought of the strange new world that one will find, is instantly familiar, and has been felt by every one.

The train toils slowly round the mountain grades, the short and powerful blasts of its squat funnel sound harsh and metallic against the sides of rocky cuts. One looks out the window and sees cut, bank, and gorge slide slowly past, the old rock wet and gleaming with the water of some buried mountain spring. The train goes slowly over the perilous and dizzy height of a wooden trestle; far below, the traveller can see and hear the clean foaming clamors of rock-bright mountain water; beside the track, before his little hut, a switchman stands looking at the train with the slow wondering gaze of the mountaineer. The little shack in which he lives is stuck to the very edge of the track above the steep and perilous ravine. His wife, a slattern with a hank of tight drawn hair, a snuff-stick in her mouth, and the same gaunt, slow wondering stare her husband has, stands in the doorway of the shack, holding a dirty little baby in her arms.

It is all so strange, so near, so far, so terrible, beautiful, and instantly familiar, that it seems to the traveller that he must have known these people forever, that he must now stretch forth his hand to them from the windows and the rich and sumptuous luxury of the pullman car,

that he must speak to them. And it seems to him that all the strange and bitter miracle of life—how, why, or in what way, he does not know—is in that instant greeting and farewell; for once seen, and lost the moment that he sees it, it is his forever and he can never forget it. And then the slow toiling train has passed these lives and faces and is gone, and there is something in his heart he cannot say.

At length the train has breached the last great wall of the soaring ranges, has made its slow and sinuous descent around the powerful bends and corkscrews of the shining rails (which now he sees above him seven times) and towards dark, the lowland country has been reached. The sun goes down behind the train a tremendous globe of orange and pollen, the soaring ranges melt swiftly into shapes of smoky and enchanted purple, night comes—great-starred and velvet-breasted night—and now the train takes up its level pounding rhythm across the piedmont swell and convolution of the mighty State.

Towards nine o'clock at night there is a pause to switch cars and change engines at a junction town. The traveller, with the same feeling of wild unrest, wonder, nameless excitement and wordless expectancy, leaves the train, walks back and forth upon the platform, rushes into the little station lunch room or out into the streets to buy cigarettes, a sandwich—really just to feel this moment's contact with another town. He sees vast flares and steamings of gigantic locomotives on the rails, the seamed, blackened, lonely faces of the engineers in the cabs of their great engines, and a little later he is rushing again across the rude, mysterious visage of the powerful, dark, and lonely earth of old Catawba.

Toward midnight there is another pause at a larger town—the last stop in Catawba—again the feeling of wild unrest and nameless joy and sorrow. The traveller gets out, walks up and down the platform, sees the vast slow flare and steaming of the mighty engine, rushes into the station, and looks into the faces of all the peo-

ple passing with the same sense of instant familiarity, greeting, and farewell,—that lonely, strange, and poignantly wordless feeling that Americans know so well. Then he is in the pullman again, the last outposts of the town have slipped away from him and the great train which all through the afternoon has travelled eastward from the mountains half across the mighty State, is now for the first time pointed northward, worldward, towards the secret borders of Virginia, towards the great world cities of his hope, the fable of his childhood legendry, and the wild and secret hunger of his heart, his spirit and his life.

Already the little town from which he came in the great hills, the faces of his kinsmen and his friends, their most familiar voices, the shapes of things he knew seem far and strange as dreams, lost at the bottom of the million-visaged sea-depth of dark time, the strange and bitter miracle of life. He cannot think that he has ever lived there in the far lost hills, or ever left them, and all his life seems stranger than the dream of time, and the great train moves on across the immense and lonely visage of America, making its great monotone that is the sound of silence and forever. And in the train, and in ten thousand little towns, the sleepers sleep upon the earth.

Then bitter sorrow, loneliness and joy come swelling to his throat—quenchless hunger rises from the adyts[1] of his life and conquers

---

1 **adyts** (ad' its): sacred, inner shrines.

him, and with wild wordless fury horsed upon his life, he comes at length, in dark mid-watches of the night, up to the borders of the old earth of Virginia.

Who has seen fury riding in the mountains? Who has known fury striding in the storm? Who has been mad with fury in his youth, given no rest or peace or certitude by fury, driven on across the earth by fury, until the great vine of the heart was broke, the sinews wrenched, the little tenement of bone, blood, marrow, brain, and feeling in which great fury raged, was twisted, wrung, depleted, worn out, and exhausted by the fury which it could not lose or put away? Who has known fury, how it came?

How have we breathed him, drunk him, eaten fury to the core, until we have him in us now and cannot lose him anywhere we go? It is a strange and subtle worm that will be forever feeding at our heart. It is a madness working in our brain, a hunger growing from the food it feeds upon, a devil moving in the conduits of our blood, it is a spirit wild and dark and uncontrollable forever swelling in our soul, and it is in the saddle now, horsed upon our lives, rowelling the spurs of its insatiate desire into our naked and defenseless sides, our owner, master, and the mad and cruel tyrant who goads us on forever down the blind and brutal tunnel of kaleidoscopic days at the end of which is nothing but the blind mouth of the pit and darkness and no more.

Then, then, will fury leave us, he will cease from those red channels of our life he has so often run, another sort of worm will work at that great vine, whereat he fed. Then, then, indeed, he must give over, fold his camp, retreat; there is no place for madness in a dead man's brain, no place for hunger in a dead man's flesh, and in a dead man's heart there is a place for no desire.

At what place of velvet-breasted night long long ago, and in what leafy darkened street of mountain summer, hearing the footsteps of approaching lovers in the night, the man's voice, low, hushed, casual, confiding, suddenly the low rich welling of a woman's laughter, tender and sensual in the dark, going, receding, fading, and then the million-noted silence of the night again? In what ancient light of fading day in a late summer; what wordless passion then of sorrow, joy, and ecstasy—was he betrayed to fury when it came? . . .

He never knew; it may have been a rock, a stone, a leaf, the moths of golden light as warm and moving in a place of magic green, it may have been the storm-wind howling in the barren trees, the ancient fading light of day in some forgotten summer, the huge unfolding mystery of undulant, on-coming night.

Oh, it might have been all this in the April and most lilac darkness of some forgotten morning as he saw the clean line of the East cleave into morning at the mountain's ridge. It may have been the first light, bird-song, an end to labor and the sweet ache and pure fatigue of the lightened shoulder as he came home at morning hearing the single lonely hoof, the jinking bottles, and the wheel upon the street again, and smelled the early morning breakfast smells, the smoking wheat-cakes, and the pungent sausages, the steaks, biscuits, grits, and fried green apples, and the brains and eggs. It may have been the coil of pungent smoke upcurling from his father's chimney, the clean sweet gardens and the peach-bloom, apples, crinkled lettuce wet with dew, bloom and cherry bloom down drifting in their magic snow within his father's orchard, and his father's giant figure awake now and astir, and moving in his house!

Oh, ever to wake at morning knowing he was there! To feel the fire-full chimney-throat roar up a-tremble with the blast of his terrific fires, to hear the first fire crackling in the kitchen range, to hear the sounds of morning in the house, the smells of breakfast and the feeling of security never to be changed! Oh, to hear him prowling like a wakened lion below, the stertorous hoarse frenzy of his furious breath; to hear the ominous muttering mounting to faint howls as with infuriated relish he prepared the roaring invective of the morning's tirade, to hear him muttering as the coal went rattling out upon the fire, to hear him growling as savagely the flame shot up the trembling chimney-throat, to hear him muttering back and forth now like a raging beast, finally to hear his giant stride racing through the house prepared now, storming to the charge, and the well-remembered howl of his awakened fury as springing to the door-way of the back-room stairs he flung it open, yelling at them to awake.

Was it in such a way, one time as he awoke, and heard below his father's lion-ramp of morning that fury came? He never knew, no more than one could weave the great web of his life back through the brutal chaos of ten thousand furious days, unwind the great vexed pattern of his life to silence, peace, and certitude in the magic land of new beginnings, no return.

He never knew if fury had lain dormant all those years, had worked secret, silent, like a madness in the blood. But later it would seem to him that fury had first filled his life, exploded, conquered, and possessed him, that he first felt it, saw it, knew the dark illimitable madness of its power, one night years later on a train across Virginia.

Study Questions

1. Three times before the train leaves the state of Catawba the traveler is deeply moved. What are the three occasions? What is the nature of the traveler's emotion?

2. As the train moves "northward, worldward," why do you think Wolfe describes the borders of Virginia as "secret"?

3. Why is the traveler leaving home? What is the nature of the "fury" that possesses him?

4. Altamont is at one end of the journey and New York at the other. What are the characteristics of each place in the traveler's mind? What do these two contrasting places symbolize?

Vocabulary

Each sentence below is based upon the selection from Thomas Wolfe's *Of Time and the River* and each contains a blank space. Only one of the five words listed below each sentence is appropriate to fill the blank.

On a separate sheet of paper, give the number of each sentence and copy the word that fits meaningfully into each **sentence context**. If you need assistance, use a dictionary.

1. The great train toils slowly down from the mountain summits with the _____ twists and turns of an enormous snake.

    exorbitant   philanthropic   sinuous   piquant   voracious

2. The slowness of the train and the stillness of the marvelous nearby hills together _____ an emotion which it is impossible to define.

    evoke   convoke   equivoque   revoke   provoke

3. The feeling is a strange and ____ one that mingles wild sorrow with joy, grief for the old world one is losing with swelling triumph for the new world that one will soon discover.

magnanimous   risque   analine   consumptive   poignant

4. The traveler feels that he should stretch forth his hand to the switchman and his wife from the window of the rich and ____ luxury of the pullman car.

dolorous   penurious   ignominious

sumptuous   monogamous

5. As the sun sets, the train takes up its level pounding rhythm through the swells and ____ of the foothills.

conjectures   constituencies   convolutions

concordances   confutations

6. Fury is a madness that works in our brain, a hunger that grows from the food it feeds upon, a devil that moves freely and easily through the ____ which carry our blood, a spirit wild and dark and uncontrollable.

embolisms   conduits   strictures   terminuses   occlusions

7. Fury is our owner and master, a mad and cruel tyrant who ____ us to keep moving on forever down the blind and brutal tunnel of days at the end of which is nothing but darkness.

razes   gleans   trusses   coifs   goads

8. The traveler imagines that he can hear his father prowling about downstairs like a wakened lion, furiously roaring in ____, hoarse breaths.

stertorous   striated   sublet   sidereal   seraphic

9. Again, the traveler imagines he can hear his father's ominous muttering, mounting to howls as he prepares the ____ he will use in this morning's session of scolding.

indigence   invective   insouciance

introversion   incarceration

New York City in the Twenties

The American sense of place also includes the city. One writer who has vividly described city life is Alfred Kazin (1915—   ). Kazin is a literary critic and teacher who grew up in the Brownsville section of Brooklyn. This part of New York City in the late 1920s was an immigrant quarter settled largely by Russian and Polish Jews. The following passages are taken from the autobiographical *A Walker in the City* (1951). Throughout this excerpt, Kazin communicates a fierce yet melancholy feeling for his tenement surroundings. During this period, horse-drawn wagons were still common on city streets. Radio and television were unknown. Where did a fourteen-year-old city youth without a back yard or front lawn play? What did he do for pastime in the heart of a crowded metropolis?

from A Walker in the City

ALFRED KAZIN

THE BLOCK: *my* block. It was on the Chester Street side of our house, between the grocery and the back wall of the old drugstore, that I was hammered into the shape of the streets. Everything beginning at Blake Avenue would always wear for me some delightful strangeness and mildness, simply because it was not of my block, *the* block, where the clang of your head sounded against the pavement when you fell in a fist fight, and the rows of store-lights on each side were pitiless, watching you. Anything away from the block was good: even a school you never went to, two blocks away: there were vegetable gardens in the park across the street. Returning from "New York," I would take the longest routes home from the subway, get off a station ahead of my own, only for the unexpectedness of walking through Betsy Head Park and hearing the gravel crunch under my feet as I went beyond the vegetable gardens, smelling the sweaty sweet dampness from the pool in summer and the dust on the leaves as I passed under the ailanthus trees. On the block itself everything rose up only to test me.

We worked every inch of it, from the cellars and the back yards to the sickening space between the roofs. Any wall, any stoop, any curving metal edge on a billboard sign made a place against which to knock a ball; any bottom rung of a fire-escape ladder a goal in basketball; any sewer cover a base; any crack in the pavement a "net" for the tense sharp tennis that we played by beating a soft ball back and forth with our hands between the squares. Betsy Head Park two blocks away would always feel slightly foreign, for it belonged to the Amboys and the Bristols and the Hopkinsons as much as it did to us. *Our* life every day was fought out on the pavement and in the gutter, up against the walls of the houses and the glass fronts of the drugstore and the grocery, in and out of the fresh steaming piles of horse manure, the wheels of passing carts and automobiles, along the iron spikes of the stairway to the cellar, the jagged edge of the open garbage cans, the crumbly steps of the old farmhouses still left on one side of the street.

As I go back to the block now, and for a moment fold my body up again in its narrow arena—there, just there, between the black of the asphalt and the old women in their kerchiefs and flowered housedresses sitting on the tawny kitchen chairs—the back wall of the drugstore still rises up to test me. Every day we smashed a small black viciously hard regulation handball against it with fanatical cuts and drives and slams, beating and slashing at it almost in hatred for the blind strength of the wall itself. I was never good enough at handball, was always practicing some trick shot that might earn me esteem, and when I was weary of trying, would often bat a ball down Chester Street just to get myself to Blake Avenue. I have this memory of playing one-o'-cat by myself in the sleepy twilight, at a moment when everyone else had left the block. The sparrows floated down from the telephone

wires to peck at every fresh pile of horse manure, and there was a smell of brine from the delicatessen store, of egg crates and of the milk scum left in the great metal cans outside the grocery, of the thick white paste oozing out from behind the fresh Hecker's Flour ad on the metal signboard. I would throw the ball in the air, hit it with my bat, then with perfect satisfaction drop the bat to the ground and run to the next sewer cover. Over and over I did this, from sewer cover to sewer cover, until I had worked my way to Blake Avenue and could see the park.

With each clean triumphant ring of my bat against the gutter leading me on, I did the whole length of our block up and down, and never knew how happy I was just watching the asphalt rise and fall, the curve of the steps up to an old farmhouse. The farmhouses themselves were streaked red on one side, brown on the other, but the steps themselves were always gray. There was a tremor of pleasure at one place; I held my breath in nausea at another. As I ran after my ball with the bat heavy in my hand, the odd successiveness of things in myself almost choked me, the world was so full as I ran—past the cobblestoned yards into the old farmhouses, where stray chickens still waddled along the stones; past the little candy store where we went only if the big one on our side of the block was out of Eskimo Pies; past the three neighboring tenements where the last of the old women sat on their kitchen chairs yawning before they went up to make supper. Then came Mrs. Rosenwasser's house, the place on the block I first identified with what was farthest from home, and strangest, because it was a "private" house; then the fences around the monument works, where black cranes rose up above the yard and you could see the smooth gray slabs that would be cut and carved into tombstones, some of them already engraved with the names and dates and family virtues of the dead.

Beyond Blake Avenue was the pool parlor outside which we waited all through the tense

September afternoons of the World's Series to hear the latest scores called off the ticker tape—and where as we waited, banging a ball against the bottom of the wall and drinking water out of empty coke bottles, I breathed the chalk off the cues and listened to the clocks ringing in the fire station across the street. There was an old warehouse next to the pool parlor; the oil on the barrels and the iron staves had the same rusty smell. A block away was the park, thick with the dusty gravel I liked to hear my shoes crunch in as I ran round and round the track; then a great open pavilion, the inside mysteriously dark, chill even in summer; there I would wait in the sweaty coolness before pushing on to the wading ring where they put up a shower on the hottest days.

——

For all those first summer walks into the city, all daily walks across the bridge[1] for years afterward, when I came to leave Brownsville at last, were efforts to understand one single half-hour at dusk, on a dark winter day, the year I was fourteen. There had been some school excursion that day to City Hall and the courts of lower New York,[2] and looking up at the green dome of the *World*[3] as we came into Park Row, I found myself separated from the class, and decided to go it across the bridge alone. I remember holding a little red volume of THE WORLD'S GREATEST SELECTED SHORT STORIES in my hand as I started out under the groined arcade of the Municipal Building and the rusty green-black terminal of the El[4] sweeping onto the bridge from Park Row—somewhere in the course of that walk

across the bridge the last of those volumes got lost for all time. Evening was coming on fast, great crowds in thick black overcoats were pounding up the staircases to the El; the whole bridge seemed to shake under the furious blows of that crowd starting for home.

Rush hour above, on every side, below: the iron wheels of the El trains shooting blue-white sparks against the black, black tracks sweeping in from Chinatown and Oliver Street under the black tar roofs and fire escapes and empty window boxes along the grimy black tenements on whose sides I could see the streaky whitewashed letters CHILDREN CRY FOR IT FLETCHER'S CASTORIA CHARLES S. FLETCHER; trolley cars bounding up into the air on each side of me, their bells clanging, clanging; cars sweeping off the bridge and

1 **bridge:** Brooklyn Bridge crosses the East River between lower Manhattan and Brooklyn.
2 **lower New York:** the southern tip of the island of Manhattan.
3 *World:* The New York *World,* one of the most influential newspapers in New York from 1883 to 1931.
4 **El:** elevated railway. The major Els have now gone underground to become subways.

from *A Walker in the City* **33**

onto the bridge in the narrow last roadways before me.

Then a long line of naked electric bulbs hung on wires above the newsstands and hot dog stands in the arcade, raw light glittering above the flaky iron rust, newsboys selling the *Evening World,* the smell of popcorn and of frankfurters sizzling on the grill. And now up a flight of metal-edged wooden steps and into the open at last, the evening coming on faster and faster, a first few flakes of snow in the air, the lights blue and hard up one side of the transparent staircases in Wall Street, dark on another; the river black, inky black; then the long hollow boom shivering the worn wooden planks under my feet as a ship passes under the bridge.

Dusk of a dark winter's day that first hour walking Brooklyn Bridge. Suddenly I felt lost and happy as I went up another flight of steps, passed under the arches of the tower, and waited, next to a black barrel, at the railing of the observation platform. The trolleys clanged and clanged; every angry stalled car below sounded its horn as, bumper to bumper, they all poked their way along the bridge; the El trains crackled and thundered over my right shoulder. A clock across the street showed its lighted face; along the fire escapes of the building were sculptured figures of runners and baseball players, of prize fighters flexing their muscles and wearing their championship belts, just as they did in the *Police Gazette.* But from that platform under the tower the way ahead was strange. Only the electric sign of the Jewish Daily *Forward,* burning high over the tenements of the East Side, suddenly stilled the riot in my heart as I saw the cables leap up to the tower, saw those great meshed triangles leap up and up, higher and still higher—Lord my Lord, when will they cease to drive me up with them in their flight?—and then, each line singing out alone the higher it came and nearer, fly flaming into the topmost eyelets of the tower.

Somewhere below they were roasting coffee, handling spices—the odor was in the pillars, in the battered wooden planks of the promenade under my feet, in the blackness upwelling from the river. A painter's scaffold dangled down one side of the tower over a spattered canvas. Never again would I walk Brooklyn Bridge without smelling that coffee, those spices, the paint on that canvas. The trolley car clanged, clanged, clanged taking me home that day from the bridge.

Study Questions

1. A writer can recreate a place by describing sensory impressions of that place. What are the different impressions of sound, smell, and sight used by Kazin? Which are pleasant images? Which are unpleasant?

2. How is color used in the passage about the Brooklyn Bridge? What effect does it have on your impression of the bridge?

3. How does Kazin's statement, "I felt lost and happy," sum up his feelings about the city?

The Modern Highway

To modern Americans travel from place to place has become common, and certainly the expressway is a familiar sight. Everyone has an impression of these long concrete or asphalt stretches which most people take for granted. But how might a creature from another planet react on seeing a string of cars speeding along a busy freeway? That question is dealt with in the following poem by May Swenson (1919—   ). A native of Utah, Swenson has become one of the most accessible of all living American poets. Her poems have appeared in hundreds of magazines from the little quarterlies and *The New Yorker* to the *Chicago Tribune* magazine. Since winning her first poetry award twenty years ago, she has published many books of poems, among them, *Half Sun Half Sleep* (1967) and *Things Taking Place* (1979).

Southbound on the Freeway

MAY SWENSON

A tourist came in from Orbitville,
parked in the air, and said:

The creatures of this star
are made of metal and glass.

Through the transparent parts   5
you can see their guts.

Their feet are round and roll
on diagrams—or long

measuring tapes—dark
with white lines.   10

They have four eyes.
The two in the back are red.

Sometimes you can see a 5-eyed
one, with a red eye turning

on the top of his head.   15
He must be special—

the others respect him,
and go slow,

when he passes, winding
among them from behind.   20

They all hiss as they glide,
like inches, down the marked

tapes. Those soft shapes,
shadowy inside

the hard bodies—are they   25
their guts or their brains?

HIGHWAY *James Rosenquist*
Rosenquist's painting, like Swenson's poem, plays on the freeway motif in modern
American culture.

Study Questions

1. How does the freeway appear to the visitor in the space ship?
2. What might make an observer from another planet think the "soft shapes" are "guts"? What might make the observer think that the shapes are "brains"? What is the irony of that line?

Barrio Life

Homesickness has been felt by almost everyone who has been away from home. Sometimes a person does not realize what home
as a sense of place means until he or she
leaves it. The next poet, Ricardo Sánchez
(1941—   ), reflects on life in the Chicano
neighborhood (barrio) of his home town, El
Paso, Texas. After college, Sánchez worked
as teacher, community leader, and editor.
He is presently Director of Chicano Studies
at the University of Utah. Among his published works is *The Liberation of a Chicano
Mind* (1971). Few writers have better conveyed the feeling for barrio life.

i yearn

RICARDO SÁNCHEZ

i yearn this morning
what i've yearned
since i left

   almost a year ago . . .

it is hollow   5
this
being away
from everyday life
in the barrios
of my homeland . . .   10
all those cities
like el paso, los angeles,
albuquerque,
denver, san antonio
   (off into chicano   15
     infinitum!);

i yearn
to hear spanish
spoken in caló—
that special way   20
chicanos roll their

  tongues
to form
words
which dart or glide;   25

i yearn
for foods
that have character
and strength—the kind
that assail yet caress   30
you with the zest of life;

more than anything,
i yearn, my people,
for the warmth of you
greeting me with "¿qué tal,   35
hermano?" [1]
and the knowing that you
  mean it
when you tell me that you love
the fact that we exist . . .   40

---

1 **qué tal hermano** (kā täl, ar män'ō): Spanish for "how
goes it, brother?"

COIFFURE *Manuel Alvarez Brava*

Collection, the Museum of Modern Art, New York. Gift of Edgar Kaufmann, Jr.

Study Questions

1. What three specific things does the speaker yearn for?
2. If you were away from home what three things would you miss most? Are they similar in any way to things named in "i yearn"?

An American Farm

One place that is a significant part of life in America is the farm. In this poem, Margaret Walker (Alexander) (1915—   ) describes a satisfied, prospering farmer.

In addition to her responsibilities as a wife, mother, and professor at Jackson State University in Mississippi, Ms. Walker is a widely published poet. Her first volume of poetry, *For My People,* was awarded the Yale Poetry Prize in 1942. In 1965, she published a novel, *Jubilee,* based on her family's experiences before, during, and after the Civil War.

Iowa Farmer

MARGARET WALKER

I talked to a farmer one day in Iowa.
We looked out far over acres of wheat.
He spoke with pride and yet not boastfully;
he had no need to fumble for his words.
He knew his land and there was love for home   5
within the soft serene eyes of his son.
His ugly house was clean against the storm;
there was no hunger deep within the heart
nor burning riveted within the bone,
but here they ate a satisfying bread.   10
Yet in the Middle West where wheat was plentiful;
where grain grew golden under sunny skies
and cattle fattened through the summer heat
I could remember more familiar sights.

Study Questions

1. In the first five lines what do you learn about the Iowa farmer's relation-ship to the place where he lives? What is the source of this relationship?

2. In lines 8, 9, and 14 how do you learn about the speaker's sense of place? How does this contrast with the farmer's sense of place?

3. What kind of bread would not be "satisfying"? What other implications do lines 4, 6, 7, and 10 have?

Composition

1. Write an essay in which you compare Thomas Wolfe's feeling of attach-ment to his home with that of Ricardo Sanchez. Or compare the descrip-tion of belonging to the land in "The Gift Outright" with "Where Mountain Lion Lay Down with Deer." For the topic chosen, summarize each au-thor's attitudes; then point out similarities and differences between the two. Conclude with a statement telling which point of view you prefer and why.

2. Examine your own feelings about the place where you live. Then write an essay expressing your personal Sense of Place. Be specific. Con-centrate on the details of your region or neighborhood. Include physical surroundings, what you see, the noises that you associate with the place, and the smells. Describe your place vividly enough so that the reader will know how you feel about it.

The Individual

Individualism was from the beginning a central fact of life for the earliest European settlers. They were products of the Protestant Reformation in Europe which gave each believer the sense of standing alone before God. Such isolation promoted a tendency toward self-contemplation. This feeling was intensified by the need for self-reliance in surviving the rigors of the wilderness. Our literature has faithfully reflected these pressures. The stress has been on individual thought and action and on the relation between the individual and society. The member of a fixed-order society has perhaps less need to puzzle over such questions. However, individuals from a democratic society can, within limits, make of themselves and of the world around them whatever their courage and imagination will permit. The selections here present a spectrum of individualisms, from the benevolent optimism of Walt Whitman to the uncertainties of Cathy Song.

I Hear America Singing

Walt Whitman (1819–1892) celebrated individuality in one of his most famous poems, "I Hear America Singing." This poem focuses on various types of people in the American democracy who have their individual songs to sing as they work. (Additional information on Whitman is included in Unit 5 on page 336.)

I Hear America Singing

WALT WHITMAN

I hear America singing, the varied carols I hear,
Those of mechanics, each one singing his as it should be
    blithe and strong,
The carpenter singing his as he measures his plank or
    beam,
The mason singing his as he makes ready for work,
    or leaves off work,
The boatman singing what belongs to him in his boat,
    the deckhand singing on the steamboat deck,   5
The shoemaker singing as he sits on his bench,
    the hatter singing as he stands,
The wood-cutter's song, the plowboy's on his way in
    the morning, or at noon intermission or at sundown,
The delicious singing of the mother, or of the young wife
    at work, or of the girl sewing or washing,
Each singing what belongs to him or her and to none else,
The day what belongs to the day—at night the
    party of young fellows, robust, friendly,   10
Singing with open mouths their strong melodious songs.

COLONIAL CUBISM *Stuart Davis*

Study Questions

1. Who are the different types of Americans mentioned by Whitman? Although their carols are "varied," what do they all have in common?
2. How many times is the word "singing" repeated? What is the effect of the repetition?

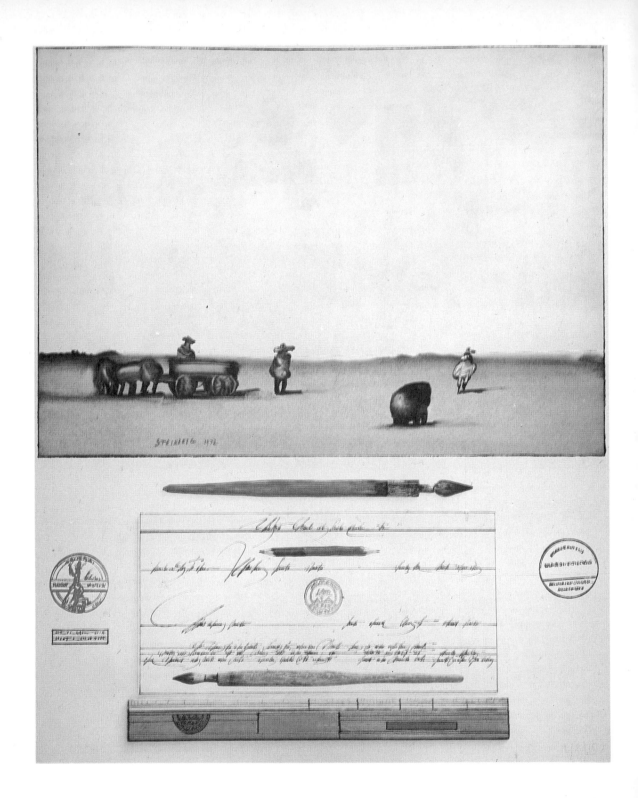

What is Individualism?

Though Alexis de Tocqueville (1805–1859) was French, the book he wrote, *Democracy in America* (1835), is a penetrating analysis of the American character. Students of America and its literature cannot afford to ignore this remarkably objective portrait. The clarity and logic of de Tocqueville's mind is evident even in translation.

Of Individualism in Democratic Countries

ALEXIS DE TOCQUEVILLE

I HAVE SHOWN how it is that in ages of equality every man seeks for his opinions within himself; I am now to show how it is that in the same ages all his feelings are turned towards himself alone. *Individualism* is a novel expression, to which a novel idea has given birth. Our fathers were only acquainted with *égoïsme* (selfishness). Selfishness is a passionate and exaggerated love of self, which leads a man to connect everything with himself and to prefer himself to everything in the world. Individualism is a mature and calm feeling, which disposes each member of the community to sever himself from the mass of his fellows and to draw apart with his family and his friends, so that after he has thus formed a little circle of his own, he willingly leaves society at large to itself. Selfishness originates in blind instinct; individualism proceeds from erroneous judgment more than from depraved feelings; it originates as much in deficiencies of mind as in perversity of heart.

Selfishness blights the germ of all virtue; individualism, at first, only saps the virtues of public life; but in the long run it attacks and destroys all others and is at length absorbed in downright selfishness. Selfishness is a vice as old as the world, which does not belong to one form of society more than to another; individualism is of democratic origin, and it threatens to spread in the same ratio as the equality of condition.

Among aristocratic nations, as families remain for centuries in the same condition, often on the same spot, all generations become, as it were, contemporaneous. A man almost always knows his forefathers and respects them; he thinks he already sees his remote descendants and he loves them. He willingly imposes duties on himself towards the former and the latter, and he will frequently sacrifice his personal gratifications to those who went before and to those who will come after him. Aristocratic institutions, moreover, have the effect of closely binding every man to several of his fellow citizens. As the classes of an aristocratic people are strongly marked and permanent, each of them is regarded by its own members as a sort of lesser country, more tangible and more cherished than the country at large. As in aristocratic communities all the citizens occupy fixed positions, one above another, the result is that each of them always sees a man above himself whose patronage is necessary to him, and below himself another man whose co-operation he may claim. Men living in aristocratic ages are therefore almost always closely attached to something placed out of their own sphere, and they are often disposed to forget themselves. It is true that in these ages the notion of human fellowship is faint and that men seldom think of sacrificing themselves for mankind; but they often sacrifice themselves for other men. In democratic times, on the contrary, when the duties of each individual to the race are much more clear, devoted service to any one man becomes more rare; the bond of human affection is extended, but it is relaxed.

Among democratic nations new families are constantly springing up, others are constantly falling away, and all that remain change their condition; the woof of time is every instant broken and the track of generations effaced.

Those who went before are soon forgotten; of those who will come after, no one has any idea: the interest of man is confined to those in close propinquity to himself. As each class gradually approaches others and mingles with them, its members become undifferentiated and lose their class identity for each other. Aristocracy had made a chain of all the members of the community, from the peasant to the king; democracy breaks that chain and severs every link of it.

As social conditions become more equal, the number of persons increases who, although they are neither rich nor powerful enough to exercise any great influence over their fellows, have nevertheless acquired or retained sufficient education and fortune to satisfy their own wants. They owe nothing to any man, they expect nothing from any man; they acquire the habit of always considering themselves as standing alone, and they are apt to imagine that their whole destiny is in their own hands.

Thus not only does democracy make every man forget his ancestors, but it hides his descendants and separates his contemporaries from him; it throws him back forever upon himself alone and threatens in the end to confine him entirely within the solitude of his own heart.

Study Questions

1. What distinction does de Tocqueville make between selfishness and individualism? How does he relate them to each other?

2. In what way had aristocracy "made a chain of all the members of the community"? How has democracy broken the chain?

3. What is de Tocqueville's attitude toward the "self-made" man?

4. Do you think de Tocqueville overstates the dangers of individualism? What evidence can you find in American life since 1835 to refute him? to support him?

The Inner Life of the Individual

The individual in a democratic society can, within limits, make of him or herself whatever courage and imagination will allow. Mature speculations, however, may produce haunting uncertainties. So it was with the poet Emily Dickinson (1830–1886). She apparently retreated from society. Her poetic vision, however, was imaginative and sharp. (Additional information on Dickinson is included in Unit 5 on page 344.)

"The Soul selects her own Society"

EMILY DICKINSON

The Soul selects her own Society—
Then—shuts the Door—
To her divine Majority—
Present no more—

Unmoved—she notes the Chariots—pausing—   5
At her low Gate—
Unmoved—an Emperor be kneeling
Upon her Mat—

I've known her—from an ample nation—
Choose One—   10
Then—close the Valves of her attention—
Like Stone—

Study Questions

1. When the Soul shuts the door (stanza 1), is the "divine Majority" then inside or outside? In either case, what is this "Majority," and why is it "divine"?

2. To what is the Soul compared in the first two stanzas?

3. How does the statement in stanza 3 add to your knowledge of the Soul? In what way does this indicate the speaker's individualism?

The Individual in the Local Community

Until he was 21, José Armas (1944—   ) was a farm worker. He now lives in Albuquerque, New Mexico, where he has taught at the University of Albuquerque and the University of New Mexico. He is founder and Managing Editor of *DeColores,* a quarterly journal, and Publisher of Pajarito Pub-lications. In addition to his writing, he is also involved in the community and has hosted a bi-weekly television program for Raza affairs. In the following short story, "A Delicate Balance," he uses fiction to examine an individual's relationship to his neighborhood.

A Delicate Balance

JOSÉ ARMAS

ROMERO ESTRADA had his home near the Golden Heights Centro where he spent a lot of time. He would get up almost every morning and clean and shave, and then after breakfast he would get his broom and go up and down the block sweeping the sidewalks for everyone. He would sweep in front of the Tortillería América, the Tres Milpas Bar, Barelas' Barbershop, the used furniture store owned by Goldstein, the corner grocery store, and Model Cities office, and the print shop. In the afternoons, he would come back and sit in the barbershop and just watch the people go by.

Sometimes, when there was no business, Barelas would let him sit in the barber chair, and Romero would love it. He would do this just about every day except Sundays and Mondays when Barelas' was closed. Over time, people got to expect Romero to do his little task of sweeping the sidewalks. When he was feeling real good, he would sweep in front of the houses on the block also.

Romero took great care to sweep cleanly, between the cracks and even between the sides of the buildings. Everything went into the gutter. The work took him the whole morning if he did it the way he wanted.

Romero was considered a little crazy by most people, but they pretty much tolerated him. Nobody minded much when he got too drunk at the Tres Milpas bar and went around telling everyone he loved them. "I love youuu," he would tell everyone.

"'*Ta bueno,* Romero, '*ta bueno. Ya vete,*"[1] they would tell him. Sometimes when he got too drunk and obnoxious, Tino, the bartender, would make him go home.

Romero received some kind of financial support, but it wasn't much. He was not given any credit by anyone because he would always forget to pay his bills. He didn't do it on purpose; he just never remembered. The business-

---

1 '*ta bueno. Ya vete:* Fine, fine. Now go away.

men preferred just to do things for him and give him things when they wanted. Barelas would trim his hair when things were slow; Tortillería América would give him *menudo* with fresh tortillas; the grocery store would give him overripe fruit and broken boxes of food that no one would buy.

When Barelas' oldest son, Seferino, graduated from high school, he went to work in his shop. Seferino took notice of Romero and came to feel sorry for him. One day, Romero was in the shop and Seferino decided to act.

"Mira, Romero. Yo te doy 50 centavos cada vez que me barras la acera. Fifty cents for every day you do the sidewalk for us. *¿Qué te parece?"* [2]

Romero thought about it carefully. *"Hecho.*

2 *¿Qué te parece?:* What do you think of that?

Done." he exclaimed. He started for home right away to get his broom.

"What did you do that for, *m'ijo,*"[3] asked Barelas.

"It don't seem right, Dad. The man works, and no one pays him for his work. Everyone should get paid for what they do."

"He don't need no pay. He has everything he needs."

"It's not the same, Dad. How would you like to do what he does and be treated the same way?"

"I'm not Romero. You don't know about these things, *m'ijo.* Romero would be unhappy if his routine was upset. Right now, everyone likes him and takes care of him. He sweeps the sidewalks because he wants something to do. Not because he wants some money."

"I'll pay him out of my money; don't worry about it."

"The money is not the point. The point is that money will not help Romero. Don't you understand that?"

"Look, Dad. Just put yourself in his place. Would you do it? Would you cut hair for nothing?"

Barelas knew his son was putting something over on him, but he didn't know how to answer. It made sense the way Seferino explained it, but it didn't seem right. On the other hand, Seferino had gone and finished high school. He must know something. Barelas didn't know many kids who had finished high school, much less gone to college. And his son was going to college in the fall. Barelas himself had never even gone to school. Maybe his son had something there; yet on the other hand. . . . Barelas had known Romero a long time. . . . Despite his uncertainty on the matter, Barelas decided to drop the issue and not say anything else about it.

Just then, Romero came back and started to sweep in front of Barelas' shop again, pushing what little dirt was left into the curb. He swept up the gutter, put the trash in a box and threw it in a garbage can.

Seferino watched with pride as Romero went about his job, and when Romero was finished Seferino went outside and told him he had done a good job and gave him his fifty cents.

Manolo was coming into the shop to get his hair cut as Seferino was giving Romero his wages. He noticed Romero with his broom. "What's going on?" he asked. Barelas shrugged his shoulders. "What's with Romero? Is he sick or something?"

"No, he's not sick," explained Seferino, who now was inside. He told Manolo the story.

"We're going to make Romero a businessman. Do you realize how much money he would make if people just paid him fifty cents a day, if everyone paid him just fifty cents? He does do a job, you know."

"Well, it makes sense," said Manolo.

"Maybe I'll ask people to do that," said Seferino. "That way the guy could make a decent wage. Do you want to help, Manolo? You can go with me to ask people to pay him."

"Well," said Manolo, "I'm not too good at asking people for money."

This did not stop Seferino. He contacted all the businesses in the neighborhood, but no one else wanted to contribute. Still, that didn't discourage Seferino either. He went on giving Romero fifty cents a day.

A couple of weeks later, Seferino heard that Romero had gotten credit at the grocery store. "See, Dad, what did I tell you? Things are getting better for him already. And look, it's only been a couple of weeks."

But, for the next week, Romero did not show up to sweep any sidewalks. He was around, but he didn't do any work for anybody. He walked around Golden Heights Centro in his best gray work pants and his slouch hat, trying his best to look important and walking right past the barbershop.

The following week, he came and asked to

3 *m'ijo:* my son.

talk with Seferino in private. They went into the back, where Barelas could not hear, and Romero informed Seferino that he wanted a raise.

"What! What do you mean a raise? You haven't worked for a week. You've only been doing this a couple of weeks, and now you want a raise?" Seferino was clearly angry, but Romero was calm and persistent. He pointed out that he had been sweeping the sidewalks for a long time—even before Seferino finished school.

"I deserve a raise," he insisted.

Seferino stared at Romero coldly. It was clearly a standoff in a labor-management confrontation.

Seferino said, "Look, maybe we should forget the whole thing. I was just trying to help you out, and now look at what you do."

Romero held his ground. "I helped you out, too. No one told me to do it, and I did it anyway. I helped you many years."

"Well, let's forget about the whole thing then," said Seferino.

"I quit then," said Romero.

"Quit!" exclaimed Seferino, laughing at the absurdity of the whole thing.

"Quit! I quit!" said Romero as he stormed out the front of the shop, passing Barelas who was cutting Pedrito's hair.

Seferino walked into the shop, shaking his head and laughing.

"Can you imagine that old guy?" he said. Barelas, for his part, did not seem too amused. He felt he could have predicted something like this would happen.

The next day, Romero was back sweeping the sidewalks again, but, when he came to the barbershop, he walked completely around it and then continued sweeping the rest of the sidewalks. After about a week of doing this everyday, he began sweeping the sidewalk all the way up to Barelas' and then pushing the trash to the sidewalk in front of the barbershop.

He had also stopped coming to the shop altogether. When he and Barelas met in the street, they would still greet each other. And Barelas would never bring up the fact that Romero kept pushing the trash in front of the shop. Things went on like that for a long time, until fall came and Seferino went off to college and stopped helping his father in the shop.

It was then that Romero began sweeping *all* the sidewalk again. He was happier then, and he even whistled and sang at his job.

Study Questions

1. At the beginning of the story what is the relationship between Romero and the people of his neighborhood? How is that relationship mutually rewarding?

2. What destroys the relationship? How is peace restored?

3. Why do you think Seferino, his father Barelas, and Romero act as they do?

4. There are different values at work in this story. How did Seferino lose the values of his parents and his community? How will this affect his trying to live in both Anglo and Chicano cultures?

5. How does the title "A Delicate Balance" relate this story to the theme of The Individual?

The Individual in Transition

Stephen Crane (1871–1900) gave up college to try newspaper work in his native New Jersey and in New York City. At twenty-four he published *The Red Badge of Courage,* the story of a young man's first battle experience in the Civil War. Crane was soon reporting war firsthand. He served as a newspaper correspondent during the Greek-Turkish War in 1897 and the Spanish-American War in 1898. The exposure and hardships he suffered as a reporter affected his health. He died of tuberculosis before reaching the age of twenty-nine.

Crane was fascinated by problems of heroism and courage wherever he found them. One background for some of his best writing was the American West. In Crane's lifetime the West was in transition from frontier to civilization. "The Bride Comes to Yellow Sky" is a story of a man who symbolizes that transition.

The Bride Comes to Yellow Sky

STEPHEN CRANE

I

THE GREAT PULLMAN was whirling onward with such dignity of motion that a glance from the window seemed simply to prove that the plains of Texas were pouring eastward. Vast flats of green grass, dull-hued spaces of mesquite and cactus, little groups of frame houses, woods of light and tender trees, all were sweeping into the east, sweeping over the horizon, a precipice.

A newly married pair had boarded this coach at San Antonio. The man's face was reddened from many days in the wind and sun, and a direct result of his new black clothes was that his brick-colored hands were constantly performing in a most conscious fashion. From time to time he looked down respectfully at his attire. He sat with a hand on each knee, like a man waiting in a barber's shop. The glances he devoted to other passengers were furtive and shy.

The bride was not pretty, nor was she very young. She wore a dress of blue cashmere, with small reservations of velvet here and there, and with steel buttons abounding. She continually twisted her head to regard her puff sleeves, very stiff, straight, and high. They embarrassed her. It was quite apparent that she had cooked, and that she expected to cook, dutifully. The blushes caused by the careless scrutiny of some passengers as she had entered the car were strange to see upon this plain, under-class countenance, which was drawn in placid, almost emotionless lines.

They were evidently very happy. "Ever been in a parlor car before?" he asked, smiling with delight.

"No," she answered; "I never was. It's fine, ain't it?"

"Great! And then after a while we'll go forward to the diner, and get a big layout. Finest meal in the world. Charge a dollar."

"Oh, do they?" cried the bride. "Charge a dollar? Why, that's too much—for us—ain't it, Jack?"

"Not this trip, anyhow," he answered bravely. "We're going to go the whole thing."

Later he explained to her about the trains. "You see, it's a thousand miles from one end of Texas to the other; and this train runs right across it, and never stops but four times." He had the pride of an owner. He pointed out to her the dazzling fittings of the coach; and in truth her eyes opened wider as she contemplated the sea-green figured velvet, the shining brass, silver, and glass, the wood that gleamed as darkly brilliant as the surface of a pool of oil. At one end a bronze figure sturdily held a support for a separated chamber, and at convenient places on the ceiling were frescoes in olive and silver.

To the minds of the pair, their surroundings reflected the glory of their marriage that morning in San Antonio; this was the environment of their new estate; and the man's face in particular beamed with an elation that made him appear ridiculous to the Negro porter. This individual at times surveyed them from afar with an amused and superior grin. On other occasions he bullied them with skill in ways that did not make it exactly plain to them that they were being bullied. He subtly used all the manners of the most unconquerable kind of snobbery. He oppressed them; but of this oppression they had small knowledge, and they speedily forgot that infrequently a number of travelers covered them with stares of derisive enjoyment. Historically there was supposed to be something infinitely humorous in their situation.

"We are due in Yellow Sky at 3:42," he said, looking tenderly into her eyes.

"Oh, are we?" she said, as if she had not been aware of it. To evince surprise at her husband's statement was part of her wifely amiability. She took from a pocket a little silver watch; and as she held it before her, and stared at it with a frown of attention, the new husband's face shone.

"I bought it in San Anton' from a friend of mine," he told her gleefully.

"It's seventeen minutes past twelve," she said, looking up at him with a kind of shy and clumsy coquetry. A passenger, noting this play, grew excessively sardonic, and winked at himself in one of the numerous mirrors.

At last they went to the dining car. Two rows of Negro waiters, in glowing white suits, surveyed their entrance with the interest, and also the equanimity, of men who had been forewarned. The pair fell to the lot of a waiter who happened to feel pleasure in steering them through their meal. He viewed them with the manner of a fatherly pilot, his countenance radiant with benevolence. The patronage, entwined with the ordinary deference, was not plain to them. And yet, as they returned to their coach, they showed in their faces a sense of escape.

To the left, miles down a long purple slope, was a little ribbon of mist where moved the keening Rio Grande. The train was approaching it at an angle, and the apex was Yellow Sky. Presently it was apparent that, as the distance from Yellow Sky grew shorter, the husband became commensurately restless. His brick-red hands were more insistent in their prominence. Occasionally he was even rather absentminded and faraway when the bride leaned forward and addressed him.

As a matter of truth, Jack Potter was beginning to find the shadow of a deed weigh upon him like a leaden slab. He, the town marshal of Yellow Sky, a man known, liked, and feared in his corner, a prominent person, had gone to San Antonio to meet a girl he believed he loved, and there, after the usual prayers, had

actually induced her to marry him, without consulting Yellow Sky for any part of the transaction. He was now bringing his bride before an innocent and unsuspecting community.

Of course people in Yellow Sky married as it pleased them, in accordance with a general custom; but such was Potter's thought of his duty to his friends, or of their idea of his duty, or of an unspoken form which does not control men in these matters, that he felt he was heinous. He had committed an extraordinary crime. Face to face with this girl in San Antonio, and spurred by his sharp impulse, he had gone headlong over all the social hedges. At San Antonio he was like a man hidden in the dark. A knife to sever any friendly duty, any form, was easy to his hand in that remote city. But the hour of Yellow Sky—the hour of daylight—was approaching.

He knew full well that his marriage was an important thing to his town. It could only be exceeded by the burning of the new hotel. His friends could not forgive him. Frequently he had reflected on the advisability of telling them by telegraph, but a new cowardice had been upon him. He feared to do it. And now the train was hurrying him toward a scene of amazement, glee, and reproach. He glanced out of the window at the line of haze swinging slowly in toward the train.

Yellow Sky had a kind of brass band, which played painfully, to the delight of the populace. He laughed without heart as he thought of it. If the citizens could dream of his prospective arrival with his bride, they would parade the band at the station and escort them, amid cheers and laughing congratulations, to his adobe home.

He resolved that he would use all the devices of speed and plainscraft in making the journey from the station to his house. Once within that safe citadel, he could issue some sort of a vocal bulletin, and then not go among the citizens until they had time to wear off a little of their enthusiasm.

The bride looked anxiously at him. "What's worrying you, Jack?"

He laughed again. "I'm not worrying, girl; I'm only thinking of Yellow Sky."

She flushed in comprehension.

A sense of mutual guilt invaded their minds and developed a finer tenderness. They looked at each other with eyes softly aglow. But Potter often laughed the same nervous laugh; the flush upon the bride's face seemed quite permanent.

The traitor to the feelings of Yellow Sky narrowly watched the speeding landscape. "We're nearly there," he said.

Presently the porter came and announced the proximity of Potter's home. He held a brush in his hand, and, with all his airy superiority gone, he brushed Potter's new clothes as the latter slowly turned this way and that way. Potter fumbled out a coin and gave it to the porter, as he had seen others do. It was a heavy and muscle-bound business, as that of a man shoeing his first horse.

The porter took their bag, and as the train began to slow they moved forward to the hooded platform of the car. Presently the two engines and their long string of coaches rushed into the station of Yellow Sky.

"They have to take water here," said Potter, from a constricted throat and in mournful cadence, as one announcing death. Before the train stopped his eye had swept the length of the platform, and he was glad and astonished to see there was none upon it but the station agent, who, with a slightly hurried and anxious air, was walking toward the water tanks. When the train had halted, the porter alighted first, and placed in position a little temporary step.

"Come on, girl," said Potter, hoarsely. As he helped her down they each laughed on a false note. He took the bag from the Negro, and bade his wife cling to his arm. As they slunk rapidly away, his hangdog glance perceived that they were unloading the two trunks, and also that the station agent, far ahead near the baggage car, had turned and was running toward him, making gestures. He laughed, and groaned as he laughed, when he noted the first effect of his marital bliss upon Yellow Sky. He gripped his wife's arm firmly to his side, and they fled. Behind them the porter stood, chuckling fatuously.

II

The California express on the Southern Railway was due at Yellow Sky in twenty-one minutes. There were six men at the bar of the Weary Gentleman Saloon. One was a drummer,[1] who talked a great deal and rapidly; three were Texans, who did not care to talk at that time; and two were Mexican sheepherders, who did not talk as a general practice in the Weary Gentleman Saloon. The barkeeper's dog lay on the board walk that crossed in front of the door. His head was on his paws, and he glanced drowsily here and there with the constant vigilance of a dog that is kicked on occasion. Across the sandy street were some vivid green grassplots, so wonderful in appearance, amid the sands that burned near them in a blazing sun, that they caused a doubt in the mind. They exactly resembled the grass mats used to represent lawns on the stage. At the cooler end of the railway station, a man without a coat sat in a tilted chair and smoked his pipe. The fresh-cut bank of the Rio Grande circled near the town, and there could be seen beyond it a great plum-colored plain of mesquite.

Save for the busy drummer and his companions in the saloon, Yellow Sky was dozing. The newcomer leaned gracefully upon the bar, and recited many tales with the confidence of a bard who has come upon a new field.

"—and at the moment that the old man fell downstairs with the bureau in his arms, the old

---

1 **drummer:** traveling salesman.

woman was coming up with two scuttles of coal, and of course—"

The drummer's tale was interrupted by a young man who suddenly appeared in the open door. He cried: "Scratchy Wilson's drunk, and has turned loose with both hands." The two Mexicans at once set down their glasses and faded out of the rear entrance of the saloon.

The drummer, innocent and jocular, answered: "All right, old man. S'pose he has? Come in and have a drink, anyhow."

But the information had made such an obvious cleft in every skull in the room that the drummer was obliged to see its importance. All had become instantly solemn. "Say," said he, mystified, "what is this?" His three companions made the introductory gesture of eloquent speech; but the young man at the door forestalled them.

"It means, my friend," he answered, as he came into the saloon, "that for the next two hours this town won't be a health resort."

The barkeeper went to the door, and locked and barred it; reaching out of the window, he pulled in heavy wooden shutters, and barred them. Immediately a solemn, chapellike gloom was upon the place. The drummer was looking from one to another.

"But say," he cried, "what is this, anyhow? You don't mean there is going to be a gunfight?"

"Don't know whether there'll be a fight or not," answered one man, grimly; "but there'll be some shootin'—some good shootin'."

The young man who had warned them waved his hand. "Oh, there'll be a fight fast enough, if anyone wants it. Anybody can get a fight out there in the street. There's a fight just waiting."

The drummer seemed to be swayed between the interest of a foreigner and a perception of personal danger.

"What did you say his name was?" he asked.

"Scratchy Wilson," they answered in chorus.

"And will he kill anybody? What are you going to do? Does this happen often? Does he rampage around like this once a week or so? Can he break in that door?"

"No; he can't break down that door," replied the barkeeper. "He's tried it three times. But when he comes you'd better lay down on the floor, stranger. He's dead sure to shoot at it, and a bullet may come through."

Thereafter the drummer kept a strict eye upon the door. The time had not yet been called for him to hug the floor, but, as a minor precaution, he sidled near to the wall. "Will he kill anybody? " he said again.

The men laughed low and scornfully at the question.

"He's out to shoot, and he's out for trouble. Don't see any good in experimentin' with him."

"But what do you do in a case like this? What do you do?"

A man responded: "Why, he and Jack Potter—"

"But," in chorus the other men interrupted, "Jack Potter's in San Anton'."

"Well, who is he? What's he got to do with it?"

"Oh, he's the town marshal. He goes out and fights Scratchy when he gets on one of these tears."

"Wow!" said the drummer, mopping his brow. "Nice job he's got."

The voices had toned away to mere whisperings. The drummer wished to ask further questions, which were born of an increasing anxiety and bewilderment; but when he attempted them, the men merely looked at him in irritation and motioned him to remain silent. A tense waiting hush was upon them. In the deep shadows of the room their eyes shone as they listened for sounds from the street. One man made three gestures at the barkeeper; and the latter, moving like a ghost, handed him a glass and a bottle. The man poured a full glass of whisky, and set down the bottle noiselessly. He gulped the whisky in a shallow, and turned again toward the door in immovable silence. The drummer saw that the barkeeper, without a sound, had taken a Winchester from beneath the bar. Later he saw this individual beckoning to him, so he tiptoed across the room.

"You better come with me back of the bar."

"No, thanks," said the drummer, perspiring; "I'd rather be where I can make a break for the back door."

Whereupon the man of bottles made a kindly but peremptory gesture. The drummer obeyed it, and, finding himself seated on a box with his head below the level of the bar, balm was laid upon his soul at sight of various zinc and copper fittings that bore a resemblance to armor plate. The barkeeper took a seat comfortably upon an adjacent box.

"You see," he whispered, "this here Scratchy Wilson is a wonder with a gun—a perfect wonder; and when he goes on the war-trail, we hunt our holes—naturally. He's about the last one of the old gang that used to hang out along the river here. He's a terror

when he's drunk. When he's sober he's all right—kind of simple—wouldn't hurt a fly—nicest fellow in town. But when he's drunk—whoo!"

There were periods of stillness. "I wish Jack Potter was back from San Anton'," said the barkeeper. "He shot Wilson up once—in the leg—and he would sail in and pull out the kinks in this thing."

Presently they heard from a distance the sound of a shot, followed by three wild yowls. It instantly removed a bond from the men in the darkened saloon. There was a shuffling of feet. They looked at each other. "Here he comes," they said.

III

A man in a maroon-colored flannel shirt, which had been purchased for purposes of decoration, and made principally by some Jewish women on the East Side of New York, rounded a corner and walked into the middle of the main street of Yellow Sky. In either hand the man held a long, heavy, blue-black revolver. Often he yelled, and these cries rang through a semblance of a deserted village, shrilly flying over the roofs in a volume that seemed to have no relation to the ordinary vocal strength of a man. It was as if the surrounding stillness formed the arch of a tomb over him. These cries of ferocious challenge rang against walls of silence. And his boots had red tops with gilded imprints, of the kind beloved in winter by little sledding boys on the hillsides of New England.

The man's face flamed in a rage begot of whisky. His eyes, rolling, and yet keen for ambush, hunted the still doorways and windows. He walked with the creeping movement of the midnight cat. As it occurred to him, he roared menacing information. The long revolvers in his hands were as easy as straws; they were moved with an electric swiftness. The little fingers of each hand played sometimes in a musician's way. Plain from the low collar of the shirt, the cords of his neck straightened and sank, straightened and sank, as passion moved him. The only sounds were his terrible invitations. The calm adobes preserved their demeanor at the passing of this small thing in the middle of the street.

There was no offer of fight—no offer of fight. The man called to the sky. There were no attractions. He bellowed and fumed and swayed his revolvers here and everywhere.

The dog of the barkeeper of the Weary Gentleman Saloon had not appreciated the advance of events. He yet lay dozing in front of his master's door. At sight of the dog, the man paused and raised his revolver humorously. At sight of the man, the dog sprang up and walked diagonally away, with a sullen head, and growling. The man yelled, and the dog broke into a gallop. As it was about to enter an alley, there was a loud noise, a whistling, and something spat the ground directly before it. The dog screamed, and, wheeling in terror, galloped headlong in a new direction. Again there was a noise, a whistling, and sand was kicked viciously before it. Fearstricken, the dog turned and flurried like an animal in a pen. The man stood laughing, his weapons at his hips.

Ultimately the man was attracted by the closed door of the Weary Gentleman Saloon. He went to it, and, hammering with a revolver, demanded drink.

The door remaining imperturbable, he picked a bit of paper from the walk, and nailed it to the framework with a knife. He then turned his back contemptuously upon this popular resort, and, walking to the opposite side of the street, and spinning there on his heel quickly and lithely, fired at the bit of paper. He missed it by a half-inch. He swore at himself, and went away. Later he comfortably fusilladed the windows of his most intimate friend. The man was playing with this town; it was a toy for him.

But still there was no offer of fight. The name of Jack Potter, his ancient antagonist, entered his mind, and he concluded that it would be a glad thing if he should go to Potter's house, and by bombardment induce him to come out and fight. He moved in the direction of his desire, chanting Apache scalp-music.

When he arrived at it, Potter's house presented the same still front as had the other adobes. Taking up a strategic position, the man howled a challenge. But this house regarded him as might a great stone god. It gave no sign. After a decent wait, the man howled further challenges, mingling with them wonderful epithets.

Presently there came the spectacle of a man churning himself into deepest rage over the immobility of a house. He fumed at it as the winter wind attacks a prairie cabin in the North. To the distance there should have gone the sound of a tumult like the fighting of two hundred Mexicans. As necessity bade him, he paused for breath or to reload his revolvers.

IV

Potter and his bride walked sheepishly and with speed. Sometimes they laughed together shamefacedly and low.

"Next corner, dear," he said finally.

They put forth the efforts of a pair walking bowed against a strong wind. Potter was about to raise a finger to point the first appearance of the new home when, as they circled the corner, they came face to face with a man in a maroon-colored shirt, who was feverishly pushing cartridges into a large revolver. Upon the instant the man dropped his revolver to the ground, and, like lightning, whipped another from its holster. The second weapon was aimed at the bridegroom's chest.

There was a silence. Potter's mouth seemed to be merely a grave for his tongue. He exhibited an instinct to at once loosen his arm from

the woman's grip, and he dropped the bag to the sand. As for the bride, her face had gone as yellow as old cloth. She was a slave to hideous rites, gazing at the apparitional snake.

The two men faced each other at a distance of three paces. He of the revolver smiled with a new and quiet ferocity.

"Tried to sneak up on me," he said. "Tried to sneak up on me!" His eyes grew more baleful. As Potter made a slight movement, the man thrust his revolver venomously forward. "No; don't you do it, Jack Potter. Don't you move a finger toward a gun just yet. Don't you move an eyelash. The time has come for me to settle with you, and I'm goin' to do it my own way, and loaf along with no interferin'. So if you don't want a gun bent on you, just mind what I tell you."

Potter looked at his enemy. "I ain't got a gun on me, Scratchy," he said. "Honest, I ain't." He was stiffening and steadying, but yet somewhere at the back of his mind a vision of the Pullman floated: the sea-green figured velvet, the shining brass, silver, and glass, the wood that gleamed as darkly brilliant as the surface of a pool of oil—all the glory of the marriage, the environment of the new estate. "You know I fight when it comes to fighting, Scratchy Wilson; but I ain't got a gun on me. You'll have to do all the shootin' yourself."

His enemy's face went livid. He stepped forward, and lashed his weapon to and fro before Potter's chest. "Don't you tell me you ain't got no gun on you, you whelp. Don't tell me no lie like that. There ain't a man in Texas ever seen you without no gun. Don't take me for no kid." His eyes blazed with light, and his throat worked like a pump.

"I ain't takin' you for no kid," answered Potter. His heels had not moved an inch backward. "I'm takin' you for a——fool. I tell you I ain't got a gun, and I ain't. If you're goin' to shoot me up, you better begin now; you'll never get a chance like this again."

So much enforced reasoning had told on Wilson's rage; he was calmer. "If you ain't got a gun, why ain't you got a gun?" he sneered. "Been to Sunday school?"

"I ain't got a gun because I've just come from San Anton' with my wife. I'm married," said Potter. "And if I'd thought there was going to be any galoots like you prowling around when I brought my wife home, I'd had a gun, and don't you forget it."

"Married!" said Scratchy, not at all comprehending.

"Yes, married. I'm married," said Potter, distinctly.

"Married?" said Scratchy. Seemingly for the first time, he saw the drooping, drowning woman at the other man's side. "No!" he said. He was like a creature allowed a glimpse of another world. He moved a pace backward, and his arm, with the revolver, dropped to his side. "Is this the lady?" he asked.

"Yes; this is the lady," answered Potter.

There was another period of silence.

"Well," said Wilson at last, slowly, "I s'pose it's all off now."

"It's all off if you say so, Scratchy. You know I didn't make the trouble." Potter lifted his valise.

"Well, I 'low it's off, Jack," said Wilson. He was looking at the ground. "Married!" He was not a student of chivalry; it was merely that in the presence of this foreign condition he was a simple child of the earlier plains. He picked up his starboard revolver, and, placing both weapons in their holsters, he went away. His feet made funnel-shaped tracks in the heavy sand.

Study Questions

1. How do Jack Potter and his bride show their uneasiness? How do the furnishings of the train and the other people aboard contribute to this picture of uneasiness?

2. Jack is also bothered by something more than newlywed nervousness. What else is on his mind? What is learned in Section II that reinforces this concern?

3. What other information is provided in Section II that foreshadows the conflict in the story?

4. Who is the antagonist in this story? Describe the antagonist's character. How does he contrast with Jack, the protagonist?

5. The fourth section contains the elements of the usual climax for "westerns"—the "showdown" between two gunmen. What makes this showdown comic and anticlimactic?

6. How does the title summarize the issues in this story? How does this reflect the theme of The Individual?

Vocabulary

A **verbal analogy** problem compares one feature which two pairs of words have in common. In the following sentence, for example, the first and second word-pairs consist of antonyms and therefore share the feature of oppositeness:

Friend is to *enemy* as *closed* is to *open*.

Besides oppositeness, the two word-pairs in a verbal analogy problem may have some other feature in common including one of these:

1. Both word-pairs may be synonyms.
   (*Correct* is to *right* as *ill* is to *sick*.)

2. Both word-pairs may show cause and effect.
   (*Mirror* is to *reflection* as *sleep* is to *rest*.)

3. Both word-pairs may show a part-to-whole relationship.
   (*Book* is to *school* as *bullet* is to *gunfight*.)

4. Each word-pair may consist of different forms of the same word.
   (*Mechanic* is to *mechanics* as *society* is to *societies*.)

When a verbal analogy problem is used in a vocabulary examination, it usually appears in an abbreviated version, with colons (:) replacing the words *is to* and *as*. For example:

friend : enemy :: closed : open

In examinations, verbal analogy problems are arranged so that the test-taker has a choice of answers.

friend : *enemy* ::
(a) washing : clean   (b) emperor : empire   (c) closed : open
(d) doubt : uncertainty   (e) trousers : clothing

Before starting the following exercise on verbal analogies, number 1-10 on a separate sheet of paper. Then, after each number, copy the word-pair that has the closest similarity to the one which appears in *italics*.

1. *Texas* : *San Antonio* ::
   (a) New Orleans : Louisiana   (b) house : bedroom
   (c) vegetables : grocery store   (d) street : sidewalk
   (e) valise : luggage

2. *majority* : *minority* ::
   (a) carol : song   (b) education : graduation
   (c) chaos : order   (d) mason : bricks
   (e) trustworthy : capable

3. *barber* : *haircut* ::
   (a) corn : farmer   (b) passenger : train
   (c) construction : carpenter   (d) legislator : law
   (e) barkeeper : saloon

4. *erroneous* : *error* ::
   (a) creative : creation   (b) melody : melodic
   (c) individualism : individuality   (d) selfishness : selfish
   (e) measurement : measure

5. *cut* : *sever* ::
   (a) stationary : moving   (b) Ohio : United States
   (c) mother : child   (d) vice : virtue
   (e) solitude : isolation

6. *cent* : *money* ::
   (a) jade : mineral   (b) ceremony : wedding
   (c) food : rice   (d) public : private
   (e) cat : mice

7. *broom* : *sweep* ::
   (a) sew : thread   (b) fruit : tree
   (c) wages : salary   (d) drum : band
   (e) car : drive

8. *management* : *labor* ::
   (a) predict : foretell   (b) hour : time
   (c) ancestor : descendant   (d) wagon : chariot
   (e) drunkenness : liquor

9. *shoemaker* : *cobbler* ::
   (a) bride : groom   (b) devil : demon
   (c) guilt : innocence   (d) revolver : firearm
   (e) landlord : rent

10. *obey* : *obedience* ::
    (a) art : artist   (b) laboratory : labor
    (c) agree : disagreement   (d) expect : expectation
    (e) aristocratic : aristocracy

The Tension Within

While the previous story by Crane focuses on the tension between society and the individual, the poem below dramatizes the tension that can take place within an individual. Inner tension can come from the effort to reconcile traditional ways with the ways of the new world. This poem written by Cathy Song describes this conflict. Cathy Song, whose mother is Chinese and father is Korean, was born and reared in Hawaii. She received her B.A. degree from Wellesley College in Massachusetts.

Lost Sister

CATHY SONG

1.

In China,
even the peasants
named their first daughters,
Jade—
the stone that in the far fields   5
could moisten the dry season,
could make men move mountains
for the healing green of the inner hills,
glistening like slices of winter melon.

And the daughters were grateful: 10
they never left home.
To move freely was a luxury
stolen from them at birth.
Instead, they gathered patience,
learning to walk in shoes   15
the size of teacups,

without breaking—
the arc of their movements
as dormant as the rooted willow,
as redundant as the farmyard hens.   20
But they travelled far
in surviving,
learning to stretch the family rice,
to quiet the demons,
the noisy stomachs.   25

      2.

There is a sister
across the ocean,
who relinquished her name,
diluting jade green
with the blue of the Pacific.   30
Rising with a tide of locusts,
she swarmed with others
to inundate another shore.
In America,
there are many roads   35
and women can stride along with men.

But in another wilderness,
the possibilities,
the loneliness,
can strangulate like jungle vines.   40
The meager provisions and sentiments
of once belonging:
fermented roots, mahjong[1] tiles and fire crackers;
cannot shake away the ghosts,
sets but a flimsy household   45
in a forest of nightless cities.
A giant snake rattles above,
spewing black clouds into your kitchen.
Dough faced landlords
slip in and out of your keyholes,   50
making claims you don't understand,
tapping into your communication systems
of laundry lines and restaurant chains.

---

1 **mahjong:** a game played with tiles.

You find you need China:
your one fragile identification,   55
a jade link
handcuffed to your wrist.

You remember your mother
who walked for centuries,
footless—   60
and like her,
you have left no footprints,
but only because
there is an ocean inbetween,
the unremitting space of your rebellion.   65

Study Questions

1. What is the time and place in the first section of the poem? How did the daughters retain their individuality and self-respect even though their movements were limited?

2. What is the time and place of the second section? What do lines 28–30 mean? What is the major difference between the two places as expressed in lines 35–40?

3. What are some of the difficulties in the new place?

4. Why do you think the speaker needs China? How does this need support her individuality?

The Creative Individual

James Baldwin (1924—   ) grew up in the Harlem section of New York City. Like many American writers before him, however, he went to Paris to work out his relationship to himself and his country. In Paris he completed the first of many novels, *Go Tell It on the Mountain,* which was published in 1953. Some of Baldwin's other novels are: *Giovanni's Room* (1956), *Another Country* (1962), and most recently *Just Above My Head* (1979). Though he is a leading contemporary writer, Baldwin is perhaps best known as a literary critic and social commentator.

Baldwin describes himself as a "public witness" to the situation of Blacks in America. His collections of essays, *Notes of a Native Son* (1955), *Nobody Knows My Name* (1961), *The Fire Next Time* (1963), and *No Name in the Street* (1972), attest to his skill as a witness. In "The Creative Dilemma," included here he presents the case for society's need of the critical artist.

The Creative Dilemma

JAMES BALDWIN

PERHAPS THE PRIMARY distinction of the artist is that he must actively cultivate that state which most men, necessarily, must avoid: the state of being alone. That all men *are,* when the chips are down, alone, is a banality—a banality because it is very frequently stated, but very rarely, on the evidence, believed. Most of us are not compelled to linger with the knowledge of our aloneness, for it is a knowledge that can paralyze all action in this world. There are, forever, swamps to be drained, cities to be created, mines to be exploited, children to be fed. None of these things can be done alone. But the conquest of the physical world is not man's only duty. He is also enjoined to conquer the great wilderness of himself. The precise role of the artist, then, is to illuminate that darkness, blaze roads through that vast forest, so that we will not, in all our doing, lose sight of its purpose, which is, after all, to make the world a more human dwelling place.

The state of being alone is not meant to bring to mind merely a rustic musing beside some silver lake. The aloneness of which I speak is much more like the aloneness of birth or death. It is like the fearful aloneness that one sees in the eyes of someone who is suffering, whom we cannot help. Or it is like the aloneness of love, the force and mystery that so many have extolled and so many have cursed, but which no one has ever understood or ever really been able to control. I put the matter this way, not out of any desire to create pity for the artist—God forbid!—but to suggest how nearly, after all, is his state the state of everyone, and in an attempt to make vivid his endeavor. The states of birth, suffering, love, and death are extreme states—extreme, universal, and inescapable. We all know this, but we would rather not know it. The artist is present to correct the delusions to which we fall prey in our attempts to avoid this knowledge.

It is for this reason that all societies have battled with that incorrigible disturber of the peace—the artist. I doubt that future societies will get on with him any better. The entire purpose of society is to create a bulwark against the inner and the outer chaos, in order to make life bearable and to keep the human race alive. And it is absolutely inevitable that when a tradition has been evolved, whatever the tradition is, the people, in general, will suppose it to have existed from before the beginning of time and will be most unwilling and indeed unable to conceive of any changes in it. They do not know how they will live without those traditions that have given them their identity. Their reaction, when it is suggested that they can or that they must, is panic. And we see this panic, I think, everywhere in the world today, from the streets of New Orleans to the grisly battleground of Algeria.[1] And a higher level of consciousness among the people is the only hope we have, now or in the future, of minimizing human damage.

The artist is distinguished from all other responsible actors in society—the politicians, legislators, educators, and scientists by the fact that he is his own test tube, his own laboratory, working according to very rigorous rules, however unstated these may be, and cannot allow any consideration to supersede his responsibility to reveal all that he can possibly discover concerning the mystery of the human

being. Society must accept some things as real; but he must always know that visible reality hides a deeper one, and that all our action and achievement rests on things unseen. A society must assume that it is stable, but the artist must know, and he must let us know, that there is nothing stable under heaven. One cannot possibly build a school, teach a child, or drive a car without taking some things for granted. The artist cannot and must not take anything for granted, but must drive to the heart of every answer and expose the question the answer hides.

I seem to be making extremely grandiloquent claims for a breed of men and women historically despised while living and acclaimed when safely dead. But, in a way, the belated honor that all societies tender their artists proves the reality of the point I am trying to make. I am really trying to make clear the nature of the artist's responsibility to his society. The peculiar nature of this responsibility is that he must never cease warring with it, for its sake and for his own. For the truth, in spite of appearances and all our hopes, is that everything is always changing and the measure of our maturity as nations and as men is how well prepared we are to meet these changes and, further, to use them for our health.

Now, anyone who has ever been compelled to think about it—anyone, for example, who has ever been in love—knows that the one face that one can never see is one's own face. One's lover—or one's brother, or one's enemy—sees the face you wear, and this face can elicit the most extraordinary reactions. We do the things we do and feel what we feel essentially because we must—we are responsible for our actions, but we rarely understand them. It goes without saying, I believe, that if we understood ourselves better, we would damage ourselves less. But the barrier between oneself and one's knowledge of oneself is high indeed. There are so many things one would rather not know! We become social creatures because

---

1 **Algeria:** Baldwin refers to the fighting then taking place in this colonial French North African country during the rebellion against France.

we cannot live any other way. But in order to become social, there are a great many other things that we must not become, and we are frightened, all of us, of those forces within us that perpetually menace our precarious security. Yet the forces are there; we cannot will them away. All we can do is learn to live with them. And we cannot learn this unless we are willing to tell the truth about ourselves, and the truth about us is always at variance with what we wish to be. The human effort is to bring these two realities into a relationship resembling reconciliation. The human beings whom we respect the most, after all—and sometimes fear the most—are those who are most deeply involved in this delicate and strenuous effort, for they have the unshakable authority that comes only from having looked on and endured and survived the worst. That nation is healthiest which has the least necessity to distrust or ostracize or victimize these people—whom, as I say, we honor, once they are gone, because somewhere in our hearts we know that we cannot live without them.

The dangers of being an American artist are not greater than those of being an artist anywhere else in the world, but they are very particular. These dangers are produced by our history. They rest on the fact that in order to conquer this continent, the particular aloneness of which I speak—the aloneness in which one discovers that life is tragic, and therefore unutterably beautiful—could not be permitted. And that this prohibition is typical of all emergent nations will be proved, I have no doubt, in many ways during the next fifty

years. This continent now is conquered, but our habits and our fears remain. And, in the same way that to become a social human being one modifies and suppresses and, ultimately, without great courage, lies to oneself about all one's interior, uncharted chaos, so have we, as a nation, modified and suppressed and lied about all the darker forces in our history. We know, in the case of the person, that whoever cannot tell himself the truth about his past is trapped in it, is immobilized in the prison of his undiscovered self. This is also true of nations. We know how a person, in such a paralysis, is unable to assess either his weaknesses or his strengths, and how frequently indeed he mistakes the one for the other. And this, I think, we do. We are the strongest nation in the Western world, but this is not for the reasons that we think. It is because we have an opportunity that no other nation has of moving beyond the Old World concepts of race and class and caste, to create, finally, what we must have had in mind when we first began speaking of the New World. But the price of this is a long look backward whence we came and an unflinching assessment of the record. For an artist, the record of that journey is most clearly revealed in the personalities of the people the journey produced. Societies never know it, but the war of an artist with his society is a lover's war, and he does, at his best, what lovers do, which is to reveal the beloved to himself and, with that revelation, to make freedom real.

Study Questions

1. According to Baldwin, what is the role of the artist in society? Why is the artist especially qualified for that role?

2. In Baldwin's view, why does society tend to reject the artist? Why is it important nevertheless for the artist to insist on playing a part in society?

3. What is Baldwin's explanation for the fact that artists are not usually honored during their lifetimes?

4. Why does Baldwin say that the artist has a special role in America?

5. What, then, is the creative dilemma of the artist? How is the relationship between an artist and society described?

Composition

1. Summarize Baldwin's essay in your own words. Be sure to include each of his points. Conclude with a statement on whether or not you agree with his position on the artist's role in society and why.

2. Baldwin makes this statement in "The Creative Dilemma": "We know, in the case of the person, that whoever cannot tell himself [herself] the truth about his [her] past is trapped in it, is immobilized in the prison of his [her] undiscovered self." Write a descriptive narrative of a situation, either real or imaginary, which supports this statement. Be sure to describe the past and tell how it trapped the person. Tell how an examination of the past provided a release. Conclude by relating this situation to the theme of The Individual.

The Individual as a Family Member

In her prolific career as an anthropologist, Margaret Mead (1901–1978) studied the biological, psychological, and sociological forces that shaped personality in simple societies such as Samoa and New Guinea. Then she used what she learned to explain lucidly how individuals learn adult roles in contemporary complex societies. Mead's autobiography of the first half of her life, *Blackberry Winter,* is the story of a spirited, courageous woman. She had an insatiable curiosity on hundreds of subjects from global pollution to women's liberation.

How does a young person develop this kind of individuality while growing up around strong personalities in a family unit? This excerpt from *Blackberry Winter* describes a grandmother who was a definite influence on the personality of Margaret Mead.

On Being a Granddaughter

MARGARET MEAD

MY PATERNAL grandmother, who lived with us from the time my parents married until she died in 1927, while I was studying anthropological collections in German museums, was the most decisive influence in my life. She sat at the center of our household. Her room—and my mother always saw to it that she had the best room, spacious and sunny, with a fireplace if possible—was the place to which we immediately went when we came in from playing or home from school. There my father went when he arrived in the house. There we did our lessons on the cherry-wood table with which she had begun housekeeping and which, later, was my dining room table for twenty-five years. There, sitting by the fire, erect and intense, she listened to us and to all of Mother's friends and to our friends. In my early childhood she was also very active—cooking, preserving, growing flowers in the garden, and attentive to all the activities of the country and the farm, including the chickens that were always invading the lawn and that I was always being called from my book to shoo away.

My mother was trustworthy in all matters that concerned our care. Grandma was trustworthy in a quite different way. She meant exactly what she said, always. If you borrowed her scissors, you returned them. In like case, Mother would wail ineffectually, "Why does everyone borrow my scissors and never return them?" and Father would often utter idle threats. But Grandma never threatened. She never raised her voice. She simply commanded respect and obedience by her complete expectation that she would be obeyed. And she never gave silly orders. She became my model when, in later life, I tried to formulate a role for the modern parent who can no longer exact obedience merely by virtue of being a parent and yet must be able to get obedience when it is necessary. Grandma never said, "Do this because Grandma says so," or "because Grandma wants you to do it." She simply said, "Do it," and I knew from her tone of voice that it was necessary.

My grandmother grew up in the little town of Winchester, in Adams County, Ohio, which two of my great-great grandfathers had founded. She was one of nine children who reached adulthood. Her father was a farmer, a small entrepreneur, a member of the state legislature, a justice of the peace, and the Methodist local preacher. His name was Richard Ramsay, and in our family there have been so many Richards that they have to be referred to as Uncle El's Richard, Grace Bradford's Richard, and so on.

My grandmother began school teaching quite young, at a time when it was still somewhat unusual for a girl to teach school. When my grandfather, who was also a teacher, came home from the Civil War, he married my grandmother and they went to college together. They also graduated together. She gave a graduation address in the morning and my grandfather, who gave one in the afternoon,

Margaret Mead's paternal grandparents.

was introduced as the husband of Mrs. Mead who spoke this morning.

My grandfather was a school superintendent who was such a vigorous innovator that exhausted school boards used to request him to leave after a one-year term—with the highest credentials—to undertake the reform of some other school. We have a few examples of my grandmother's letters to him while they were engaged, including admonitions not to go on picnics on the Sabbath. He died when my father was six. Two days later the principal took his place and my grandmother took the principal's place. From then on she taught, sometimes in high school, sometimes small children, until she came to live with us when my parents married. It was the small children in whom she was most interested, and I have the notes she took on the schools she observed during a visit to Philadelphia before my parents' marriage.

She understood many things that are barely recognized in the wider educational world even today. For example, she realized that arithmetic is injurious to young minds and so, after I had learned my tables, she taught me

Margaret Mead and her mother.

to kindergarten, for Grandma believed in training the hands early, though not with too fine work, and the year I was eight, when I went to school for a half-day in the fourth grade in Swarthmore, she taught me until I went to high school and even then helped me with my lessons when my teachers were woefully inadequate, as they often were. I never expected any teacher to know as much as my parents or my grandmother did. Although my grandmother had no Greek, she had a good deal of Latin, and I remember that once, on the Fourth of July, she picked up one of my brother's Latin texts because she had never read Sallust.

She was conscious of the developmental differences between boys and girls and considered boys to be much more vulnerable and in need of patience from their teachers than were girls of the same age. This was part of the background of my learning the meaning of gender. And just as Grandma thought boys were more vulnerable, my father thought it was easier for girls to do well in school, and so he always required me to get two and a half points higher than my brother in order to win the same financial bonus.

Grandma had no sense at all of ever having been handicapped by being a woman. I think she played as strong a role among her brothers and sisters as her elder brother, who was a famous Methodist preacher. Between them they kept up an active relationship with their parents in Winchester and, returning often for visits, they supervised, stimulated, and advised the less adventurous members of the family. This has now become my role among some of the descendants of my grandmother's sisters, who still live in various small towns and large cities in Ohio.

Grandma was a wonderful storyteller, and she had a set of priceless, individually tailored anecdotes with which American grandparents of her day brought up children. There was the story of the little boys who had been taught absolute, quick obedience. One day when they

algebra. She also understood the advantages of learning both inductively and deductively. On some days she gave me a set of plants to analyze; on others, she gave me a description and sent me out to the woods and meadows to collect examples, say, of the "mint family." She thought that memorizing mere facts was not very important and that drill was stultifying. The result was that I was not well drilled in geography or spelling. But I learned to observe the world around me and to note what I saw—to observe flowers and children and baby chicks. She taught me to read for the sense of what I read and to enjoy learning.

With the exception of the two years I went

were out on the prairie, their father shouted, "Fall down on your faces!" They did, and the terrible prairie fire swept over them *and they weren't hurt.* There was also the story of three boys at school, each of whom received a cake sent from home. One hoarded his, and the mice ate it; one ate all of his, and he got sick; and who do you think had the best time?— why, of course, the one who shared his cake with his friends. Then there was the little boy who ran away from home and stayed away all day. When he came home after supper, he found the family sitting around the fire and nobody said a word. Not a word. Finally, he couldn't stand it anymore and said, "Well, I see you have the same old cat!" And there was one about a man who was so lazy he would rather starve than work. Finally, his neighbors decided to bury him alive. On the way to the cemetery they met a man with a wagonload of unshelled corn. He asked where they were going. When they told him that they were going to bury that no-good man alive, the owner of the corn took pity on him and said, "I tell you what. I will give you this load of corn. All you will have to do is shell it." But the lazy man said, "Drive on, boys!"

Because Grandma did so many things with her hands, a little girl could always tag after her, talking and asking questions and listening. Side by side with Grandma, I learned to peel apples, to take the skin off tomatoes by plunging them into scalding water, to do simple embroidery stitches, and to knit. Later, during World War I, when I had to cook for the whole household, she taught me a lot about cooking, for example, just when to add a lump of butter, something that always had to be concealed from Mother, who thought that cooking with butter was extravagant.

While I followed her about as she carried out the endless little household tasks that she took on, supplementing the work of the maids or doing more in between maids—and we were often in between—she told me endless tales about Winchester. She told me about her

school days and about the poor children who used to beg the cores of apples from the rich children who had whole apples for lunch. She told me about Em Eiler, who pushed Aunt Lou off a rail fence into a flooded pasture lot; about Great-aunt Louisian, who could read people's minds and tell them everything they had said about her and who had been a triplet and so small when she was born that she would fit into a quart cup; about Grace, who died from riding a trotting horse too hard, which wasn't good for girls; and about the time Lida cut off Anna Louise's curls and said, "Now they won't say 'pretty little girl' anymore." My great-grandfather used to say such a long grace, she told me, that one of her most vivid memories was of standing, holding a log she had started to put on the fire, for what seemed to be hours for fear of interrupting him. All this was as real to me as if I had lived it myself. I think that if anyone had tried to repeat the Bridie Murphy case,[1] I could easily have impersonated, in trance, the child and girl my grandmother had been.

One of the stories I loved most was about the time the Confederate soldiers came through the village and shot down the flag. In the face of the danger, my grandmother's younger sister ran out and held the flag aloft. It was only another Barbara Frietchie[2] episode and the story gained a great deal from the fact that we had learned to recite, "'Shoot, if you must, this old gray head,/But spare your country's flag,' she said." But this particular Barbara Frietchie had been young and was my great-aunt. Later, I tried to immortalize her in a story called "A Strip of Old Glory," which was published in the Doylestown High School magazine, of which I was the editor.

I never saw Winchester until recently,

---

1 **Bridie Murphy case:** a celebrated case where a woman under hypnosis claimed to remember events in the life of a much earlier ancestor, Bridie Murphy.
2 **Barbara Frietchie:** subject of a ballad by John Greenleaf Whittier, she supposedly hung out a Union flag in defiance of confederate troops during the Civil War.

when the town was holding its sesquicentennial celebration. I took my daughter with me, and as we walked through the streets, I looked at houses that were completely familiar. I saw the house in which my great-grandparents had lived and in which my father's cousin Cally had heard the sound of a ghostly coffin bumping on the stairs until her mother made her get down on her knees and promise never again to indulge in that strange, outlandish, Aunt-Louisian kind of behavior. I saw the house in which the Bradfords had lived and where they had been such warm hosts to the next generation. And I recognized the sites of the fires. For part of the history of Winchester, a little town that never grew, is written in fire.

I was treated as an honored guest in a handsome house with peacocks on the lawn that had been bought by a successful man who had returned from a large city to buy the house where he had once been the stableboy. The husband of one of my cousins also was being honored for his success, and people told me how pleased they were; as a boy he had been so poor, they explained, that he had had to ride a horse bareback to school. One of the peculiarities of the little town, which was never reflected in my grandmother's stories because she saw life ethically and not in class terms, was its incredible snobbishness. This came home to me as I watched how people with strange ticks and deformities seldom seen in a city entered the house humbly in order to shake the hands of the guests of a leading citizen who now owned the garage, as once her father had owned the livery stable.

My grandmother was indifferent to social class, but in her stories she told me about poor people, unfortunate people, people who were better off, and no-count people who drank or gambled or deserted their wives and children. Her own family, for all their pride and their handsome noses, had a fair number of charming, no-count men in each generation and, appropriately, a fair number of women who married the same kind of men. There were a number of stern, impressive women and an occasional impressive man, but a lot of weak ones, too—that is the family picture. My cousins suspect that our great-grandfather was not a very strong character, but that he was kept in hand by our great-grandmother.

This indifference to social class irritated my mother, who used to complain that Grandma could get interested in the most ordinary people. Sometimes she went on a holiday to the seaside. When she came home she told us endless narratives about the lives of the ordinary people with whom she sat on the steps of the seaside hotel. This used to make Mother mutter. Grandma and Mother looked a good deal alike. They were of the same height and weight, and had similar enough features so that people often mistook them for mother and daughter. This, too, did not please Mother.

Mother never ceased to resent the fact that Grandma lived with us, but she gave her her due. Grandma never "interfered"—never tried to teach the children anything religious that had not previously been introduced by my mother, and in disagreements between my mother and father she always took my mother's side. When my father threatened to leave my mother, Grandma told him firmly that she would stay with her and the children.

When Grandma was angry, she sat and held her tongue. I used to believe that this involved some very mysterious internal, anatomical trick. She was so still, so angry, and so determined not to speak, not to lose her temper. And she never did. But not losing her temper came out of her eyes like fire. Years later, when I was given a picture of her as a young woman, I felt that I had looked very like her at the same age. But when I actually compared pictures of me with the one of her, I looked milky mild. Not until the birth of her great-great-granddaughter, my daughter's daughter Sevanne Margaret, did that flashing glance reappear in the family. Looking at her black eyes, inherited from her Armenian father, I see again shining out of them the flash of Martha Ramsay's furiousness.

I think it was my grandmother who gave me my ease in being a woman. She was unquestionably feminine—small and dainty and pretty and wholly without masculine protest or feminist aggrievement. She had gone to college when this was a very unusual thing for a girl to do, she had a firm grasp of anything she paid attention to, she had married and had a child, and she had a career of her own. All this was true of my mother, as well. But my mother was filled with passionate resentment about the condition of women, as perhaps my grandmother might have been had my grandfather lived and had she borne five children and had little opportunity to use her special gifts and training. As it was, the two women I knew best were mothers and had professional training. So I had no reason to doubt that brains were suitable for a woman. And as I had my father's kind of mind—which was also his mother's—I learned that the mind is not sex-typed.

The content of my conscience came from my mother's concern for other people and the state of the world and from my father's insistence that the only thing worth doing is to add to the store of exactly known facts. But the strength of my conscience came from Grandma, who meant what she said. Perhaps nothing is more valuable for a child than living with an adult who is firm and loving—and Grandma was loving. I loved the feel of her soft skin, but she would never let me give her an extra kiss when I said good night.

After I left home I used to write long letters to Grandma, and later, when I went to Samoa, it was for Grandma that I tried to make clear what I was doing. She was not entirely happy with my choice of a career; she thought that botany would have been better than savages. Even though she herself hardly ever went to church— she had decided that she had gone to church enough—she taught me to treat all people as the children of God. But she had no way to include in her conception of human beings the unknown peoples of distant South Sea islands. When I was a child and would come into her room with my hair flying, she would tell me that I looked like the wild man of Borneo. For her, that was only a figure of speech.

Throughout my childhood she talked a great deal about teachers, about their problems and conflicts, and about those teachers who could never close the schoolhouse door behind them. The sense she gave me of what teachers are like, undistorted by my own particular experience with teachers, made me want to write my first book about adolescents in such a way that the teachers of adolescents would understand it. Grandma always wanted to understand things, and she was willing to listen or read until she did. There was only one subject, she decided rather fastidiously, that she did not wish to pursue. That was birth control.

Margaret Mead in Samoa, 1925.

At eighty, she said, she did not need to know about it.

When I returned from Samoa, Grandma had already left for Fairhope, Alabama, where she had taken my two younger sisters to an experimental school. So I never had a chance to follow up the letters I wrote her from Samoa with long talks through which she would have understood more about what I was doing, and I would have learned more about how to say things useful to teachers.

In her later years she had devoted herself with almost single-minded passion to my sister Elizabeth, the one of us who was least like the rest. At the end of that year in Fairhope, Elizabeth graduated from high school. I have a vision of her standing in her white graduation dress in the garden where Grandma was sitting. I am sure Grandma felt that her hardest task—protecting and educating Elizabeth—was finished. She died on the way home, while she was visiting a favorite niece in Ohio.

The closest friends I have made all through life have been people who also grew up close to a loved and loving grandmother or grandfather.

Study Questions

1. Mead states that her grandmother was the "most decisive influence" in her life. What are some of the grandmother's traits and talents which made such a strong impression on Margaret Mead?
2. Which of the grandmother's activities were not typical for her time?
3. How does the grandmother teach her granddaughter to "observe the world" around her? Of what value was this to Margaret Mead as an anthropologist?
4. In what ways does the grandmother instill an appreciation for past family history?

Composition

1. Choose the selection from this section which you think best expresses "The Individual" theme. Tell why it is the best expression of individualism. Use examples from the selection to support your position. Conclude by stating how the chosen selection corresponds to your own idea of individualism.
2. Based on Margaret Mead's description of her grandmother, write a character sketch of an individual who has influenced you in some way. Select a family member or some other individual you have known well. Include enough information about the person so that your reader will know how you feel about the person's influence.

The American Dream

One cannot define the American Dream precisely because it has taken such a variety of forms. The dream has usually involved conceptions of freedom and justice and equality (though the meaning of these words has ranged widely). More often than not, it has included material prosperity. Whatever the variations in the content of the dream, there has been one constant: the time of its fulfillment. The American Dream is a dream of the future. As such it implies the ideas of progress and change. What the twentieth-century American looks forward to may be quite different from the goal of William Bradford or even of Thomas Jefferson. Most of us have dreamed not so much of a time when things were better as of a time when things will be better.

The selections included in The American Dream section are versions of the dream as recorded by Americans through some five centuries. The earliest, from the Iroquois Law of the Great Peace, includes some of the principles that were later included in other American documents. The Mayflower Compact expresses a dream more by implication than by statement. Yet, the people who subscribed to it clearly felt that they were engaged in an effort to establish a better order of society than their parents had known. The Declaration of Independence, written a century and a half later, states the hopes of a new nation. These hopes are expressed both in terms of the tyranny which was being rejected and of the justice

which was being declared. Realizing the dream, however, requires more than a declaration of intent—as Maya Angelou tells us in her autobiographical *I Know Why the Caged Bird Sings.* Sometimes, as we see in Fitzgerald's "Winter Dreams," one doesn't know what dream to pursue. Abstract and elusive as the dream may be, Americans can still say, with Martin Luther King, Jr. "I have a dream." We are still seeking.

America the Beautiful

Katharine Lee Bates (1859–1929) was a
Professor of English at Wellesley College,
who is best remembered for the composition
of "America the Beautiful" in 1895, for
which she has been immortalized. The
poem's image of America is quite idealistic,
as dreams sometimes are. However, it so
poignantly expresses our nation's aspirations
that it has become an unofficial national
anthem.

America the Beautiful

KATHARINE LEE BATES

O beautiful for spacious skies,
  For amber waves of grain,
For purple mountain majesties
  Above the fruited plain!
    America! America!   5
  God shed His grace on thee
And crown thy good with brotherhood
  From sea to shining sea!

O beautiful for pilgrim feet,
  Whose stern, impassioned stress   10
A thoroughfare for freedom beat
  Across the wilderness!
    America! America!
  God mend thine every flaw,
Confirm thy soul in self-control,   15
  Thy liberty in law!

O beautiful for heroes proved
  In liberating strife,
Who more than self their country loved,
  And mercy more than life!   20
    America! America!
  May God thy gold refine
Till all success be nobleness
  And every gain divine!

O beautiful for patriot dream   25
  That sees beyond the years
Thine alabaster cities gleam
  Undimmed by human tears!
    America! America!
  God shed His grace on thee   30
And crown thy good with brotherhood
  From sea to shining sea!

Study Questions

1. The first half of each stanza describes a different kind of beauty in America. What are these four kinds of beauty? Why do you think they are presented in this order?

2. The second half of each stanza begins with the "America! America!" refrain. How do the subsequent lines of each refrain fit the stanza in which they appear? How are they repetitious? How do they differ?

3. How does the poem as a whole summarize the idea of The American Dream?

A Dream of Peace

In the late fourteenth century five Indian nations came together to establish the Iroquois Confederacy. These nations were the Seneca, Mohawk, Oneida, Onondaga, and Cayuga. The constitution, or Law of the Great Peace, which they adopted in 1390 is still in force today, and its council fire has never been extinguished. The principles of justice and community responsibility in the Constitution of the Iroquois Confederacy served as a model for the United States Constitution in 1787. A portion of those laws is included here.

from The Law of the Great Peace

IROQUOIS CONFEDERACY

With the statesmen of the League of Five Nations, I plant the Tree of Great Peace. I plant it in your territory, Atotarho, and the Onondaga Nation: in the territory of you who are Firekeepers. I name the tree *Tsioneratasekowa,* the Great White Pine.

Under the shade of this Tree of Great Peace, we spread the soft, white, feathery down of the

Globe Thistle as seats for you, Atotarho, and your cousin statesmen.

We place you upon those seats, spread soft with the feathery down of the Globe Thistle, there beneath the shade of the spreading branches of the Tree of Great Peace. There shall you sit and watch the Fire of the League of Five Nations. All the affairs of the League shall be transacted at this place before you, Atotarho and your cousin statesmen, by the statesmen of the League of Five Nations. Roots have spread out from the Tree of Great Peace, one to the north, one to the east, one to the south, and one to the west. These are the Great White Roots, and their nature is Peace and Strength. If any man or any nation of the Five Nations shall obey the laws of the Great Peace (Kaianerekowa), and shall make this known to the statesmen of the League, they may trace back the roots to the Tree. If their minds are clean, and if they are obedient and promise to obey the wishes of the Council of the League, they

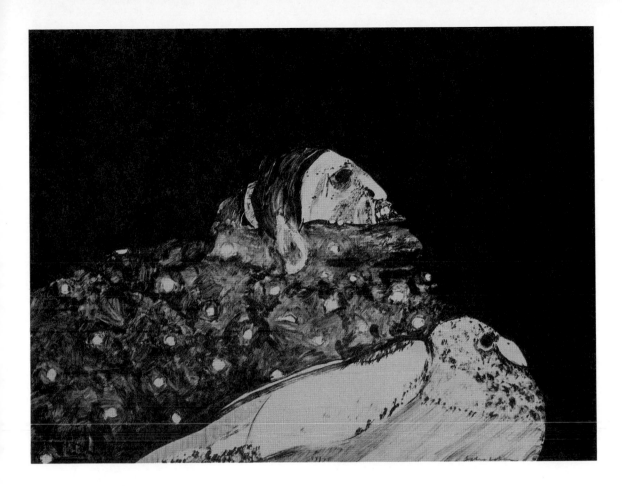

shall be welcomed to take shelter beneath the Great Evergreen Tree.

We place at the top of the Tree of Great Peace an eagle, who is able to see afar. If he sees in the distance any danger threatening, he will at once warn the people of the League.

THANKSGIVING

Whenever the statesmen of the League shall assemble for the purpose of holding a council, the Onondaga statesmen shall open it by expressing their gratitude to their cousin statesmen, and greeting them, and they shall make an address and offer thanks to the earth where men dwell, to the streams of water, the pools and the lakes, to the maise and the fruits, to the medicinal herbs and trees, to the forest trees for their usefulness, and to the animals that serve as food and give their pelts for clothing, to the great winds and the lesser winds, to the Thunderers; to the Sun, the mighty warrior; to the moon, to the messengers of the Creator who reveals his wishes, and to the Great Creator who dwells in the heavens above who gives all the things useful to men, and who is the source and the ruler of health and life.

Then shall the Onondaga statesmen declare the Council open.

The Council shall not sit after darkness has set in.

A NEW CHIEF

When a candidate chief is to be installed, he shall furnish four strings of shells or wampum one span in length bound together at one end. Such will constitute the evidence of his pledge to the chiefs of the League that he will live according to the Constitution of the Great Peace and exercise justice in all affairs. When the pledge is furnished, the Speaker of the Council must hold the shell strings in his hand and address the opposite side of the Council Fire, and he shall begin his address saying:

"Now behold him. He has now become a chief of the League. See how splendid he looks."

An address may then follow. At the end of it he shall send the bunch of shell strings to the opposite side, and they shall be received as evidence of the pledge. Then shall the opposite side say:

"We now do crown you with the sacred emblem of the deer's antlers, the emblem of your chieftainship.

You shall now become a mentor of the people of the Five Nations. The thickness of your skin shall be seven spans, which is to say that you shall be proof against anger, offensive actions, and criticism. Your heart shall be filled with peace and good will. Your mind shall be filled with a yearning for the welfare of the people of the League. With endless patience you shall carry out your duty and your firmness shall be tempered with tenderness for your people. Neither anger nor fury shall find lodging in your mind. All your words and actions shall be marked with calm deliberation. In all your deliberations in the Council of the League, in all your efforts at law-making, in all your official acts, self-interest shall be cast away. Do not cast over your shoulder behind you the warnings of your nephews and nieces should they chide you for any error or wrong you may do, but return to the way of the Great Law which is right and just. Look and listen for the welfare of the whole people, and have always in view not only the present, but also the coming generations, even those whose faces are yet beneath the surface of the ground—the unborn of the future Nation."

Study Questions

1. What is the purpose of the great tree planted in the Onondaga nation at approximately the center of the Confederacy?
2. What are the requirements for outsiders to be welcomed by the Council?
3. What is the purpose of the thanksgiving ritual at the beginning of each Council meeting?
4. What conduct is required of a chief?
5. On the basis of this excerpt from the constitution, what do you learn about the people of the Iroquois Confederacy?

A Dream of a New Life

The Mayflower Compact grew out of an error in navigation. By their patent from the Virginia Company in London, the Pilgrims were granted lands and privileges in the Virginia Colony, but storms and miscalculations led to a landing on Cape Cod. Immediately some of the passengers began to argue that the patent was no longer valid and to declare themselves free of obligation to Pilgrim leaders. Since some unity of purpose seemed necessary for survival, the Pilgrims drew up the historic document printed below. The original copy was lost. Our best source now is the text included in *The History of Plymouth Plantation* by William Bradford (1590?–1657), a long-time governor of the colony.

The Mayflower Compact

WILLIAM BRADFORD

I SHALL A LITTLE return back, and begin with a combination made by them before they came ashore; being the first foundation of their government in this place. Occasioned partly by the discontented and mutinous speeches that some of the strangers amongst them had let fall from them in the ship: That when they came ashore they would use their own liberty, for none had power to command them, the patent they had being for Virginia and not for New England, which belonged to another government, with which the Virginia Company had nothing to do. And partly that such an act by them done, this their condition considered, might be as firm as any patent, and in some respects more sure.

The form was as followeth:
[The Mayflower Compact]
In the Name of God, Amen.

We whose names are underwritten, the loyal subjects of our dread Sovereign Lord King James, by the grace of God of Great Britain, France, and Ireland King, Defender of the Faith, etc.

Having undertaken, for the glory of God and advancement of the Christian faith and honor of our King and country, a voyage to plant the first colony in the northern parts of Virginia, do by these presents solemnly and mutually in the presence of God and one of another, covenant and combine ourselves together into a civil body politic, for our better ordering and preservation and furtherance of the ends aforesaid; and by virtue hereof to enact, constitute, and frame such just and equal laws, ordinances, acts, constitutions, and offices, from time to time, as shall be thought most meet and convenient for the general good of the colony, unto which we promise all due submission and obedience. In witness whereof we have hereunder subscribed our names at Cape Cod, the 11th of November, in the year of the reign of our Sovereign Lord King James, of England, France and Ireland the eighteenth, and of Scotland the fifty-fourth. *Anno Domini* 1620.

After this they chose, or rather confirmed, Mr. John Carver (a man godly and well approved amongst them) their Governor for that year. And after they had provided a place for their goods, or common store (which were long in unlading for want of boats, foulness of the winter weather and sickness of divers) and begun some small cottages for their habitation; as time would admit, they met and consulted of laws and orders, both for their civil and military government as the necessity of their condition did require, still adding thereunto as urgent occasion in several times, and as cases did require.

Study Questions

1. Why did the people on the *Mayflower* draw up an agreement before going ashore?

2. What is the stated purpose of making the Compact? What specific provisions does the Compact make for governing the colony?

3. Which phrases in the Compact foreshadow aspects of the American Dream? Explain why.

A Dream of a New Nation

A century and a half after the Mayflower
Compact, the Continental Congress, meeting in Philadelphia on June 11, 1776,
appointed a committee of five to write a Declaration of Independence. The Committee
asked Thomas Jefferson to compose a draft.
It was substantially his composition which
was adopted with some revisions on July 4.
Possibly no other nation has produced at its
inception a document so clear, eloquent, and
universally appealing. The American Dream
as expressed in the Declaration of Independence has inspired oppressed people everywhere.

The Declaration of Independence

THOMAS JEFFERSON

WHEN, IN THE COURSE of human
events, it becomes necessary for one
people to dissolve the political bands
which have connected them with another, and
to assume, among the powers of the earth, the
separate and equal station to which the laws of
nature and of nature's God entitle them, a decent respect to the opinions of mankind requires that they should declare the causes
which impel them to the separation.

We hold these truths to be self-evident:—
That all men are created equal; that they are
endowed by their Creator with certain unalienable rights; that among these are life, liberty,
and the pursuit of happiness. That, to secure
these rights, governments are instituted among
men, deriving their just powers from the consent of the governed; that, whenever any form
of government becomes destructive of these
ends, it is the right of the people to alter or to
abolish it, and to institute new government,
laying its foundation on such principles, and
organizing its powers in such form, as to them
shall seem most likely to effect their safety and
happiness. Prudence, indeed, will dictate that
governments long established should not be
changed for light and transient causes; and accordingly all experience hath shown that
mankind are more disposed to suffer while
evils are sufferable, than to right themselves by
abolishing the forms to which they are accustomed. But when a long train of abuses and

usurpations, pursuing invariably the same object, evinces a design to reduce them under absolute despotism, it is their right, it is their duty, to throw off such government, and to provide new guards for their future security. Such has been the patient sufferance of these colonies; and such is now the necessity which constrains them to alter their former systems of government. The history of the present King of Great Britain is a history of repeated injuries and usurpations, all having in direct object the establishment of an absolute tyranny over these states. To prove this, let facts be submitted to a candid world.

He has refused his assent to laws, the most wholesome and necessary for the public good.

He has forbidden his governors to pass laws of immediate and pressing importance, unless suspended in their operation till his assent should be obtained; and when so suspended, he has utterly neglected to attend to them.

He has refused to pass other laws for the accommodation of large districts of people, unless those people would relinquish the right of representation in the legislature—a right inestimable to them and formidable to tyrants only.

He has called together legislative bodies at places unusual, uncomfortable, and distant from the depository of their public records, for the sole purpose of fatiguing them into compliance with his measures.

He has dissolved representative houses repeatedly, for opposing with manly firmness his invasions on the rights of the people.

He has refused for a long time, after such dissolutions, to cause others to be elected; whereby the legislative powers, incapable of annihilation, have returned to the people at large for their exercise; the State remaining in the meantime exposed to all the dangers of invasions from without, and convulsions within.

He has endeavored to prevent the population of these States; for that purpose obstruct-

ing the laws for naturalization of foreigners; refusing to pass others to encourage their migrations hither, and raising the conditions of new appropriations of lands.

He has obstructed the administration of justice, by refusing his assent to laws for establishing judiciary powers.

He has made judges dependent on his will alone, for the tenure of their offices, and the amount and payment of their salaries.

He has erected a multitude of new offices, and sent hither swarms of officers to harass our people and eat out their substance.

He has kept among us, in times of peace, standing armies without the consent of our legislatures.

He has affected to render the military independent of and superior to the civil power.

He has combined with others to subject us to a jurisdiction foreign to our constitutions, and unacknowledged by our laws; giving his assent to their acts of pretended legislation:

For quartering large bodies of armed troops among us;

For protecting them, by a mock trial, from punishment for any murders which they should commit on the inhabitants of these States;

For cutting off our trade with all parts of the world;

For imposing taxes on us without our consent;

For depriving us, in many cases, of the benefits of trial by jury;

For transporting us beyond seas to be tried for pretended offenses;

For abolishing the free system of English laws in a neighboring province, establishing therein an arbitrary government, and enlarging its boundaries so as to render it at once an example and fit instrument for introducing the same absolute rule into these colonies;

For taking away our charters, abolishing our most valuable laws, and altering, fundamentally, the forms of our governments;

For suspending our own legislatures, and declaring themselves invested with power to legislate for us in all cases whatsoever.

He has abdicated government here, by declaring us out of his protection and waging war against us.

He has plundered our seas, ravaged our coasts, burned our towns, and destroyed the lives of our people.

He is at this time transporting large armies of foreign mercenaries to complete the works of death, desolation, and tyranny, already begun with circumstances of cruelty and perfidy scarcely paralleled in the most barbarous ages, and totally unworthy the head of a civilized nation.

He has constrained our fellow citizens taken captive on the high seas to bear arms against their country, to become the executioners of their friends and brethren, or to fall themselves by their hands.

He has excited domestic insurrection among us, and has endeavored to bring on the inhabitants of our frontiers the merciless Indian savages, whose known rule of warfare is an undistinguished destruction of all ages, sexes, and conditions.

In every stage of these oppressions we have petitioned for redress in the most humble terms; our repeated petitions have been answered only by repeated injury. A prince whose character is thus marked by every act which may define a tyrant is unfit to be the ruler of a free people.

Nor have we been wanting in our attentions to our British brethren. We have warned them from time to time of attempts by their legislature to extend an unwarrantable jurisdiction over us. We have reminded them of the circumstances of our emigration and settlement here. We have appealed to their native justice and magnanimity; and we have conjured them, by the ties of our common kindred, to disavow these usurpations, which would inevitably interrupt our connections and correspondence. They, too, have been deaf to the voice of justice and of consanguinity. We must, therefore, acquiesce in the necessity which denounces our separation, and hold them, as we hold the rest of mankind, enemies in war, in peace friends.

We, therefore, the Representatives of the United States of America, in General Congress assembled, appealing to the Supreme Judge of the world for the rectitude of our intentions, do, in the name and by the authority of the good people of these colonies, solemnly publish and declare, That these united Colonies are, and of right ought to be, free and independent states; that they are absolved from all allegiance to the British crown, and that all political connection between them and the state of Great Britain is, and ought to be, totally dissolved; and that, as free and independent states, they have full power to levy war, conclude peace, contract alliances, establish commerce, and to do all other acts and things which independent states may of right do. And for the support of this declaration, with a firm reliance on the protection of Divine Providence, we mutually pledge to each other our lives, our fortunes, and our sacred honor.

Study Questions

1. The structure of the Declaration is basically a deductive argument: it starts with an assertion, makes a major and a minor premise, follows with particulars, and ends with a concluding statement. What is the as-

sertion in the first paragraph? What are the two premises in the second paragraph? What are the indictments which serve as evidence? In the final paragraph what is the declaration resulting from these indictments?

2. Commenting on the choice of Jefferson to write the Declaration, John Adams (later our second President) said that Jefferson was known for his "peculiar felicity of expression," for example, "in the course of human events." What are some other examples of Jefferson's talent for expressing ideas?

3. Why might this document be inspirational to other oppressed peoples? Find examples in the Declaration to support your position.

Composition

1. In a brief essay, summarize The American Dream as it is expressed by Bates, the Iroquois Confederacy, Bradford, and Jefferson. Each of these dreams is for a nation or group of people. Show how they are similar, or how they differ. Conclude by telling to what extent the dreams have come true.

2. Write your own version of what you dream for the country. Tell how your dream would improve present conditions. Also include what you think the possibilities are for its implementation.

A Dream Deferred

What happens when a dream is postponed? One of the most prolific writers in America, Langston Hughes (1902–1967), examines that idea in the following poem. Hughes wrote in every genre: poetry, short stories, novels, drama, biography, and essay. He also wrote children's books and did translations of literature in Spanish. He was the first Black American to consistently earn his living by writing. Hughes also did much to promote and encourage other Black writers during his fifty years of productivity. Hughes was born in Joplin, Missouri, lived in Mexico for a while and in Harlem. The power and rhythms of the blues and jazz are reflected in Hughes's poetry.

Lenox Avenue[1] *Mural*

LANGSTON HUGHES

HARLEM

What happens to a dream deferred?
  Does it dry up
  like a raisin in the sun?
  Or fester like a sore—
  And then run?   5

  Does it stink like rotten meat?
  Or crust and sugar over—
  like a syrupy sweet?

  Maybe it just sags
  like a heavy load.   10

  Or does it explode?

GOOD MORNING

Good morning, daddy!
I was born here, he said,
watched Harlem grow

until colored folks spread   15
from river to river
across the middle of Manhattan
out of Penn Station
dark tenth of a nation,
planes from Puerto Rico,   20
and holds of boats, chico,
up from Cuba Haiti Jamaica,
in busses marked New York
from Georgia Florida Louisiana
to Harlem Brooklyn the Bronx   25
but most of all to Harlem
dusky sash across Manhattan
I've seen them come dark
  wondering
  wide-eyed   30
  dreaming
out of Penn Station—
but the trains are late.

The gates open—
but there're bars   35

---

1 **Lenox Avenue:** a main street in Harlem.

at each gate.
    What happens
    to a dream deferred?
Daddy, ain't you heard?

SAME IN BLUES

I said to my baby,   40
Baby, take it slow.
I can't, she said, I can't!
I got to go!
    There's a certain
    amount of traveling   45
    in a dream deferred.
Lulu said to Leonard,
I want a diamond ring.
Leonard said to Lulu,
You won't get a . . . thing!   50
    A certain
    amount of nothing
    in a dream deferred.
Daddy, daddy, daddy,
All I want is you.   55
You can have me, baby—
but my lovin' days is through.
    A certain
    amount of impotence
    in a dream deferred.   60
Three parties
On my party line—
But that third party,
Lord, ain't mine!
    There's liable   65
    to be confusion
    in a dream deferred.

TOMBSTONES *Jacob Lawrence* 1942
Jacob Lawrence, a Black American artist, portrays in this
painting the theme and images articulated in Hughes's poem.

From river to river
Uptown and down,
There's liable to be confusion   70
when a dream gets kicked around.
You talk like
they don't kick
dreams around
Downtown.   75
I expect they do—
But I'm talking about
Harlem to you!

LETTER

Dear Mama,
    Time I pay rent and get my food   80
and laundry I don't have much left
but here is five dollars for you
to show you I still appreciates you.
My girl-friend send her love and say
she hopes to lay eyes on you sometime in life.   85
Mama, it has been raining cats and dogs up
here. Well, that is all so I will close.
    Your son baby
        Respectable as ever,
            Joe   90

ISLAND

Between two rivers,
North of the park,
Like darker rivers
The streets are dark.

Black and white,   95
Gold and brown—
Chocolate-custard
Pie of a town.
Dream within a dream
Our dream deferred.   100

Good morning, daddy!
Ain't you heard?

Study Questions

1. What are the possibilities offered in answer to the question in the first line? What is common to each of the images?

2. In lines 13–31 what is being described? What dream did they have?

3. What happens to the dream? How is this implied in lines 33–36? Lines 40–78 duplicate the style of blues songs. Why is this style and tone appropriate for the topic?

4. What is the effect of the "letter"? How does it reinforce other parts of the poem?

5. How does the final section, "Island," sum up the theme, repeat certain images, and add new ones?

Winter Dreams

F. Scott Fitzgerald (1896–1940) developed a desire for much more than his family background seemed to promise. Romance, glamour, wealth, success—these became his goals. He achieved them all, but at a heavy cost. From his home in St. Paul, Minnesota, he went to boarding school and then to Princeton University. He was an officer in World War I and published *The Great Gatsby* in 1925. This highly praised novel portrayed the dream of wealth and fast living which characterized the Roaring Twenties.

Unfortunately, Fitzgerald was continually in financial trouble. He often had to use his talent on inferior but marketable stories to cover ever-mounting debts. Nevertheless, in his best work, as "Winter Dreams" shows, Fitzgerald was a great writer who examined a part of The American Dream.

Winter Dreams

F. SCOTT FITZGERALD

I

SOME OF THE CADDIES were poor as sin and lived in one-room houses with a neurasthenic[1] cow in the front yard, but Dexter Green's father owned the second-best grocery-store in Black Bear—the best one was "The Hub," patronized by the wealthy people from Sherry Island—and Dexter caddied only for pocket-money.

In the fall when the days became crisp and gray, and the long Minnesota winter shut down like the white lid of a box, Dexter's skis moved over the snow that hid the fairways of the golf course. At these times the country gave him a feeling of profound melancholy—it offended him that the links should lie in enforced fallowness, haunted by ragged sparrows for the long season. It was dreary, too, that on the tees where the gay colors fluttered in summer there were now only the desolate sand-boxes knee-deep in crusted ice. When he crossed the hills the wind blew cold as misery, and if the sun was out he tramped with his eyes squinted up against the hard dimensionless glare.

In April the winter ceased abruptly. The snow ran down into Black Bear Lake scarcely tarrying for the early golfers to brave the season with red and black balls. Without elation, without an interval of moist glory, the cold was gone.

Dexter knew that there was something dismal about this Northern spring, just as he

---

1 **neurasthenic:** suffering from nervous exhaustion or overwork.

Scott and Zelda Fitzgerald soon after their marriage in 1920. They were a handsome but troubled couple, much like the characters in Scott's novels and stories.

knew there was something gorgeous about the fall. Fall made him clinch his hands and tremble and repeat idiotic sentences to himself, and make brisk abrupt gestures of command to imaginary audiences and armies. October filled him with hope which November raised to a sort of ecstatic triumph, and in this mood the fleeting brilliant impressions of the summer at Sherry Island were ready grist to his mill. He became a golf champion and defeated Mr. T. A. Hedrick in a marvellous match played a hundred times over the fairways of his imagination, a match each detail of which he changed about untiringly—sometimes he won with almost laughable ease, sometimes he came up magnificently from behind. Again, stepping from a Pierce-Arrow automobile, like Mr. Mortimer Jones, he strolled frigidly into the lounge of the Sherry Island Golf Club—or perhaps, surrounded by an admiring crowd, he gave an exhibition of fancy diving from the springboard of the club raft. . . . Among those who watched him in open-mouthed wonder was Mr. Mortimer Jones.

And one day it came to pass that Mr. Jones—himself and not his ghost—came up to Dexter with tears in his eyes and said that Dexter was the——best caddy in the club, and wouldn't he decide not to quit if Mr. Jones made it worth his while, because every other ——caddy in the club lost one ball a hole for him—regularly—

"No, sir," said Dexter decisively, "I don't want to caddy any more." Then, after a pause: "I'm too old."

"You're not more than fourteen. Why the devil did you decide just this morning that you wanted to quit? You promised that next week you'd go over to the State tournament with me."

"I decided I was too old."

Dexter handed in his "A Class" badge, collected what money was due him from the caddy-master, and walked home to Black Bear Village.

"The best——caddy I ever saw," shouted Mr. Mortimer Jones over a drink that afternoon. "Never lost a ball! Willing! Intelligent! Quiet! Honest! Grateful!"

The little girl who had done this was eleven—beautifully ugly as little girls are apt to be who are destined after a few years to be inexpressibly lovely and bring no end of misery to a great number of men. The spark, however, was perceptible. There was a general ungodliness in the way her lips twisted down at the corners when she smiled, and in the—Heaven help us!—in the almost passionate quality of her eyes. Vitality is born early in such women. It was utterly in evidence now, shining through her thin frame in a sort of glow.

She had come eagerly out on to the course at nine o'clock with a white linen nurse and five small new golf-clubs in a white canvas bag which the nurse was carrying. When Dexter first saw her she was standing by the caddy house, rather ill at ease and trying to conceal the fact by engaging her nurse in an obviously unnatural conversation graced by startling and irrelevant grimaces from herself.

"Well, it's certainly a nice day, Hilda," Dexter heard her say. She drew down the corners of her mouth, smiled, and glanced furtively around, her eyes in transit falling for an instant on Dexter.

Then to the nurse:

"Well, I guess there aren't very many people out here this morning, are there?"

The smile again—radiant, blatantly artificial—convincing.

"I don't know what we're supposed to do now," said the nurse, looking nowhere in particular.

"Oh, that's all right. I'll fix it up."

Dexter stood perfectly still, his mouth slightly ajar. He knew that if he moved forward a step his stare would be in her line of vision—if he moved backward he would lose his full view of her face. For a moment he had not realized how young she was. Now he remembered having seen her several times the year before—in bloomers.

Suddenly, involuntarily, he laughed, a short abrupt laugh—then, startled by himself, he turned and began to walk quickly away.

"Boy!"

Dexter stopped.

"Boy—"

Beyond question he was addressed. Not only that, but he was treated to that absurd smile, that preposterous smile—the memory of which at least a dozen men were to carry into middle age.

"Boy, do you know where the golf teacher is?"

"He's giving a lesson."

"Well, do you know where the caddy master is?"

"He isn't here yet this morning."

"Oh." For a moment this baffled her. She stood alternately on her right and left foot.

"We'd like to get a caddy," said the nurse. "Mrs. Mortimer Jones sent us out to play golf, and we don't know how without we get a caddy."

Here she was stopped by an ominous glance from Miss Jones, followed immediately by the smile.

"There aren't any caddies here except me," said Dexter to the nurse, "and I got to stay here in charge until the caddy-master gets here."

"Oh."

Miss Jones and her retinue now withdrew, and at a proper distance from Dexter became involved in a heated conversation, which was concluded by Miss Jones taking one of the clubs and hitting it on the ground with violence. For further emphasis she raised it again and was about to bring it down smartly upon the nurse's bosom, when the nurse seized the club and twisted it from her hands.

"You damn little mean old *thing!*" cried Miss Jones wildly.

Another argument ensued. Realizing that the elements of the comedy were implied in the scene, Dexter several times began to laugh, but each time restrained the laugh before it reached audibility. He could not resist the monstrous conviction that the little girl was justified in beating the nurse.

The situation was resolved by the fortuitous appearance of the caddy-master, who was appealed to immediately by the nurse.

"Miss Jones is to have a little caddy, and this one says he can't go."

"Mr. McKenna said I was to wait here till you came," said Dexter quickly.

"Well, he's here now." Miss Jones smiled cheerfully at the caddy-master. Then she dropped her bag and set off at a haughty mince toward the first tee.

"Well?" The caddy-master turned to Dexter. "What you standing there like a dummy for? Go pick up the young lady's clubs."

"I don't think I'll go out to-day," said Dexter.

"You don't—"

"I think I'll quit."

The enormity of his decision frightened him. He was a favorite caddy, and the thirty dollars a month he earned through the summer were not to be made elsewhere around the lake. But he had received a strong emotional shock, and his perturbation required a violent and immediate outlet.

It is not so simple as that, either. As so frequently would be the case in the future, Dexter was unconsciously dictated to by his winter dreams.

II

Now, of course, the quality and the seasonability of these winter dreams varied, but the stuff of them remained. They persuaded Dexter several years later to pass up a business course at the State university—his father, prospering now, would have paid his way—

for the precarious advantage of attending an older and more famous university in the East, where he was bothered by his scanty funds. But do not get the impression, because his winter dreams happened to be concerned at first with musings on the rich, that there was anything merely snobbish in the boy. He wanted not association with glittering things and glittering people—he wanted the glittering things themselves. Often he reached out for the best without knowing why he wanted it—and sometimes he ran up against the mysterious denials and prohibitions in which life indulges. It is with one of those denials and not with his career as a whole that this story deals.

He made money. It was rather amazing. After college he went to the city from which Black Bear Lake draws its wealthy patrons. When he was only twenty-three and had been there not quite two years, there were already people who liked to say: "Now *there's* a boy—" All about him rich men's sons were peddling bonds precariously, or investing patrimonies precariously, or plodding through the two dozen volumes of the "George Washington Commercial Course," but Dexter borrowed a thousand dollars on his college degree and his confident mouth, and bought a partnership in a laundry.

It was a small laundry when he went into it but Dexter made a speciality of learning how the English washed fine woollen golf-stockings without shrinking them, and within a year he was catering to the trade that wore knickerbockers. Men were insisting that their Shetland hose and sweaters go to his laundry just as they had insisted on a caddy who could find golf-balls. A little later he was doing their wives' lingerie as well—and running five branches in different parts of the city. Before he was twenty-seven he owned the largest string of laundries in his section of the country. It was then that he sold out and went to New York. But the part of his story that concerns us goes back to the days when he was making his first big success.

When he was twenty-three Mr. Hart—one of the gray-haired men who like to say "Now there's a boy"—gave him a guest card to the Sherry Island Golf Club for a week-end. So he signed his name one day on the register, and that afternoon played golf in a foursome with Mr. Hart and Mr. Sandwood and Mr. T. A. Hedrick. He did not consider it necessary to remark that he had once carried Mr. Hart's bag over this same links, and that he knew every trap and gully with his eyes shut—but he found himself glancing at the four caddies who trailed them, trying to catch a gleam or gesture that would remind him of himself, that would lessen the gap which lay between his present and his past.

It was a curious day, slashed abruptly with fleeting, familiar impressions. One minute he had the sense of being a trespasser—in the next he was impressed by the tremendous superiority he felt toward Mr. T. A. Hedrick, who was a bore and not even a good golfer any more.

Then, because of a ball Mr. Hart lost near the fifteenth green, an enormous thing happened. While they were searching the stiff grasses of the rough there was a clear call of "Fore!" from behind a hill in their rear. And as they all turned abruptly from their search a bright new ball sliced abruptly over the hill and caught Mr. T. A. Hedrick in the abdomen.

"By Gad!" cried Mr. T. A. Hedrick, "they ought to put some of these crazy women off the course. It's getting to be outrageous."

A head and a voice came up together over the hill:

"Do you mind if we go through?"

"You hit me in the stomach!" declared Mr. Hedrick wildly.

"Did I?" The girl approached the group of men. "I'm sorry. I yelled 'Fore!'"

Her glance fell casually on each of the men—then scanned the fairway for her ball.

"Did I bounce into the rough?"

It was impossible to determine whether this question was ingenuous or malicious. In a moment, however, she left no doubt, for as her partner came up over the hill she called cheerfully:

"Here I am! I'd have gone on the green except that I hit something."

As she took her stance for a short mashie shot, Dexter looked at her closely. She wore a blue gingham dress, rimmed at throat and shoulders with a white edging that accentuated her tan. The quality of exaggeration, of thinness, which had made her passionate eyes and down-turning mouth absurd at eleven, was gone now. She was arrestingly beautiful. The color in her cheeks was centred like the color in a picture—it was not a "high" color, but a sort of fluctuating and feverish warmth, so shaded that it seemed at any moment it would recede and disappear. This color and the mobility of her mouth gave a continual impression of flux, of intense life, of passionate vitality—balanced only partially by the sad luxury of her eyes.

She swung her mashie impatiently and without interest, pitching the ball into a sand-pit on the other side of the green. With a quick, insincere smile and a careless "Thank you!" she went on after it.

"That Judy Jones!" remarked Mr. Hedrick on the next tee, as they waited—some moments—for her to play on ahead. "All she needs is to be turned up and spanked for six months and then to be married off to an old-fashioned cavalry captain."

"My God, she's good-looking!" said Mr. Sandwood, who was just over thirty.

"Good-looking!" cried Mr. Hedrick contemptuously, "she always looks as if she wanted to be kissed! Turning those big cow-eyes on every calf in town!"

It was doubtful if Mr. Hedrick intended a reference to the maternal instinct.

"She'd play pretty good golf if she'd try," said Mr. Sandwood.

"She has no form," said Mr. Hedrick solemnly.

"She has a nice figure," said Mr. Sandwood.

"Better thank the Lord she doesn't drive a swifter ball," said Mr. Hart, winking at Dexter.

Later in the afternoon the sun went down with a riotous swirl of gold and varying blues and scarlets, and left the dry, rustling night of Western summer. Dexter watched from the veranda of the Golf Club, watched the even overlap of the waters in the little wind, silver molasses under the harvest-moon. Then the moon held a finger to her lips and the lake became a clear pool, pale and quiet. Dexter put on his bathing-suit and swam out to the farthest raft, where he stretched dripping on the wet canvas of the springboard.

There was a fish jumping and a star shining and the lights around the lake were gleaming. Over on a dark peninsula a piano was playing the songs of last summer and of summers before that—songs from "Chin-Chin" and "The Count of Luxemburg" and "The Chocolate Soldier"—and because the sound of a piano over a stretch of water had always seemed beautiful to Dexter he lay perfectly quiet and listened.

The tune the piano was playing at that moment had been gay and new five years before when Dexter was a sophomore at college. They had played it at a prom once when he could not afford the luxury of proms, and he had stood outside the gymnasium and listened. The sound of the tune precipitated in him a sort of ecstasy and it was with that ecstasy he viewed what happened to him now. It was a mood of intense appreciation, a sense that, for once, he was magnificently attuned to life and that everything about him was radiating a brightness and a glamour he might never know again.

A low, pale oblong detached itself suddenly from the darkness of the Island, spitting forth the reverberate sound of a racing motor-boat. Two white streamers of cleft water rolled themselves out behind it and almost immediately the boat was beside him, drowning out the hot tinkle of the piano in the drone of its spray. Dexter raising himself on his arms was aware of a figure standing at the wheel, of two dark eyes regarding him over the lengthening space of water—then the boat had gone by and was sweeping in an immense and purposeless circle of spray round and round in the middle of the lake. With equal eccentricity one of the circles flattened out and headed back toward the raft.

"Who's that?" she called, shutting off her motor. She was so near now that Dexter could see her bathing-suit, which consisted apparently of pink rompers.

The nose of the boat bumped the raft, and as the latter tilted rakishly he was precipitated toward her. With different degrees of interest they recognized each other.

"Aren't you one of those men we played through this afternoon?" she demanded.

He was.

"Well, do you know how to drive a motor-boat? Because if you do I wish you'd drive this one so I can ride on the surf-board behind. My name is Judy Jones"—she favored him with an absurd smirk—rather, what tried to be a smirk, for, twist her mouth as she might, it was not grotesque, it was merely beautiful—"and I live in a house over there on the Island, and in that house there is a man waiting for me. When he drove up at the door I drove out of the dock because he says I'm his ideal."

There was a fish jumping and a star shining and the lights around the lake were gleaming. Dexter sat beside Judy Jones and she explained how her boat was driven. Then she was in the water, swimming to the floating surf-board with a sinuous crawl. Watching her was without effort to the eye, watching a branch waving or a sea-gull flying. Her arms, burned to butternut, moved sinuously among the dull platinum ripples, elbow appearing first, casting the forearm back with a cadence of falling water, then reaching out and down, stabbing a path ahead.

They moved out into the lake; turning,

Dexter saw that she was kneeling on the low rear of the now uptilted surf-board.

"Go faster," she called, "fast as it'll go."

Obediently he jammed the lever forward and the white spray mounted at the bow. When he looked around again the girl was standing up on the rushing board, her arms spread wide, her eyes lifted toward the moon.

"It's awful cold," she shouted. "What's your name?"

He told her.

"Well, why don't you come to dinner tomorrow night?"

His heart turned over like the flywheel of the boat, and, for the second time, her casual whim gave a new direction to his life.

III

Next evening while he waited for her to come down-stairs, Dexter peopled the soft deep summer room and the sun-porch that opened from it with the men who had already loved Judy Jones. He knew the sort of men they were—the men who when he first went to college had entered from the great prep schools with graceful clothes and the deep tan of healthy summers. He had seen that, in one sense, he was better than these men. He was newer and stronger. Yet in acknowledging to himself that he wished his children to be like them he was admitting that he was but the rough, strong stuff from which they eternally sprang.

When the time had come for him to wear good clothes, he had known who were the best tailors in America, and the best tailors in America had made him the suit he wore this evening. He had acquired that particular reserve peculiar to his university, that set it off from other universities. He recognized the value to him of such a mannerism and he had adopted it; he knew that to be careless in dress and manner required more confidence than to be careful. But carelessness was for his children. His mother's name had been Krimslich. She was a Bohemian of the peasant class and she had talked broken English to the end of her days. Her son must keep to the set patterns.

At a little after seven Judy Jones came down-stairs. She wore a blue silk afternoon dress, and he was disappointed at first that she had not put on something more elaborate. This feeling was accentuated when, after a brief greeting, she went to the door of a butler's pantry and pushing it open called: "You can serve dinner, Martha." He had rather expected that a butler would announce dinner, that there would be a cocktail. Then he put these thoughts behind him as they sat down side by side on a lounge and looked at each other.

"Father and mother won't be here," she said thoughtfully.

He remembered the last time he had seen her father, and he was glad the parents were not to be here to-night—they might wonder who he was. He had been born in Keeble, a Minnesota village fifty miles farther north, and he always gave Keeble as his home instead of Black Bear Village. Country towns were well enough to come from if they weren't inconveniently in sight and used as footstools by fashionable lakes.

They talked of his university, which she had visited frequently during the past two years, and of the near-by city which supplied Sherry Island with its patrons, and whither Dexter would return next day to his prospering laundries.

During dinner she slipped into a moody depression which gave Dexter a feeling of uneasiness. Whatever petulance she uttered in her throaty voice worried him. Whatever she smiled at—at him, at a chicken liver, at nothing—it disturbed him that her smile could have no root in mirth, or even in amusement. When the scarlet corners of her lips curved

down, it was less a smile than an invitation to a kiss.

Then, after dinner, she led him out on the dark sun-porch and deliberately changed the atmosphere.

"Do you mind if I weep a little?" she said.

"I'm afraid I'm boring you," he responded quickly.

"You're not. I like you. But I've just had a terrible afternoon. There was a man I cared about, and this afternoon he told me out of a clear sky that he was poor as a church-mouse. He'd never even hinted it before. Does this sound horribly mundane?"

"Perhaps he was afraid to tell you."

"Suppose he was," she answered. "He didn't start right. You see, if I'd thought of him as poor—well, I've been mad about loads of poor men, and fully intended to marry them all. But in this case, I hadn't thought of him that way, and my interest in him wasn't strong enough to survive the shock. As if a girl calmly informed her fiancé that she was a widow. He might not object to widows, but—

"Let's start right," she interrupted herself suddenly. "Who are you, anyhow?"

For a moment Dexter hesitated. Then:

"I'm nobody," he announced. "My career is largely a matter of futures."

"Are you poor?"

"No," he said frankly, "I'm probably making more money than any man my age in the Northwest. I know that's an obnoxious remark, but you advised me to start right."

There was a pause. Then she smiled and the corners of her mouth drooped and an almost imperceptible sway brought her closer to him, looking up into his eyes. A lump rose in Dexter's throat, and he waited breathless for the experiment, facing the unpredictable compound that would form mysteriously from the elements of their lips. Then he saw—she communicated her excitement to him, lavishly, deeply, with kisses that were not a promise but

a fulfilment. They aroused in him not hunger demanding renewal but surfeit that would demand more surfeit . . . kisses that were like charity, creating want by holding back nothing at all.

It did not take him many hours to decide that he had wanted Judy Jones ever since he was a proud, desirous little boy.

IV

It began like that—and continued, with varying shades of intensity, on such a note right up to the dénouement. Dexter surrendered a part of himself to the most direct and unprincipled personality with which he had ever come in contact. Whatever Judy wanted, she went after with the full pressure of her charm. There was no divergence of method, no jockeying for position or premeditation of effects—there was a very little mental side to any of her affairs. She simply made men conscious to the highest degree of her physical loveliness. Dexter had no desire to change her. Her deficiencies were knit up with a passionate energy that transcended and justified them.

When, as Judy's head lay against his shoulder that first night, she whispered, "I don't know what's the matter with me. Last night I thought I was in love with a man and tonight I think I'm in love with you—" —it seemed to him a beautiful and romantic thing to say. It was the exquisite excitability that for the moment he controlled and owned. But a week later he was compelled to view this same quality in a different light. She took him in her roadster to a picnic supper, and after supper she disappeared, likewise in her roadster, with another man. Dexter became enormously upset and was scarcely able to be decently civil to the other people present. When she assured him that she had not kissed the other man, he knew she was lying—yet he was glad that she had taken the trouble to lie to him.

He was, as he found before the summer ended, one of a varying dozen who circulated about her. Each of them had at one time been favored above all others—about half of them still basked in the solace of occasional sentimental revivals. Whenever one showed signs of dropping out through long neglect, she granted him a brief honeyed hour, which encouraged him to tag along for a year or so longer. Judy made these forays upon the helpless and defeated without malice, indeed half unconscious that there was anything mischievous in what she did.

When a new man came to town every one dropped out—dates were automatically cancelled.

The helpless part of trying to do anything about it was that she did it all herself. She was not a girl who could be "won" in the kinetic sense—she was proof against cleverness, she was proof against charm; if any of these assailed her too strongly she would immediately resolve the affair to a physical basis, and under the magic of her physical splendor the strong as well as the brilliant played her game and not their own. She was entertained only by the gratification of her desires and by the direct exercise of her own charm. Perhaps from so much youthful love, so many youthful lovers, she had come, in self-defense, to nourish herself wholly from within.

Succeeding Dexter's first exhilaration came restlessness and dissatisfaction. The helpless ecstasy of losing himself in her was opiate rather than tonic. It was fortunate for his work during the winter that those moments of ecstasy came infrequently. Early in their acquaintance it had seemed for a while that there was a deep and spontaneous mutual attraction—that first August, for example—three days of long evenings on her dusky veranda, of strange wan kisses through the late afternoon, in shadowy alcoves or behind the protecting trellises of the garden arbors, of mornings when she was fresh as a dream and almost shy at meeting him in the clarity of the rising day.

There was all the ecstasy of an engagement about it, sharpened by his realization that there was no engagement. It was during those three days that, for the first time, he had asked her to marry him. She said "maybe some day," she said "kiss me," she said "I'd like to marry you," she said "I love you"—she said—nothing.

The three days were interrupted by the arrival of a New York man who visited at her house for half September. To Dexter's agony, rumor engaged them. The man was the son of the president of a great trust company. But at the end of a month it was reported that Judy was yawning. At a dance one night she sat all evening in a motor-boat with a local beau, while the New Yorker searched the club for her frantically. She told the local beau that she was bored with her visitor, and two days later he left. She was seen with him at the station, and it was reported that he looked very mournful indeed.

On this note the summer ended. Dexter was twenty-four, and he found himself increasingly in a position to do as he wished. He joined two clubs in the city and lived at one of them. Though he was by no means an integral part of the stag-lines at these clubs, he managed to be on hand at dances where Judy Jones was likely to appear. He could have gone out socially as much as he liked—he was an eligible young man, now, and popular with down-town fathers. His confessed devotion to Judy Jones had rather solidified his position. But he had no social aspirations and rather despised the dancing men who were always on tap for the Thursday or Saturday parties and who filled in at dinners with the younger married set. Already he was playing with the idea of going East to New York. He wanted to take Judy Jones with him. No disillusion as to the world in which she had grown up could cure his illusion as to her desirability.

Remember that—for only in the light of it can what he did for her be understood.

Eighteen months after he first met Judy Jones he became engaged to another girl. Her name was Irene Scheerer, and her father was one of the men who had always believed in Dexter. Irene was light-haired and sweet and honorable, and a little stout, and she had two suitors whom she pleasantly relinquished when Dexter formally asked her to marry him.

Summer, fall, winter, spring, another summer, another fall—so much he had given of his active life to the incorrigible lips of Judy Jones. She had treated him with interest, with encouragement, with malice, with indifference, with contempt. She had inflicted on him the innumerable little slights and indignities possible in such a case—as if in revenge for having ever cared for him at all. She had beckoned him and yawned at him and beckoned him again and he had responded often with bitterness and narrowed eyes. She had brought him ecstatic happiness and intolerable agony of spirit. She had caused him untold inconvenience and not a little trouble. She had insulted him, and she had ridden over him, and she had played his interest in her against his interest in his work—for fun. She had done everything to him except to criticise him—this she had not done—it seemed to him only because it might have sullied the utter indifference she manifested and sincerely felt toward him.

When autumn had come and gone again it occurred to him that he could not have Judy Jones. He had to beat this into his mind but he convinced himself at last. He lay awake at night for a while and argued it over. He told himself the trouble and the pain she had caused him, he enumerated her glaring deficiencies as a wife. Then he said to himself that he loved her, and after a while he fell asleep. For a week, lest he imagined her husky voice over the telephone or her eyes opposite him at lunch, he worked hard and late, and at night he went to his office and plotted out his years.

At the end of a week he went to a dance and cut in on her once. For almost the first time since they had met he did not ask her to sit out with him or tell her that she was lovely. It hurt him that she did not miss these things—that was all. He was not jealous when he saw that there was a new man to-night. He had been hardened against jealousy long before.

He stayed late at the dance. He sat for an hour with Irene Scheerer and talked about books and about music. He knew very little about either. But he was beginning to be master of his own time now, and he had a rather priggish notion that he—the young and already fabulously successful Dexter Green—should know more about such things.

That was in October, when he was twenty-five. In January, Dexter and Irene became engaged. It was to be announced in June, and they were to be married three months later.

The Minnesota winter prolonged itself interminably, and it was almost May when the winds came soft and the snow ran down into Black Bear Lake at last. For the first time in over a year Dexter was enjoying a certain tranquillity of spirit. Judy Jones had been in Florida, and afterward in Hot Springs, and somewhere she had been engaged, and somewhere she had broken it off. At first, when Dexter had definitely given her up, it had made him sad that people still linked them together and asked for news of her, but when he began to be placed at dinner next to Irene Scheerer people didn't ask him about her any more—they told him about her. He ceased to be an authority on her.

May at last. Dexter walked the streets at night when the darkness was damp as rain, wondering that so soon, with so little done, so much of ecstasy had gone from him. May one year back had been marked by Judy's poignant, unforgivable, yet forgiven turbulence—it had been one of those rare times when he fancied she had grown to care for him. That old penny's worth of happiness he had spent for this bushel of content. He knew that Irene would be no more than a curtain spread behind him, a hand moving among gleaming tea-cups, a voice calling to children . . . fire and loveliness were gone, the magic of nights and the wonder of the varying hours and seasons . . . slender lips, down-turning, dropping to his lips and bearing him up into a heaven of eyes. . . . The thing was deep in him. He was too strong and alive for it to die lightly.

In the middle of May when the weather balanced for a few days on the thin bridge that led to deep summer he turned in one night at Irene's house. Their engagement was to be announced in a week now—no one would be surprised at it. And to-night they would sit together on the lounge at the University Club and look on for an hour at the dancers. It gave him a sense of solidity to go with her—she was so sturdily popular, so intensely "great."

He mounted the steps of the brownstone house and stepped inside.

"Irene," he called.

Mrs. Scheerer came out of the living-room to meet him.

"Dexter," she said, "Irene's gone upstairs with a splitting headache. She wanted to go with you but I made her go to bed."

"Nothing serious, I—"

"Oh, no. She's going to play golf with you in the morning. You can spare her for just one night, can't you, Dexter?"

Her smile was kind. She and Dexter liked each other. In the living-room he talked for a moment before he said good-night.

Returning to the University Club, where he had rooms, he stood in the doorway for a moment and watched the dancers. He leaned against the doorpost, nodded at a man or two—yawned.

"Hello, darling."

The familiar voice at his elbow startled him. Judy Jones had left a man and crossed the room to him—Judy Jones, a slender enamelled doll in cloth of gold: gold in a band at her head, gold in two slipper points at her dress's hem.

The fragile glow of her face seemed to blossom as she smiled at him. A breeze of warmth and light blew through the room. His hands in the pockets of his dinner-jacket tightened spasmodically. He was filled with a sudden excitement.

"When did you get back?" he asked casually.

"Come here and I'll tell you about it."

She turned and he followed her. She had been away—he could have wept at the wonder of her return. She had passed through enchanted streets, doing things that were like provocative music. All mysterious happenings, all fresh and quickening hopes, had gone away with her, come back with her now.

She turned in the doorway.

"Have you a car here? If you haven't, I have."

"I have a coupé."

In then, with a rustle of golden cloth. He slammed the door. Into so many cars she had stepped—like this—like that—her back against the leather, so—her elbow resting on the door—waiting. She would have been soiled long since had there been anything to soil her—except herself—but this was her own self outpouring.

With an effort he forced himself to start the car and back into the street. This was nothing, he must remember. She had done this before, and he had put her behind him, as he would have crossed a bad account from his books.

He drove slowly down-town and, affecting abstraction, traversed the deserted streets of the business section, peopled here and there where a movie was giving out its crowd or where consumptive or pugilistic youth lounged in front of pool halls. The clink of glasses and the slap of hands on the bars issued from saloons, cloisters of glazed glass and dirty yellow light.

She was watching him closely and the silence was embarrassing, yet in this crisis he could find no casual word with which to profane the hour. At a convenient turning he began to zigzag back toward the University Club.

"Have you missed me?" she asked suddenly.

"Everybody missed you."

He wondered if she knew of Irene Scheerer. She had been back only a day—her absence had been almost contemporaneous with his engagement.

"What a remark!" Judy laughed sadly—without sadness. She looked at him searchingly. He became absorbed in the dashboard.

"You're handsomer than you used to be," she said thoughtfully. "Dexter, you have the most rememberable eyes."

He could have laughed at this, but he did not laugh. It was the sort of thing that was said to sophomores. Yet it stabbed at him.

"I'm awfully tired of everything, darling." She called every one darling, endowing the endearment with careless, individual camaraderie. "I wish you'd marry me."

The directness of this confused him. He should have told her now that he was going to marry another girl, but he could not tell her. He could as easily have sworn that he had never loved her.

"I think we'd get along," she continued, on the same note, "unless probably you've forgotten me and fallen in love with another girl."

Her confidence was obviously enormous. She had said, in effect, that she found such a thing impossible to believe, that if it were true he had merely committed a childish indiscretion—and probably to show off. She would forgive him, because it was not a matter of any moment but rather something to be brushed aside lightly.

"Of course you could never love anybody but me," she continued, "I like the way you love me. Oh, Dexter, have you forgotten last year?"

"No, I haven't forgotten."

"Neither have I!"

Was she sincerely moved—or was she carried along by the wave of her own acting?"

"I wish we could be like that again," she said, and he forced himself to answer:

"I don't think we can."

"I suppose not. . . . I hear you're giving Irene Scheerer a violent rush."

There was not the faintest emphasis on the name, yet Dexter was suddenly ashamed.

"Oh, take me home," cried Judy suddenly; "I don't want to go back to that idiotic dance—with those children."

Then, as he turned up the street that led to the residence district, Judy began to cry quietly to herself. He had never seen her cry before.

The dark street lightened, the dwellings of the rich loomed up around them, he stopped his coupé in front of the great white bulk of the Mortimer Joneses' house, somnolent, gorgeous, drenched with the splendor of the damp moonlight. Its solidity startled him. The strong walls, the steel of the girders, the breadth and beam and pomp of it were there only to bring out the contrast with the young beauty beside him. It was sturdy to accentuate her slightness—as if to show what a breeze could be generated by a butterfly's wing.

He sat perfectly quiet, his nerves in wild clamor, afraid that if he moved he would find her irresistibly in his arms. Two tears had rolled down her wet face and trembled on her upper lip.

"I'm more beautiful than anybody else," she said brokenly, "why can't I be happy?" Her moist eyes tore at his stability—her mouth turned slowly downward with an exquisite sadness: "I'd like to marry you if you'll have me, Dexter. I suppose you think I'm not worth having, but I'll be so beautiful for you, Dexter."

A million phrases of anger, pride, passion, hatred, tenderness fought on his lips. Then a perfect wave of emotion washed over him, carrying off with it a sediment of wisdom, of convention, of doubt, of honor. This was his girl who was speaking, his own, his beautiful, his pride.

"Won't you come in?" He heard her draw in her breath sharply.

Waiting.

"All right," his voice was trembling, "I'll come in."

V

It was strange that neither when it was over nor a long time afterward did he regret that night. Looking at it from the perspective of ten years, the fact that Judy's flare for him endured just one month seemed of little importance. Nor did it matter that by his yielding he subjected himself to a deeper agony in the end and gave serious hurt to Irene Scheerer and to Irene's parents, who had befriended him. There was nothing sufficiently pictorial about Irene's grief to stamp itself on his mind.

Dexter was at bottom hard-minded. The attitude of the city on his action was of no importance to him, not because he was going to leave the city, but because any outside attitude on the situation seemed superficial. He was completely indifferent to popular opinion. Nor, when he had seen that it was no use, that he did not possess in himself the power to move fundamentally or to hold Judy Jones, did he bear any malice toward her. He loved her, and he would love her until the day he was too old for loving—but he could not have her. So he tasted the deep pain that is reserved only for the strong, just as he had tasted for a little while the deep happiness.

Even the ultimate falsity of the grounds upon which Judy terminated the engagement that she did not want to "take him away" from Irene—Judy, who had wanted nothing else—did not revolt him. He was beyond any revulsion or any amusement.

He went East in February with the intention of selling out his laundries and settling in New York—but the war came to America in March and changed his plans. He returned to the West, handed over the management of the business to his partner, and went into the first officers' training-camp in late April. He was one of those young thousands who greeted the war with a certain amount of relief, welcoming the liberation from webs of tangled emotion.

VI

This story is not his biography, remember, although things creep into it which have nothing to do with those dreams he had when he was young. We are almost done with them and with him now. There is only one more incident to be related here, and it happens seven years farther on.

It took place in New York, where he had done well—so well that there were no barriers too high for him. He was thirty-two years old, and, except for one flying trip immediately after the war, he had not been West in seven years. A man named Devlin from Detroit came into his office to see him in a business way, and then and there this incident occurred, and closed out, so to speak, this particular side of his life.

"So you're from the Middle West," said the man Devlin with careless curiosity. "That's funny—I thought men like you were probably born and raised on Wall Street. You know—wife of one of my best friends in Detroit came from your city. I was an usher at the wedding."

Dexter waited with no apprehension of what was coming.

"Judy Simms," said Devlin with no particular interest; "Judy Jones she was once."

"Yes, I knew her." A dull impatience spread over him. He had heard, of course, that she was married—perhaps deliberately he had heard no more.

"Awfully nice girl," brooded Devlin meaninglessly, "I'm sort of sorry for her."

"Why?" Something in Dexter was alert, receptive, at once.

"Oh, Lud Simms has gone to pieces in a way. I don't mean he ill-uses her, but he drinks and runs around——"

"Doesn't she run around?"

"No. Stays at home with her kids."

"Oh."

"She's a little too old for him," said Devlin.

"Too old!" cried Dexter. "Why, man, she's only twenty-seven."

He was possessed with a wild notion of rushing out into the streets and taking a train to Detroit. He rose to his feet spasmodically.

"I guess you're busy," Devlin apologized quickly. "I didn't realize——"

"No, I'm not busy," said Dexter, steadying his voice. "I'm not busy at all. Not busy at all. Did you say she was—twenty-seven? No, I said she was twenty-seven."

"Yes, you did," agreed Devlin dryly.

"Go on, then. Go on."

"What do you mean?"

"About Judy Jones."

Devlin looked at him helplessly.

"Well, that's—I told you all there is to it. He treats her like the devil. Oh, they're not going to get divorced or anything. When he's particularly outrageous she forgives him. In fact, I'm inclined to think she loves him. She was a pretty girl when she first came to Detroit."

A pretty girl! The phrase struck Dexter as ludicrous.

"Isn't she—a pretty girl, any more?"

"Oh, she's all right."

"Look here," said Dexter, sitting down suddenly, "I don't understand. You say she was a 'pretty girl' and now you say she's 'all right.' I don't understand what you mean—Judy Jones wasn't a pretty girl, at all. She was a great beauty. Why, I knew her, I knew her. She was——"

Devlin laughed pleasantly.

"I'm not trying to start a row," he said. "I think Judy's a nice girl and I like her. I can't understand how a man like Lud Simms could fall madly in love with her, but he did." Then he added: "Most of the women like her."

Dexter looked closely at Devlin, thinking wildly that there must be a reason for this, some insensitivity in the man or some private malice.

"Lots of women fade just like *that,*" Devlin snapped his fingers. "You must have seen it happen. Perhaps I've forgotten how pretty she was at her wedding. I've seen her so much since then, you see. She has nice eyes."

A sort of dullness settled down upon Dexter. For the first time in his life he felt like getting very drunk. He knew that he was laughing loudly at something Devlin had said, but he did not know what it was or why it was funny. When, in a few minutes, Devlin went he lay down on his lounge and looked out the window at the New York sky-line into which the sun was sinking in dull lovely shades of pink and gold.

He had thought that having nothing else to lose he was invulnerable at last—but he knew that he had just lost something more, as surely as if he had married Judy Jones and seen her fade away before his eyes.

The dream was gone. Something had been taken from him. In a sort of panic he pushed the palms of his hands into his eyes and tried to bring up a picture of the waters lapping on Sherry Island and the moonlit veranda, and

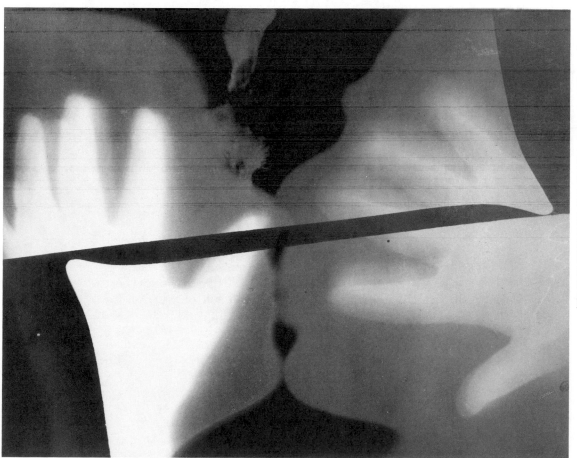

RAYOGRAPH *Man Ray* 1922

gingham on the golf-links and the dry sun and the gold color of her neck's soft down. And her mouth damp to his kisses and her eyes plaintive with melancholy and her freshness like new fine linen in the morning. Why, these things were no longer in the world! They had existed and they existed no longer.

For the first time in years the tears were streaming down his face. But they were for himself now. He did not care about mouth and eyes and moving hands. He wanted to care, and he could not care. For he had gone away and he could never go back any more. The gates were closed, the sun was gone down, and there was no beauty but the gray beauty of steel that withstands all time. Even the grief he could have borne was left behind in the country of illusion, of youth, of the richness of life, where his winter dreams had flourished.

"Long ago," he said, "long ago, there was something in me, but now that thing is gone. Now that thing is gone, that thing is gone. I cannot cry. I cannot care. That thing will come back no more."

Study Questions

1. Why does Dexter Green resign from caddying at the end of Part I? How does this resignation help keep his dream alive?

2. In Parts II and III Dexter has three further encounters with Judy Jones. What do we learn about her? What is her effect on Dexter?

3. In Parts IV and V we are able to compare Judy Jones with another girl, Irene Scheerer. What are the differences between them? Why do you think Dexter chooses Judy? To what extent is he surprised by the end of his engagement to Judy?

4. In Part VI Dexter's dream of Judy is destroyed by the man from Detroit. How does he know that the dream is finally dead?

5. Carefully reread the first three paragraphs of the story and the last three. What is the nature of Dexter's dream? How is it symbolized by Judy Jones?

Vocabulary

Each item in this exercise begins with a sentence or group of sentences based on "Winter Dreams." Every passage contains one *italicized* word and is followed by five word choices. From these choices, select an **antonym** whose meaning is most nearly opposite to that of the *italicized* word. Write your answers on a separate sheet of paper. If you are in doubt about the meaning of any word, use a dictionary.

1. In April the winter ceased abruptly and without *elation,* without an interval of moist glory, the cold was gone.

   dryness   notice   hurry   sadness   joy

2. She drew down the corners of her mouth, smiled, and glanced *furtively* around, her eyes in transit falling for an instant on Dexter.

   boldly   slowly   grimly   timidly   cheerfully

3. The situation was resolved by the *fortuitous* appearance of the caddy-master, who was appealed to by the nurse.

   accidental   early   unlucky   planned   belated

4. When she asked, "Did I bounce the ball into the rough?" it was impossible to determine whether the question was *ingenuous.*

   stupid   honest   deceitful   serious   unnecessary

5. "I've had a terrible afternoon," Judy said. "A man I cared about told me out of a clear sky that he was poor as a church-mouse. Does that sound horribly *mundane?*"

   unselfish   spiritual   thoughtful   routine   amazing

6. "I'm probably making more money than any other man my age in the Northwest," said Dexter. "I know that's an *obnoxious* remark, but you advised me to start right."

   modest   sophisticated   original   ordinary   pleasant

7. She had done everything to him except criticize him. This she had not done, it seemed to him, only because it might have *sullied* the utter indifference she felt toward him.

   concealed   cleansed   preserved   continued   softened

8. He stopped his coupe in front of the great white bulk of the Mortimer Jones' house, *somnolent,* gorgeous, drenched with moonlight splendor.

   uncared-for   alert   well-lighted   humble   unimpressive

9. Devlin said, "She was a pretty girl when she first came to Detroit."—A pretty girl? The phrase struck Dexter as *ludicrous.*

   laughable   appropriate   heartbreaking   unsurprising
   essential

10. Dexter looked closely at Devlin, thinking wildly that there must be some reason for this, some insensitivity or some private *malice.*

    purpose   misunderstanding   kindness   affection   jealousy

A Dream of Equality

While some young Americans had romantic dreams like Dexter Green's in "Winter Dreams," other young people had more practical longings. The young Black woman in the following excerpt from *I Know Why the Caged Bird Sings* (1969), demonstrates the determination and courage that have also been part of the American Dream. After this first job, Maya Angelou (1926—   ) went on to become a dancer, actress, poet, and writer of original scripts for television and film. However, she is perhaps best known for her best-selling autobiographical series. In addition to *I Know Why the Caged Bird Sings,* it also includes *Gather Together in My Name, Singing, Swinging, and Getting Merry Like Christmas,* and *Heart of a Woman.*

from I Know Why the Caged Bird Sings

MAYA ANGELOU

LATER, MY ROOM had all the cheeriness of a dungeon and the appeal of a tomb. It was going to be impossible to stay there, but leaving held no attraction for me, either. Running away from home would be anticlimactic after Mexico, and a dull story after my month in the car lot. But the need for change bulldozed a road down the center of my mind.

I had it. The answer came to me with the suddenness of a collision. I would go to work. Mother wouldn't be difficult to convince; after all, in school I was a year ahead of my grade

and Mother was a firm believer in self-sufficiency. In fact, she'd be pleased to think that I had that much gumption, that much of her in my character. (She liked to speak of herself as the original "do-it-yourself girl.")

Once I had settled on getting a job, all that remained was to decide which kind of job I was most fitted for. My intellectual pride had kept me from selecting typing, shorthand or filing as subjects in school, so office work was ruled out. War plants and shipyards demanded birth certificates, and mine would reveal me to be fifteen, and ineligible for work. So the well-paying defense jobs were also out. Women had replaced men on the streetcars as conductors and motormen, and the thought of sailing up and down the hills of San Francisco in a dark-blue uniform, with a money changer at my belt, caught my fancy.

Mother was as easy as I had anticipated. The world was moving so fast, so much money was being made, so many people were dying in Guam, and Germany, that hordes of strangers became good friends overnight. Life was cheap and death entirely free. How could she have the time to think about my academic career?

To her question of what I planned to do, I replied that I would get a job on the streetcars. She rejected the proposal with: "They don't accept colored people on the streetcars."

I would like to claim an immediate fury which was followed by the noble determination to break the restricting tradition. But the truth is, my first reaction was one of disappointment. I'd pictured myself, dressed in a neat blue serge suit, my money changer swinging jauntily at my waist, and a cheery smile for the passengers which would make their own work day brighter.

From disappointment, I gradually ascended the emotional ladder to haughty indignation, and finally to that state of stubbornness where the mind is locked like the jaws of an enraged bulldog.

I would go to work on the streetcars and wear a blue serge suit. Mother gave me her support with one of her usual terse asides, "That's what you want to do? Then nothing beats a trial but a failure. Give it everything you've got. I've told you many times, 'Can't do is like Don't Care.' Neither of them have a home."

Translated, that meant there was nothing a person can't do, and there should be nothing a human being didn't care about. It was the most positive encouragement I could have hoped for.

In the offices of the Market Street Railway Company, the receptionist seemed as surprised to see me there as I was surprised to find the interior dingy and the décor drab. Somehow I had expected waxed surfaces and carpeted floors. If I had met no resistance, I might have decided against working for such a poor-mouth-looking concern. As it was, I explained that I had come to see about a job. She asked, was I sent by an agency, and when I replied that I was not, she told me they were only accepting applicants from agencies.

The classified pages of the morning papers had listed advertisements for motorettes and conductorettes and I reminded her of that. She gave me a face full of astonishment that my suspicious nature would not accept.

"I am applying for the job listed in this morning's *Chronicle* and I'd like to be presented to your personnel manager." While I spoke in supercilious accents, and looked at the room as if I had an oil well in my own backyard, my armpits were being pricked by millions of hot pointed needles. She saw her escape and dived into it.

"He's out. He's out for the day. You might call tomorrow and if he's in, I'm sure you can see him." Then she swiveled her chair around on its rusty screws and with that I was supposed to be dismissed.

"May I ask his name?"

She half turned, acting surprised to find me still there.

"His name? Whose name?"

"Your personnel manager."

We were firmly joined in the hypocrisy to play out the scene.

"The personnel manager? Oh, he's Mr. Cooper, but I'm not sure you'll find him here tomorrow. He's . . . Oh, but you can try."

"Thank you."

"You're welcome."

And I was out of the musty room and into the even mustier lobby. In the street I saw the receptionist and myself going faithfully through paces that were stale with familiarity, although I had never encountered that kind of situation before and, probably, neither had she. We were like actors who, knowing the play by heart, were still able to cry afresh over the old tragedies and laugh spontaneously at the comic situations.

The miserable little encounter had nothing to do with me, the me of me, any more than it had to do with that silly clerk. The incident was a recurring dream, concocted years before by stupid whites and it eternally came back to haunt us all. The secretary and I were like Hamlet and Laertes in the final scene, where, because of harm done by one ancestor to another, we were bound to duel to the death. Also because the play must end somewhere.

I went further than forgiving the clerk, I accepted her as a fellow victim of the same puppeteer.

On the streetcar, I put my fare into the box and the conductorette looked at me with the usual hard eyes of white contempt. "Move into the car, please move on in the car." She patted her money changer.

Her Southern nasal accent sliced my meditation and I looked deep into my thoughts. All lies, all comfortable lies. The receptionist was not innocent and neither was I. The whole charade we had played out in that crummy waiting room had directly to do with me, Black, and her, white.

I wouldn't move into the streetcar but stood on the ledge over the conductor, glaring. My mind shouted so energetically that the announcement made my veins stand out, and my mouth tighten into a prune.

I WOULD HAVE THE JOB. I WOULD BE A CONDUCTORETTE AND SLING A FULL MONEY CHANGER FROM MY BELT. I WOULD.

The next three weeks were a honeycomb of determination with apertures for the days to go in and out. The Negro organizations to whom I appealed for support bounced me back and forth like a shuttlecock on a badminton court. Why did I insist on that particular job? Openings were going begging that paid nearly twice the money. The minor officials with whom I was able to win an audience thought me mad. Possibly I was.

Downtown San Francisco became alien and cold, and the streets I had loved in a personal familiarity were unknown lanes that twisted with malicious intent. Old buildings, whose gray rococo façades housed my memories of the Forty-Niners, and Diamond Lil, Robert Service, Sutter and Jack London, were then imposing structures viciously joined to keep me out. My trips to the streetcar office were of the frequency of a person on salary. The struggle expanded. I was no longer in conflict only with the Market Street Railway but with the marble lobby of the building which housed its offices, and elevators and their operators.

During this period of strain Mother and I began our first steps on the long path toward mutual adult admiration. She never asked for reports and I didn't offer any details. But every morning she made breakfast, gave me carfare and lunch money, as if I were going to work. She comprehended the perversity of life, that in the struggle lies the joy. That I was no glory seeker was obvious to her, and that I had to exhaust every possibility before giving in was also clear.

On my way out of the house one morning she said, "Life is going to give you just what you put in it. Put your whole heart in everything you do, and pray, then you can wait." Another time she reminded me that "God helps those who help themselves." She had a store of aphorisms which she dished out as the occasion demanded. Strangely, as bored as I was with clichés, her inflection gave them something new, and set me thinking for a little while at least. Later when asked how I got my job, I was never able to say exactly. I only knew that one day, which was tiresomely like all the others before it, I sat in the Railway office, ostensibly waiting to be interviewed. The receptionist called me to her desk and shuffled a bundle of papers to me. They were job application forms. She said they had to be

filled in triplicate. I had little time to wonder if I had won or not, for the standard questions reminded me of the necessity for dexterous lying. How old was I? List my previous jobs, starting from the last held and go backward to the first. How much money did I earn, and why did I leave the position? Give two references (not relatives).

Sitting at a side table my mind and I wove a cat's ladder of near truths and total lies. I kept my face blank (an old art) and wrote quickly the fable of Marguerite Johnson, aged nineteen, former companion and driver for Mrs. Annie Henderson (a White Lady) in Stamps, Arkansas.

I was given blood tests, aptitude tests, physical coordination tests, and Rorschachs, then on a blissful day I was hired as the first Negro on the San Francisco streetcars.

Mother gave me the money to have my blue serge suit tailored, and I learned to fill out work cards, operate the money changer and punch transfers. The time crowded together and at an End of Days I was swinging on the back of the rackety trolley, smiling sweetly and persuading my charges to "step forward in the car, please."

For one whole semester the streetcars and I shimmied up and scooted down the sheer hills of San Francisco. I lost some of my need for the Black ghetto's shielding-sponge quality, as I clanged and cleared my way down Market Street, with its honky-tonk homes for homeless sailors, past the quiet retreat of Golden Gate Park and along closed undwelled-in-looking dwellings of the Sunset District.

My work shifts were split so haphazardly that it was easy to believe that my superiors had chosen them maliciously. Upon mentioning my suspicions to Mother, she said, "Don't worry about it. You ask for what you want, and you pay for what you get. And I'm going to show you that it ain't no trouble when you pack double."

She stayed awake to drive me out to the car barn at four thirty in the mornings, or to pick me up when I was relieved just before dawn. Her awareness of life's perils convinced her that while I would be safe on the public conveyances, she "wasn't about to trust a taxi driver with her baby."

When the spring classes began, I resumed my commitment with formal education. I was so much wiser and older, so much more independent, with a bank account and clothes that I had bought for myself, that I was sure that I had learned and earned the magic formula which would make me a part of the gay life my contemporaries led.

Not a bit of it. Within weeks, I realized that my schoolmates and I were on paths moving diametrically away from each other. They were concerned and excited over the approaching football games, but I had in my immediate past raced a car down a dark and foreign Mexican mountain. They concentrated great interest on who was worthy of being student body president, and when the metal bands would be removed from their teeth, while I remembered sleeping for a month in a wrecked automobile and conducting a streetcar in the uneven hours of the morning.

Without willing it, I had gone from being ignorant of being ignorant to being aware of being aware. And the worst part of my awareness was that I didn't know what I was aware of. I knew I knew very little, but I was certain that the things I had yet to learn wouldn't be taught to me at George Washington High School.

Study Questions

1. Why does Angelou persist in trying to get the job despite the obstacles?
2. How does the struggle to obtain the job establish a mutual admiration between the mother and daughter?
3. Even though Angelou returns to school after her experience as a conductorette, how has she changed as a person? What does she mean by, "I had gone from being ignorant of being ignorant to being aware of being aware"?
4. In what way is this story related to the poem, "Lenox Avenue Mural"?

The March for a Dream

Even though Martin Luther King, Jr., (1929–1968) was a theologian and writer, he is remembered most for his considerable ability as an orator. He was foremost a skilled Black Baptist preacher. Born in Atlanta, the son and grandson of Baptist ministers, he was graduated from Morehouse College. Later, he received the Ph.D. from Boston University. King wrote several books. Among them are: *Stride Toward Freedom* (1958), *Strength to Love* (1963), and *Why We Can't Wait* (1964).

On August 28, 1963, over 200,000 people marched on Washington, D.C. for a common purpose, to bring the needed pressure to pass a civil rights law. When the marchers came to a halt before the Lincoln Memorial, various leaders addressed the crowd. Martin Luther King, Jr., gave the speech included here. This speech, about his undying dream of imperishable rights and opportunities, has since become legendary. A few months later President Kennedy sent Congress the strongest civil rights bill in American history. It became law in 1964—the same year King received the Nobel Peace Prize. He was the youngest person ever to win that award. Four years later he was assassinated in Memphis, Tennessee, where he was leading a demonstration for striking garbage workers.

I Have a Dream

MARTIN LUTHER KING, JR.

. . . Five score years ago, a great American, in whose symbolic shadow we stand, signed the Emancipation Proclamation. This momentous decree came as a great beacon light of hope to millions of Negro slaves who had been seared in the flames of withering injustice. It came as a joyous daybreak to end the long night of captivity.

But one hundred years later, we must face the tragic fact that the Negro is still not free. One hundred years later, the life of the Negro is still sadly crippled by the manacles of segregation and the chains of discrimination. One hundred years later, the Negro lives on a lonely island of poverty in the midst of a vast ocean of material prosperity. One hundred years later, the Negro is still languished in the corners of American society and finds himself an exile in his own land. So we have come here today to dramatize an appalling condition.

In a sense we have come to our Nation's Capital to cash a check. When the architects of our Republic wrote the magnificent words of the Constitution and the Declaration of Independence, they were signing a promissory note to which every American was to fall heir. This note was a promise that all men would be guaranteed the unalienable rights of life, liberty, and the pursuit of happiness.

It is obvious today that America has defaulted on this promissory note insofar as her citizens of color are concerned. Instead of honoring this sacred obligation, America has given the Negro people a bad check; a check which has come back marked "insufficient funds." But we refuse to believe that the bank of justice is bankrupt. We refuse to believe that there are insufficient funds in the great vaults of opportunity of this nation. So we have come to cash this check—a check that will give us upon demand the riches of freedom and the security of justice. We have also come to this hallowed spot to remind America of the fierce urgency of now. This is no time to engage in the luxury of cooling off or to take the tranquilizing drug of gradualism. Now is the time to make real the promises of Democracy. Now is the time to rise from the dark and desolate valley of segregation to the sunlit path of racial justice. Now is the time to open the doors of opportunity to all of God's children. Now is the time to lift our nation from the quicksands of racial injustice to the solid rock of brotherhood.

It would be fatal for the nation to overlook the urgency of the moment and to underestimate the determination of the Negro. This sweltering summer of the Negro's legitimate discontent will not pass until there is an invigorating autumn of freedom and equality. 1963 is not an end, but a beginning. Those who hope that the Negro needed to blow off steam and will be content will have a rude awakening if the Nation returns to business as usual. There will be neither rest nor tranquility in America until the Negro is granted his citizenship rights. The whirlwinds of revolt will continue to shake the foundations of our Nation until the bright day of justice emerges.

But there is something that I must say to my people who stand on the warm threshold which leads into the palace of justice. In the process of gaining our rightful place we must not be guilty of wrongful deeds. Let us not seek to satisfy our thirst for freedom by drinking from the cup of bitterness and hatred. We must forever conduct our struggle on the high plane of dignity and discipline. We must not allow our creative protest to degenerate into physical violence. Again and again we must rise to the majestic heights of meeting physical force with soul force. The marvelous new militancy which has engulfed the Negro community must not lead us to a distrust of all white people, for many of our white brothers, as evidenced by their presence here today, have come to realize that their destiny is tied up with our destiny and their freedom is inextricably bound to our freedom. We cannot walk alone.

And as we walk, we must make the pledge that we shall march ahead. We cannot turn back. There are those who are asking the devotees of civil rights, "when will you be satisfied?" We can never be satisfied as long as the Negro is the victim of the unspeakable horrors of police brutality. We can never be satisfied as long as our bodies, heavy with the fatigue of travel, cannot gain lodging in the motels of the highways and the hotels of the cities. We cannot be satisfied as long as the Negro's basic mobility is from a smaller ghetto to a larger one. We can never be satisfied as long as a Negro in Mississippi cannot vote and a Negro in New York believes he has nothing for which to vote. No, no we are not satisfied, and we will not be satisfied until justice rolls down like water and righteousness like a mighty stream.

I am not unmindful that some of you have come here out of great trials and tribulations. Some of you have come fresh from narrow jail cells. Some of you have come from areas where your quest for freedom left you battered by the storms of persecution and staggered by the winds of police brutality. You have been the veterans of creative suffering. Continue to

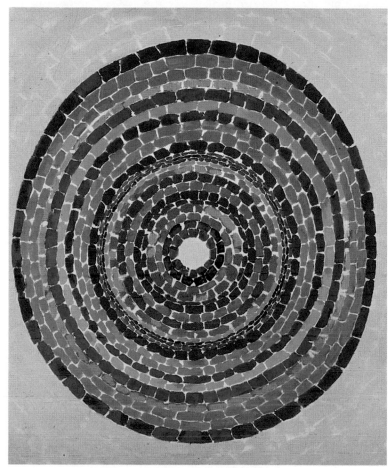

FLOWERS AT THE JEFFERSON MEMORIAL *Alma Thomas*

work with the faith that unearned suffering is redemptive.

Go back to Mississippi, go back to South Carolina, go back to Georgia, go back to Louisiana, go back to the slums and ghettos of our northern cities, knowing that somehow this situation can and will be changed. Let us not wallow in the valley of despair.

I say to you today, my friends, that in spite of the difficulties and frustrations of the moment I still have a dream. It is a dream deeply rooted in the American dream.

I have a dream that one day this nation will rise up and live out the true meaning of its creed: "We hold these truths to be self-evident; that all men are created equal."

I have a dream that one day on the red hills of Georgia the sons of former slaves and the sons of former slaveowners will be able to sit down together at the table of brotherhood.

I have a dream that one day even the state of Mississippi, a desert state sweltering with the heat of injustice and oppression, will be transformed into an oasis of freedom and justice.

I have a dream that my four little children will one day live in a nation where they will not be judged by the color of their skin but by the content of their character.

I have a dream today.

I have a dream that one day the state of Alabama, . . . will be transformed into a situation where little black boys and black girls will be able to join hands with little white boys and white girls and walk together as sisters and brothers.

I have a dream today.

I have a dream that one day every valley shall be exalted, every hill and mountain shall be made low, the rough places will be made plains, and the crooked places will be made straight, and the glory of the Lord shall be revealed, and all flesh shall see it together.

This is our hope. This is the faith with which I return to the South. With this faith we will be able to hew out of the mountain of despair a stone of hope. With this faith we will be able to transform the jangling discords of our nation into a beautiful symphony of brotherhood. With this faith we will be able to work together, to pray together, to struggle together, to go to jail together, to stand up for freedom together, knowing that we will be free one day.

This will be the day when all of God's children will be able to sing with new meaning "My country 'tis of thee, sweet land of liberty, of thee I sing. Land where my fathers died, land of the pilgrim's pride, from every mountainside, let freedom ring."

And if America is to be a great nation this must become true. So let freedom ring from the prodigious hilltops of New Hampshire. Let freedom ring from the mighty mountains of New York. Let freedom ring from the heightening Alleghenies of Pennsylvania!

Let freedom ring from the snowcapped Rockies of Colorado!

Let freedom ring from the curvaceous peaks of California!

But not only that—let freedom ring from Stone Mountain of Georgia!

Let freedom ring from every hill and mole hill of Mississippi. From every mountainside, let freedom ring.

When we let freedom ring, when we let it ring from every village and every hamlet, from every state and every city, we will be able to speed up that day when all of God's children, black men and white men, Jews and Gentiles, Protestants and Catholics, will be able to join hands and sing in the words of that old Negro spiritual, "Free at last! Free at last! Thank God almighty, we are free at last!"

Study Questions

1. A traditional characteristic of good Black Baptist sermons is the generous use of metaphors. Find the metaphors in the first two paragraphs of "I Have a Dream." In the third paragraph King introduces another metaphor which continues for two paragraphs. What is it? Why is it effective? Other techniques used by King are alliteration (dignity and discipline) and repetition. Find examples of these two techniques.

2. King used allusions to familiar songs, speeches, and the *Bible*. What are these allusions? Why are they effective? ineffective?

3. What aspects of The American Dream is King referring to? What approach does he suggest to achieve this dream?

Dream as Vision

This unit ends with an essay which describes an old man's way of seeing into the meaning of his own humanity. The writer of the essay is N. Scott Momaday (1934—   ), a Cherokee/Kiowa Indian who was born in Oklahoma and grew up on reservations in the Southwest. He was awarded the Pulitzer Prize for his novel, *House Made of Dawn* (1968). Momaday has taught American literature at the University of California and at Stanford University where he received his doctorate.

Momaday is also a poet, *The Gourd Dancer* (1976), and the author of another novel, *The Way to Rainy Mountain* (1969).

A Vision Beyond Time and Place

N. SCOTT MOMADAY

W HEN MY FATHER was a boy, an old man used to come to (my grandfather) Mammedaty's house and pay his respects. He was a lean old man in braids and was impressive in his age and bearing. His name was Cheney, and he was an arrowmaker. Every morning, my father tells me, Cheney would paint his wrinkled face, go out, and pray aloud to the rising sun. In my mind I can see that man as if he were there now. I like to watch him as he makes his prayer. I know where he stands and where his voice goes on the rolling grasses and where the sun comes up on the land. There, at dawn, you can feel the silence. It is cold and clear and deep like water. It takes hold of you and will not let you go.

I often think of old man Cheney, and of his daily devotion to the sun. He died before I was born, and I never knew where he came from or what of good and bad entered into his life. But I think I know who he was, essentially, and what his view of the world meant to him and to me. He was a man who saw very deeply into the distance, I believe, one whose vision extended far beyond the physical boundaries of his time and place. He perceived the wonder and meaning of Creation itself. In his mind's eye he could integrate all the realities and illusions of the earth and sky; they became for him profoundly intelligible and whole.

Once, in the first light, I stood where Cheney has stood, next to the house which my grandfather Mammedaty had built on a rise of land near Rainy Mountain Creek, and watched the sun come out of the black horizon of the world. It was an irresistible and awesome emergence, as waters gather to the flood, of weather and of light. I could not have been more sensitive to the cold nor to the heat which came upon it. And I could not have *foreseen* the break of day. The shadows on the rolling plains became large and luminous in a moment, impalpable, then faceted, dark and distinct again as they were run through with splinters of light. And the sun itself, when it appeared, was pale and immense, original in the deepest sense of the word. It is no wonder, I thought, that an old man should pray to it. It is no wonder . . . and yet, of course, wonder is the principal part of such a vision. Cheney's prayer was an affirmation of his wonder and regard, a testament to the realization of a quest for vision.

This native vision, this gift of seeing truly, with wonder and delight, into the natural world, is informed by a certain attitude of reverence and self-respect. It is a matter of extrasensory as well as sensory perception, I believe. In addition to the eye, it involves the intelligence, the instinct, and the imagination. It is the perception not only of objects and forms but also of essences and ideals, as in this Chippewa song:

as my eyes
search
the prairie
I feel the summer
in the spring

Even as the singer sees into the immediate landscape, he perceives a now and future dimension that is altogether remote, yet nonetheless real and inherent within it, a quality of evanescence and evolution, a state at once of being and of becoming. He beholds what is there; nothing of the scene is lost upon him. In the integrity of his vision he is wholly in possession of himself and of the world around him; he is quintessentially alive.

Most Indian people are able to see in these terms. Their view of the world is peculiarly native and distinct, and it determines who and what they are to a great extent. It is indeed the basis upon which they identify themselves as individuals and as a race. There is something of genetic significance in such a thing, perhaps, an element of being which resides in the blood and which is, after all, the very nucleus of the self. When old man Cheney looked into the sunrise, he saw as far into himself, I suspect, as he saw into the distance. He knew certainly of his existence and of his place in the scheme of things.

In contrast, most of us in this society are afflicted with a kind of cultural nearsightedness. Our eyes, it may be, have been trained too long upon the superficial, and *artificial,* aspects of our environment; we do not see beyond the buildings and billboards that seem at times to be the monuments of our civilization, and consequently we fail to see into the nature and meaning of our own humanity. Now, more than ever, we might do well to enter upon a vision quest of our own, that is, a quest after vision itself. And in this the Indian stands to lead by his example. For with respect to such things as a sense of heritage, of a vital continuity in terms of origin and of destiny, a profound investment of the mind and spirit in the oral traditions of literature, philosophy, and religion—those things, in short, which constitute his vision of the world—the Indian is perhaps the most culturally secure of all Americans.

As I see him, that old man, he walks very slowly to the place where he will make his prayer, and it is always the same place, a small mound where the grass is sparse and the hard red earth shows through. He limps a little, with age, but when he plants his feet he is tall and straight and hard. The bones are fine and prominent in his face and hands. And his face is painted. There are red and yellow bars under his eyes, neither bright nor sharply defined on the dark, furrowed skin, but soft and organic, the colors of sandstone and of pollen. His long braids are wrapped with blood-red cloth. His eyes are deep and open to the wide world. At sunrise, precisely, they catch fire and close, having seen. The low light descends upon him. And when he lifts his voice, it enters upon the silence and carries there, like the call of a bird.

Study Questions

1. How does Momaday describe Cheney? Why do you think he has such a vivid image of a person he's never actually seen?

2. What does Momaday say is the essence of Cheney? What does Cheney's view of the world mean to Momaday?

3. Momaday's language is poetic in describing the sunrise in the third paragraph. Find examples of alliteration and euphony.

4. How, according to Momaday, are most people afflicted with cultural nearsightedness? How does this contrast with the idea of the verse from the Chippewa song?

5. What is the "quest after vision itself" that Momaday recommends?

Vocabulary

A **verbal analogy** problem compares one feature which two pairs of words have in common. In this sentence, for example, the first and second word-pairs consist of antonyms and therefore share the feature of oppositeness:

Heat is to *cold* as *security* is to *risk.*

Besides oppositeness, the two word-pairs in a verbal analogy problem may have some other feature in common, including one of these:

1. Both word-pairs may be synonyms.
(*Change* is to *alter* as *basis* is to *foundation.*)

2. Both word-pairs may show cause and effect.
(*Tax* is to *revenue* as *poverty* is to *deprivation.*)

3. Both word-pairs may show a part-to-whole relationship.
(*City* is to *state* as *power* is to *government.*)

4. Each word-pair may consist of different forms of the same word.
(*Hope* is to *hopes* as *constitution* is to *constitutions.*)

When a verbal analogy problem is used in a vocabulary examination, it usually appears in an abbreviated version, with colons (:) replacing the words *is to* and *as.*

heat : cold :: light : dark

In an examination, verbal analogy problems are arranged so that the test-taker has a choice of answers.

heat : cold ::
(a) plunder : ravage   (b) judiciary : power
(c) obstruct : prevent   (d) light : dark   (e) protection : safety

Before starting the following exercise on verbal analogies, number 1-8 on a separate sheet of paper. Then, after each number, copy the word-pair that has the closest similarity to the one which appears in *italics*.

1. *soft : hard* ::
 (a) dream : vision   (b) beginning : end   (c) stand : pray
 (d) war : soldier   (e) purple : mountain

2. *liberty : freedom* ::
 (a) health : life   (b) amber : grain   (c) east : west
 (d) thunder : wind   (e) requirement : necessity

3. *declare : declaration* ::
 (a) independence : independent   (b) bank : bankrupt
 (c) submit : submission   (d) happy : happiness
 (e) equality : equal

4. *sun : light* ::
 (a) patriotic : hero   (b) shell : ocean   (c) tyrant : injustice
 (d) payment : wampum   (e) tomb : cemetery

5. *receptionist : receive* ::
 (a) pride : proud   (b) militant : military   (c) consent : consensus
 (d) conductor : conduct   (e) spiritual : spirit

6. *postpone : defer* ::
 (a) determination : despair   (b) distant : remote   (c) glory : divine
 (d) hope : creed   (e) superior : inferior

7. *foreign : native* ::
 (a) culture : heritage   (b) struggle : triumph   (c) heir : inheritance
 (d) manacles : chains   (e) success : failure

8. *dog : collie* ::
 (a) eagle : bird   (b) newspaper : advertisement
 (c) fulfill : fulfillment   (d) blood : veins   (e) game : badminton

Study Questions

1. The Sense of Place frequently involves conflicting emotions. What is the conflict in the selections by the following writers: Thomas Wolfe, Leslie Silko, Alfred Kazin, and Robert Frost?

2. Compare the "fury" of Thomas Wolfe's young man with Dexter Green's dream in Fitzgerald's "Winter Dreams." What do the two young men have in common? How do they differ?

3. The Declaration of Independence, now in the National Archives at Washington, is still an electrifying and revolutionary document. President Kennedy said in a speech, "To read it today is to hear a trumpet call. For that declaration unleashed not merely a revolution against the British, but a revolution in human affairs." Do you agree with this statement? What is your personal reaction to the Declaration? Why is its message meaningful to you?

4. The selections by Maya Angelou and Margaret Mead are both autobiographical. Compare these two people using examples from what they have written. How are their experiences similar? How do they differ?

5. Many of the selections included here overlap two or all three themes. How do the selections by the following writers overlap more than one theme: Thomas Wolfe, Ricardo Sanchez, Cathy Song, James Baldwin, Langston Hughes, N. Scott Momaday? What does this overlapping of themes imply about American writers?

Composition

1. De Tocqueville argues that democratic individualism tends to isolate, even alienate one from the rest of the world. Write an essay in which you agree or disagree with that argument. Use examples from the selections in this unit to support your position.

2. Imagine yourself in George Percy's situation—arriving in a strange place. Or recall a time when you visited a new place (city, foreign country, unsettled area, new school, or some other place entirely new to you). Write an essay in which you describe your first reaction. Contrast it to a similar familiar place. Give your reader a vivid picture of the place, the people, and your reactions to them.

2

A New Land

A NEW LAND

THE TITLE of this unit is subject to some qualification. To the colonists who came to Virginia in 1607 and Massachusetts in 1620, America was indeed a new land. To the people already living here, on the other hand, it was an old country with established social and cultural traditions. In order to represent those traditions, selections from Native American oral literature have been included in this unit.

American literature written in English begins with the Virginia and Massachusetts colonists. You have already observed the start of the Virginia Colony through the eyes of George Percy (page 11), and in this unit you will read a further account of Virginia in the writing of William Byrd. The most impressive outpouring of literary expression during the early colonial years, however, came from those highminded religious refugees who settled in Massachusetts. The selections in this unit reflect that fact.

Some account of Puritan attitudes and beliefs may be helpful in appreciating their literature. Three centuries separate us from these pious men and women. Their world is not our

A map of New York city as it was in 1660 (then known as New Amsterdam).

world, and we cannot approach them as if they were our contemporaries. They lived for many years in a land which bore little resemblance to the paved Massachusetts of today. They had no cities, supermarkets, factories, or movies; no television, football, baseball, basketball, automobiles, planes, or trains; no plumbing, central heating, cold war, or space probes; no United Nations—the list is endless. They did have a harsh climate and crudely made houses. Also, these colonists tried to develop a self-sufficient economy and, hence, competed directly with Native Americans for use of the land. This created hostilities on both sides.

Not only the early colonists' living conditions but their habits of thought as well were different from ours. Such a term as "religious freedom," for instance, did not mean for them the unrestricted choice among varieties of worship or nonworship, which we take for granted. Rather it meant the opportunity to enforce their particular form of Puritan worship in a whole community, unchallenged by the English Church or the English monarch.

In Puritan belief all men and women are corrupted by the original sin of Adam and Eve, and all are predestined for Hell except a few chosen arbitrarily by God. Thus, the Puritans saw human beings as creatures driven by their own natures to evil deeds and in constant need of restraint. It was a strict doctrine. Yet the Puritans lived by it willingly, even joyfully, and made it a source of strength. Believing firmly that they were performing the will of God, they were enabled to act with power and to endure all manner of hardship.

This stern and serious view of life naturally carried over into Puritan writing. In our time we tend to regard fiction, poetry, and drama as "literature" to the exclusion of other forms. But the Puritans felt that art has value only as a means of presenting some moral or religious

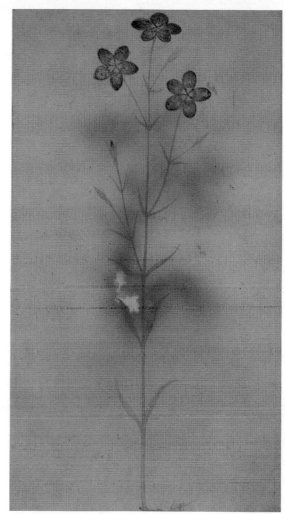

AMERICAN WILDFLOWER *John White*
Between 1577 and 1590 John White, a British artist, was sent by Sir Walter Raleigh to accompany three expeditions to the new world to make a permanent pictorial record of fauna, flora, and the customs of the Native Americans.

truth, and they were suspicious of writing which might be "mere entertainment." For them a sermon, a history, or a political document was a proper form of literary expression. Poetry was acceptable so long as it remained morally serious.

Navaho: The Night Chant

The Navaho *Night Chant* is an elaborate series of rituals, songs, and prayers descending from ancient oral tradition. Lasting up to nine days in full performance, it serves simultaneously as therapy for one who is ill and as a religious occasion for performers and observers. The song given below is the morning prayer for the third day of the ceremony. It is what is known as a Blessing Way song, in which the chanter prays for a "patient" to be restored to a harmonious, healthful relationship with the forces of nature.

Native American petrogylphs: ancient rock carvings and paintings.

Night Chant/Blessing Way

NAVAHO

Tségihi
House made of dawn.
House made of evening light.
House made of dark cloud.
House made of male rain.
House made of dark mist.   5
House made of female rain.
House made of pollen.
House made of grasshoppers.
Dark cloud is at the door.
The trail out of it is dark cloud.   10
The zigzag lightning stands high upon it.
Male Deity!
Your offering I make.

I have prepared a smoke for you.
Restore my feet for me.   15
Restore my legs for me.
Restore my body for me.
Restore my mind for me.
This very day take out your spell for me.
Your spell remove for me.   20
You have taken it away for me.
Far off it has gone.
Happily I recover.
Happily my interior becomes cool.
Happily I go forth.   25
My interior feeling cool, may I walk.
No longer sore, may I walk.

Impervious to pain, may I walk.
With lively feelings, may I walk.
As it used to be long ago, may I walk.   30
Happily may I walk.
Happily, with abundant dark clouds, may I walk.
Happily, with abundant showers, may I walk.
Happily, with abundant plants, may I walk.
Happily, on a trail of pollen, may I walk.   35
Happily may I walk.
Being as it used to be long ago, may I walk.
May it be beautiful before me.
May it be beautiful behind me.
May it be beautiful below me.   40
May it be beautiful above me.
May it be beautiful all around me.
In beauty it is finished.

Study Questions

1. In the first section of the song (lines 1–14) why is the singer making an offering? What do the cloud and lightning foretell?

2. For what does the supplicant, or "patient," ask? How will the answer to the prayer be revealed?

3. What does this prayer tell you about the Navaho conception of life?

4. What phrasing gives the song the feeling of a prayer?

Algonkin: Poem of Lament

Among the many surviving Native American legends is this poem concerning an Algonkin woman who probably lived near what is now Maine, at a time prior to the arrival of the first European. It is apparently the lament of a young woman marooned on an island by jealous rivals, "false friends."

Like all oral literature, this song is one of many versions passed anonymously from generation to generation. And as is the case with all translations it can only approximate the tone and meaning of the original. Yet the universal qualities of human feeling remain for all to appreciate.

Now I Am Left

ALGONKIN

A duck decoy used by Native Americans in hunting.

Now I am left on this lonely island to die—
No one to hear the sound of my voice.
Who will bury me when I die?
Who will sing my death-song for me?
My false friends leave me here to die alone;   5
Like a wild beast, I am left on this island to die.
I wish the wind spirit would carry my cry to my love!
My love is as swift as the deer; he would speed through the
    forest to find me;
Now I am left on this lonely island to die.
I wish the spirit of air would carry my breath to my love.   10
My love's canoe, like the sunlight, would shoot through the
    water to my side,
But I am left on this lonely island to die, with no one to pity
    me but the little birds.
My love is brave and strong; but, when he hears my fate, his
    stout heart will break;
And I am on this lonely island to die.
Now the night comes on, and all is silent but the owl.   15
He sings a mournful song to his mate, in pity for me.
I will try to sleep.
I wish the night spirit to hear my song; he will tell my love
    of my fate; and when I awake, I shall see the one I love.
I am on this lonely island to die.

Study Questions

1. The speaker is singing her sad words to herself, but three times she pleads for some kind of divine force to alert her lover to her plight. What are the three appeals?
2. Besides dreading the sheer likelihood of death itself, the speaker laments the absence of what customs normally associated with death?
3. In lines 8, 11, and 13, what qualities does the speaker attribute to her lover?
4. Find examples of the speaker's feeling for nature.
5. In what ways does this poem resemble traditional ballads or folk songs?

Composition

1. Write an essay comparing the storytelling method of this poem with the method of a short story or novel. What significant differences can you find? What are the advantages and disadvantages of each method?
2. Like most ballads this poem tells only a small part of the story, leaving the reader to imagine the rest. Write your own version of the young woman's story: show how she comes to be on the island, what happens to her there, and how her situation is resolved.

William Bradford   1590-1657

The first English settlers in Massachusetts are familiarly known to us as the Pilgrims. In 1609, to escape religious persecution in England, the Pilgrims fled to Holland. In 1620 they came to America in the *Mayflower*. A leader of those hardy settlers was William Bradford. He was one of the group who entered Plymouth Bay in a heavy snowstorm and made the famous landing there. From 1621 until his death he served almost continuously as elected governor of the Plymouth Colony.

During those years he slowly compiled *The History of Plymouth Plantation,* the primary source book for Pilgrim life. The following excerpt from that work shows the courage and faith which helped the Pilgrims to survive.

from The History of Plymouth Plantation

WILLIAM BRADFORD

BEING THUS ARRIVED at Cape Cod the 11th of November, and necessity calling them to look out a place for habitation (as well as the master's and mariners' importunity); they having brought a large shallop with them out of England, stowed in quarters in the ship, they now got her out and set their carpenters to work to trim her up; but being much bruised and shattered in the ship with foul weather, they saw she would be long in mending. Whereupon a few of them tendered themselves to go by land and discover those nearest places, whilst the shallop was in mending; and the rather because as they went into that harbor there seemed to be an opening some two or three leagues off, which the master judged to be a river. It was conceived there might be some danger in the attempt, yet seeing them resolute, they were permitted to go, being sixteen of them well armed under the conduct of Captain Standish, having such instructions given them as was thought meet.

They set forth the 15th of November; and when they had marched about the space of a mile by the seaside, they espied five or six persons with a dog coming towards them, who were savages;[1] but they fled from them and ran up into the woods, and the English followed them, partly to see if they could speak with them, and partly to discover if there might not be more of them lying in ambush. But the Indians seeing themselves thus followed, they again forsook the woods and ran away on the sand as hard as they could, so as they could not come near them but followed them by the track of their feet sundry miles and saw that

1 **savages:** Europeans were unaccustomed to the lifestyle of the people residing in this country and sometimes called them savages.

they had come the same way. So, night coming on, they made their rendezvous and set out their sentinels, and rested in quiet that night; and the next morning followed their track till they had headed a great creek and so left the sands, and turned another way into the woods. But they still followed them by guess, hoping to find their dwellings; but they soon lost both them and themselves, falling into such thickets as were ready to tear their clothes and armor in pieces; but were most distressed for want of drink. But at length they found water and refreshed themselves, being the first New England water they drunk of, and was now in great thirst as pleasant unto them as wine or beer had been in foretimes.

Afterwards they directed their course to come to the other shore, for they knew it was a neck of land they were to cross over, and so at length got to the seaside and marched to this supposed river, and by the way found a pond of clear, fresh water, and shortly after a good quantity of clear ground where the Indians had formerly set corn, and some of their graves. And proceeding further they saw new stubble where corn had been set the same year; also they found where lately a house had been, where some planks and a great kettle was remaining, and heaps of sand newly paddled with their hands. Which, they digging up, found in them divers fair Indian baskets filled with corn, and some in ears, fair and good, of

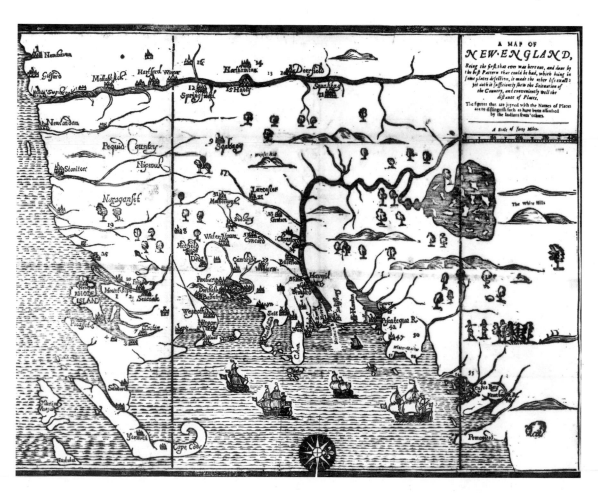

divers colors, which seemed to them a very goodly sight (having never seen any such before). This was near the place of that supposed river they came to seek, unto which they went and found it to open itself into two arms with a high cliff of sand in the entrance but more like to be creeks of salt water than any fresh, for aught they saw; and that there was good harborage for their shallop, leaving it further to be discovered by their shallop, when she was ready. So, their time limited them being expired, they returned to the ship lest they should be in fear of their safety; and took with them part of the corn and buried up the rest. And so, like the men from Eshcol, carried with them of the fruits of the land and showed their brethren;[2] of which, and their return, they were marvelously glad and their hearts encouraged.

After this, the shallop being got ready, they set out again for the better discovery of this place, and the master of the ship desired to go himself. So there went some thirty men but found it to be no harbor for ships but only for boats. There was also found two of their houses covered with mats, and sundry of their implements in them, but the people were run away and could not be seen. Also there was

---

2 like the men . . . brethren: See the *Bible,* Numbers 13:23-26.

AMERICAN BUTTERFLY *John White*

found more of their corn and of their beans of various colors; the corn and beans they brought away, purposing to give them full satisfaction when they should meet with any of them as, about some six months afterward they did, to their good content.

And here is to be noted a special providence of God, and a great mercy to this poor people, that here they got seed to plant them corn the next year, or else they might have starved, for they had none nor any likelihood to get any till the season had been past, as the sequel did manifest. Neither is it likely they had had this, if the first voyage had not been made, for the ground was now all covered with snow and hard frozen; but the Lord is never wanting unto His in their greatest needs; let His holy name have all the praise.

The month of November being spent in these affairs, and much foul weather falling in, the 6th of December they sent out their shallop again with ten of their principal men and some seamen, upon further discovery, intending to circulate that deep bay of Cape Cod. The weather was very cold and it froze so hard as the spray of the sea lighting on their coats, they were as if they had been glazed. Yet that night betimes they got down into the bottom of the bay, and as they drew near the shore they saw some ten or twelve Indians very busy about something. They landed about a league or two from them; and had much ado to put ashore anywhere—it lay so full of flats. Being landed, it grew late and they made themselves a barricado with logs and boughs as well as they could in the time, and set out their sentinel and betook them to rest, and saw the smoke of the fire the savages made that night. When morning was come they divided their company, some to coast along the shore in the boat, and the rest marched through the woods to see the land, if any fit place might be for their dwelling. They came also to the place where they saw the Indians the night before, and found they had been cutting up a great fish like a grampus, being some two inches thick of fat like a hog, some pieces whereof they had left by the way. And the shallop found two more of these fishes dead on the sands, a thing usual after storms in that place, by reason of the great flats of sand that lie off.

So they ranged up and down all that day, but found no people, nor any place they liked. When the sun grew low, they hasted out of the woods to meet with their shallop, to whom they made signs to come to them into a creek hard by, the which they did at high water; of which they were very glad, for they had not seen each other all that day since the morning. So they made them a barricado as usually they did every night, with logs, stakes and thick pine boughs, the height of a man, leaving it open to leeward, partly to shelter them from the cold and wind (making their fire in the middle and lying round about it) and partly to defend them from any sudden assaults of the savages, if they should surround them; so being very weary, they betook them to rest. But about midnight they heard a hideous and great cry, and their sentinel called "Arm! arm!" So they bestirred them and stood to their arms and shot off a couple of muskets, and then the noise ceased. They concluded it was a company of wolves or such like wild beasts, for one of the seamen told them he had often heard such a noise in Newfoundland.

So they rested till about five of the clock in the morning; for the tide, and their purpose to go from thence, made them be stirring betimes. So after prayer they prepared for breakfast, and it being day dawning it was thought best to be carrying things down to the boat. But some said it was not best to carry the arms down, others said they would be the readier, for they had lapped them up in their coats from the dew; but some three or four would not carry theirs till they went themselves. Yet as it fell out, the water being not high enough, they laid them down on the bank side and came up to breakfast.

From hence they departed and coasted all along but discerned no place likely for harbor; and therefore hasted to a place that their pilot (one Mr. Coppin who had been in the country before) did assure them was a good harbor, which he had been in, and they might fetch it before night; of which they were glad for it began to be foul weather.

After some hours' sailing it began to snow and rain, and about the middle of the afternoon the wind increased and the sea became very rough, and they broke their rudder, and it was as much as two men could do to steer her with a couple of oars. But their pilot bade them be of good cheer for he saw the harbor; but the storm increasing, and night drawing on, they bore what sail they could to get in, while they could see. But herewith they broke their mast in three pieces and their sail fell overboard in a very grown sea, so as they had like to have been cast away. Yet by God's mercy they recovered themselves, and having the flood[3] with them, struck into the harbor.

---

3 **flood:** the rising, incoming tide.

AMERICAN WILD DUCK *John White*

But when it came to, the pilot was deceived in the place, and said the Lord be merciful unto them for his eyes never saw that place before; and he and the master's mate would have run her ashore in a cove full of breakers before the wind. But a lusty seaman which steered bade those which rowed, if they were men, about with her or else they were all cast away; the which they did with speed. So he bid them be of good cheer and row lustily, for there was a fair sound before them, and he doubted not but they should find one place or other where they might ride in safety. And though it was very dark and rained sore, yet in the end they got under the lee of a small island and re-mained there all that night in safety. But they knew not this to be an island till morning, but were divided in their minds; some would keep the boat for fear they might be amongst the Indians, others were so wet and cold they could not endure but got ashore, and with much ado got fire (all things being so wet); and the rest were glad to come to them, for after midnight the wind shifted to the north-west and it froze hard.

But though this had been a day and night of much trouble and danger unto them, yet God gave them a morning of comfort and refreshing (as usually He doth to His children) for the next day was a fair, sunshining day, and

Plymouth meeting house, built in 1683.

they found themselves to be on an island secure from the Indians, where they might dry their stuff, fix their pieces and rest themselves; and gave God thanks for His mercies in their manifold deliverances. And this being the last day of the week, they prepared there to keep the Sabbath.

On Monday they sounded the harbor and found it fit for shipping, and marched into the land and found divers cornfields and little running brooks, a place (as they supposed) fit for situation.[4] At least it was the best they could find, and the season and their present necessity made them glad to accept of it. So they returned to their ship again with this news to the rest of their people, which did much comfort their hearts.

On the 15th of December they weighed anchor to go to the place they had discovered, and came within two leagues of it, but were fain to bear up again; but the 16th day, the wind came fair, and they arrived safe in this harbor. And afterwards took better view of the place, and resolved where to pitch their dwelling; and the 25th day began to erect the first house for common use to receive them and their goods.

---

4 **On Monday . . . situation:** This is the only contemporary account of the landing at Plymouth.

Study Questions

1. After the Pilgrims land what problems do they face? How do they deal with these problems?
2. What is the English attitude toward the Indians? What is the Indian attitude toward the English? How does Bradford justify taking the Indians' corn?
3. Bradford obviously sees the events he describes as part of some larger pattern of meaning. What does he see as the source of that meaning? What is the pattern he sees?

Vocabulary

With the passage of time, fashions in language change, just as fashions in clothing do. Thoughtful people do not consider the costumes of 1620 either better or worse than the clothes we wear today, but simply different. Language specialists recommend that we take the same neutral attitude toward changes in language.

Nevertheless, the differences between earlier forms of English and the English we speak sometimes present problems in interpretation. These problems can often be overcome through **paraphrasing**—restating in our own terms—the troublesome passages we find in reading selections written centuries ago. For example:

> The Indians forsook the woods and ran away, so as they could not come near them but followed them by the track of their feet sundry miles.

Paraphrasing such a sentence involves several steps:

1. Read the entire sentence through slowly, usually more than once. Place the sentence in context—that is, take into account how this event relates to what has already happened as well as to what will occur later.

2. Realize that the meanings of key words may differ from those which first come to mind, and consult a dictionary to select synonyms for words that are unclear.

3. Add or subtract words whenever doing so will clarify the passage.

4. Rearrange any words or phrases whose original sequence interferes with full understanding.

Using this procedure will help the reader restate, or paraphrase, most confusing passages:

> Abandoning the woods, the Indians avoided the Pilgrims by running away; but the Pilgrims followed the Indians' footprints for several miles.

On a separate sheet of paper, practice the paraphrasing process with the following sentences adapted from *The History of Plymouth Plantation*.

1. The explorers still followed them by guess; but they soon lost both them and themselves, falling into such thickets as were ready to tear their clothes and armor in pieces; but were most distressed for want of drink.

2. Here they got seed to plant them corn the next year, or else they might have starved, for they had none, nor any likelihood to get any till the season had been past, as the sequel did manifest.

3. The 6th of December they sent out their shallop again with ten of their principal men and some seamen, upon further discovery, intending to circulate that deep bay of Cape Cod.

4. They hasted out of the woods to meet with their shallop, to whom they made signs to come to them into a creek hard by, the which they did at high water.

5. They rested till about five of the clock in the morning; for the tide, and their purpose to go from thence, made them be stirring betimes.

William Byrd 1674-1744

William Byrd was a Virginia plantation owner and lawyer, educated in England and widely traveled abroad. Byrd spent about ten years in England as colonial agent and thirty years as an influential leader in the Virginia governor's council. He managed a vast property, totaling 179,000 acres. On one of his estates he laid out the city of Richmond. Like George Washington and Thomas Jefferson, he was a slave owner, but he disliked human bondage and wished to see its abolition.

As a hobby, Byrd kept secret diaries of his frequent trips into the backwoods country. After his death Byrd's secret diaries were discovered and published at various times between 1841 and 1958. His best-known writing is the witty and satirical *History of the Dividing Line Run in the Year 1728*. It is his journal of the survey establishing the official boundary between Virginia and North Carolina. The following entries from that journal describe Dismal Swamp—a heavily forested, almost impenetrable, undrained area of about 600 square miles between the two states.

from A History of the Dividing Line

WILLIAM BYRD

March 14, 1728

BEFORE NINE of the clock this morning the provisions, bedding and other necessaries were made up into packs for the men to carry on their shoulders into the Dismal. They were victualed[1] for eight days at full allowance, nobody doubting but that would be abundantly sufficient to carry them through that inhospitable place; nor indeed was it possible for the poor fellows to stagger under more. As it was, their loads weighed from sixty to seventy pounds, in just proportion to the strength of those who were to bear them.

---

1 **victualed** (vit' ld): supplied with food.

'Twould have been unconscionable to have saddled them with burdens heavier than that, when they were to lug them through a filthy bog, which was hardly practicable with no burden at all. Besides this luggage at their backs, they were obliged to measure the distance, mark the trees, and clear the way for the surveyors every step they went. It was really a pleasure to see with how much cheerfulness they undertook, and with how much spirit they went through all this drudgery. For their greater safety, the commissioners took care to furnish them with Peruvian bark, rhubarb and hipocoacanah,[2] in case they might happen in that wet journey to be taken with fevers or fluxes.

Although there was no need of example to inflame persons already so cheerful, yet to enter the people with the better grace, the author and two more of the commissioners accompanied them half a mile into the Dismal. The skirts of it were thinly planted with dwarf reeds and gall bushes, but when we got into the Dismal itself, we found the reeds grew there much taller and closer, and, to mend the matter, were so interlaced with bamboo briers that there was no scuffling through them without the help of pioneers. At the same time we found the ground moist and trembling under our feet like a quagmire, insomuch that it was an easy matter to run a ten-foot pole up to the head in it without exerting any uncommon strength to do it. Two of the men, whose burdens were the least cumbersome, had orders to march before with their tomahawks and clear the way in order to make an opening for the surveyors. By their assistance we made a shift to push the line half a mile in three hours, and then reached a small piece of firm land, about a hundred yards wide, standing up above the rest like an island. Here the people were glad to lay down their loads and take a little refreshment, while the happy man whose lot it was to carry the jug of rum began already, like Aesop's bread-carriers,[3] to find it grow a good deal lighter.

After reposing about an hour, the commissioners recommended vigor and constancy to their fellow travelers, by whom they were answered with three cheerful huzzas, in token of obedience. This ceremony was no sooner over but they took up their burdens and attended the motion of the surveyors, who, though they worked with all their might, could reach but one mile farther, the same obstacles still attending them which they had met with in the morning. However small this distance may seem to such as are used to travel at their ease, yet our poor men, who were obliged to work with an unwieldy load at their backs, had reason to think it a long way; especially in a bog where they had no firm footing, but every step made a deep impression which was instantly filled with water. At the same time they were laboring with their hands to cut down the reeds, which were ten feet high, their legs were hampered with the briers. Besides, the weather happened to be very warm, and the tallness of the reeds kept off every friendly breeze from coming to refresh them. And indeed it was a little provoking to hear the wind whistling among the branches of the white cedars, which grew here and there amongst the reeds, and at the same time not have the comfort to feel the least breath of it.

In the meantime the three commissioners returned out of the Dismal the same way they went in and having joined their brethren proceeded that night as far as Mr. Wilson's. This worthy person lives within sight of the Dismal, in the skirts whereof his stocks range and maintain themselves all the winter, and yet he knew as little of it as he did of Terra Australis Incognita.[4] He told us a Canterbury tale of a

---

2 **hipocoacanah:** healing herbs.

3 **Aesop's bread-carriers:** In the fable the traveler who chooses the bread-filled baskets has the heaviest load until the bread is eaten, leaving his baskets empty.
4 **Terra Australis Incognita:** unfamiliar land to the south, as Australia is designated on 18th-century maps.

North Briton whose curiosity spurred him a long way into this great desert, as he called it, near twenty years ago, but he having no compass nor seeing the sun for several days together wandered about till he was almost famished; but at last he bethought himself of a secret his countrymen make use of to pilot themselves in a dark day. He took a fat louse out of his collar and exposed it to the open day on a piece of white paper which he brought along with him for his journal. The poor insect, having no eyelids turned himself about till he found the darkest part of the heavens, and so made the best of his way towards the north. By this direction he steered himself safe out, and gave such a frightful account of the monsters he saw and the distresses he underwent that no mortal since has been hardy enough to go upon the like dangerous discovery.

A Narrow Escape from a Snake

March 17, 1728

Since the surveyors had entered the Dismal, they had laid eyes on no living creature: neither bird nor beast, insect nor reptile came in view. Doubtless the eternal shade that broods over this mighty bog and hinders the sunbeams from blessing the ground makes it an uncomfortable habitation for anything that has life. Not so much as a Zealand frog could endure so aguish a situation. It had one beauty, however, that delighted the eye, though at the expense of all the other senses: the moisture of the soil preserves a continual verdure, and makes every plant an evergreen, but at the same time the foul damps ascend without ceasing, corrupt the air, and render it unfit for respiration. Not even a turkey buzzard will venture to fly over it, no more than the Italian vultures will over the filthy Lake Avernus,[5] or the birds in the Holy Land over the Salt Sea where Sodom and Gomorrah formerly stood.

In these sad circumstances, the kindest thing we could do for our suffering friends was to give them a place in the Litany.[6] Our chaplain, for his part, did his office and rubbed us up with a seasonable sermon. This was quite a new thing to our brethren of North Carolina, who live in a climate where no clergyman can breathe any more than spiders in Ireland.

For want of men in holy orders, both the members of the council and justices of the peace are empowered by the laws of that country to marry all those who will not take one another's word; but for the ceremony of christening their children, they trust that to chance. If a parson come in their way, they will crave a cast of his office, as they call it, else they are content their offspring should remain as arrant pagans as themselves. They account it among their greatest advantages that they are not priest-ridden, not remembering that the clergy is rarely guilty of bestriding such as have the misfortune to be poor. One thing may be said for the inhabitants of that province, that they are not troubled with any religious fumes and have the least superstition of any people living. They do not know Sunday from any other day, any more than Robinson Crusoe did, which would give them a great advantage were they given to be industrious. But they keep so many Sabbaths every week that their disregard of the seventh day has no manner of cruelty in it, either to servants or cattle.

---

5 **Lake Avernus:** near Naples; considered by the ancients as an entrance to Hell and from whose waters arose vile-smelling vapors that supposedly killed birds.
6 **Litany** (lit′ n ē): a religious ritual.

It was with some difficulty we could make our people quit the good cheer they met with at this house, so it was late before we took our departure; but to make us amends, our landlord was so good as to conduct us ten miles on our way, as far as the Cypress Swamp, which drains itself into the Dismal. Eight miles beyond that we forded the waters of the Coropeak, which tend the same way as do many others on that side. In six miles more we reached the plantation of Mr. Thomas Spight, a grandee of North Carolina. We found the good man upon his crutches, being crippled with the gout in both his knees. Here we flattered ourselves we should by this time meet with good tiding of the surveyors, but had reckoned, alas! without our host: on the contrary, we were told the Dismal was at least thirty miles wide in that place. However, as nobody could say this on his own knowledge, we ordered guns to be fired and a drum to be beaten, but received no answer, unless it was from that prating nymph Echo,[7] who, like a loquacious wife, will always have the last word, and sometimes return three for one.

---

7 **Echo:** In Greek mythology, she grieved so long for love of the beautiful youth, Narcissus, that only her voice remained.

Study Questions

1. Byrd describes many features of Dismal Swamp. What are the explicit details that enable the reader to visualize the place? Why do these details justify the name "Dismal"?

2. Byrd includes Mr. Wilson's tale of the North Briton lost in Dismal Swamp and remarks about the way in which North Carolinians observe Sunday. Why do you think these details are included?

3. What are the character traits of Byrd and the other surveyors ("commissioners") as revealed in these journal entries? How do the men demonstrate consideration, foresight, leadership, persistence, and industry? Find examples.

4. Byrd builds up and exaggerates the foul-smelling air in Dismal Swamp. Find other examples of Byrd's use of hyperbole.

John Winthrop   1588-1649

Although Plymouth was the first important English settlement in New England, it was soon overshadowed by a larger neighbor. In 1630 the group properly called Puritans arrived in Salem. They had a Royal Charter for the lands around Massachusetts Bay and began rapidly to spread through what is now metropolitan Boston. Eventually Plymouth was formally incorporated into the Massachusetts Bay Colony.

John Winthrop's position in the Massachusetts Bay Colony was similar to Bradford's in the Plymouth Colony. Winthrop was elected governor before the departure from England and served repeatedly there-after as either governor or deputy governor. In office or out, he was an important individual in his community. More rigid and authoritarian than Bradford, Winthrop often found himself engaged in bitter controversy. In 1645, for example, he was put on trial for exceeding the authority of his office. He was acquitted. Immediately upon hearing the verdict he spoke to the court, delivering the following speech which has been called "the classic expression of Puritan political theory." In the speech Winthrop defines the Puritan theory of how people should be governed.

Speech to the General Court

JOHN WINTHROP

I SUPPOSE SOMETHING may be expected from me, upon this charge that is befallen me, which moves me to speak now to you. Yet I intend not to intermeddle in the proceedings of the Court, or with any of the persons concerned therein. Only I bless God that I see an issue of this troublesome business. I also acknowledge the justice of the Court, and, for mine own part, I am well satisfied, I was publicly charged, and I am publicly and legally acquitted, which is all I did expect or desire.

And though this be sufficient for my justification before men, yet not so before God, who hath seen so much amiss in my dispensations (and even in this affair) as calls me to be humble. For to be publicly and criminally charged in this Court is a matter of humiliation (and I desire to make a right use of it), notwithstanding I be thus acquitted. If her father had spit in her face (saith the Lord concerning Miriam), should she not have been ashamed seven days? Shame had lien upon her, whatever the occasion had been. I am unwilling to stay you from your urgent affairs; yet give me leave (upon this special occasion) to speak a little more to this assembly. It may be of some good use, to inform and rectify the judgments of some of the people, and may prevent such distempers as have arisen amongst us.

The great questions that have troubled the country are about the authority of the magistrates and the liberty of the people. It is yourselves who have called us to this office; and being called by you, we have our authority from God, in way of an ordinance, such as hath the image of God eminently stamped upon it, the contempt and violation whereof hath been vindicated with examples of divine vengeance. I entreat you to consider that when you choose magistrates, you take them from among yourselves, men subject to like passions as you are. Therefore, when you see infirmities in us, you should reflect upon your own; and that would make you bear the more with us, and not be severe censurers of the failings of your magistrates, when you have continual experience of the like infirmities in yourselves and others. We account him a good servant who breaks not his covenant. The covenant between you and us is the oath you have taken of us, which is to this purpose, that we shall govern you and judge your causes by the rules of God's law and our own, according to our best skill. When you agree with a workman to build you a ship or house,

JOHN WINTHROP, 1640

etc., he undertakes as well for his skill as for his faithfulness, for it is his profession, and you pay him for both. But when you call one to be a magistrate, he doth not profess nor undertake to have sufficient skill for that office, nor can you furnish him with gifts, etc.; therefore you must run the hazard of his skill and ability. But if he fail in faithfulness, which by his oath he is bound unto, that he must answer for. If it fall out that the case be clear to common apprehension and the rule clear also, if he transgress here, the error is not in the skill but in

the evil of the will: it must be required of him. But if the case be doubtful or the rule doubtful to men of such understanding and parts as your magistrates are, if your magistrates should err here, yourselves must bear it.

For the other point concerning liberty, I observe a great mistake in the country about that. There is a twofold liberty—natural (I mean as our nature is now corrupt), and civil or federal. The first is common to man, with beasts and other creatures. By this, man, as he stands in relation to man simply, hath liberty to do what he lists;[1] it is a liberty to evil as well as to good. This liberty is incompatible and inconsistent with authority, and cannot endure the least restraint of the most just authority. The exercise and maintaining of this liberty makes men grow more evil and in time to be worse than brute beasts: *omnes sumus licentia deteriores.*[2] This is that great enemy of truth and peace, that wild beast, which all the ordinances of God are bent against to restrain and subdue it.

The other kind of liberty I call civil or federal; it may also be termed moral, in reference to the covenant between God and man in the moral law, and the politic covenants and constitutions amongst men themselves. This liberty is the proper end and object of authority and cannot subsist without it; and it is a liberty to that only which is good, just, and honest. This liberty you are to stand for, with the haz-

1 lists: pleases.
2 *omnes . . . deteriores:* the first part of the sentence is the English equivalent of this Latin phrase.

ard not only of your goods, but of your lives, if need be. Whatsoever crosseth this is not authority, but a distemper thereof. This liberty is maintained and exercised in a way of subjection to authority; it is of the same kind of liberty wherewith Christ hath made us free. The woman's own choice makes such a man her husband; yet being so chosen, he is her lord, and she is to be subject to him, yet in a way of liberty, not of bondage; and a true wife accounts her subjection her honor and freedom, and would not think her condition safe and free but in her subjection to her husband's authority. Such is the liberty of the church under the authority of Christ, her king and husband; his yoke is so easy and sweet to her as a bride's ornaments; and if through frowardness[3] or wantonness, etc., she shake it off at any time, she is at no rest in her spirit until she take it up again; and whether her lord smiles upon her and embraceth her in his arms, or whether he frowns or rebukes, or smites her, she apprehends the sweetness of his love in all, and is refreshed, supported, and instructed by every such dispensation of his authority over her. On the other side, ye know who they are that complain of this yoke and say, let us break their bands, etc., we will not have this man to rule over us.

Even so, brethren, it will be between you and your magistrates. If you stand for your natural, corrupt liberties and will do what is good in your own eyes, you will not endure the least weight of authority, but will murmur, and oppose, and be always striving to shake off that yoke. But if you will be satisfied to enjoy such civil and lawful liberties, such as Christ allows you, then will you quietly and cheerfully submit unto that authority which is set over you, in all the administrations of it, for your good. Wherein, if we fail at any time, we hope we shall be willing by God's assistance, to hearken to good advice from any of you or in any way of God. So shall your liberties be preserved, in upholding the honor and power of authority amongst you.

---

3 **frowardness:** stubborn willfulness.

Study Questions

1. What are the two political questions which, according to Winthrop, most concern the people of his time?

2. Winthrop says that there are circumstances under which people may justly complain of the actions of their magistrates. What are they? Under what circumstances does he say they may not complain?

3. In the system of government described by Winthrop, who is the ultimate source of authority? What is Winthrop's assumption concerning the nature of humanity? What part in the government do the people play? What part do the elected officials play?

4. What are the two kinds of liberty defined by Winthrop? What is the relationship between the two liberties?

5. How would you feel about living under the government John Winthrop describes?

Anne Bradstreet   1612-1672

Anne Bradstreet was the first American to have a volume of poetry published. Born in England, she and her new husband, Simon Bradstreet arrived in 1630 as members of John Winthrop's settlers on Massachusetts Bay. In addition to her public duties as wife of the governor of the colony and her responsibilities as the mother of eight children, she also found the time to compose several thousand lines of verse. Some of these verses were secretly taken to London by her brother-in-law. They were published there anonymously in 1650 under the title *The Tenth Muse Lately Sprung Up in America.* Perhaps Anne Bradstreet anticipated little approval of a female poet in Puritan New England. In the prologue to one of her long poems in that first volume she wrote:

I am obnoxious to each carping tongue
Who says my hand a needle better fits;
A poet's pen all scorn I should thus wrong,
For such despite they cast on female wits.
If what I do prove well, it won't advance;
They'll say it's stol'n, or else it was by chance.

Two of her poems, from a later work, are printed here. The first is a tribute to her relationship with her husband, and the second a declaration of her efforts as a poet.

To My Dear and Loving Husband

ANNE BRADSTREET

If ever two were one, then surely we;
If ever man were loved by wife, then thee;
If ever wife was happy in a man,
Compare with me, ye women, if you can.
I prize thy love more than whole mines of gold,   5
Or all the riches that the East doth hold.
My love is such that rivers cannot quench,
Nor ought but love from thee give recompense.
Thy love is such I can no way repay,
The heavens reward thee manifold, I pray.   10
Then while we live in love let's so persevere
That when we live no more we may live ever.

MRS. JACOB CONKLIN *T. Skynner* c. 1845

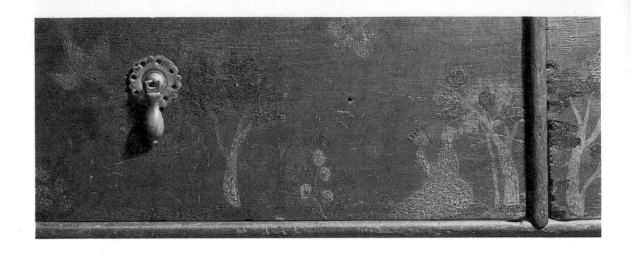

The Author to Her Book

ANNE BRADSTREET

Thou ill-formed offspring of my feeble brain,
Who after birth didst by my side remain,
Till snatched from thence by friends, less wise than true,
Who thee abroad, exposed to public view,
Made thee in rags, halting to th' press to trudge,   5
Where errors were not lessened (all may judge).
At thy return my blushing was not small,
My rambling brat (in print) should mother call,
I cast thee by as one unfit for light,
Thy visage was so irksome in my sight;   10
Yet being mine own, at length affection would
Thy blemishes amend, if so I could:
I washed thy face, but more defects I saw,
And rubbing off a spot still made a flaw.
I stretched thy joints to make thee even feet,   15
Yet still thou run'st more hobbling than is meet;
In better dress to trim thee was my mind,
But nought save homespun cloth i' th' house I find.
In this array 'mongst vulgars may'st thou roam.

In critic's hands beware thou dost not come,   20
And take thy way where yet thou art not known;
If for thy father asked, say thou hadst none;
And for thy mother, she alas is poor,
Which caused her thus to send thee out of door.

Study Questions

1. The first four lines of "To My Dear and Loving Husband" express the husband and wife's love and happiness. State in your own words the meaning of these lines.

2. What are the three comparisons the speaker makes in the three rhymed couplets (lines 5 through 10) in "To My Dear and Loving Husband"?

3. The final two lines of "To My Dear and Loving Husband" lift the statement of their love to an everlasting level. What do the last two lines mean to you?

4. What is the central metaphor for "The Author to Her Book"? Find examples which reinforce this metaphor.

5. The word "vulgars" in "The Author to Her Book" means the public. What warning does Bradstreet give in lines 19–21?

6. What is the humor in the last two lines of "The Author to Her Book"?

Composition

1. Write an expository essay based on one of the concerns expressed by Anne Bradstreet. Identify the concern and tell how she feels about it. Conclude by expressing your own opinion of her concern.

2. Write a poem of 10–15 lines. Use a central metaphor as Bradstreet does in "The Author to Her Book." Make sure that each comparison represents the metaphor accurately.

Mary White Rowlandson 1635?-1678?

In 1675, after years of uneasy relations, war broke out between the European settlers in New England and three of the more powerful Indian groups. The conflict has come to be known as King Philip's War, named after the Wampanoag chief, Metacomet, whom the English called King Philip.

In one of the early battles Chief Metacomet's forces captured, among others, Mary White Rowlandson. After eleven weeks and five days of captivity, Rowlandson was ransomed. Subsequently she wrote a vivid account of her adventures which was published in 1682 after her death. Its full title was *The Sovereignty and Goodness of God, Together with the Faithfulness of His Promises Displayed: Being a Narrative of the Captivity and Restoration of Mrs. Mary Rowlandson.*

Her story was the first of hundreds of "captivity narratives" which appeared in America over the next century and a half. Initially these stories were, like Rowlandson's, written to demonstrate "The Sovereignty and Goodness of God." As time went on, however, the religious motive tended to disappear, and wild stories were cranked out to satisfy a market for thrills and chills.

Captivity Narrative

MARY ROWLANDSON

ON THE TENTH of February, 1675, came the Indians with great numbers upon Lancaster. Their first coming was about sunrising. Hearing the noise of some guns, we looked out; several houses were burning and the smoke ascending to Heaven. There were five persons taken in one house, the father, and the mother and a sucking child, they knocked on the head; the other two they took and carried away alive. There were two others, who being out of their Garrison upon some occasion were set upon; one was knocked on the head, the other escaped. Another there was who running along was shot and wounded and fell down; he begged of them his life, promising them money (as they told me) but they would not hearken to him.

At length they came and beset our own house, and quickly it was the most doleful day that ever mine eyes saw. The house stood upon the edge of a hill; some of the Indians got behind the hill, others into the barn, and others behind anything that could shelter them; from all which places they shot against the house, so that the bullets seemed to fly like hail, and quickly they wounded one man among us, then another, and then a third. About two hours (according to my observation, in that amazing time) they had been about the house before they prevailed to fire it (which they did with flax and hemp, which they brought out of the barn, and there being no defense about the house, only two flankers at two opposite corners and one of them not finished), they fired it once, and one ventured out and quenched it, but they quickly fired it again, and that took. . . . The Lord hereby would make us the more to acknowledge his hand, and to see that our help is always in Him. But out we must go, the fire increasing, and coming along behind us, roaring, and the Indians gaping before us with their guns, spears and hatchets to devour us. . . . The Indians laid hold of us, pulling me one way, and the children another, and said, come go along with us. I told them they would kill me. They answered if I were willing to go along with them, they would not hurt me.

Oh the doleful sight that now was to behold at this house! *Come, behold the works of the Lord, what dissolations he has made in the earth.* Of thirty-seven persons who were in this one house, none escaped either present death, or a bitter captivity, save only one, who might say as he, Job 1:15, *and I only am escaped alone to tell the news.* . . . Yet the Lord by his almighty power preserved a number of us from death, for there were twenty-four of us taken alive and carried captive.

I had often said before this, that if the Indians should come, I should choose rather to be killed by them than taken alive, but when it came to the trial my mind changed; their glittering weapons so daunted my spirit, that I chose rather to go along with those (as I may say) ravenous beasts, than that moment to end my days. That I may the better declare what happened to me during that grievous captivity, I shall particularly speak of the several removes we had up and down the wilderness.

Now away we must go with those barbarous creatures, with our bodies wounded and bleeding, and our hearts no less than our bodies. About a mile we went that night, up upon a hill within sight of the town, where they intended to lodge. There was hard by a vacant house (deserted by the English before for fear of the Indians). I asked them whether I might not lodge in the house that night to which they answered, "What will you love Englishmen still?" This was the most doleful night that ever my eyes saw. Oh the roaring, and singing and dancing and yelling of those black creatures in the night which made the place a lively resemblance of hell. And miserable was the waste of horses, cattle, sheep, swine, calves, lambs, roasting pigs, and fowl (which they had plundered in the town) some roasting, some lying and burning, and some boiling to feed our merciless enemies; who were joyful enough though we were disconsolate. To add to the dolefulness of the former day, and the dismalness of the present night, my thoughts ran upon my losses and sad bereaved condition. All was gone, my husband gone (at least separated from me, he being in the bay, and to add to my grief, the Indians told me they would kill him as he came homeward), my children gone, my relations and friends gone, our house and home and all our comforts within door and without, all was gone (except my life), and I knew not but the next moment that might go too. There remained nothing to me but one poor wounded babe, and it seemed at present worse than death that it was in such a pitiful condition, bespeaking compassion, and I had no refreshment for it, nor suitable things to revive it. Little do many think what is the savageness and brutishness of this barbarous enemy, even those that seem to profess more than others among them, when the English have fallen into their hands.

But now, the next morning, I must turn my back upon the town and travel with them into the vast and desolate wilderness. I knew not whither. It is not my tongue or pen can express the sorrows of my heart and bitterness of my spirit that I had at this departure, but God was with me, in a wonderful manner, carrying me along and bearing up my spirit that it did not quite fail. One of the Indians carried my poor wounded babe upon a horse. It went moaning all along, "I shall die, I shall die." I went on foot after it, with sorrow that cannot be expressed. At length I took it off the horse and carried it in my arms till my strength failed, and I fell down with it. Then they set me upon a horse with my wounded child in my lap, and there being no furniture upon the horse's back, as we were going down a steep hill, we both fell over the horse's head, at which they, like inhumane creatures, laughed, and rejoiced to see it, though I thought we should there have ended our days as overcome with so many difficulties. But the Lord renewed my strength still and carried me along that I might see more of his power; yea, so much that I could never have thought of had I not experienced it.

After this it quickly began to snow, and when night came on, they stopped. And now down I must sit in the snow by a little fire and a few boughs behind me with my sick child in my lap, and calling much for water, being now (through the wound) fallen into a violent fever. My own wound also growing so stiff that I could scarce sit down or rise up, yet so it must be that I must sit all this cold winter night upon the cold, snowy ground with my sick child in my arms, looking that every hour would be the last of its life, and having no Christian friend near me either to comfort or help me. Oh, I may see the wonderful power of God, that my spirit did not utterly sink under my affliction. Still, the Lord upheld me with his gracious and merciful spirit, and we were both alive to see the light of the next morning.

The morning being come, they prepared to go on their way. One of the Indians got up upon a horse, and they set me up behind him with my poor sick babe in my lap. A very wearisome and tedious day I had of it, what with my own wound and my child's being so exceedingly sick and in a lamentable condition with her wound. It may be easily judged what a poor feeble condition we were in, there being not the least crumb of refreshment that came within either of our mouths from Wednesday night to Saturday night except only a little cold water. This day, in the after-noon, about an hour by sun, we came to the place where they intended, an Indian town, called Wenimesset, northward of Quabaug. When we had come, oh the number of pagans (now merciless enemies) that there came about me, that I may say as David, Psal. 27:13, *I had fainted, unless I had believed.* The next day was the Sabbath. I then remembered how careless I had been of God's holy time, how many Sabbaths I had lost and misspent, and how evilly I had walked in God's sight, which lay so close unto my spirit that it was easy for me to see how righteous it was with God to cut off the thread of my life and cast me out of his presence forever. Yet the Lord still showed mercy to me and upheld me, and as He wounded me with one hand, so He healed me with the other. This day there came to me one Robert Pepper (a man belonging to Roxbury) who was taken in Captain Beers' fight and had been now a considerable time with the Indians, and up with them almost as far as Albany to see King Philip, as he told me, and had now very lately come into these parts. Hearing that I was in this Indian town, he obtained leave to come and see me. He told me he himself was wounded in the leg at Captain Beers' fight, and was not able some time to go, but as they carried him, and as he took oak leaves and laid to his wound, and through the blessing of God, he was able to travel again. Then I took oak leaves and laid them to my side, and with the blessing of God, it cured me also. Yet, before the cure was wrought, I may say, as it is in Psal. 38:5,6. *My wounds stink and are corrupt, I am troubled, I am bowed down greatly, I go mourning all the day long.* I sat much alone with a poor wounded child in my lap which moaned night and day, having nothing to revive the body or cheer the spirits of her. . . . About two hours in the night, my sweet babe, like a lamb, departed this life on Feb. 18, 1675, it being about six years and five months old. . . . In the morning, when they understood that my child was dead, they sent for me home to my master's wigwam . . . I went to take up my dead child in my arms to carry it with me, but they bid me let it alone. There was no resisting, but go I must and leave it. When I had been at my master's wigwam, I took the first opportunity I could get to go look after my dead child. When I came, I asked them what they had done with it. Then they told me it was upon the hill. Then they went and showed me where it was. I saw the ground was newly dug, and there they told me they had buried it. There I left that child in the wilderness, and must commit it, and myself also in this wilderness condition, to Him who is above all.

It was their usual manner to remove, when they had done any mischief, lest they should be found out: and so they did at this time. We went about three or four miles, and there they built a great wigwam, big enough to hold an hundred Indians, which they did in preparation for a great day of dancing. They would say now amongst themselves, that the Governor would be so angry for his loss at Sudbury, that he would send no more about the captives, which made me grieve and tremble. My sister being not far from the place where we now were, and hearing that I was here, desired her master to let her come and see me, and he was willing to do it, and would go with her: but she being ready before him, told him she would go before. She was come within a mile or two of the place. Then he overtook her, and began to rant as if he had been mad, and made her go back again in the rain so that I never saw her till I saw her in Charlestown. But the Lord requited many of their ill doings, for this Indian her master, was hanged afterward at Boston. The Indians now began to come from all quarters, against their merry dancing day. Among some of them came one Goodwife Kettle: I told her my heart was so heavy that it was ready to break. So is mine too said she, but yet said, I hope we shall hear some good news shortly. I could hear how earnestly my sister desired to see me, and I as earnestly desired to see her. Yet neither of us could get an opportunity. My daughter was also now about a mile off, and I had not seen her in nine or ten weeks, as I had not seen my sister since our first taking. I earnestly desired them to let me go and see them. Yea, I entreated, begged, and persuaded them, but to let me see my daughter; and yet so hard hearted were they, that they would not suffer it. They made use of their tyrannical power while they had it, but through the Lord's wonderful mercy, their time was now but short. . . .

On Tuesday morning they called their General Court (as they call it) to consult and determine, whether I should go home or no. And they all as one man did seemingly consent to it, that I should go home, except Philip, who would not come among them.

But before I go any further, I would take leave to mention a few remarkable passages of providence, which I took special notice of in my afflicted time. . . .

I cannot but remember how the Indians derided the slowness and dullness of the English army, in its setting out. For after the desolations at Lancaster and Medfield, as I went along with them, they asked me when I thought the English army would come after them. I told them I could not tell. It may be they will come in May, said they. Thus did they scoff at us, as if the English would be a quarter of a year getting ready. . . .

But to return again to my going home, where we may see a remarkable change of providence. At first they were all against it, except my husband would come for me, but afterwards they assented to it, and seemed much to rejoice in it. Some asked me to send them some bread, others some tobacco, others shaking me by the hand, offering me a hood and scarf to ride in, not one moving hand or tongue against it. Thus hath the Lord answered my poor desire, and the many earnest requests of others put up unto God for me. . . . So I took my leave of them, and in coming along my heart melted into tears, more than all the while I was with them, and I was almost swallowed up with the thoughts that ever I should go home again.

I can remember the time, when I used to sleep quietly, without workings in my thoughts, whole nights together, but now it is other ways with me. When all are fast asleep about me and no eye open but His who ever waketh, my thoughts are upon things past, upon the awful dispensation of the Lord towards us, upon His wonderful power and might in carrying us through so many difficulties, in returning us in safety, and suffering none to hurt us. I remember in the night season, how the other day I was in the midst of thousands of enemies, and nothing but death before me. It is then hard work to persuade myself, that ever I should be satisfied with bread again. But now we are fed with the finest of the wheat, and, as I may say, with honey out of the rock. Instead of the husk, we have the fatted calf. The thoughts of these things in the particulars of them, and of the love and goodness of God towards us make it true of me what David said of himself, Psal. 6:5. *I watered my couch with my tears.* Oh! The wonderful power of God that mine eyes have seen, affording matter enough for my thoughts to run in, that when others are sleeping mine eyes are weeping.

I have seen the extreme vanity of this world. One hour I have been in health and wealth, wanting nothing. But the next hour, in sickness and wounds and death, having nothing but sorrow and affliction.

Before I knew what affliction meant, I was ready sometimes to wish for it. When I lived in prosperity, having the comforts of the world about me, my relations by me, my heart cheerful, and taking little care for anything, and yet, seeing many whom I preferred before myself under many trials and afflictions, in sickness, weakness, poverty, losses, crosses, and cares of the world, I should be sometimes jealous least I should have my portion in this life,

and that Scripture would come to my mind, Heb. 12:6 *For whom the Lord loveth he chasteneth, and scourgeth every son whom he receiveth.* But now I see the Lord had His time to scourge and chasten me. The portion of some is to have their afflictions by drops, now one drop and then another, but the dregs of the cup, the wine of astonishment, like a sweeping rain that leaveth no food, did the Lord prepare to be my portion. Affliction I wanted, and affliction I had, full measure (I thought) pressed down and running over. Yet I see, when God calls a person to anything, and through so many difficulties, yet He is fully able to carry them through and make them see, and say they have been gainers thereby. And I hope I can say in some measure, as David did, *It is good for me that I have been afflicted.* The Lord hath showed me the vanity of these outward things. That they are the vanity of vanities, and vexation of spirit, that they are but a shadow, a blast, a bubble, and things of no continuance. That we must rely on God himself, and our whole dependence must be upon Him. If trouble from smaller matters begins to arise in me, I have something at hand to check myself with, and say, "Why am I troubled?" It was but the other day that if I had had the world, I would have given it for my freedom or to have been a servant to a Christian. I have learned to look beyond present and smaller troubles, and to be quieted under them, as Moses said, Exod. 14:13. *Stand still and see the salvation of the Lord.*

Study Questions

1. Describe the circumstances of Mary Rowlandson's capture. What does she suffer during her captivity?
2. What is Mary Rowlandson's interpretation of her ordeal?
3. Why do you think captivity narratives became so popular?

Vocabulary

When we encounter an unfamiliar word in reading, it is often possible to figure out its general meaning through the use of **context clues**, words and ideas that precede or follow the unfamiliar word. For example:

At length the Indians came and *beset* our house, shooting at it so that the bullets flew like hail.

In this sentence based on Mary Rowlandson's story, the context clue "shooting at (the house) so that the bullets flew like hail" makes it a good guess that the word *beset* means "attacked."

A. On a separate sheet of paper, copy the *italicized* words from the following sentences based on Rowlandson's report of her experiences. Study the context clues in each sentence carefully. Decide upon a general meaning for each word you have copied, then write your answers.

 1. After they had tried for about two hours, the Indians finally *prevailed* in setting the house afire.
 2. The Indians' weapons so *daunted* my spirit that I chose to go along with them rather than end my days immediately.
 3. They roasted, boiled, or simply burned the horses, cattle, sheep, and other farm animals which they had *plundered* in the town.
 4. Our enemies were joyful enough though we were *disconsolate*.
 5. Adding to the general dismalness, my thoughts ran upon my losses and my sad *bereaved* condition.
 6. A very wearisome and *tedious* day I had of it, what with my own wound and my child's being so sick.
 7. My cure was *wrought* after I had taken oaken leaves and laid them on my side.
 8. The Lord *requited* their ill doings; they were later punished.
 9. At first the Indians were all against my going home, except my husband would come for me; but afterward they *assented* to it.

B. When you have completed Exercise A, use a dictionary to check each written definition. Keep in mind that some dictionary entries include more than one definition. Direct your attention to the definition that fits the context of the sentence. Rewrite any incorrect answers.

Edward Taylor   1642?-1729

For over two centuries Edward Taylor was remembered as a Puritan minister who served a small Massachusetts community for some sixty years. But in 1937 a scholar found Taylor's four-hundred-page manuscript of poems in the Yale University Library. It had been deposited there by the poet's grandson when Taylor forbade publication by his immediate heirs. Since that discovery critics have acclaimed Taylor as the best American poet prior to the nineteenth century.

Taylor apparently learned much from English religious poets like John Donne and George Herbert. However, his poetry also has a definite American flavor—especially in its use of images taken from daily life in New England. In order to give the reader an example of American language before spelling and capitalization were standardized, "Huswifery" has been printed as Taylor wrote it. The second poem, "Meditation Six," has been modernized.

Huswifery

EDWARD TAYLOR

Make me, O Lord, thy Spining Wheele compleat;
   Thy Holy Worde my Distaff make for mee.
Make mine Affections thy Swift Flyers neate,
   And make my Soule thy holy Spoole to bee.
   My Conversation make to be thy Reele,   5
   And reele the yarn thereon spun of thy Wheele.

Make me thy Loome then, knit therein this Twine:
   And make thy Holy Spirit, Lord, winde quills:
Then weave the Web thyselfe. The yarn is fine.
   Thine Ordinances make my Fulling Mills.   10
   Then dy the same in Heavenly Colours Choice,
   All pinkt with Varnish't Flowers of Paradise.

Then cloath therewith mine Understanding, Will,
  Affections, Judgment, Conscience, Memory;
My Words and Actions, that their shine may fill   15
  My wayes with glory and thee glorify.
  Then mine apparell shall display before yee
  That I am Cloathd in Holy robes for glory.

Meditation Six

EDWARD TAYLOR

CANTICLES 2:1: *I am . . . the lily of the valleys.*

Am I thy gold? Or purse, Lord, for thy wealth,
  Whether in mine or mint refined for thee?
I'm counted so, but count me o'er thyself,
  Lest gold washed face, and brass in heart I be.
  I fear my touchstone[1] touches when I try   5
  Me and my counted gold too overly.

Am I new minted by thy stamp indeed?
  Mine eyes are dim; I cannot clearly see.
Be thou my spectacles that I may read
  Thine image and inscription stamped on me.   10
  If thy bright image do upon me stand,
  I am a golden angel[2] in thy hand.

Lord, make my soul thy plate: thine image bright
  Within the circle of the same enfoil.
And on its brims in golden letters write   15
  Thy superscription in an holy style.
  Then I shall be thy money, thou my hoard:
  Let me thy angel be, be thou my Lord.

---

1 **touchstone:** stone used to test purity of gold.
2 **golden angel:** an English coin in use at the time. Imprinted on it
was the archangel Michael slaying the dragon.

Study Questions

1. In order to understand "Huswifery," you should know how the spinning process works. What is the meaning of the following terms: *distaff, flyers, spool, reel, loom, quills, web, fulling mills, pinked?*

2. What is the central metaphor of each of the poems? Find examples of the comparisons in "Huswifery," and in "Meditation Six."

3. At the end of "Huswifery," what has happened on both sides of the comparison?

4. In the first stanza of "Meditation Six," Taylor expresses a doubt about the comparison. What is the nature of his doubt? In the second stanza what is the help he seeks to resolve the doubt? How will he know if his doubt is groundless?

5. Several words in "Meditation Six" have double meanings. Identify them and explain their double meanings.

6. "Meditation Six" discusses a spiritual matter in terms of material economics. Is this technique appropriate? Inappropriate?

Vocabulary

A **verbal analogy** problem compares one feature which two pairs of words have in common. For example, the two word-pairs may consist of antonyms and therefore share the feature of oppositeness.

True is to *false* as *comfort* is to *pain.*

The two word-pairs in a verbal analogy problem may have some other feature in common, including any one of these:

1. Both word-pairs may be synonyms.
   (*Defect* is to *flaw* as *carry* is to *bear.*)

2. Both word-pairs may show cause and effect.
   (*Fire* is to *smoke* as *loom* is to *cloth.*)

3. Both word-pairs may show a part-to-whole relationship.
   (*Cow* is to *cattle* as *cedar* is to *evergreen.*)

4. Each word-pair may consist of different forms of the same word.
   (*Persuade* is to *persuasion* as *intend* is to *intention.*)

In a vocabulary examination, a verbal analogy problem usually appears in an abbreviated version, like this:

true : false :: comfort : pain

Or, instead of being worked out completely, the problem may be arranged to provide the test-taker with a choice of answers. For example:

true : *false* ::
(a) doleful : unhappy   (b) lightning : rain   (c) comfort : pain
(d) sentinel : alarm   (e) pagan : heathen

Number 1–10 on a separate sheet of paper. Then, after each number, copy the word-pair that has the closest similarity to the one which appears in *italics*. Write your answers like this:

comfort : pain

1. *dawn* : *sunset* ::
   (a) plant : seed   (b) judgment : acquittal   (c) bow : arrow
   (d) evil : good   (e) famished : hungry
2. *affliction* : *suffering* ::
   (a) sickness : health   (b) marriage : husband
   (c) mile : travel   (d) leg : knee   (e) safe : secure
3. *pray* : *prayer* ::
   (a) happily : happy   (b) dispense : dispensation   (c) just : justify
   (d) meditation : meditate   (e) beauty : beautiful
4. *grasshopper* : *insect* ::
   (a) sand : seaside   (b) merciful : cruel   (c) year : May
   (d) repair : mend   (e) weapon : tomahawk
5. *spin* : *yarn* ::
   (a) quench : water   (b) chaplain : clergyman
   (c) mint : money   (d) apparel : scarf   (e) gun : bullet
6. *god* : *deity* ::
   (a) pollen : flower   (b) naught : anything   (o) boat : rudder
   (d) swamp : marsh   (e) cool : warm
7. *bread* : *food* ::
   (a) family : sister   (b) die : live   (c) wigwam : building
   (d) bird : owl   (e) see : eyes
8. *does* : *doth* ::
   (a) goodwife : goodwives   (b) brothers : brethren
   (c) thy : your   (d) babe : baby   (e) brass : brazen
9. *dye* : *color* ::
   (a) obey : command   (b) gun : musket   (c) child : children
   (d) paddle : row   (e) print : book
10. *heaven* : *hell* ::
    (a) captivity : freedom   (b) riches : gold
    (c) resolute : determined   (d) storm : weather   (e) entreat : beg

Jonathan Edwards   1703-1758

Jonathan Edwards was a great and formidable Puritan mind. When he was born the power of the Puritan ministers had already faded. Nevertheless, he tried as a Congregational minister to recapture the rigorous principles of the first settlers. Although he had some success, he was rejected by his own congregation in Northampton, Massachusetts. He spent his last years as a missionary to the Stockbridge Indians. In January, 1758, he became president of the College of New Jersey (Princeton University) but died of smallpox within three months.

Edwards is best known for his powerful sermon, "Sinners in the Hands of an Angry God," preached at Enfield, Connecticut, on July 8, 1741. Although his manner in the pulpit was quiet and matter-of-fact, his words shook the souls of the congregation. One listener that day described the scene, "There was such a breathing of distress, and weeping, that the preacher was obliged to speak to the people and desire silence, that he might be heard." The following passage from this sermon shows why the listeners were so deeply moved.

from Sinners in the Hands of an Angry God

JONATHAN EDWARDS

T HE BOW OF GOD'S wrath is bent, and the arrow made ready on the string, and justice bends the arrow at your heart, and strains the bow, and it is nothing but the mere pleasure of God, and that of an angry God, without any promise or obligation at all, that keeps the arrow one moment from being made drunk with your blood. Thus all you that never passed under a great change of heart, by the mighty power of the Spirit of God upon your souls; all you that were never born again, and made new creatures, and raised from being dead in sin, to a state of new, and before altogether unexperienced light and life, are in the hands of an angry God. However you may have reformed your life in many things, and may have had religious affections, and may keep up a form of religion in your families and closets, and in the house of God, it is nothing but his mere pleasure that keeps you from being this moment swallowed up in everlasting destruction. However unconvinced you may now be of the truth of what you hear, by and by you will be fully convinced of it. Those that are gone from being in the like circumstances with you, see that it was so with them; for destruction came suddenly upon most of them; when they expected nothing of it, and while they were saying, peace and safety: now they see, that those things on which they depended for peace and safety, were nothing but thin air and empty shadows.

The God that holds you over the pit of hell, much as one holds a spider, or some loathsome insect over the fire, abhors you, and is dreadfully provoked: his wrath towards you burns like fire; he looks upon you as worthy of nothing else, but to be cast into the fire; he is of purer eyes than to bear to have you in his sight; you are ten thousand times more abominable in his eyes, than the most hateful venomous serpent is in ours. You have offended him infinitely more than ever a stubborn rebel did his prince; and yet it is nothing but his hand that holds you from falling into the fire every moment. It is to be ascribed to nothing else, that you did not go to hell the last night; that you were suffered to awake again in this world, after you closed your eyes to sleep. And there is no other reason to be given, why you have not dropped into hell since you arose in the morning, but that God's hand has held you up. There is no other reason to be given why you have not gone to hell, since you have sat here in the house of God, provoking his pure eyes by your sinful wicked manner of attending his solemn worship. Yea, there is nothing else that is to be given as a reason why you do not this very moment drop down into hell.

O sinner! Consider the fearful danger you are in: it is a great furnace of wrath, a wide and bottomless pit, full of the fire of wrath, that you are held over in the hand of that God, whose wrath is provoked and incensed as much against you, as against many of the damned in hell. You hang by a slender thread, with the flames of divine wrath flashing about it, and ready every moment to singe it, and burn it asunder; and you have no interest in any Mediator, and nothing to lay hold of to save yourself, nothing to keep off the flames of wrath, nothing of your own, nothing that you ever have done, nothing that you can do, to induce God to spare you one moment.

Study Questions

1. Which people, according to Edwards, are in danger of being punished by God's arrow?

2. What does Edwards mean when he says only the "pleasure of God" will keep the arrow from striking the sinners' hearts?

3. Describe the "pit" over which God is holding the sinner. How many times is the word "fire" used in this context? the word "flames"?

4. Most of the sermon depicts a God of wrath. Where is there any implication that God is merciful?

5. The sermon expresses three basic Puritan tenets: a) God's absolute sovereignty (God is all-powerful and asserts His influence in every event of human life); b) original sin (as a result of Adam and Eve's eating the

forbidden fruit, all humanity is naturally and completely wicked); c) predestination (human fate is predetermined by God). Find examples of these beliefs in the sermon.

Composition

1. Imagine you were among Edwards's congregation hearing this sermon. Write a short essay explaining your reaction to it. Use examples from the sermon to tell why you think Edwards is too reasonable or unreasonable with his parishioners.

2. Write a description of a place, either real or imaginary. Use as many graphic details as possible in order to affect the reaction of your readers. It could be a frightening place (such as Edwards' image of hell as the fire in the pit) or a happy place.

Vocabulary

Synonyms are words whose meanings are either similar or identical. Theoretically, then, synonyms should have equal value in the expression of ideas. In practice, however, that is seldom true. Consider the first sentence of "Sinners in the Hands of an Angry God":

The bow of God's *wrath* (anger) is bent, and the arrow made ready on the string, and justice bends the arrow at your heart . . .

The *italicized* word, *wrath,* and the parenthesized word, *anger,* both mean "strong displeasure." The two words may seem interchangeable, but they are not. *Anger* is defined as "strong, but general and usually temporary displeasure." *Wrath,* on the other hand, means "fierce anger that demands vengeance or punishment." Of the two synonyms, then, the second has a far more intense meaning than the first. It is therefore better suited for Jonathan Edwards's purpose which was to put the fear of God into members of his congregation.

The following passages from "Sinners in the Hands of an Angry God" contain *italicized* words, each followed by a synonym enclosed in parentheses. Copy each pair of words. Then, with the help of a dictionary, tell why the intensity of the word Edwards chose for his sermon makes it more appropriate than the other word.

1. All you that were never born again, and raised from being *dead* (deceased) in sin are in the hands of an angry God.

2. The God that holds you over the pit of hell, much as one holds a spider or some *loathsome* (offensive) insect over the fire . . .

3. . . . *abhors* (hates) you, and is dreadfully provoked.

4. You are ten thousand times more *abominable* (repellent) in his eyes than the most hateful venomous serpent is in ours.

5. You have *offended* (displeased) him infinitely more than ever a stubborn rebel did his prince.

6. God is *incensed* (annoyed) as much against you . . .

2 REVIEW

Study Questions

1. The selections from Native American oral literature are from two different groups. Compare the tone and subject matter of these selections. What similarities do they have? How do they differ?

2. Both William Bradford and William Byrd describe explorations of unfamiliar places. What are the similarities in the two descriptions? How do they differ? What are the attitudes of the people involved? What do they see along the way? How do they respond to their adventures?

3. Anne Bradstreet and Edward Taylor were both seventeenth-century poets. However, the poetry they wrote was quite different. Find examples of their differences in subject matter and tone. Why do you think they wrote such different poetry? Use examples from their work or biographical information to support your position.

4. Would you be more or less happy in Puritan society than in your present community? What are the differences in daily occupations and personal freedom? How does the sense of purpose in life differ from then to now?

Composition

1. Either directly or by implication the Puritan selections deal with ideas of history, religion, government, personal freedom, faith and love, courage, race relations, literary expression—they describe a way of life. Using examples from these selections, write an analysis of the Puritan character. Tell how the Puritans lived and how they behaved towards others. Also include what they thought about. Conclude with a statement on the kind of people they were as revealed in their writings.

2. A number of the selections in this unit (the Algonkin poem, Bradford, Byrd, Rowlandson) tell or imply stories of adventure. Keeping in mind the events of these stories, write the story of an adventure that you know about. Be sure to tell how the adventure came about and what happened. Conclude by telling how the adventure ended.

3

A New Nation

THE FIRST WRITERS in America were preoccupied with religious issues and problems related to settling in a new land. However, the later colonial writers were deeply concerned with political matters. As the wilderness became more tractable, the early European settlers not only survived but prospered. They gradually found it easier to think about their present world instead of a future one after death.

Additional pressures for change were created by the shifting population and political repression. What had begun as a tightly knit band of dedicated persons lost much of its unity and zeal in the second and third generations. As the population grew, so too did a need for a national identity and the freedom to express that identity. However, the English government displayed an insensitivity to colonial problems and colonial pride. That insensitivity, coupled with the emergence of an American identity, ultimately provoked the American Revolution and resulted in the birth of a new nation.

The writers in the period roughly between 1775 and 1815, then, increasingly felt that this new nation resulted as much from hard work as from God's providence. Certainly they were repeatedly irritated by political interference from England. The colonial mind was open to new influences and new attitudes.

From England as early as 1690 came John Locke's *Two Treatises of Government* to argue that government is a contract between the people and their rulers. Later the French philosopher Jean Jacques Rousseau reinforced this concept in *The Social Contract* (1762). Rousseau stressed the principle that a government derives its authority from the consent of the

A Front VIEW of YALE-COLLEGE, and the COLLEGE CHAPEL, in NEW-HAVEN.

A compendious History of Yale-College, and a general Account of the Course of Studies pursued by the Students.

NEW-HAVEN: PRINTED BY DANIEL BOWEN, in CHAPEL-STREET; where every Kind of PRINTING is performed with Dispatch, and in the neatest Manner.

people it governs. These political ideas were part of that broad movement in European thought known as the Enlightenment. The thinkers of the Enlightenment suggested that people are actually rational beings capable of making their own decisions and of progressing by their own efforts to a better condition in life. Benjamin Franklin, Thomas Jefferson, and Thomas Paine were all deeply influenced by these ideas, as were the African slaves and other Americans. This influence is apparent in the literature represented in this unit.

At the same time, other voices were being heard—Patrick Henry with his ringing patriotism, Abigail Adams with her concern for women's rights, and Benjamin Banneker with his pointed attack on racial prejudice.

Benjamin Franklin   1706-1790

To some Benjamin Franklin is the first and best example of the American success story. Franklin draws a picture of himself in his *Autobiography,* arriving in Philadelphia to seek his fortune with one dollar in his pocket and a loaf of bread under each arm. This image has inspired countless young people. On the other hand, his critics have complained that Franklin was obsessed with "getting ahead" in material things. As a result of his strong influence, some say, the national character suffers from this drive for material acquisitions at the expense of spiritual or inner growth.

Franklin's accomplishments were indeed astounding. In Philadelphia he organized the fire department and the first paid police force. He introduced fire insurance, and caused the streets to be paved, swept, and lighted (radical innovations for the time). He started the first circulating library in America. He founded the American Philosophical Society, a scholarly organization for "Improving Natural Knowledge." He also founded a school which later became the University of Pennsylvania. He held public office on municipal, state, federal, and international levels. He was a superb diplomat and statesman during the years of the American revolution and early independence. His experiments with lightning began the intelligent study of electricity. He studied and composed music, played four instruments, and invented the glass harmonica—for which Mozart and Beethoven wrote pieces. Not only did he invent the "Franklin" stove, but at the age of eighty-three he invented bifocal glasses. His collected manuscripts now number more than sixteen thousand items.

Franklin was also celebrated as a wit. In the following satirical essay he writes about the English use of German mercenary troops (from a region called Hesse) to fight against

Dr Benjamin Franklin, F. R. S.
Sometime Governor of Pennsylvan
Aged 84

This classic profile of Franklin is regarded as the last likeness done before his death in 1790 at the age of 84.

the Americans. The ruler of Hesse reportedly was paid thirty guineas for every Hessian soldier killed. The author clearly means to horrify as well as amuse in this hoax letter.

The Sale of the Hessians

BENJAMIN FRANKLIN

From the Count de Schaumbergh[1] to the Baron Hohendorf, Commanding the Hessian Troops in America

Rome, February 18, 1777

Monsieur Le Baron:

On my return from Naples, I received at Rome your letter of the 27th December of last year. I have learned with unspeakable pleasure the courage our troops exhibited at Trenton,[2] and you cannot imagine my joy on being told that of the 1950 Hessians engaged in the fight, but 345 escaped. There were just 1605 men[3] killed, and I cannot sufficiently commend your prudence in sending an exact list of the dead to my minister in London. This precaution was the more necessary, as the report sent to the English ministry does not give but 1455 dead. This would make 483,450 florins[4] instead of 643,500 which I am entitled to demand under our convention. You will comprehend the prejudice which such an error would work in my finances, and I do not doubt you will take the necessary pains to prove that Lord North's[5] list is false and yours correct.

The court of London objects that there were a hundred wounded who ought not to be in-cluded in the list, nor paid for as dead; but I trust you will not overlook my instructions to you on quitting Cassel[6], and that you will not have tried by human succor to recall the life of the unfortunates whose days could not be lengthened but by the loss of a leg or an arm. That would be making them a pernicious present, and I am sure they would rather die than live in a condition no longer fit for my service. I do not mean by this that you should assassinate them; we should be humane, my

---

1 **Schaumbergh:** The real Count de Schaumbergh was an agent for the British in buying soldiers in Germany; Franklin makes him the Hessian ruler.
2 **Trenton:** in New Jersey; place of defeat of Hessian troops by Revolutionary Army on Christmas Day, 1776.
3 **1605 men:** The casualty figures are exaggerated.
4 **florins:** English coins.
5 **Lord North:** British Prime Minister during the American Revolution.

6 **Cassel:** chief town in Hesse-Nassau province, Prussia.

dear Baron, but you may insinuate to the surgeons with entire propriety that a crippled man is a reproach to their profession, and that there is no wiser course than to let every one of them die when he ceases to be fit to fight.

I am about to send to you some new recruits. Don't economize them. Remember glory before all things. Glory is true wealth. There is nothing degrades the soldier like the love of money. He must care only for honor and reputation, but this reputation must be acquired in the midst of dangers. A battle gained without costing the conqueror any blood is an inglorious success, while the conquered cover themselves with glory by perishing with their arms in their hands. Do you remember that of the three hundred Lacedaemonians who defended the defile of Thermopylae, not one returned? How happy should I

be could I say the same of my brave Hessians!

It is true that their king, Leonidas, perished with them; but things have changed, and it is no longer the custom for princes of the empire to go and fight in America for a cause with which they have no concern. And besides, to whom should they pay the thirty guineas per man if I did not stay in Europe to receive them? Then, it is necessary also that I be ready to send recruits to replace the men you lose. For this purpose I must return to Hesse. It is true, grown men are becoming scarce there, but I will send you boys. Besides, the scarcer the commodity the higher the price. I am assured that the women and little girls have begun to till our lands, and they get on not badly. You did right to send back to Europe that Dr. Crumerus who was so successful in curing dysentery. Don't bother with a man

who is subject to looseness of the bowels. That disease makes bad soldiers. One coward will do more mischief in an engagement than ten brave men will do good. Better that they burst in their barracks than fly in a battle, and tarnish the glory of our arms. Besides, you know that they pay me as killed for all who die from disease, and I don't get a farthing for runaways. My trip to Italy, which has cost me enormously, makes it desirable that there should be a great mortality among them. You will therefore promise promotion to all who expose themselves; you will exhort them to seek glory in the midst of dangers; you will say to Major Maundorff that I am not at all content with his saving the 345 men who escaped the massacre of Trenton. Through the whole campaign he has not had ten men killed in consequence of his orders. Finally, let it be your principal object to prolong the war and avoid a decisive engagement on either side, for I have made arrangements for a grand Italian opera, and I do not wish to be obliged to give it up. Meantime I pray God, my dear Baron de Hohendorf, to have you in his holy and gracious keeping.

Study Questions

1. What arrangement for payment of dead Hessians had been made between the English ministry and the Count? In the battle of Trenton about thirty Hessians were actually killed and about 950 taken prisoner. What is the effect of Franklin's hyperbolic figure for this battle?

2. What ironic effect does Franklin achieve by having the Count write from Rome (not Germany) and refer to his plans to attend an opera performance?

3. Why is the use of the words "humane" in the second paragraph and "glory" in the third paragraph ironic?

4. Explain the irony in the reference to Leonidas and the defense of Thermopylae.

5. What does the final sentence in the essay mean?

Vocabulary

Benjamin Franklin offered the following advice about writing:

> The words used should be the most expressive that the language affords, provided that they are the most generally understood. Nothing should be expressed in two words that can be expressed in one. . . . The whole should be smooth, clear, and short, for the contrary qualities are displeasing.

As earlier selections in this book demonstrate, most eighteenth-century authors did not follow Franklin's advice. Instead, they used what modern readers think of as **elevated language**: long, complicated sentences; frequent comparisons involving the characters and events of the *Bible*, mythology, and ancient history; and sophisticated vocabulary.

Here is one explanation for the widespread use of this kind of writing style in Colonial America: Although most children of the time were taught to read and write at an elementary level, opportunities for more advanced forms of education were usually available only to members of wealthy or aristocratic classes. As in Europe, advanced education emphasized Latin, Greek, classical literature and history, philosophy, and similar subjects. Most books of the period were written, and read, only by people who had this type of educational background, which prepared them for communication through elevated language.

Benjamin Franklin was one of the exceptions to this general rule. A self-educated man, he wrote for "the average American Colonist," the person who had achieved literacy but who had not gone far beyond that.

It appears that Franklin used elevated language in "The Sale of the Hessians." Actually, he did not. In this selection, he only mimicked that writing style for the purpose of satirizing the self-important and heartless aristocrat who was the imaginary author.

A. Assume that instead of using mock elevated language, Franklin had followed his own advice as quoted above when he wrote this selection. How might he have shortened and clarified the two sentences below? On a separate sheet of paper, paraphrase the sentences in the simplest, most direct way you can. If you have had no previous experience with paraphrasing, start by reading the explanation of the process on pages 137–38.

1. The court of London objects that there were a hundred wounded who ought not to be included in the list, nor paid for as dead; but I trust you will not overlook my instructions to you on quitting Cassel, and that you will not have tried by human succor to recall the life of the unfortunates whose days could not be lengthened but by the loss of a leg or an arm.

2. Finally, let it be your principal object to prolong the war and avoid a decisive engagement on either side, for I have made arrangements for a grand Italian opera, and I do not wish to be obliged to give it up.

B. If Franklin had not been mimicking elevated language for a satiric purpose, then, he would probably have substituted ordinary synonyms for most of the following difficult words in this selection. Tell what synonyms he could have used. Consult a dictionary as needed, making sure that your choices of synonyms fit the contexts in which they appear.

prudence *(paragraph 1)*   inglorious *(paragraph 3)*
pernicious *(paragraph 2)*   commodity *(paragraph 4)*
reproach *(paragraph 2)*   exhort *(paragraph 4)*

From 1733 to 1758 Franklin published an annual almanac under the fictional name of Richard Saunders, or "Poor Richard." In addition to the usual information on the stars and the weather, he inserted numerous proverbs and bits of practical advice. These sayings originally came from a wide variety of earlier books of aphorisms and proverbs, but Franklin compressed, sharpened, and Americanized them. The almanacs were enormously popular, and the phrase, "as Poor Richard says" inserted after each proverb, became famous. The samples below were chosen at random from various editions of Franklin's almanac.

from Poor Richard's Almanac

BENJAMIN FRANKLIN

Courteous Readers,

Your kind and charitable assistance last year, in purchasing so large an impression of my Almanacs, has made my circumstances much more easy in the world, and requires my grateful acknowledgment. My wife has been enabled to get a pot of her own, and is no longer obliged to borrow one from a neighbor; nor have we ever since been without something of our own to put in it. She has also got a pair of shoes, two new shifts, and a new warm petticoat; and for my part, I have bought a second-hand coat, so good, that I am now not ashamed to go to town or be seen there. These things have rendered her temper so much more pacific than it used to be, that I may say, I have slept more, and more quietly within this last year, than in the three foregoing years put together. Accept my hearty thanks therefore, and my sincere wishes for your health and prosperity.

Early to bed, early to rise, makes a man healthy, wealthy, and wise.

God helps them that help themselves.

A word to the wise is enough.

Fish and visitors smell in three days.

The used key is always bright.

Lost time is never found again.

The sleeping fox catches no poultry.

He that falls in love with himself has no rivals.

One today is worth two tomorrows.

Little strokes fell great oaks.

Since thou are not sure of a minute, throw not away an hour.

Beware of little expenses; a small leak will sink a great ship.

Fools make feasts and wise men eat them.

When the well's dry, they know the worth of water.

If you would know the worth of money, go and try to borrow some.

Make hay while the sun shines.

He that lieth down with dogs shall rise up with fleas.

'Tis hard for an empty bag to stand upright.

The worst wheel of the cart makes the most noise.

If you would have your business done, go; if not, send.

Study Questions

1. What common theme underlies the advice in many of these proverbs?
2. Find the references to rural life which would have been familiar to Franklin's almanac readers and may have accounted for the popularity of the proverbs.
3. How do these sayings impress a modern reader? Are you critical of any? Why?
4. When does a proverb become a cliché? How does a saying retain its freshness? How does it lose its punch?

Composition

1. Write an essay in which you compare the virtues stressed by Franklin with those emphasized by Jonathan Edwards (p. 160). Tell whether or not the person following Franklin's advice would also be living by Edwards' advice. Use examples from each selection to support your position.
2. Select one of Franklin's proverbs as a starting point. Write a narrative essay or short short story around it so that your fictional anecdote will illustrate the point of the proverb. The result might be similar to an Aesop fable. It can be humorous or serious. Franklin's "Sleeping fox catches no poultry," for example, sounds like the concluding line of an Aesop fable.

Patrick Henry   1736-1799

Patrick Henry was a self-educated lawyer from the back country of Virginia. He served as legislator and governor in his home state and was instrumental in adding the Bill of Rights to the Federal Constitution. He was also one of the most outspoken and revolutionary colonists. On March 23, 1775, he delivered his famous "liberty or death" speech to the Virginia Assembly of Delegates. His words on that occasion were prophetic. Less than a month later, at the battles of Lexington and Concord, the Minutemen fired "the shot heard round the world." (See "Concord Hymn," page 231.)

Speech in the Virginia Convention

March 23, 1775

PATRICK HENRY

NO MAN THINKS more highly than I do of the patriotism, as well as abilities, of the very worthy gentlemen who have just addressed the house. But different men often see the same subject in different lights; and therefore, I hope it will not be thought disrespectful to those gentlemen, if, entertaining, as I do, opinions of a character very opposite to theirs, I shall speak forth my sentiments freely, and without reserve. This is no time for ceremony. The question before the house is one of awful moment to this country. For my own part, I consider it as nothing less than a question of freedom or slavery. And in proportion to the magnitude of the subject, ought to be the freedom of debate. It is only in this way that we can hope to arrive at truth, and fulfill the great responsibility which we hold to God and our country. Should I keep back my opinions at such a time, through fear of giving offense, I should consider myself guilty of treason toward my country, and of an act of disloyalty toward the majesty of Heaven, which I revere above all earthly kings.

Mr. President, it is natural to man to indulge in the illusions of hope. We are apt to shut our eyes against a painful truth—and listen to the song of that siren, till she transforms us into beasts.[1] Is this the part of wise men, engaged in a great and arduous struggle for liberty? Are we disposed to be of the number of those, who having eyes, see not, and having ears, hear not, the things which so nearly concern their temporal salvation? For my part, whatever anguish of spirit it may cost, I am willing to know the whole truth; to know the worst, and to provide for it.

I have but one lamp by which my feet are guided; and that is the lamp of experience. I know of no way of judging the future but by the past. And judging by the past, I wish to know what there has been in the conduct of the British ministry for the last ten years to justify those hopes with which gentlemen have been pleased to solace themselves and the house? Is it that insidious smile with which our petition has been lately received? Trust it not, sir; it will prove a snare to your feet. Suffer not yourselves to be betrayed with a kiss. Ask yourselves how this gracious reception of our petition comports with those warlike preparations which cover our waters and darken our land. Are fleets and armies necessary to a work of love and reconciliation? Have we shown ourselves so unwilling to be reconciled that force must be called in to win back our love? Let us not deceive ourselves, sir. These are the implements of war and subjugation—the last arguments to which kings resort. I ask gentlemen, sir, what means this martial array, if its purpose be not to force us to submission? Can gentlemen assign any other possible motive for it? Has Great Britain any enemy in this quarter of the world to call for all this accumulation of navies and armies? No sir, she has none. They are meant for us: they can be meant for no other. They are sent over to bind and rivet upon us those chains which the British ministry have been so long

forging. And what have we to oppose to them? Shall we try argument? Sir, we have been trying that for the last ten years. Have we anything new to offer upon the subject? Nothing. We have held the subject up in every light of which it is capable; but it has been all in vain. Shall we resort to entreaty and humble supplication? What terms shall we find which have not been already exhausted? Let us not, I beseech you, sir, deceive ourselves longer. Sir, we have done everything that could be done, to avert the storm which is now coming on. We have petitioned—we have remonstrated—we have supplicated—we have prostrated ourselves before the throne, and have implored its interposition to arrest the tyrannical hands of the ministry and parliament. Our petitions have been slighted; our remonstrances have produced additional violence and insult; our supplications have been disregarded; and we have been spurned, with contempt, from the foot of the throne. In vain, after these things, may we indulge the fond[2] hope of peace and reconciliation. *There is no longer any room for hope.* If we wish to be free—if we mean to preserve inviolate those inestimable privileges for which we have been so long contending—if we mean not basely to abandon the noble struggle in which we have been so long engaged, and which we have pledged ourselves never to abandon until the glorious object of our contest shall be obtained—we must fight!—I repeat it, sir, we must fight! An appeal to arms and to the God of Hosts, is all that is left us!

They tell us, sir, that we are weak—unable to cope with so formidable an adversary. But when shall we be stronger? Will it be the next week, or the next year? Will it be when we are totally disarmed, and when a British guard shall be stationed in every house? Shall we gather strength by irresolution and inaction? Shall we acquire the means of effectual resist-

---

1 **listen . . . beasts:** in Greek mythology the sirens lured sailors to destruction by their sweet song.

2 **fond:** foolish.

ance by lying supinely on our backs, and hugging the delusive phantom of Hope, until our enemies shall have bound us hand and foot? Sir, we are not weak, if we make a proper use of those means which the God of nature hath placed in our power. Three millions of people, armed in the holy cause of liberty, and in such a country as that which we possess, are invincible by any force which our enemy can send against us. Besides, sir, we shall not fight our battles alone. There is a just God who presides over the destinies of nations; and who will raise up friends to fight our battles for us. The battle, sir, is not to the strong alone; it is to the vigilant, the active, the brave. Besides, sir, we have no election.[3] If we were base enough to

desire it, it is now too late to retire from the contest. There is no retreat but in submission and slavery! Our chains are forged; their clanking may be heard on the plains of Boston! The war is inevitable—and let it come! I repeat it, sir, let it come!

It is in vain, sir, to extenuate the matter. Gentlemen may cry, peace, peace—but there is no peace. The war is actually begun! The next gale that sweeps from the north will bring to our ears the clash of resounding arms! Our brethren are already in the field! Why stand we here idle? What is it that gentlemen wish? What would they have? Is life so dear, or peace so sweet, as to be purchased at the price of chains and slavery? Forbid it, Almighty God! I know not what course others may take; but as for me, give me liberty, or give me death!

---

3 **election:** choice.

Study Questions

1. What does Henry say is his guiding principle in judging the present situation?
2. Before stating his own conclusion, Henry disposes of other possible courses of action. What are these other possibilities, and how does he dispose of them?
3. What is Henry's proposed action? How does he justify it?
4. Taking this speech as a model, how would you plan a speech to persuade your classmates to take a certain action?

Vocabulary

Many words have **multiple meanings**. The only way to decide which one of their definitions is intended is to see or hear the words in use. Patrick Henry's speech contains many examples of such multiple-meaning words. For example:

An appeal to *arms* and to the God of Hosts, is all that is *left* us.

In this sentence the word *arms* refers to weapons or warfare. In a different sentence, the same word could refer to upper limbs of the human body. Similarly, in this sentence *left* means "remaining to"; but in another sentence, *left* could be an antonym for *right*.

Column One, below, contains a series of phrases and clauses either quoted from or based upon Patrick Henry's speech. Each phrase or clause contains one *italicized* word. On a separate sheet of paper, define each italicized word as Patrick Henry was using it. Then, in Column Two, find a different definition for each italicized word.

COLUMN ONE
1. an *act* of disloyalty
2. if we were *base* enough to desire it
3. to *cope* with so formidable an adversary
4. is life so *dear* or peace so sweet
5. *entertaining,* as I do, opposite opinions
6. of awful *moment* to this country
7. is this the *part* of wise men
8. Listen to the song of that *siren*
9. we have held the *subject* up in every light
10. it has all been in *vain*

COLUMN TWO
A. a brief interval of time
B. conceited; unduly proud
C. the chief ingredient with which a mixture is prepared
D. a person who owes allegiance to a ruler
E. costly; high-priced
F. the line on the head along which hair is divided during combing
G. a loud warning signal
H. a major division within a play or opera
I. extending hospitality
J. a garment similar to a mantle or cloak

Thomas Paine   1737-1809

The first man to use the phrase, "the United States of America," in print was Thomas Paine, a native of England. Benjamin Franklin, who was in London as commissioner of the colonies, recognized Paine as "an ingenious, worthy young man." Franklin persuaded him to try his luck in America. In 1774 Paine arrived in Philadelphia and, with a letter of introduction from Franklin, soon became editor of the new *Pennsylvania Magazine.* Almost immediately his career as a crusader for political freedom began. One of his first pieces in the magazine concerned the oppressed state of women, certainly radical for the year 1775. Paine wrote:

If we take a survey of ages and of countries, we shall find the women, almost—without exception—at all times, and in all places, adored and oppressed. Man, who has never neglected an opportunity of exerting his power, in paying homage to their beauty, has always availed himself of their weakness. He has been at once their tyrant and their slave . . . If a woman were to defend the cause of her sex, she might address [man] in the following manner: "How great is your injustice? . . . Our duties are different from yours, but they are not therefore less difficult to fulfill, or of less consequence to society . . . Permit our names to be some time pronounced, beyond the narrow circle in which we live . . ."[1]

An ardent patriot in action as well as in words, Paine enlisted in the Revolutionary Army. While he was with General Washington's forces during their forced retreat across New Jersey, Paine wrote the first in a series of pamphlets, each entitled

The American Crisis and signed "Common Sense." On Christmas Eve, 1776, Washington and his army crossed the Delaware River and launched a surprise attack against the enemy near Trenton. Washington ordered that Paine's new pamphlet (printed on page 180) be read to the troops before they set out. The essay not only encouraged the soldiers and helped them to their victory in the battle at Trenton, but it also rallied public sentiment behind Washington and his army.

[1]*Pennsylvania Magazine.* Vol 1, August 1775, pp. 362–364.

from The American Crisis

THOMAS PAINE

T HESE ARE THE TIMES that try men's souls. The summer soldier and the sunshine patriot will, in this crisis, shrink from the service of his country; but he that stands it *now,* deserves the love and thanks of man and woman. Tyranny, like hell, is not easily conquered; yet we have this consolation with us, that the harder the conflict, the more glorious the triumph. What we obtain too cheap, we esteem too lightly: it is dearness only that gives everything its value. Heaven knows how to put a proper price upon its goods; and it would be strange indeed if so celestial an article as FREEDOM should not be highly rated. Britain, with an army to enforce her tyranny, has declared that she has a right (*not only to* TAX) but "to BIND *us in* ALL CASES WHATSOEVER"; and if being *bound in that manner* is not slavery, then is there not such a thing as slavery upon earth. Even the expression is impious; for so unlimited a power can belong only to God.

Whether the independence of the continent was declared too soon, or delayed too long, I will not now enter into as an argument; my own simple opinion is, that had it been eight months earlier it would have been much better. We did not make a proper use of last winter; neither could we, while we were in a dependent state. However, the fault, if it were one, was all our own; we have none to blame but ourselves. But no great deal is lost yet. All that Howe[1] has been doing for this month past is rather a ravage than a conquest, which the spirit of the Jerseys[2] a year ago would have quickly repulsed, and which time and a little resolution will soon recover.

I have as little superstition in me as any man living; but my secret opinion has ever been, and still is, that God Almighty will not give up a people to military destruction, or leave them unsupportedly to perish, who have so earnestly and so repeatedly sought to avoid the calamities of war, by every decent method which wisdom could invent. Neither have I so much of the infidel in me as to suppose that He has relinquished the government of the world, and given us up to the care of devils; and as I do not, I cannot see on what grounds the king of Britain can look up to heaven for help against us: a common murderer, a highwayman, or a housebreaker, has as good a pretense as he.

It is surprising to see how rapidly a panic will sometimes run through a country. All nations and ages have been subject to them: Britain has trembled like an ague at the report of a French fleet of flat-bottomed boats; and in the 14th century the whole English army, after ravaging the kingdom of France, was driven back like men petrified with fear; and this brave exploit was performed by a few broken forces collected and headed by a woman, Joan of Arc. Would that heaven might inspire some Jersey maid to spirit up her countrymen, and save her fair fellow sufferers from ravage and ravishment! Yet panics, in some cases, have their uses; they produce as much good as hurt.

---

1 **Howe:** Sir William Howe was the British commander-in-chief in America (1775–1778).

2 **Jerseys:** East and West Jersey, later united as the state of New Jersey.

WASHINGTON CROSSING THE DELAWARE *Larry Rivers* 1953

Their duration is always short; the mind soon grows through them, and acquires a firmer habit than before. But their peculiar advantage is, that they are the touchstones of sincerity and hypocrisy, and bring things and men to light, which might otherwise have lain forever undiscovered. In fact, they have the same effect on secret traitors which an imaginary apparition would have upon a private murderer. They sift out the hidden thoughts of man, and hold them up in public to the world. Many a disguised Tory[3] has lately shown his head, that shall penitentially solemnize with curses the day on which Howe arrived upon the Delaware.

I once felt all that kind of anger, which a man ought to feel, against the mean principles that are held by the Tories: A noted one, who kept a tavern at Amboy, was standing at his door, with as pretty a child in his hand, about eight or nine years old, as I ever saw, and after speaking his mind as freely as he thought was prudent, finished with this unfatherly expression, *"Well! give me peace in my day."* Not a man lives on the continent but fully believes that a separation must some time or other finally take place, and a generous parent should have said, *"If there must be trouble, let it be in my*

---

3 **Tory**: in America at that time, those loyal to England.

day, that my child may have peace"; and this single reflection, well applied, is sufficient to awaken every man to duty. Not a place upon earth might be so happy as America. Her situation is remote from all the wrangling world, and she has nothing to do but to trade with them. A man can distinguish himself between temper and principle; and I am as confident as I am that God governs the world, that America will never be happy till she gets clear of foreign dominion. Wars, without ceasing, will break out till that period arrives, and the continent must in the end be conqueror; for though the flame of liberty may sometimes cease to shine, the coal can never expire.

America did not, nor does not want force; but she wanted a proper application of that force. Wisdom is not the purchase of a day, and it is no wonder that we should err at the first setting off. From an excess of tenderness, we were unwilling to raise an army, and trusted our cause to the temporary defense of a well-meaning militia. A summer's experience has now taught us better; yet with those troops, while they were collected, we were able to set bounds to the progress of the enemy, and thank God! they are again assembling. I always considered militia as the best troops in the world for a sudden exertion, but they will not do for a long campaign. Howe, it is probable, will make an attempt on this city;[4] should he fail on this side the Delaware, he is ruined. If he succeeds, our cause is not ruined. He stakes all on his side against a part on ours; admitting he succeeds, the consequences will be that armies from both ends of the continent will march to assist their suffering friends in the middle states; for he cannot go everywhere—it is impossible. I consider Howe as the greatest enemy the Tories have; he is bringing a war into their country, which, had it not been for him and partly for themselves, they had been clear of. Should he now be expelled, I wish with all the devotion of a Christian, that the names of Whig[5] and Tory may never more be mentioned; but should the Tories give him encouragement to come, or assistance if he come, I as sincerely wish that our next year's arms may expel them from the continent, and the Congress appropriate their possessions to the relief of those who have suffered in well-doing. A single successful battle next year will settle the whole. America could carry on a two years' war by the confiscation of the property of disaffected persons, and be made happy by their expulsion. Say not that this is revenge; call it rather the soft resentment of a suffering people, who, having no object in view but the *good* of *all,* have staked their *own all* upon a seemingly doubtful event. Yet it is folly to argue against determined hardness; eloquence may strike the ear, and the language of sorrow draw forth the tear of compassion, but nothing can reach the heart that is steeled with prejudice.

Quitting this class of men, I turn with the warm ardor of a friend to those who have nobly stood, and are yet determined to stand the matter out: I call not upon a few, but upon all: not on *this* State or *that* State, but on *every* State: up and help us; lay your shoulders to the wheel; better have too much force than too little, when so great an object is at stake. Let it be told to the future world, that in the depth of winter, when nothing but hope and virtue could survive, that the city and the country alarmed at one common danger, came forth to meet and to repulse it. Say not that thousands are gone—turn out your tens of thousands; throw not the burden of the day upon Providence, but "*show your faith by your works,*" that God may bless you. It matters not where you live, or what rank of life you hold, the evil or the blessing will reach you all. The far and the near, the home counties and the back, the rich and the poor, will suffer or rejoice alike. The heart that feels not now is dead; the blood of his children will curse his cowardice

---

4 **this city:** Philadelphia.

5 **Whig:** those favoring an independent America.

STUDY FOR WASHINGTON CROSSING THE DELAWARE *Larry Rivers* 1953

from *The American Crisis* 183

who shrinks back at a time when a little might have saved the whole and made *them* happy: I love the man that can smile in trouble, that can gather strength from distress and grow brave by reflection. It is the business of little minds to shrink; but he whose heart is firm, and whose conscience approves his conduct, will pursue his principles unto death. My own line of reasoning is to myself as straight and clear as a ray of light. Not all the treasures of the world, so far as I believe, could have induced me to support an offensive war, for I think it murder; but if a thief breaks into my house, burns and destroys my property, and kills or threatens to kill me or those that are in it, and to *"bind me in all cases whatsoever"* to his absolute will, am I to suffer it? What signifies it to me whether he who does it is a king or a common man; my countryman or not my countryman; whether it be done by an individual villain, or an army of them? If we reason to the root of things we shall find no difference; neither can any just cause be assigned why we should punish in the one case and pardon in the other. Let them call me rebel and welcome—I feel no concern from it; but I should suffer the misery of devils, were I to make a whore of my soul by swearing allegiance to one whose character is that of a sottish, stupid, stubborn, worthless, brutish man. I conceive likewise a horrid idea in receiving mercy from a being, who at the last day shall be shrieking to the rocks and mountains to cover him, and fleeing with terror from the orphan, the widow, and the slain of America.

There are cases which cannot be overdone by language, and this is one. There are persons, too, who see not the full extent of the evil which threatens them; they solace themselves with hopes that the enemy, if he succceed, will be merciful. It is the madness of folly to expect mercy from those who have refused to do justice; and even mercy, where conquest is the object, is only a trick of war. The cunning of the fox is as murderous as the violence of the

wolf, and we ought to guard equally against both. Howe's first object is, partly by threats and partly by promises, to terrify or seduce the people to deliver up their arms and receive mercy. The ministry recommended the same plan to Gage,[6] and this is what the Tories call making their peace, *"a peace which passeth all understanding,"*[7] indeed!" A peace which would be the immediate forerunner of a worse ruin than any we have yet thought of. Ye men of Pennsylvania, do reason upon these things! Were the back counties to give up their arms, they would fall an easy prey to the Indians, who are all armed: this perhaps is what some Tories would not be sorry for. Were the home counties to deliver up their arms, they would be exposed to the resentment of the back counties, who would then have it in their power to chastise their defection at pleasure. And were any one State to give up its arms, *that* State must be garrisoned by all Howe's army of Britons and Hessians[8] to preserve it from the anger of the rest. Mutual fear is the principal link in the chain of mutual love; and woe be to that State that breaks the compact. Howe is mercifully inviting you to barbarous destruction, and men must be either rogues or fools that will not see it. I dwell not upon the vapors of imagination; I bring reason to your ears, and, in language as plain as A B C, hold up truth to your eyes.

I thank God that I fear not. I see no real cause for fear. I know our situation well, and can see the way out of it. While our army was collected, Howe dared not risk a battle; and it is no credit to him that he decamped from the White Plains,[9] and waited a mean opportunity to ravage the defenseless Jerseys; but it is great

---

6 **Gage:** Thomas Gage (1721–1787) preceded General Howe as commander-in-chief of the British forces.
7 **a peace . . . understanding:** See the *Bible,* Philippians 4:7.
8 **Hessians:** the mercenary troops hired by the British. (See p. 169)
9 **the White Plains:** area north of New York City where Howe's troops met with Washington in an indecisive battle on October 28, 1776.

credit to us, that with a handful of men, we sustained an orderly retreat for near a hundred miles, brought off our ammunition, all our fieldpieces, the greatest part of our stores, and had four rivers to pass. None can say that our retreat was precipitate; for we were near three weeks in performing it, that the country might have time to come in. Twice we marched back to meet the enemy, and remained out till dark. The sign of fear was not seen in our camp, and had not some of the cowardly and disaffected inhabitants spread false alarms through the country, the Jerseys had never been ravaged. Once more we are again collected and collecting, our new army at both ends of the continent is recruiting fast, and we shall be able to open the next campaign with sixty thousand men, well-armed and clothed. This is our situation, and who will may know it. By perseverance and fortitude we have the prospect of a glorious issue; by cowardice and submission, the sad choice of a variety of evils: a ravaged country—a depopulated city—habitations without safety, and slavery without hope—our homes turned into barracks and bawdyhouses for Hessians—and a

STUDY FOR WASHINGTON CROSSING THE DELAWARE
Larry Rivers 1953

future race to provide for, whose fathers we shall doubt of. Look on this picture and weep over it! and if there yet remains one thoughtless wretch who believes it not, let him suffer it unlamented.

COMMON SENSE
December 23, 1776

Study Questions

1. What consolation does Paine give to hard-pressed Americans who support the overthrow of tyranny? How does his quotation of the British statement, "to BIND us in ALL CASES WHATSOEVER," support his statement of the issue?

2. Find examples of statements that would be especially emotion-charged for Paine's audience in the year 1776. Where, on the other hand, are his points realistic and practical?

3. What are the different implications of the two statements: "Give me peace in my day" and "If there must be trouble, let it be in my day, that my child may have peace" (pages 181–182)?

4. Paine says, "Nothing can reach the heart that is steeled with prejudice." Explain why you agree or disagree with this statement.

5. Analyze the wording in Paine's first sentence. Why does it still have such an impact? Try rewriting it to see if other wordings are equally effective.

Why is the imagery in the second sentence, "summer soldier" and "sunshine patriot," so appropriate? Point out other examples of Paine's effective use of figurative language. Tell why each is effective and appropriate.

Composition

1. In a brief essay summarize the points in Paine's essay which are particularly relevant to Americans today. Look for points which reinforce a belief in the democratic spirit.

2. Select a custom, practice, or institution of which you disapprove; for example, final exams, required courses, or curfews. Write an article for the school paper in which you persuade readers to your point of view. Present a rational, carefully balanced argument addressed to readers who are as well informed as you are.

Vocabulary

Both Thomas Paine and Benjamin Franklin wrote for "the average American Colonist." For that reason, both authors used simpler, more direct words than those chosen by most writers of their time. Another way in which Paine and Franklin appealed to their reading audience was by turning out great quantities of quotable sayings, or "words of wisdom," which were immensely popular at the end of the eighteenth century.

The English language contains many synonyms for quotable sayings: *adage, aphorism, epigram, maxim, proverb,* and *saw.* All these terms signify concise statements which seem to express general truths or principles. Of the six, the term that applies best to Paine's sayings is **aphorism**, defined as "an artfully phrased saying which appears to have been developed only after lengthy and serious deliberation." For example:

> It is the madness of folly to expect mercy from those who have refused to do justice; and even mercy, where conquest is the object, is only a trick of war.

Like some other kinds of quotable sayings, an aphorism is first created to serve just one specific situation at one specific time. But an aphorism carries such a ring of truth that it seems equally appropriate in many other circumstances during many other periods.

Even though the preceding selection from Paine's *The American Crisis* is brief, it contains no fewer than twenty aphorisms.

A. As one evidence of their artful phrasing, Paine's aphorisms frequently include figures of speech. On a separate sheet of paper, tell which of the following aphorisms contain similes and which contain metaphors. Also tell what things are being compared in the simile or metaphor.

1. Though the flame of liberty may sometimes cease to shine, the coal can never expire.

2. Tyranny, like hell, is not easily conquered.

3. The cunning of the fox is as murderous as the violence of the wolf, and we ought to guard equally against both.

4. Heaven knows how to put a proper price upon its goods; and it would be strange indeed if so celestial an article as FREEDOM should not be highly rated.

5. Mutual fear is the principal link in the chain of mutual love.

B. Despite Thomas Paine's habitual use of a simple vocabulary, a few words in some of his aphorisms are not so widely understood today as they were two centuries ago. Examples of such words are *italicized* below.

   Give your opinion of the meaning of these words suggested by their context. Compare your opinions with the actual definitions which appear in a dictionary.

   1. What we obtain too cheap, we esteem too lightly; it is *dearness* only that gives everything its value.

   2. Eloquence may strike the ear, and the language of sorrow draw forth the tear of *compassion,* but nothing can reach the heart that is steeled with prejudice.

   3. (Panics) have the same effect on secret traitors which an imaginary *apparition* would have upon a private murderer: they sift out the hidden thoughts of man, and hold them up in public to the world.

   4. I love the man that can smile in trouble, that can gather strength from distress and grow brave by *reflection.*

   5. The harder the conflict, the more glorious the *triumph.*

C. In a dictionary, find the word *epigram.* Disregard the definition that applies to a type of poem. Concentrate entirely on the definition which applies to a short quotable saying. With this definition in mind, compare the tone of Thomas Paine's aphorisms with that of the sayings from *Poor Richard's Almanac* (page 173). Then tell briefly why most of Benjamin Franklin's sayings in that book may more properly be called *epigrams* than *aphorisms.*

Phillis Wheatley   1753?-1784

The child who was later named Phillis Wheatley was born in Senegal on the west coast of Africa. She was captured at age five or six and brought to Boston on a slave ship in 1761. There she was purchased at the auction block by John Wheatley, a prosperous merchant, as a gift for his wife. The little girl's exceptional intelligence encouraged the Wheatleys to give her an education superior to that of most females in her day. She quickly mastered English and Latin. At age thirteen she wrote her first poem and began to read her works in the drawing rooms of Boston society. In 1770, she published her first poem. Recognition came quickly.

In London she was lionized as "The Sable Muse." In 1773 her first book, *Poems on Various Subjects, Religious and Moral,* was published there. After Phillis Wheatley was freed, she married John Peters, another free Black. Phillis Wheatley's poetry was used by abolitionists in the 19th century to combat the mythology of racial inferiority. One of her poems in which she expressed her love of freedom appears below. It was dedicated to William Legge, Earl of Dartmouth, after his appointment in 1773 as British Secretary of State for the colonies.

To the Right Honourable William, Earl of Dartmouth

PHILLIS WHEATLEY

HAIL, happy day, when, smiling like the morn,
Fair *Freedom* rose *New-England* to adorn:
The northern clime beneath her genial ray,
Dartmouth, congratulates thy blissful sway:
Elate with hope her race no longer mourns,   5
Each soul expands, each grateful bosom burns,
While in thine hand with pleasure we behold
The silken reins, and *Freedom's* charms unfold.
Long lost to realms beneath the northern skies
She shines supreme, while hated *faction* dies: 10
Soon as appear'd the *Goddess* long desir'd;
Sick at the view, she lanquish'd and expir'd;
Thus from the splendors of the morning light
The owl in sadness seeks the caves of night.

No more, *America,* in mournful strain   15
Of wrongs, and grievance unredress'd complain,
No longer shalt thou dread the iron chain,
Which wanton *Tyranny* with lawless hand
Had made, and with it meant t' enslave the land.

Should you, my lord, while you peruse my song,   20
Wonder from whence my love of *Freedom* sprung,
Whence flow these wishes for the common good,
By feeling hearts alone best understood,
I, young in life, by seeming cruel fate
Was snatch'd from *Afric's* fancy'd happy seat: 25
What pangs excruciating must molest,
What sorrows labour in my parent's breast?
Steel'd was that soul and by no misery mov'd
That from a father seiz'd his babe belov'd:
Such, such my case. And can I then but pray   30
Others may never feel tyrannic sway?

For favours past, great Sir, our thanks are due,
And thee we ask thy favours to renew,
Since in thy pow'r, as in thy will before,
To sooth the griefs, which thou did'st once deplore.   35
May heav'nly grace the sacred sanction give
To all thy works, and thou for ever live
Not only on the wings of fleeting *Fame,*
Though praise immortal crowns the patriot's name,
But to conduct to heav'ns refulgent[1] fane,   40
May fiery coursers sweep th' ethereal plain,
And bear thee upwards to that blest abode,
Where, like the prophet, thou shalt find thy God.

---

1 **refulgent:** brilliant.

Study Questions

1. In the first stanza, addressed to Lord Dartmouth, what are the speaker's reasons for welcoming his appointment? What are the "reins" (line 8)? Why does he hold them?

2. In the third stanza what biographical details does the speaker give to re-inforce her point? What was the parents' reaction to the loss of their child? Who seized the father's babe?

3. The final stanza concentrates on religious images. What reward does the speaker say Lord Dartmouth can expect if he promotes freedom in America?

Abigail Smith Adams   1744-1818

Abigail Smith Adams was the wife of John Adams, a signer of the Declaration of Independence and later our second president. In her own right and through influence on her husband, she played a significant role in the founding of this country. Her many eloquent letters give a vivid picture of life during the times of the revolution and the early republic.

On March 31, 1776, while the Continental Congress was moving toward the Declaration, Abigail Adams wrote to her husband urging him forward and expressing a special concern for the rights of women in the new nation:

I long to hear that you have declared an independence—and by the way in the new Code of Laws which I suppose it will be necessary for you to make I desire you would Remember the Ladies, and be more generous and favorable to them than your ancestors. Do not put such unlimited power into the hands of the Husbands. Remember all Men would be tyrants if they could. If particular care and attention is not paid to the Ladies we are determined to foment a Rebellion, and will not hold ourselves bound by any Laws in which we have no voice, or Representation.

A month later she returned to this theme in a letter showing how capably and judiciously she combined personal and domestic cares with a feeling for the general welfare.

Letter to Her Husband

ABIGAIL SMITH ADAMS

Braintree

May 7, 1776

How many are the solitary hours I spend, ruminating upon the past and anticipating the future whilst you, overwhelmed with the cares of state, have but few moments you can devote to any individual. All domestic pleasures and enjoyments are absorbed in the great and important duty you owe your country "for our country is, as it were, a secondary god and the first and greatest parent. It is to be preferred to parents, wives, children, friends and all things; the gods only excepted. For if our country perishes, it is as impossible to save an individual as to preserve one of the fingers of a mortified hand." Thus do I suppress every wish and silence every murmur, acquiescing in a painful separation from the companion of my youth and the friend of my heart.

I believe it is near ten days since I wrote you a line. I have not felt in a humor to entertain you. If I had taken up my pen, perhaps some unbecoming invective might have fallen from it; the eyes of our rulers have been closed and a lethargy has seized almost every member. I fear a fatal security has taken possession of them. Whilst the building is in flame, they tremble at the expense of water to quench it. In short, two months have elapsed since the evacuation of Boston, and very little has been done in that time to secure it or the harbor from future invasion until the people are all in a flame, and no one among us that I have heard of even mentions expense. They think universally that there has been an amazing neglect somewhere. Many have turned out as volunteers to work upon Nodles Island, and many more would go upon Nantasket if it was once set on foot. "It is a maxim of state that power and liberty are like heat and moisture; where they are well mixed everything prospers; where they are single, they are destructive."

A government of more stability is much wanted in this colony, and they are ready to receive it from the hands of the Congress, and since I have begun with maxims of state, I will add another: A people may let a king fall, yet still remain a people, but if a king lets his people slip from him, he is no longer a king. And as this is most certainly our case, why not proclaim to the world in decisive terms your own importance?

Shall we not be despised by foreign powers for hesitating so long at a word?

I cannot say that I think you very generous to the ladies, for whilst you are proclaiming peace and good will to men, emancipating all nations, you insist upon retaining an absolute power over wives. But you must remember that arbitrary power is like most other things which are very hard, very liable to be broken—and notwithstanding all your wise laws and maxims, we have it in our power not only to free ourselves but to subdue our masters, and without violence throw both your natural and legal authority at our feet—

"Charm by accepting, by submitting sway
Yet have our humor most when we obey."

I thank you for several letters which I have received since I wrote last. They alleviate a tedious absence, and I long earnestly for a Saturday evening and experience a similar pleasure to that which I used to find in the return of my friend upon that day after a week's absence. The idea of a year dissolves all my philosophy.

Our little ones, whom you so often recommend to my care and instruction, shall not be deficient in virtue or probity if the precepts of a mother have their desired effect, but they would be doubly enforced could they be indulged with the example of a father constantly before them; I often point them to their sire

"Engaged in a corrupted state
Wrestling with vice and faction."

Study Questions

1. How does Abigail Adams explain the necessity for separation from her husband?
2. Why has she not written for ten days?
3. What advice does she have for John Adams?
4. How does she make use of the perilous times in educating their children?
5. What does this letter tell you about the character of Abigail Adams?

Thomas Jefferson   1743-1826

The epitaph Jefferson wrote for himself lists only three highlights from his brilliant career:

> Here Was Buried
> Thomas Jefferson
> Author of the Declaration of
> American Independence,
> of the Statute of Virginia
> for Religious Freedom,
> and Father of the
> University of Virginia.

Jefferson was a successful lawyer and an accomplished architect. He designed his estate at Monticello, the Mall in Washington, and the University of Virginia. He was also a statesman and diplomat, a classical and linguistic scholar: he knew Latin, French, Italian, Greek, Spanish, and Old English. He was an agricultural theorist, an inventor (calendars, clocks, storm windows, plows), and, above all, the third President of the United States. Yet the three achievements Jefferson chose for his gravestone go to the heart of his greatest legacy, the ideal of the free person. Each of them stands for one essential element of the ideal: the Declaration, for freedom of the person; the Virginia statute, for freedom of the individual conscience; the University, for freedom of the mind. Jefferson argued that the best hope for the preservation and growth of society was education.

Jefferson's bold vision and clear thought can be seen in his many writings. These include the Declaration of Independence (page 85), parts of the Bill of Rights, numerous state and national documents. He also had a voluminous correspondence (18,000 letters), and in 1785 published *Notes on the State of Virginia.* The selection that follows from that publication emphasizes Jefferson the thinker or philosopher and reflects his concern for total emancipation.

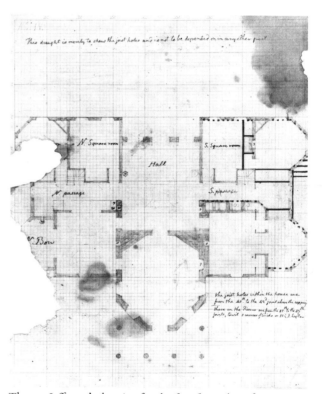

Thomas Jefferson's drawing for the first floor plan of Monticello.

from Notes on the State of Virginia

THOMAS JEFFERSON

IT IS DIFFICULT to determine on the standard by which the manners of a nation may be tried, whether *catholic*[1] or *particular.* It is more difficult for a native to bring to that standard the manners of his own nation, familiarized to him by habit. There must doubtless be an unhappy influence on the manners of our people produced by the existence of slavery among us. The whole commerce between master and slave is a perpetual exercise of the most boisterous passions, the most unremitting despotism on the one part, and degrading submissions on the other. Our children see this, and learn to imitate it; for man is an imitative animal. This quality is the germ of all education in him. From his cradle to his grave he is learning to do what he sees others do. If a parent could find no motive either in his philanthropy or his self-love, for restraining the intemperance of passion towards his slave, it should always be a sufficient one that his child is present. But generally it is not sufficient. The parent storms, the child looks on, catches the lineaments of wrath, puts on the same airs in the circle of smaller slaves, gives a loose to the worst of passions, and thus nursed, educated, and daily exercised in tyranny, cannot but be stamped by it with odious peculiarities. The man must be a prodigy[2] who can retain his manners and morals undepraved by such circumstances. And with what execration[3] should the statesman be loaded, who, permitting one half the citizens thus to trample on the rights of the other, transforms those into despots, and these into enemies, destroys the morals of the one part, and the *amor patriae*[4] of the other. For if a slave can have a country in this world, it must be any other in preference to that in which he is born to live and labor for another; in which he must lock up the faculties of his nature, contribute as far as depends on his individual endeavors to the evanishment[5] of the human race, or entail his own miserable condition on the endless generations proceeding from him. With the morals of the people, their industry also is destroyed. For in a warm climate, no man will labor for himself who can make another labor for him. This is so true, that of the proprietors of slaves a very small proportion indeed are ever seen to labor. And can the liberties of a nation be thought secure when we have removed their only firm basis, a conviction in the minds of the people that these liberties are the gift of God? That they are not to be violated but with His wrath? Indeed I tremble for my country when I reflect that God is just; that his justice cannot sleep forever; that considering numbers, nature and natural means only, a revolution of the wheel of fortune, and exchange of situation is among possible events; that it may become probably by supernatural interference! The Almighty has no attribute which can take side with us in such a contest. But it is impossible to be temperate and to pursue this subject through the various considerations of policy, of morals, of history natural and civil. We must be contented to hope they will force their way into every one's mind. I think a change already

---

1 **catholic:** general; all-inclusive.
2 **prodigy:** person with exceptional talents.
3 **execration:** loathing; abhorrence.

4 **amor patriae:** love of country; patriotism.
5 **evanishment:** disappearance.

perceptible, since the origin of the present revolution. The spirit of the master is abating, that of the slave rising from the dust, his condition mollifying, the way I hope preparing, under the auspices of heaven, for a total emancipation, and that this is disposed, in the order of events, to be with the consent of the masters, rather than by their extirpation.[6]

---

6 **extirpation**: complete destruction.

Study Questions

1. What does Jefferson see as the damaging effect ("perpetual exercise") the existence of slavery produces in masters and in slaves?
2. What human tendency does Jefferson see as the "germ of all education"?
3. What parallel does Jefferson draw between the statesman and the parent?
4. Where does Jefferson hope that a change in attitude toward slavery will begin?
5. How do you think men such as Thomas Jefferson, George Washington, and William Byrd could own slaves yet also profess so strongly that slavery was wrong?

Vocabulary

Each item below contains one *italicized* word taken from Thomas Jefferson's *Notes on the State of Virginia*. The *italicized* word is followed by five choices. For example:

degrading: lowering   assisting   recalling   elevating   believing

From among the five choices, select an **antonym**, the one word whose meaning is most nearly opposite to that of the *italicized* word. Write your answers on a separate sheet of paper.

1. *perpetual:* horrible   specific   momentary   dignified   false
2. *prodigy:* moron   winner   cheapskate   genius   wallflower
3. *abate:* rebel   pursue   enjoy   allow   increase
4. *mollify:* convince   irritate   equalize   advance   borrow
5. *execration:* misbehavior   politeness   luck   delay   blessing

Benjamin Banneker   1731-1806

Benjamin Banneker was one of the most intellectual and versatile people in colonial America. Though his father was a slave, his mother was free, and the offspring of free women were also free. He inherited a small farm near Baltimore and taught himself mathematics, astronomy, and engineering. He was also a poet and naturalist. President George Washington appointed him a member of the commission to lay out the District of Columbia, the new capital. He built a wooden clock thought to be the first accurate one made in America. At the age of sixty Banneker had sufficiently developed his calculations of the heavenly bodies to enable him to write his first almanac for the year 1792. Thomas Jefferson, then the nation's first Secretary of State, had written that Blacks "could scarcely be found capable of . . . comprehending . . . Euclid." In response, Banneker sent a manuscript copy of his almanac to Jefferson. Banneker's cover letter sent with the almanac is printed below. In it he challenged America's most famous slaveholder to evaluate his position on freedom and liberty "for all" and helped to make public the intellectual capabilities of African-Americans.

Letter to Thomas Jefferson

BENJAMIN BANNEKER

Maryland, Baltimore County

Near Ellicotts' Lower Mills,

August 19th, 1791

Thomas Jefferson, Secretary of State.

Sir:—I am fully sensible of the greatness of that freedom, which I take with you on the present occasion, a liberty which seemed to me scarcely allowable, when I reflected on that distinguished and dignified station in which you stand, and the almost general prejudice and prepossession which is so prevalent in the world against those of my complexion.

I suppose it is a truth too well attested to you, to need a proof here, that we are a race of beings who have long labored under the abuse and censure of the world, that we have long been considered rather as brutish than human, and scarcely capable of mental endowments.

Sir, I hope I may safely admit, in consequence of that report which hath reached me,

HEAD OF A NEGRO *John Singleton Copley* late 1700s

that you are a man far less inflexible in sentiments of this nature than many others, that you are measurably friendly and well disposed towards us, and that you are willing and ready to lend your aid and assistance to our relief, from those many distresses and numerous calamities, to which we are reduced.

Now, sir, if this is founded in truth, I apprehend you will readily embrace every opportunity to eradicate that train of absurd and false ideas and opinions, which so generally prevails with respect to us, and that your sentiments are concurrent with mine, which are that one universal Father hath given Being to us all, and that He hath not only made us all of one flesh, but that He hath also without partiality afforded us all the same sensations, and endowed us all with the same faculties, and that however variable we may be in society or religion, however diversified in situation or color, we are all of the same family, and stand in the same relation to Him.

Sir, if these are sentiments of which you are fully persuaded, I hope you cannot but acknowledge, that it is the indispensable duty of those who maintain for themselves the rights of human nature, and who profess the obligations of christianity, to extend their power and influence to the relief of every part of the human race, from whatever burden or oppression they may unjustly labor under, and this I apprehend a full conviction of the truth and obligation of these principles should lead all to.

Sir, I have long been convinced that if your love for yourselves and for those inesteemable laws, which preserve to you the rights of human nature, was found on sincerity, you could not but be solicitous that every individual of whatever rank or distinction, might with you equally enjoy the blessings thereof, neither could you rest satisfied, short of the most active diffusion of your exertions in order to their promotions from any state of degradation to which the unjustifiable cruelty and barbarism of men have reduced them.

Sir, I freely and cheerfully acknowledge that I am of the African race, and in that color which is natural to them of the deepest dye, and it is under a sense of the most profound gratitude to the Supreme Ruler of the universe that I now confess to you that I am not under that state of tyrannical thraldom and inhuman captivity to which too many of my brethren are doomed; but that I have abundantly tasted of the fruition of those blessings which proceed from that free and unequalled liberty with which you are favored and which, I hope you will willingly allow you have received from the immediate hand of that Being, from whom proceedeth every good and perfect gift.

Sir, suffer me to recall to your mind that time in which the arms and tyranny of the British Crown were exerted with every powerful effort in order to reduce you to a State of Servitude, look back I entreat you on the variety of dangers to which you were exposed; reflect on that time in which every human aid appeared unavailable, and in which even hope and fortitude wore the aspect of inability to the conflict and you cannot but be led to a serious and grateful sense of your miraculous and providential preservation; you cannot but acknowledge that the present freedom and tranquility which you enjoy you have mercifully received and that it is the peculiar blessing of Heaven.

This sir, was a time in which you clearly saw into the injustice of a state of slavery and in which you had just apprehensions of the horrors of its condition, it was now, sir, that your abhorrence thereof was so excited, that you publicly held forth this true and valuable doctrine, which is worthy to be recorded and remembered in all succeeding ages. "We hold these truths to be self-evident, that all men are created equal, and that they are endowed by their creator with certain unalienable rights, that among these are life, liberty and the pursuit of happiness."

Here, sir, was a time in which your tender feelings for yourselves had engaged you thus to declare, you were then impressed with proper ideas of the great valuation of liberty and the free possession of those blessings to which you were entitled by nature; but, sir, how pitiable is it to reflect that although you were so fully convinced of the benevolence of the Father of mankind and of his equal and impartial distribution of those rights and privileges which he had conferred upon them, that you should at the same time counteract his mercies in detaining by fraud and violence so numerous a part of my brethren under groaning captivity and cruel oppression, that you should at the same time be found guilty of that most criminal act which you professedly detested in others with respect to yourselves.

Sir, I suppose that your knowledge of the situation of my brethren is too extensive to need a recital here; neither shall I presume to prescribe methods by which they may be relieved, otherwise than by recommending to you and all others to wean yourselves from those narrow prejudices which you have imbibed with respect to them and as Job proposed to his friends, "put your souls in their souls' stead," thus shall your hearts be enlarged with kindness and benevolence towards them, and thus shall you need neither the direction of myself or others, in what manner to proceed herein. . . .

B. Banneker

Study Questions

1. In the first two paragraphs what is the "general prejudice" and "abuse and censure" Banneker refers to? What do you think he means by "we have long been considered . . . brutish . . ."?

2. Why does Banneker feel that Jefferson particularly would be responsive to the mistreatment of African-Americans?

3. In paragraphs 4 and 6, Banneker presents two different reasons why African-Americans should be treated the same as other Americans. What are the reasons?

4. What is the "state of tyrannical thraldom and inhuman captivity" Banneker talks about in paragraph 7?

5. In paragraph 10, Banneker accuses Jefferson of being guilty. What does he say Jefferson is guilty of? and why?

6. Why do you think Banneker would send this letter to Jefferson along with a handwritten copy of his almanac? Why do you think Banneker begins each paragraph with "Sir"?

Composition

1. In a short essay, summarize Banneker's letter using modern language and terms. For example, instead of "inhuman captivity" use the word "slavery." Be sure to include each point Banneker makes.

2. Write a reply from Thomas Jefferson to Benjamin Banneker's letter. Be sure to acknowledge each of Banneker's points. Respond to Banneker's accusation of guilt and tell what you think of the almanac.

THE SKATER *Gilbert Stuart* 1782

Hector St. John de Crèvecoeur   1735-1813

"What then is the American, this new [person]?" The question has been asked ever since the nation began its struggle for existence. It was a French immigrant who attempted the answer in the first literary definition of the American character. In 1782 Michel Guillaume Jean de Crèvecoeur published in England a collection of twelve essays entitled *Letters from an American Farmer,* under the name J. Hector St. Jean. These essays contain de Crèvecoeur's observations of America's effect on what he called the "new man." He had made such observations during wide travels in the American colonies and ten years' residence on a frontier farm in Orange County, New York. Included here is part of the third essay in *Letters from an American Farmer.* It represents an eloquent expression of that American Dream which has inspired so many pioneers and immigrants. These people sought and continue to seek in the New World a life of opportunity, individual liberty and self-development unhampered by Old World social and political restraints. De Crèvecoeur's essay articulates that emerging American spirit and character.

This Is an American

HECTOR ST. JOHN DE CRÈVECOEUR

WHAT ATTACHMENT can a poor European emigrant have for a country where he had nothing? The knowledge of the language, the love of a few kindred as poor as himself, were the only cords that tied him: his country is now that which gives him land, bread, protection, and consequence. *Ubi panis ibi patria*[1] is the motto of all emigrants. What then is the American, this new man? He is either an European, or the descendant of an European, hence that strange mixture of blood, which you will find in no other country. I could point out to you a family whose grandfather was an Englishman, whose wife was Dutch, whose son married a French woman, and whose present four sons have now four wives of different nations. *He* is an American, who, leaving behind him all his ancient prejudices and manners, receives new ones from the new mode of life he has embraced, the new government he obeys, and the new rank he holds. He becomes an American by being received in the broad lap of our great *Alma Mater.*[2] Here individuals of all nations are melted into a new race of men, whose labors and posterity will one day cause great changes in the world. Americans are the western pilgrims, who are carrying along with

---

1 *Ubi . . . patria:* "Where bread is, there is one's country."

2 *Alma Mater:* "beloved mother."

them that great mass of arts, sciences, vigor, and industry which began long since in the east; they will finish the great circle. The Americans were once scattered all over Europe; here they are incorporated into one of the finest systems of population which has ever appeared, and which will hereafter become distinct by the power of the different climates they inhabit. The American ought therefore to love this country much better than that wherein either he or his forefathers were born. Here the rewards of his industry follow with equal steps the progress of his labor; his labor is founded on the basis of nature, *self-interest;* can it want a stronger allurement? Wives and children, who before in vain demanded of him a morsel of bread, now, fat and frolicsome, gladly help their father to clear those fields whence exuberant crops are to arise to feed and to clothe them all; without any part being claimed, either by a despotic prince, a rich abbot, or a mighty lord. Here religion demands but little of him; a small voluntary salary to the minister, and gratitude to God; can he refuse these? The American is a new man, who acts upon new principles; he must therefore entertain new ideas, and form new opinions. From involuntary idleness, servile dependence, penury, and useless labor, he has passed to toils of a very different nature, rewarded by ample subsistence.—This is an American.

Study Questions

1. What did the European immigrants to this country bring with them that shaped the character of the American? What did they leave behind in Europe which also helped determine the character of this new individual?

2. Why do you think de Crevecoeur defined Americans as "either an European, or the descendant of an European"? What about other ethnic groups?

3. What are the reasons de Crevecoeur gives for Americans to love this country more than the country of their ancestors?

4. How does de Crevecoeur describe the new American? How is this description consistent with characteristics of the American Dream?

Study Questions

1. Based on the information contained in Abigail Adams's letter, how do her concerns reflect those of Anne Bradstreet (page 146) and Phillis Wheatley (page 188)?

2. How does some of Franklin's advice in "Poor Richard's Almanac" demonstrate the self-made man to which de Tocqueville (page 45) objected?

3. Paine's writings are said to have served as models in substance and language for the Declaration of Independence (page 85). Although Paine himself did not work with the committee which drafted the document, he was closely associated with Jefferson while it was being composed. Compare the Declaration with Paine's essay. Where do you find Paine's principles incorporated into the Declaration? Find examples of similarities in language. For example, in the indictment of George III we read, "declaring themselves invested with power to legislate for us in all cases whatsoever" (page 87). Paine uses the phrase, "to bind us in all cases whatsoever" (page 180).

4. Compare Paine's definition of "tyranny" and "freedom" with Phillis Wheatley's use of the same words (page 189). Then compare Jefferson's and Banneker's attitudes toward freedom.

5. Using writers in this unit as examples, discuss the eighteenth-century version of the American Dream. Define which aspect of the American Dream the writers emphasize directly or indirectly.

Composition

1. Literature of the Independence period has been called literature of persuasion. In an essay apply this statement to the selections in this Unit. In a short introductory paragraph explain your objective. Then in a separate paragraph for each author explain what main point or points each writer is trying to persuade the audience to accept. In a concluding paragraph explain what concerns the writers have in common.

2. Follow Banneker's example and write a letter to a well-known political figure with whom you disagree or agree on a current national issue. You should first state the issue clearly and then give reasons for your point of view. You might conclude by requesting action. Be as specific as possible.

4

A New Literature

A NEW LITERATURE

IN THE YEARS following the Revolution, Americans became very self-conscious about their cultural status in the world. Many felt we would be truly independent only when we had produced a literature to express the national character. Some argued that we needed an American epic, after the manner of Homer and Virgil, to give us the desired eminence. This argument resulted in several ambitious poems about the discovery and colonization of the New World—very long and very dull.

Other writers, like Ralph Waldo Emerson, declared that we should forget European models and create new forms to express our new country. One new form, introduced in the eighteenth century, was the slave narrative, which received wide acclaim with the publication in 1845 of *Narrative of the Life of Frederick Douglass, an American Slave.*

However, American writers were more creative in their experiments with standard European forms than in establishing new ones. Edgar Allan Poe mastered the art of suspense in such short stories as "The Pit and the Pendulum," "The Telltale Heart," and "The Cask of Amontillado." Nathaniel Hawthorne gave the traditional gothic romance a particularly American flavor in *The Scarlet Letter.* And Herman Melville matched the vastness of the

FUR TRADERS DESCENDING THE MISSOURI *(detail) George Caleb Bingham*

American landscape with his immense novel *Moby Dick*, which is perhaps more popular today than in Melville's time.

During this period of the nineteenth century, more attention was being given to the imaginative forms which are traditionally thought of as literature. However, American writers continued to comment on political and social issues. William Cullen Bryant not only wrote poetry, but was also a journalist concerned with the abolitionist issue. Elizabeth Cady Stanton wrote a *Declaration of Sentiments,* modeled closely after the *Declaration of Independence,* to officially begin the Women's Rights Movement.

It was during this experimental period that American writers began to develop a recognizable identity. That identity was based on their common spirit in the thematic treatment of subjects. All of the writers had the American Sense of Place, were concerned with the problems of the Individual in a democratic society, and shared the knowledge of a Dream whose fulfillment was in the future.

In short, the first half of the nineteenth century was a time for discovering the great possibilities of an American Literature.

HIAWATHA *Thomas Eakins* 1871

Washington Irving   1783-1859

Washington Irving is chiefly remembered for two stories, "Rip Van Winkle" and "The Legend of Sleepy Hollow." He also wrote the comic *Knickerbocker's History of New York* and a great many other works during a long career. Irving was the first American author to be widely acclaimed on both sides of the Atlantic.

Frequently he sought out old tales and legends which he could recreate for his readers. "Rip Van Winkle" is one of these. Irving adapts an old German legend about a goatherd named Peter Klaus. The new American tale is about a shiftless, but amiable huband named Rip Van Winkle. Both Klaus and Rip fall asleep for twenty years. To the basic outline of the old story Irving adds details of American local color.

Rip Van Winkle

WASHINGTON IRVING

WHOEVER HAS MADE a voyage up the Hudson must remember the Kaatskill mountains. They are a dismembered branch of the great Appalachian family, and are seen away to the west of the river, swelling up to a noble height, and lording it over the surrounding country. Every change of season, every change of weather, indeed, every hour of the day, produces some change in the magical hues and shapes of these mountains, and they are regarded by all the good wives, far and near, as perfect barometers. When the weather is fair and settled, they are clothed in blue and purple, and print their bold outlines on the clear evening sky; but, sometimes, when the rest of the landscape is cloudless, they will gather a hood of gray vapors about their summits, which, in the last rays of the setting sun, will glow and light up like a crown of glory.

At the foot of these fairy mountains, the voyager may have descried the light smoke curling up from a village, whose shingle roofs gleam among the trees, just where the blue tints of the upland melt away into the fresh green of the nearer landscape. It is a little village, of great antiquity, having been founded by some of the Dutch colonists, in the early times of the province, just about the beginning of the government of the good Peter Stuyvesant[1] (may he rest in peace!), and there were some of the houses of the original settlers standing within a few years, built of small yellow bricks brought from Holland, having latticed windows and gable fronts, surmounted with weathercocks.

In that same village, and in one of these very houses (which, to tell the precise truth, was sadly timeworn and weather-beaten), there lived many years since, while the country was yet a province of Great Britain, a simple good-natured fellow, of the name of Rip Van Winkle. He was a descendant of the Van Winkles who figured so gallantly in the chivalrous days of Peter Stuyvesant, and accompanied him to the siege of Fort Christina. He inherited, however, but little of the martial character of his ancestors. I have observed that he was a simple good-natured man; he was, moreover, a kind neighbor, and an obedient henpecked husband. Indeed, to the latter circumstance might be owing that meekness of spirit which gained him such universal popularity; for those men are most apt to be obsequious and conciliating abroad who are under the discipline of shrews at home. Their tempers, doubtless, are rendered pliant and malleable in the fiery furnace of domestic tribulation; and a curtain lecture is worth all the sermons in the world for teaching the virtues of patience and long-suffering. A termagant wife may, therefore, in some respects, be considered a tolerable blessing; and if so, Rip Van Winkle was thrice blessed.

Certain it is, that he was a great favorite among all the good wives of the village, who, as usual, with the amiable sex, took his part in all family squabbles; and never failed, whenever they talked those matters over in their evening gossipings, to lay all the blame on Dame Van Winkle. The children of the village, too, would shout with joy whenever he approached. He assisted at their sports, made their playthings, taught them to fly kites and shoot marbles, and told them long stories of ghosts, witches, and Indians. Whenever he went dodging about the village, he was surrounded by a troop of them, hanging on his skirts, clambering on his back, and playing a thousand tricks on him with impunity; and not a dog would bark at him throughout the neighborhood.

The great error in Rip's composition was an insuperable aversion to all kinds of profitable labor. It could not be from the want of assiduity or perseverance; for he would sit on a wet rock, with a rod as long and heavy as a Tartar's[2] lance, and fish all day without a murmur, even though he should not be encouraged by a single nibble. He would carry a fowling piece[3] on his shoulder for hours together, trudging through woods and swamps, and up hill and down dale, to shoot a few squirrels or wild pigeons. He would never refuse to assist a neighbor even in the roughest toil, and was a foremost man at all country frolics for husking Indian corn, or building stone fences; the women of the village, too, used to employ him to run their errands, and to do such little odd jobs as their less obliging husbands would not do for them. In a word Rip was ready to attend to anybody's business but his own; but as to doing family duty, and keeping his farm in order, he found it impossible.

In fact, he declared it was of no use to work on his farm; it was the most pestilent little piece of ground in the whole country; every-

---

1 **Peter Stuyvesant** (Stī′ və sənt) 1592–1672: last governor of the Dutch colony making up what is now New York, New Jersey, and Delaware.

2 **Tartar:** one of the Mongolian peoples who conquered Asia and eastern Europe.
3 **fowling piece:** old-fashioned gun for shooting fowl.

thing about it went wrong, and would go wrong, in spite of him. His fences were continually falling to pieces; his cow would either go astray or get among the cabbages; weeds were sure to grow quicker in his field than anywhere else; the rain always made a point of setting in just as he had some outdoor work to do; so that though his patrimonial estate[4] had dwindled away under his management, acre by acre, until there was little more left than a mere patch of Indian corn and potatoes, yet it was the worst-conditioned farm in the neighborhood.

His children, too, were as ragged and wild as if they belonged to nobody. His son Rip, an urchin begotten in his own likeness, promised to inherit the habits, with the old clothes of his father. He was generally seen trooping like a colt at his mother's heels, equipped in a pair of his father's castoff galligaskins,[5] which he had much ado to hold up with one hand, as a fine lady does her train in bad weather.

Rip Van Winkle, however, was one of those happy mortals, of foolish, well-oiled dispositions, who take the world easy, eat white bread or brown, whichever can be got with least thought or trouble, and would rather starve on a penny than work for a pound. If left to himself, he would have whistled life away in perfect contentment; but his wife kept continually dinning in his ears about his idleness, his carelessness, and the ruin he was bringing on his family. Morning, noon, and night, her tongue was incessantly going, and everything he said or did was sure to produce a torrent of household eloquence. Rip had but one way of replying to all lectures of the kind, and that, by frequent use, had grown into a habit. He shrugged his shoulders, shook his head, cast up his eyes, but said nothing. This, however, always provoked a fresh volley from his wife; so that he was fain to draw off his forces, and take to the outside of the house—the only side

which, in truth, belongs to a henpecked husband.

Rip's sole domestic adherent was his dog Wolf, who was as much henpecked as his master; for Dame Van Winkle regarded them as companions in idleness, and even looked upon Wolf with an evil eye, as the cause of his master's going so often astray. True it is, in all points of spirit befitting an honorable dog, he was as courageous an animal as ever scoured the woods—but what courage can withstand the everduring and all-besetting terrors of a woman's tongue? The moment Wolf entered the house his crest fell, his tail drooped to the ground, or curled between his legs, he sneaked about with a gallows air, casting many a sidelong glance at Dame Van Winkle, and at the least flourish of a broomstick or ladle, he would fly to the door with yelping precipitation.

Times grew worse and worse with Rip Van Winkle as years of matrimony rolled on; a tart temper never mellows with age, and a sharp tongue is the only edged tool that grows keener with constant use. For a long while he used to console himself, when driven from home, by frequenting a kind of perpetual club of the sages, philosophers, and other idle personages of the village; which held its sessions on a bench before a small inn, designated by a rubicund[6] portrait of His Majesty George the Third.[7] Here they used to sit in the shade through a long lazy summer's day, talking listlessly over village gossip, or telling endless sleepy stories about nothing. But it would have been worth any statesman's money to have heard the profound discussions that sometimes took place, when by chance an old newspaper fell into their hands from some passing traveler. How solemnly they would listen to the contents, as drawled out by Derrick Van Bummel, the schoolmaster, a dapper learned little man, who was not to be daunted by the most gigantic word in the dictionary;

---

4 **patrimonial** (pat' rə mō' nē əl) **estate:** land left by one's ancestors.
5 **galligaskins** (gal' ə gas' kənz): knee breeches.

6 **rubicund** (rü' bə kund): reddish; ruddy.
7 **George the Third:** King of England from 1760–1820.

and how sagely they would deliberate upon public events some months after they had taken place.

The opinions of this junto[8] were completely controlled by Nicholas Vedder, a patriarch of the village, and landlord of the inn, at the door of which he took his seat from morning till night, just moving sufficiently to avoid the sun and keep in the shade of a large tree; so that the neighbors could tell the hour by his movements as accurately as by a sundial. It is true he was rarely heard to speak, but smoked his pipe incessantly. His adherents, however (for every great man has his adherents), perfectly understood him, and knew how to gather his opinions. When anything that was read or related displeased him, he was observed to smoke his pipe vehemently, and to send forth short, frequent and angry puffs; but when pleased, he would inhale the smoke slowly and tranquilly, and emit it in light and placid clouds; and sometimes, taking the pipe from his mouth, and letting the fragrant vapor curl about his nose, would gravely nod his head in token of perfect approbation.

From even this stronghold the unlucky Rip was at length routed by his termagant wife, who would suddenly break in upon the tranquillity of the assemblage and call the members all to naught; nor was that august personage, Nicholas Vedder himself, sacred from the daring tongue of this terrible virago, who charged him outright with encouraging her husband in habits of idleness.

Poor Rip was at last reduced almost to despair; and his only alternative, to escape from the labor of the farm and clamor of his wife, was to take gun in hand and stroll away into the woods. Here he would sometimes seat himself at the foot of a tree, and share the contents of his wallet with Wolf, with whom he sympathized as a fellow sufferer in persecution. "Poor Wolf," he would say, "thy mistress leads thee a dog's life of it; but never

mind, my lad, whilst I live thou shalt never want a friend to stand by thee!" Wolf would wag his tail, look wistfully in his master's face, and if dogs can feel pity I verily believe he reciprocated the sentiment with all his heart.

In a long ramble of the kind on a fine autumnal day, Rip had unconsciously scrambled to one of the highest parts of the Kaatskill mountains. He was after his favorite sport of squirrel shooting, and the still solitudes had echoed and re-echoed with the reports of his gun. Panting and fatigued, he threw himself, late in the afternoon, on a green knoll, covered with mountain herbage, that crowned the brow of a precipice. From an opening between the trees he could overlook all the lower country for many a mile of rich woodland. He saw at a distance the lordly Hudson, far, far below him, moving on its silent but majestic course, with the reflection of a purple cloud, or the sail of a lagging bark, here and there sleeping on its glassy bosom, and at last losing itself in the blue highlands.

On the other side he looked down into a deep mountain glen, wild, lonely, and shagged, the bottom filled with fragments from the impending cliffs, and scarcely lighted by the reflected rays of the setting sun. For some time Rip lay musing on this scene; evening was gradually advancing; the mountains began to throw their long blue shadows over the valleys; he saw that it would be dark long before he could reach the village, and he heaved a heavy sigh when he thought of encountering the terrors of Dame Van Winkle.

As he was about to descend, he heard a voice from a distance, hallooing, "Rip Van Winkle! Rip Van Winkle!" He looked round, but could see nothing but a crow winging its solitary flight across the mountain. He thought his fancy must have deceived him, and turned again to descend, when he heard the same cry ring through the still evening air; "Rip Van Winkle! Rip Van Winkle!"—at the same time Wolf bristled up his back, and giving a low growl, skulked to his master's side, looking

---

8 junto (jun′ tō): clique; secret group.

fearfully down into the glen. Rip now felt a vague apprehension stealing over him; he looked anxiously in the same direction, and perceived a strange figure slowly toiling up the rocks, and bending under the weight of something he carried on his back. He was surprised to see any human being in this lonely and unfrequented place, but supposing it to be someone of the neighborhood in need of his assistance, he hastened down to yield it.

On nearer approach he was still more surprised at the singularity of the stranger's appearance. He was a short square-built old fellow, with thick bushy hair, and a grizzled beard. His dress was of the antique Dutch fashion—a cloth jerkin strapped round the waist—several pair of breeches, the outer one of ample volume, decorated with rows of buttons down the sides, and bunches at the knees. He bore on his shoulder a stout keg that seemed full of liquor and made signs for Rip to approach and assist him with the load. Though rather shy and distrustful of this new acquaintance, Rip complied with his usual alacrity; and mutually relieving one another, they clambered up a narrow gully, apparently the dry bed of a mountain torrent. As they ascended, Rip every now and then heard long rolling peals, like distant thunder, that seemed to issue out of a deep ravine, or rather cleft, between lofty rocks, toward which their rugged path conducted. He paused for an instant, but supposing it to be the muttering of one of those transient thundershowers which often take place in mountain heights, he proceeded. Passing through the ravine, they came to a hollow, like a small amphitheater, surrounded by perpendicular precipices, over the brinks of which impending trees shot their branches, so that you only caught glimpses of the azure sky and the bright evening cloud. During the whole time Rip and his companion had labored on in silence; for though the former marveled greatly what could be the object of carrying a keg of liquor up this wild mountain, yet there was something strange and incomprehensible about the unknown that inspired awe and checked familiarity.

On entering the amphitheater, new objects of wonder presented themselves. On a level spot in the center was a company of odd-looking personages playing at ninepins.[9] They were dressed in a quaint outlandish fashion; some wore short doublets, others jerkins, with long knives in their belts, and most of them had enormous breeches, of similar style with that of the guide's. Their visages, too, were peculiar: one had a large beard, broad face, and small piggish eyes: the face of another seemed to consist entirely of nose, and was surmounted by a white sugar-loaf hat, set off with a little red cock's tail. They all had beards, of various shapes and colors. There was one who seemed to be the commander. He was a stout old gentleman, with a weather-beaten countenance; he wore a laced doublet, broad belt and hanger,[10] high crowned hat and feather, red stockings, and high-heeled shoes, with roses[11] in them. The whole group reminded Rip of the figures in an old Flemish painting, in the parlor of Dominic Van Shaick, the village

---

9 **ninepins:** a bowling game with nine pins.
10 **hanger:** a short sword.
11 **roses:** ribbons in a rose-shaped arrangement.

parson, and which had been brought over from Holland at the time of the settlement.

What seemed particularly odd to Rip was, though these folks were evidently amusing themselves, yet they maintained the gravest faces, the most mysterious silence, and were, withal, the most melancholy party of pleasure he had ever witnessed. Nothing interrupted the stillness of the scene but the noise of the balls, which, whenever they were rolled, echoed along the mountains like rumbling peals of thunder.

As Rip and his companion approached them, they suddenly desisted from their play, and stared at him with such fixed statuelike gaze, and such strange, uncouth, lackluster countenances, that his heart turned within him, and his knees smote together. His companion now emptied the contents of the keg into large flagons, and made signs to him to wait upon the company. He obeyed with fear and trembling; they quaffed the liquor in profound silence, and then returned to their game.

By degrees Rip's awe and apprehension subsided. He even ventured, when no eye was fixed upon him, to taste the beverage, which he found had much of the flavor of excellent Hollands.[12] He was naturally a thirsty soul, and was soon tempted to repeat the draught. One taste provoked another; and he reiterated his visits to the flagon so often that at length his senses were overpowered, his eyes swam in his head, his head gradually declined, and he fell into a deep sleep.

---

12 **Hollands:** gin made in Holland.

On waking, he found himself on the green knoll whence he had first seen the old man of the glen. He rubbed his eyes—it was a bright sunny morning. The birds were hopping and twittering among the bushes, and the eagle was wheeling aloft, and breasting the pure mountain breeze. "Surely," thought Rip, "I have not slept here all night." He recalled the occurrences before he fell asleep. The strange man with a keg of liquor—the mountain ravine—the wild retreat among the rocks—the woebegone party at ninepins—the flagon—"Oh! that flagon! that wicked flagon!" thought Rip—"what excuse shall I make to Dame Van Winkle!"

He looked round for his gun, but in place of the clean well-oiled fowling piece, he found an old firelock lying by him, the barrel encrusted with rust, the lock falling off, and the stock worm-eaten. He now suspected that the grave roysters of the mountain had put a trick upon him, and, having dosed him with liquor, had robbed him of his gun. Wolf, too, had disappeared, but he might have strayed away after a squirrel or partridge. He whistled after him and shouted his name, but all in vain; the echoes repeated his whistle and shout, but no dog was to be seen.

He determined to revisit the scene of the last evening's gambol, and if he met with any of the party, to demand his dog and gun. As he rose to walk, he found himself stiff in the joints, and wanting in his usual activity. "These mountain beds do not agree with me," thought Rip, "and if this frolic should lay me up with a fit of the rheumatism, I shall have a blessed time with Dame Van Winkle." With

some difficulty he got down into the glen: he found the gully up which he and his companion had ascended the preceding evening; but to his astonishment a mountain stream was now foaming down it, leaping from rock to rock, and filling the glen with babbling murmurs. He, however, made shift to scramble up its sides, working his toilsome way through thickets of birch, sassafras, and witch hazel, and sometimes tripped up or entangled by the wild grapevines that twisted their coils or tendrils from tree to tree, and spread a kind of network in his path.

At length he reached to where the ravine had opened through the cliffs to the amphitheater; but no traces of such opening remained. The rocks presented a high, impenetrable wall over which the torrent came tumbling in a sheet of feathery foam, and fell into a broad deep basin, black from the shadows of the surrounding forest. Here, then, poor Rip was brought to a stand. He again called and whistled after his dog; he was only answered by the cawing of a flock of idle crows, sporting high in air about a dry tree that overhung a sunny precipice; and who, secure in their elevation, seemed to look down and scoff at the poor man's perplexities. What was to be done? The morning was passing away, and Rip felt famished for want of his breakfast. He grieved to give up his dog and gun; he dreaded to meet his wife; but it would not do to starve among the mountains. He shook his head, shouldered the rusty firelock, and, with a heart full of trouble and anxiety, turned his steps homeward.

As he approached the village he met a number of people, but none whom he knew, which somewhat surprised him, for he had thought himself acquainted with everyone in the country round. Their dress, too, was of a different fashion from that to which he was accustomed. They all stared at him with equal marks of surprise, and whenever they cast their eyes upon him, invariably stroked their chins. The constant recurrence of this gesture induced

Rip, involuntarily, to do the same, when, to his astonishment, he found his beard had grown a foot long!

He had now entered the skirts of the village. A troop of strange children ran at his heels, hooting after him, and pointing at his gray beard. The dogs, too, not one of which he recognized for an old acquaintance, barked at him as he passed. The very village was altered; it was larger and more populous. There were rows of houses which he had never seen before, and those which had been his familiar haunts had disappeared. Strange names were over the doors—strange faces at the windows—everything was strange. His mind now misgave him; he began to doubt whether both he and the world around him were not bewitched. Surely this was his native village, which he had left but the day before. There stood the Kaatskill mountains—there ran the silver Hudson at a distance—there was every hill and dale precisely as it had always been—Rip was sorely perplexed—"That flagon last night," thought he, "has addled my poor head sadly!"

It was with some difficulty that he found the way to his own house, which he approached with silent awe, expecting every moment to hear the shrill voice of Dame Van Winkle. He found the house gone to decay—the roof fallen in, the windows shattered, and the doors off the hinges. A half-starved dog that looked like Wolf was skulking about it. Rip called him by name, but the cur snarled, showed his teeth, and passed on. This was an unkind cut indeed—"My very dog," sighed poor Rip, "has forgotten me!"

He entered the house, which, to tell the truth, Dame Van Winkle had always kept in neat order. It was empty, forlorn, and apparently abandoned. This desolateness overcame all his connubial fears—he called loudly for his wife and children—the lonely chambers rang for a moment with his voice, and then all again was silence.

He now hurried forth, and hastened to his

old resort, the village inn—but it too was gone. A large rickety wooden building stood in its place, with great gaping windows, some of them broken and mended with old hats and petticoats, and over the door was painted, "The Union Hotel, by Jonathan Doolittle." Instead of the great tree that used to shelter the quiet little Dutch inn of yore, there now was reared a tall naked pole, with something on the top that looked like a red nightcap, and from it was fluttering a flag, on which was a singular assemblage of stars and stripes—all this was strange and incomprehensible. He recognized on the sign, however, the ruby face of King George, under which he had smoked so many a peaceful pipe; but even this was singularly metamorphosed. The red coat was changed for one of blue and buff, a sword was held in the hand instead of a scepter, the head was decorated with a cocked hat, and underneath was painted in large characters,

GENERAL WASHINGTON

There was, as usual, a crowd of folk about the door, but none that Rip recollected. The very character of the people seemed changed. There was a busy, bustling, disputatious tone about it, instead of the accustomed phlegm and drowsy tranquillity. He looked in vain for the sage Nicholas Vedder, with his broad face, double chin, and fair long pipe, uttering clouds of tobacco smoke instead of idle speeches; or Van Bummel, the schoolmaster, doling forth the contents of an ancient newspaper. In place of these, a lean, bilious-looking fellow, with his pockets full of handbills, was haranguing vehemently about rights of citizens—elections—members of congress—liberty—Bunker's Hill—heroes of seventy-six—and other words, which were a perfect Babylonish jargon to the bewildered Van Winkle.

The appearance of Rip, with his long grizzled beard, his rusty fowling piece, his uncouth dress, and an army of women and children at his heels, soon attracted the attention of the tavern politicians. They crowded round him, eyeing him from head to foot with great curiosity. The orator bustled up to him, and, drawing him partly aside, inquired "on which side he voted?" Rip stared in vacant stupidity. Another short but busy little fellow pulled him by the arm, and, rising on tiptoe, inquired in his ear, "Whether he was Federal or Democrat?" Rip was equally at a loss to comprehend the question; when a knowing, self-important old gentleman, in a sharp cocked hat, made his way through the crowd, putting them to the right and left with his elbows as he passed, and planting himself before Van Winkle, with one arm akimbo, the other resting on his cane, his keen eyes and sharp hat penetrating, as it were, into his very soul, demanded in an austere tone, "what brought him to the election with a gun on his shoulder, and a mob at his heels, and whether he meant to breed a riot in the village?"—"Alas! gentlemen," cried Rip, somewhat dismayed, "I am a poor, quiet man, a native of the place, and a loyal subject of the king, God bless him!"

Here a general shout burst from the bystanders—"A tory! a tory! a spy! a refugee! hustle him! away with him!" It was with great difficulty that the self-important man in the cocked hat restored order; and, having assumed a tenfold austerity of brow, demanded again of the unknown culprit, what he came there for, and whom he was seeking? The poor man humbly assured him that he meant no harm, but merely came there in search of some of his neighbors, who used to keep about the tavern.

"Well—who are they?—name them."

Rip bethought himself a moment, and inquired, "Where's Nicholas Vedder?"

There was a silence for a little while, when an old man replied, in a thin piping voice, "Nicholas Vedder! why, he is dead and gone these eighteen years! There was a wooden tombstone in the churchyard that used to tell all about him, but that's rotten and gone too."

"Where's Brom Dutcher?"

"Oh, he went off to the army in the beginning of the war; some say he was killed at the storming of Stony Point—others say he was drowned in a squall at the foot of Antony's Nose.[13] I don't know—he never came back again."

"Where's Van Brummel, the schoolmaster?"

"He went off to the wars too, was a great militia general, and is now in congress."

Rip's heart died away at hearing of these sad changes in his home and friends, and finding himself thus alone in the world. Every answer puzzled him too, by treating of such enormous lapses of time, and of matters which he could not understand: war—congress—Stony Point; he had no courage to ask after any more friends, but cried out in despair, "Does nobody here know Rip Van Winkle?"

"Oh, Rip Van Winkle!" exclaimed two or three, "Oh, to be sure! that's Rip Van Winkle yonder, leaning against the tree."

Rip looked, and beheld a precise counterpart of himself, as he went up the mountain: apparently as lazy, and certainly as ragged. The poor fellow was now completely confounded. He doubted his own identity, and whether he was himself or another man. In the midst of his bewilderment, the man in the cocked hat demanded who he was, and what was his name?

"God knows," exclaimed he, at his wit's end; "I'm not myself—I'm somebody else—that's me yonder—no—that's somebody else got into my shoes—I was myself last night, but I fell asleep on the mountain, and they've changed my gun, and everything's changed, and I'm changed, and I can't tell what's my name, or who I am!"

The bystanders began now to look at each other, nod, wink significantly, and tap their fingers against their foreheads. There was a whisper, also, about securing the gun, and keeping the old fellow from doing mischief, at

the very suggestion of which the self-important man in the cocked hat retired with some precipitation. At this critical moment a fresh comely woman pressed through the throng to get a peep at the gray-bearded man. She had a chubby child in her arms, which, frightened at his looks, began to cry. "Hush, Rip," cried she, "hush, you little fool; the old man won't hurt you." The name of the child, the air of the mother, the tone of her voice, all awakened a train of recollection in his mind. "What is your name, my good woman?" asked he.

"Judith Gardenier."

"And your father's name?"

"Ah, poor man, Rip Van Winkle was his name, but it's twenty years since he went away from home with his gun, and never has been heard of since—his dog came home without him; but whether he shot himself, or was carried away by the Indians, nobody can tell. I was then but a little girl."

Rip had but one question more to ask; but he put it with a faltering voice:

"Where's your mother?"

"Oh, she too had died but a short time since; she broke a blood vessel in a fit of passion at a New England peddler."

There was a drop of comfort, at least, in this intelligence. The honest man could contain himself no longer. He caught his daughter and her child in his arms. "I am your father!" cried he—"Young Rip Van Winkle once—old Rip Van Winkle now!—Does nobody know poor Rip Van Winkle?"

All stood amazed, until an old woman, tottering out from among the crowd, put her hand to her brow, and peering under it in his face for a moment, exclaimed, "Sure enough! it is Rip Van Winkle—it is himself! Welcome home again, old neighbor—Why, where have you been these twenty long years?"

Rip's story was soon told, for the whole twenty years had been to him but as one night. The neighbors stared when they heard it; some were seen to wink at each other, and put their

---

13 **Stony Point . . . Antony's Nose:** battle sites in the Revolutionary War.

tongues in their cheeks: and the self-important man in the cocked hat, too, when the alarm was over, had returned to the field, screwed down the corners of his mouth, and shook his head—upon which there was a general shaking of the head throughout the assemblage.

It was determined, however, to take the opinion of old Peter Vanderdonk, who was seen slowly advancing up the road. He was a descendant of the historian of that name, who wrote one of the earliest accounts of the province. Peter was the most ancient inhabitant of the village, and well versed in all the wonderful events and traditions of the neighborhood. He recollected Rip at once, and corroborated his story in the most satisfactory manner. He assured the company that it was a fact, handed down from his ancestor the historian, that the Kaatskill mountains had always been haunted by strange beings. That it was affirmed that the great Hendrick Hudson, the first discoverer of the river and country, kept a kind of vigil there every twenty years, with his crew of the *Half Moon;* being permitted in this way to revisit the scenes of his enterprise, and keep a guardian eye upon the river, and the great city called by his name. That his father had once seen them in their old Dutch dresses playing at ninepins in a hollow of the mountain; and that he himself had heard, one summer afternoon, the sound of their balls like distant peals of thunder.

To make a long story short, the company broke up and returned to the more important concerns of the election. Rip's daughter took him home to live with her; she had a snug, well-furnished house, and a stout cheery farmer for a husband, whom Rip recollected for one of the urchins that used to climb upon his back. As to Rip's son and heir, who was the ditto of himself, seen leaning against the tree, he was employed to work on the farm; but evinced an hereditary disposition to attend to anything else but his business.

Rip now resumed his old walks and habits; he soon found many of his former cronies, though all rather the worse for the wear and tear of time; and preferred making friends among the rising generation, with whom he soon grew into great favor.

Having nothing to do at home, and being arrived at that happy age when a man can be idle with impunity, he took his place once more on the bench at the inn door, and was reverenced as one of the patriarchs of the village, and a chronicle of the old times "before the war." It was sometime before he could get into the regular track of gossip, or could be made to comprehend the strange events that had taken place during his torpor. How that there had been a revolutionary war—that the country had thrown off the yoke of old England—and that, instead of being a subject of His Majesty George the Third, he was now a free citizen of the United States. Rip, in fact, was no politician; the changes of states and empires made but little impression on him; but there was one species of despotism under which he had long groaned, and that was—petticoat government. Happily that was at an end; he had got his neck out of the yoke of matrimony, and could go in and out whenever he pleased, without dreading the tyranny of Dame Van Winkle. Whenever her name was mentioned, however, he shook his head, shrugged his shoulders, and cast up his eyes; which might pass either for an expression of resignation to his fate, or joy at his deliverance.

He used to tell his story to every stranger that arrived at Mr. Doolittle's hotel. He was observed, at first, to vary on some points every time he told it, which was, doubtless, owing to his having so recently awakened. It at last settled down precisely to the tale I have related, and not a man, woman, or child in the neighborhood, but knew it by heart. Some always pretended to doubt the reality of it, and insisted that Rip had been out of his head, and that this was one point on which he always remained flighty. The old Dutch inhabitants, however, almost universally gave it full credit. Even to this day they never hear a thunderstorm of a summer afternoon about the Kaatskill, but they say Hendrick Hudson and his crew are at their game of ninepins; and it is a common wish of all henpecked husbands in the neighborhood, when life hangs heavy on their hands, that they might have a quieting draught out of Rip Van Winkle's flagon.

Study Questions

1. What is the daily life like in Rip's village at the beginning of the story? How does this compare with Rip's personal life?

2. What is the attitude of the people in the village toward Rip?

3. At what point in the story does Rip's long sleep begin? How does the reader learn that Rip is about to sleep?

4. In the course of his dream Rip sees people and actions which seem unusual. Describe these people. What is Rip's reaction to them?

5. When Rip comes home after sleeping for twenty years, he finds many changes. What are these changes and what do they mean?

6. "Rip Van Winkle" is one of the most popular short stories ever written by an American. Why do you think it has retained popularity for so long?

Vocabulary

Buried somewhere in the average dictionary entry is a skeletal outline of the history of the word being defined. The name for this brief historic outline is **etymology**. The etymology can be located by markers called brackets [ ]:

> pay (pā) v. to give money in exchange for goods or services; to discharge a debt or obligation [<ME *payen* <OF *paier* <Med L *pacare*, "to satisfy," <L *pacare*, "to pacify," < *pax*, "peace"]

To dig the meaning out of an etymology, a person must be able to decipher the symbols and abbreviations often used to keep the outline brief. The symbol < stands for the word *from*. Each *italicized* word gives a spelling of the word as it was used in an earlier language. Terms in quotation marks represent meanings other than the one now used in English. Abbreviations in the etymology of *pay* are these: ME = Middle English (used from the mid-12th century to the 15th); OF = Old French; Med L = Medieval Latin; L = Ancient or Classical Latin (dating from the time of the Roman Empire).

If all the information contained in the etymology of *pay* were written out instead of summarized and abbreviated, it would read this way:

[The modern English word *pay* comes from the Middle English word *payen*. This word was adapted from the Old French word *paier,* which had previously been borrowed from the Medieval Latin word *pacare,* meaning "to satisfy." *Pacare,* in turn, had been adopted from Ancient Latin, in which it meant "to pacify, or to make peace with." This word was one form of the Latin term *pax,* which meant "peace." (Thus the etymology of *pay* originally suggested a way of keeping peace with people to whom one owes money.)]

The etymology of pay is fairly typical of those for many modern English words that have some relationship to money. But there are many exceptions, including gold:

> gold (gōld) *n.* a soft, yellow chemical element whose beauty and rarity combine to make it highly valuable; the most malleable and ductile of metals; a symbol for money or riches [<ME *gold*<OE *gold*]

Like *pay,* this word comes from Middle English. But prior to the 12th century, it had been an Old English word, not one borrowed from other European languages. The word has not undergone any spelling changes or alterations in meaning.

A. Find the etymology for each of these words:

fortune   land   property   treasure   wealth

Patterning your answers after the model shown for pay, write interpretations of these etymologies on a separate sheet of paper.

B. Some etymologies hold surprises in store. Without knowing the etymology of *pay,* hardly anyone would associate that word with peace. The etymologies of the following words have similarly strange historical connections in meaning:

extort   miser   money   mortgage   sum

Find out whether the etymologies given by your dictionary reveal these words' unexpected origins. If so, describe each of these unusual etymological associations. But first give the definition for each word.

William Cullen Bryant   1794-1878

William Cullen Bryant was the first important poet in the newly independent United States of America. For nearly ten years he practiced law near his home in western Massachusetts. He was never completely happy in that profession, however, and continued to write poems and essays. In 1829, he was appointed editor of the New York *Evening Post.* He spent the rest of his life developing the *Post* into one of the country's leading national newspapers. As a powerful editor and an effective champion of liberal causes from abolition of slavery to trade unionism, Bryant was a respected public figure. His enduring fame, however, rests on his poetry.

"Thanatopsis" is not only Bryant's best known poem but also one of his earliest. He wrote a first draft in 1811 when he was not quite seventeen years old. When it was published six years later, he achieved immediate fame. The title comes from the Greek and means "contemplation of death."

SPRING BLOSSOMS *George Inness*

Thanatopsis

WILLIAM CULLEN BRYANT

To him who in the love of Nature holds
Communion with her visible forms, she speaks
A various language; for his gayer hours
She has a voice of gladness, and a smile
And eloquence of beauty, and she glides   5
Into his darker musings, with a mild
And healing sympathy, that steals away
Their sharpness, ere he is aware. When thoughts
Of the last bitter hour come like a blight
Over thy spirit, and sad images   10
Of the stern agony, and shroud, and pall,
And breathless darkness, and the narrow house,
Make thee to shudder, and grow sick at heart;—
Go forth, under the open sky, and list
To Nature's teachings, while from all around—   15
Earth and her waters, and the depths of air—
Comes a still voice—Yet a few days, and thee
The all-beholding sun shall see no more
In all his course; nor yet in the cold ground,
Where thy pale form was laid, with many tears,   20
Nor in the embrace of ocean, shall exist
Thy image. Earth, that nourished thee, shall claim
Thy growth, to be resolved to earth again,
And, lost each human trace, surrendering up
Thine individual being, shalt thou go   25
To mix forever with the elements,
To be a brother to the insensible rock
And to the sluggish clod, which the rude swain
Turns with his share, and treads upon. The oak
Shall send his roots abroad, and pierce thy mold.   30

Yet not to thine eternal resting place
Shalt thou retire alone, nor couldst thou wish
Couch more magnificent. Thou shalt lie down
With patriarchs of the infant world—with kings,
The powerful of the earth—the wise, the good,   35
Fair forms, and hoary seers of ages past,
All in one mighty sepulcher. The hills
Rock-ribbed and ancient as the sun,—the vales
Stretching in pensive quietness between;
The venerable woods—rivers that move   40
In majesty, and the complaining brooks
That make the meadows green; and, poured round all,
Old Ocean's gray and melancholy waste,—
Are but the solemn decorations all
Of the great tomb of man. The golden sun,   45
The planets, all the infinite host of heaven,
Are shining on the sad abodes of death,
Through the still lapse of ages. All that tread
The globe are but a handful to the tribes
That slumber in its bosom.—Take the wings   50
Of morning, pierce the Barcan[1] wilderness,
Or lose thyself in the continuous woods
Where rolls the Oregon,[2] and hears no sound,
Save his own dashings—yet the dead are there:
And millions in those solitudes, since first   55
The flight of years began, have laid them down
In their last sleep—the dead reign there alone.
So shalt thou rest, and what if thou withdraw
In silence from the living, and no friend
Take note of thy departure? All that breathe   60
Will share thy destiny. The gay will laugh
When thou art gone, the solemn brood of care
Plod on, and each one as before will chase
His favorite phantom; yet all these shall leave
Their mirth and their employments, and shall come   65
And make their bed with thee. As the long train
Of ages glide away, the sons of men,
The youth in life's green spring, and he who goes
In the full strength of years, matron and maid,
The speechless babe, and the gray-headed man—   70
Shall one by one be gathered to thy side,
By those, who in their turn shall follow them.

---

1 **Barcan**: Barca was an ancient desert country of North Africa; here the adjective describes a part of the United States.
2 **Oregon**: now the Columbia River in the northwest United States.

So live, that when thy summons comes to join
The innumerable caravan, which moves
To that mysterious realm, where each shall take   75
His chamber in the silent halls of death,
Thou go not, like the quarry slave at night,
Scourged to his dungeon, but, sustained and soothed
By an unfaltering trust, approach thy grave,
Like one who wraps the drapery of his couch   80
About him, and lies down to pleasant dreams.

Study Questions

1. In lines 1–8, what is Nature described as capable of doing? Under what circumstances?

2. Bryant uses several different images to describe death in lines 8–12. What are they? Why are they effective? ineffective?

3. What are "Nature's teachings" (line 15)?

4. In lines 31–72 Nature begins a second statement. What does Nature say about "the great tomb of man"?

5. In the first part of the poem Bryant calls death a "blight" which makes one "shudder, and grow sick at heart." In the final section (lines 73–81) Nature describes death as "pleasant dreams" and urges us to accept it with calm dignity. What details in the poem lead to this conclusion?

Vocabulary

The title "Thanatopsis" means "a view of death." This word originated when forms of two Ancient Greek words were put together: *thanato(s),* meaning "death," and *opsis,* meaning "a sight, a view, or an appearance of."

The name **combining form** is given to any basic word which can be put together with additional letters to create another term, as has been done here with *thanato(s)* and *opsis.*

Two other words in William Cullen Bryant's poem which contain combining forms are *patriarch* and *matron.* The former is derived from Greek and the latter from Latin. But the two words have closely related meanings: *patri* is a form of the word for "father"; *matri* is a form of the word for "mother."

With the help of a dictionary, explain how the definition of each word below relates in some way to the meaning "father" or "mother":

patriarch	patrimony	patriot	matriarchy	matrix
patrilineal	patronymic	matron	matricide	matrimony

Ralph Waldo Emerson   1803-1882

Ralph Waldo Emerson was the great
prophet of America. Other writers had, like
de Crèvecoeur, sensed from the beginning of
the Republic that the American was a new
person, and some had agreed with de
Tocqueville that the natural field of poetic
vision in a democracy is not the past but
the future. It was Emerson, however, who
stated these ideas most persuasively and elo-
quently. In the introduction to his essay
Nature (1836) he asked, "Why should we
grope among the dry bones of the past?" He
urged Americans to begin with observation
and appreciation of the natural world
around them and to build their own "original relation to the universe." In "The
American Scholar" (1837), Emerson called
for Americans to create a new kind of literature which would not be slavishly indebted
to European models. "The American
Scholar" was, as Oliver Wendell Holmes
said, our "intellectual Declaration of Independence."

Emerson subsequently became the central
figure of the group of Concord-Boston
writers known as Transcendentalists.
According to Transcendentalism, reality is
not the material world we see immediately
around us; it is spiritual. To apprehend this
spiritual reality we must *transcend* our material surroundings. It is one's duty, Emerson
believed, to resist the pressure of society and
to obey internal dictates. This philosophy of
responsible individualism is given its most
dynamic form in the essay "Self-Reliance."

MAX SCHMITT IN A SINGLE SCULL   *Thomas Eakins*
Thomas Eakins captures the spirit and themes of rugged
individualism and self-reliance in a series of famous
American paintings of his friends boating.

from Self-Reliance

RALPH WALDO EMERSON

THERE IS A TIME in every man's education when he arrives at the conviction that envy is ignorance; that imitation is suicide; that he must take himself for better for worse as his portion; that though the wide universe is full of good, no kernel of nourishing corn can come to him but through his toil bestowed on that plot of ground which is given to him to till. The power which resides in him is new in nature, and none but he knows what that is which he can do, nor does he know until he has tried. Not for nothing one face, one character, one fact, makes much impression on him, and another none. This sculpture in the memory is not without preestablished harmony. The eye was placed where one ray should fall, that it might testify of that particular ray. We but half express ourselves, and are ashamed of that divine idea which each of us represents. It may be safely trusted as proportionate and of good issues, so it be faithfully imparted, but God will not have his work made manifest by cowards. A man is relieved and gay when he has put his heart into his work and done his best; but what he has said or done otherwise shall give him no peace. It is a deliverance which does not deliver. In the attempt his genius deserts him; no muse befriends; no invention, no hope.

Trust thyself: every heart vibrates to that iron string. Accept the place the divine providence has found for you, the society of your contemporaries, the connection of events. Great men have always done so, and confided themselves childlike to the genius of their age, betraying their perception that the absolutely trustworthy was seated at their heart, working through their hands, predominating in all their being. And we are now men, and must accept in the highest mind the same transcendent destiny; and not minors and invalids in a protected corner, not cowards fleeing before a revolution, but guides, redeemers and benefactors, obeying the Almighty effort and advancing on Chaos and the Dark.

What pretty oracles nature yields us on this text in the face and behavior of children, babes, and even brutes! That divided and rebel mind, that distrust of a sentiment because our arithmetic has computed the strength and means opposed to our purpose, these have not. Their mind being whole, their eye is as yet unconquered, and when we look in their faces we are disconcerted. Infancy conforms to nobody; all conform to it; so that one babe commonly makes four or five out of the adults who prattle and play to it. So God has armed youth and puberty and manhood no less with its own piquancy and charm, and made it enviable and gracious and its claims not to be put by, if it will stand by itself. Do not think the youth has no force, because he cannot speak to you and me. Hark! in the next room his voice is sufficiently clear and emphatic. It seems he knows how to speak to his contemporaries. Bashful or bold then, he will know how to make us seniors very unnecessary.

The nonchalance of boys who are sure of a dinner, and would disdain as much as a lord to do or say aught to conciliate one, is the healthy attitude of human nature. A boy is in the parlor what the pit is in the playhouse; independent, irresponsible, looking out from his corner on such people and facts as pass by, he tries and sentences them on their merits, in the swift, summary way of boys, as good, bad, interesting, silly, eloquent, troublesome. He cumbers himself never about consequences, about interests; he gives an independent, genuine verdict. You must court him; he does not court you. But the man is as it were clapped into jail by his consciousness. As soon as he has once acted or spoken with *éclat*[1] he is a committed person, watched by the sympathy or the hatred of hundreds, whose affections must now enter into his account. There is no Lethe[2] for this. Ah, that he could pass again into his neutrality! Who can thus avoid all pledges and, having observed, observe again from the same unaffected, unbiased, unbribable, unaffrighted innocence, must always be formidable. He would utter opinions on all passing affairs, which being seen to be not private but necessary, would sink like darts into the ear of men and put them in fear.

These are the voices which we hear in solitude, but they grow faint and inaudible as we enter into the world. Society everywhere is in conspiracy against the manhood of every one of its members. Society is a joint-stock company, in which the members agree, for the better securing of his bread to each shareholder, to surrender the liberty and culture of the eater. The virtue in most request is conformity. Self-reliance is its aversion. It loves not realities and creators, but names and customs.

Whoso would be a man must be a nonconformist. He who would gather immortal palms[3] must not be hindered by the name of goodness, but must explore if it be goodness. Nothing is at last sacred but the integrity of your own mind. Absolve you to yourself, and you shall have the suffrage of the world. I remember an answer which when quite young I was prompted to make to a valued adviser who was wont to importune me with the dear old doctrines of the church. On my saying, "What have I to do with the sacredness of traditions, if I live wholly from within?" my friend suggested—"But these impulses may be from below, not from above." I replied, "They do not seem to me to be such; but if I am the Devil's child, I will live then from the Devil." No law can be sacred to me but that of my nature. Good and bad are but names very readily transferable to that or this; the only right is what is after my constitution; the only wrong what is against it. A man is to carry himself in the presence of all opposition as if everything were titular and ephemeral but he. I am ashamed to think how easily we capitulate to badges and names, to large societies and dead institutions. Every decent and well-spoken individual affects and sways me more than is right. I ought to go upright and vital, and speak the rude truth in all ways. If malice and vanity wear the coat of philanthropy, shall that pass? If an angry bigot assumes this bountiful cause of Abolition, and comes to me with his last news from Barbadoes,[4] why should I not say to him, "Go love thy infant; love thy wood chopper; be good-natured and modest; have that grace; and never varnish your hard, uncharitable ambition with this incredible tenderness for black folk a thousand miles off. Thy love afar is spite at home." Rough and graceless would be such greeting, but truth is handsomer than the affection of love. Your goodness must have some edge to it—else it is none. The doctrine of hatred must be preached, as the counteraction of the doctrine of love, when that pules and whines. I shun father and mother and wife and brother when my genius calls me. I would write on the lintels of the doorpost, *Whim.* I hope it is somewhat better than whim at last, but we cannot spend the day in explanation. Expect me not to show cause why I seek or why I

---

1 *éclat* (ā klá'): a French word meaning "burst of light"; in English, "brilliant public success."
2 **Lethe** (lē' thē): in Greek mythology, a river whose waters produced forgetfulness.
3 palms: rewards for success.

4 **Barbadoes** (bär bā' dōz): island in the West Indies where slavery was abolished in 1834.

STUDY FOR "THE PAIR-OARED SHELL" *Thomas Eakins*

exclude company. Then again, do not tell me, as a good man did today, of my obligation to put all poor men in good situations. Are they *my* poor? I tell thee, thou foolish philanthropist, that I grudge the dollar, the dime, the cent I give to such men as do not belong to me and to whom I do not belong. There is a class of persons to whom by all spiritual affinity I am bought and sold; for them I will go to prison if need be; but your miscellaneous popular charities; the education at college of fools; the building of meetinghouses to the vain end to which many now stand; alms to sots, and the thousandfold Relief Societies;—though I confess with shame I sometimes succumb and give the dollar, it is a wicked dollar, which by and by I shall have the manhood to withhold.

Virtues are, in the popular estimate, rather the exception than the rule. There is the man *and* his virtues. Men do what is called a good action, as some piece of courage or charity, much as they would pay a fine in expiation of daily nonappearance on parade. Their works are done as an apology or extenuation of their living in the world—as invalids and the insane pay a high board. Their virtues are penances. I do not wish to expiate, but to live. My life is for itself and not for a spectacle. I much prefer that it should be of a lower strain, so it be genuine and equal, than that it should be glittering and unsteady. I wish it to be sound and sweet, and not to need diet and bleeding. I ask primary evidence that you are a man, and refuse this appeal from the man to his actions. I know that for myself it makes no difference whether I do or forbear those actions which are reckoned excellent. I cannot consent to pay for a privilege where I have intrinsic right.

from *Self-Reliance* **227**

Few and mean as my gifts may be, I actually am, and do not need for my own assurance or the assurance of my fellows any secondary testimony.

What I must do is all that concerns me, not what the people think. This rule, equally arduous in actual and in intellectual life, may serve for the whole distinction between greatness and meanness. It is the harder because you will always find those who think they know what is your duty better than you know it. It is easy in the world to live after the world's opinion; it is easy in solitude to live after our own; but the great man is he who in the midst of the crowd keeps with perfect sweetness the independence of solitude.

The objection to conforming to usages that have become dead to you is that it scatters your force. It loses your time and blurs the impression of your character. If you maintain a dead church, contribute to a dead Bible society, vote with a great party either for the government or against it, spread your table like base housekeepers—under all these screens I have difficulty to detect the precise man you are; and of course so much force is withdrawn from your proper life. But do your work, and I shall know you. Do your work, and you shall reinforce yourself. A man must consider what a blindman's buff is this game of conformity. If I know your sect I anticipate your argument. I hear a preacher announce for his text and topic the expediency of one of the institutions of his church. Do I not know beforehand that not possibly can he say a new and spontaneous word? Do I not know that with all this ostentation of examining the grounds of the institution he will do no such thing? Do I not know that he is pledged to himself not to look but at one side, the permitted side, not as a man, but as a parish minister? He is a retained attorney, and these airs of the bench[5] are the emptiest affectation. Well, most men have bound their eyes with one or another handkerchief, and attached themselves to some one of these communities of opinion. This conformity makes them not false in a few particulars, authors of a few lies, but false in all particulars. Their every truth is not quite true. Their two is not the real two, their four not the real four; so that every word they say chagrins us and we know not where to begin to set them right. Meantime nature is not slow to equip us in the prison-uniform of the party to which we adhere. We come to wear one cut of face and figure, and acquire by degrees the gentlest asinine expression. There is a mortifying experience in particular, which does not fail to wreak itself also in the general history; I mean "the foolish face of praise,"[6] the forced smile which we put on in company where we do not feel at ease, in answer to conversation which does not interest us. The muscles, not spontaneously moved but moved by a low usurping willfulness, grow tight about the outline of the face, with the most disagreeable sensation.

For nonconformity the world whips you with its displeasure. And therefore a man must know how to estimate a sour face. The bystanders look askance on him in the public street or in the friend's parlor. If this aversion had its origin in contempt and resistance like his own he might well go home with a sad countenance; but the sour faces of the multitude, like their sweet faces, have no deep cause, but are put on and off as the wind blows and a newspaper directs. Yet is the discontent of the multitude more formidable than that of the senate and the college. It is easy enough for a firm man who knows the world to brook the rage of the cultivated classes. Their rage is decorous and prudent, for they are timid, as being very vulnerable themselves. But when to their feminine rage the indignation of the people is added, when the ignorant and the poor are aroused, when the unintelligent brute force

---

5 **bench:** seat on which a judge sits.

6 "the . . . praise": a quotation from Alexander Pope, an English poet (1688–1744).

that lies at the bottom of society is made to growl and mow, it needs the habit of magnanimity and religion to treat it godlike as a trifle of no concernment.

The other terror that scares us from self-trust is our consistency; a reverence for our past act or word because the eyes of others have no other data for computing our orbit than our past acts, and we are loth to disappoint them.

But why should you keep your head over your shoulder? Why drag about this corpse of your memory, lest you contradict somewhat you have stated in this or that public place? Suppose you should contradict yourself; what then? It seems to be a rule of wisdom never to rely on your memory alone, scarcely even in acts of pure memory, but to bring the past for judgment into the thousand-eyed present, and live ever in a new day. In your metaphysics you have denied personality to the Deity, yet when the devout motions of the soul come, yield to them heart and life, though they should clothe God with shape and color. Leave

your theory, as Joseph his coat in the hand of the harlot,[7] and flee.

A foolish consistency is the hobgoblin of little minds, adored by little statesmen and philosophers and divines. With consistency a great soul has simply nothing to do. He may as well concern himself with his shadow on the wall. Speak what you think now in hard words and tomorrow speak what tomorrow thinks in hard words again, though it contradict everything you said today.—"Ah, so you shall be sure to be misunderstood." Is it so bad then to be misunderstood? Pythagoras was misunderstood, and Socrates, and Jesus, and Luther, and Copernicus, and Galileo, and Newton,[8] and

7 **Joseph . . . harlot:** See the *Bible*, Genesis 39:12.
8 **Pythagoras . . . Newton:** Pythagoras (582?–500? B.C.), a Greek philosopher, mathematician, and astronomer. Socrates, a Greek philosopher of the 5th century B.C. Martin Luther (1483–1546), a German leader of the Protestant Reformation. Nicolaus Copernicus (1473–1543), a Polish astronomer who published his theory that planets revolve around the sun. Galileo (1564–1642), an Italian astronomer, mathematician, and physicist. Isaac Newton (1642–1727), an English mathematician ·and physicist.

JOHN BIGLEN IN A SINGLE SCULL *Thomas Eakins*

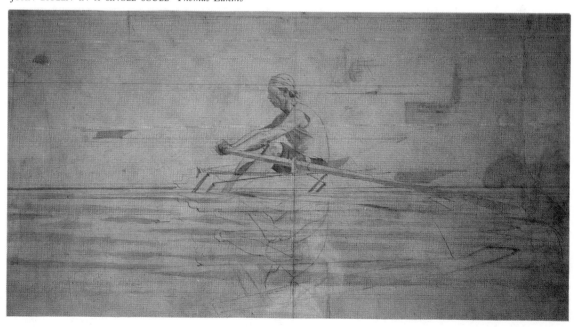

every pure and wise spirit that ever took flesh. To be great is to be misunderstood. . . .

The populace think that your rejection of popular standards is a rejection of all standard, and mere antinomianism;[9] and the bold sensualist will use the name of philosophy to gild his crimes. But the law of consciousness abides. There are two confessionals, in one or the other of which we must be shriven.[10] You may fulfill your round of duties by clearing yourself in the *direct,* or in the *reflex* way. Consider whether you have satisfied your relations to father, mother, cousin, neighbor, town, cat, and dog—whether any of these can upbraid you. But I may also neglect this reflex standard and absolve me to myself. I have my own stern claims and perfect circle. It denies the name of duty to many offices that are called duties. But if I can discharge its debts it enables me to dispense with the popular code. If any one imagines that this law is lax, let him keep its commandment one day.

And truly it demands something god-like in him who has cast off the common motives of humanity and has ventured to trust himself for a taskmaster. High be his heart, faithful his will, clear his sight, that he may in good earnest be doctrine, society, law, to himself, that a simple purpose may be to him as strong as iron necessity is to others! . . .

---

9 **antinomianism** (ant i nō′ me ə niz əm): a religious doctrine which says that moral laws are not binding for the Christian who has been saved by the grace of God.
10 **shriven:** confessed and forgiven.

Study Questions

1. What discovery of the self, according to Emerson, is crucial in the development of one's education?
2. Emerson says, "Infancy conforms to nobody . . . But the man is as it were clapped into jail by his consciousness." What characteristics of the child and the youth does Emerson admire? What happens to these characteristics to bring about the change which Emerson calls being "clapped into jail"?
3. "Trust thyself," says Emerson. What does he find are the two great social barriers to this self-trust?
4. In discussing conformity Emerson declares, "The doctrine of hatred must be preached, as the counteraction of the doctrine of love, when that pules and whines" (page 226). Read the whole paragraph carefully. What do you think Emerson means?
5. Some readers have interpreted Emerson's doctrine of self-reliance to mean that one should act entirely as one pleases, accepting no restraints whatever. In the final two paragraphs in this selection, where does Emerson say restraints should come from?

Emerson was a poet as well as an essayist. The "Concord Hymn" was written as a tribute to those who fought for American independence. The second poem, "Brahma," is a philosophical poem which grew out of Emerson's reading in the Hindu literature of India. In Hindu theology, Brahma is the supreme creative principle in the universe. The poem illustrates an aspect of the transcendentalist philosophy.

Concord Hymn

(Sung at the completion of the Battle Monument, July 4, 1837)

RALPH WALDO EMERSON

By the rude bridge that arched the flood,
   Their flag to April's breeze unfurled,
Here once the embattled farmers stood
   And fired the shot heard round the world.

The foe long since in silence slept;   5
   Alike the conqueror silent sleeps;
And Time the ruined bridge has swept
   Down the dark stream which seaward creeps.

On this green bank, by this soft stream,
   We set today a votive[1] stone;   10
That memory may their deed redeem,
   When, like our sires, our sons are gone.

Spirit, that made those heroes dare
   To die, and leave their children free,
Bid Time and Nature gently spare   15
   The shaft we raise to them and thee.

---

1 **votive** (vō′ tiv): done because of a vow.

Brahma

RALPH WALDO EMERSON

If the red slayer thinks he slays,
    Or if the slain think he is slain,
They know not well the subtle ways
    I keep, and pass, and turn again.

Far or forgot to me is near;   5
    Shadow and sunlight are the same;
The vanished gods to me appear;
    And one to me are shame and fame.

They reckon ill who leave me out;
    When me they fly, I am the wings;   10
I am the doubter and the doubt,
    And I the hymn the Brahmin[1] sings.

The strong gods pine for my abode,
    And pine in vain the sacred Seven;[2]
But thou, meek lover of the good!   15
    Find me, and turn thy back on heaven.

---

1 **Brahmin**: member of the priestly caste.
2 **sacred Seven**: in Hindu theology, the seven highest saints.

Study Questions

1. Each of the four stanzas in the "Concord Hymn" is a complete statement. What does each statement say?
2. Who is the speaker in the poem "Brahma"? Who is the audience?
3. The meaning of "Brahma" is contained in a series of paradoxes, or apparent contradictions. Identify them and explain the nature of the contradictions.

FLIGHT AND PURSUIT *William Rimmer* 1872

One of the most haunting and original imaginative paintings of the 19th century is Rimmer's *Flight and Pursuit.* Although it is not Brahman in purpose, it does indicate some basic paradoxes of living: "the panicked flight of an assassin/victim, man/conscience, good/evil down the endless corridors of the mind/time."

4. Why, from the point of view of "Brahma," are these paradoxes not really contradictions at all?

Composition

1. Emerson recorded his thoughts in a notebook. He built up his essays from accumulations of many short statements. As a result, the essays are full of quotable statements or aphorisms. From "Self Reliance" select one of these aphoristic sentences. Write an essay on that sentence explaining exactly what you think Emerson meant. In justifying your interpretation be sure to cite supporting evidence from the rest of the essay.

2. Write a description of some person you know, or know of, who is truly self-reliant in the Emersonian sense. Document your case with specific references to Emerson's essay.

Nathaniel Hawthorne   1804-1864

Nathaniel Hawthorne was as much concerned with the American past as Emerson was with the American future. He was born in Salem, home of the infamous Witchcraft Trials in 1692. In his preface to the *Scarlet Letter* (1850), Hawthorne reflected half humorously on his ties with two ancestors:

Doubtless, however, either of these stern and black-browed Puritans would have thought it quite a sufficient retribution for his sins, that, after so long a lapse of years, the old trunk of the family tree, with so much venerable moss upon it, should have borne, as its topmost bough, an idler like myself. No aim that I have ever cherished, would they recognize as laudable; no success of mine . . . would they deem otherwise than worthless, if not positively disgraceful. "What is he?" murmers one gray shadow of my forefathers to the other. "A writer of storybooks! What kind of a business in life,—what mode of glorifying God, or being serviceable to mankind in his day and generation,—may that be? Why the degenerate fellow might as well have been a fiddler!" Such are the compliments bandied between my great-grandsires and myself, across the gulf of time! And yet, let them scorn me as they will, strong traits of their nature have intertwined themselves with mine.

Most of Hawthorne's stories illustrate his lifelong fascination with the Puritan sense of sin, guilt, and moral responsibility. "Young Goodman Brown" is no exception. Here the story of a young man's terrifying night journey becomes an allegory of everyone's search for love and faith in a world seemingly full of wickedness and doubt.

NATHANIEL HAWTHORNE *Charles Osgood* 1840

Young Goodman Brown

NATHANIEL HAWTHORNE

YOUNG GOODMAN[1] BROWN came forth at sunset into the street at Salem village; but put his head back, after crossing the threshold, to exchange a parting kiss with his young wife. And Faith, as the wife was aptly named, thrust her own pretty head into the street, letting the wind play with the pink ribbons of her cap while she called to Goodman Brown.

"Dearest heart," whispered she, softly and rather sadly, when her lips were close to his ear, "prithee put off your journey until sunrise and sleep in your own bed tonight. A lone woman is troubled with such dreams and such thoughts that she's afeared of herself sometimes. Pray tarry with me this night dear husband, of all nights in the year."

"My love and my Faith," replied young Goodman Brown, "of all nights in the year, this one night must I tarry away from thee. My journey, as thou callest it, forth and back again, must needs be done 'twixt now and sunrise. What, my sweet, pretty wife, dost thou doubt me already, and we but three months married?"

"Then God bless you!" said Faith, with the pink ribbons; "and may you find all well when you come back."

"Amen!" cried Goodman Brown. "Say thy prayers, dear Faith, and go to bed at dusk, and no harm will come to thee."

So they parted; and the young man pursued his way until, being about to turn the corner by the meetinghouse, he looked back and saw the head of Faith still peeping after him with a melancholy air, in spite of her pink ribbons.

"Poor little Faith!" thought he, for his heart smote him. "What a wretch am I to leave her on such an errand! She talks of dreams, too. Methought as she spoke there was trouble in her face, as if a dream had warned her what work is to be done tonight. But no, no; 'twould kill her to think it. Well, she's a

---

1 **Goodman**: A term often used to designate a farmer or other man of property without rank.

blessed angel on earth; and after this one night I'll cling to her skirts and follow her to heaven."

With this excellent resolve for the future, Goodman Brown felt himself justified in making more haste on his present evil purpose. He had taken a dreary road, darkened by all the gloomiest trees of the forest, which barely stood aside to let the narrow path creep through, and closed immediately behind. It was all as lonely as could be; and there is this peculiarity in such a solitude, that the traveler knows not who may be concealed by the innumerable trunks and the thick boughs overhead; so that with lonely footsteps he may yet be passing through an unseen multitude.

"There may be a devilish Indian behind every tree," said Goodman Brown to himself; and he glanced fearfully behind him as he added, "What if the devil himself should be at my very elbow!"

His head being turned back, he passed a crook of the road, and, looking forward again, beheld the figure of a man, in grave and decent attire, seated at the foot of an old tree. He arose at Goodman Brown's approach and walked onward side by side with him.

"You are late, Goodman Brown," said he. "The clock of the Old South was striking as I came through Boston, and that is full fifteen minutes agone."

"Faith kept me back awhile," replied the young man, with a tremor in his voice, caused by the sudden appearance of his companion, though not wholly unexpected.

It was now deep dusk in the forest, and deepest in that part of it where these two were journeying. As nearly as could be discerned, the second traveler was about fifty years old, apparently in the same rank of life as Goodman Brown, and bearing a considerable resemblance to him, though perhaps more in expression than features. Still they might have been taken for father and son. And yet, though the elder person was as simply clad as the younger, and as simple in manner too, he had

an indescribable air of one who knew the world, and who would not have felt abashed at the governor's dinner table or in King William's court, were it possible that his affairs should call him thither. But the only thing about him that could be fixed upon as remarkable was his staff, which bore the likeness of a great black snake, so curiously wrought that it might almost be seen to twist and wriggle itself like a living serpent. This, of course, must have been an ocular deception,[2] assisted by the uncertain light.

"Come, Goodman Brown," cried his fellow traveler, "this is a dull pace for the beginning of a journey. Take my staff, if you are so soon weary."

"Friend," said the other, exchanging his slow pace for a full stop, "having kept covenant by meeting thee here, it is my purpose now to return whence I came. I have scruples touching the matter thou wot'st[3] of."

"Sayest thou so?" replied he of the serpent, smiling apart. "Let us walk on, nevertheless, reasoning as we go; and if I convince thee not thou shalt turn back. We are but a little way in the forest yet."

"Too far! too far!" exclaimed the goodman, unconsciously resuming his walk. "My father never went into the woods on such an errand, nor his father before him. We have been a race of honest men and good Christians since the days of the martyrs; and shall I be the first of the name of Brown that ever took this path and kept"—

"Such company, thou wouldst say," observed the elder person, interpreting his pause. "Well said, Goodman Brown! I have been as well acquainted with your family as with ever a one among the Puritans; and that's no trifle to say. I helped your grandfather, the constable, when he lashed the Quaker woman so smartly through the streets of Salem; and it was I that brought your father a pitch-pine

---

2 **ocular deception:** optical illusion.
3 **wot'st:** knows.

knot, kindled at my own hearth, to set fire to an Indian village, in King Philip's War.[4] They were my good friends, both; and many a pleasant walk have we had along this path, and returned merrily after midnight. I would fain be friends with you for their sake."

"If it be as thou sayest," replied Goodman Brown, "I marvel they never spoke of these matters; or, verily, I marvel not, seeing that the least rumor of the sort would have driven them from New England. We are a people of prayer, and good works to boot, and abide no such wickedness."

"Wickedness or not," said the traveler with the twisted staff, "I have a very general acquaintance here in New England. The deacons of many a church have drunk the communion wine with me; the selectmen of divers towns make me their chairman; and a majority of the Great and General Court[5] are firm supporters of my interest. The governor and I, too—But these are state secrets."

"Can this be so?" cried Goodman Brown, with a stare of amazement at his undisturbed companion. "Howbeit, I have nothing to do with the governor and council; they have their own ways, and are no rule for a simple husbandman like me. But, were I to go on with thee, how should I meet the eye of that good old man, our minister, at Salem village? Oh, his voice would make me tremble both Sabbath day and lecture day."

Thus far the elder traveler had listened with due gravity; but now burst into a fit of irrepressible mirth, shaking himself so violently that his snakelike staff actually seemed to wriggle in sympathy.

"Ha! ha! ha!" shouted he again and again; then composing himself, "Well, go on, Good-

man Brown, go on; but, prithee, don't kill me with laughing."

"Well, then, to end the matter at once," said Goodman Brown, considerably nettled, "there is my wife, Faith. It would break her dear little heart; and I'd rather break my own."

"Nay, if that be the case," answered the other, "e'en go thy ways, Goodman Brown. I would not for twenty old women like the one hobbling before us that Faith should come to any harm."

As he spoke he pointed his staff at a female figure on the path, in whom Goodman Brown recognized a very pious and exemplary dame, who had taught him his catechism in youth, and was still his moral and spiritual adviser, jointly with the minister and Deacon Gookin.

"A marvel, truly, that Goody[6] Cloyse should be so far in the wilderness at nightfall," said he. "But with your leave, friend, I shall take a cut through the woods until we have left this Christian woman behind. Being a stranger to you, she might ask whom I was consorting with and whither I was going."

"Be it so," said his fellow traveler. "Betake you the woods, and let me keep the path."

Accordingly the young man turned aside, but took care to watch his companion, who advanced softly along the road until he had come within a staff's length of the old dame. She, meanwhile, was making the best of her way, with singular speed for so aged a woman, and mumbling some indistinct words—a prayer, doubtless—as she went. The traveler put forth his staff and touched her withered neck with what seemed the serpent's tail.

"The devil!" screamed the pious old lady.

"Then Goody Cloyse knows her old friend?" observed the traveler, confronting her and leaning on his writhing stick.

"Ah, forsooth, and is it your worship indeed?" cried the good dame. "Yea, truly is it, and in the very image of my old gossip, Good-

---

4 **King Philip's War:** (1675–1676) war between the New England colonists and Indians. The Indian groups were united by the chief whom the English called King Philip.

5 **Great and General Court:** the legislature of Massachusetts in colonial times.

6 **Goody:** form of goodwife, a term of address for a woman of low rank.

man Brown, the grandfather of the silly fellow that now is. But—would your worship believe it?—my broomstick hath strangely disappeared, stolen, as I suspect, by that unhanged witch, Goody Cory, and that, too, when I was all anointed with the juice of smallage, and cinquefoil, and wolfsbane."[7]

"Mingled with fine wheat and the fat of a newborn babe," said the shape of old Goodman Brown.

"Ah, your worship knows the recipe," cried the old lady, cackling aloud. "So, as I was saying, being all ready for the meeting, and no horse to ride on, I made up my mind to foot it; for they tell me there is a nice young man to be taken into communion tonight. But now your good worship will lend me your arm, and we shall be there in a twinkling."

"That can hardly be," answered her friend. "I may not spare you my arm, Goody Cloyse; but here is my staff, if you will."

So saying, he threw it down at her feet, where, perhaps, it assumed life, being one of the rods which its owner had formerly lent to the Egyptian magi. Of this fact, however, Goodman Brown could not take cognizance. He had cast up his eyes in astonishment, and, looking down again, beheld neither Goody Cloyse nor the serpentine staff, but this fellow traveler alone, who waited for him as calmly as if nothing had happened.

"That old woman taught me my catechism," said the young man; and there was a world of meaning in this simple comment.

They continued to walk onward, while the elder traveler exhorted his companion to make good speed and persevere in the path, discoursing so aptly that his arguments seemed rather to spring up in the bosom of his auditor than to be suggested by himself. As they went, he plucked a branch of maple to serve for a walking stick, and began to strip it of the twigs and little boughs, which were wet with evening dew. The moment his fingers touched them

they became strangely withered and dried up as with a week's sunshine. Thus the pair proceeded, at a good free pace, until suddenly, in a gloomy hollow of the road, Goodman Brown sat himself down on the stump of a tree and refused to go any farther.

"Friend," said he, stubbornly, "my mind is made up. Not another step will I budge on this errand. What if a wretched old woman do choose to go to the devil when I thought she was going to heaven: is that any reason why I should quit my dear Faith and go after her?"

"You will think better of this by and by," said his acquaintance, composedly. "Sit here and rest yourself a while; and when you feel like moving again, there is my staff to help you along."

Without more words, he threw his companion the maple stick, and was as speedily out of sight as if he had vanished into the deepening gloom. The young man sat a few moments by the roadside, applauding himself greatly, and thinking with how clear a conscience he should meet the minister in his morning walk, nor shrink from the eye of good old Deacon Gookin. And what calm sleep would be his that very night, which was to have been spent so wickedly, but so purely and sweetly now, in the arms of Faith! Amidst these pleasant and praiseworthy meditations, Goodman Brown heard the tramp of horses along the road, and deemed it advisable to conceal himself within the verge of the forest, conscious of the guilty purpose that had brought him thither, though now so happily turned from it.

On came the hoof tramps and the voices of the riders, two grave old voices, conversing soberly as they drew near. These mingled sounds appeared to pass along the road, within a few yards of the young man's hiding place; but, owing doubtless to the depth of the gloom at that particular spot, neither the travelers nor their steeds were visible. Though their figures brushed the small boughs by the wayside, it could not be seen that they intercepted, even for a moment, the faint gleam from the strip of

---

7 smallage . . . wolfsbane: plants and herbs.

bright sky athwart which they must have passed. Goodman Brown alternately crouched and stood on tiptoe, pulling aside the branches and thrusting forth his head as far as he durst without discerning so much as a shadow. It vexed him the more, because he could have sworn, were such a thing possible, that he recognized the voices of the minister and Deacon Gookin, jogging along quietly, as they were wont to do, when bound to some ordination or ecclesiastical council. While yet within hearing, one of the riders stopped to pluck a switch.

"Of the two, reverend sir," said the voice like the deacon's, "I had rather miss an ordination dinner than tonight's meeting. They tell me that some of our community are to be here from Falmouth and beyond, and others from Connecticut and Rhode Island, besides several of the Indian powwows,[8] who, after their fashion, know almost as much deviltry as the best of us. Moreover, there is a goodly young woman to be taken into communion."

"Mighty well, Deacon Gookin!" replied the solemn old tones of the minister. "Spur up, or we shall be late. Nothing can be done, you know, until I get on the ground."

The hoofs clattered again; and the voices, talking so strangely in the empty air, passed on through the forest, where no church had ever been gathered or solitary Christian prayed. Whither, then, could these holy men be journeying so deep into the heathen wilderness? Young Goodman Brown caught hold of a tree for support, being ready to sink down on the ground, faint and overburdened with the heavy sickness of his heart. He looked up to the sky, doubting whether there really was a heaven above him. Yet there was the blue arch, and the stars brightening in it.

"With heaven above and Faith below, I will yet stand firm against the devil!" cried Goodman Brown.

While he still gazed upward into the deep

arch of the firmament and had lifted his hands to pray, a cloud, though no wind was stirring, hurried across the zenith and hid the brightening stars. The blue sky was still visible, except directly overhead, where this black mass of cloud was sweeping swiftly northward. Aloft in the air, as if from the depths of the cloud, came a confused and doubtful sound of voices. Once the listener fancied that he could distinguish the accents of townspeople of his own, men and women, both pious and ungodly, many of whom he had met at the communion table, and had seen others rioting at the tavern. The next moment, so indistinct were the sounds, he doubted whether he had heard aught but the murmur of the old forest, whispering without a wind. Then came a stronger swell of those familiar tones, heard daily in the sunshine at Salem village, but never until now from a cloud of night. There was one voice, of a young woman, uttering lamentations, yet with an uncertain sorrow, and entreating for some favor, which, perhaps, it would grieve her to obtain; and all the unseen multitude, both saints and sinners, seemed to encourage her onward.

"Faith!" shouted Goodman Brown, in a voice of agony and desperation; and the echoes of the forest mocked him, crying, "Faith! Faith!" as if bewildered wretches were seeking her all through the wilderness.

The cry of grief, rage, and terror was yet piercing the night, when the unhappy husband held his breath for a response. There was a scream, drowned immediately in a louder murmur of voices, fading into far-off laughter, as the dark cloud swept away, leaving the clear and silent sky above Goodman Brown. But something fluttered lightly down through the air and caught on the branch of a tree. The young man seized it, and beheld a pink ribbon.

"My Faith is gone!" cried he, after one stupefied moment. "There is no good on earth; and sin is but a name. Come, devil; for to thee is this world given."

And, maddened with despair, so that he

8 **powwows**: medicine men.

laughed loud and long, did Goodman Brown grasp his staff and set forth again, at such a rate that he seemed to fly along the forest path rather than to walk or run. The road grew wilder and drearier and more faintly traced, and vanished at length, leaving him in the heart of the dark wilderness, still rushing onward with the instinct that guides mortal man to evil. The whole forest was peopled with frightful sounds—the creaking of the trees, the howling of wild beasts, and the yell of Indians; while sometimes the wind tolled like a distant church bell, and sometimes gave a broad roar around the traveler, as if all Nature were laughing him to scorn. But he was himself the chief horror of the scene, and shrank not from its other horrors.

"Ha! ha! ha!" roared Goodman Brown when the wind laughed at him. "Let us hear which will laugh loudest. Think not to frighten me with your deviltry. Come witch, come wizard, come Indian powwow, come devil himself, and here comes Goodman Brown. You may as well fear him as he fear you."

In truth all through the haunted forest there could be nothing more frightful than the figure of Goodman Brown. On he flew among the black pines, brandishing his staff with frenzied gestures, now giving vent to an inspiration of horrid blasphemy, and now shouting forth such laughter as set all the echoes of the forest laughing like demons around him. The fiend in his own shape is less hideous than when he rages in the breast of man. Thus sped the demoniac on his course, until, quivering among the trees, he saw a red light before him, as when the felled trunks and branches of a clearing have been set on fire, and throw up their lurid blaze against the sky, at the hour of midnight. He paused, in a lull of the tempest that had driven him onward, and heard the swell of what seemed a hymn, rolling solemnly from a distance with the weight of many voices. He knew the tune; it was a familiar one in the choir of the village meeting-house. The verse died heavily away, and was lengthened by a chorus, not of human voices, but of all the sounds of the benighted wilderness pealing in awful harmony together. Goodman Brown cried out, and his cry was lost to his own ear by its unison with the cry of the desert.

In the interval of silence he stole forward until the light glared full upon his eyes. At one extremity of an open space, hemmed in by the dark wall of the forest, arose a rock, bearing some rude, natural resemblance either to an altar or a pulpit, and surrounded by four blazing pines, their tops aflame, their stems untouched, like candles at an evening meeting. The mass of foliage that had overgrown the summit of the rock was all on fire, blazing high into the night and fitfully illuminating the whole field. Each pendant twig and leafy festoon was in a blaze. As the red light arose and fell, a numerous congregation alternately shone forth, then disappeared in shadow, and again grew, as it were, out of the darkness, peopling the heart of the solitary woods at once.

"A grave and dark-clad company," quoth Goodman Brown.

In truth they were such. Among them, quivering to and fro between gloom and splendor, appeared faces that would be seen next day at the council board of the province, and others which, Sabbath after Sabbath, looked devoutly heavenward, and benignantly over the crowded pews, from the holiest pulpits in the land. Some affirm that the lady of the governor was there. At least there were high dames well known to her, and wives of honored husbands, and widows, a great multitude, and ancient maidens, all of excellent repute, and fair young girls, who trembled lest their mothers should espy them. Either the sudden gleams of light flashing over the obscure field bedazzled Goodman Brown, or he recognized a score of the church members of Salem village famous for their especial sanctity. Good old Deacon Gookin had arrived, and waited at the skirts of that venerable saint, his revered pastor. But, irreverently consorting with these grave, reputable, and pious people, these elders of the church, these chaste dames and dewy virgins, there were men of dissolute lives and women of spotted fame, wretches given over to all mean and filthy vice, and suspected even of horrid crimes. It was strange to see that the good shrank not from the wicked, nor were the sinners abashed by the saints. Scattered also among their pale-faced enemies were the Indian priests, or powwows, who had often scared their native forest with more hideous incantations than any known to English witchcraft.

"But where is Faith?" thought Goodman Brown; and, as hope came into his heart, he trembled.

Another verse of the hymn arose, a slow and mournful strain, such as the pious love, but joined to words which expressed all that our nature can conceive of sin, and darkly hinted at far more. Unfathomable to mere mortals is the lore of fiends. Verse after verse was sung; and still the chorus of the desert swelled between like the deepest tone of a mighty organ; and with the final peal of that dreadful anthem there came a sound, as if the roaring wind, the rushing streams, the howling beasts, and every other voice of the unconcerted wilderness were mingling and according with the voice of guilty man in homage to the prince of all. The four blazing pines threw up a loftier flame, and obscurely discovered shapes and visages of horror on the smoke wreaths above the impious assembly. At the same moment the fire on the rock shot redly forth and formed a glowing arch above its base, where now appeared a figure. With reverence be it spoken, the figure bore no slight similitude, both in garb and manner, to some grave divine of the New England churches.

"Bring forth the converts!" cried a voice that echoed through the field and rolled into the forest.

At the word, Goodman Brown stepped forth from the shadow of the trees and approached the congregation, with whom he felt a loathful brotherhood by the sympathy of all that was wicked in his heart. He could have well-nigh sworn that the shape of his own dead father beckoned him to advance, looking downward from a smoke wreath, while a woman, with dim features of despair, threw out her hand to warn him back. Was it his mother? But he had no power to retreat one step, nor to resist, even in thought, when the minister and good old Deacon Gookin seized his arms and led him to the blazing rock. Thither came also the slender form of a veiled female, led between Goody Cloyse, that pious teacher of the catechism, and Martha Carrier, who had received the devil's promise to be queen of hell. A rampant hag was she. And there stood the proselytes[9] beneath the canopy of fire.

"Welcome, my children," said the dark figure, "to the communion of your race. Ye have found thus young your nature and your destiny. My children, look behind you!"

They turned; and flashing forth, as it were, in a sheet of flame, the fiend worshipers were seen; the smile of welcome gleamed darkly on every visage.

"There," resumed the sable form, "are all whom ye have reverenced from youth. Ye deemed them holier than yourselves, and shrank from your own sin, contrasting it with their lives of righteousness and prayerful aspirations heavenward. Yet here are they all in my worshiping assembly. This night it shall be granted you to know their secret deeds: how hoary-bearded elders of the church have whispered wanton words to the young maids of their households; how many a woman, eager for widows' weeds, has given her husband a drink at bedtime and let him sleep his last sleep in her bosom; how beardless youths have made haste to inherit their fathers' wealth; and how fair damsels—blush not, sweet ones—have dug

---

9 **proselytes:** converts.

little graves in the garden, and bidden me, the sole guest, to an infant's funeral. By the sympathy of your human hearts for sin ye shall scent out all the places—whether in church, bedchamber, street, field, or forest—where crime has been committed, and shall exult to behold the whole earth one stain of guilt, one mighty blood spot. Far more than this. It shall be yours to penetrate, in every bosom, the deep mystery of sin, the fountain of all wicked arts, and which inexhaustibly supplies more evil impulses than human power—than my power at its utmost—can make manifest in deeds. And now, my children, look upon each other."

They did so; and, by the blaze of the hell-kindled torches, the wretched man beheld his Faith, and the wife her husband, trembling before that unhallowed altar.

"Lo, there ye stand, my children," said the figure, in a deep and solemn tone, almost sad with its despairing awfulness, as if his once angelic nature could yet mourn for our miserable race. "Depending upon one another's hearts, ye had still hoped that virtue were not all a dream. Now are ye undeceived. Evil is the nature of mankind. Evil must be your only happiness. Welcome again, my children, to the communion of your race."

"Welcome," repeated the fiend worshipers, in one cry of despair and triumph.

And there they stood, the only pair, as it seemed, who were yet hesitating on the verge of wickedness in this dark world. A basin was hollowed, naturally, in the rock. Did it contain water, reddened by the lurid light? or was it blood? or, perchance, a liquid flame? Herein did the shape of evil dip his hand and prepare to lay the mark of baptism upon their foreheads, that they might be partakers of the mystery of sin, more conscious of the secret guilt of others, both in deed and thought, than they could now be of their own. The husband cast one look at his pale wife, and Faith at him. What polluted wretches would the next glance show them to each other, shuddering alike at what they disclosed and what they saw!

"Faith! Faith!" cried the husband, "look up to heaven, and resist the wicked one."

Whether Faith obeyed he knew not. Hardly had he spoken when he found himself amid calm night and solitude, listening to a roar of the wind which died heavily away through the forest. He staggered against the rock, and felt it chill and damp; while a hanging twig, that had been on fire, besprinkled his cheek with the coldest dew.

The next morning young Goodman Brown came slowly into the street of Salem village, staring around him like a bewildered man. The good old minister was taking a walk along the graveyard to get an appetite for breakfast and meditate his sermon, and bestowed a blessing, as he passed, on Goodman Brown. He shrank from the venerable saint as if to avoid an anathema.[10] Old Deacon Gookin was at domestic worship, and the holy words of his prayer were heard through the open window. "What God doth the wizard pray to?" quoth Goodman Brown. Goody Cloyse, that excellent old Christian, stood in the early sunshine at her own lattice, catechizing a little girl who had brought her a pint of morning's milk. Goodman Brown snatched away the child as from the grasp of the fiend himself. Turning the corner by the meetinghouse, he spied the head of Faith, with the pink ribbons, gazing anxiously forth, and bursting into such joy at sight of him that she skipped along the street and almost kissed her husband before the whole village. But Goodman Brown looked sternly and sadly into her face, and passed on without a greeting.

Had Goodman Brown fallen asleep in the forest and only dreamed a wild dream of a witch-meeting?

Be it so if you will; but, alas! it was a dream of evil omen for young Goodman Brown. A stern, a sad, a darkly meditative, a distrustful, if not a desperate man did he become from the

---

10 **anathema:** a cursed or damned person.

night of that fearful dream. On the Sabbath day, when the congregation were singing a holy psalm, he could not listen because an anthem of sin rushed loudly upon his ear and drowned all the blessed strain. When the minister spoke from the pulpit with power and fervid eloquence, and, with his hand on the open Bible, of the sacred truths of our religion, and of saintlike lives and triumphant deaths, and of future bliss or misery unutterable, then did Goodman Brown turn pale, dreading lest the roof should thunder down upon the gray blasphemer and his hearers. Often, awaking suddenly at midnight, he shrank from the bosom of Faith; and at morning or eventide, when the family knelt down at prayer, he scowled and muttered to himself, and gazed sternly at his wife, and turned away. And when he had lived long, and was borne to his grave a hoary corpse, followed by Faith, an aged woman, and children and grandchildren, a goodly procession, besides neighbors not a few, they carved no hopeful verse upon his tombstone, for his dying hour was gloom.

Detail from MOONLIT COVE *A.P. Ryder*

Study Questions

1. As the story opens, Young Goodman Brown is leaving home for an overnight journey. How is the purpose of the journey foreshadowed?
2. How do you know who the man is Goodman Brown meets in the forest?
3. After joining his traveling companion, Goodman Brown begins to show hesitation and finally resolves not to continue. What causes him to change his mind and go on?
4. Who are the people Goodman Brown finds at the forest meeting? How does the devil explain this?
5. How does the meeting end?
6. "Young Goodman Brown" is an allegory, that is, a story in which specific settings and characters represent general or universal meanings. What is the universal meaning of this story? Find evidence in the story to support your answer.

Vocabulary

Almost everytime we master one previously unfamiliar English word, our general knowledge of the language automatically makes it possible for us to use additional forms of that same word. Take, for example, the term *goodman* in the title of Nathaniel Hawthorne's story: "a male head of household; a courteous title of address for a male." Learning that definition automatically enables us to couple it with our already-existing knowledge of other forms in which the second syllable can appear—*men, man's, men's*—and to use different forms of *goodman* in various sentences.

The process by which a word can be altered so that it will be grammatically suitable in a number of different speech and writing situations is called **inflection**. Different inflectional systems are used with different parts of speech. Here are a few examples of the most frequently used inflectional systems in our language:

Nouns: Add *s* to form a plural (*devil* + *s* = *devils*), or *'s* to form the singular possessive (*devil's*), or *s'* to form the plural possessive (*devils'*).

Verbs: Add *ed* to form the past tense (*gather* + *ed* = *gathered*).

Adjectives: Add *er* to make the comparative form (*dark* + *er* = *darker*), or *est* to make the superlative form (*darkest*).

Adverbs: Add *er* to make the comparative form (*early* + *er* = *earlier*), or *est* to make the superlative form (*earliest*).

Ranking high among the English words which undergo the most complete changes when they are inflected are pronouns such as *I, he, they,* and *her.*

In the following exercise you will inflect a number of ordinary English words in order to make each one suitable for use in its sentence context. The exercise consists of a partial summary of the story of "Young Goodman Brown" printed with a number of *italicized* words enclosed in parentheses. For example:

> At sunset, Young Goodman Brown parted from (1. *he*) wife, Faith. He went into the forest to meet an older man who had (2. *invite*) him there to attend a strange, evil religious service.

The words *he* and *invite* are both incorrect, not in terms of meaning, but in terms of inflection for the contexts in which they appear. For the exercise below write both the number and the correctly inflected form of each such *italicized* word. For example:

1. his
2. invited

Brown immediately began to regret coming to the forest. He (1. *want*) to turn back. But before he could leave, (2. *him*) experienced one of the (3. *great*) surprises that he had ever had: His childhood catechism teacher, Goody Cloyse, (4. *appear*). She recognized the (5. *old*) of the two men in the forest as the devil and greeted him warmly as her master. Then down the path (6. *come*) Brown's minister and Deacon Gookin, both supposedly fine, virtuous (7. *man*). Brown could scarcely believe (8. *he*) eyes when these three pious hypocrites set out to worship the devil.

Nevertheless, Brown (9. *remain*) firm in his decision to go no farther. But (10. *he*) decision changed quickly when he discovered that Faith, the (11. *dear*) person in the world to him, would be among the people (12. *attend*) the meeting.

Brown then went forward and joined the congregation of (13. *devil-worshiper*). Among them he (14. *see*) many of the leading citizens of his community, all the (15. *good*) and most pious people he had ever (16. *know*). Every one of (17. *they*) took part in the singing of several (18. *hymn*) to the devil.

Henry Wadsworth Longfellow   1807-1882

Henry Wadsworth Longfellow was a popular American poet, here and in Europe. He remains the only American to be honored with a commemorative bust in the Poet's Corner of Westminster Abbey in London. A vast general public still acclaims such poems as "Paul Revere's Ride," "The Village Blacksmith," *Evangeline, The Song of Hiawatha,* and *The Courtship of Miles Standish.*

Longfellow was born in Portland, Maine and published his first poem there in the local paper at age thirteen. At age eighteen he was offered one of the first American professorships in modern languages at Bowdoin College. In 1836 he became professor of French and Spanish at Harvard.

My Lost Youth

HENRY WADSWORTH LONGFELLOW

Often I think of the beautiful town
  That is seated by the sea;
Often in thought go up and down
The pleasant streets of that dear old town,
  And my youth comes back to me.   5
    And a verse of a Lapland song
    Is haunting my memory still:
    "A boy's will is the wind's will,
And the thoughts of youth are long, long thoughts."

I can see the shadowy lines of its trees,   10
  And catch, in sudden gleams,
The sheen of the far-surrounding seas,
And islands that were the Hesperides[1]
  Of all my boyish dreams.
    And the burden of that old song,   15
    It murmurs and whispers still:
    "A boy's will is the wind's will,
And the thoughts of youth are long, long thoughts."

---

1 **Hesperides** (he sper' ə dēz'): in Greek mythology, a garden where golden apples grew, guarded by nymphs.

I remember the black wharves and the slips,
   And the sea tides tossing free;   20
And Spanish sailors with bearded lips,
And the beauty and mystery of the ships,
   And the magic of the sea.
     And the voice of that wayward song
     Is singing and saying still: 25
     "A boy's will is the wind's will,
And the thoughts of youth are long, long thoughts."

I remember the bulwarks by the shore,
   And the fort upon the hill;
The sunrise gun, with its hollow roar,   30
The drumbeat repeated o'er and o'er,
   And the bugle wild and shrill.
     And the music of that old song
     Throbs in my memory still:
     "A boy's will is the wind's will,   35
And the thoughts of youth are long, long thoughts."

I remember the sea fight far away,
    How it thundered o'er the tide!
And the dead captains, as they lay
In their graves, o'erlooking the tranquil bay   40
    Where they in battle died.
        And the sound of that mournful song
        Goes through me with a thrill:
        "A boy's will is the wind's will,
And the thoughts of youth are long, long thoughts."   45

I can see the breezy dome of groves,
    The shadows of Deering's Woods;
And the friendships old and the early loves
Come back with a Sabbath sound, as of doves
    In quiet neighborhoods.   50
        And the verse of that sweet old song,
        It flutters and murmurs still:
        "A boy's will is the wind's will,
And the thoughts of youth are long, long thoughts."

I remember the gleams and glooms that dart   55
    Across the schoolboy's brain;
The song and the silence in the heart,
That in part are prophecies, and in part
    Are longings wild and vain.
        And the voice of that fitful song   60
        Sings on, and is never still:
        "A boy's will is the wind's will,
And the thoughts of youth are long, long thoughts."

There are things of which I may not speak;
    There are dreams that cannot die;   65
There are thoughts that make the strong heart weak,
And bring a pallor into the cheek,
    And a mist before the eye.
        And the words of that fatal song
        Come over me like a chill: 70
        "A boy's will is the wind's will,
And the thoughts of youth are long, long thoughts."

Strange to me now are the forms I meet
    When I visit the dear old town;
But the native air is pure and sweet,   75
And the trees that o'ershadow each well-known street,
    As they balance up and down,
        Are singing the beautiful song,
        Are sighing and whispering still:
        "A boy's will is the wind's will,   80
And the thoughts of youth are long, long thoughts."

And Deering's Woods are fresh and fair,
    And with joy that is almost pain
My heart goes back to wander there,
And among the dreams of the days that were,   85
    I find my lost youth again.
        And the strange and beautiful song,
        The groves are repeating it still:
        "A boy's will is the wind's will,
And the thoughts of youth are long, long thoughts."   90

Study Questions

1. What details does the speaker give about the town? Find evidence that he is more concerned with the emotions aroused in his mind than what the town was like.

2. Why is the two-line refrain from the Lapland song suitable to the main idea Longfellow communicates? Explain the metaphor. How is a boy's "will" similar to the "wind's will"? What does "will" mean here?

3. The speaker has not actually seen the Hesperides (line 13), but why is the allusion a good one here?

4. The seventh line in each stanza contains a key word, usually a verb, which sums up the feeling established in the stanza. For example, in the first stanza, "haunting" sums up the feeling that was begun earlier with "often in thought" and "comes back to me." Or, in the second stanza, the verbs "murmurs and whispers" echo the fleeting, dream quality of "shadowy," "sudden gleams," and "boyish dreams." Find this technique in the other stanzas.

The Tide Rises, the Tide Falls

HENRY WADSWORTH LONGFELLOW

The tide rises, the tide falls,
The twilight darkens, the curlew calls;
Along the sea sands damp and brown
The traveler hastens toward the town,
    And the tide rises, the tide falls.   5

Darkness settles on roofs and walls,
But the sea, the sea in the darkness calls;
The little waves, with their soft, white hands,
Efface the footprints in the sands,
    And the tide rises, the tide falls.   10

The morning breaks; the steeds in their stalls
Stamp and neigh, as the hostler[1] calls;
The day returns, but nevermore
Returns the traveler to the shore,
    And the tide rises, the tide falls.   15

---

1 **hostler** (hos′ lər, os′ lər): person who takes care of horses
at an inn.

Study Questions

1. At what time of day do the events in the poem take place? What happened to the traveler between the first and third stanzas? Explain the "footprints."

2. What kind of sea is this one—cruel, kind, or indifferent? Why?

3. A slow melancholy tone is produced by prolonging the refrain line, forcing the reader to read the line solemnly. What other techniques are used to present the idea that the poem is making a comforting statement about the cycle of life and death?

4. Both "My Lost Youth" and "The Tide Rises, the Tide Falls" include references to the sea. What is the attitude towards the sea in each of the two poems?

Composition

1. Write a brief essay in which you compare the poems written by Longfellow and Bryant about death. Tell what similarities and differences the poems have in tone and rhythmical pattern. Support your statement with examples from the poem.

2. Write a narrative in which you describe a place or event from earlier in your life. Tell why you have fond memories of the place or event. Include enough details so that your reader understands how you feel about it.

Elizabeth Cady Stanton   1815-1902

At an early age in Johnstown, New York, Elizabeth Cady resolved to reform laws that placed women in a lower civil, social, and political status than men. In 1840 when she was married to Henry Stanton, a prominent abolitionist, they agreed not to include the word "obey" in the ceremony. She and Lucretia C. Mott organized the first women's rights convention in Seneca Falls, New York in 1848. The Declaration of Sentiments which she wrote for that convention was unanimously adopted by the group. For forty years after that Elizabeth Cady Stanton worked closely with Susan B. Anthony and other suffragists to bring about amendments to laws granting women's rights in salaries, joint guardianship of children, and property ownership. They also advocated the radical idea that women be allowed to vote. Stanton helped compile the first half of the six-volume *History of Woman Suffrage* (1881–1922). She also published her autobiography, *Eighty Years and More,* in 1898. The following statement, consciously modeled after the Declaration of Independence, points out omissions in that historic document.

Declaration of Sentiments

ELIZABETH CADY STANTON

WHEN, IN THE COURSE of human events, it becomes necessary for one portion of the family of man to assume among the people of the earth a position different from that which they have hitherto occupied, but one to which the laws of nature and of nature's God entitle them, a decent respect to the opinions of mankind requires that they should declare the causes that impel them to such a course.

We hold these truths to be self-evident: that all men and women are created equal; that they are endowed by their Creator with certain inalienable rights, that among these are life, liberty, and the pursuit of happiness; that to secure these rights governments are instituted, deriving their just powers from the consent of the governed. Whenever any form of government becomes destructive of these ends, it is the right of those who suffer from it to refuse allegiance to it, and to insist upon the institution of a new government, laying its foundation on such principles, and organizing its powers in such form as to them shall seem most likely to effect their safety and happiness. Prudence, indeed, will dictate that governments long established should not be changed for light and transient causes; and accordingly, all experience hath shown that mankind are more disposed to suffer, while evils are sufferable, than to right themselves by abolishing the forms to which they were accustomed. But when a long train of abuses and usurpations, pursuing invariably the same object evinces a

"MOTHER AND DAUGHTER" *William Shew* 1850

design to reduce them under absolute despotism, it is their duty to throw off such government, and to provide new guards for their future security. Such has been the patient sufferance of the women under this government, and such is now the necessity which constrains them to demand the equal station to which they are entitled.

The history of mankind is a history of repeated injuries and usurpations on the part of man toward woman, having in direct object the establishment of an absolute tyranny over her. To prove this, let facts be submitted to a candid world.

He has never permitted her to exercise her inalienable right to the elective franchise.

He has compelled her to submit to laws, in the formation of which she had no voice.

He has withheld from her the rights which are given to the most ignorant and degraded men—both natives and foreigners.

Having deprived her of this first right of a citizen, the elective franchise, thereby leaving her without representation in the halls of legislation, he has oppressed her on all sides.

He has made her, if married, in the eye of the law, civilly dead.

He has taken from her all right in property, even to the wages she earns.

He has made her, morally, an irresponsible being, as she can commit many crimes with impunity, provided they be done in the presence of her husband. In the covenant of marriage, she is compelled to promise obedience to her husband, he becoming, to all intents and purposes, her master—the law giving him power to deprive her of her liberty, and to administer chastisement.

He has so framed the laws of divorce, as to what shall be the proper causes of divorce; in case of separation, to whom the guardianship of the children shall be given; as to be wholly regardless of the happiness of woman—the law, in all cases, going upon a false supposition of the supremacy of man, and giving all power into his hands.

After depriving her of all rights as a married woman, if single and the owner of property, he has taxed her to support a government which recognizes her only when her property can be made profitable to it.

He has monopolized nearly all the profitable employments, and from those she is permitted to follow, she receives but a scanty remuneration.

He closes against her all the avenues to wealth and distinction, which he considers most honorable to himself. As a teacher of theology, medicine, or law, she is not known.

He has denied her the facilities for obtaining a thorough education—all colleges being closed against her.

He allows her in Church, as well as State, but a subordinate position, claiming Apostolic authority for her exclusion from the ministry, and, with some exceptions, from any public participation in the affairs of the Church.

He has created a false public sentiment, by giving to the world a different code of morals for men and women, by which moral delinquencies which exclude women from society, are not only tolerated but deemed of little account in man.

He has usurped the prerogative of Jehovah himself, claiming it as his right to assign for her a sphere of action, when that belongs to her conscience and to her God.

He has endeavored, in every way that he could, to destroy her confidence in her own powers, to lessen her self-respect, and to make her willing to lead a dependent and abject life.

Now, in view of this entire disfranchisement of one-half the people of this country, their social and religious degradation,—in view of the unjust laws above mentioned, and because women do feel themselves aggrieved, oppressed, and fraudulently deprived of their most sacred rights, we insist that they have immediate admission to all the rights and privileges which belong to them as citizens of the United States.

In entering upon the great work before us,

we anticipate no small amount of misconception, misrepresentation, and ridicule; but we shall use every instrumentality within our powers to effect our object. We shall employ agents, circulate tracts, petition the state and national legislatures, and endeavor to enlist the pulpit and the press in our behalf. We hope this Convention will be followed by a series of Conventions, embracing every part of the country.

Firmly relying upon the final triumph of the Right and the True, we do this day affix our signatures to this declaration.

Lucretia Mott
Harriet Cady Eaton
Margaret Pryor
Elizabeth Cady Stanton
Eunice Newton Foote
Mary Ann McClintock

Study Questions

1. In modeling this statement after the Declaration of Independence, why do you think the word "Independence" was changed to "Sentiments" in the title?
2. How do the first two paragraphs differ from the opening of the Declaration of Independence? (page 85).
3. The Declaration of Independence contains a long list of charges against the King of Great Britain, all beginning with the pronoun "He." In Stanton's long list of charges, to whom does "He" refer?
4. Why do you think Stanton's proposals met with such great opposition in 1848? Which of her proposals are still being opposed today?

Vocabulary

Antonyms are words that have exactly opposite or approximately opposite meanings. Each group of four words in this exercise contains two antonyms along with two other words. For example:

suffrage   guardianship   exception   disfranchisement

In this case, the antonyms are *suffrage* (the right to vote) and *disfranchisement* (denial of the rights of citizenship, particularly the right to vote). Therefore, even though the two words' meanings are not exactly opposite, they are the two words in the group closest to being antonyms. Consult a dictionary for the meanings of any unfamiliar words below. Then copy the two antonyms from each series.

1. despotic   candid   degraded   evasive
2. delinquency   chastisement   impunity   misconception
3. abject   equal   glorified   transient
4. abuse   affix   declare   remove
5. prerogative   impediment   right   instrumentality
6. grant   usurp   occupy   dictate
7. assurance   irresponsibility   prudence   endowment
8. derived   aggrieved   encouraged   deemed

Sojourner Truth   1795-1883

Sojourner Truth was born into slavery in Hurley, New York. When that state emancipated its slaves in 1827, she gained her freedom. At the age of forty-six, to mark a change in her career, she dropped her slave name, Isabella, and called herself Sojourner Truth. She stopped working as a domestic and started traveling throughout the country as a speaker and fund raiser for abolitionist and feminist causes. At the Women's Rights Convention in Akron, Ohio, in 1851, she made the following extemporaneous speech. She was responding to a number of male speakers who opposed granting freedom to women. Her powerful words were recorded by Frances Gage.

Sojourner Truth

Ain't I a Woman?

SOJOURNER TRUTH

WELL, CHILDREN, where there is so much racket there must be something out of kilter. I think that 'twixt the Negroes of the South and the women at the North, all talking about rights, the white men will be in a fix pretty soon. But what's all this here talking about?

That man over there says that women need to be helped into carriages, and lifted over ditches, and to have the best place everywhere. Nobody ever helps me into carriages, or over mud-puddles, or gives me any best place! And ain't I a woman? Look at me! Look at my arm! I have ploughed and planted, and gathered into barns, and no man could head me! And ain't I a woman? I could work as much and eat as much as a man—when I could get it—and bear the lash as well! And ain't I a woman? I have borne thirteen children, and seen them most all sold off to slavery, and when I cried out with my mother's grief, none but Jesus heard me! And ain't I a woman?

Then they talk about this thing in the head; what's this they call it? [Intellect, someone whispers.] That's it, honey. What's that got to do with women's rights or Negro's rights? If my cup won't hold but a pint, and yours holds a quart, wouldn't you be mean not to let me have my little half-measure full?

Then that little man in black there, he says women can't have as much rights as men, 'cause Christ wasn't a woman! Where did your Christ come from? Where did your Christ come from? From God and a woman! Man had nothing to do with Him.

If the first woman God ever made was strong enough to turn the world upside down all alone, these women together ought to be able to turn it back, and get it right side up again! And now they is asking to do it, the men better let them.

Obliged to you for hearing me, and now old Sojourner ain't got nothing more to say.

Study Questions

1. Sojourner Truth follows a pattern in replying to the previous speakers. First, she rephrases the point, then refutes it. In the second paragraph what is her answer to the man who has stated women are delicate and require special treatment?

2. What are the other arguments offered by various men in the audience? How does she refute them? To the man who argued that justification for male superiority was Christ's manhood, what does Sojourner Truth say?

3. What does she say about "Eve's sin"?

4. Why is the speech effective? ineffective?

Edgar Allan Poe   1809-1849

Edgar Allan Poe was a master of the suspenseful short story and originator of the detective story. He led a life which was almost as unusual as his writing. Poe was born in Boston but orphaned before the age of three. The John Allans, a wealthy Virginia tobacco family, took him in, and he took their name as his own middle name. Although Poe did well scholastically, his gambling debts and John Allan's meager financial support forced Poe to leave the University of Virginia after only one year. He returned to Boston and enlisted in the Army. During this time his first literary work, *Tamerlane and Other Poems,* was published. After a brief military career Poe focused directly on writing. His revised *Poems* appeared in 1831, but he soon turned to fiction and won recognition for his magazine stories and articles. He worked as an editor for a number of popular magazines and received a few prizes for his stories. Yet his personal life continued to be a struggle with poverty. He married Virginia Clemm in 1836 and supported both her and her mother until Virginia died. As his life became increasingly difficult, Poe sought to escape from it, often through alcohol. The circumstances of his death in Baltimore have never been clear.

Poe's stories and poems are often set in remote times and places, isolated from the usual concerns of society. His heroes frequently use an uncanny combination of reason and intuition to help them escape from strange, terrifying predicaments. "The Pit and the Pendulum" (1842) is told from the first person point of view by the man who experiences the terror of a ghastly imprisonment.

The Pit and the Pendulum

EDGAR ALLAN POE

I WAS SICK—sick unto death with that long agony; and when they at length unbound me, and I was permitted to sit, I felt that my senses were leaving me. The sentence—the dread sentence of death—was the last of distinct accentuation which reached my ears. After that, the sound of the inquisitorial voices seemed merged in one dreamy indeterminate hum. It conveyed to my soul the idea of *revolution*—perhaps from its association in fancy with the burr of a mill wheel. This only for a brief period; for presently I heard no more. Yet, for a while, I saw; but with how terrible an exaggeration! I saw the lips of the black-robed judges. They appeared to me white—whiter than the sheet upon which I trace these words—and thin even to grotesqueness; thin with the intensity of their expression of firmness—of immoveable resolution—of stern contempt of human torture. I saw that the decrees of what to me was Fate were still issuing from those lips. I saw them writhe with a deadly locution. I saw them fashion the syllables of my name; and I shuddered because no sound succeeded. I saw, too, for a few moments of delirious horror, the soft and nearly imperceptible waving of the sable draperies which enwrapped the walls of the apartment. And then my vision fell upon the seven tall candles upon the table. At first they wore the aspect of charity, and seemed white slender angels who would save me; but then, all at once, there came a most deadly nausea over my spirit, and I felt every fiber in my frame thrill as if I had touched the wire of a galvanic battery, while the angel forms became meaningless specters, with heads of flame, and I saw that from them there would be no help. And then there stole into my fancy, like a rich musical note, the thought of what sweet rest there must be in the grave. The thought came gently and stealthily, and it seemed long before it attained full appreciation; but just as my spirit came at length properly to feel and entertain it, the figures of the judges vanished, as if magically, from before me; the tall candles sank into nothingness; their flames went out utterly; the blackness of darkness supervened; all sensations appeared swallowed up in a mad rushing descent as of the soul into Hades. Then silence, and stillness, and night were the universe.

I had swooned; but still will not say that all of consciousness was lost. What of it there remained I will not attempt to define, or even to describe; yet all was not lost. In the deepest slumber—no! In delirium—no! In a swoon—no! In death—no! even in the grave all *is not* lost. Else there is no immortality for man. Arousing from the most profound of slumbers, we break the gossamer web of *some* dream. Yet in a second afterward (so frail may that web have been), we remember not that we have dreamed. In the return to life from the swoon there are two stages; first, that of the sense of mental or spiritual; secondly, that of the sense of physical, existence. It seems probable that if, upon reaching the second stage, we could recall the impressions of the first, we should find these impressions eloquent in memories of the gulf beyond. And that gulf is—what? How at least shall we distinguish its shadows from those of the tomb? But if the impressions of what I have termed the first stage, are not, at will, recalled, yet, after long interval, do they not come unbidden, while we marvel whence they come? He who has never swooned is not he who finds strange palaces and wildly familiar faces in coals that glow; is not he who beholds floating in mid-air the sad visions that the many may not view; is not he who ponders over the perfume of some novel flower—is not he whose brain grows bewildered with the meaning of some musical cadence which has never before arrested his attention.

Amid frequent and thoughtful endeavors to remember; amid earnest struggles to regather some token of the state of seeming nothingness into which my soul had lapsed, there have been moments when I have dreamed of success; there have been brief, very brief periods when I have conjured up remembrances which the lucid reason of a later epoch assures me could have had reference only to that condition of seeming unconsciousness. These shadows of memory tell, indistinctly, of tall figures that lifted and bore me in silence down— down—still down—till a hideous dizziness oppressed me at the mere idea of the interminableness of the descent. They tell also of a vague horror at my heart, on account of that heart's unnatural stillness. Then comes a sense of sudden motionlessness throughout all things; as if those who bore me (a ghastly train!) had outrun, in their descent, the limits of the limitless, and paused from the wearisomeness of their toil. After this I call to mind flatness and dampness; and then all is *madness*—the madness of a memory which busies itself among forbidden things.

Very suddenly there came back to my soul motion and sound—the tumultuous motion of the heart, and, in my ears, the sound of its beating. Then a pause in which all is blank. Then again sound, and motion, and touch—a tingling sensation pervading my frame. Then the mere consciousness of existence, without thought—a condition which lasted long. Then, very suddenly, *thought,* and shuddering terror, and earnest endeavor to comprehend my true state. Then a strong desire to lapse into insensibility. Then a rushing revival of soul and a successful effort to move. And now a full memory of the trial, of the judges, of the sable draperies, of the sentence, of the sickness, of the swoon. Then entire forgetfulness of all that followed; of all that a later day and much earnestness of endeavor have enabled me vaguely to recall.

So far, I had not opened my eyes. I felt that I lay upon my back, unbound. I reached out my hand, and it fell heavily upon something damp and hard. There I suffered it to remain for many minutes, while I strove to imagine where and *what* I could be. I longed, yet dared not to employ my vision. I dreaded the first glance at objects around me. It was not that I feared to look upon things horrible, but that I grew aghast lest there should be *nothing* to see. At length, with a wild desperation at heart, I quickly unclosed my eyes. My worst thoughts, then, were confirmed. The blackness of eternal night encompassed me. I struggled for breath. The intensity of the darkness seemed to oppress and stifle me. The atmosphere was intolerably close. I still lay quietly, and made effort to exercise my reason. I brought to mind the inquisitorial proceedings, and attempted from that point to deduce my real condition. The sentence had passed; and it appeared to me that a very long interval of time had since elapsed. Yet not for a moment did I suppose myself actually dead. Such a supposition, notwithstanding what we read in fiction, is altogether inconsistent with real existence;—but where and in what state was I? The condemned to death, I knew, perished usually at the autos-da-fé,[1] and one of these had been held on the very night of the day of my trial. Had I been remanded to my dungeon, to await the next sacrifice, which would not take place for many months? This I at once saw could not be. Victims had been in immediate demand.

---

1 **autos-da-fe** (ô′ tōz də fa′): ceremonies of the Inquisition at which judgment was pronounced on heretics; execution followed.

Moreover, my dungeon, as well as all the condemned cells at Toledo,[2] had stone floors, and light was not altogether excluded.

A fearful idea now suddenly drove the blood in torrents upon my heart, and for a brief period, I once more relapsed into insensibility. Upon recovering, I at once started to my feet, trembling convulsively in every fiber. I thrust my arms wildly above and around me in all directions. I felt nothing; yet dreaded to move a step, lest I should be impeded by the walls of a *tomb*. Perspiration burst from every pore, and stood in cold big beads upon my forehead. The agony of suspense grew at length intolerable, and I cautiously moved forward, with my arms extended, and my eyes straining from their sockets, in the hope of catching some faint ray of light. I proceeded for many paces; but still all was blackness and vacancy. I breathed more freely. It seemed evident that mine was not, at least, the most hideous of fates.

And now, as I still continued to step cautiously onward, there came thronging upon my recollection, a thousand vague rumors of the horrors of Toledo. Of the dungeons there had been strange things narrated—fables I had always deemed them—but yet strange, and too ghastly to repeat, save in a whisper. Was I left to perish of starvation in this subterranean world of darkness; or what fate, perhaps even more fearful, awaited me? That the result would be death, and a death of more than customary bitterness, I knew too well the character of my judges to doubt. The mode and the hour were all that occupied or distracted me.

My outstretched hands at length encountered some solid obstruction. It was a wall, seemingly of stone masonry—very smooth, slimy, and cold. I followed it up; stepping with all the careful distrust with which certain antique narratives had inspired me. This process, however, afforded me no means of ascertaining the dimensions of my dungeon; as I might

make its circuit, and return to the point whence I set out, without being aware of the fact; so perfectly uniform seemed the wall. I therefore sought the knife which had been in my pocket, when led into the inquisitorial chamber; but it was gone; my clothes had been exchanged for a wrapper of coarse serge. I had thought of forcing the blade in some minute crevice of the masonry, so as to identify my point of departure. The difficulty, nevertheless, was but trivial; although, in the disorder of my fancy, it seemed at first insuperable. I tore a part of the hem from the robe and placed the fragment at full length, and at right angles to the wall. In groping my way around the prison, I could not fail to encounter this rag upon completing the circuit. So, at least I thought: but I had not counted upon the extent of the dungeon, or upon my own weakness. The ground was moist and slippery. I staggered onward for some time, when I stumbled and fell. My excessive fatigue induced me to remain prostrate; and sleep soon overtook me as I lay.

Upon awaking, and stretching forth an arm, I found beside me a loaf and a pitcher with water. I was too much exhausted to reflect upon this circumstance, but ate and drank with avidity. Shortly afterward, I resumed my tour around the prison, and with much toil, came at last upon the fragment of the serge. Up to the period when I fell I had counted fifty-two paces, and upon resuming my walk, I had counted forty-eight more;—when I arrived at the rag. There were in all, then, a hundred paces; and, admitting two paces to the yard, I presumed the dungeon to be fifty yards in circuit. I had met, however, with many angles in the wall, and thus I could form no guess at the shape of the vault; for vault I could not help supposing it to be.

I had little object—certainly no hope—in these researches; but a vague curiosity prompted me to continue them. Quitting the wall, I resolved to cross the area of the enclosure. At first I proceeded with extreme cau-

---

2 **Toledo:** city in central Spain.

tion, for the floor, although seemingly of solid material, was treacherous with slime. At length, however, I took courage, and did not hesitate to step firmly; endeavoring to cross in as direct a line as possible. I had advanced some ten or twelve paces in this manner, when the remnant of the torn hem of my robe became entangled between my legs. I stepped on it, and fell violently on my face.

In the confusion attending my fall, I did not immediately apprehend a somewhat startling circumstance, which yet, in a few seconds afterward, and while I still lay prostrate, arrested my attention. It was this—my chin rested upon the floor of the prison, but my lips and the upper portion of my head, although seemingly at a less elevation than the chin, touched nothing. At the same time my forehead seemed bathed in a clammy vapor, and the peculiar smell of decayed fungus arose to my nostrils. I put forward my arm, and shuddered to find that I had fallen at the very brink of a circular pit, whose extent, of course, I had no means of ascertaining at the moment. Groping about the masonry just below the margin, I succeeded in dislodging a small fragment, and let it fall into the abyss. For many seconds I hearkened to its reverberations as it dashed against the sides of the chasm in its descent; at length there was a sullen plunge into water, succeeded by loud echoes. At the same moment there came a sound resembling the quick opening, and as rapid closing of a door overhead, while a faint gleam of light flashed suddenly through the gloom, and as suddenly faded away.

I saw clearly the doom which had been prepared for me, and congratulated myself upon the timely accident by which I had escaped. Another step before my fall, and the world had seen me no more. And the death just avoided, was of that very character which I had regarded as fabulous and frivolous in the tales respecting the Inquisition. To the victims of its tyranny, there was the choice of death with its direst physical agonies, or death with its most

hideous moral horrors. I had been reserved for the latter. By long suffering my nerves had been unstrung, until I trembled at the sound of my own voice, and had become in every respect a fitting subject for the species of torture which awaited me.

Shaking in every limb, I groped my way back to the wall; resolving there to perish rather than risk the terrors of the wells, of which my imagination now pictured many in various positions about the dungeon. In other conditions of mind I might have had courage to end my misery at once by a plunge into one of these abysses; but now I was the veriest of cowards. Neither could I forget what I had read of these pits—that the *sudden* extinction of life formed no part of their most horrible plan.

Agitation of spirit kept me awake for many long hours; but at length I again slumbered. Upon arousing, I found by my side, as before, a loaf and a pitcher of water. A burning thirst consumed me, and I emptied the vessel at a draught. It must have been drugged; for scarcely had I drunk, before I became irresistibly drowsy. A deep sleep fell upon me—a sleep like that of death. How long it lasted of course, I know not; but when, once again, I unclosed my eyes, the objects around me were visible. By a wild sulphurous luster, the origin of which I could not at first determine, I was enabled to see the extent and aspect of the prison.

In its size I had been greatly mistaken. The whole circuit of its walls did not exceed twenty-five yards. For some minutes this fact occasioned me a world of vain trouble; vain indeed! for what could be of less importance, under the terrible circumstances which environed me, than the mere dimensions of my dungeon? But my soul took a wild interest in trifles, and I busied myself in endeavors to account for the error I had committed in my measurement. The truth at length flashed upon me. In my first attempt at exploration I had counted fifty-two paces, up to the period when I fell; I must then have been within a pace or two of the fragment of serge; in fact, I had

nearly performed the circuit of the vault. I then slept, and upon awaking, I must have returned upon my steps—thus supposing the circuit nearly double what it actually was. My confusion of mind prevented me from observing that I began my tour with the wall to the left, and ended it with the wall to the right.

I had been deceived, too, in respect to the shape of the enclosure. In feeling my way I had found many angles, and thus deduced an idea of great irregularity; so potent is the effect of total darkness upon one arousing from lethargy or sleep! The angles were simply those of a few slight depressions, or niches, at odd intervals. The general shape of the prison was square. What I had taken for masonry seemed now to be iron, or some other metal, in huge plates, whose sutures or joints occasioned the depression. The entire surface of this metallic enclosure was rudely daubed in all the hideous and repulsive devices to which the charnel[3] superstition of the monks has given rise. The figures of fiends in aspects of menace, with skeleton forms, and other more really fearful images, overspread and disfigured the walls. I observed that the outlines of these monstrosities were sufficiently distinct, but that the colors seemed faded and blurred, as if from the effects of a damp atmosphere. I now noticed the floor, too, which was of stone. In the center yawned the circular pit from whose jaws I had escaped; but it was the only one in the dungeon.

All this I saw indistinctly and by much effort: for my personal condition had been greatly changed during slumber. I now lay upon my back, and at full length, on a species of low framework of wood. To this I was securely bound by a long strap resembling a surcingle.[4] It passed in many convolutions about my limbs and body, leaving at liberty only my head, and my left arm to such extent that I could, by dint of much exertion, supply myself with food from an earthen dish which lay by my side on the floor. I saw, to my horror, that the pitcher had been removed. I say to my horror; for I was consumed with intolerable thirst. This thirst it appeared to be the design of my persecutors to stimulate: for the food in the dish was meat pungently seasoned.

Looking upward, I surveyed the ceiling of my prison. It was some thirty or forty feet overhead, and constructed much as the side walls. In one of its panels a very singular figure riveted my whole attention. It was the painted figure of Time as he is commonly represented, save that, in lieu of a scythe, he held what, at a casual glance, I supposed to be the pictured image of a huge pendulum such as we see on antique clocks. There was something, however, in the appearance of this machine which caused me to regard it more attentively. While I gazed directly upward at it (for its position was immediately over my own) I fancied that I saw it in motion. In an instant afterward the fancy was confirmed. Its sweep was brief, and of course slow. I watched it for some minutes, somewhat in fear, but more in wonder. Wearied at length with observing its dull movement, I turned my eyes upon the other objects in the cell.

A slight noise attracted my notice, and, looking to the floor, I saw several enormous rats traversing it. They had issued from the well, which lay just within view to my right. Even then, while I gazed, they came up in troops, hurriedly, with ravenous eyes, allured by the scent of the meat. From this it required much effort and attention to scare them away.

It might have been half an hour, perhaps even an hour (for I could take but imperfect note of time), before I again cast my eyes upward. What I then saw confounded and amazed me. The sweep of the pendulum had increased in extent by nearly a yard. As a natural consequence, its velocity was also much greater. But what mainly disturbed me was the idea that it had perceptibly *descended*. I now

---

3 **charnel:** gruesome; a house where the bones of the dead are placed.
4 **surcingle** (sér′ sing gəl): a strap, usually used to secure a pack, blanket, or saddle to a horse.

observed—with what horror it is needless to say—that its nether extremity was formed of a crescent of glittering steel, about a foot in length from horn to horn; the horns upward, and the under edge evidently as keen as that of a razor. Like a razor also, it seemed massy and heavy, tapering from the edge into a solid and broad structure above. It was appended to a weighty rod of brass, and the whole *hissed* as it swung through the air.

I could no longer doubt the doom prepared for me by monkish ingenuity in torture. My cognizance of the pit had become known to the inquisitorial agents—*the pit,* whose horrors had been destined for so bold a recusant[5] as myself—*the pit,* typical of hell, and regarded by rumor as the Ultima Thule[6] of all their punishments. The plunge into this pit I had avoided by the merest of accidents, and I knew that surprise, or entrapment into torment, formed an important portion of all the grotesquerie of these dungeon deaths. Having failed to fall, it was no part of the demon plan to hurl me into the abyss; and thus (there being no alternative) a different and a milder destruction awaited me. Milder! I half smiled in my agony as I thought of such application of such a term.

What boots it to tell of the long, long hours of horror more than mortal, during which I counted the rushing vibrations of the steel! Inch by inch—line by line—with a descent only appreciable at intervals that seemed ages—down and still down it came! Days passed—it might have been that many days passed—ere it swept so closely over me as to fan me with its acrid breath. The odor of the sharp steel forced itself into my nostrils. I prayed—I wearied heaven with my prayer for its more speedy descent. I grew frantically mad, and struggled to force myself upward against the sweep of the fearful scimitar. And

then I fell suddenly calm, and lay smiling at the glittering death, as a child at some rare bauble.

There was another interval of utter insensibility; it was brief; for, upon again lapsing into life there had been no perceptible descent in the pendulum. But it might have been long; for I knew there were demons who took note of my swoon, and who could have arrested the vibration at pleasure. Upon my recovery, too, I felt very—oh, inexpressibly sick and weak, as if through long inanition.[7] Even amid the agonies of that period, the human nature craved food. With painful effort I outstretched my left arm as far as my bonds permitted, and took possession of the small remnant which had been spared me by the rats. As I put a portion of it within my lips, there rushed to my mind a half-formed thought of joy—of hope. Yet what business had I with hope? It was, as I say, a half-formed thought—man has many such which are never completed. I felt that it was of joy—of hope; but I felt also that it had perished in its formation. In vain I struggled to perfect—to regain it. Long suffering had nearly annihilated all my ordinary powers of mind. I was an imbecile—an idiot.

The vibration of the pendulum was at right angles to my length. I saw that the crescent was designed to cross the region of the heart. It would fray the serge of my robe—it would return and repeat its operations—again—and again. Notwithstanding its terrifically wide sweep (some thirty feet or more) and the hissing vigor of its descent sufficient to sunder these very walls of iron, still the fraying of my robe would be all that, for several minutes, it would accomplish. And at this thought I paused. I dared not go farther than this reflection. I dwelt upon it with a pertinacity of attention—as if, in so dwelling, I could arrest *here* the descent of the steel. I forced myself to ponder upon the sound of the crescent as it should pass across the garment—upon the

---

5 **recusant** (rek′ yə zənt, ri kuuz nt): nonconformist, particularly in religious practice.
6 **Ultima Thule** (ul′ tə mə thü′ lē): the most extreme example.

---

7 **inanition** (in′ ə nish′ ən): exhaustion from lack of food.

peculiar thrilling sensation which friction of cloth produces on the nerves. I pondered upon all this frivolity until my teeth were on edge.

Down—steadily down it crept. I took a frenzied pleasure in contrasting its downward with its lateral velocity. To the right—to the left—far and wide—with the shriek of a damned spirit; to my heart with the stealthy pace of the tiger! I alternately laughed and howled as the one or the other idea grew predominant.

Down—certainly, relentlessly down! It vibrated within three inches of my bosom! I struggled violently, furiously, to free my left arm. This was free only from the elbow to the hand. I could reach the latter, from the platter beside me, to my mouth, with great effort, but no farther. Could I have broken the fastenings above the elbow I would have seized and attempted to arrest the pendulum. I might as well have attempted to arrest an avalanche!

Down—still unceasingly—still inevitably down! I gasped and struggled at each vibration. I shrunk convulsively at its every sweep. My eyes followed its outward or upward whirls with the eagerness of the most unmeaning despair; they closed themselves spasmodically at the descent, although death would have been a relief, oh! how unspeakable! Still I quivered in every nerve to think how slight a sinking of the machinery would precipitate that keen, glistening ax upon my bosom. It was *hope* that prompted the nerve to quiver—the frame to shrink. It was *hope*—the hope that triumphs on the rack—that whispers to the death-condemned even in the dungeons of the Inquisition.

I saw that some ten or twelve vibrations would bring the steel in actual contact with my robe, and with this observation there suddenly came over my spirit all the keen, collected calmness of despair. For the first time during many hours—or perhaps days—I *thought.* It now occurred to me that the bandage, or surcingle, which enveloped me, was *unique.* I was tied by no separate cord. The first

stroke of the razorlike crescent athwart any portion of the band, would so detach it that it might be unwound from my person by means of my left hand. But how fearful, in that case, the proximity of the steel! the result of the slightest struggle, how deadly! Was it likely, moreover, that the minions of the torturer had not foreseen and provided for this possibility! Was it probable that the bandage crossed my bosom in the track of the pendulum? Dreading to find my faint, and, as it seemed, my last hope frustrated, I so far elevated my head as to obtain a distinct view of my breast. The surcingle enveloped my limbs and body close in all directions—*save in the path of the destroying crescent.*

Scarcely had I dropped my head back into its original position, when there flashed upon my mind what I cannot better describe than as the unformed half of that idea of deliverance to which I have previously alluded, and of which a moiety[8] only floated indeterminately through my brain when I raised food to my burning lips. The whole thought was now present—feeble, scarcely sane, scarcely definite—but still entire. I proceeded at once, with the nervous energy of despair, to attempt its execution.

For many hours the immediate vicinity of the low framework upon which I lay, had been literally swarming with rats. They were wild, bold, ravenous; their red eyes glaring upon me as if they waited but for motionlessness on my part to make me their prey. "To what food," I thought, "have they been accustomed in the well?"

They had devoured, in spite of all my efforts to prevent them, all but a small remnant of the contents of the dish. I had fallen into an habitual seesaw, or wave of the hand about the platter: and, at length, the unconscious uniformity of the movement deprived it of effect. In their voracity the vermin frequently fastened their sharp fangs in my fingers. With the particles of

8 moiety (moi′ ə tē′): a part.

the oily and spicy viand which now remained, I thoroughly rubbed the bandage wherever I could reach it; then, raising my hand from the floor, I lay breathlessly still.

At first the ravenous animals were startled and terrified at the change—at the cessation of movement. They shrank alarmedly back; many sought the well. But this was only for a moment. I had not counted in vain upon their voracity. Observing that I remained without motion, one or two of the boldest leaped upon the framework and smelt at the surcingle. This seemed the signal for a general rush. Forth from the well they hurried in fresh troops. They clung to the wood—they overran it, and leaped in hundreds upon my person. The measured movement of the pendulum disturbed them not at all. Avoiding its strokes they busied themselves with the anointed bandage. They pressed—they swarmed upon me in ever accumulating heaps. They writhed upon my throat; their cold lips sought my own; I was half stifled by their thronging pressure; disgust, for which the world has no name, swelled my bosom, and chilled, with a heavy clamminess, my heart. Yet one minute, and I felt that the struggle would be over. Plainly I perceived the loosening of the bandage. I knew that in more than one place it must be already severed. With a more than human resolution I lay *still*.

Nor had I erred in my calculations—nor had I endured in vain. I at length felt that I was *free*. The surcingle hung in ribands from my body. But the stroke of the pendulum already pressed upon my bosom. It had divided the serge of the robe. It had cut through the linen beneath. Twice again it swung, and a sharp sense of pain shot through every nerve. But the moment of escape had arrived. At a wave of my hand my deliverers hurried tumultuously away. With a steady movement—cautious, sidelong, shrinking, and slow—I slid from the embrace of the bandage and beyond the reach of the scimitar. For the moment, at least, *I was free*.

Free!—and in the grasp of the Inquisition! I had scarcely stepped from my wooden bed of horror upon the stone floor of the prison, when the motion of the hellish machine ceased and I beheld it drawn up, by some invisible force, through the ceiling. This was a lesson which I took desperately to heart. My every motion was undoubtedly watched. Free!—I had but escaped death in one form of agony, to be delivered unto worse than death in some other. With that thought I rolled my eyes nervously around on the barriers of iron that hemmed me in. Something unusual—some change which, at first, I could not appreciate distinctly—it was obvious, had taken place in the apartment. For many minutes of a dreamy and trembling abstraction, I busied myself in vain, unconnected conjecture. During this period, I became aware, for the first time, of the origin of the sulphurous light which illumined the cell. It proceeded from a fissure, about half an inch in width, extending entirely around the prison at the base of the walls, which thus appeared, and were, completely separated from the floor. I endeavored, but of course in vain, to look through the aperture.

As I arose from the attempt, the mystery of the alteration in the chamber broke at once upon my understanding. I have observed that, although the outlines of the figures upon the walls were sufficiently distinct, yet the colors seemed blurred and indefinite. These colors had now assumed, and were momentarily assuming, a startling and most intense brilliancy, that gave to the spectral and fiendish portraitures an aspect that might have thrilled even firmer nerves than my own. Demon eyes, of a wild and ghastly vivacity, glared upon me in a thousand directions, where none had been visible before, and gleamed with the lurid luster of a fire that I could not force my imagination to regard as unreal.

Unreal!—Even while I breathed there came to my nostrils the breath of the vapor of heated iron! A suffocating odor pervaded the prison! A deeper glow settled each moment in the eyes that glared at my agonies! A richer tint of crimson diffused itself over the pictured horrors of blood. I panted! I gasped for breath! There could be no doubt of the design of my tormentors—oh! most unrelenting! oh! most demoniac of men! I shrank from the glowing metal to the center of the cell. Amid the thought of the fiery destruction that impended, the idea of the coolness of the well came over my soul like balm. I rushed to its deadly brink. I threw my straining vision below. The glare from the enkindled roof illumined its inmost recesses. Yet, for a wild moment, did my spirit refuse to comprehend the meaning of what I saw. At length it forced—it wrestled its way into my soul—it burned itself in upon my shuddering reason.—Oh! for a voice to speak!—oh! horror!—oh! any horror but this! With a shriek, I rushed from the margin, and buried my face in my hands—weeping bitterly.

The heat rapidly increased, and once again I looked up, shuddering as with a fit of the ague. There had been a second change in the cell—and now the change was obviously in the *form*. As before, it was in vain that I, at first, endeavored to appreciate or understand what was taking place. But not long was I left in doubt. The Inquisitorial vengeance had been hurried by my twofold escape, and there was to be no more dallying with the King of Terrors. The room had been square. I saw that two of its iron angles were now acute—two, consequently, obtuse. The fearful difference quickly increased with a low rumbling or moaning sound. In an instant the apartment had shifted its form into that of a lozenge.[9] But the alteration stopped not here—I neither hoped nor desired it to stop. I could have clasped the red walls to my bosom as a garment of eternal peace. "Death," I said, "any death but that of the pit!" Fool! might I have not known that *into the pit* it was the object of the burning iron to urge me? Could I resist its glow? or, if even that, could I withstand its pressure? And now, flatter and flatter grew the lozenge, with a rapidity that left me no time for contemplation. Its center, and of course, its greatest width, came just over the yawning gulf. I shrank back—but the closing walls pressed me resistlessly onward. At length for my seared and writhing body there was no longer an inch of foothold on the firm floor of the prison. I struggled no more, but the agony of my soul found vent in one loud, long, and final scream of despair. I felt that I tottered upon the brink—I averted my eyes—.

There was a discordant hum of human voices! There was a loud blast as of many trumpets! There was a harsh grating as of a thousand thunders! The fiery walls rushed back! An outstretched arm caught my own as I fell, fainting, into the abyss. It was that of General Lasalle. The French army had entered Toledo. The Inquisition was in the hands of its enemies.

---

9 **lozenge** (loz′ inj): diamond-shape.

Study Questions

1. This story is a monologue. Every thought and action is described from the prisoner's point of view. How does this consistency in point of view contribute to the suspense and movement of events? Are you ever bored by the tale? Why or why not?

2. What clues are there early in the story which suggest that the prisoner survived? How does Poe make us forget or disregard these clues?

3. Each type of torture is carefully interwoven with the previous one. How is the utter blackness tied in with the fiery walls? Why is the prisoner drugged? Why is the food highly seasoned? How often are the rats described before they jump onto the cot? Why are the size and shape of the cell mentioned several times? What is the effect of these details?

4. Find the three successive short paragraphs, all starting with the same word. How are these repetitions, the brevity of the sentences, and the frequent dashes appropriate to the prisoner's emotional state and the movement of the pendulum?

5. To what extent is the rescue improbable or unrealistic? Why, then, is it acceptable?

Composition

1. Consider what purpose the story might have beyond its obvious one of creating relentless suspense. Near the middle of the story there are indications of a more general meaning for "pit" and "pendulum." People often have to choose between two equally serious evils, the pit or the pendulum, the frying pan or the fire. Write a brief summary discussing the general condition suggested by this story. Use examples from the story to reinforce your points.

2. Write a brief narrative in which you use a first-person narrator describing a frightening situation or predicament. For example, the narrator might be accidentally locked in a deserted house, lost in a graveyard at night, stranded in a beach house in the winter, stalled in a car on a country lane during a thunderstorm. Try to maintain a consistent point of view and to evoke a specific response from your reader.

Vocabulary

Each noun in Column One below designates something featured in "The Pit and the Pendulum." In Column Two, an approximate **synonym** is given for each noun in Column One. The synonyms are not given in the same order as the words in Column One. From Column Two select the best synonym for each word in Column One.

COLUMN ONE	COLUMN TWO
1. abyss	A. guess
2. aperture	B. blade
3. cognizance	C. opening
4. conjecture	D. time
5. epoch	E. nearness
6. fissure	F. pit
7. pertinacity	G. crack
8. proximity	H. rats
9. scimitar	I. knowledge
10. vermin	J. stubbornness

Of Poe's total output of forty-eight poems, "To Helen" is one of his most famous and most debated.

To Helen

EDGAR ALLAN POE

Helen, thy beauty is to me
  Like those Nicéan barks of yore,
That gently, o'er a perfumed sea,
  The weary, wayworn wanderer[1] bore
  To his own native shore.   5

On desperate seas long wont to roam,
  Thy hyacinth hair,[2] thy classic face,
Thy Naiad[3] airs have brought me home
  To the glory that was Greece,
  And the grandeur that was Rome.   10

Lo! in yon brilliant window niche
  How statuelike I see thee stand,
The agate lamp within thy hand!
  Ah, Psyche,[4] from the regions which
  Are Holy Land!   15

1 **wanderer:** suggesting Ulysses from Homer's *Odyssey.*
2 **hyacinth hair:** a Homeric phrase used to describe luxuriant, curling hair.
3 **Naiad** (nā′ ad nı′ ad): in Greek legend, a graceful water nymph who resembled a beautiful maiden.
4 **Psyche** (sī′ kē): the Greek princess loved by Cupid; also the Greek word for "soul."

This poem is one of the few in which Poe's foremost objective is to explore an idea logically; consequently, he depends less on musical effects here than in the other two poems.

Sonnet—To Science

EDGAR ALLAN POE

Science! true daughter of Old Time thou art!
   Who alterest all things with thy peering eyes.
Why preyest thou thus upon the poet's heart,
   Vulture, whose wings are dull realities?
How should he love thee? or how deem thee wise,   5
   Who wouldst not leave him in his wandering
To seek for treasure in the jeweled skies,
   Albeit he soared with an undaunted wing?
Hast thou not dragged Diana[1] from her car?[2]
   And driven the Hamadryad[3] from the wood   10
To seek a shelter in some happier star?
   Hast thou not torn the Naiad from her flood,
The Elfin from the green grass, and from me
The summer dream beneath the tamarind tree?[4]

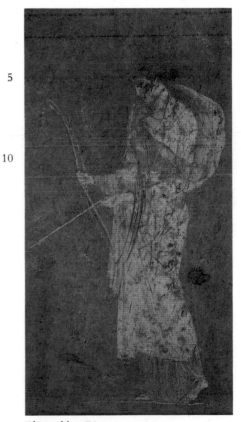

The goddess Diana,
from an ancient Roman fresco.

---

1 **Diana**: goddess of nature, the hunt, and the moon.
2 **car**: poetic term for chariot; here, the moon.
3 **Hamadryad** (ham' ə drī' əd): a nymph of the woods.
4 **tamarind tree**: a tropical tree with beautiful flowers and delicious fruit.

Study Questions

To Helen

1. In the first stanza, to what is Helen's beauty compared? What effect does her beauty have on the speaker?

2. What details in stanza two develop the images of beauty and ships that are introduced in the first stanza?

3. Throughout the poem Poe uses allusions to classical names and places, as well as certain kinds of images to create the impression of a far-off, idealized, unreal woman like a Greek statue. Point out words in lines 7, 8, and 12 which contribute to this impression. In what line of the poem is the woman described as if she were a statue of a saint?

4. Do you think the poem praises a living woman, a past lady (such as the legendary Helen of Troy), or an ideal heroine?

5. This poem was actually written to a Mrs. Jane Stanard, the mother of one of Poe's schoolmates. She died when Poe was only fifteen, and Poe once described her as "the first purely ideal love of my soul." Does this information alter the meaning of the poem? Why or why not?

6. Much of the effect and ultimately the meaning of the poem is derived from its rich verbal music. That is, the total effect of images and sounds impresses the reader more than isolated, specific details do. How do alliteration, rhyme scheme, and line length contribute to the over-all effect?

Sonnet—To Science

1. What specific words or phrases indicate the speaker's critical attitude toward factual science? For example, why are the "eyes" of science "peering" (line 2)?

2. In lines 6–8 what activity of a poet is desirable?

3. In lines 9–14 how does a poet see nature? How does science see nature?

The City in the Sea

EDGAR ALLAN POE

Lo! Death has reared himself a throne
In a strange city lying alone
Far down within the dim West,
Where the good and the bad and the worst and the best
Have gone to their eternal rest.   5
There shrines and palaces and towers
(Time-eaten towers that tremble not!)
Resemble nothing that is ours.
Around, by lifting winds forgot,
Resignedly beneath the sky   10
The melancholy waters lie.

No rays from the holy heaven come down
On the long nighttime of that town;
But light from out the lurid[1] sea
Streams up the turrets silently—   15
Gleams up the pinnacles far and free—
Up domes—up spires—up kingly halls—
Up fanes[2]—up Babylonlike[3] walls—
Up shadowy long-forgotten bowers
Of sculptured ivy and stone flowers—   20
Up many and many a marvelous shrine
Whose wreathèd friezes intertwine
The viol, the violet, and the vine.
Resignedly beneath the sky
The melancholy waters lie.   25
So blend the turrets and shadows there
That all seem pendulous in air,
While from a proud tower in the town
Death looks gigantically down.

There open fanes and gaping graves   30
Yawn level with the luminous waves
But not the riches there that lie

---

1 **lurid:** having the ghastly appearance of fire veiled by clouds or smoke.
2 **fanes:** temples.
3 **Babylonlike:** Babylon was an ancient Asian city. The walls of Babylon became legendary for their size.

In each idol's diamond eye—
Not the gaily jeweled dead
Tempt the waters from their bed;   35
For no ripples curl, alas!
Along that wilderness of glass—
No swellings tell that winds may be
Upon some far-off happier sea—
No heavings hint that winds have been   40
On seas less hideously serene.

But lo, a stir is in the air!
The wave—there is a movement there!
As if the towers had thrust aside,
In slightly sinking, the dull tide—   45
As if their tops had feebly given
A void within the filmy Heaven.
The waves have now a redder glow—
The hours are breathing faint and low—
And when, amid no earthly moans,   50
Down, down that town shall settle hence,
Hell, rising from a thousand thrones,
Shall do it reverence.[4]

---

4 **Hell . . . reverence:** See the *Bible,* Isaiah 14:9.

Study Questions

1. In stanza one, who rules the dream city? What does Poe say about the townspeople? Why is it appropriate for the city to lie in the west? Explain how towers can be "Time-eaten" (line 7).

2. What details of architecture are mentioned in the poem? What kinds of buildings are present? Are there any slums or shabby houses? What sort of city, then, is envisioned?

3. The eeriness of the dead city is produced, in part, by the use of light. Find phrases in the first thirteen lines that record the absence of light. What kind of light is described in the remainder of the poem?

4. If this city is meant to describe a kind of death, what is the nature of this death? What is the chief torture in the doomed city? How do the many negatives ("no," "not," "nothing") contribute to this torture?

5. Poe's earlier titles for this poem were "The Doomed City" and "The City of Sin." Which of the three titles is best for the text of the poem? Why?

Henry David Thoreau   1817-1862

Over a century ago Henry David Thoreau tried a variety of occupations for brief periods in his native Massachusetts. He worked in his father's pencil-making business, served as general handyman to the Emerson family, taught school, lectured, and occasionally surveyed for neighboring farmers. What he enjoyed most was dividing his days into tasks that fed his body and alloting the other half to feed his mind. Thoreau read, wrote, and meditated. His life work, amounting to twenty volumes of diaries, journals, and essays concerning what he saw and thought, places him among the great figures in American literary and intellectual history.

During his lifetime, however, Thoreau was not always a popular figure. In 1849 he published his most controversial essay, "Civil Disobedience." In it he described his one-day imprisonment in 1845 for refusing to pay a poll tax levied by a government, which supported slavery and the Mexican War. In this essay, which influenced later activist thinkers such as Mahatma Gandhi and Martin Luther King, Jr., Thoreau wrote:

That government is best which governs not at all . . . for a single man can bend it to his will . . . . I ask for, not at once no government but *at once* a better government . . . . Can there not be a government in which majorities do not virtually decide right and wrong, but conscience? . . . I think that we should be men first, and subjects afterwards. It is not desirable to cultivate a respect for the law, so much as for the right. The only obligation which I have a right to assume is to do at any time what I think right . . . . The State never intentionally confronts a man's sense, intellectual or moral, but only his body, . . . There will never be a

really free and enlightened State until the State comes to recognize the individual as a higher and independent power, from which all its own power and authority are derived, and treats him accordingly.

Thoreau's belief in the importance of the individual led him to launch an experiment in living. On July 4, 1845, he walked about a mile and a half from his home in Concord to Walden Pond where he built a cabin by himself at a total cost of $28.12\frac{1}{2}$. There the rugged individualist lived for two years in seclusion. He was not a hermit during the two years, for he went to Concord almost daily and had scores of visitors. The two years resulted in his writing *Walden, or Life in the Woods,* his own declaration of independence.

In the second chapter of *Walden* printed here, Thoreau speaks directly to the reader as though merely conducting a conversation. His thoughts, however, are loftier—or deeper—than the title and the conversational style seem to indicate.

A drawing of Henry Thoreau by one of his friends.

Where I Lived and What I Lived For

from WALDEN

HENRY DAVID THOREAU

AT A CERTAIN SEASON of our life we are accustomed to consider every spot as the possible site of a house. I have thus surveyed the country on every side within a dozen miles of where I live. In imagination I have bought all the farms in succession, for all were to be bought, and I knew their price. I walked over each farmer's premises, tasted his wild apples, discoursed on husbandry with him, took his farm at his price, at any price, mortgaging it to him in my mind; even put a higher price on it—took everything but a deed of it—took his word for his deed, for I dearly love to talk—cultivated it, and him too to some extent, I trust, and withdrew when I had enjoyed it long enough, leaving him to carry it on. This experience entitled me to be regarded as a sort of real-estate broker by my friends. Wherever I sat, there I might live, and the landscape radiated from me accordingly. What is a house but a *sedes*[1], a seat?—better if a country seat. I discovered many a site for a house not likely to be soon improved, which some might have thought too far from the village, but to my eyes the village was too far from it. Well, there I might live, I said; and there I did live, for an hour, a summer and a winter life; saw how I could let the years run off, buffet the winter through, and see the spring come in. The future inhabitants of this region, wherever they may place their houses, may be sure that they have been anticipated.

An afternoon sufficed to lay out the land into orchard, wood, lot, and pasture, and to decide what fine oaks or pines should be left to stand before the door, and whence each blasted tree could be seen to the best advantage; and then I let it lie, fallow perchance, for a man is rich in proportion to the number of things which he can afford to let alone.

My imagination carried me so far that I even had the refusal of several farms—the refusal was all I wanted—but I never got my fingers burned by actual possession. The nearest that I came to actual possession was when I bought the Hollowell place, and had begun to sort my seeds, and collected materials with which to make a wheelbarrow to carry it on or off with; but before the owner gave me a deed of it, his wife—every man has such a wife—changed her mind and wished to keep it, and he offered me ten dollars to release him. Now, to speak the truth, I had but ten cents in the world, and it surpassed my arithmetic to tell, if I was that man who had ten cents, or who had a farm, or ten dollars, or all together. However, I let him keep the ten dollars and the farm too, for I had carried it far enough; or rather, to be generous, I sold him the farm for just what I gave for it, and, as he was not a rich man, made him a present of ten dollars, and still had my ten cents, and seeds, and materials for a wheelbarrow left. I found thus that I had been a rich man without any damage to my poverty. But I retained the landscape, and I have since annually carried off what it yielded without a wheelbarrow. . . .

---

1 *sedes:* the Latin word has a double meaning, "seat" or "dwelling place."

The real attractions of the Hollowell farm, to me, were: its complete retirement, being about two miles from the village, half a mile from the nearest neighbor, and separated from the highway by a broad field; its bounding on the river, which the owner said protected it by its fogs from frosts in the spring, though that was nothing to me; the gray color and ruinous state of the house and barn, and the dilapidated fences, which put such an interval between me and the last occupant; the hollow and lichen-covered apple trees, gnawed by rabbits, showing what kind of neighbors I should have; but above all, the recollection I had of it from my earliest voyages up the river, when the house was concealed behind a dense grove of red maples, through which I heard the house-dog bark. I was in haste to buy it, before the proprietor finished getting out some rocks, cutting down the hollow apple trees, and grubbing up some young birches which had sprung up in the pasture, or, in short, had made any more of his improvements. To enjoy these advantages I was ready to carry it on; like Atlas,[2] to take the world on my shoulders—I never heard what compensation he received for that—and do all those things which had no other motive or excuse but that I might pay for it and be unmolested in my possession of it; for I knew all the while that it would yield the most abundant crop of the kind I wanted, if I could only afford to let it alone. But it turned out as I have said.

All that I could say, then, with respect to farming on a large scale—I have always cultivated a garden—was that I had had my seeds ready. Many think that seeds improve with age. I have no doubt that time discriminates between the good and the bad; and when at last I shall plant, I shall be less likely to be disappointed. But I would say to my fellows, once for all, As long as possible live free and uncommitted. It makes but little difference whether you are committed to a farm or the county jail. . . .

The present was my next experiment of this kind, which I purpose to describe more at length, for convenience putting the experience of two years into one. As I have said, I do not propose to write an ode to dejection, but to brag as lustily as chanticleer in the morning, standing on his roost, if only to wake my neighbors up.

When first I took up my abode in the woods, that is, began to spend my nights as well as days there, which by accident, was on Independence Day, or the Fourth of July, 1845, my house was not finished for winter, but was merely a defense against the rain, without plastering or chimney, the walls being of rough, weather-stained boards, with wide chinks, which made it cool at night. The upright white hewn studs and freshly planed door and window casings gave it a clean and airy look, especially in the morning, when its timbers were saturated with dew, so that I fancied that by noon some sweet gum would exude from them. To my imagination it retained throughout the day more or less of this auroral character, reminding me of a certain house on a mountain which I had visited a year before. This was an airy and unplastered cabin, fit to entertain a traveling god, and where a goddess might trail her garments. The winds which passed over my dwelling were such as sweep over the ridges of mountains, bearing the broken strains, or celestial parts only, of terrestrial music. The morning wind forever blows, the poem of creation is uninterrupted; but few are the ears that hear it. Olympus[3] is but the outside of the earth everywhere.

The only house I had been the owner of before, if I except a boat, was a tent, which I used occasionally when making excursions in the summer, and this is still rolled up in my garret; but the boat, after passing from hand to

---

2 **Atlas:** in Greek mythology, a demigod supposed to support the heavens on his shoulders.

3 **Olympus:** a mountain in Greece; in legend the home of the gods.

hand, has gone down the stream of time. With this more substantial shelter about me, I had made some progress toward settling in the world. This frame, so slightly clad, was a sort of crystallization around me, and reacted on the builder. It was suggestive somewhat as a picture in outlines. I did not need to go outdoors to take the air, for the atmosphere within had lost none of its freshness. It was not so much within doors as behind a door where I sat, even in the rainiest weather. The Harivansa[4] says, "An abode without birds is like a meat without seasoning." Such was not my abode, for I found myself suddenly neighbor to the birds; not by having imprisoned one, but having caged myself near them. I was not only nearer to some of those which commonly frequent the garden and the orchard, but to those wilder and more thrilling songsters of the forest which never, or rarely, serenade a villager—the wood thrush, the veery, the scarlet tanager, the field sparrow, the whippoorwill, and many others.

I was seated by the shore of a small pond, about a mile and a half south of the village of Concord and somewhat higher than it, in the midst of an extensive wood between that town and Lincoln,[5] and about two miles south of that our only field known to fame, Concord Battle Ground;[6] but I was so low in the woods that the opposite shore, half a mile off, like the rest, covered with wood, was my most distant horizon. For the first week, whenever I looked out on the pond it impressed me like a tarn high up on the side of a mountain, its bottom far above the surface of other lakes, and, as the sun arose, I saw it throwing off its nightly clothing of mist, and here and there, by degrees, its soft ripples or its smooth reflecting surface was revealed, while the mists, like ghosts, were stealthily withdrawing in every direction into the woods, as at the breaking up of some nocturnal conventicle. The very dew seemed to hang upon the trees later into the day than usual, as on the sides of mountains.

This small lake was of most value as a neighbor in the intervals of a gentle rainstorm in August, when, both air and water being perfectly still, but the sky overcast, midafternoon had all the serenity of evening, and the wood thrush sang around, and was heard from shore to shore. A lake like this is never smoother than at such a time; and the clear portion of the air above it being shallow and darkened by clouds, the water, full of light and reflections, becomes a lower heaven itself so much the more important. From a hilltop nearby, where the wood had been recently cut off, there was a pleasing vista southward across the pond, through a wide indentation in the hills which form the shore there, where their opposite sides sloping toward each other suggested a stream flowing out in that direction through a wooded valley, but stream there was none. That way I looked between and over the near green hills to some distant and higher ones in the horizon, tinged with blue. Indeed, by standing on tiptoe I could catch a glimpse of some of the peaks of the still bluer and more distant mountain ranges in the northwest, those true-blue coins from heaven's own mint, and also of some portion of the village. But in other directions, even from this point, I could not see over or beyond the woods which surrounded me. It is well to have some water in your neighborhood, to give buoyancy to and float the earth. One value even of the smallest well is that when you look into it you see that earth is not continent but insular. This is as important as that it keeps butter cool. When I looked across the pond from this peak toward the Sudbury meadows, which in time of flood I distinguished elevated perhaps by a mirage in their seething valley, like a coin in a basin, all the earth beyond the pond appeared like a thin

---

4 **Harivansa** (or Harivansha): a Hindu classic poem about the deity Krishna.

5 **Lincoln**: small town in Massachusetts between Concord and Sudbury, which is mentioned in the next paragraph.

6 **Concord Battle Ground**: See Emerson's poem "Concord Hymn" (p. 231).

crust insulated and floated even by this small sheet of intervening water, and I was reminded that this on which I dwelt was but *dry land.*

Though the view from my door was still more contracted, I did not feel crowded or confined in the least. There was pasture enough for my imagination. The low shrub oak plateau to which the opposite shore arose stretched away toward the prairies of the West and the steppes of Tartary,[7] affording ample room for all the roving families of men. "There are none happy in the world but beings who enjoy freely a vast horizon,"—said Damodara,[8] when his herds required new and larger pastures. . . .

Every morning was a cheerful invitation to make my life of equal simplicity, and I may say innocence, with Nature herself. I have been as sincere a worshiper of Aurora[9] as the Greeks. I got up early and bathed in the pond; that was a religious exercise, and one of the best things which I did. They say that characters were engraven on the bathing tub of King Tching-thang to this effect: "Renew thyself completely each day; do it again, and again, and forever again." I can understand that. Morning brings back the heroic ages. I was as much affected by the faint hum of a mosquito making its invisible and unimaginable tour through my apartment at earliest dawn, when I was sitting with door and windows open, as I could be by any trumpet that ever sang of fame. It was Homer's requiem; itself an Iliad and Odyssey in the air, singing its own wrath and wanderings.[10] There was something cosmical about it; a standing advertisement, till forbidden, of the everlasting vigor and fertility of the world. The morning, which is the most memorable season of the day, is the awakening hour. Then there is least somnolence in us; and for an hour, at least, some part of us awakes which slumbers all the rest of the day and night. Little is to be expected of that day, if it can be called a day, to which we are not awakened by our Genius, but by the mechanical nudgings of some servitor, are not awakened by our own newly acquired force and aspirations from within, accompanied by the undulations of celestial music, instead of factory bells, and a fragrance filling the air—to a higher life than we fell asleep from; and thus the darkness bear its fruit, and prove itself to be good, no less than the light. That man who does not believe that each day contains an earlier, more sacred, and auroral hour than he has yet profaned has despaired of life, and is pursuing a descending and darkening way. After a partial cessation of his sensuous life, the soul of man, or its organs rather, are reinvigorated each day, and his Genius tries again what noble life it can make. All memorable events, I should say, transpire in morning time and in a morning atmosphere. The Vedas[11] say, "All intelligences awake with the morning." Poetry and art, and the fairest and most memorable of the actions of men, date from such an hour. All poets and heroes, like Memnon,[12] are the children of Aurora, and emit their music at sunrise. To him whose elastic and vigorous thought keeps pace with the sun, the day is a perpetual morning. It matters not what the clocks say or the attitudes and labors of men. Morning is when I am awake and there is a dawn in me. Moral reform is the effort to throw off sleep. Why is it that men give so poor an account of their day if they have not been slumbering? They are not such poor calculators. If they had not been overcome with drowsiness, they would have performed something. The millions are awake enough for physical labor; but only one in a million is

---

7 **Tartary** (or **Tatary**): an indefinite region in northern Asia and Europe, extending from the Sea of Japan to the Dnieper River.

8 **Damodara**: another name for the Hindu god Krishna.

9 **Aurora**: Greek goddess of dawn.

10 **wrath and wanderings**: Homer's *Iliad* concerns the "wrath" of Achilles, and the *Odyssey* tells of the "wanderings" of Odysseus.

11 **Vedas**: collection of sacred Hindu literature.

12 **Memnon**: in Greek mythology, the King of the Ethiopians whom Zeus made immortal. Memnon's statue at Thebes was supposed to emit musical notes at dawn.

awake enough for effective intellectual exertion, only one in a hundred millions to a poetic or divine life. To be awake is to be alive. I have never yet met a man who was quite awake. How could I have looked him in the face?

We must learn to reawaken and keep ourselves awake, not by mechanical aids, but by an infinite expectation of the dawn, which does not forsake us in our soundest sleep. I know of no more encouraging fact than the unquestionable ability of man to elevate his life by a conscious endeavor. It is something to be able to paint a particular picture, or to carve a statue, and so to make a few objects beautiful; but it is far more glorious to carve and paint the very atmosphere and medium through which we look, which morally we can do. To affect the quality of the day, that is the highest of arts. Every man is tasked to make his life, even in its details, worthy of the contemplation of his most elevated and critical hour. If we refused, or rather used up, such paltry information as we get, the oracles would distinctly inform us how this might be done.

I went to the woods because I wished to live deliberately, to front only the essential facts of life, and see if I could not learn what it had to teach, and not, when I came to die, discover that I had not lived. I did not wish to live what was not life, living is so dear; nor did I wish to practice resignation, unless it was quite necessary. I wanted to live deep and suck out all the marrow of life, to live so sturdily and Spartanlike[13] as to put to rout all that was not life, to cut a broad swath and shave close, to drive life into a corner, and reduce it to its lowest terms, and, if it proved to be mean, why then to get the whole and genuine meanness of it, and publish its meanness to the world; or if it were sublime, to know it by experience, and be able to give a true account of it in my next excursion. For most men, it appears to me, are in a strange uncertainty about it, whether it is of the devil or of God, and have *somewhat hastily* concluded that it is the chief end of man here to "glorify God and enjoy him forever."[14]

Still we live meanly, like ants; though the fable tells us that we were long ago changed into men; like pygmies we fight with cranes; it is error upon error, and clout upon clout, and our best virtue has for its occasion a superfluous and evitable wretchedness. Our life is frittered away by detail. An honest man has hardly need to count more than his ten fingers, or in extreme cases he may add his ten toes, and lump the rest. Simplicity, simplicity, simplicity! I say, let your affairs be as two or three, and not a hundred or a thousand; instead of a million count half a dozen, and keep your accounts on your thumbnail. In the midst of this chopping sea of civilized life such are the clouds and storms and quicksands and thousand-and-one items to be allowed for, that a man has to live, if he would not founder and go to the bottom and not make his port at all, by dead reckoning,[15] and he must be a great calculator indeed who succeeds. Simplify, simplify. Instead of three meals a day, if it be necessary eat but one; instead of a hundred dishes, five; and reduce other things in proportion. Our life is like a German Confederacy,[16] made up of petty states, with its boundary forever fluctuating, so that even a German cannot tell you how it is bounded at any moment. The nation itself, with all its so-called internal improvements, which, by the way are all external and superficial, is just such an unwieldy and overgrown establishment, cluttered with furniture and tripped up by its own traps, ruined by luxury and heedless expense, by want of calculation and a worthy aim, as the million households in the land; and the only cure for

---

13 **Spartanlike:** The inhabitants of the ancient Greek city-state of Sparta were famed for their courage, discipline, and frugality.

14 "glorify . . . forever": from the Presbyterian book of beliefs, *Westminster Shorter Catechism*.

15 **dead reckoning:** nautical term for a method of positioning a ship without using the more reliable method of astronomical observation.

16 **German Confederacy:** In 1815, the first ineffective alliance of German territories.

it, as for them, is in a rigid economy, a stern and more than Spartan simplicity of life and elevation of purpose. It lives too fast. Men think that it is essential that the *Nation* have commerce, and export ice, and talk through a telegraph, and ride thirty miles an hour, without a doubt, whether *they* do or not; but whether we should live like baboons or like men, is a little uncertain. If we do not get out sleepers,[17] and forge rails, and devote days and nights to the work, but go to tinkering upon our *lives* to improve *them,* who will build railroads? And if railroads are not built, how shall we get to heaven in season? But if we stay at home and mind our business, who will want railroads? We do not ride on the railroad; it rides upon us. Did you ever think what those sleepers are that underlie the railroad? Each one is a man, an Irishman, or a Yankee man. The rails are laid on them, and they are covered with sand, and the cars run smoothly over them. They are sound sleepers, I assure you. And every few years a new lot is laid down and run over; so that, if some have the pleasure of riding on a rail, others have the misfortune to be ridden upon. And when they run over a man that is walking in his sleep, a supernumerary sleeper in the wrong position, and wake him up, they suddenly stop the cars, and make a hue and cry about it, as if this were an exception. I am glad to know that it takes a gang of men for every five miles to keep the sleepers down and level in their beds as it is, for this is a sign that they may sometime get up again.

Why should we live with such hurry and waste of life? We are determined to be starved before we are hungry. Men say that a stitch in time saves nine, and so they take a thousand stitches today to save nine tomorrow. As for *work,* we haven't any of any consequence. We have the Saint Vitus's dance,[18] and cannot possibly keep our heads still. If I should only give a few pulls at the parish bell rope, as for a fire, that is, without setting the bell,[19] there is hardly a man on his farm in the outskirts of Concord, notwithstanding that press of engagements which was his excuse so many times this morning, nor a boy, nor a woman, I might almost say, but would forsake all and follow that sound, not mainly to save property from the flames, but, if we will confess the truth, much more to see it burn, since burn it must, and we, be it known, did not set it on fire—or to see it put out, and have a hand in it, if that is done as handsomely; yes, even if it were the parish church itself. Hardly a man takes a half-hour's nap after dinner, but when he wakes he holds up his head and asks, "What's the news?" as if the rest of mankind has stood his sentinels. Some give directions to be waked every half-hour, doubtless for no other purpose; and then, to pay for it, they tell what they have dreamed. After a night's sleep the news is as indispensable as the breakfast. "Pray tell me anything new that has happened to a man anywhere on this globe"—and he reads it over his coffee and rolls, that a man has had his eyes gouged out this morning on the Wachito River;[20] never dreaming the while that he lives in the dark unfathomed mammoth cave of this world, and has but the rudiment of an eye himself.

For my part, I could easily do without the post office. I think that there are very few important communications made through it. To speak critically, I never received more than one or two letters in my life—I wrote this some years ago—that were worth the postage. The penny post is, commonly, an institution through which you seriously offer a man that penny for his thoughts which is so often safely offered in jest. And I am sure that I never read any memorable news in a newspaper. If we

---

17 **sleepers**: wooden beams to which railway tracks are riveted.
18 **Saint Vitus's dance**: a nervous disorder accompanied by spasmodic twitchings.
19 **setting the bell**: A "few pulls" would sound an alarm. A slow, complete pull would rotate the bell (or "set it") and only toll it.
20 **Wachito River** (or **Ouachita** or **Washita**): in Arkansas.

read of one man robbed, or murdered, or killed by accident, or one house burned, or one vessel wrecked, or one steamboat blown up, or one cow run over on the Western Railroad,[21] or one mad dog killed, or one lot of grasshoppers in the winter—we never need read of another. One is enough. If you are acquainted with the principle, what do you care for myriad instances and applications? To a philospher all *news,* as it is called, is gossip, and they who edit and read it are old women over their tea. Yet not a few are greedy after this gossip. There was such a rush, as I hear, the other day at one of the offices to learn the foreign news by the last arrival, that several large squares of plate glass belonging to the establishment were broken by the pressure— news which I seriously think a ready wit might write a twelvemonth, or twelve years, beforehand with sufficient accuracy. . . .

Shams and delusions are esteemed for soundest truths, while reality is fabulous. If men would steadily observe realities only, and not allow themselves to be deluded, life, to compare it with such things as we know, would be like a fairy tale and the Arabian Nights' Entertainments. If we respected only what is inevitable and has a right to be, music and poetry would resound along the streets. When we are unhurried and wise, we perceive that only great and worthy things have any permanent and absolute existence, that petty fears and petty pleasures are but the shadow of the reality. This is always exhilarating and sublime. By closing the eyes and slumbering, and consenting to be deceived by shows, men establish and confirm their daily life of routine and habit everywhere, which still is built on purely illusory foundations. Children, who play life, discern its true law and relations more clearly than men, who fail to live it worthily, but who think that they are wiser by experience, that is, by failure. . . .

Let us spend one day as deliberately as Nature, and not be thrown off the track by every nutshell and mosquito's wing that falls on the rails. Let us rise early and fast, or break fast, gently and without perturbation; let company come and let company go, let the bells ring and the children cry—determined to make a day of it. Why should we knock under and go with the stream? Let us not be upset and overwhelmed in that terrible rapid and whirlpool called a dinner, situated in the meridian shallows. Weather this danger and you are safe, for the rest of the way is down hill. With unrelaxed nerves, with morning vigor, sail by it, looking another way, tied to the mast like Ulysses.[22] If the engine whistles, let it whistle till it is hoarse for its pains. If the bell rings, why should we run? We will consider what kind of music they are like. Let us settle ourselves, and work and wedge our feet downward through the mud and slush of opinion, and prejudice, and tradition, and delusion, and appearance, that alluvion which covers the globe, through Paris and London, through New York and Boston and Concord, through Church and State, through poetry and philosophy and religion, till we come to a hard bottom and rocks in place, which we can call *reality,* and say, "This is, and no mistake"; and then begin, having a *point d'appui,*[23] below freshet and frost and fire, a place where you might found a wall or a state, or set a lamppost safely, or perhaps a gauge, not a Nilometer,[24] but a Realometer,[25] that future ages might know how deep a freshet of shams and appearances had gathered from time to time. If you stand right fronting and face to face to a fact, you will see the sun glimmer on both its surfaces, as if it were a cimeter, and feel its sweet

21 **Western Railroad:** from Boston to Troy, N.Y.

22 tied . . . **Ulysses:** After Ulysses had avoided Charybdis (the "whirlpool" Thoreau mentions a few lines earlier), he had himself tied to the mast of his ship in order not to fall victim to the Sirens' songs. Sailors who heard the songs were irresistibly drawn to destruction in the whirlpool.
23 *point d'appui* (pwan dä pwē´): French for "point of support" or "basis of operation."
24 **Nilometer:** instrument used on the Nile for measuring rising flood waters.
25 **Realometer:** Thoreau's coined word to pun on Nilometer and to emphasize the "real" as against the material.

edge dividing you through the heart and marrow, and so you will happily conclude your mortal career. Be it life or death, we crave only reality. If we are really dying, let us hear the rattle in our throats and feel cold in the extremities; if we are alive, let us go about our business.

Time is but the stream I go a-fishing in. I drink at it; but while I drink I see the sandy bottom and detect how shallow it is. Its thin current slides away, but eternity remains. I would drink deeper; fish in the sky, whose bottom is pebbly with stars. I cannot count one. I know not the first letter of the alphabet.

I have always been regretting that I was not as wise as the day I was born. The intellect is a cleaver; it discerns and rifts its way into the secret of things. I do not wish to be any more busy with my hands than is necessary. My head is hands and feet. I feel all my best faculties concentrated in it. My instinct tells me that my head is an organ for burrowing, as some creatures use their snout and forepaws, and with it I would mine and burrow my way through these hills. I think that the richest vein is somewhere hereabouts; so by the divining rod and thin rising vapors I judge; and here I will begin to mine.

Study Questions

1. The selection begins with a discussion of the advantages and disadvantages of owning property and Thoreau's imaginary purchases. What reason did he state for not purchasing the Hollowell farm? Why was Thoreau willing to purchase the Hollowell farm despite his desire to live "free and uncommitted"? How did Thoreau benefit from the farm though he did not purchase it?

2. Thoreau's most direct statement of why he went to the woods is: "I went to the woods because I wished to live deliberately, to front only the essential facts of life." Find examples in the selection which support that statement.

3. Why does Thoreau consider the location of his cabin by the pond's shore as ideal as any faraway, exotic place?

4. What are Thoreau's objections to the way most people spend their lives?

5. Thoreau describes many of his experiences by alluding to natural phenomena, for example, "Morning is when I am awake and there is dawn in me." Find other examples of figurative language which allude to natural occurrences.

Composition

1. One hundred years after the Walden experiment, the following paragraph appeared in *The Atlantic Monthly*:

   In July, 1945, we celebrated the centennial of Henry David Thoreau's retirement to Walden Pond. Almost twice as many people as usual made the pilgrimage to Concord, to see the shrine containing his furniture, and to Walden, where they had the privilege of adding a rock to the cairn where his hut once stood and of opening a box lunch in the picnic ground that stands as his monument. The American Museum of Natural History staged a Walden Pond exhibit. *The Saturday Evening Post* ran an illustrated article. And to add the final mortuary touch, a professor of English published a slim volume called *Walden Revisited*. All in all, it was a typical American literary centennial. Henry Thoreau would probably not have enjoyed it.[1]

   Write a reply to Mr. Hyman in which you explain why you agree or disagree with his view that Thoreau would probably not have enjoyed the celebration. Find examples in the selection by Thoreau to support your position.

2. For a friend, write a description of a favorite place (either real or imaginary) where you go (or would like to go) to be alone. Be sure to include its location, a description of what it looks like, what you do there and what it means to you.

---

[1] Stanley Edgar Hyman, "Henry Thoreau in Our Time," *The Atlantic Monthly,* November, 1946, p. 137.

Frederick Douglass   1817-1895

A classic of early nineteenth-century American literature is Frederick Douglass' narrative about his life as a slave. Douglass was born in 1817 in Maryland. He was taught the rudiments of reading and writing by a kindly slavemaster's wife. When she was reminded of the laws against educating slaves, she stopped. Douglass cleverly continued his learning by challenging local schoolboys to reading and writing duels. He escaped slavery in 1838 and continued to educate himself. In 1841 at an anti-slavery meeting in New Bedford, Massachusetts, he described his brutal experiences as a slave. His eloquence and intellect put him at once in the forefront of the abolitionist crusade. He soon became a paid lecturer and later founded a newspaper, *The North Star*. In 1846, his supporters paid his Maryland master 150 pounds (about $500.00) to make him legally a free man. Douglass eventually asked for something more than freedom—he demanded Black equality as well. In his many articles, books, and speeches he also advocated women's rights, temperance, and fair treatment of all working class people.

   Douglass wrote three autobiographies. An excerpt from the first one, published in 1845, is included here. It is considered a classic in the genre known as the slave narrative. Not only is it a moving and well-written account of a slave's experiences, it is also the story of an extraordinary human.

from Narrative of the Life of Frederick Douglass

FREDERICK DOUGLASS

MY MASTER and myself had quite a number of differences. He found me unsuitable to his purpose. . . . One of my greatest faults was that of letting his horse run away, and go down to his father-in-law's farm, which was about five miles from St. Michael's. I would then have to go after it. My reason for this kind of carelessness, or carefulness, was, that I could always get something to eat when I went there. Master William Hamilton, my master's father-in-law, always gave his slaves enough to eat. I never left there hungry, no matter how great the need of my speedy return. Master Thomas at length said he would stand it no longer. I had lived with him nine months, during which time he had given me a number of severe whippings, all to no good purpose. He resolved to put me out, as he said, to be broken; and, for this purpose, he let me for one year to a man named Edward Covey.

Mr. Covey was a poor man, a farm-renter. He rented the place upon which he lived, as also the hands with which he tilled it. Mr. Covey had acquired a very high reputation for breaking young slaves, and this reputation was of immense value to him. It enabled him to get his farm tilled with much less expense to himself than he could have had it done without such a reputation. Some slaveholders thought it not much loss to allow Mr. Covey to have their slaves one year, for the sake of the training to which they were subjected, without any other compensation. He could hire young help with great ease, in consequence of this reputation. Added to the natural good qualities of Mr. Covey, he was a professor of religion—a pious soul—a member and a class-leader in the Methodist church. All of this added weight to his reputation as a "nigger-breaker." I was aware of all the facts, having been made acquainted with them by a young man who had lived there. I nevertheless made the change gladly; for I was sure of getting enough to eat, which is not the smallest consideration to a hungry man.

I left Master Thomas's house, and went to live with Mr. Covey, on the 1st of January, 1833. I was now, for the first time in my life, a field hand. . . . If at any one time of my life more than another, I was made to drink the bitterest dregs of slavery, that time was during the first six months of my stay with Mr. Covey. We were worked in all weathers. It was never too hot or too cold; it could never rain, blow, hail, or snow, too hard for us to work in the field. Work, work, work, was scarcely more the order of the day than of the night. The longest days were too short for him, and the shortest nights too long for him. I was somewhat unmanageable when I first went there, but a few months of this discipline tamed me. Mr. Covey succeeded in breaking me. I was broken in body, soul, and spirit. My natural elasticity was crushed, my intellect languished, the disposition to read departed, the cheerful spark that lingered about my eye died; the dark night of slavery closed in upon me; and behold a man transformed into a brute!

Sunday was my only leisure time. I spent this in a sort of beast-like stupor, between sleep and wake, under some large tree. At times I would rise up, a flash of energetic freedom would dart through my soul, accompanied with a faint beam of hope, that flickered for a moment, and then vanished. I sank down again, mourning over my wretched condition. I was sometimes prompted to take my life, and that of Covey, but was prevented by a combination of hope and fear. My sufferings on this plantation seem now like a dream rather than a stern reality.

Our house stood within a few rods of the Chesapeake Bay, whose broad bosom was ever white with sails from every quarter of the habitable globe. Those beautiful vessels, robed in purest white, so delightful to the eye of freemen, were to me so many shrouded ghosts, to terrify and torment me with thoughts of my wretched condition. I have often, in the deep stillness of a summer's Sabbath, stood all alone upon the lofty banks of that noble bay, and traced, with saddened heart and tearful eye, the countless number of sails moving off to the mighty ocean. The sight of these always affected me powerfully. My thoughts would compel utterance; and there, with no audience but the Almighty, I would pour out my soul's complaint, in my rude way, with an apostrophe to the moving multitude of ships:

"You are loosed from your moorings, and are free; I am fast in my chains, and am a slave! You move merrily before the gentle gale, and I sadly before the bloody whip! You are freedom's swift-winged angels, that fly round the world; I am confined in bands of iron! O that I were free! O, that I were on one of your gallant decks, and under your protecting wing! Alas! betwixt me and you, the turbid waters roll. Go on, go on. O that I could also go! Could I but swim! If I could fly! O, why was I born a man, of whom to make a brute! The glad ship is gone; she hides in the dim distance. I am left in the hottest hell of unending slavery. O God, save me! God, deliver me! Let me be free! Is there any God? Why am I a slave? I will run away. I will not stand it. Get caught, or get clear, I'll try it. . . . I have only one life to lose. I had as well be killed running as die standing. Only think of it; one hundred miles straight north, and I am free! Try it? Yes! God helping me, I will. It cannot be that I shall live and die a slave. I will take to the water. This very bay shall yet bear me into freedom. The steamboats steered in a north-east course from North Point. I will do the same; and when I get to the head of the bay, I will turn my canoe adrift, and walk straight through Delaware into Pennsylvania. When I get there, I shall not be required to have a pass; I can travel without being disturbed. Let but the first opportunity offer, and, come what will, I am off. Meanwhile, I will try to bear up under the yoke. I am not the only slave in the world. Why should I fret? I can bear as much as any of them. Besides, I am but a boy, and all boys are bound to some one. It may be that my misery in slavery will only increase my happiness when I get free. There is a better day coming."

Thus I used to think, and thus I used to speak to myself; goaded almost to madness at one moment, and at the next reconciling myself to my wretched lot.

I have already intimated that my condition was much worse, during the first six months of my stay at Mr. Covey's, than in the last six. The circumstances leading to the change in Mr. Covey's course toward me form an epoch in my humble history. You have seen how a man was made a slave; you shall see how a slave was made a man.

On one of the hottest days of the month of August, 1833, Bill Smith, William Hughes, a slave named Eli, and myself, were engaged in fanning wheat. Hughes was clearing the fanned wheat from before the fan. Eli was turning, Smith was feeding, and I was carrying wheat to the fan. The work was simple, requiring strength rather than intellect; yet, to one entirely unused to such work, it came very hard. About three o'clock of that day, I broke down; my strength failed me; I was seized with a violent aching of the head, attended with extreme dizziness; I trembled in every limb. Finding what was coming, I nerved myself up, feeling it would never do to stop work. I stood as long as I could stagger to the hopper with grain. When I could stand no longer, I fell, and felt as if held down by an immense weight. The fan of course stopped; every one had his own work to do; and no one could do the work of the other, and have his own go on at the same time.

Mr. Covey was at the house, about one hundred yards from the treading-yard where we were fanning. On hearing the fan stop, he left immediately, and came to the spot where we were. He hastily inquired what the matter was. Bill answered that I was sick, and there was no one to bring wheat to the fan. I had by this time crawled away under the side of the post and rail-fence by which the yard was enclosed, hoping to find relief by getting out of the sun. He then asked where I was. He was told by one of the hands. He came to the spot, and, after looking at me awhile, asked me what was the matter. I told him as well as I could, for I scarce had strength to speak. He then gave me a savage kick in the side, and told me to get up. I tried to do so, but fell back in the attempt. He gave me another kick, and again told me to rise. I again tried, and succeeded in gaining my feet; but, stooping to get the tub with which I was feeding the fan, I again staggered and fell. While down in this situation, Mr. Covey took up the hickory slat with which Hughes had been striking off the half-bushel measure, and with it gave me a heavy blow upon the head, making a large wound, and the blood ran freely; and with this again told me to get up. I made no effort to comply, having now made up my mind to let him do his worst. In a short time after receiving this blow, my head grew better. Mr. Covey had now left me to my fate. . . .

I spent [the next] day mostly in the woods, having the alternative before me,—to go home and be whipped to death, or stay in the woods and be starved to death. That night, I fell in with Sandy Jenkins, a slave with whom I was somewhat acquainted. Sandy had a free wife who lived about four miles from Mr. Covey's; and it being Saturday, he was on his way to see her. I told him my circumstances, and he very kindly invited me to go home with him. I went home with him, and talked this whole matter over, and got his advice as to what course it was best for me to pursue. I found Sandy an old adviser. He told me, with great solemnity, I must go back to Covey; but that before I went, I must go with him into another part of the woods, where there was a certain *root,* which, if I would take some of it with me, carrying it *always on my right side,* would render it impossible for Mr. Covey, or any other white man, to whip me. He said he had carried it for years; and since he had done so, he had never received a blow, and never expected to while he carried it. I at first rejected the idea, that the simple carrying of a root in my pocket would have any such effect as he had said, and was not disposed to take it; but Sandy impressed the necessity with much earnestness, telling me it could do no harm, if it did no good.

To please him, I at length took the root, and, according to his direction, carried it upon my right side. This was Sunday morning. I immediately started for home; and upon entering the yard gate, out came Mr. Covey on his way to meeting. He spoke to me very kindly, bade me drive the pigs from a lot nearby, and passed on towards the church. Now, this singular conduct of Mr. Covey really made me begin to think that there was something in the *root* which Sandy had given me; and had it been on any other day than Sunday, I could have attributed the conduct to no other cause than the influence of that *root;* and as it was, I was half inclined to think the *root* to be something more than I at first had taken it to be.

All went well till Monday morning. On this morning, the virtue of the *root* was fully tested. Long before daylight, I was called to go and rub, curry, and feed, the horses. I obeyed, and was glad to obey. But whilst thus engaged, whilst in the act of throwing down some blades from the loft, Mr. Covey entered the stable with a long rope; and just as I was half out of the loft, he caught hold of my legs, and was about tying me. As soon as I found what he was up to, I gave a sudden spring, and as I did so, he holding to my legs, I was brought sprawling on the stable floor. Mr. Covey seemed now to think he had me, and could do what he pleased; but at this moment—from whence came the spirit I don't know—I resolved to fight; and, suiting my action to the resolution, I seized Covey hard by the throat; and as I did so, I rose. He held on to me, and I to him. My resistance was so entirely unexpected, that Covey seemed taken all aback. He trembled like a leaf. This gave me assurance, and I held him. . . . He asked me if I meant to persist in my resistance. I told him I did, come what might; that he had used me like a brute for six months, and that I was determined to be used so no longer. With that, he strove to drag me to a stick that was lying just out of the stable door. He meant to knock me down. But just as he was leaning over to get the stick, I seized him with both hands by his collar, and brought him by a sudden snatch to the ground. By this time, Bill came. Covey called upon him for assistance. Bill wanted to know what he could do. Covey said, "Take hold of him, take hold of him!" Bill said his master hired him out to work, and not to help to whip me; so he left Covey and myself to fight our own battle out. We were at it for nearly two hours. Covey at length let me go, puffing and blowing at a great rate, saying that if I had not resisted, he would not have whipped me half so much. The truth was, that he had not whipped me at all. I considered him as getting entirely the worst end of the bargain; for he had drawn no blood from me, but I had from him. The whole six months afterwards, that I spent with Mr. Covey, he never laid the weight of his finger upon me in anger. He would occasionally say, he didn't want to get hold of me again. "No," thought I, "you need not; for you will come off worse than you did before."

This battle with Mr. Covey was the turning-point in my career as a slave. It rekindled the few expiring embers of freedom, and revived within me a sense of my own manhood. It recalled the departed self-confidence, and inspired me again with a determination to be free. The gratification afforded by the triumph was a full compensation for whatever else might follow, even death itself. He only can understand the deep satisfaction which I experienced, who has himself repelled by force the bloody arm of slavery. I felt as I never felt before. It was a glorious resurrection, from the tomb of slavery, to the heaven of freedom. My long-crushed spirit rose, cowardice departed, bold defiance took its place; and I now resolved that, however long I might remain a slave in form, the day had passed forever when I could be a slave in fact. I did not hesitate to let it be known of me, that the white man who expected to succeed in whipping, must also succeed in killing me.

From this time I was never again what might be called fairly whipped, though I remained a slave four years afterwards. I had several fights, but was never whipped.

Study Questions

1. Why is Douglass sent to Edward Covey's farm by his former master, Thomas Auld?
2. During his Sunday leisure time why did Douglass admire the ships in Chesapeake Bay?
3. What happens to change Douglass' final six months with Covey?
4. What does Douglass mean by the statement, "However long I might remain a slave in form, the day had passed forever when I could be a slave in fact"?
5. Why do you think Douglass was able to get away with this resistance to Covey?

Composition

1. Frederick Douglass wrote a great many letters to friends and people he admired. Write a letter such as Douglass might have written to Emerson praising or condemning "Self-Reliance." Select two or three specific points in "Self-Reliance" for Douglass to comment on. Make sure that Douglass' attitude is consistent with the information you have about him.
2. Frederick Douglass was an extraordinary human who succeeded despite seemingly insurmountable barriers. Write a description of someone extraordinary whom you know, or know about. Tell what the obstacles were which this person had to overcome. Tell how she or he managed to overcome the obstacles. Conclude by describing her or his achievement.

Vocabulary

A **suffix** is a letter or series of letters added to the end of a word (a) to change the word's meaning, (b) to create a derivative of the word, or, most often, (c) to do both.

1. In a dictionary, find the meanings of these two suffixes: *-ation* and *-tion.* Write these meanings on a separate sheet of paper.
2. a. Find and copy a short definition for each of the following words:

   compensate   gratify   resolve
   determine   intimidate   violate

   b. After having defined each of the above words, write its derivative as formed by the addition of either *-ation* or *-tion,* whichever suffix is used to change that verb into a noun. For example:

   combine: to join or mix together
   combination
   (Note that as in *combination,* the addition of a suffix may require an adjustment in the spelling of the original word.)

Frances Watkins Harper   1825-1911

Although she was free, Frances Watkins Harper never forgot that other Blacks were enslaved. She was born in Baltimore and educated in Pennsylvania and Ohio. For many years she was an effective lecturer and poetic orator for the Anti-Slavery Society. She began her literary career with the publication of *Poems on Miscellaneous Subjects* in 1854. This popular book went through twenty editions by 1874. She also wrote short stories and a novel, *Iola Leroy* (1892). Frances Harper is best remembered for her anti–slavery poetry which was so effective in her abolitionist work. The following poem depicts in style and tone the effectiveness of her poetical oratory.

Bury Me in a Free Land

FRANCES WATKINS HARPER

Make me a grave where'er you will,
In a lowly plain, or a lofty hill;
Make it among earth's humblest graves,
But not in a land where men are slaves.

I could not rest if around my grave   5
I heard the steps of a trembling slave;
His shadow above my silent tomb
Would make it a place of fearful gloom.

I could not rest if I heard the tread
Of a coffle[1] gang to the shambles[2] led,   10
And the mother's shriek of wild despair
Rise like a curse on the trembling air.

I could not sleep if I saw the lash
Drinking her blood at each fearful gash,
And I saw her babes torn from her breast,   15
Like trembling doves torn from their parent nest.

I'd shudder and start if I heard the bay
Of bloodhounds seizing their human prey,
And I heard the captive plead in vain
As they bound afresh his galling chain.   20

---

1 **coffle:** group of slaves chained together.
2 **shambles:** a slaughterhouse or scene of mass destruction.

If I saw young girls from their mother's arms
Bartered and sold for their youthful charms,
My eye would flash with a mournful flame,
My death-paled cheek grow red with shame.

I would sleep, dear friends, where bloated might   25
Can rob no man of his dearest right;
My rest shall be calm in any grave
Where none can call his brother a slave.

I ask no monument, proud and high,
To arrest the gaze of the passers-by;   30
All that my yearning spirit craves,
Is bury me not in a land of slaves.

Study Questions

1. In this poem, Harper contemplates her death and burial. What are her concerns?
2. How does the speaker make her feeling about slavery vivid for the reader?
3. Why do you think this poem was effective in the anti-slavery movement?

Herman Melville   1819-1891

At an early age, Herman Melville decided
to go to sea. For five years, between 1839
and 1844, he was a sailor acquiring a rich
experience and reading constantly in his
spare time. Encouraged by family and
friends to describe his adventures, Melville
wrote *Typee* (1846). This fictionalized account of his brief stay in the Marquesas
Islands became a popular success. He then
exploited his sailing life in three more
loosely autobiographical narratives: *Omoo,
Redburn,* and *White-Jacket.* These made him
a well-known literary figure.

Melville was ambitious to be more than
an adventure writer. He aspired to probe
the very secrets of God and nature. In 1851
his masterpiece, *Moby Dick,* was published.
Moby Dick is a story in which a whaling
voyage becomes the image of man's struggle
against the forces of the universe. This is
considered one of the world's great books.
When it was first published, its philosophy
and its symbolism baffled many readers.
They preferred the straightforward sea
stories they had come to expect from
Melville. After his next novel, *Pierre* (1852),
had also failed with the public, Melville felt
estranged from American society. He
refused to write what the public wanted, and
they refused to read what he gave them.
This estrangement is reflected in the story
that follows, "Bartleby the Scrivener" (1853).
Although Melville was yet to write most of
his poetry and his fine short novel, *Billy
Budd,* he never regained his early popularity.
Only since the 1920s has his greatness been
rediscovered. Like Bartleby, Melville was
asleep "with kings and counselors" before
the world knew him for the great writer he
was.

Bartleby the Scrivener

A STORY OF WALL STREET

HERMAN MELVILLE

I AM A RATHER elderly man. The nature of my avocations, for the last thirty years, has brought me into more than ordinary contact with what would seem an interesting and somewhat singular set of men, of whom, as yet, nothing, that I know of, has ever been written—I mean, the law-copyist, or scriveners. I have known very many of them, professionally and privately, and, if I pleased, could relate divers histories, at which good-natured gentlemen might smile, and sentimental souls might weep. But I waive the biographies of all other scriveners, for a few passages in the life of Bartleby, who was a scrivener, the strangest I ever saw, or heard of. While, of other law-copyists, I might write the complete life, of Bartleby nothing of that sort can be done. I believe that no materials exist for a full and satisfactory biography of this man. It is an irreparable loss to literature. Bartleby was one of those beings of whom nothing is ascertainable, except from the original sources, and, in his case, those are very small. What my own astonished eyes saw of Bartleby, *that* is all I know of him, except, indeed, one vague report, which will appear in the sequel.

Ere introducing the scrivener, as he first appeared to me, it is fit I make some mention of myself, my employees, my business, my chambers, and general surroundings; because some such description is indispensable to an adequate understanding of the chief character about to be presented. *Imprimis:*[1] I am a man who, from his youth upwards, has been filled with a profound conviction that the easiest way of life is the best. Hence, though I belong to a profession proverbially energetic and nervous, even to turbulence, at times, yet nothing of that sort have I ever suffered to invade my peace. I am one of those unambitious lawyers who never addresses a jury, or in any way draws down public applause; but, in the cool tranquillity of a snug retreat, do a snug business among rich men's bonds, and mortgages, and title deeds. All who know me, consider me an eminently *safe* man. The late John Jacob Astor,[2] a personage little given to poetic enthusiasm, had no hesitation in pronouncing my first grand point to be prudence; my next, method. I do not speak it in vanity, but simply record the fact, that I was not unemployed in my profession by the late John Jacob Astor; a name which, I admit, I love to repeat; for it hath a rounded and orbicular sound to it, and rings like unto bullion. I will freely add, that I was not insensible to the late John Jacob Astor's good opinion.

Some time prior to the period at which this little history begins, my avocations had been largely increased. The good old office, now extinct in the State of New York, of a Master in Chancery, had been conferred upon me. It was not a very arduous office, but very pleasantly remunerative. I seldom lose my temper; much more seldom indulge in dangerous indignation at wrongs and outrages; but, I must be permitted to be rash here, and declare, that I

---

1 **Imprimis** (im pri′ məs): Latin for "in the first place."

2 **John Jacob Astor**: financier and fur merchant (1763–1848).

consider the sudden and violent abrogation of the office of Master in Chancery, by the new constitution, as a——premature act; inasmuch as I had counted upon a life-lease of the profits, whereas I only received those of a few short years. But this is by the way.

My chambers were up stairs, at No.—Wall Street. At one end, they looked upon the white wall of the interior of a spacious skylight shaft, penetrating the building from top to bottom.

This view might have been considered rather tame than otherwise, deficient in what landscape painters call "life." But, if so, the view from the other end of my chambers offered at least, a contrast, if nothing more. In that direction, my windows commanded an unobstructed view of a lofty brick wall, black by age and everlasting shade; which wall required no spyglass to bring out its lurking beauties, but, for the benefit of all nearsighted spectators, was pushed up to within ten feet of my windowpanes. Owing to the great height of the surrounding buildings, and my chambers being on the second floor, the interval between this wall and mine not a little resembled a huge square cistern.

At the period just preceding the advent of Bartleby, I had two persons as copyists in my employment, and a promising lad as an office boy. First, Turkey; second, Nippers; third, Ginger Nut. These may seem names the like of which are not usually found in the Directory. In truth, they were nicknames, mutually conferred upon each other by my three clerks, and were deemed expressive of their respective persons or characters. Turkey was a short, pursy[3] Englishman, of about my own age—that is, somewhere not far from sixty. In the morning, one might say, his face was of a fine florid hue, but after twelve o'clock, meridian—his dinner hour—it blazed like a grate full of Christmas coals; and continued blazing—but, as it were, with a gradual wane—till six o'clock, P.M., or thereabouts; after which, I

3 **pursy**: short-winded and fat.

saw no more of the proprietor of the face, which, gaining its meridian with the sun, seemed to set with it, to rise, culminate, and decline the following day, with the like regularity and undiminished glory. There are many singular coincidences I have known in the course of my life, not the least among which was the fact that, exactly when Turkey displayed his fullest beams from his red and radiant countenance, just then, too, at that critical moment, began the daily period when I considered his business capacities as seriously disturbed for the remainder of the twenty-four hours. Not that he was absolutely idle, or averse to business, then; far from it. The difficulty was, he was apt to be altogether too energetic. There was a strange, inflamed, flurried, flighty recklessness of activity about him. He would be incautious in dipping his pen into his inkstand. All his blots upon my documents were dropped there after twelve o'clock, meridian. Indeed, not only would he be reckless, and sadly given to making blots in the afternoon, but, some days, he went further, and was rather noisy. At such times, too, his face flamed with augmented blazonry, as if cannel coal[4] had been heaped on anthracite. He made an unpleasant racket with his chair; spilled his sandbox;[5] in mending his pens, impatiently split them all to pieces, and threw them on the floor in a sudden passion; stood up, and leaned over his table, boxing his papers about in a most indecorous manner, very sad to behold in an elderly man like him. Nevertheless, as he was in many ways a most valuable person to me, and all the time before twelve o'clock, meridian, was the quickest, steadiest creature, too, accomplishing a great deal of work in a style not easily to be matched—for these reasons, I was willing to overlook his eccentricities, though, indeed, occasionally, I remonstrated with him. I did this very gently,

4 **cannel coal**: a brightly burning coal.
5 **sandbox**: container holding sand for sprinkling on wet ink.

however, because, though the civilest, nay, the blandest and most reverential of men in the morning, yet, in the afternoon, he was disposed, upon provocation, to be slightly rash with his tongue—in fact, insolent. Now, valuing his morning services as I did, and resolved not to lose them—yet, at the same time, made uncomfortable by his inflamed ways after twelve o'clock—and being a man of peace, unwilling by my admonitions to call forth unseemly retorts from him, I took upon me, one Saturday noon (he was always worse on Saturdays) to hint to him, very kindly, that, perhaps, now that he was growing old, it might be well to abridge his labors; in short, he need not come to my chambers after twelve o'clock, but, dinner over, had best go home to his lodging, and rest himself till teatime. But no; he insisted upon his afternoon devotions. His countenance became intolerably fervid, as he oratorically assured me—gesticulating with a long ruler at the other end of the room—that if his services in the morning were useful, how indispensable, then, in the afternoon?

"With submission, sir," said Turkey, on this occasion, "I consider myself your right-hand man. In the morning I but marshal and deploy my columns; but in the afternoon I put myself at their head, and gallantly charge the foe, thus"—and he made a violent thrust with the ruler.

"But the blots, Turkey," intimated I.

"True; but, with submission, sir, behold these hairs! I am getting old. Surely, sir, a blot or two of a warm afternoon is not to be severely urged against gray hairs. Old age—even if it blot the page—is honorable. With submission, sir, we *both* are getting old."

This appeal to my fellow feeling was hardly to be resisted. At all events, I saw that go he would not. So, I made up my mind to let him stay, resolving, nevertheless, to see to it that, during the afternoon, he had to do with my less important papers.

Nippers, the second on my list, was a whiskered, sallow, and, upon the whole,

rather piratical-looking young man, of about five and twenty. I always deemed him the victim of two evil powers—ambition and indigestion. The ambition was evinced by a certain impatience of the duties of a mere copyist, an unwarrantable usurpation of strictly professional affairs, such as the original drawing up of legal documents. The indigestion seemed betokened in an occasional nervous testiness and grinning irritability, causing the teeth to audibly grind together over mistakes committed in copying; unnecessary maledictions, hissed, rather than spoken, in the heat of business; and especially by a continual discontent with the height of the table where he worked. Though of a very ingenious mechanical turn, Nippers could never get this table to suit him. He put chips under it, blocks of various sorts, bits of pasteboard, and at last went so far as to attempt an exquisite adjustment, by final pieces of folded blotting paper. But no invention would answer. If, for the sake of easing his back, he brought the table lid at a sharp angle well up towards his chin, and wrote there like a man using the steep roof of a Dutch house for his desk, then he declared that it stopped the circulation in his arms. If now he lowered the table to his waistbands, and stooped over it in writing, then there was a sore aching in his back. In short, the truth of the matter was, Nippers knew not what he wanted. Or, if he wanted anything, it was to be rid of a scrivener's table altogether. Among the manifestations of his diseased ambition was a fondness he had for receiving visits from certain ambiguous-looking fellows in seedy coats, whom he called his clients. Indeed, I was aware that not only was he, at times, considerable of a ward-politician, but he occasionally did a little business at the Justices' courts, and was not unknown on the steps of the Tombs.[6] I have good reason to believe, however, that one individual who called upon him at my chambers, and who, with a grand air, he insisted was his client, was no

---

6 the Tombs: a prison.

other than a dun, and the alleged title deed, a bill. But, with all his failings, and the annoyances he caused me, Nippers, like his compatriot Turkey, was a very useful man to me; wrote a neat, swift hand; and, when he chose, was not deficient in a gentlemanly sort of deportment. Added to this, he always dressed in a gentlemanly sort of way; and so, incidentally, reflected credit upon my chambers. Whereas, with respect to Turkey, I had much ado to keep him from being a reproach to me. His clothes were apt to look oily, and smell of eating houses. He wore his pantaloons very loose and baggy in summer. His coats were execrable; his hat was not to be handled. But while the hat was a thing of indifference to me, inasmuch as his natural civility and deference, as a dependent Englishman, always led him to doff it the moment he entered the room, yet his coat was another matter. Concerning his coats, I reasoned with him; but with no effect. The truth was, I suppose, that a man with so small an income could not afford to sport such a lustrous face and a lustrous coat at one and the same time. As Nippers once observed, Turkey's money went chiefly for red ink. One winter day I presented Turkey with a highly respectable-looking coat of my own—a padded gray coat, of a most comfortable warmth, and which buttoned straight up from the knee to the neck. I thought Turkey would appreciate the favor, and abate his rashness and obstreperousness of afternoons. But no; I verily believe that buttoning himself up in so downy and blanketlike a coat had a pernicious effect upon him—upon the same principle that too much oats are bad for horses. In fact, precisely as a rash, restive horse is said to feel his oats, so Turkey felt his coat. It made him insolent. He was a man whom prosperity harmed.

Though, concerning the self-indulgent habits of Turkey, I had my own private surmises, yet, touching Nippers, I was well persuaded that, whatever might be his faults in other respects, he was, at least, a temperate young man. But, indeed, nature herself seemed to have

been his vintner,[7] and, at his birth, charged him so thoroughly with an irritable, brandy-like disposition, that all subsequent potations[8] were needless. When I consider how, amid the stillness of my chambers, Nippers would sometimes impatiently rise from his seat, and, stooping over his table, spread his arms wide apart, seize the whole desk, and move it, and jerk it, with a grim, grinding motion on the floor, as if the table were a perverse voluntary agent, intent on thwarting and vexing him, I plainly perceive that, for Nippers, brandy and water were altogether superfluous.

It was fortunate for me that, owing to its peculiar cause—indigestion—the irritability and consequent nervousness of Nippers were mainly observable in the morning, while in the afternoon he was comparatively mild. So that, Turkey's paroxysms only coming on about twelve o'clock, I never had to do with their eccentricities at one time. Their fits relieved each other, like guards. When Nippers's was on, Turkey's was off; and vice versa. This was a good natural arrangement, under the circumstances.

Ginger Nut, the third on my list, was a lad, some twelve years old. His father was a car-man, ambitious of seeing his son on the bench instead of a car, before he died. So he sent him to my office, as student at law, errand boy, cleaner and sweeper, at the rate of one dollar a week. He had a little desk to himself, but he did not use it much. Upon inspection, the drawer exhibited a great array of the shells of various sorts of nuts. Indeed, to this quick-witted youth, the whole noble science of the law was contained in a nutshell. Not the least among the employments of Ginger Nut, as well as one which he discharged with the most alacrity, was his duty as cake and apple purveyor for Turkey and Nippers. Copying law papers being proverbially a dry, husky sort of business, my two scriveners were fain to

moisten their mouths very often with Spitzenburgs,[9] to be had at the numerous stalls nigh the Custom House and Post Office. Also, they sent Ginger Nut very frequently for that peculiar cake—small, flat, round, and very spicy—after which he had been named by them. Of a cold morning, when business was but dull, Turkey would gobble up scores of these cakes, as if they were mere wafers—indeed, they sell them at the rate of six or eight for a penny—the scrape of his pen blending with the crunching of the crisp particles in his mouth. Of all the fiery afternoon blunders and

7 **vintner:** wine merchant.
8 **potations:** alcoholic drinks.

9 **Spitzenburgs:** A spitzenburg is a kind of apple.

flurried rashnesses of Turkey, was his once moistening a ginger cake between his lips, and clapping it on to a mortgage, for a seal. I came within an ace of dismissing him then. But he mollified me by making an Oriental bow, and saying—

"With submission, sir, it was generous of me to find you in stationery of my own account."

Now my original business—that of a conveyancer and title hunter, and drawer-up of recondite[10] documents of all sorts—was considerably increased by receiving the master's office. There was now great work for scriveners. Not only must I push the clerks already with me, but I must have additional help.

In answer to my advertisement, a motionless young man one morning stood upon my office threshold, the door being open, for it was summer. I can see that figure now—pallidly neat, pitiably respectable, incurably forlorn! It was Bartleby.

After a few words touching his qualifications, I engaged him, glad to have among my corps of copyists a man of so singularly sedate an aspect, which I thought might operate beneficially upon the flighty temper of Turkey, and the fiery one of Nippers.

---

10 **recondite** (reK′ ən dit, ri kon′ dit): obscure; hard to understand.

I should have stated before that ground glass folding doors divided my premises into two parts, one of which was occupied by my scriveners, the other by myself. According to my humor, I threw open these doors, or closed them. I resolved to assign Bartleby a corner by the folding doors, but on my side of them, so as to have this quiet man within easy call, in case any trifling thing was to be done. I placed his desk close up to a small side window in that part of the room, a window which originally had afforded a lateral view of certain grimy back yards and bricks, but which, owing to subsequent erections, commanded at present no view at all, though it gave some light. Within three feet of the panes was a wall, and the light came down from far above, between two lofty buildings, as from a very small opening in a dome. Still further to a satisfactory arrangement, I procured a high green folding screen, which might entirely isolate Bartleby from my sight, though not remove him from my voice. And thus, in a manner, privacy and society were conjoined.

At first, Bartleby did an extraordinary quantity of writing. As if long famishing for something to copy, he seemed to gorge himself on my documents. There was no pause for digestion. He ran a day and night line, copying by sunlight and by candlelight. I should have been quite delighted with his application, had he been cheerfully industrious. But he wrote on silently, palely, mechanically.

It is, of course, an indispensable part of a scrivener's business to verify the accuracy of his copy, word by word. Where there are two or more scriveners in an office, they assist each other in this examination, one reading from the copy, the other holding the original. It is a very dull, wearisome, and lethargic affair. I can readily imagine that, to some sanguine[11] temperaments, it would be altogether intoler-able. For example, I cannot credit that the mettlesome poet, Byron,[12] would have contentedly sat down with Bartleby to examine a law document of, say five hundred pages, closely written in a crimpy hand.

Now and then, in the haste of business, it had been my habit to assist in comparing some brief document myself, calling Turkey or Nippers for this purpose. One object I had, in placing Bartleby so handy to me behind the screen, was, to avail myself of his services on such trivial occasions. It was on the third day, I think, of his being with me, and before any necessity had arisen for having his own writing examined, that, being much hurried to complete a small affair I had in hand, I abruptly called to Bartleby. In my haste and natural expectancy of instant compliance, I sat with my head bent over the original on my desk, and my right hand sideways, and somewhat nervously extended with the copy, so that, immediately upon emerging from his retreat, Bartleby might snatch it and proceed to business without the least delay.

In this very attitude did I sit when I called to him, rapidly stating what it was I wanted him to do—namely, to examine a small paper with me. Imagine my surprise, nay, my consternation, when, without moving from his privacy, Bartleby, in a singularly mild, firm voice, replied, "I would prefer not to."

I sat awhile in perfect silence, rallying my stunned faculties. Immediately it occurred to me that my ears had deceived me, or Bartleby had entirely misunderstood my meaning. I repeated my request in the clearest tone I could assume; but in quite as clear a one came the previous reply, "I would prefer not to."

"Prefer not to," echoed I, rising in high excitement, and crossing the room with a stride. "What do you mean? Are you moonstruck? I want you to help me prepare this

---

11 **sanguine** (sang' gwən): here, active; cheerful, energetic.

12 **Byron**: George Gordon, Lord Byron (1788–1824), a British poet noted for his nervous, energetic character.

sheet here—take it," and I thrust it towards him.

"I would prefer not to," said he.

I looked at him steadfastly. His face was leanly composed; his gray eye dimly calm. Not a wrinkle of agitation rippled him. Had there been the least uneasiness, anger, impatience or impertinence in his manner; in other words, had there been any thing ordinarily human about him, doubtless I should have violently dismissed him from the premises. But as it was, I should have as soon thought of turning my pale plaster-of-paris bust of Cicero out of doors. I stood gazing at him awhile, as he went on with his own writing, and then reseated myself at my desk. This is very strange, thought I. What had one best do? But my business hurried me. I concluded to forget the matter for the present, reserving it for my future leisure. So calling Nippers from the other room, the paper was speedily examined.

A few days after this, Bartleby concluded four lengthy documents, being quadruplicates of a week's testimony taken before me in my High Court of Chancery. It became necessary to examine them. It was an important suit, and great accuracy was imperative. Having all things arranged, I called Turkey, Nippers, and Ginger Nut, from the next room, meaning to place the four copies in the hands of my four clerks, while I should read from the original. Accordingly, Turkey, Nippers, and Ginger Nut had taken their seats in a row, each with his document in his hand, when I called to Bartleby to join this interesting group.

"Bartleby! quick, I am waiting."

I heard a slow scrape of his chair legs on the uncarpeted floor, and soon he appeared standing at the entrance of his hermitage.

"What is wanted?" said he, mildly.

"The copies, the copies," said I, hurriedly. "We are going to examine them. There"— and I held towards him the fourth quadruplicate.

"I would prefer not to," he said, and gently disappeared behind the screen.

For a few moments I was turned into a pillar of salt,[13] standing at the head of my seated column of clerks. Recovering myself, I advanced towards the screen, and demanded the reason for such extraordinary conduct.

"*Why* do you refuse?"

"I would prefer not to."

With any other man I should have flown outright into a dreadful passion, scorned all further words, and thrust him ignominiously from my presence. But there was something about Bartleby that not only strangely disarmed me, but, in a wonderful manner, touched and disconcerted me. I began to reason with him.

"These are your own copies we are about to examine. It is laborsaving to you, because one examination will answer for your four papers. It is common usage. Every copyist is bound to help examine his copy. Is it not so? Will you not speak? Answer!"

"I prefer not to," he replied in a flutelike tone. It seemed to me that, while I had been addressing him, he carefully revolved every statement that I made; fully comprehended the meaning; could not gainsay[14] the irresistible conclusion; but, at the same time, some paramount consideration prevailed with him to reply as he did.

"You are decided, then, not to comply with my request—a request made according to common usage and common sense?"

He briefly gave me to understand, that on that point my judgment was sound. Yes: his decision was irreversible.

It is not seldom the case that, when a man is browbeaten in some unprecedented and violently unreasonable way, he begins to stagger in his own plainest faith. He begins, as it were, vaguely to surmise that, wonderful as it may be, all the justice and all the reason is on the other side. Accordingly, if any disinterested

---

13 **pillar of salt:** See the *Bible,* Genesis 19:26.
14 **gainsay:** dispute or deny.

persons are present, he turns to them for some reinforcement for his own faltering mind.

"Turkey," said I, "what do you think of this? Am I not right?"

"With submission, sir," said Turkey, in his blandest tone, "I think that you are."

"Nippers," said I, "what do *you* think of it?"

"I think I should kick him out of the office."

(The reader, of nice[15] perceptions, will here perceive that, it being morning, Turkey's answer is couched in polite and tranquil terms, but Nippers replies in ill-tempered ones. Or, to repeat a previous sentence, Nippers's ugly mood was on duty, and Turkey's off.)

"Ginger Nut," said I, willing to enlist the smallest suffrage[16] in my behalf, "what do *you* think of it?"

"I think, sir, he's a little *luny*," replied Ginger Nut, with a grin.

"You hear what they say," said I, turning towards the screen, "come forth and do your duty."

But he vouchsafed no reply. I pondered a moment in sore perplexity. But once more business hurried me. I determined again to postpone the consideration of this dilemma to my future leisure. With a little trouble we made out to examine the papers without Bartleby, though at every page or two Turkey deferentially dropped his opinion, that this proceeding was quite out of the common; while Nippers, twitching in his chair with a dyspeptic nervousness, ground out, between his set teeth, occasional hissing maledictions against the stubborn oaf behind the screen. And for his (Nippers's) part, this was the first and the last time he would do another man's business without pay.

Meanwhile Bartleby sat in his hermitage, oblivious to everything but his own peculiar business there.

Some days passed, the scrivener being employed upon another lengthy work. His late remarkable conduct led me to regard his ways narrowly. I observed that he never went to dinner; indeed, that he never went anywhere. As yet I had never, of my personal knowledge, known him to be outside of my office. He was a perpetual sentry in the corner. At about eleven o'clock though, in the morning, I noticed that Ginger Nut would advance toward the opening in Bartleby's screen, as if silently beckoned thither by a gesture invisible to me where I sat. The boy would then leave the office, jingling a few pence, and reappear with a handful of gingernuts, which he delivered in the hermitage, receiving two of the cakes for his trouble.

He lives, then, on gingernuts, thought I; never eats a dinner, properly speaking; he must be a vegetarian, then; but no; he never eats even vegetables, he eats nothing but gingernuts. My mind then ran on in reveries concerning the probable effects upon the human constitution of living entirely on gingernuts. Gingernuts are so called, because they contain ginger as one of their peculiar constituents, and the final flavoring one. Now, what was ginger? A hot, spicy thing. Was Bartleby hot and spicy? Not at all. Ginger, then, had no effect upon Bartlebly. Probably he preferred it should have none.

Nothing so aggravates an earnest person as a passive resistance. If the individual so resisted be of a not inhumane temper, and the resisting one perfectly harmless in his passivity, then, in the better moods of the former, he will endeavor charitably to construe to his imagination what proves impossible to be solved by his judgment. Even so, for the most part, I regarded Bartleby and his ways. Poor fellow! thought I, he means no mischief; it is plain he intends no insolence; his aspect sufficiently evinces that his eccentricities are involuntary. He is useful to me. I can get along with him. If I turn him away, the chances are he will fall in with some less indulgent employer, and then

---

15 **nice:** precise; accurate.
16 **suffrage** (suf′ rij): vote.

he will be rudely treated, and perhaps driven forth miserably to starve. Yes. Here I can cheaply purchase a delicious self-approval. To befriend Bartleby; to humor him in his strange willfulness, will cost me little or nothing, while I lay up in my soul what will eventually prove a sweet morsel for my conscience. But this mood was not invariable with me. I felt strangely goaded on to encounter him in new opposition—to elicit some angry spark from him answerable to my own. But, indeed, I might as well have essayed to strike fire with my knuckles against a bit of Windsor soap.[17] But one afternoon the evil impulse in me mastered me, and the following little scene ensued:

"Bartleby," said I, "when those papers are all copied, I will compare them with you."

"I would prefer not to."

"How? Surely you do not mean to persist in that mulish vagary?"

No answer.

I threw open the folding doors nearby, and, turning upon Turkey and Nippers, exclaimed:

"Bartleby a second time says, he won't examine his papers. What do you think of it, Turkey?"

It was afternoon, be it remembered. Turkey sat glowing like a brass boiler; his bald head steaming; his hands reeling among his blotted papers.

"Think of it?" roared Turkey; "I think I'll just step behind his screen, and black his eyes for him!"

So saying, Turkey rose to his feet and threw his arms into a pugilistic position. He was hurrying away to make good his promise, when I detained him, alarmed at the effect of incautiously rousing Turkey's combativeness after dinner.

"Sit down, Turkey," said I, "and hear what Nippers has to say. What do you think of it, Nippers? Would I not be justified in immediately dismissing Bartleby?"

"Excuse me, that is for you to decide, sir. I think his conduct quite unusual, and, indeed, unjust, as regards Turkey and myself. But it may only be a passing whim."

"Ah," exclaimed I, "you have strangely changed your mind, then—you speak very gently of him now."

"All beer," cried Turkey; "gentleness is effects of beer—Nippers and I dined together today. You see how gentle *I* am, sir. Shall I go and black his eyes?"

"You refer to Bartleby, I suppose. No, not today, Turkey," I replied; "pray, put up your fists."

I closed the doors, and again advanced towards Bartleby. I felt additional incentives tempting me to my fate. I burned to be rebelled against again. I remembered that Bartleby never left the office.

"Bartleby," said I, "Ginger Nut is away; just step around to the Post Office, won't you? (it was but a three minutes' walk), and see if there is anything for me."

"I would prefer not to."

"You *will* not?"

"I *prefer* not."

I staggered to my desk, and sat there in a deep study. My blind inveteracy returned. Was there any other thing in which I could procure myself to be ignominiously repulsed by this lean, penniless wight?[18]—my hired clerk? What added thing is there, perfectly reasonable, that he will be sure to refuse to do?

"Bartleby!"

No answer.

"Bartleby," in a louder tone.

No answer.

"Bartleby," I roared.

Like a very ghost, agreeably to the laws of magical invocation, at the third summons, he appeared at the entrance of his hermitage.

"Go to the next room, and tell Nippers to come to me."

"I prefer not to," he respectfully and slowly said, and mildly disappeared.

---

17 **Windsor soap:** a fragrant brown soap.

18 **wight:** person.

"Very good, Bartleby," said I, in a quiet sort of serenely severe self-possessed tone, intimating the unalterable purpose of some terrible retribution very close at hand. At the moment I half intended something of the kind. But upon the whole, as it was drawing towards my dinner hour, I thought it best to put on my hat and walk home for the day, suffering much from perplexity and distress of mind.

Shall I acknowledge it? The conclusion of this whole business was, that it soon became a fixed fact of my chambers, that a pale young scrivener, by the name of Bartleby, had a desk there; that he copied for me at the usual rate of four cents a folio (one hundred words); but he was permanently exempt from examining the work done by him, that duty being transferred to Turkey and Nippers, out of compliment, doubtless, to their superior acuteness; moreover, said Bartleby was never, on any account, to be dispatched on the most trivial errand of any sort; and that even if entreated to take upon him such a matter, it was generally understood that he would "prefer not to"—in other words, that he would refuse point blank.

As days passed on, I became considerably reconciled to Bartleby. His steadiness, his freedom from all dissipation, his incessant industry (except when he chose to throw himself into a standing reverie behind his screen), his great stillness, his unalterableness of demeanor under all circumstances, made him a valuable acquisition. One prime thing was this—*he was always there*—first in the morning, continually through the day, and the last at night. I had a singular confidence in his honesty. I felt my most precious papers perfectly safe in his hands. Sometimes, to be sure, I could not, for the very soul of me, avoid falling into sudden spasmodic passions with him. For it was exceeding difficult to bear in mind all the time those strange peculiarities, privileges, and unheard of exemptions, forming the tacit stipulations on Bartleby's part under which he remained in my office. Now and then, in the eagerness of dispatching pressing business, I would inadvertently summon Bartleby, in a short, rapid tone, to put his finger, say, on the incipient tie of a bit of red tape with which I was about compressing some papers. Of course, from behind the screen the usual answer, "I prefer not to," was sure to come; and then, how could a human creature, with the common infirmities of our nature, refrain from bitterly exclaiming upon such perverseness—such unreasonableness. However, every added repulse of this sort which I received only tended to lessen the probability of my repeating the inadvertence.

Here it must be said, that according to the custom of most legal gentlemen occupying chambers in densely populated law buildings, there were several keys to my door. One was kept by a woman residing in the attic, which person weekly scrubbed and daily swept and dusted my apartments. Another was kept by Turkey for convenience sake. The third I sometimes carried in my own pocket. The fourth I knew not who had.

Now, one Sunday morning, I happened to go to Trinity Church, to hear a celebrated preacher, and finding myself rather early on the ground I thought I would walk round to my chambers for a while. Luckily I had my key with me; but upon applying it to the lock, I found it resisted by something inserted from the inside. Quite surprised, I called out; when to my consternation a key was turned from within; and thrusting his lean visage at me, and holding the door ajar, the apparition of Bartleby appeared, in his shirt sleeves, and otherwise in a strangely tattered dishabille,[19] saying quietly that he was sorry, but he was deeply engaged just then, and—preferred not admitting me at present. In a brief word or two, he moreover added, that perhaps I had better walk round the block two or three times, and by that time he would probably have concluded his affairs.

Now, the utterly unsurmised appearance of

---

19 **dishabille** (dis' ə bēl'): state of undress.

Bartleby, tenanting my law chambers of a Sunday morning, with his cadaverously gentlemanly nonchalance, yet withal firm and self-possessed, had such a strange effect upon me, that incontinently I slunk away from my own door, and did as desired. But not without sundry twinges of impotent rebellion against the mild effrontery of this unaccountable scrivener. Indeed, it was his wonderful mildness chiefly, which not only disarmed me, but unmanned me as it were. For I consider that one, for the time, is sort of unmanned when he tranquilly permits his hired clerk to dictate to him, and order him away from his own premises. Furthermore, I was full of uneasiness as to what Bartleby could possibly be doing in my office in his shirt sleeves, and in an otherwise dismantled condition of a Sunday morning. Was anything amiss going on? Nay, that was out of the question. It was not to be thought of for a moment that Bartleby was an immoral person. But what could he be doing there?—copying? Nay again, whatever might be his eccentricities, Bartleby was an eminently decorous person. He would be the last man to sit down to his desk in any state approaching to nudity. Besides, it was Sunday; and there was something about Bartleby that forbade the supposition that he would by any secular occupation violate the proprieties of the day.

Nevertheless, my mind was not pacified; and full of a restless curiosity, at last I returned to the door. Without hindrance I inserted my key, opened it, and entered. Bartleby was not to be seen. I looked round anxiously, peeped behind his screen; but it was very plain that he was gone. Upon more closely examining the place, I surmised that for an indefinite period Bartleby must have ate, dressed, and slept in my office, and that, too, without plate, mirror, or bed. The cushioned seat of a rickety old sofa in one corner bore the faint impress of a lean, reclining form. Rolled away under his desk, I found a blanket; under the empty grate, a blacking box and brush; on a chair, a tin basin, with soap and a ragged towel; in a newspaper a few crumbs of gingernuts and a morsel of cheese. Yes, thought I, it is evident enough that Bartleby has been making his home here, keeping bachelor's hall all by himself. Immediately then the thought came sweeping across me, what miserable friendlessness and loneliness are here revealed! His poverty is great; but his solitude, how horrible! Think of it. Of a Sunday, Wall Street is deserted as Petra;[20] and every night of every day it is an emptiness. This building, too, which of weekdays hums with industry and life, at nightfall echoes with sheer vacancy, and all through Sunday is forlorn. And here Bartleby makes his home; sole spectator of a solitude which he has seen all populous—a sort of innocent and transformed Marius brooding among the ruins of Carthage![21]

For the first time in my life a feeling of overpowering stinging melancholy seized me. Before, I had never experienced aught but a not unpleasing sadness. The bond of a common humanity now drew me irresistibly to gloom. A fraternal melancholy! For both I and Bartleby were sons of Adam. I remembered the bright silks and sparkling faces I had seen that day, in gala trim, swanlike sailing down the Mississippi of Broadway; and I contrasted them with the pallid copyist, and thought to myself, Ah, happiness courts the light, so we deem the world is gay; but misery hides aloof, so we deem that misery there is none. These sad fancyings—chimeras, doubtless, of a sick and silly brain—led on to other and more special thoughts, concerning the eccentricities of Bartleby. Presentiments of strange discoveries hovered round me. The scrivener's pale form appeared to me laid out, among uncaring strangers, in its shivering winding sheet.

---

20 **Petra:** ancient ruined city in Jordan.
21 **Marius . . . Carthage:** Gaius Marius (155–86 B.C.) was a Roman general who had been victorious in African campaigns and then was banished from Rome.

Suddenly I was attracted by Bartleby's closed desk, the key in open sight left in the lock.

I mean no mischief, seek the gratification of no heartless curiosity, thought I; besides, the desk is mine, and its contents, too, so I will make bold to look within. Everything was methodically arranged, the papers smoothly placed. The pigeonholes were deep, and removing the files of documents, I groped into their recesses. Presently I felt something there, and dragged it out. It was an old bandanna handkerchief, heavy and knotted. I opened it, and saw it was a savings bank.

I now recalled all the quiet mysteries which I had noted in the man. I remembered that he never spoke but to answer; that, though at intervals he had considerable time to himself, yet I had never seen him reading—no, not even a newspaper; that for long periods he would stand looking out, at his pale window behind the screen, upon the dead brick wall; I was quite sure he never visited any refectory or eating house; while his pale face clearly indicated that he never drank beer like Turkey, or tea and coffee even, like other men; that he never went anywhere in particular that I could learn; never went out for a walk, unless, indeed, that was the case at present; that he had declined telling who he was, or whence he came, or whether he had any relatives in the world; that though so thin and pale, he never complained of ill-health. And more than all, I remembered a certain unconscious air of pallid—how shall I call it?—of pallid haughtiness, say, or rather an austere reserve about him, which had positively awed me into my tame compliance with his eccentricities, when I had feared to ask him to do the slightest incidental thing for me, even though I might know, from his long-continued motionlessness, that behind his screen he must be standing in one of those dead-wall reveries of his.

Revolving all these things, and coupling them with the recently discovered fact, that he made my office his constant abiding place and home, and not forgetting of his morbid moodiness; revolving all these things, a prudential feeling began to steal over me. My first emotions had been those of pure melancholy and sincerest pity; but just in proportion as the forlornness of Bartleby grew and grew to my imagination, did that same melancholy merge into fear, that pity into repulsion. So true it is, and so terrible, too, that up to a certain point the thought or sight of misery enlists our best affections; but, in certain special cases, beyond that point it does not. They err who would assert that invariably this is owing to the inherent selfishness of the human heart. It rather proceeds from a certain hopelessness of remedying excessive and organic ill. To a sensitive being, pity is not seldom pain. And when at last it is perceived that such pity cannot lead to effectual succor, common sense bids the soul be rid of it. What I saw that morning persuaded me that the scrivener was the victim of innate and incurable disorder. I might give alms to his body; but his body did not pain him; it was his soul that suffered, and his soul I could not reach.

I did not accomplish the purpose of going to Trinity Church that morning. Somehow, the things I had seen disqualified me for the time from churchgoing. I walked homeward, thinking what I would do with Bartleby. Finally, I resolved upon this—I would put certain calm questions to him the next morning, touching his history, etc., and if he declined to answer them openly and unreservedly (and I supposed he would prefer not), then to give him a twenty-dollar bill over and above whatever I might owe him, and tell him his services were no longer required; but that if in any other way I could assist him, I would be happy to do so, especially if he desired to return to his native place, wherever that might be, I would willingly help to defray the expenses. Moreover, if, after reaching home, he found himself at any time in want of aid, a letter from him would be sure of a reply.

The next morning came.

"Bartleby," said I, gently calling to him behind his screen.

No reply.

"Bartleby," said I, in a still gentler tone, "come here; I am not going to ask you to do anything you would prefer not to do—I simply wish to speak to you."

Upon this he noiselessly slid into view.

"Will you tell me, Bartleby, where you were born?"

"I would prefer not to."

"Will you tell me *anything* about yourself?"

"I would prefer not to."

"But what reasonable objection can you have to speak to me? I feel friendly towards you."

He did not look at me while I spoke, but kept his glance fixed upon my bust of Cicero, which, as I then sat, was directly behind me, some six inches above my head.

"What is your answer, Bartleby," said I, after waiting a considerable time for a reply, during which his countenance remained immovable, only there was the faintest conceivable tremor of the white attenuated mouth.

"At present I prefer to give no answer," he said, and retired into his hermitage.

It was rather weak in me I confess, but his manner, on this occasion, nettled me. Not only did there seem to lurk in it a certain calm disdain, but his perverseness seemed ungrateful, considering the undeniable good usage and indulgence he had received from me.

Again I sat ruminating what I should do. Mortified as I was at his behavior, and resolved as I had been to dismiss him when I entered my office, nevertheless I strangely felt something superstitious knocking at my heart, and forbidding me to carry out my purpose, and denouncing me for a villain if I dared to breathe one bitter word against this forlornest of mankind. At last, familiarly drawing my chair behind his screen, I sat down and said: "Bartleby, never mind, then, about revealing your history; but let me entreat you, as a friend, to comply as far as may be with the usages of this office. Say now, you will help to examine papers tomorrow or next day: in short, say now, that in a day or two you will begin to be a little reasonable:—say so, Bartleby."

"At present I would prefer not to be a little reasonable," was his mildly cadaverous reply.

Just then the folding doors opened, and Nippers approached. He seemed suffering from an unusually bad night's rest, induced by severer indigestion than common. He overheard those final words of Bartleby.

"*Prefer not, eh?*" gritted Nippers—"I'd *prefer* him, if I were you, sir," addressing me—"I'd *prefer* him; I'd give him preferences, the stubborn mule! What is it, sir, pray, that he *prefers* not to do now?"

Bartleby moved not a limb.

"Mr. Nippers," said I, "I'd prefer that you would withdraw for the present."

Somehow, of late, I had got into the way of involuntarily using this word "prefer" upon all sorts of not exactly suitable occasions. And I trembled to think that my contact with the scrivener had already and seriously affected me in a mental way. And what further and deeper aberration might it not yet produce? This apprehension had not been without efficacy in determining me to summary measures.

As Nippers, looking very sour and sulky, was departing, Turkey blandly and deferentially approached.

"With submission, sir," said he, "yesterday I was thinking about Bartleby here, and I think that if he would but prefer to take a quart of good ale every day, it would do much towards mending him, and enabling him to assist in examining his papers."

"So you have got the word, too," said I, slightly excited.

"With submission, what word, sir?" asked Turkey, respectfully crowding himself into the contracted space behind the screen, and by so doing, making me jostle the scrivener.

"What word, sir?"

"I would prefer to be left alone here," said Bartleby, as if offended at being mobbed in his privacy.

"*That's* the word, Turkey," said I—"*that's* it."

"Oh, *prefer?* oh yes—queer word. I never use it myself. But, sir, as I was saying, if he would but prefer—"

"Turkey," interrupted I, "you will please withdraw."

"Oh certainly, sir, if you prefer that I should."

As he opened the folding door to retire, Nippers at his desk caught a glimpse of me, and asked whether I would prefer to have a certain paper copied on blue paper or white. He did not in the least roguishly accent the word "prefer." It was plain that it involuntarily rolled from his tongue. I thought to myself, surely I must get rid of a demented man, who already has in some degree turned the tongues, if not the heads of myself and clerks. But I thought it prudent not to break the dismission at once.

The next day I noticed that Bartleby did nothing but stand at his window in his dead-wall reverie. Upon asking him why he did not write, he said that he had decided upon doing no more writing.

"Why, how now? what next?" exclaimed I, "do no more writing?"

"No more."

"And what is the reason?"

"Do you not see the reason for yourself," he indifferently replied.

I looked steadfastly at him, and perceived that his eyes looked dull and glazed. Instantly it occurred to me, that his unexampled diligence in copying by his dim window for the first few weeks of his stay with me might have temporarily impaired his vision.

I was touched. I said something in condolence with him. I hinted that of course he did wisely in abstaining from writing for a while; and urged him to embrace that opportunity of taking wholesome exercise in the open air. This, however, he did not do. A few days after this, my other clerks being absent, and being in a great hurry to dispatch certain letters by the mail, I thought that, having nothing else earthly to do, Bartleby would surely be less inflexible than usual, and carry these letters to the post office. But he blankly declined. So, much to my inconvenience, I went myself.

Still added days went by. Whether Bartleby's eyes improved or not, I could not say. To all appearance, I thought they did. But when I asked him if they did, he vouchsafed no answer. At all events, he would do no copying. At last, in reply to my urgings, he informed me that he had permanently given up copying.

"What!" exclaimed I; "suppose your eyes should get entirely well—better than ever before—would you not copy then?"

"I have given up copying," he answered, and slid aside.

He remained as ever, a fixture in my chamber. Nay—if that were possible—he became still more of a fixture than before. What was to be done? He would do nothing in the office; why should he stay there? In plain fact, he had now become a millstone[22] to me, not only useless as a necklace, but afflictive to bear. Yet I was sorry for him. I speak less than truth when I say that, on his own account, he occasioned me uneasiness. If he would but have named a single relative or friend, I would instantly have written, and urged their taking the poor fellow away to some convenient retreat. But he seemed alone, absolutely alone in the universe. A bit of wreck in the mid-Atlantic. At length, necessities connected with my business tyrannized over all other considerations. Decently as I could, I told Bartleby that in six days' time he must unconditionally leave the office. I warned him to take measures, in the interval, for procuring some other abode. I offered to assist him in this endeavor, if he himself would but take

---

22 **millstone:** here, a heavy burden.

the first step towards a removal. "And when you finally quit me, Bartleby," added I, "I shall see that you go not away entirely unprovided. Six days from this hour, remember."

At the expiration of that period, I peeped behind the screen, and lo! Bartleby was there.

I buttoned up my coat, balanced myself; advanced slowly towards him, touched his shoulder, and said, "The time has come; you must quit this place; I am sorry for you; here is money; but you must go."

"I would prefer not," he replied, with his back still towards me.

"You *must*."

He remained silent.

Now I had an unbounded confidence in this man's common honesty. He had frequently restored to me sixpences and shillings carelessly dropped upon the floor, for I am apt to be very reckless in such shirt-button affairs. The proceeding, then, which followed will not be deemed extraordinary.

"Bartleby," said I, "I owe you twelve dollars on account; here are thirty-two; the odd twenty are yours—Will you take it?" and I handed the bills towards him.

But he made no motion.

"I will leave them here, then," putting them under a weight on the table. Then taking my hat and cane and going to the door, I tranquilly turned and added—"After you have removed your things from these offices, Bartleby, you will of course lock the door—since everyone is now gone for the day but you—and if you please, slip your key underneath the mat, so that I may have it in the morning. I shall not see you again; so good-by to you. If, hereafter, in your new place of abode, I can be of any service to you, do not fail to advise me by letter. Good-by, Bartleby, and fare you well."

But he answered not a word; like the last column of some ruined temple, he remained standing mute and solitary in the middle of the otherwise deserted room.

As I walked home in a pensive mood, my vanity got the better of my pity. I could not but highly plume myself on my masterly management in getting rid of Bartleby. Masterly I call it, and such it must appear to any dispassionate thinker. The beauty of my procedure seemed to consist in its perfect quietness. There was no vulgar bullying, no bravado of any sort, no choleric hectoring,[23] and striding to and fro across the apartment, jerking out vehement commands for Bartleby to bundle himself off with his beggarly traps.[24] Nothing of the kind. Without loudly bidding Bartleby depart—as an inferior genius might have done—I *assumed* the ground that depart he must; and upon that assumption built all I had to say. The more I thought over my procedure, the more I was charmed with it. Nevertheless, next morning, upon awakening, I had my doubts—I had somehow slept off the fumes of vanity. One of the coolest and wisest hours a man has, is just after he awakes in the morning. My procedure seemed as sagacious as ever—but only in theory. How it would prove in practice—there was the rub. It was truly a beautiful thought to have assumed Bartleby's departure; but, after all, that assumption was simply my own, and none of Bartleby's. The great point was, not whether I had assumed that he would quit me, but whether he would prefer so to do. He was more a man of preference than assumptions.

After breakfast, I walked down town, arguing the probabilities pro and con. One moment I thought it would prove a miserable failure, and Bartleby would be found all alive at my office as usual; the next moment it seemed certain that I should find his chair empty. And so I kept veering about. At the corner of Broadway and Canal Street, I saw quite an excited group of people standing in earnest conversation.

"I'll take odds he doesn't," said a voice as I passed.

---

23 **choleric** (kol′ ər ik) **hectoring**: angry bullying.
24 **traps**: baggage.

"Doesn't go?—done!" said I, "put up your money."

I was instinctively putting my hand in my pocket to produce my own, when I remembered that this was an election day. The words I had overheard bore no reference to Bartleby, but to the success or nonsuccess of some candidate for the mayoralty. In my intent frame of mind, I had, as it were, imagined that all Broadway shared in my excitement, and were debating the same question with me. I passed on, very thankful that the uproar of the street screened my momentary absent-mindedness.

As I had intended, I was earlier than usual at my office door. I stood listening for a moment. All was still. He must be gone. I tried the knob. The door was locked. Yes, my procedure had worked to a charm; he indeed must be vanished. Yet a certain melancholy mixed with this: I was almost sorry for my brilliant success. I was fumbling under the door mat for the key, which Bartleby was to have left there for me, when accidentally my knee knocked against a panel, producing a summoning sound, and in response a voice came to me from within—"Not yet; I am occupied."

It was Bartleby.

I was thunderstruck. For an instant I stood like the man who, pipe in mouth, was killed one cloudless afternoon long ago in Virginia, by summer lightning; at his own warm open window he was killed, and remained leaning out there upon the dreamy afternoon, till someone touched him, when he fell.

"Not gone!" I murmured at last. But again obeying that wondrous ascendancy which the inscrutable scrivener had over me, and from which ascendancy, for all my chafing, I could not completely escape, I slowly went downstairs and out into the street, and while walking round the block, considered what I should next do in this unheard-of perplexity. Turn the man out by an actual thrusting I could not; to drive him away by calling him hard names would not do; calling in the police was an unpleasant idea; and yet, permit him to enjoy his cadaverous triumph over me—this, too, I could not think of. What was to be done? or, if nothing could be done, was there anything further that I could *assume* in this matter? Yes, as before I had prospectively assumed that Bartleby would depart, so now I might retrospectively assume that departed he was. In the legitimate carrying out of this assumption, I might enter my office in a great hurry, and pretending not to see Bartleby at all, walk straight against him as if he were air. Such a proceeding would in a singular degree have the appearance of a homethrust. It was hardly possible that Bartleby could withstand such an application of the doctrine of assumptions. But upon second thoughts the success of the plan seemed rather dubious. I resolved to argue the matter over with him again.

"Bartleby," said I, entering the office, with a quietly severe expression, "I am seriously displeased. I am pained, Bartleby. I had thought better of you. I had imagined you of such a gentlemanly organization, that in any delicate dilemma a slight hint would suffice—in short, an assumption. But it appears I am deceived. "Why," I added, unaffectedly starting, "you have not even touched that money yet," pointing to it, just where I had left it the evening previous.

He answered nothing.

"Will you, or will you not, quit me?" I now demanded in a sudden passion, advancing close to him.

"I would prefer *not* to quit you," he replied gently emphasizing the *not*.

"What earthly right have you to stay here? Do you pay any rent? Do you pay my taxes? Or is this property yours?"

He answered nothing.

"Are you ready to go on and write now? Are your eyes recovered? Could you copy a small paper for me this morning? or help examine a few lines? or step round to the post office? In a word, will you do anything at all, to give a coloring to your refusal to depart the premises?"

He silently retired into his hermitage.

I was now in such a state of nervous resentment that I thought it but prudent to check myself at present from further demonstrations. Bartleby and I were alone. I remembered the tragedy of the unfortunate Adams and the still more unfortunate Colt in the solitary office of the latter; and how poor Colt, being dreadfully incensed by Adams, and imprudently permitting himself to get wildly excited, was at unawares hurried into his fatal act—an act which certainly no man could possibly deplore more than the actor himself. Often it had occurred to me in my ponderings upon the subject, that had that altercation taken place in the public street, or at a private residence, it would not have terminated as it did. It was the circumstance of being alone in a solitary office, upstairs, of a building entirely unhallowed by humanizing domestic associations—an uncarpeted office, doubtless, of a dusty, haggard sort of appearance—this it must have been, which greatly helped to enhance the irritable desperation of the hapless Colt.

But when this old Adam of resentment rose in me and tempted me concerning Bartleby, I grappled him and threw him. How? Why, simply by recalling the divine injunction: "A new commandment give I unto you, that ye love one another." [25] Yes, this it was that saved me. Aside from higher considerations, charity often operates as a vastly wise and prudent principle—a great safeguard to its possessor. Men have committed murder for jealousy's sake, and anger's sake, and hatred's sake, and selfishness' sake, and spiritual pride's sake; but no man, that ever I heard of, ever committed a diabolical murder for sweet charity's sake. Mere self-interest, then, if no better motive can be enlisted, should, especially with high-tempered men, prompt all beings to charity and philanthropy. At any rate, upon the occasion in question, I strove to drown my exasperated feelings toward the scrivener by benevolently construing his conduct. Poor fellow, poor fellow! thought I, he don't mean anything; and besides, he has seen hard times, and ought to be indulged.

I endeavored, also, immediately to occupy myself, and at the same time to comfort my despondency. I tried to fancy, that in the course of the morning, at such time as might prove agreeable to him, Bartleby, of his own free accord, would emerge from his hermitage and take up some decided line of march in the direction of the door. But no. Half-past twelve o'clock came; Turkey began to glow in the face, overturn his inkstand, and become generally obstreperous; Nippers abated down into quietude and courtesy; Ginger Nut munched his noon apple; and Bartleby remained standing at his window in one of his profoundest dead-wall reveries. Will it be credited? Ought I to acknowledge it? That afternoon I left the office without saying one further word to him.

Some days now passed, during which, at leisure intervals I looked a little into "Edwards on the Will," [26] and "Priestley on Necessity." [27] Under the circumstances, those books induced a salutary feeling. Gradually I slid into the persuasion that these troubles of mine, touching the scrivener, had been all predestinated from eternity, and Bartleby was billeted upon me for some mysterious purpose of an all-wise Providence, which it was not for a mere mortal like me to fathom. Yes, Bartleby, stay there behind your screen, thought I; I shall persecute you no more; you are harmless and noiseless as any of these old chairs; in short, I never feel so private as when I know you are here. At last I see it, I feel it; I penetrate to the predestined purpose of my life. I am content. Others may have loftier parts to enact; but my mission in this world, Bartleby, is to furnish you with office room for such period as you may see fit to remain.

---

25 "A new . . . another": See the Bible, John 13:24.

26 "Edwards . . . Will": a work by Jonathan Edwards (1703–1758) called *The Freedom of the Will.*
27 "Priestley . . . Necessity": Joseph Priestley (1733–1804) an English theologian and scientist.

I believe that this wise and blessed frame of mind would have continued with me, had it not been for the unsolicited and uncharitable remarks obtruded upon me by my professional friends who visited the rooms. But thus it often is, that the constant friction of illiberal minds wears out at last the best resolves of the more generous. Though to be sure, when I reflected upon it, it was not strange that people entering my office should be struck by the peculiar aspect of the unaccountable Bartleby, and so be tempted to throw out some sinister observations concerning him. Sometimes an attorney, having business with me, and calling at my office, and finding no one but the scrivener there, would undertake to obtain some sort of precise information from him touching my whereabouts; but without heeding his idle talk, Bartleby would remain standing immovable in the middle of the room. So after contemplating him in that position for a time, the attorney would depart, no wiser than he came.

Also, when a reference was going on, and the room full of lawyers and witnesses, and business driving fast, some deeply occupied legal gentleman present, seeing Bartleby wholly unemployed, would request him to run round to his (the legal gentleman's) office and fetch some papers for him. Thereupon, Bartleby would tranquilly decline, and yet remain idle as before. Then the lawyer would give a great stare, and turn to me. And what could I say? At last I was made aware that all through the circle of my professional acquaintance, a whisper of wonder was running round, having reference to the strange creature I kept at my office. This worried me very much. And as the idea came upon me of his possibly turning out a long-lived man, and keep occupying my chambers, and denying my authority; and perplexing my visitors; and scandalizing my professional reputation; and casting a general gloom over the premises; keeping soul and body together to the last upon his savings (for doubtless he spent but half a dime a day), and in the end perhaps outlive me, and claim possession of my office by right of his perpetual occupancy: as all these dark anticipations crowded upon me more and more, and my friends continually intruded their relentless remarks upon the apparition in my room; a great change was wrought in me. I resolved to gather all my faculties together, and forever rid me of this intolerable incubus.[28]

Ere revolving any complicated project, however, adapted to this end, I first simply suggested to Bartleby the propriety of his permanent departure. In a calm and serious tone, I commended the idea to his careful and mature consideration. But, having taken three days to meditate upon it, he apprised me, that his original determination remained the same; in short, that he still preferred to abide with me.

What shall I do? I now said to myself, buttoning up my coat to the last button. What shall I do? What ought I to do? What does conscience say I *should* do with this man, or, rather, ghost. Rid myself of him, I must; go, he shall. But how? You will not thrust him, the poor, pale, passive mortal—you will not thrust such a helpless creature out of your door? You will not dishonor yourself by such cruelty? No, I will not, I cannot do that. Rather would I let him live and die here, and then mason up his remains in the wall. What, then, will you do? For all your coaxing, he will not budge. Bribes he leaves under your own paperweight on your table; in short, it is quite plain that he prefers to cling to you.

Then something severe, something unusual must be done. What! surely you will not have him collared by a constable, and commit his innocent pallor to the common jail? And upon what ground could you procure such a thing to be done?—a vagrant, is he? What! he a vagrant, a wanderer, who refuses to budge? It is because he will *not* be a vagrant, then, that

---

28 **incubus** (ing'kyə bəs, in'kyə bəs): haunting spirit.

you seek to count him *as* a vagrant. That is too absurd. No visible means of support: there I have him. Wrong again: for indubitably he *does* support himself, and that is the only unanswerable proof that any man can show of his possessing the means to do so. No more, then. Since he will not quit me, I must quit him. I will change my offices; I will move elsewhere, and give him fair notice, that if I find him on my new premises I will then proceed against him as a common trespasser.

Acting accordingly, next day I thus addressed him: "I find these chambers too far from the City Hall; the air is unwholesome. In a word, I propose to remove my offices next week, and shall no longer require your services. I tell you this now, in order that you may seek another place."

He made no reply, and nothing more was said.

On the appointed day I engaged carts and men, proceeded to my chambers, and, having but little furniture, everything was removed in a few hours. Throughout, the scrivener remained standing behind the screen, which I directed to be removed the last thing. It was withdrawn; and, being folded up like a huge folio, left him the motionless occupant of a naked room. I stood in the entry watching him a moment, while something from within me upbraided me.

I re-entered, with my hand in my pocket—and—and my heart in my mouth.

"Good-by, Bartleby; I am going—good-by, and God some way bless you; and take that," slipping something in his hand. But it dropped upon the floor, and then—strange to say—I tore myself from him whom I had so longed to be rid of.

Established in my new quarters, for a day or two I kept the door locked, and started at every footfall in the passages. When I returned to my rooms, after any little absence, I would pause at the threshold for an instant, and attentively listen, ere applying my key. But these fears were needless. Bartleby never came nigh me.

I thought all was going well, when a perturbed-looking stranger visited me, inquiring whether I was the person who had recently occupied rooms at No. — Wall Street.

Full of forebodings, I replied that I was.

"Then, sir," said the stranger, who proved a lawyer, "you are responsible for the man you left there. He refuses to do any copying; he refuses to do anything; he says he prefers not to; and he refuses to quit the premises."

"I am very sorry, sir," said I, with assumed tranquillity, but an inward tremor, "but, really, the man you allude to is nothing to me—he is no relation or apprentice of mine, that you should hold me responsible for him."

"In mercy's name, who is he?"

"I certainly cannot inform you. I know nothing about him. Formerly I employed him as a copyist; but he has done nothing for me now for some time past."

"I shall settle him, then—good morning, sir."

Several days passed, and I heard nothing more; and, though I often felt a charitable prompting to call at the place and see poor Bartleby, yet a certain squeamishness, of I know not what, withheld me.

All is over with him, by this time, thought I, at last, when, through another week, no further intelligence reached me. But, coming to my room the day after, I found several persons waiting at my door in a high state of nervous excitement.

"That's the man—here he comes," cried the foremost one, whom I recognized as the lawyer who had previously called upon me alone.

"You must take him away, sir, at once," cried a portly person among them, advancing upon me, and whom I knew to be the landlord of No.—Wall Street. "These gentlemen, my tenants, cannot stand it any longer; Mr. B——," pointing to the lawyer, "has turned him out of his room, and he now persists in haunting the building generally, sitting upon the banisters of the stairs by day, and sleeping in the entry by night. Everybody is concerned; clients are leaving the offices; some fears are entertained of a mob; something you must do, and that without delay."

Aghast at this torrent, I fell back before it, and would fain have locked myself in my new quarters. In vain I persisted that Bartleby was nothing to me—no more than to anyone else. In vain—I was the last person known to have anything to do with him, and they held me to the terrible account. Fearful, then, of being exposed in the papers (as one person present obscurely threatened), I considered the matter, and, at length, said, that if the lawyer would give me a confidential interview with the scrivener, in his (the lawyer's) own room, I would, that afternoon, strive my best to rid them of the nuisance they complained of.

Going upstairs to my old haunt, there was Bartleby silently sitting upon the banister at the landing.

"What are you doing here, Bartleby?" said I.

"Sitting upon the banister," he mildly replied.

I motioned him into the lawyer's room, who then left us.

"Bartleby" said I, "are you aware that you are the cause of great tribulation to me, by persisting in occupying the entry after being dismissed from the office?"

No answer.

"Now one of two things must take place. Either you must do something, or something must be done to you. Now what sort of business would you like to engage in? Would you like to re-engage in copying for someone?"

"No; I would prefer not to make any change."

"Would you like a clerkship in a dry-goods store?"

"There is too much confinement about that. No, I would not like a clerkship; but I am not particular."

"Too much confinement," I cried, "why you keep yourself confined all the time!"

"I would prefer not to take a clerkship," he rejoined, as if to settle that little item at once.

"How would a bartender's business suit you? There is no trying of the eyesight in that."

"I would not like it at all; though, as I said before, I am not particular."

His unwonted wordiness inspirited me. I returned to the charge.

"Well, then, would you like to travel through the country collecting bills for the merchants? That would improve your health."

"No, I would prefer to be doing something else."

"How then, would going as a companion to Europe, to entertain some young gentleman with your conversation—how would that suit you?"

"Not at all. It does not strike me that there is anything definite about that. I like to be stationary. But I am not particular."

"Stationary you shall be, then," I cried, now losing all patience, and, for the first time in all my exasperating connection with him, fairly flying into a passion. "If you do not go away from these premises before night, I shall feel bound—indeed, I *am* bound—to—to—to quit the premises myself!" I rather absurdly concluded, knowing not with what possible threat to try to frighten his immobility into compliance. Despairing of all further efforts, I was precipitately leaving him, when a final thought occurred to me—one which had not been wholly unindulged before.

"Bartleby," said I, in the kindest tone I could assume under such exciting circumstances, "will you go home with me now—not to my office, but my dwelling—and remain there till we can conclude upon some convenient arrangement for you at our leisure? Come, let us start now, right away."

"No: at present I would prefer not to make any change at all."

I answered nothing; but, effectually dodging everyone by the suddenness and rapidity of my flight, rushed from the building, ran up Wall Street towards Broadway, and jumping into the first omnibus, was soon removed from pursuit. As soon as tranquillity returned, I distinctly perceived that I had now done all that I possibly could, both in respect to the demands of the landlord and his tenants, and with regard to my own desire and sense of duty, to benefit Bartleby, and shield him from rude persecution. I now strove to be entirely carefree and quiescent; and my conscience justified me in the attempt; though, indeed, it was not so successful as I could have wished. So fearful was I of being again hunted out by the incensed landlord and his exasperated tenants, that, surrendering my business to Nippers, for a few days, I drove about the upper part of the town and through the suburbs, in my rockaway;[29] crossed over to Jersey City and Hoboken, and paid fugitive visits to Manhattanville and Astoria. In fact, I almost lived in my rockaway for the time.

When again I entered my office, lo, a note from the landlord lay upon the desk. I opened it with trembling hands. It informed me that the writer had sent to the police, and had Bartleby removed to the Tombs as a vagrant. Moreover, since I knew more about him than anyone else, he wished me to appear at that place, and make a suitable statement of the facts. These tidings had a conflicting effect upon me. At first I was indignant; but, at last, almost approved. The landlord's energetic, summary disposition had led him to adopt a procedure which I do not think I would have decided upon myself; and yet, as a last resort, under such peculiar circumstances, it seemed the only plan.

As I afterwards learned, the poor scrivener, when told that he must be conducted to the Tombs, offered not the slightest obstacle, but,

29 **rockaway**: a carriage.

in his pale, unmoving way, silently acquiesced.

Some of the compassionate and curious bystanders joined the party; and headed by one of the constables arm in arm with Bartleby, the silent procession filed its way through all the noise, and heat, and joy of the roaring thoroughfares at noon.

The same day I received the note, I went to the Tombs, or, to speak more properly, the Halls of Justice. Seeking the right officer, I stated the purpose of my call, and was informed that the individual I described was, indeed, within. I then assured the functionary that Bartleby was a perfectly honest man, and greatly to be compassionated, however unaccountably eccentric. I narrated all I knew, and closed by suggesting the idea of letting him remain in as indulgent confinement as possible, till something less harsh might be done—though, indeed, I hardly knew what. At all events, if nothing else could be decided upon, the almshouse must receive him. I then begged to have an interview.

Being under no disgraceful charge, and quite serene and harmless in all his ways, they had permitted him freely to wander about the prison, and, especially, in the enclosed grass-platted yards thereof. And so I found him there, standing all alone in the quietest of the yards, his face towards a high wall, while all around, from the narrow slits of the jail windows, I thought I saw peering out upon him the eyes of murderers and thieves.

"Bartleby!"

"I know you," he said, without looking round—"and I want nothing to say to you."

"It was not I that brought you here, Bartleby," said I, keenly pained at his implied suspicion. "And to you, this should not be so vile a place. Nothing reproachful attaches to you by being here. And see, it is not so sad a place as one might think. Look, there is the sky, and here is the grass."

"I know where I am," he replied, but would say nothing more, and so I left him.

As I entered the corridor again, a broad meatlike man, in an apron, accosted me, and, jerking his thumb over his shoulder, said—"Is that your friend?"

"Yes."

"Does he want to starve? If he does, let him live on the prison fare, that's all."

"Who are you?" asked I, not knowing what to make of such an unofficially speaking person in such a place.

"I am the grub-man. Such gentlemen as have friends here, hire me to provide them with something good to eat."

"Is this so?" said I, turning to the turnkey. He said it was.

"Well, then," said I, slipping some silver into the grub-man's hands (for so they called him), "I want you to give particular attention to my friend there; let him have the best dinner you can get. And you must be as polite to him as possible."

"Introduce me, will you?" said the grub-man, looking at me with an expression which seemed to say he was all impatience for an opportunity to give a specimen of his breeding.

Thinking it would prove of benefit to the scrivener, I acquiesced; and, asking the grub-man his name, went up with him to Bartlebly.

"Bartleby, this is a friend; you will find him very useful to you."

"Your sarvant, sir, your sarvant," said the grub-man, making a low salutation behind his apron. "Hope you find it pleasant here, sir; nice grounds—cool apartments—hope you'll stay with us some time—try to make it agreeable. What will you have for dinner today?"

"I prefer not to dine today," said Bartleby, turning away. "It would disagree with me; I am unused to dinners." So saying, he slowly moved to the other side of the enclosure, and took up a position fronting the dead-wall.

"How's this?" said the grub-man, addressing me with a stare of astonishment. "He's odd, ain't he?"

"I think he is a little deranged," said I, sadly.

"Deranged? deranged is it? Well, now, upon my word, I thought that friend of yourn was a gentleman forger; they are always pale and genteel-like, them forgers. I can't help pity 'em—can't help it, sir. Did you know Monroe Edwards?" he added, touchingly, and paused. Then, laying his hand piteously on my shoulder, sighed, "he died of consumption at Sing-Sing. So you weren't acquainted with Monroe?"

"No, I was never socially acquainted with any forgers. But I cannot stop longer. Look to my friend yonder. You will not lose by it. I will see you again."

Some few days after this, I again obtained admission to the Tombs, and went through the corridors in quest of Bartleby; but without finding him.

"I saw him coming from his cell not long ago," said a turnkey, "may be he's gone to loiter in the yards."

So I went in that direction.

"Are you looking for the silent man?" said another turnkey, passing me. "Yonder he lies—sleeping in the yard there. 'Tis not twenty minutes since I saw him lie down."

The yard was entirely quiet. It was not accessible to the common prisoners. The surrounding walls, of amazing thickness, kept off all sounds behind them. The Egyptian character of the masonry weighed upon me with its gloom. But a soft imprisoned turf grew under foot. The heart of the eternal pyramids, it seemed, wherein, by some strange magic, through the clefts, grass seed, dropped by birds, had sprung.

Strangely huddled at the base of the wall, his knees drawn up, and lying on his side, his head touching the cold stones, I saw the wasted Bartleby. But nothing stirred. I paused; then went close up to him; stooped over, and saw that his dim eyes were open; otherwise he seemed profoundly sleeping. Something prompted me to touch him. I felt his hand, when a tingling shiver ran up my arm and down my spine to my feet.

The round face of the grub-man peered upon me now. "His dinner is ready. Won't he dine today, either? Or does he live without dining?"

"Lives without dining," said I, and closed the eyes.

"Eh!—He's asleep, ain't he?"

"With kings and counselors,"[30] murmured I.

There would seem little need for proceeding further in this history. Imagination will readily supply the meager recital of poor Bartleby's interment. But, ere parting with the reader, let me say, that if this little narrative has sufficiently interested him, to awaken curiosity as to who Bartleby was, and what manner of life he led prior to the present narrator's making his acquaintance, I can only reply, that in such curiosity I fully share, but am wholly unable to gratify it. Yet here I hardly know whether I should divulge one little item of rumor, which came to my ear a few months after the scrivener's decease. Upon what basis it rested, I

___

30 "With kings and counselors": See the *Bible*, Job 3:13-14.

could never ascertain; and hence, how true it is I cannot now tell. But, inasmuch as this vague report has not been without a certain suggestive interest to me, however sad, it may prove the same with some others; and so I will briefly mention it. The report was this: that Bartleby had been a subordinate clerk in the Dead Letter Office at Washington, from which he had been suddenly removed by a change in the administration. When I think over this rumor, hardly can I express the emotions which seize me. Dead letters! does it not sound like dead men? Conceive a man by nature and misfortune prone to a pallid hopelessness, can any business seem more fitted to heighten it than that of continually handling these dead letters, and assorting them for the flames? For by the cartload they are annually burned. Sometimes from out the folded paper the pale clerk takes a ring—the finger it was meant for, perhaps, molders in the grave; a bank note sent in swiftest charity—he whom it would relieve, nor eats nor hungers any more; pardon for those who died despairing; hope for those who died unhoping; good tidings for those who died stifled by unrelieved calamities. On errands of life, these letters speed to death.

Ah, Bartleby! Ah, humanity!

Study Questions

1. In the first five pages of the story, Melville introduces the lawyer/narrator and the three office clerks. Who are they? How is each character described? To what extent are the three clerks comic and eccentric?

2. How does the narrator depict the routine of the business world before Bartleby's arrival?

3. In what ways does Bartleby's arrival affect his co-workers and the lawyer?

4. Although Bartleby's manner might be considered exasperating, how does Melville arouse sympathy for him?

5. Since the lawyer cannot persuade Bartleby to leave the office, what does he do in order to rid himself of Bartleby? What happens to Bartleby then?

6. In the first paragraph of the story the narrator says, "What my own astonished eyes saw of Bartleby, that is all I know of him, except, indeed, one vague report which will appear in the sequel." What is that vague report? What does it contribute to the understanding of Bartleby?
7. Walls or barriers in this story become symbols. Find examples of walls. What is the double meaning in the name "Wall Street"? (Note the subtitle of the story.) What, then, do walls symbolize here?

Vocabulary

A **prefix** is a letter or series of letters added at the beginning of a word (a) to change the word's meaning in some way, (b) to create a derivative of the word, or most often, (c) to do both.

One of the most common prefixes in English is *un-*, which gives any word to which it is attached the opposite, or negative of its original meaning. For example:

un- + co-operative = unco-operative; *the negative* of co-operative
un- + usual = unusual = *not* usual: *the opposite* of usual

Unlike *un-*, many other prefixes have more than one meaning. An example of these is the prefix *in-*, which has two entirely different major definitions:

In- can mean "in, into, within, or inside.":

intrude: come or go *in* (when not wanted)
inspect: look *into*
inward: *within;* toward the *inside*

In-, like *un-*, can reverse the meaning of the word to which it is added, making that word mean the opposite, or negative, of what it originally meant:

invariable: *the opposite* of variable; *not* variable
indefinite: *the negative* of definite: *not* definite

1. On a separate sheet of paper, tell which of the two meanings listed above for the prefix *in-* applies to each of the following words taken from "Bartleby the Scrivener":

   incautious   inhumane   inquire   intimate   involuntary

2. With the help of a dictionary give a brief definition for the following "*in-*words" used. Tell how each *in-* prefix changes the base word.

   inadvertent   indecorous   indignant   inherent   instinct
   incontinent   indifferent   indubitably   innate   interment

4 REVIEW

Study Questions

1. "Young Goodman Brown" and "The Pit and the Pendulum" are both stories in which the central character has a terrifying experience. Compare these two stories regarding point of view, effect on the reader, and what you think each story means.

2. What is the similarity between "Thanatopsis" and the statement in "Bartleby the Scrivener" that Bartleby "sleeps with kings and counselors"?

3. In what ways do Thoreau, Douglass, Harper, and Stanton exemplify individualism?

4. How do you think Emerson and Thoreau would have responded to Bartleby's "prefer not to"? Use examples from "Self-Reliance" and "Where I Lived and What I Lived For" to support your answers.

5. Compare the poetry of Edgar Allan Poe with the poetry of Henry Wadsworth Longfellow. How are their poems similar in use of imagery, metrical patterns, subject, tone? How do they differ?

Composition

1. Choose one of the three major themes from Unit 1 (The Sense of Place, The Individual, The American Dream). Write an essay showing how that theme is reflected in at least three selections from this unit. Your essay should begin with a definition of the theme. After pointing out specific examples of the theme in three works, you should conclude with comments on the different ways in which your three authors present the theme.

2. "Rip Van Winkle," *Walden,* Douglass' *Narrative,* and "Bartleby the Scrivener" all present interesting individuals. Write an account of an unusual individual whom you know or know about. Describe the person, giving specific examples of his or her appearance and manners and actions. Try to explain why he or she is interesting to you.

5

A New Maturity

A NEW MATURITY

IN the period between the Civil War and the first World War—roughly 1865 to 1915—America matured as a nation. Having to cope with the devastation of a Civil War and the problems of post-war reconstruction took both strength and maturity. Abraham Lincoln, whose vision of reunification helped preserve the nation, was assassinated. The country, however, survived and prospered during this period of internal strife and chaos. Industry flourished, railroads were built, and

The Capitol Building, Washington, D.C., during its construction.

immigration increased. This growth was reflected in the emergence of an urban civilization. The invention of new machinery and technologies spurred the exploitation and development of natural resources. America was changing.

Likewise, American writers reflected this period of tension and change. Henry James depicted the rise and ruin of recognizable American characters. While James combined American and European settings in his work, other writers—such as Mark Twain, Kate Chopin, and Mary E. Wilkins Freeman—focused on the populace in various regions of the United States. Walt Whitman, in his poetry, sang of an emerging nation and spirit.

W. E. B. Du Bois began his lifetime work of urging America to live up to its expressed ideals and commenting on its failure to do so.

While these writers celebrated the American character in its many forms, the population moved westward. This westward movement increased the agony of displaced Native Americans, as reflected in Chief Joseph's speech protesting the brutal treatment of his Nez Percé people.

The American Literature of this period was characterized by an increasing realism, a concern for the realities of living in chaotic, changing times. The emerging modern American literature, much like the nation itself, struggled toward a new maturity.

Abraham Lincoln   1809-1865

Abraham Lincoln's simplicity, modesty, and humor are evident in this excerpt from the autobiographical sketch he wrote in 1859, just before he was elected President:

I was born February 12, 1809, in Hardin County, Kentucky. My parents were both born in Virginia, of undistinguished families—second families, perhaps I should say. My mother, who died in my tenth year, was of a family of the name of Hanks, . . . My paternal grandfather, Abraham Lincoln, emigrated from Rockingham County, Virginia, to Kentucky about 1781 or 1782, where a year or two later he was killed by the Indians, . . .

My father, at the death of his father, was but six years of age, and he grew up literally without education. He removed from Kentucky to what is now Spencer County, Indiana, in my eighth year. . . . There I grew up. There were some schools, so called, but no qualification was ever required of a teacher beyond "readin', writin', and cipherin'" to the rule of three. . . . Of course, when I came of age I did not know much. . . . I have not been to school since. The little advance I now have upon this store of education, I have picked up from time to time under the pressure of necessity.

I was raised to farm work, which I continued till I was twenty-two. . . . I was elected a captain of volunteers [during the Black Hawk War] a success which gave me more pleasure than any I have had since. I ran for the legislature the same year (1832), and was beaten—the only time I ever have been beaten by the people. The next and three succeeding biennial elections, I was elected to the legislature. During this legislative period I had studied law, and removed to Springfield to practice it. In 1846 I was once elected to the lower House of Congress. . . . I was losing interest in politics when the repeal of the Missouri Compromise[1] aroused me again.

---

[1] Missouri Compromise: a set of laws adopted in 1820 to maintain the balance between slave and non-slave states.

What I have done since then is pretty well known.

As shown by his manner of writing this sketch and his famous speeches, Lincoln was a wise and masterful writer. His most famous utterance was the Gettysburg Address, delivered on November 19, 1863. The occasion was the dedication of a national cemetery on the site of one of the most bloody and decisive battles of the Civil War.

Gettysburg Address

ABRAHAM LINCOLN

FOURSCORE AND SEVEN YEARS ago our fathers brought forth on this continent a new nation, conceived in liberty, and dedicated to the proposition that all men are created equal.

Now we are engaged in a great civil war, testing whether that nation, or any nation so conceived and so dedicated can long endure. We are met on a great battlefield of that war. We have come to dedicate a portion of that field as a final resting place for those who here gave their lives that that nation might live. It is altogether fitting and proper that we should do this.

But, in a larger sense, we cannot dedicate—we cannot consecrate—we cannot hallow—this ground. The brave men, living and dead, who struggled here, have consecrated it far above our poor power to add or detract. The world will little note nor long remember what we say here, but it can never forget what they did here. It is for us, the living, rather, to be dedicated here to the unfinished work which they who fought here have thus far so nobly advanced. It is rather for us to be here dedicated to the great task remaining before us—that from these honored dead we take increased devotion to that cause for which they gave the last full measure of devotion; that we here highly resolve that these dead shall not have died in vain; that this nation, under God, shall have a new birth of freedom; and that government of the people, by the people, for the people, shall not perish from the earth.

Study Questions

1. In his speech Lincoln moves from past to present to future. Point out where this movement occurs. What is the common subject that holds the three divisions of time together?

2. The movement of the speech through time is reinforced by a progression of images linking the existence of the nation with the human cycle of birth, baptism, life, death, and rebirth. Trace this progression by pointing out the words which contain these images. Discuss the appropriateness of this imagery to the speech as a whole.

3. Why do you think the Gettysburg Address is especially memorable? Why is it especially effective for oral delivery?

Elizabeth Keckley   1825-1905

For the first thirty years of her life, Elizabeth Keckley was a slave. In 1855, with the help of friends, she purchased her freedom and embarked on a career as a fashionable dressmaker. After settling in Washington, she became seamstress and close friend of Mrs. Abraham Lincoln. It was Elizabeth Keckley who comforted Mary Todd Lincoln when her husband was assassinated. During her years in the White House, Keckley founded the Contraband Relief Association. This organization, for which she traveled to raise funds, offered assistance to former slaves. In 1868 Keckley published her autobiography with the title *Behind the Scenes, or Thirty Years a Slave, and Four Years in the White House.* The selection below is taken from that book.

The Death of President Lincoln

ELIZABETH KECKLEY

THE DAYS PASSED without any incident of particular note disturbing the current of life. On Friday morning, April 14th—alas! what American does not remember the day—I saw Mrs. Lincoln but for a moment. She told me that she was to attend the theater that night with the President, but I was not summoned to assist her in making her toilette. Sherman had swept from the northern border of Georgia through the heart of the Confederacy down to the sea, striking the death-blow to the rebellion. Grant had pursued General Lee beyond Richmond, and the army of Virginia, that had made such stubborn resistance, was crumbling to pieces. Fort Sumter had fallen;—the stronghold first wrenched from the Union, and which had braved the fury of Federal guns for so many years, was restored to the Union; the end of the war was near at hand, and the great pulse of the loyal North thrilled with joy. The dark war-cloud was fading, and a white-robed angel seemed to hover in the sky, whispering "Peace—peace on earth, good-will toward men!" Sons, brothers, fathers, friends, sweethearts were coming home. Soon the white tents would be folded, the volunteer army be disbanded, and tranquillity again reign. Happy, happy day!—happy at least to those who fought under the banner of the Union. There was great rejoicing throughout the North. From the Atlantic to the Pacific, flags were gayly thrown to the breeze, and at night every city blazed with its tens of thousand lights. But scarcely had the fireworks ceased to play, and the lights been taken down from the windows, when the lightning flashed the most appalling news over the magnetic wires. "The President has been murdered!" spoke the swift-winged messenger, and the loud huzza died upon the lips. A nation suddenly paused in the midst of festivity, and stood paralyzed with horror—transfixed with awe.

Oh, memorable day! Oh, memorable night! Never before was joy so violently contrasted with sorrow.

At 11 o'clock at night I was awakened by an old friend and neighbor, Miss M. Brown, with the startling intelligence that the entire Cabinet had been assassinated, and Mr. Lincoln shot, but not mortally wounded. When I heard the words I felt as if the blood had been frozen in my veins, and that my lungs must collapse for the want of air. Mr. Lincoln shot! the Cabinet assassinated! What could it mean? The streets were alive with wondering, awe-stricken people. Rumors flew thick and fast, and the wildest reports came with every new arrival. The words were repeated with blanched cheeks and quivering lips. I waked Mr. and Mrs. Lewis, and told them that the President was shot, and that I must go to the White House. I could not remain in a state of uncertainty. I felt that the house would not hold me. They tried to quiet me, but gentle words could not calm the wild tempest. They quickly dressed themselves, and we sallied out into the street to drift with the excited throng. We walked rapidly towards the White House, and on our way passed the residence of Secretary Seward, which was surrounded by armed soldiers, keeping back all intruders with the point of the bayonet. We hurried on, and as we approached the White House, saw that it too was surrounded with soldiers. Every entrance was strongly guarded, and no one was permitted to pass. The guard at the gate told us that Mr. Lincoln had not been brought home, but refused to give any other information. More excited than ever, we wandered down the street. Grief and anxiety were making me weak, and as we joined the outskirts of a large crowd, I began to feel as meek and humble as a penitent child. A gray-haired old man was passing. I caught a glimpse of his face, and it seemed so full of kindness and sorrow that I

gently touched his arm, and imploringly asked:

"Will you please, sir, to tell me whether Mr. Lincoln is dead or not?"

"Not dead," he replied, "but dying. God help us!" and with a heavy step he passed on.

"Not dead, but dying! then indeed God help us!"

We learned that the President was mortally wounded—that he had been shot down in his box at the theater, and that he was not expected to live till morning; when we returned home with heavy hearts. I could not sleep. I wanted to go to Mrs. Lincoln, as I pictured her wild with grief; but then I did not know where to find her, and I must wait till morning. Never did the hours drag so slowly. Every moment seemed an age, and I could do nothing but walk about and hold my arms in mental agony.

Morning came at last, and a sad morning was it. The flags that floated so gayly yesterday now were draped in black, and hung in silent folds at half-mast. The President was dead, and a nation was mourning for him. Every house was draped in black, and every face wore a solemn look. People spoke in subdued tones, and glided whisperingly, wonderingly, silently about the streets.

About eleven o'clock on Saturday morning a carriage drove up to the door, and a messenger asked for "Elizabeth Keckley."

"Who wants her?" I asked.

"I come from Mrs. Lincoln. If you are Mrs. Keckley, come with me immediately to the White House."

I hastily put on my shawl and bonnet, and was driven at a rapid rate to the White House. Everything about the building was sad and solemn. I was quickly shown to Mrs. Lincoln's room, and on entering, saw Mrs. L. tossing uneasily about upon a bed. The room was darkened, and the only person in it besides the widow of the President was Mrs. Secretary Welles, who had spent the night with her. Bowing to Mrs. Welles, I went to the bedside.

"Why did you not come to me last night, Elizabeth—I sent for you?" Mrs. Lincoln asked in a low whisper.

"I did try to come to you, but I could not find you," I answered, as I laid my hand upon her hot brow.

I afterwards learned, that when she had partially recovered from the first shock of the terrible tragedy in the theater, Mrs. Welles asked:

"Is there no one, Mrs. Lincoln, that you desire to have with you in this terrible affliction?"

"Yes, send for Elizabeth Keckley. I want her just as soon as she can be brought here."

Three messengers, it appears, were successively despatched for me, but all of them mistook the number and failed to find me.

Shortly after entering the room on Saturday morning, Mrs. Welles excused herself, as she said she must go to her own family, and I was left alone with Mrs. Lincoln.

She was nearly exhausted with grief, and when she became a little quiet, I asked and received permission to go into the Guests'

Room, where the body of the President lay in state. When I crossed the threshold of the room, I could not help recalling the day on which I had seen little Willie lying in his coffin where the body of his father now lay. I remembered how the President had wept over the pale beautiful face of his gifted boy, and now the President himself was dead. The last time I saw him he spoke kindly to me, but alas! the lips would never move again. The light had faded from his eyes, and when the light went out the soul went with it. What a noble soul was his—noble in all the noble attributes of God! Never did I enter the solemn chamber of death with such palpitating heart and trembling footsteps as I entered it that day. No common mortal had died. The Moses of my people had fallen in the hour of his triumph. Fame had woven her choicest chaplet[1] for his brow. Though the brow was cold and pale in death, the chaplet should not fade, for God had studded it with the glory of the eternal stars.

---

1 **chaplet:** wreath or garland for the head.

Study Questions

1. Under what circumstances does Elizabeth Keckley receive the news of President Lincoln's assassination? What causes her delay in seeing Mary Lincoln?

2. Describe Keckley's feelings about President Lincoln.

3. How does Keckley's description make the reader feel the impact of the assassination?

Walt Whitman   1819-1892

Walt Whitman is one of the most original poets America has produced. In his themes as well as his techniques, he jarred a reading public that had been accustomed to the traditional topics and regular stanzas of such New England poets as Bryant and Longfellow. Whitman's individualism is evident in much of his life. He was born in a small farming community on Long Island, New York. His father moved the family of nine children to Brooklyn in 1823. There Walt Whitman attended public school for five years, ending his formal education at the age of ten. Between jobs as a journeyman printer and as editor of various New York papers, he taught in a country school on Long Island and did carpentry in Brooklyn. His education was obtained from wide reading in public libraries, attending lectures on astronomy, and going to the opera.

In 1855 Whitman published his now famous book of poems, *Leaves of Grass,* which he helped typeset and had privately financed. Every poem he wrote, no matter where it was first published, eventually appeared in one of the eight subsequent editions of *Leaves of Grass* until the book grew from twelve poems to hundreds. The public began to notice *Leaves of Grass* and, before Whitman's death, he was hailed as a unique voice in American literature.

In his subject matter Whitman is comprehensive, trying to show his readers that any subject can become poetry if it is deeply felt. Whitman aimed to stir in his readers an honest feeling for life itself, an acceptance of just being alive and experiencing the immediate excitement of life. To coincide with his frankness and unconventionality in subject matter, Whitman developed a revolutionary poetic form called free verse. Free verse is important in that it liberated poetry from dependence on strict meter and regular rhymes and stanzas. However, it is not free from all poetic discipline, but rather substitutes a careful rhythmic sound pattern in each phrase, line, and stanza. Indeed, because of Whitman's example, poets since World War I have made a wide range of experience and freer verse forms characteristic of their poetry. (Additional information on Whitman is included in Unit 1 on page 42.)

A rare photograph of Walt Whitman.

A Noiseless Patient Spider

WALT WHITMAN

A noiseless patient spider,
I marked where on a little promontory it stood isolated,
Marked how to explore the vacant vast surrounding,
It launched forth filament, filament, filament, out of itself,
Ever unreeling them, ever tirelessly speeding them.   5

And you O my soul where you stand,
Surrounded, detached, in measureless oceans of space,
Ceaselessly musing, venturing, throwing, seeking the spheres to connect them,
Till the bridge you will need be formed, till the ductile[1] anchor hold,
Till the gossamer thread you fling catch somewhere, O my soul.   10

---

1 **ductile:** drawn out into a thin thread.

Study Questions

1. The first stanza (entirely about the spider) sets up an elaborate parallel or comparison with the second (about the human soul). What words in the second stanza correspond to the spider's "filaments"? What effect is achieved by repeating the words "filament" and "ever" in the first stanza?

2. The spider is "isolated" and in a "vacant vast surrounding." What words reveal that the soul is also alone?

3. The spider's task is "to explore." What does the soul do that is comparable?

4. In what ways are the types of activities of the spider and the soul different? Which is more exploratory and tentative?

5. Explain Whitman's conception of the soul. What kinds of things might the soul be trying to "connect" or "catch"?

One's-Self I Sing

WALT WHITMAN

One's-self I sing, a simple separate person,
Yet utter the word Democratic, the word En-Masse.[1]

Of physiology from top to toe I sing,
Not physiognomy alone nor brain alone is worthy for the Muse,[2]
   I say the Form complete is worthier far,
The Female equally with the Male I sing.

Of Life immense in passion, pulse, and power,
Cheerful, for freest action formed under the laws divine,
The Modern Man I sing.

1 **En-masse** (en mas'): in a group; all together.
2 **Muse**: in Greek myths, one of the nine goddesses of
the fine arts and sciences.

Study Questions

1. In the first stanza Whitman says he sings praises of both the "separate person" and "the word En-Masse." Explain the paradox; how do you think a person can sing of both?

2. In stanza two what subject does the poet say is worth writing about? What is the difference between "physiology" and "physiognomy"?

3. In stanza three what kind of life for the "Modern Man" is Whitman praising?

4. Although this poem is written in free verse, certain poetic disciplines are recognizable. In addition to the pattern established by the word "Of," what other words are repeated? Where do you find alliteration? Why might Whitman have capitalized certain words within lines?

There Was a Child Went Forth

WALT WHITMAN

There was a child went forth every day,
And the first object he looked upon, that object he became,
And that object became part of him for the day or a certain part of the day,
Or for many years or stretching cycles of years.

The early lilacs became part of this child,   5
And grass and white and red morning-glories, and white and red
   clover, and the song of the phoebe-bird,
And the Third-month[1] lambs and the sow's pink-faint litter,
   and the mare's foal and the cow's calf,
And the noisy brood of the barnyard or by the mire of the pond-side,
And the fish suspending themselves so curiously below there,
   and beautiful curious liquid,
And the water-plants with their graceful flat heads, all became part of him.   10

The field-sprouts of Fourth-month and Fifth-month became part of him,
Winter-grain sprouts and those of the light yellow corn,
   and the esculent roots[2] of the garden,
And the apple-trees covered with blossoms and the fruit
   afterward, and wood-berries, and the commonest weeds by the road,
And the old drunkard staggering home from the outhouse
   of the tavern whence he had lately risen,
And the schoolmistress that passed on her way to the school,   15
And the friendly boys that passed, and the quarrelsome boys,
And the tidy and fresh-cheeked girls, and the barefoot Negro boy and girl,
And all the changes of city and country wherever he went.

His own parents, he that had fathered him and she that had
   conceived him in her womb and birthed him,
They gave this child more of themselves than that,   20
They gave him afterward every day, they became part of him.

The mother at home quietly placing the dishes on the supper-table,
The mother with mild words, clean her cap and gown,
   a wholesome odor falling off her person and clothes as she walks by,

---

1 **Third-month**: Whitman often numbered the months this way in accordance with
the Quaker objection to using the names of the pagan gods Janus, Mars, etc.
(Whitman was of Quaker background.)
2 **esculent roots**: edible vegetables.

The father, strong, self-sufficient, manly, mean, angered, unjust,
The blow, the quick loud word, the tight bargain, the crafty lure,   25
The family usages, the language, the company, the furniture,
    the yearning and swelling heart,
Affection that will not be gainsaid,[3] the sense of what is
    real, the thought if after all it should prove unreal,
The doubts of day-time and the doubts of night-time, the curious whether
    and how,
Whether that which appears so is so, or is it all flashes and specks?
Men and women crowding fast in the streets, if they are not flashes and
    specks what are they?   30
The streets themselves and the façades of houses, and goods in the win-
    dows,
Vehicles, teams, the heavy-planked wharves, the huge crossing at the fer-
    ries,
The village on the highland seen from afar at sunset, the river between,
Shadows, aureola[4] and mist, the light falling on roofs and
    gables of white or brown two miles off,
The schooner near by sleepily dropping down the tide, the
    little boat slack-towed astern,   35
The hurrying tumbling waves, quick-broken crests, slapping,
The strata of colored clouds, the long bar of maroon-tint away
    solitary by itself, the spread of purity it lies motionless in,
The horizon's edge, the flying sea-crow, the fragrance of salt
    marsh and shore mud,
These became part of that child who went forth every day,
    and who now goes, and will always go forth every day.

3 **gainsaid**: denied, contradicted, disputed.
4 **aureola** (also *aureole*): halo effect around the sun when seen through mist: any encircling ring
of light.

Study Questions

1. As Whitman says in the introductory stanza, any object a child sees will
   have a permanent effect on his or her individuality. In the second
   stanza, how do the sights and sounds noticed by the child reflect youthful fascination?

2. How do the child's first observations of other people in stanza three differ from more mature observations in later stanzas?

3. In which lines does philosophical questioning begin? Where is there more mature awareness of the beauty of landscapes? In what way is the description of nature at the end of the poem different from the way nature is described at the beginning?

4. How do time changes and settings parallel the growth of the child?

5. Compare Whitman's concept of a human being in this poem with that in "One's-Self I Sing."

Vocabulary

Frequent use of **compound words** is a conspicuous feature of "There Was a Child Went Forth" by Walt Whitman. "A compound word is a single word composed of two or more words joined together, either with or without a hyphen. The basic purpose of a compound word is to express an idea that is entirely different, either in meaning or grammatical function, from that expressed by the unconnected component words (*red coat,* a garment; *red-coat,* a soldier)."[1]

There are three major rules that govern the formation of compound words found in Whitman's poem:

1. Traditionally, two or more words making a compound word should be written as one, with no hyphen. For example:

afterward	became	upon
barnyard	quarrelsome	itself

2. If two or more words are to be joined as a single adjective preceding (but usually *not* following) the noun it modifies, the words should be hyphenated, for example:

Third-month lambs   the sow's *pink-faint* litter

Other compounds should, of course, be hyphenated if they are presented that way in a standard contemporary dictionary.

3. When neither of the foregoing rules is applicable, words should not be joined in any way, no matter how closely associated their meanings may be.

A. On the next page is a list of paired words. Each pair is followed by a number indicating the line in which they can be found in "There Was a Child Went Forth":

---

1 Alice M. Ball, *The Compounding and Hyphenation of English Words* (New York: Funk and Wagnalls Co., 1951), p. 3.

a far (33)   motion less (37)
fresh cheeked (17)   quick broken (36)
gain said (27)   red clover (6)
them selves (31)   salt marsh (38)
light yellow (12)   sun set (33)

Find each pair of words in the poem. Then using a separate sheet of paper, copy each word-pair as a solid compound, as a hyphenated compound, or as separate words, according to the way Whitman wrote them. After each word-pair you copy, write 1, 2, or 3 to tell which rule given above Whitman followed in writing these words.

B. Perhaps the most changeable element in English spelling is that involving compound words. A pair of closely associated words written separately in one generation may be hyphenated in the next, only to become a solid compound in the third—or vice versa. For example, *apple-tree*, a hyphenated compound in the Whitman poem, is now written as two separate words: *apple tree*. For this reason, not all the rules Whitman followed in compounding words can be assumed to apply in our time. Again, find word-pairs as they are printed in "There Was a Child Went Forth":

bare foot (17)   morning glories (6)
cow's calf (7)   school mistress (15)
day time (28)   self sufficient (24)
field sprouts (11)   supper table (22)
heavy planked (32)   winter grain (12)

But this time trust only one of the rules listed at the beginning of this lesson: *Rule 2*. If this rule applies, copy the word-pair as Whitman presents it, and after the word-pair, write 2 as you did earlier.

Check all other word-pairs in the dictionary. Write these according to its guidance. If the dictionary does not present a wordpair as either a solid or a hyphenated compound, follow *Rule 3*. After each word-pair, write the number of the rule you have followed, disregarding whether Whitman followed the same rule.

Emily Dickinson   1830-1886

Emily Dickinson is an example of one who followed Thoreau's advice to "Explore thyself," to "be a Columbus to whole new continents and worlds within you." After a brief period of education away from home at Mount Holyoke Seminary (later College), she secluded herself in the family home at Amherst, Massachusetts. In a letter written in 1862, she said of herself:

You ask of my Companions—Hills—Sir—and the Sundown—and a Dog—large as myself. They are better than Beings—because they know—but do not tell—and the noise in the Pool, at Noon—excels my Piano. I have a Brother and Sister—My Mother does not care for thought—and Father, too busy with his Briefs—to notice what we do—He buys me many Books—but begs me not to read them—because he fears they joggle the Mind.

Her life was dull only on the surface. The inner adventures recorded in her poems show one of the great spirits of the age.

Emily Dickinson's literary career was as private as the rest of her activity. In 1862 she sent a few poems to the well-known man of letters, Thomas Wentworth Higginson. Higginson was struck by her genius and became her friend and counselor. However, he was puzzled by the irregular verse and feared their public reception. She accepted his verdict and thereafter wrote for herself and a few intimate friends. During her lifetime only seven poems were published and those without her consent. Yet she is now considered one of America's foremost poets.

At her death Emily Dickinson left behind close to 1800 poems, some neatly sewn together in little packets but many on odd scraps of paper. (Further information on Dickinson is included in Unit 1 on page 47.)

"Success is counted sweetest"

EMILY DICKINSON

Success is counted sweetest
By those who ne'er succeed.
To comprehend a nectar
Requires sorest need.

Not one of all the purple Host   5
Who took the Flag today
Can tell the definition
So clear of Victory

As he defeated—dying—
On whose forbidden ear   10
The distant strains of triumph
Burst agonized and clear!

Study Questions

1. In the first stanza who, according to the speaker, finds success most sweet? Why do they understand the "nectar" of success?

2. In the second and third stanzas the poet gives a specific example of the general statement made in the first stanza. What is the example?

3. How are the victors described in the second stanza? To what does the word "purple" allude?

4. Why does the one who is defeated clearly understand victory? How does the description in the last stanza help to explain lines 3 and 4?

5. Summarize the main idea of this poem.

"Because I could not stop for Death"

EMILY DICKINSON

Because I could not stop for Death—
He kindly stopped for me—
The Carriage held but just Ourselves—
And Immortality.

We slowly drove—He knew no haste   5
And I had put away
My labor and my leisure too,
For His Civility—

We passed the School where Children strove
At Recess—in the Ring—   10
We passed the Fields of Gazing Grain—
We passed the Setting Sun—

Or rather—He passed Us—
The Dews drew quivering and chill—
For only Gossamer,[1] my Gown—   15
My Tippet[2]—only Tulle[3]—

We paused before a House that seemed
A Swelling of the Ground—
The Roof was scarcely visible—
The Cornice[4]—in the Ground—   20

Since then—'tis Centuries—and yet
Feels shorter than the Day
I first surmised the Horses' Heads
Were toward Eternity—

---

1 **Gossamer:** a thin, gauzelike material.
2 **Tippet:** a scarf or shawl covering the neck and shoulders.
3 **Tulle** (tül): a thin, silk net material.
4 **Cornice:** ridge around the top of a house, just beneath the roof.

EQUIVALENT *Alfred Stieglitz*

Study Questions

1. Death is frequently described as a terrifying grim reaper with a scythe. How is death described in this poem?

2. If the journey in the carriage is a sustained metaphor for the journey through life, explain the symbolic significance of the visual images of school children, grain, and sun.

3. What is the "House" in line 17?

4. The last stanza registers a time change. Where is the speaker in this stanza?

5. Describe the speaker's attitude toward death in this poem.

6. This poem has sometimes been published without the fourth stanza. What effect would this omission have on your appreciation of the poem?

"After great pain, a formal feeling comes"

EMILY DICKINSON

After great pain, a formal feeling comes—
The Nerves sit ceremonious, like Tombs—
The stiff Heart questions was it He, that bore,
And Yesterday, or Centuries before?

The Feet, mechanical, go round—   5
Of Ground, or Air, or Ought—
A Wooden way
Regardless grown,
A Quartz contentment, like a stone—

This is the Hour of Lead—   10
Remembered, if outlived,
As Freezing persons, recollect the Snow—
First—Chill—then Stupor—then the letting go—

Study Questions

1. In this poem pain, either emotional or physical, is described. What kind of pain do words such as "formal," "ceremonious," and "stiff" suggest?

2. How does reference to parts of the body help the reader to recognize the depth of the pain? What contrast is provided by the way in which parts of the body are described?

3. Pain is felt, yet the imagery of the second stanza is all nonfeeling. What are the images used? Why are they effective? ineffective?

4. How does the image of freezing in the last stanza serve to complete and intensify the speaker's account of the pain?

Composition

1. In a short essay explain how Emily Dickinson uses concrete images to describe abstract experiences or feelings. Use examples from her poetry to support your position.

2. In a brief narrative describe how Emily Dickinson's poems express the theme of The Individual. Include the poem from Unit 1 (page 47) also. Tie in the quotation from Thoreau used in the headnote, (page 344).

Samuel Langhorne Clemens   1835-1910

Samuel Clemens (Mark Twain) in 1908.

Samuel Langhorne Clemens wrote under the name, "Mark Twain." Clemens grew up in Hannibal, Missouri, where he early acquired the lore of the Mississippi River which filled his writings. Later, he worked for a time as a printer. He then went west to become first a journalist and eventually a writer of humorous sketches. Pieces like "The Celebrated Jumping Frog of Calaveras County" (1865) were so well-received that he decided on a literary career. With the publication of *Tom Sawyer* (1876) and *Huckleberry Finn* (1884) he established himself as a signal figure in American letters. Ernest Hemingway was later moved to say, "All modern American literature comes from one book by Mark Twain called *Huckleberry Finn*. . . . There was nothing before. There has been nothing as good since."

Extravagant as this claim may seem, it reminds us of Clemens's two great contributions to the literature of this country: local language and humor. Instead of the formal English of earlier writers, he wrote English as it was actually spoken in this country. In so doing, he completed the "intellectual Declaration of Independence" begun by Emerson in "The American Scholar." And he used our familiar language to make us laugh. "The Invalid's Story" shows how he did it. (Further information on Clemens is included in Unit 1 on page 17.)

The Invalid's Story

SAMUEL LANGHORNE CLEMENS

I SEEM SIXTY and married, but these effects are due to my condition and sufferings, for I am a bachelor, and only forty-one. It will be hard for you to believe that I, who am now but a shadow, was a hale, hearty man two short years ago—a man of iron, a very athlete!—yet such is the simple truth. But stranger still than this fact is the way in which I lost my health. I lost it through helping to take care of a box of guns on a two-hundred-mile railway journey one winter's night. It is the actual truth, and I will tell you about it.

I belong in Cleveland, Ohio. One winter's night, two years ago, I reached home just after dark, in a driving snowstorm, and the first thing I heard when I entered the house was that my dearest boyhood friend and schoolmate, John B. Hackett, had died the day before, and that his last utterance had been a desire that I would take his remains home to his poor old father and mother in Wisconsin. I was greatly shocked and grieved, but there was no time to waste in emotions; I must start at once. I took the card, marked "Deacon Levi Hackett, Bethlehem, Wisconsin," and hurried off through the whistling storm to the railway station. Arrived there I found the long white-pine box which had been described to me; I fastened the card to it with some tacks, saw it put safely aboard the express car, and then ran into the eating room to provide myself with a sandwich and some cigars. When I returned, presently, there was my coffin box *back again,* apparently, and a young fellow examining around it, with a card in his hands, and some tacks and a hammer! I was astonished and puzzled. He began to nail on his card, and I rushed out to the express car, in a good deal of a state of mind, to ask for an explanation. But no—there was my box, all right, in the express car; it hadn't been disturbed. [The fact is that without my suspecting it a prodigious mistake had been made. I was carrying off a box of *guns* which that young fellow had come to the station to ship to a rifle company in Peoria, Illinois, and *he* had got my corpse!] Just then the conductor sang out "All aboard," and I jumped into the express car and got a comfortable seat on a bale of buckets. The expressman was there, hard at work—a plain man of fifty, with a simple, honest, good-natured face, and a breezy, practical heartiness in his general style. As the train moved off a stranger skipped into the car and set a package of peculiarly mature and capable Limburger cheese on one end of my coffin box—I mean my box of guns. That is to say, I know *now* that it was Limburger cheese, but at that time I never had heard of the article in my life, and of course was wholly ignorant of its character. Well, we sped through the wild night, the bitter storm raged on, a cheerless misery stole over me, my heart went down, down, down! The old expressman made a brisk remark or two about the tempest and the arctic weather, slammed his sliding doors to, and bolted them, closed his window down tight, and then went bustling around, here and there and yonder, setting things to rights, and all the time contentedly humming "Sweet By and By," in a low tone, and flatting a good deal. Presently I began to detect a most evil and searching odor stealing about on the frozen air. This depressed my spirits still more, because of course I attributed it to my poor departed friend. There was something infinitely saddening about his calling himself to my remembrance in this dumb, pathetic way, so it was hard to keep the tears back. Moreover, it distressed me on account of the old expressman, who, I was afraid, might notice it. However, he went humming tranquilly on, and gave no sign; and for this I was grateful. Grateful, yes, but still uneasy; and soon I began to feel more and more uneasy every minute, for every minute that went by that odor thickened up the more, and got to be more and more gamy and hard to stand. Presently, having got things arranged to his satisfaction, the expressman got some wood and made up a tremendous fire in his stove. This distressed me more than I can tell, for I could not but feel that it was a mistake. I was sure that the effect would be deleterious upon my poor departed friend. Thompson—the expressman's name was Thompson, as I found out in the course of the night—now went poking around his car, stopping up whatever stray cracks he could find, remarking that it didn't make any difference what kind of night it was outside, he calculated to make *us* comfortable, anyway. I said nothing, but I believed he was not choosing the right way. Meantime he was humming to himself just as before; and meantime, too, the stove was getting hotter and hotter, and the place closer and closer. I felt myself growing pale and qualmish, but grieved in silence and said nothing. Soon I noticed that the "Sweet By and By" was gradually fading out; next it ceased altogether, and there was an ominous stillness. After a few moments Thompson said—

"Pfew! I reckon it ain't no cinnamon 't I've loaded up thish-yer stove with!"

He gasped once or twice, then moved toward the cof—gun box, stood over that Limburger cheese part of a moment, then came back and sat down near me, looking a good deal impressed. After a contemplative pause, he said, indicating the box with a gesture—

"Friend of yourn?"

"Yes," I said with a sigh.

"He's pretty ripe, *ain't* he!"

Nothing further was said for perhaps a couple of minutes, each being busy with his own thoughts; then Thompson said, in a low, awed voice—

"Sometimes it's uncertain whether they're really gone or not—*seem* gone, you know—body warm, joints limber and so, although you *think* they're gone, you don't really know. I've had cases in my car. It's perfectly awful, becuz *you* don't know what minute they'll rise up and look at you!" Then, after a pause, and slightly lifting his elbow toward the box,— "But *he* ain't in no trance! No, sir, I go bail for *him!*"

We sat some time, in meditative silence, listening to the wind and the roar of the train; then Thompson said, with a good deal of feeling:

"Well-a-well, we've all got to go, they ain't no getting around it. Man that is born of woman is of few days and far between, as Scriptur' says. Yes, you look at it any way you want to, it's awful solemn and cur'us: they ain't *nobody* can get around it; *all's* got to go—just *everybody,* as you may say. One day you're hearty and strong"—here he scrambled to his feet and broke a pane and stretched his nose out at it a moment or two, then sat down again while I struggled up and thrust my nose out at the same place, and this we kept on doing every now and then—"and next day he's cut down like the grass, and the places which knowed him then knows him no more forever, as Scriptur' says. Yes'n-deedy, it's awful solemn and cur'us; but we've all got to go, one time or another; they ain't no getting around it."

There was another long pause; then—

"What did he die of?"

I said I didn't know.

"How long has he been dead?"

It seemed judicious to enlarge the facts to fit the probabilities; so I said:

"Two or three days."

But it did no good; for Thompson received it with an injured look which plainly said,

"Two or three *years,* you mean." Then he went right along, placidly ignoring my statement, and gave his views at considerable length upon the unwisdom of putting off burials too long. Then he lounged off toward the box, stood a moment, then came back on a sharp trot and visited the broken pane, observing:

"'Twould 'a' ben a dum sight better, all around, if they'd started him along last summer."

Thompson sat down and buried his face in his red silk handkerchief, and began to slowly sway and rock his body like one who is doing his best to endure the almost unendurable. By this time the fragrance—if you may call it fragrance—was just about suffocating, as near as you can come at it. Thompson's face was turning gray; I knew mine hadn't any color left in it. By and by Thompson rested his forehead in his left hand, with his elbow on his knee, and sort of waved his red handkerchief toward the box with his other hand, and said:

"I've carried a many a one of 'em—some of 'em considerable overdue, too—but, lordy, he just lays over 'em all!—and does it *easy.* Cap, they was heliotrope[1] to *him!*"

This recognition of my poor friend gratified me, in spite of the sad circumstances, because it had so much the sound of a compliment.

Pretty soon it was plain that something had got to be done. I suggested cigars. Thompson thought it was a good idea. He said:

"Likely it'll modify him some."

We puffed gingerly along for a while, and tried hard to imagine that things were improved. But it wasn't any use. Before very long, and without any consultation, both cigars were quietly dropped from our nerveless fingers at the same moment. Thompson said, with a sigh:

"No, Cap, it don't modify him worth a cent. Fact is, it makes him worse, becuz it

appears to stir up his ambition. What do you reckon we better do, now?"

I was not able to suggest anything; indeed, I had to be swallowing and swallowing all the time, and did not like to trust myself to speak. Thompson fell to maundering, in a desultory and low-spirited way, about the miserable experiences of this night; and he got to referring to my poor friend by various titles—sometimes military ones, sometimes civil ones; and I noticed that as fast as my poor friend's effectiveness grew, Thompson promoted him accordingly—gave him a bigger title. Finally he said:

"I've got an idea. Suppos'n' we buckle down to it and give the Colonel a bit of a shove toward t'other end of the car?—about ten foot, say. He wouldn't have so much influence, then, don't you reckon?"

I said it was a good scheme. So we took in a good fresh breath at the broken pane, calculating to hold it till we got through; then we went there and bent over that deadly cheese and took a grip on the box. Thompson nodded "All ready," and then we threw ourselves forward with all our might; but Thompson slipped, and slumped down with his nose on the cheese, and his breath got loose. He gagged and gasped, and floundered up and made a break for the door, pawing the air and saying hoarsely, "Don't hender me!—gimme the road! I'm a-dying; gimme the road!" Out on the cold platform I sat down and held his head awhile, and he revived. Presently he said:

"Do you reckon we started the Gen'rul any?"

I said no; we hadn't budged him.

"Well, then, *that* idea's up the flume. We got to think up something else. He's suited wher' he is, I reckon; and if that's the way he feels about it, and has made up his mind that he don't wish to be disturbed, you bet he's a-going to have his own way in the business. Yes, better leave him right wher' he is, long as he wants it so; becuz he holds all the trumps, don't you know, and so it stands to reason that

---

1 heliotrope (hē' lē ə trōp): a fragrant purple flower.

the man that lays out to alter his plans for him is going to get left."

But we couldn't stay out there in that mad storm; we should have frozen to death. So we went in again and shut the door, and began to suffer once more and take turns at the break in the window. By and by, as we were starting away from a station where we had stopped a moment Thompson pranced in cheerily, and exclaimed:

"We're all right, now! I reckon we've got the Commodore this time. I judge I've got the stuff here that'll take the tuck out of him."

It was carbolic acid. He had a carboy[2] of it. He sprinkled it all around everywhere; in fact he drenched everything with it, rifle box, cheese and all. Then we sat down, feeling pretty hopeful. But it wasn't for long. You see the two perfumes began to mix, and then— well, pretty soon we made a break for the door; and out there Thompson swabbed his face with his bandanna and said in a kind of disheartened way:

"It ain't no use. We can't buck agin *him.* He just utilizes everything we put up to modify him with, and gives it his own flavor and plays it back on us. Why, Cap, don't you know, it's as much as a hundred times worse in there now than it was when he first got a-going. I never *did* see one of 'em warm up to his work so, and take such a dumnation interest in it. No, sir, I never did, as long as I've ben on the road; and I've carried a many a one of 'em, as I was telling you."

We went in again after we were frozen pretty stiff; but my, we couldn't *stay* in, now. So we just waltzed back and forth, freezing, and thawing, and stifling, by turns. In about an hour we stopped at another station; and as we left it Thompson came in with a bag, and said—

"Cap, I'm a-going to chance him once more—just this once; and if we don't fetch him this time, the thing for us to do, is to just

throw up the sponge and withdraw from the canvass. That's the way *I* put it up."

He had brought a lot of chicken feathers, and dried apples, and leaf tobacco, and rags, and old shoes, and sulphur, and asafetida,[3] and one thing or another; and he piled them on a breadth of sheet iron in the middle of the floor, and set fire to them.

When they got well started, I couldn't see, myself, how even the corpse could stand it. All that went before was just simply poetry to that smell—but mind you, the original smell stood up out of it just as sublime as ever—fact is, these other smells just seemed to give it a better hold; and my, how rich it was! I didn't make these reflections there—there wasn't time—made them on the platform. And breaking for the platform, Thompson got suffocated and fell; and before I got him dragged out, which I did by the collar, I was mighty near gone myself. When we revived, Thompson said dejectedly:

"We got to stay out here, Cap. We got to do it. They ain't no other way. The Governor wants to travel alone, and he's fixed so he can outvote us."

And presently he added:

"And don't you know, we're *pisoned.* It's *our* last trip, you can make up your mind to it. Typhoid fever is what's going to come of this. I feel it a-coming right now. Yes, sir, we're elected, just as sure as you're born."

We were taken from the platform an hour later, frozen and insensible, at the next station, and I went straight off into a virulent fever, and never knew anything again for three weeks. I found out, then, that I had spent that awful night with a harmless box of rifles and a lot of innocent cheese; but the news was too late to save *me;* imagination had done its work, and my health was permanently shattered; neither Bermuda nor any other land can ever bring it back to me. This is my last trip; I am on my way home to die.

---

2 **carboy:** glass container.

3 **asafetida** (as efid′ ed ē): strong-smelling resin.

Study Questions

1. How, according to the narrator, did he lose his health?
2. What two accidents lead to the narrator's misadventure?
3. How does the reader know by the end of the first paragraph that this is a tall tale? What humorous details indicate this?
4. This story is what today would be called a "sick" joke. What information does Clemens include so that the reader will be able to laugh and not be appalled?
5. There are two styles of writing in the story, the straightforward, correct prose of the narrator and the racy colloquial speech of the expressman. How does Clemens use these contrasting styles to produce humor?

Vocabulary

Much of the humor in "The Invalid's Story" springs from Clemens's skillful use of **euphemisms** and **circumlocution.**

A euphemism is a comparatively pleasant word or phrase substituted for a harsh or unpleasant one. The word *remains* is a euphemism when it is substituted for the word *corpse.* "We've all got to *go*" is a euphemism when it replaces "We've all got to *die.*"

The term *circumlocution* is defined as "any roundabout expression." Euphemisms, then, constitute a subcategory of circumlocutions. However, circumlocutions also include other kinds of indirect expressions, especially those which use more words than necessary and those in which word choice has a more elegant tone than that of ordinary language. For example:

Plain Statement: I was sorry my friend's corpse had begun to smell decayed.
Circumlocution: There was something infinitely saddening about his calling himself to my remembrance in this dumb, pathetic way.

Not all circumlocutions are long-winded and framed in elegant language. For example:

Plain Statement: "I have put really foul-smelling stuff in this stove!"
Circumlocution: "I reckon it ain't no cinnamon 't I've loaded up thish-yer stove with."

Find at least five examples of euphemism or circumlocution in Clemens's "The Invalid's Story." Then convert each one into a rephrased plain, straightforward statement.

Chief Joseph · 1841-1904

Gold was discovered in the peaceful Wallowa Valley in the 1860s. Soon, miners' towns crowded out the Native American villages. Several Nez Percé chiefs signed over tribal lands to the miners, but, following the example of his father, Chief Joseph did not sign the treaty. Enormous pressures, eventually leading to war, were brought against Chief Joseph. During the fighting, Chief Joseph led his people over more than a thousand miles under terrible conditions. He finally surrendered on the battlefield, but never gave up the struggle of trying to convince the government to treat Native Americans the same as other Americans. The speech below is one of those efforts.

Let Me Be a Free Man

CHIEF JOSEPH (In-mut-too-yah-lat-lat)

MY FRIENDS, I have been asked to show you my heart. I am glad to have a chance to do so. I want the white people to understand my people. Some of you think an Indian is like a wild animal. This is a great mistake. I will tell you all about our people, and then you can judge whether an Indian is a man or not. I believe much trouble and blood would be saved if we opened our hearts more. I will tell you in my way how the Indian sees things. The white man has more words to tell you how they look to him, but it does not require many words to speak the truth. What I have to say will come from my heart, and I will speak with a straight tongue. Ah-cum-kin-i-ma-me-hut (the Great Spirit) is looking at me, and will hear me.

My name is In-mut-too-yah-lat-lat (Thunder traveling over the Mountains). I am chief of the Wal-lam-wat-kin band of Chute-pa-lu, or Nez Percés (nose-pierced Indians). I was born in eastern Oregon, thirty-eight winters ago. My father was chief before me. When a young man, he was called Joseph by Mr. Spaulding, a missionary. He died a few years ago. He left a good name on earth. He advised me well for my people. . . .

We did not know there were other people besides the Indian until about one hundred winters ago, when some men with white faces came to our country. They brought many things with them to trade for furs and skins. They brought tobacco, which was new to us. They brought guns with flint stones on them, which frightened our women and children. Our people could not talk with these white-faced men, but they used signs which all people understand. These men were Frenchmen, and they called our people "Nez Percés," because they wore rings in their noses for ornaments. Although very few of our people wear them now, we are still called by the same name. These French trappers said a great many things to our fathers, which have been planted in our hearts. Some were good for us, but some were bad. Our people were divided in opinion about these men. Some thought they taught more bad than good. An Indian respects a brave man, but he despises a coward. He loves a straight tongue, but he hates a forked tongue. The French trappers told us some truths and some lies.

The first white men of your people who came to our country were named Lewis and Clark. They also brought many things that our people had never seen. They talked straight, and our people gave them a great feast, as a proof that their hearts were friendly. These men were very kind. They made presents to our chiefs and our people made presents to them. We had a great many horses, of which we gave them what they needed, and they gave us guns and tobacco in return. All the Nez Percés made friends with Lewis and Clark, and agreed to let them pass through their country, and never to make war on white men. This promise the Nez Percés have never broken. No white man can accuse them of bad faith, and speak with a straight tongue. It has always been the pride of the Nez Percés that they were the friends of the white men. When my father was a young man there came to our country a white man (Rev. Mr. Spaulding) who talked spirit law. He won the affections of our people because he spoke good things to them. At first he did not say anything about white men wanting to settle on our lands. Nothing was said about that until about twenty winters ago, when a number of white people came into our country and built houses and made farms. At first our people made no complaint. They thought there was room enough for all to live in peace, and they were learning many things from the white men that seemed to be good. But we soon found that the white men were growing rich very fast, and

were greedy to possess everything the Indian had. My father was the first to see through the schemes of the white men, and he warned his tribe to be careful about trading with them. He had suspicion of men who seemed anxious to make money. I was a boy then, but I remember well my father's caution. He had sharper eyes than the rest of our people.

Next there came a white officer (Governor Stevens), who invited all the Nez Percés to a treaty council. After the council was opened he made known his heart. He said there were a great many white people in our country, and many more would come; that he wanted the land marked out so that the Indians and white men could be separated. If they were to live in peace it was necessary, he said, that the Indians should have a country set apart for them, and in that country they must stay. My father, who represented his band, refused to have anything to do with the council, because he wished to be a free man. He claimed that no man owned any part of the earth, and a man could not sell what he did not own.

Mr. Spaulding took hold of my father's arm and said, "Come and sign the treaty." My father pushed him away, and said: "Why do you ask me to sign away my country? It is your business to talk to us about spirit matters and not to talk to us about parting with our land." Governor Stevens urged my father to sign his treaty, but he refused. "I will not sign your paper," he said; "you go where you please, so do I; you are not a child, I am no child; I can think for myself. No man can think for me. I have no other home than this. I will not give it up to any man. My people would have no home. Take away your paper. I will not touch it with my hand."

My father left the council. Some of the chiefs of the other bands of the Nez Percés signed the treaty, and then Governor Stevens gave them presents of blankets. My father cautioned his people to take no presents, for "after a while," he said, "they will claim that you have accepted pay for your country." Since

Chief Joseph, chief of the Nez Percé Indians.

A New Maturity

that time four bands of the Nez Percés have received annuities[1] from the United States. My father was invited to many councils, and they tried hard to make him sign the treaty, but he was firm as the rock, and would not sign away his home. His refusal caused a difference among the Nez Percés.

Eight years later (1863) was the next treaty council. A chief called Lawyer, because he was a great talker, took the lead in this council, and sold nearly all the Nez Percés country. My father was not there. He said to me: "When you go into council with the white man, always remember your country. Do not give it away. The white man will cheat you out of your home. I have taken no pay from the United States. I have never sold our land." In this treaty Lawyer acted without authority from our band. He had no right to sell the Wallowa (winding water) country. That had always belonged to my father's own people, and the other bands had never disputed our right to it. No other Indians ever claimed Wallowa.

In order to have all people understand how much land we owned, my father planted poles around it and said:

"Inside is the home of my people—the white man may take the land outside. Inside this boundary all our people were born. It circles around the graves of our fathers, and we will never give up these graves to any man."

The United States claimed they had bought all the Nez Percés country outside the Lapwai Reservation, from Lawyer and other chiefs, but we continued to live on this land in peace until eight years ago, when white men began to come inside the bounds my father had set. We warned them against this great wrong, but they would not leave our land, and some bad blood was raised. The white men represented that we were going upon the warpath. They reported many things that were false.

The United States Government again asked

for a treaty council. My father had become blind and feeble. He could no longer speak for his people. It was then that I took my father's place as chief. In this council I made my first speech to white men. I said to the agent who held the council:

"I did not want to come to this council, but I came hoping that we could save blood. The white man has no right to come here and take our country. We have never accepted any presents from the Government. Neither Lawyer nor any other chief had authority to sell this land. It has always belonged to my people. It came unclouded to them from our fathers, and we will defend this land as long as a drop of Indian blood warms the hearts of our men."

The agent said he had orders, from the Great White Chief at Washington, for us to go upon the Lapwai Reservation, and that if we obeyed he would help us in many ways. "You must move to the agency," he said. I answered him: "I will not. I do not need your help; we have plenty, and we are contented and happy if the white man will let us alone. The reservation is too small for so many people with all their stock. You can keep your presents; we can go to your towns and pay for all we need; we have plenty of horses and cattle to sell, and we won't have any help from you; we are free now; we can go where we please. Our fathers were born here. Here they lived, here they died, here are their graves. We will never leave them." The agent went away, and we had peace for a little while.

Soon after this my father sent for me. I saw he was dying. I took his hand in mine. He said: "My son, my body is returning to mother earth, and my spirit is going very soon to see the Great Spirit Chief. When I am gone, think of your country. You are the chief of these people. They look to you to guide them. Always remember that your father never sold this country. You must stop your ears whenever you are asked to sign a treaty selling your home. A few years more, and white men will be all around you. They have their eyes on this

---

1 **annuities:** sums of money paid every year.

Last camp of the Nez Percé Indians.

land. My son, never forget my dying words. This country holds your father's body. Never sell the bones of your father and your mother." I pressed my father's hand and told him I would protect his grave with my life. My father smiled and passed away to the spirit land.

I buried him in that beautiful valley of winding waters. I love that land more than all the rest of the world. A man who would not love his father's grave is worse than a wild animal.

For a short time we lived quietly. But this could not last. White men had found gold in the mountains around the land of winding water. They stole many horses from us, and we could not get them back because we were Indians. . . . I labored hard to avoid trouble and bloodshed. We gave up some of our country to the white men, thinking that then we could

have peace. We were mistaken. The white man would not let us alone. We could have avenged our wrongs many times, but we did not. Whenever the Government has asked us to help them against other Indians, we have never refused. When the white men were few and we were strong we could have killed them all off, but the Nez Percés wished to live at peace.

If we have not done so, we have not been to blame. I believe that the old treaty has never been correctly reported. If we ever owned the land we own it still, for we never sold it. In the treaty councils the commissioners have claimed that our country had been sold to the Government. Suppose a white man should come to me and say, "Joseph, I like your horses, and I want to buy them." I say to him, "No, my horses suit me, I will not sell them." Then he goes to my neighbor, and says to him:

"Joseph has some good horses. I want to buy them, but he refuses to sell." My neighbor answers, "Pay me the money, and I will sell you Joseph's horses." The white man returns to me and says, "Joseph, I have bought your horses, and you must let me have them." If we sold our lands to the government, this is the way they were bought. . . .

I only ask of the Government to be treated as all other men are treated. If I can not go to my own home, let me have a home in some country where my people will not die so fast. I would like to go to Bitter Root Valley. There my people would be healthy; where they are now they are dying. Three have died since I left my camp to come to Washington. . . .

Let me be a free man—free to travel, free to stop, free to work, free to trade where I choose, free to choose my own teachers, free to follow the religion of my fathers, free to think and talk and act for myself—and I will obey every law, or submit to the penalty.

Whenever the white man treats an Indian as they treat each other, then we will have no more wars. We shall all be alike—brothers of one father and one mother, with one sky above us and one country around us, and one government for all. Then the Great Spirit Chief who rules above will smile upon this land, and send rain to wash out the bloody spots made by brothers' hands from the face of the earth. For this time the Indian race are waiting and praying. I hope no more groans of wounded men and women will ever go to the ear of the Great Spirit Chief above, and that all people may be one people.

In-mut-too-yah-lat-lat has spoken for his people.

Study Questions

1. Why does Chief Joseph say he is speaking?
2. How do Chief Joseph's people react to the first people with white faces (the French) to come into Nez Percé country?
3. What promise did the Nez Percés make to Lewis and Clark? What did Governor Stevens propose?
4. Why did Chief Joseph's father repeatedly refuse to sign the treaties? What do you think Chief Joseph means by the statement, "A man who would not love his father's grave is worse than a wild animal"?
5. What happened after the death of the elder Chief Joseph?
6. Why do you think Chief Joseph's requests are reasonable? unreasonable?

Vocabulary

As Europeans took over territory after territory in North America, they adopted Native American names for many of the plants, trees, animals, and foods they were encountering for the first time.

Three out of four of the Native American words used by speakers of English today were taken from the fifty-odd Algonkin (Algonquian) languages. When the Puritans arrived at Plymouth, Algonkin tongues were spoken throughout an area stretching from the Rocky Mountains eastward to the

Atlantic, and from Labrador southward to North Carolina and Tennessee. Tribes using these languages included the Abnaki, Cree, Delaware, Massachuset, Narraganset, Ojibwa, Powhatan, and Passamaquoddy.

Predominance of Algonkin word borrowings over those from other Native American languages can be partly accounted for by the fact that these languages were the first encountered by the Europeans as they settled on the Atlantic Coast. Once Algonkin terms had been applied to the unfamiliar fauna, flora, and foods, they tended to remain in the language even though names for these same things from other language families were encountered later on.

"*Wigwam,* an Algonkin term, appears in English as early as 1628, not long after the beginning of the New England colonization. The first citation for the Plains Indians' term *tepee* is 1835, when explorers and settlers were pushing across the Mississippi. *Hogan,* the Navaho word for a dwelling, [did] not put in an appearance until 1871"[1]

English borrowings from Amerindian languages other than those of the Algonkin group include some words absorbed during the Lewis and Clark Expedition (1804–06), to which Chief Joseph refers. "It is quite natural that in the notebooks of that expedition one would find such statements as 'These natives have a large quantity of this root bread which they call *commass'*"[2] (now spelled *camas:* a Western plant with blue or white flowers and edible bulbs).

At first glance, modern English terms based on Amerindian words often seem barely related to their actual roots. For example, the word *hickory* is based upon the Native American term *pawcohiccora,* which sounds quite different. There are two principal reasons for such discrepancies: (1) Many sounds in Native American languages have no equivalents in English and, therefore, had to be adapted. (2) Many Native American words were much longer than speakers of English could manage conveniently and, therefore, were shortened.

In a collegiate dictionary, find the etymologies for these words:

opossum	persimmon	(corn)pone	skunk
pecan	poke(weed)	sequoia	succotash

In some of these etymologies, you are likely to find two unfamiliar words: *Proto-Algonkin* and *unattested. Proto-Algonkin* is defined as "the earliest reconstructed ancestor of the family of Algonkin languages" (see above). Used in etymologies, *unattested* designates a word form whose existence cannot be proved by written evidence (printed transcriptions of the languages are rare).

---

1 Albert H. Marckwardt, *American English* (New York: Oxford University Press, 1958), pp. 26–27.
2 *Ibid.,* p. 22.

Henry James   1843-1916

Born in New York, Henry James grew up
in a family which divided its time between
Europe and America. He was educated in
Germany, France, England, Switzerland, and
Italy as well as the United States. He knew
the languages of all these countries. As a
small boy he wandered among the paintings
in the Louvre as casually as a child today
might watch a television program. He was
taken to the theater in London and Paris.
He found French and English magazines in
the family living room. As an adult, he
lived for a time in Rome and Paris before
settling in London. It is little wonder that
he wrote about the frontier between the
Old European World and the New World,
rather than about life in the Wild West or
in a small American town.

   Historically, of course, America has always had a close relationship with Europe.
A long procession of writers from Benjamin
Franklin to Ernest Hemingway and James
Baldwin have discovered some part of their
American identity by going to Europe. And,
as they did in James's time, American tour-
ists still make the European pilgrimage in
huge numbers. This is the world of Henry
James. His most characteristic story deals
with Americans traveling or living in Europe and concerns the misunderstandings,
comic or tragic, which arise between people
from different cultural backgrounds. "Four
Meetings" is the story of an American who
does *not* travel in Europe; yet it is very
much a story about what Europe and
America sometimes mean to each other.

Henry James in 1906

Four Meetings

HENRY JAMES

I SAW HER only four times, but I remember them vividly; she made an impression upon me. I thought her very pretty and very interesting—a charming specimen of a type. I am very sorry to hear of her death; and yet, when I think of it, why should I be sorry? The last time I saw her she was certainly not——But I will describe all our meetings in order.

I

The first one took place in the country, at a little tea-party, one snowy night. It must have been some seventeen years ago. My friend Latouche, going to spend Christmas with his mother, had persuaded me to go with him, and the good lady had given in our honour the entertainment of which I speak. To me it was really entertaining; I had never been in the depths of New England at that season. It had been snowing all day and the drifts were knee-high. I wondered how the ladies had made their way to the house; but I perceived that at Grimwinter a conversazione offering the attraction of two gentlemen from New York was felt to be worth an effort.

Mrs. Latouche in the course of the evening asked me if I "didn't want to" show the photographs to some of the young ladies. The photographs were in a couple of great portfolios, and had been brought home by her son, who, like myself, was lately returned from Europe. I looked round and was struck with the fact that most of the young ladies were provided with an object of interest more absorbing than the most vivid sunpicture. But there was a person standing alone near the mantelshelf, and looking round the room with a small, gentle smile which seemed at odds, somehow, with her isolation. I looked at her a moment, and then said, "I should like to show them to that young lady."

"Oh yes," said Mrs. Latouche, "she is just the person. She doesn't care for flirting; I will speak to her."

I rejoined that if she did not care for flirting, she was, perhaps, not just the person; but Mrs. Latouche had already gone to propose the photographs to her.

"She's delighted," she said, coming back. "She is just the person, so quiet and so bright." And then she told me the young lady was, by name, Miss Caroline Spencer, and with this she introduced me.

Miss Caroline Spencer was not exactly a beauty, but she was a charming little figure. She must have been close upon thirty, but she was made almost like a little girl, and she had the complexion of a child. She had a very pretty head, and her hair was arranged as nearly as possible like the hair of a Greek bust, though indeed it was to be doubted if she had ever seen a Greek bust. She was "artistic," I suspected, so far as Grimwinter allowed such tendencies. She had a soft, surprised eye, and thin lips, with very pretty teeth. Round her neck she wore what ladies call, I believe, a "ruche," fastened with a very small pin in pink coral, and in her hand she carried a fan made of plaited straw and adorned with pink ribbon. She wore a scanty black silk dress. She spoke with a kind of soft precision, showing her white teeth between her narrow but tender-looking lips, and she seemed extremely pleased, even a little fluttered, at the prospect of my demonstrations. These went forward very smoothly, after I had moved the portfolios out of their corner and placed a couple of chairs near a lamp. The photographs were usually things I knew,—large views of Switzerland, Italy, and Spain, landscapes, copies of famous buildings, pictures and statues. I said what I could about them, and my companion, looking at them as I held them up, sat perfectly still, with her straw fan raised to her underlip. Occasionally, as I laid one of the pictures down, she said very softly, "Have you seen that place?" I usually answered that I had seen it several times (I had been a great traveller), and then I felt that she looked at me askance for a moment with her pretty eyes. I had asked her at the outset whether she had been to Europe; to this she answered, "No, no, no," in a little quick, confidential whisper. But after that, though she never took her eyes off the pictures, she said so little that I was afraid she was bored. Accordingly, after we had finished one portfolio, I offered, if she desired it, to desist. I felt that she was not bored, but her reticence puzzled me and I wished to make her speak. I turned round to look at her, and saw that there was a faint flush in each of her cheeks. She was waving her little fan to and fro. Instead of looking at me she fixed her eyes upon the other portfolio, which was leaning against the table.

"Won't you show me that?" she asked, with a little tremor in her voice. I could almost have believed she was agitated.

"With pleasure," I answered, "if you are not tired."

"No, I am not tired," she affirmed. "I like it—I love it."

And as I took up the other portfolio she laid her hand upon it, rubbing it softly.

"And have you been here too?" she asked.

On my opening the portfolio it appeared that I had been there. One of the first photographs was a large view of the Castle of Chillon, on the Lake of Geneva.

"Here," I said, "I have been many a time. Is it not beautiful?" And I pointed to the perfect reflection of the rugged rocks and pointed towers in the clear, still water. She did not say, "Oh, enchanting!" and push it away to see the next picture. She looked awhile, and then she asked if it was not where Bonivard, about whom Byron wrote, was confined. I assented, and tried to quote some of Byron's verses, but in this attempt I succeeded imperfectly.

She fanned herself a moment and then repeated the lines correctly, in a soft, flat, and yet agreeable voice. By the time she had finished, she was blushing. I complimented her and told her she was perfectly equipped for visiting Switzerland and Italy. She looked at me askance again, to see whether I was serious, and I added, that if she wished to recognize Byron's descriptions she must go abroad speedily; Europe was getting sadly dis-Byronised.

"How soon must I go?" she asked.

"Oh, I will give you ten years."

"I think I can go within ten years," she answered very soberly.

"Well," I said, "you will enjoy it immensely; you will find it very charming." And just then I came upon a photograph of some nook in a foreign city which I had been very fond of, and which recalled tender memories. I discoursed (as I suppose) with a certain eloquence; my companion sat listening, breathless.

"Have you been *very* long in foreign lands?" she asked, some time after I had ceased.

"Many years," I said.

"And have you traveled everywhere?"

"I have traveled a great deal. I am very fond of it; and, happily, I have been able."

Again she gave me her sidelong gaze. "And do you know the foreign languages?"

"After a fashion."

"Is it hard to speak them?"

"I don't believe you would find it hard," I gallantly responded.

"Oh, I shouldn't want to speak—I should only want to listen," she said. Then, after a pause, she added—"They say the French theater is so beautiful."

"It is the best in the world."

"Did you go there very often?"

"When I was first in Paris I went every night."

"Every night!" And she opened her clear eyes very wide. "That to me is—" and she hesitated a moment—"is very wonderful." A few minutes later she asked—"Which country do you prefer?"

"There is one country I prefer to all others. I think you would do the same."

She looked at me a moment, and then she said softly—"Italy?"

"Italy," I answered softly, too; and for a moment we looked at each other. She looked as pretty as if, instead of showing her photographs, I had been making love to her. To increase the analogy, she glanced away, blushing. There was a silence, which she broke at last by saying—

"That is the place, which—in particular—I thought of going to."

"Oh, that's the place—that's the place!" I said.

She looked at two or three photographs in silence. "They say it is not so dear."[1]

"As some other countries? Yes, that is not the least of its charms."

"But it is all very dear, is it not?"

"Europe, you mean?"

"Going there and traveling. That has been the trouble. I have very little money. I give lessons," said Miss Spencer.

"Of course one must have money," I said, "but one can manage with a moderate amount."

"I think I should manage. I have laid something by, and I am always adding a little to it.

---

1 **dear**: here, costly.

It's all for that." She paused a moment, and then went on with a kind of suppressed eagerness, as if telling me the story were a rare, but a possibly impure, satisfaction. "But it has not been only the money; it has been everything. Everything has been against it. I have waited and waited. It has been a mere castle in the air. I am almost afraid to talk about it. Two or three times it has been a little nearer, and then I have talked about it and it has melted away. I have talked about it too much," she said, hypocritically; for I saw that such talking was now a small tremulous ecstasy. "There is a lady who is a great friend of mine; she doesn't want to go; I always talk to her about it. I tire her dreadfully. She told me once she didn't know what would become of me. I should go crazy if I did not go to Europe, and I should certainly go crazy if I did."

"Well," I said, "you have not gone yet, and nevertheless you are not crazy."

She looked at me a moment, and said—"I am not so sure. I don't think of anything else. I am always thinking of it. It prevents me from thinking of things that are nearer home—things that I ought to attend to. That is a kind of craziness."

"The cure for it is to go," I said.

"I have a faith that I shall go. I have a cousin in Europe!" she announced.

We turned over some more photographs, and I asked her if she had always lived at Grimwinter.

"Oh, no, sir," said Miss Spencer. "I have spent twenty-three months in Boston."

I answered, jocosely, that in that case foreign lands would probably prove a disappointment to her; but I quite failed to alarm her.

"I know more about them than you might think," she said, with her shy, neat little smile. "I mean by reading; I have read a great deal. I have not only read Byron; I have read histories and guide-books. I know I shall like it!"

"I understand your case," I rejoined. "You have the native American passion—the passion for the picturesque. With us, I think, it is pri-mordial—antecedent to experience. Experience comes and only shows us something we have dreamed of."

"I think that is very true," said Caroline Spencer. "I have dreamed of everything; I shall know it all!"

"I am afraid you have wasted a great deal of time."

"Oh yes, that has been my great wickedness."

The people about us had begun to scatter; they were taking their leave. She got up and put out her hand to me, timidly, but with a peculiar brightness in her eyes.

"I am going back there," I said, as I shook hands with her. "I shall look out for you."

"I will tell you," she answered, "if I am disappointed."

And she went away, looking delicately agitated and moving her little straw fan.

II

A few months after this I returned to Europe, and some three years elapsed. I had been living in Paris, and, toward the end of October, I went from that city to Havre, to meet my sister and her husband, who had written me that they were about to arrive there. On reaching Havre I found that the steamer was already in; I was nearly two hours late. I repaired directly to the hotel, where my relatives were already established. My sister had gone to bed, exhausted and disabled by her voyage; she was a sadly incompetent sailor, and her sufferings on this occasion had been extreme. She wished, for the moment, for undisturbed rest, and was unable to see me more than five minutes; so it was agreed that we should remain at Havre until the next day. My brother-in-law, who was anxious about his wife, was unwilling to leave her room; but she insisted upon his going out with me to take a walk and recover his

land legs. The early autumn day was warm and charming, and our stroll through the bright colored, busy streets of the old French seaport was sufficiently entertaining. We walked along the sunny, noisy quays[2] and then turned into a wide, pleasant street which lay half in sun and half in shade—a French provincial street, that looked like an old water color drawing: tall, gray, steep-roofed, red-gabled, many-storied houses; green shutters on windows and old scroll-work above them; flower pots in balconies and white-capped women in doorways. We walked in the shade;

2 **quays** (kēz): a paved bank or artificial landing place for loading and unloading ships.

all this stretched away on the sunny side of the street and made a picture. We looked at it as we passed along; then, suddenly, my brother-in-law stopped—pressing my arm and staring. I followed his gaze and saw that we had paused just before coming to a café, where, under an awning, several tables and chairs were disposed upon the pavement. The windows were open behind; half-a-dozen plants in tubs were ranged beside the door; the pavement was besprinkled with clean bran. It was a nice little, quiet, old-fashioned café; inside, in the comparative dusk, I saw a stout, handsome woman, with pink ribbons in her cap, perched up with a mirror behind her back, smiling at someone who was out of sight. All this, however, I perceived afterwards; what I first observed was a lady sitting alone, outside, at one of the little marble-topped tables. My brother-in-law had stopped to look at her. There was something on the little table, but she was leaning back quietly, with her hands folded, looking down the street, away from us. I saw her only in something less than profile; nevertheless, I instantly felt that I had seen her before.

"The little lady of the steamer!" exclaimed my brother-in-law.

"Was she on your steamer?" I asked.

"From morning till night. She was never sick. She used to sit perpetually at the side of the vessel with her hands crossed that way, looking at the eastward horizon."

"Are you going to speak to her?"

"I don't know her. I never made acquaintance with her. I was too seedy. But I used to watch her and—I don't know why—to be interested in her. She's a dear little Yankee woman. I have an idea she is a school mistress taking a holiday—for which her scholars have made up a purse."

She turned her face a little more into profile, looking at the steep, gray house-fronts opposite to her. Then I said—"I shall speak to her myself."

"I wouldn't; she is very shy," said my brother-in-law.

"My dear fellow, I know her. I once showed her photographs at a tea party."

And I went up to her. She turned and looked at me, and I saw she was in fact Miss Caroline Spencer. But she was not so quick to recognize me; she looked startled. I pushed a chair to the table and sat down.

"Well," I said, "I hope you are not disappointed!"

She stared, blushing a little; then she gave a small jump which betrayed recognition.

"It was you who showed me the photographs—at Grimwinter!"

"Yes, it was I. This happens very charmingly, for I feel as if it were for me to give you

a formal reception here—an official welcome. I talked to you so much about Europe."

"You didn't say too much. I am so happy!" she softly exclaimed.

Very happy she looked. There was no sign of her being older; she was as gravely, decently, demurely pretty as before. If she had seemed before a thin-stemmed, mild-hued flower of Puritanism, it may be imagined whether in her present situation this delicate bloom was less apparent. Beside her an old gentleman was drinking absinthe; behind her the *dame de comptoir*[3] in the pink ribbons was calling "Alcibiade! Alcibiade!" to the long aproned waiter. I explained to Miss Spencer that my companion had lately been her shipmate, and my brother-in-law came up and was introduced to her. But she looked at him as if

---

3 *dame de comptoir* (däm de komptwä): cashier.

she had never seen him before, and I remembered that he had told me that her eyes were always fixed upon the eastward horizon. She had evidently not noticed him, and, still timidly smiling, she made no attempt whatever to pretend that she had. I stayed with her at the café door, and he went back to the hotel and to his wife. I said to Miss Spencer that this meeting of ours in the first hour of her landing was really very strange, but that I was delighted to be there and receive her first impressions.

"Oh, I can't tell you," she said; "I feel as if I were in a dream. I have been sitting here for an hour, and I don't want to move. Everything is so picturesque. I don't know whether the coffee has intoxicated me; it's so delicious."

"Really," said I, "if you are so pleased with this poor prosaic Havre, you will have no admiration left for better things. Don't spend your admiration all the first day; remember it's your intellectual letter of credit. Remember all the beautiful places and things that are waiting for you; remember that lovely Italy!"

"I'm not afraid of running short," she said gayly, still looking at the opposite houses. "I could sit here all day, saying to myself that here I am at last. It's so dark, and old, and different."

"By the way," I inquired, "how come you to be sitting here? Have you not gone to one of the inns?" For I was half amused, half alarmed at the good conscience with which this delicately pretty woman had stationed herself in conspicuous isolation on the edge of the sidewalk.

"My cousin brought me here," she answered. "You know I told you I had a cousin in Europe. He met me at the steamer this morning."

"It was hardly worth his while to meet you if he was to desert you so soon."

"Oh, he has only left me for half-an-hour," said Miss Spencer. "He has gone to get my money."

"Where is your money?"

She gave a little laugh. "It makes me feel very fine to tell you! It is in some circular notes."

"And where are your circular notes?"

"In my cousin's pocket."

This statement was very serenely uttered, but—I can hardly say why—it gave me a sensible chill. At the moment I should have been utterly unable to give the reason of this sensation, for I knew nothing of Miss Spencer's cousin. Since he was her cousin, the presumption was in his favour. But I felt suddenly uncomfortable at the thought that, half-an-hour after her landing, her scanty funds should have passed into his hands.

"Is he to travel with you?" I asked.

"Only as far as Paris. He is an art student in Paris. I wrote to him that I was coming, but I never expected him to come off to the ship. I supposed he would only just meet me at the train in Paris. It is very kind of him. But he *is* very kind—and very bright."

I instantly became conscious of an extreme curiosity to see this bright cousin who was an art student.

"He is gone to the banker's?" I asked.

"Yes, to the banker's. He took me to an hotel—such a queer, quaint, delicious little place, with a court in the middle, and a gallery all round, and a lovely landlady, in such a beautifully fluted cap, and such a perfectly fitting dress! After a while we came out to walk to the banker's, for I haven't got any French money. But I was very dizzy from the motion of the vessel, and I thought I had better sit down. He found this place for me here, and he went off to the the banker's himself. I am to wait here till he comes back."

It may seem very fantastic, but it passed through my mind that he would never come back. I settled myself in my chair beside Miss Spencer and determined to await the event. She was extremely observant; there was something touching in it. She noticed everything that the movement of the street brought before us—the peculiarities of costume, the shapes of

vehicles, the big Norman horses, the fat priests, the shaven poodles. We talked of these things, and there was something charming in her freshness of perception and the way her book-nourished fancy recognised and welcomed everything.

"And when your cousin comes back what are you going to do?" I asked.

She hesitated a moment. "We don't quite know."

"When do you go to Paris? If you go by the four o'clock train I may have the pleasure of making the journey with you."

"I don't think we shall do that. My cousin thinks I had better stay here a few days."

"Oh!" said I; and for five minutes said nothing more. I was wondering what her cousin was, in vulgar parlance, "up to." I looked up and down the street, but saw nothing that looked like a bright American art-student. At last I took the liberty of observing that Havre was hardly a place to choose as one of the aesthetic stations of a European tour. It was a place of convenience, nothing more; a place of transit, through which transit should be rapid. I recommended her to go to Paris by the afternoon train, and meanwhile to amuse herself by driving to the ancient fortress at the mouth of the harbor—that picturesque, circular structure which bore the name of Francis the First and looked like a small castle of St. Angelo. (It has lately been demolished.)

She listened with much interest; then for a moment she looked grave.

"My cousin told me that when he returned he should have something particular to say to me, and that we could do nothing or decide nothing until I should have heard it. But I will make him tell me quickly, and then we will go to the ancient fortress. There is no hurry to get to Paris; there is plenty of time."

She smiled with her softly severe little lips

as she spoke those last words. But I, looking at her with a purpose, saw just a tiny gleam of apprehension in her eye.

"Don't tell me," I said, "that this wretched man is going to give you bad news!"

"I suspect it is a little bad, but I don't believe it is very bad. At any rate, I must listen to it."

I looked at her again an instant. "You didn't come to Europe to listen," I said. "You came to see!" But now I was sure her cousin would come back; since he had something disagreeable to say to her, he certainly would turn up. We sat a while longer, and I asked her about her plans of travel. She had them on her fingers' ends, and she told over the names with a kind of solemn distinctness: from Paris to Dijon and to Avignon, from Avignon to Marseilles and the Cornice road; thence to Genoa, to Spezia, to Pisa, to Florence, to Rome. It apparently had never occurred to her that there could be the least incommodity in her traveling alone; and since she was unprovided with a companion I of course scrupulously abstained from disturbing her sense of security.

At last her cousin came back. I saw him turn towards us out of a side street, and from the moment my eyes rested upon him I felt that this was the bright American art student. He wore a slouch hat and a rusty black velvet jacket, such as I had often encountered in the Rue Bonaparte. His shirt collar revealed a large section of a throat which, at a distance, was not strikingly statuesque. He was tall and lean; he had red hair and freckles. So much I had time to observe while he approached the café, staring at me with natural surprise from under his umbrageous coiffure. When he came up to us I immediately introduced myself to him as an old acquaintance of Miss Spencer. He looked at me hard with a pair of little red eyes, then he made me a solemn bow in the French fashion, with his sombrero.

"You were not on the ship?" he said.

"No, I was not on the ship. I have been in Europe these three years."

He bowed once more, solemnly, and motioned me to be seated again. I sat down, but it was only for the purpose of observing him an instant—I saw it was time I should return to my sister. Miss Spencer's cousin was a queer fellow. Nature had not shaped him for a Raphaelesque or Byronic attire, and his velvet doublet and naked throat were not in harmony with his facial attributes. His hair was cropped close to his head; his ears were large and ill-adjusted to the same. He had a lackadaisical carriage and a sentimental droop which were peculiarly at variance with his keen, strange-colored eyes. Perhaps I was prejudiced, but I thought his eyes treacherous. He said nothing for some time; he leaned his hands on his cane and looked up and down the street. Then at last, slowly lifting his cane and pointing with it, "That's a very nice bit," he remarked, softly. He had his head on one side, and his little eyes were half closed. I followed the direction of his stick; the object it indicated was a red cloth hung out of an old window. "Nice bit of colour," he continued; and without moving his head he transferred his half-closed gaze to me. "Composes well," he pursued. "Make a nice thing." He spoke in a hard, vulgar voice.

"I see you have a great deal of eye," I replied. "Your cousin tells me you are studying art." He looked at me in the same way without answering, and I went on with deliberate urbanity—"I suppose you are at the studio of one of those great men."

Still he looked at me, and then he said softly—"Gérôme."

"Do you like it?" I asked.

"Do you understand French?" he said.

"Some kinds," I answered.

He kept his little eyes on me; then he said—"J'adore la peinture!"[4]

"Oh, I understand that kind!" I rejoined. Miss Spencer laid her hand upon her cousin's arm with a little pleased and fluttered movement; it was delightful to be among people who were on such easy terms with foreign tongues. I got up to take leave, and asked Miss Spencer where, in Paris, I might have the honor of waiting upon her. To what hotel would she go?

She turned to her cousin inquiringly and he honored me again with his little languid leer. "Do you know the Hôtel des Princes?"

"I know where it is."

"I shall take her there."

"I congratulate you," I said to Caroline Spencer. "I believe it is the best inn in the world; and in case I should still have a moment to call upon you here, where are you lodged?"

"Oh, it's such a pretty name," said Miss Spencer, gleefully. "À la Belle Normande."

As I left them her cousin gave me a great flourish with his picturesque hat.

---

4 **J'adore la peinture** (zhädôr lä pentyr): I like painting.

III

My sister, as it proved, was not sufficiently restored to leave Havre by the afternoon train; so that, as the autumn dusk began to fall, I found myself at liberty to call at the sign of the Fair Norman. I must confess that I had spent much of the interval in wondering what the disagreeable thing was that my charming friend's disagreeable cousin had been telling her. The "Belle Normande" was a modest inn in a shady bystreet, where it gave me satisfaction to think Miss Spencer must have encountered local colour in abundance. There was a crooked little court, where much of the hospitality of the house was carried on; there was a staircase climbing to bedrooms on the outer side of the wall; there was a small trickling

fountain with a stucco statuette in the midst of it; there was a little boy in a white cap and apron cleaning copper vessels at a conspicuous kitchen door; there was a chattering landlady, neatly laced, arranging apricots and grapes into an artistic pyramid upon a pink plate. I looked about, and on a green bench outside of an open door labelled *Salle à Manger,*[5] I perceived Caroline Spencer. No sooner had I looked at her than I saw that something had happened since the morning. She was leaning back on her bench, her hands were clasped in her lap, and her eyes were fixed upon the landlady, at the other side of the court, manipulating her apricots.

But I saw she was not thinking of apricots. She was staring absently, thoughtfully; as I came near her I perceived that she had been crying. I sat down on the bench beside her before she saw me; then, when she had done so, she simply turned round, without surprise, and rested her sad eyes upon me. Something very bad indeed had happened; she was completely changed.

I immediately charged her with it. "Your cousin has been giving you bad news; you are in great distress."

For a moment she said nothing, and I supposed that she was afraid to speak, lest her tears should come back. But presently I perceived that in the short time that had elapsed since my leaving her in the morning she had shed them all, and that she was now softly stoical—intensely composed.

"My poor cousin is in distress," she said at last. "His news was bad." Then, after a brief hesitation—"He was in terrible want of money."

"In want of yours, you mean?"

"Of any that he could get—honestly. Mine was the only money."

"And he has taken yours?"

She hesitated again a moment, but her glance, meanwhile, was pleading. "I gave him what I had."

I have always remembered the accent of those words as the most angelic bit of human utterance I had ever listened to; but then, almost with a sense of personal outrage,

---

5 *Salle à Manger:* dining room.

I jumped up. "Good heavens!" I said, "do you call that getting it honestly?"

I had gone too far; she blushed deeply. "We will not speak of it," she said.

"We *must* speak of it," I answered, sitting down again. "I am your friend; it seems to me you need one. What is the matter with your cousin?"

"He is in debt."

"No doubt! But what is the special fitness of your paying his debts?"

"He has told me all his story; I am very sorry for him."

"So am I! But I hope he will give you back your money."

"Certainly he will; as soon as he can."

"When will that be?"

"When he has finished his great picture."

"My dear young lady, confound his great picture! Where is this desperate cousin?"

She certainly hesitated now. Then—"At his dinner," she answered.

I turned about and looked through the open door into the *salle à manger*. There, alone at the end of a long table, I perceived the object of Miss Spencer's compassion—the bright young art student. He was dining too attentively to notice me at first; but in the act of setting down a well-emptied wine glass he caught sight of my observant attitude. He paused in his repast, and, with his head on one side and his meager jaws slowly moving, fixedly returned my gaze. Then the landlady came lightly brushing by with her pyramid of apricots.

"And that nice little plate of fruit is for him?" I exclaimed.

Miss Spencer glanced at it tenderly. "They do that so prettily!" she murmured.

I felt helpless and irritated. "Come now, really," I said; "do you approve of that long strong fellow accepting your funds?" She looked away from me; I was evidently giving her pain. The case was hopeless; the long strong fellow had "interested" her.

"Excuse me if I speak of him so unceremoniously," I said. "But you are really too generous, and he is not quite delicate enough. He made his debts himself—he ought to pay them himself."

"He has been foolish," she answered; "I know that. He has told me everything. We had a long talk this morning; the poor fellow threw himself upon my charity. He has signed notes to a large amount."

"The more fool he!"

"He is in extreme distress; and it is not only himself. It is his poor wife."

"Ah, he has a poor wife?"

"I didn't know it—but he confessed everything. He married two years since, secretly."

"Why secretly?"

Caroline Spencer glanced about her, as if she feared listeners. Then softly, in a little impressive tone—"She was a Countess!"

"Are you very sure of that?"

"She has written me a most beautiful letter."

"Asking you for money, eh?"

"Asking me for confidence and sympathy," said Miss Spencer. "She has been disinherited by her father. My cousin told me the story and she tells it in her own way, in the letter. It is like an old romance. Her father opposed the marriage and when he discovered that she had secretly disobeyed him he cruelly cast her off. It is really most romantic. They are the oldest family in Provence."

I looked and listened, in wonder. It really seemed that the poor woman was enjoying the "romance" of having a discarded Countess-cousin, out of Provence, so deeply as almost to lose the sense of what the forfeiture of her money meant for her.

"My dear young lady," I said, "you don't want to be ruined for picturesqueness' sake?"

"I shall not be ruined. I shall come back before long to stay with them. The Countess insists upon that."

"Come back! You are going home, then?"

She sat for a moment with her eyes lowered, then with an heroic suppression of a faint tremor of the voice—"I have no money for traveling!" she answered.

"You gave it *all* up?"

"I have kept enough to take me home."

I gave an angry groan, and at this juncture Miss Spencer's cousin, the fortunate possessor of her sacred savings and of the hand of the Provençal Countess, emerged from the little dining room. He stood on the threshold for an instant, removing the stone from a plump apricot which he had brought away from the table; then he put the apricot into his mouth, and while he let it sojourn there, gratefully, stood looking at us, with his long legs apart and his hands dropped into the pockets of his velvet jacket. My companion got up, giving him a thin glance which I caught in its passage, and which expressed a strange commixture of resignation and fascination—a sort of perverted exaltation. Ugly, vulgar, pretentious, dishonest as I thought the creature, he had appealed successfully to her eager and tender imagination. I was deeply disgusted, but I had no warrant to interfere, and at any rate I felt that it would be vain.

The young man waved his hand with a pictorial gesture. "Nice old court," he observed. "Nice mellow old place. Good tone in that brick. Nice crooked old staircase."

Decidedly, I couldn't stand it; without responding I gave my hand to Caroline Spencer. She looked at me an instant with her little white face and expanded eyes, and as she showed her pretty teeth I suppose she meant to smile.

"Don't be sorry for me," she said, "I am very sure I shall see something of this dear old Europe yet."

I told her that I would not bid her goodbye—I should find a moment to come back the next morning. Her cousin, who had put on his sombrero again, flourished it off at me by way of a bow—upon which I took my departure.

The next morning I came back to the inn, where I met in the court the landlady, more loosely laced than in the evening. On my asking for Miss Spencer,—"*Partie*,[6] monsieur," said the hostess. "She went away last night at ten o'clock, with her—her—not her husband, eh?—in fine her *Monsieur*. They went down to the American ship." I turned away; the poor girl had been about thirteen hours in Europe.

IV

I myself, more fortunate, was there some five years longer. During this period I lost my friend Latouche, who died of a malarious fever

---

6 *Partie:* left.

during a tour in the Levant. One of the first things I did on my return was to go up to Grimwinter to pay a consolatory visit to his poor mother. I found her in deep affliction, and I sat with her the whole of the morning that followed my arrival (I had come in late at night), listening to her tearful descant and singing the praises of my friend. We talked of nothing else, and our conversation terminated only with the arrival of a quick little woman who drove herself up to the door in a "carry-all," and whom I saw toss the reins upon the horse's back with the briskness of a startled sleeper throwing back the bed clothes. She jumped out of the carry-all and she jumped into the room. She proved to be the minister's wife and the great town gossip, and she had evidently, in the latter capacity, a choice morsel to communicate. I was as sure of this as I was that poor Mrs. Latouche was not absolutely too bereaved to listen to her. It seemed to me discreet to retire; I said I believed I would go and take a walk before dinner.

"And, by the way," I added, "if you will tell me where my old friend Miss Spencer lives I will walk to her house."

The minister's wife immediately responded. Miss Spencer lived in the fourth house beyond the Baptist church; the Baptist church was the one on the right, with that queer green thing over the door; they called it a portico, but it looked more like an old-fashioned bedstead.

"Yes, do go and see poor Caroline," said Mrs. Latouche. "It will refresh her to see a strange face."

"I should think she had had enough of strange faces!" cried the minister's wife.

"I mean, to see a visitor," said Mrs. Latouche, amending her phrase.

"I should think she had had enough of visitors!" her companion rejoined. "But *you* don't mean to stay ten years," she added, glancing at me.

"Has she a visitor of that sort?" I inquired, perplexed.

"You will see the sort!" said the minister's wife. "She's easily seen; she generally sits in the front yard. Only take care what you say to her, and be very sure you are polite."

"Ah, she is so sensitive?"

The minister's wife jumped up and dropped me a curtsey—a most ironical curtsey.

"That's what she is, if you please. She's a Countess!"

And pronouncing this word with the most scathing accent, the little woman seemed fairly to laugh in the Countess's face. I stood a moment, staring, wondering, remembering.

"Oh, I shall be very polite!" I cried; and grasping my hat and stick, I went on my way.

I found Miss Spencer's residence without difficulty. The Baptist church was easily identified, and the small dwelling near it, of a rusty white, with a large central chimney stack and a Virginia creeper, seemed naturally and properly the abode of a frugal old maid with a taste for the picturesque. As I approached I slackened my pace, for I had heard that some one was always sitting in the front yard, and I wished to reconnoitre. I looked cautiously over the low white fence which separated the small garden space from the unpaved street; but I descried nothing in the shape of a Countess. A small straight path led up to the crooked door step, and on either side of it was a little grass plot, fringed with currant bushes. In the middle of the grass, on either side, was a large quince tree, fully of antiquity and contortions, and beneath one of the quince trees were placed a small table and a couple of chairs. On the table lay a piece of unfinished embroidery and two or three books in bright-colored paper covers. I went in at the gate and paused half-way along the path, scanning the place for some farther token of its occupant, before whom—I could hardly have said why—I hesitated abruptly to present myself. Then I saw that the poor little house was very shabby. I felt a sudden doubt of my right to intrude; for curiosity had been my motive, and curiosity here seemed singularly indelicate. While I hesitated, a figure appeared in the open door way and stood there looking at me. I immediately recognized Caroline Spencer, but she looked at me as if she had never seen me before. Gently, but gravely and timidly, I advanced to the door step, and then I said, with an attempt at friendly badinage—

"I waited for you over there to come back, but you never came."

"Waited where, sir!" she asked softly, and her light-colored eyes expanded more than before.

She was much older; she looked tired and wasted.

"Well," I said, "I waited at Havre."

She stared; then she recognized me. She smiled and blushed and clasped her two hands together. "I remember you now," she said. "I remember that day." But she stood there, neither coming out nor asking me to come in. She was embarrassed.

I, too, felt a little awkward. I poked my stick into the path. "I kept looking out for you, year after year," I said.

"You mean in Europe?" murmured Miss Spencer.

"In Europe, of course! Here, apparently, you are easy enough to find."

She leaned her hand against the unpainted door post, and her head fell a little to one side. She looked at me for a moment without speaking, and I thought I recognized the expression that one sees in women's eyes when tears are rising. Suddenly she stepped out upon the cracked slab of stone before the threshold and closed the door behind her. Then she began to smile intently, and I saw that her teeth were as pretty as ever. But there had been tears too.

"Have you been there ever since?" she asked, almost in a whisper.

"Until three weeks ago. And you—you never came back?"

Still looking at me with her fixed smile, she put her hand behind her and opened the door again. "I am not very polite," she said. "Won't you come in?"

"I am afraid I incommode you."

"Oh no!" she answered, smiling more than ever. And she pushed back the door, with a sign that I should enter.

I went in, following her. She led the way to a small room on the left of the narrow hall, which I supposed to be her parlour, though it was at the back of the house, and we passed the closed door of another apartment which apparently enjoyed a view of the quince trees. This one looked out upon a small wood shed and two clucking hens. But I thought it very pretty, until I saw that its elegance was of the most frugal kind; after which, presently, I thought it prettier still, for I had never seen faded chintz and old mezzotint engravings, framed in varnished autumn leaves, disposed in so graceful a fashion. Miss Spencer sat down on a very small portion of the sofa, with her hands tightly clasped in her lap. She looked ten years older, and it would have sounded very perverse now to speak of her as pretty. But I thought her so; or at least I thought her touching. She was peculiarly agitated. I tried to appear not to notice it; but suddenly, in the most inconsequent fashion—it was an irresistible memory of our little friendship at Havre—I said to her—"I do incommode you. You are distressed."

She raised her two hands to her face, and for a moment kept it buried in them. Then, taking them away—"It's because you remind me . . ." she said.

"I remind you, you mean, of that miserable day at Havre?"

She shook her head. "It was not miserable. It was delightful."

"I never was so shocked as when, on going back to your inn the next morning, I found you had set sail again."

She was silent a moment; and then she

said—"Please let us not speak of that."

"Did you come straight back here?" I asked.

"I was back here just thirty days after I had gone away."

"And here you have remained every since?"

"Oh yes!" she said gently.

"When are you going to Europe again?"

This question seemed brutal; but there was something that irritated me in the softness of her resignation, and I wished to extort from her some expression of impatience.

She fixed her eyes for a moment upon a small sun spot on the carpet; then she got up and lowered the window blind a little, to o-bliterate it. Presently, in the same mild voice, answering my question, she said—"Never!"

"I hope your cousin repaid you your money."

"I don't care for it now," she said, looking away from me.

"You don't care for your money?"

"For going to Europe."

"Do you mean that you would not go if you could?"

"I can't—I can't," said Caroline Spencer. "It is all over; I never think of it."

"He never repaid you, then!" I exclaimed.

"Please—please," she began.

But she stopped; she was looking toward the door. There had been a rustling and a sound of steps in the hall.

I also looked toward the door, which was open, and now admitted another person—a lady who paused just within the threshold. Behind her came a young man. The lady looked at me with a good deal of fixedness—long enough for my glance to receive a vivid impression of herself. Then she turned to Caroline Spencer, and, with a smile and a strong foreign accent—

"Excuse my interruption!" she said. "I knew not you had company—the gentleman came in so quietly."

With this, she directed her eyes toward me again.

She was very strange; yet my first feeling was that I had seen her before. Then I perceived that I had only seen ladies who were very much like her. But I had seen them very far away from Grimwinter, and it was an odd sensation to be seeing her here. Whither was it the sight of her seemed to transport me? To some dusky landing before a shabby Parisian *quatrième*—to an open door revealing a greasy antechamber, and to Madame leaning over the banisters while she holds a faded dressing-gown together and bawls down to the portress to bring up her coffee. Miss Spencer's visitor was a very large woman, of middle age, with a plump, dead-white face and hair drawn back *à la chinoise*. She had a small, penetrating eye, and what is called in French an agreeable smile. She wore an old pink cashmere dressing gown, covered with white embroideries, and, like the figure in my momentary vision, she was holding it together in front with a bare and rounded arm and a plump and deeply dimpled hand.

"It is only to spick about my *café*," she said to Miss Spencer with her agreeable smile. "I should like it served in the garden under the leetle tree."

The young man behind her had now stepped into the room, and he also stood looking at me. He was a pretty-faced little fellow, with an air of provincial foppishness—a tiny Adonis of Grimwinter. He had a small, pointed nose, a small, pointed chin, and, as I observed, the most diminutive feet. He looked at me foolishly, with his mouth open.

"You shall have your coffee," said Miss Spencer, who had a faint red spot in each of her cheeks.

"It is well!" said the lady in the dressing gown. "Find your bouk," she added, turning to the young man.

He looked vaguely round the room. "My grammar, d'ye mean?" he asked, with a helpless intonation.

But the large lady was looking at me

curiously, and gathering in her dressing gown with her white arm.

"Find your bouk, my friend," she repeated.

"My poetry, d'ye mean?" said the young man, also gazing at me again.

"Never mind your bouk," said his companion. "Today we will talk. We will make some conversation. But we must not interrupt. Come," and she turned away. "Under the leetle tree," she added, for the benefit of Miss Spencer.

Then she gave me a sort of salutation, and a "Monsieur!"—with which she swept away again, followed by the young man.

Caroline Spencer stood there with her eyes fixed upon the ground.

"Who is that?" I asked.

"The Countess, my cousin."

"And who is the young man?"

"Her pupil, Mr. Mixter."

This description of the relation between the two persons who had just left the room made me break into a little laugh. Miss Spencer looked at me gravely.

"She gives French lessons; she has lost her fortune."

"I see," I said. "She is determined to be a burden to no one. That is very proper."

Miss Spencer looked down on the ground again. "I must go and get the coffee," she said.

"Has the lady many pupils?" I asked.

"She has only Mr. Mixter. She gives all her time to him."

At this I could not laugh, though I smelt provocation. Miss Spencer was too grave. "He pays very well," she presently added, with simplicity. "He is very rich. He is very kind. He takes the Countess to drive." And she was turning away.

"You are going for the Countess's coffee?" I said.

"If you will excuse me a few moments."

"Is there no one else to do it?"

She looked at me with the softest serenity. "I keep no servants."

"Can she not wait upon herself?"

"She is not used to that."

"I see," said I, as gently as possible. "But before you go, tell me this: who is this lady?"

"I told you about her before—that day. She is the wife of my cousin, whom you saw."

"The lady who was disowned by her family in consequence of her marriage?"

"Yes; they have never seen her again. They have cast her off."

"And where is her husband?"

"He is dead."

"And where is your money?"

The poor girl flinched; there was something too methodical in my questions. "I don't know," she said wearily.

But I continued a moment. "On her husband's death this lady came over here?"

"Yes, she arrived one day."

"How long ago?"

"Two years."

"She has been here ever since?"

"Every moment."

"How does she like it?"

"Not at all."

"And how do *you* like it?"

Miss Spencer laid her face in her two hands an instant, as she had done ten minutes before. Then, quickly, she went to get the Countess's coffee.

I remained alone in the little parlour; I wanted to see more—to learn more. At the end of five minutes the young man whom Miss Spencer had described as the Countess's pupil came in. He stood looking at me for a moment with parted lips. I saw he was a very rudimentary young man.

"She wants to know if you won't come out there?" he observed at last.

"Who wants to know?"

"The Countess. That French lady."

"She has asked you to bring me?"

"Yes, sir," said the young man feebly, looking at my six feet of stature.

I went out with him, and we found the Countess sitting under one of the little quince trees in front of the house. She was drawing a needle through the piece of embroidery which she had taken from the small table. She pointed graciously to the chair beside her and I seated myself. Mr. Mixter glanced about him, and then sat down in the grass at her feet. He gazed upward, looking with parted lips from the Countess to me.

"I am sure you speak French," said the Countess, fixing her brilliant little eyes upon me.

"I do, madam, after a fashion," I answered, in the lady's own tongue.

"*Voila!*" she cried most expressively. "I knew it so soon as I looked at you. You have been in my poor dear coutnry."

"A long time."

"You know Paris?"

"Thoroughly, madam." And with a certain conscious purpose I let my eyes meet her own.

She presently, hereupon, moved her own and glanced down at Mr. Mixter. "What are we talking about?" she demanded of her attentive pupil.

He pulled his knees up, plucked at the grass with his hand, stared, blushed a little. "You are talking French," said Mr. Mixter.

"*La belle découverte!*" said the Countess. "Here are ten months," she explained to me, "that I am giving him lessons. Don't put yourself out not to say he's a fool; he won't understand you."

"I hope your other pupils are more gratifying," I remarked.

"I have no others. They don't know what French is in this place; they don't want to know. You may therefore imagine the pleasure it is to me to meet a person who speaks it like yourself." I replied that my own pleasure was not less, and she went on drawing her stitches through her embroidery, with her little finger curled out. Every few moments she put her eyes close to her work, near-sightedly. I thought her a very disagreeable person; she was coarse, affected, dishonest, and no more a Countess than I was a caliph. "Talk to me of Paris," she went on. "the very name of it gives me an emotion! How long since you were there?"

"Two months ago."

"Happy man! Tell me something about it. What were they doing? Oh, for an hour of the boulevard!"

"They were doing about what they are always doing—amusing themselves a good deal."

"At the theaters, eh?" sighed the Countess. "At the *cafés-concerts*—at the little tables in front of the doors? *Quelle existence!* You know I am a Parisienne, monsieur," she added, "—to my finger-tips."

"Miss Spencer was mistaken, then," I ventured to rejoin, "in telling me that you are a Provençale."

She stared a moment, then she put her nose to her embroidery, which had a dingy, desultory aspect. "Ah, I am a Provençale by birth; but I am a Parisienne by—inclination."

"And by experience, I suppose?" I said.

She questioned me a moment with her hard

little eyes. "Oh, experience! I could talk of experience if I wished. I never expected, for example, that experience had *this* in store for me." And she pointed with her bare elbow, and with a jerk of her head, at everything that surrounded her—at the little white house, the quince-tree, the rickety paling, even at Mr. Mixter.

"You are in exile!" I said smiling.

"You may imagine what it is!! These two years that I have been here I have passed hours—hours! One gets used to things, and sometimes I think I have got used to this. But there are some things that are always beginning over again. For example, my coffee."

"Do you always have coffee at this hour?" I inquired.

She tossed back her head and measured me.

"At what hour would you prefer me to have it? I must have my little cup after breakfast."

"Ah, you breakfast at this hour?"

"At mid-day—*comme cela se fait.* Here they breakfast at a quarter past seven. That 'quarter past' is charming!"

"But you were telling me about your coffee," I observed, sympathetically.

"My *cousine* can't believe in it; she can't understand it. She's an excellent girl; but that little cup of black coffee, with a drop of cognac, served at this hour—they exceed her comprehension. So I have to break the ice every day, and it takes the coffee the time you see to arrive. And when it arrives, monsieur! If I don't offer you any of it you must not take it ill. It will be because I know you have drunk it on the boulevard."

I resented extremely this scornful treatment of poor Caroline Spencer's humble hospitality; but I said nothing, in order to say nothing uncivil. I only looked on Mr. Mixter, who had clasped his arms round his knees and was watching my companion's demonstrative graces in solemn fascination. She presently saw that I was observing him; she glanced at me with a little bold explanatory smile. "You know, he adores me," she murmured, putting her nose into her tapestry again. I expressed the promptest credence and she went on. "He dreams of becoming my lover! Yes, it's his dream. He has read a French novel; it took him six months. But ever since that he has thought himself the hero, and me the heroine!"

Mr. Mixter had evidently not an idea that he was being talked about; he was too preoccupied with the ecstasy of contemplation. At this moment Caroline Spencer came out of the house, bearing a coffee pot on a little tray. I noticed that on her way from the door to the table she gave me a single quick, vaguely appealing glance. I wondered what it signified; I felt that it signified a sort of half-frightened longing to know what, as a man of the world who had been in France, I thought of the Countess. It made me extremely uncomfortable. I could not tell her that the Countess was very possibly the runaway wife of a little hairdresser. I tried suddenly, on the contrary, to show a high consideration for her. But I got up; I couldn't stay longer. It vexed me to see Caroline Spencer standing there like a waiting-maid.

"You expect to remain some time at Grimwinter?" I said to the Countess.

She gave a terrible shrug.

"Who knows? Perhaps for years. When one is in misery! . . . *Chère belle,*" she added, turning to Miss Spencer, "you have forgotten the cognac!"

I detained Caroline Spencer as, after looking a moment in silence at the little table, she was turning away to procure this missing delicacy. I silently gave her my hand in farewell. She looked very tired, but there was a strange hint of prospective patience in her severely mild little face. I thought she was rather glad I was going. Mr. Mixter had risen to his feet and was pouring out the Countess's coffee. As I went back past the Baptist church I reflected that poor Miss Spencer had been right in her presentiment that she should still see something of that dear old Europe.

Study Questions

1. During her first meeting with the narrator how does Caroline Spencer reveal her attitude toward Europe? How is this attitude reinforced later by the description of her behavior on board ship?

2. What causes Spencer to cut short her long awaited visit to Europe? What is the narrator's view of these circumstances?

3. On their fourth meeting what is the narrator's view of Caroline Spencer's situation? On what details does he base his judgment?

4. What does the reader learn about the narrator? What type of person is he?

5. James does not allow Caroline Spencer to tell her own story, nor does he tell the story himself. Instead he uses an observer who has only limited knowledge of what happens. How does this perspective shape the story?

6. At the end of the story the narrator reflects "that poor Miss Spencer had been right in her presentiment that she should still see something of that dear old Europe." This conclusion has been described as "one of the most pitiless sentences ever penned by [a human hand]." To what extent is that a valid interpretation? How does the final sentence sum up the story?

Vocabulary

A major feature of Henry James's literary style is **understatement**. Understatement is deliberately restrained and *un*emphatic wording.

Two elements almost always found in understated writing or speech are euphemisms and circumlocutions. A euphemism is a relatively pleasant word substituted for an unpleasant one, such as the term *deceased* used in place of the word *dead*. A circumlocution is any roundabout way of saying something—such as "The Countess *looked* at me *with a good deal of fixedness*" in place of "The Countess *stared* at me." As this example indicates, circumlocutions tend to be more wordy than plain, straightforward statements. Circumlocutions also tend to use more elegant language than that found in direct statements.

In addition to euphemisms and circumlocutions, understatement commonly includes litotes. The term *litotes* is defined as "a figure of speech in which affirmative ideas are expressed by the negation of their opposites"— as in the statement "I succeeded *im*perfectly" when the meaning is "I did not do very well."

As you work with the following exercises involving these three components of understatement, consult a dictionary for the meanings of any words you do not already know. Write all your answers on a separate sheet of paper.

Fire and Ice

ome ay the world will end in fire,
ome ay in ice.
From what I've tated of deire
I hold with thoe who favor fire.
But if it had to perih twice,
I think I know enough of hate
To know that for detruction ice
I alo great
And would uffice.

1. ~~And where is your money~~ Miss Spencer finished, there was something too *methodical* in my questions.

B. Each of the sentences below contains one or more examples of litotes. For example:

I said nothing in order to say *nothing uncivil.*

Reword each sentence, eliminating as many negative words as possible and making it more straightforward. For example:

I kept silent to avoid speaking rudely.

1. It had apparently never occurred to her that there would be the least incommodity in her traveling alone.
2. His velvet doublet and naked throat were not in harmony with his facial attributes.
3. Mrs. Latouche was not absolutely too bereaved to listen to gossip.
4. "Don't put yourself out not to say he's a fool; he won't understand you."

C. All or part of each understated sentence below consists of circumlocution, either with or without euphemism and/or litotes. For example:

I repaired directly to the hotel, where my relatives were already.

Rewrite each sentence in a simpler, more direct way. For example

I went straight to the hotel, where my relatives were already.

1. I was alarmed at the good conscience with which this delicately pretty woman had stationed herself in conspicuous isolation on the edge of the sidewalk.
2. I had no warrant to interfere, and at any rate I felt that it would be vain.
3. I felt a sudden doubt of my right to intrude; curiosity seemed indelicate.

Mary E. Wilkins Freeman   1852-1930

Mary E. Wilkins Freeman spent the first fifty years of her life in Massachusetts and Vermont. Those years in New England provide the background for the short stories which assured her reputation. Freeman is particularly noted for her deft character studies of solitary, strong-willed women. The following story, set in late nineteenth-century New England, concerns just such an individual. Though long considered a minor writer, Freeman has recently been rediscovered. Among her twenty volumes of fiction are *A Humble Romance* (1887), *A New England Nun* (1891), and *Edgewater People* (1918).

A Church Mouse

MARY E. WILKINS FREEMAN

I NEVER HEARD of a woman's bein' saxton."[1]

"I dun' know what difference that makes; I don't see why they shouldn't have women saxtons as well as men saxtons, for my part, nor nobody else neither. They'd keep dusted 'nough sight cleaner. I've seen the dust layin' on my pew thick enough to write my name in a good many times, an' ain't said nothin' about it. An' I ain't goin' to say nothin' now again Joe Sowen, now he's dead an' gone. He did jest as well as most men do.

Men git in a good many places where they don't belong, an' where they set as awkward as a cow on a hen-roost, jest because they push in ahead of women. I ain't blamin' 'em; I s'pose if I could push in I should, jest the same way. But there ain't no reason that I can see, nor nobody else neither, why a woman shouldn't be saxton."

Hetty Fifield stood in the rowen[2] hay field before Caleb Gale. He was a deacon, the chairman of the selectmen,[3] and the rich and influential man of the village. One looking at him

---

1 **saxton:** local pronunciation of *sexton,* person who takes care of church property and rings the church bell.

2 **rowen** (rau' ən): stubble; cut hay.

3 **selectmen:** citizens elected to town council.

would not have guessed it. There was nothing imposing about his lumbering figure in his calico shirt and baggy trousers. However, his large face, red and moist with perspiration, scanned the distant horizon with a stiff and reserved air; he did not look at Hetty.

"How'd you go to work to ring the bell?" said he. "It would have to be tolled, too, if anybody died."

"I'd jest as lief ring that little meetin'-house bell as to stan' out here an' jingle a cow-bell," said Hetty; "an' as for tollin', I'd jest as soon toll the bell for Methusaleh, if he was livin' here! I'd laugh if I ain't got strength 'nough for that."

"It takes a kind of a knack."

"If I ain't got as much knack as old Joe Sowen ever had, I'll give up the ship."

"You couldn't tend the fires."

"Couldn't tend the fires—when I've cut an' carried in all the wood I've burned for forty year! Couldn't keep the fires a-goin' in them two little wood-stoves!"

"It's consider'ble work to sweep the meetin'-house."

"I guess I've done 'bout as much work as to sweep that little meetin'-house, I ruther guess I have."

"There's one thing you ain't thought of."

"What's that?"

"Where'd you live? All old Sowen got for bein' saxton was twenty dollar a year an' we couldn't pay a woman so much as that. You couldn't have enough to pay for your livin' anywheres."

"Where am I goin' to live whether I'm saxton or not?"

Caleb Gale was silent.

There was a wind blowing, the rowen hay drifted round Hetty like a brown-green sea touched with ripples of blue and gold by the asters and goldenrod. She stood in the midst of it like a Mayweed that had gathered a slender toughness through the long summer; her brown cotton gown clung about her like a wilting leaf, outlining her harsh little form.

She was as sallow as a squaw, and she had pretty black eyes; they were bright, although she was old. She kept them fixed upon Caleb. Suddenly she raised herself upon her toes; the wind caught her dress and made it blow out; her eyes flashed. "I tell you where I'm goin' to live," said she. *"I'm goin' to live in the meetin'-house."*

Caleb looked at her. *"Goin' to live in the meetin'-house!"*

"Yes, I be."

"Live in the meetin'-house!"

"I'd like to know why not."

"Why—you couldn't—live in the meetin'-house. You're crazy."

Caleb flung out the rake which he was holding, and drew it in full of rowen. Hetty moved around in front of him; he raked imperturbably; she moved again right in the path of the rake; then he stopped. "There ain't no sense in such talk."

"All I want is jest the east corner of the back gall'ry, where the chimbly goes up. I'll set up my cookin'-stove there, an' my bed, an' I'll curtain it off with my sunflower quilt, to keep off the wind."

"A cookin'-stove an' a bed in the meetin'-house!"

"Mis' Grout she give me that cookin'-stove, an' that bed I've allers slept on, before she died. She give 'em to me before Mary Anne Thomas, an' I moved 'em out. They air settin' out in the yard now, an' if it rains that stove an' that bed will be spoilt. It looks some like rain now. I guess you'd better give me the meetin'-house key right off."

"You don't think you can move that cookin'-stove an' that bed into the meetin'-house—I ain't goin' to stop to hear such talk."

"My worsted-work, all my mottoes I've done, an' my wool flowers, air out there in the yard."

Caleb raked. Hetty kept standing herself about until he was forced to stop or gather her in with the rowen hay. He looked straight at her and scowled; the perspiration trickled down his cheeks. "If I go up to the house can Mis' Gale git me the key to the meetin'-house?" said Hetty.

"No, she can't."

"Be you goin' up before long?"

"No, I ain't." Suddenly Caleb's voice changed: it had been full of stubborn vexation, now it was blandly argumentative. "Don't you see it ain't no use talkin' such nonsense, Hetty? You'd better go right along, an' make up your mind it ain't to be thought of."

"Where be I goin' tonight, then?"

"Tonight?"

"Yes; where be I a-goin'?"

"Ain't you got any place to go to?"

"Where do you s'pose I've got any place? Them folks air moving' into Mis' Grout's house, an' they as good as told me to clear out. I ain't got no folks to take me in. I dun' know where I'm goin'; mebbe I can go to your house?"

Caleb gave a start. "We've got company to home," said he, hastily. "I'm 'fraid Mis' Gale wouldn't think it was convenient."

Hetty laughed. "Most everybody in the town has got company," said she.

Caleb dug his rake into the ground as if it were a hoe; then he leaned on it and stared at the horizon. There was a fringe of yellow birches on the edge of the hay field; beyond them was a low range of misty blue hills. "You ain't got no place to go to, then?"

"I dun' know of any. There ain't no poor-house here, an' I ain't got no folks."

Caleb stood like a statue. Some crows flew cawing over the field. Hetty waited. "I s'pose that key is where Mis' Gale can find it?" she said, finally.

Caleb turned and threw out his rake with a jerk. "She knows where 'tis; it's hangin' up behind the settin'-room door. I s'pose you can stay there tonight, as long as you ain't got no other place. We shall have to see what can be done."

Hetty scuttled off across the field. "You mustn't take no stove nor bed into the meetin'-house," Caleb called after her; "we can't have that, nohow."

Hetty went on as if she did not hear.

The goldenrod at the sides of the road was turning brown; the asters were in their prime, blue and white ones; here and there were rows of thistles with white tops. The dust was thick; Hetty, when she emerged from Caleb's house, trotted along in a cloud of it. She did not look to the right or left; she kept her small eager face fixed straight ahead, and moved forward like some little animal with the purpose to which it was born strong within it.

Presently she came to a large cottage house on the right of the road; there she stopped. The front yard was full of furniture, tables and chairs standing among the dahlias and clumps of marigolds. Hetty leaned over the fence at one corner of the yard and inspected a little knot of household goods set aside from the others. There was a small cooking-stove, a hair trunk, a yellow bedstead stacked up against the fence, and a pile of bedding. Some children in the yard stood in a group and eyed Hetty. A woman appeared in the door—she was small, there was a black smutch on her face, which was haggard with fatigue, and she scowled in the sun as she looked over at Hetty. "Well, got a place to stay in?" said she, in an unexpectedly deep voice.

"Yes, I guess so," replied Hetty.

"I dun' know how in the world I can have you. All the beds will be full—I expect his mother some tonight, an' I'm dreadful stirred up anyhow."

"Everybody's havin' company; I never see anything like it." Hetty's voice was inscrutable. The other woman looked sharply at her.

"You've got a place, ain't you?" she asked, doubtfully.

"Yes, I have."

At the left of this house, quite back from the road, was a little unpainted cottage, hardly more than a hut. There was smoke coming out of the chimney, and a tall youth lounged in the door. Hetty, with the woman and children staring after her, struck out across the field in the little foot path towards the cottage. "I wonder if she's goin' to stay there?" the woman muttered, meditating.

The youth did not see Hetty until she was quite near him; then he aroused suddenly as if from sleep, and tried to slink off around the cottage. But Hetty called after him. "Sammy," she cried, "Sammy, come back here. I want you!"

"What d'ye want?"

"Come back here!"

The youth lounged back sulkily, and a tall woman came to the door. She bent out of it anxiously to hear Hetty.

"I want you to come an' help me move my stove an' things," said Hetty.

"Where to?"

"Into the meeetin'-house."

"The meetin'-house."

"Yes, the meetin'-house."

The woman in the door had sodden hands; behind her arose the steam of a washtub. She and the youth stared at Hetty, but surprise was too strong an emotion for them to grasp firmly.

"I want Sammy to come right over an' help me," said Hetty.

"He ain't strong enough to move a stove," said the woman.

"Ain't strong enough!"

"He's apt to git lame."

"Most folks are. Guess I've got lame. Come right along, Sammy!"

"He ain't able to lift much."

"I s'pose he's able to be lifted, ain't he?"

"I dun' know what you mean."

"The stove don't weigh nothin'," said Hetty; "I could carry it myself if I could git hold of it. Come, Sammy!"

Hetty turned down the path, and the youth moved a little way after her, as if perforce. Then he stopped, and cast an appealing glance back at his mother. Her face was distressed. "Oh, Sammy, I'm afraid you'll git sick," said she.

"No, he ain't goin' to git sick," said Hetty. "Come, Sammy." And Sammy followed her down the path.

It was four o'clock then. At dusk Hetty had her gay sunflower quilt curtaining off the chimney corner of the church gallery; her stove and little bedstead were set up, and she had entered upon a life which endured successfully for three months. All that time a storm brewed; then it broke; but Hetty sailed in her own course for the three months.

It was on a Saturday that she took up her habitation in the meeting-house. The next morning, when the boy who had been supplying the dead sexton's place came and shook the door, Hetty was prompt on the other side. "Deacon Gale said for you to let me in so I could ring the bell," called the boy.

"Go away," responded Hetty. "I'm goin' to ring the bell; I'm saxton."

Hetty rang the bell with vigor, but she made a wild, irregular jangle at first; at the last it was better. The village people said to each other that a new hand was ringing. Only a few knew that Hetty was in the meeting-house. When the congregation had assembled and saw that gaudy tent pitched in the house of the Lord and the resolute little pilgrim at the door of it, there was a commotion. The farmers and their wives were stirred out of their Sabbath decorum. After the service was over, Hetty, sitting in a pew corner of the gallery, her little face dark and watchful against the flaming background of her quilt, saw the people below gathering in groups, whispering, and looking at her.

Presently the minister, Caleb Gale, and the other deacon came up the gallery stairs. Hetty sat stiffly erect. Caleb Gale went up to the sunflower quilt, slipped it aside, and looked in. He turned to Hetty with a frown. Today his dignity was supported by important witnesses. "Did you bring that stove an' bedstead here?"

Hetty nodded.

"What made you do such a thing?"

"What was I goin' to do if I didn't? How's a

woman as old as me goin' to sleep in a pew, an' go without a cup of tea?"

The men looked at each other. They withdrew to another corner of the gallery and conferred in low tones; then they went downstairs and out of the church. Hetty smiled when she heard the door shut. When one is hard pressed, one, however simple, gets wisdom as to vantage points. Hetty comprehended hers perfectly. She was the propounder of a problem; as long as it was unguessed, she was sure of her foothold as propounder. This little village in which she had lived all her life had removed the shelter from her head; she being penniless, it was beholden to provide her another; she asked it what. When the old woman with whom she had lived died, the town promptly seized the estate for taxes—none had been paid for years. Hetty had not laid up a cent; indeed, for the most of the time she had received no wages. There had been no money in the house; all she had gotten for her labor for a sickly, impecunious old woman was a frugal board. When the old woman died, Hetty gathered in the few household articles for which she had stipulated, and made no complaint. She walked out of the house when the new tenants came in; all she asked was, "What are you going to do with me?" This little settlement of narrow-minded, prosperous farmers, however hard a task charity might be to them, could not turn an old woman out into the fields and highways to seek for food as they would a Jersey cow. They had their Puritan consciences, and her note of distress would sound louder in their ears than the Jersey's bell echoing down the valley in the stillest night. But the question as to Hetty Fifield's disposal was a hard one to answer. There was no almshouse in the village, and no private family was willing to take her in. Hetty was strong and capable; although she was old, she could well have paid for her food and shelter by her labor; but this could not secure her an entrance even among this hard working and thrifty people, who would ordinarily grasp quickly enough at service without

wage in dollars and cents. Hetty had somehow gotten for herself an unfortunate name in the village. She was held in the light of a long thorned brier among the beanpoles, or a fierce little animal with claws and teeth bared. People were afraid to take her into their families; she had the reputation of always taking her own way, and never heeding the voice of authority. "I'd take her in an' have her give me a lift with the work," said one sickly farmer's wife; "but near's I can find out, I couldn't never be sure that I'd get molasses in the beans, nor saleratus[4] in my sour milk cakes, if she took a notion not to put it in. I don't dare to risk it."

Stories were about concerning Hetty's authority over the old woman with whom she had lived. "Old Mis' Grout never dared to say her soul was her own," people said. Then Hetty's sharp, sarcastic sayings were repeated; the justice of them made them sting. People did not want a tongue like that in their homes.

Hetty as a church sexton was directly opposed to all their ideas of church decorum and propriety in general; her pitching her tent in the Lord's house was almost sacrilege. But what could they do? Hetty jangled the Sabbath bells for the three months; once she tolled the bell for an old man, and it seemed by the sound of the bell as if his long, calm years had swung by in a weak delirium; but people bore it. She swept and dusted the little meeting-house, and she garnished the walls with her treasures of worsted-work. The neatness and the garniture went far to quiet the dissatisfaction of the people. They had a crude taste. Hetty's skill in fancy-work was quite celebrated. Her wool flowers were much talked of, and young girls tried to copy them. So these wreaths and clusters of red and blue and yellow wool roses and lilies hung as acceptably between the meeting-house windows as pictures of saints in a cathedral.

---

4 **saleratus:** baking soda.

Hetty hung a worsted motto over the pulpit; on it she set her chiefest treasure of art, a white wax cross with an ivy vine trailing over it, all covered with silver frost-work. Hetty always surveyed this cross with a species of awe; she felt the irresponsibility and amazement of a genius at his own work.

When she set it on the pulpit, no queen casting her rich robes and her jewels upon a shrine could have surpassed her in generous enthusiasm. "I guess when they see that they won't say no more," she said.

But the people, although they shared Hetty's admiration for the cross, were doubtful. They, looking at it, had a double vision of a little wax Virgin upon an altar. They wondered if it savored of popery. But the cross remained, and the minister was mindful not to jostle it in his gestures.

It was three months from the time Hetty took up her abode in the church, and a week before Christmas, when the problem was solved. Hetty herself precipitated the solution. She prepared a boiled dish in the meeting-house, upon a Saturday, and the next day the odors of turnip and cabbage were strong in the senses of the worshippers. They sniffed and looked at one another. This superseding the legitimate savor of the sanctuary, the fragrance of peppermint lozenges and wintergreen, the breath of Sunday clothes, by the homely weekday odors of kitchen vegetables, was too much for the sensibilities of the people. They looked indignantly around at Hetty, sitting before her sunflower hanging, comfortable from her good dinner of the day before, radiant with the consciousness of a great plateful of cold vegetables in her tent for her Sabbath dinner.

Poor Hetty had not many comfortable dinners. The selectmen doled out a small weekly sum to her, which she took with dignity as being her hire; then she had a mild forage in the neighbors' cellars and kitchens, of poor apples and stale bread and pie, paying for it in teaching her art of worsted-work to the daughters. Her Saturday's dinner had been a banquet to her: she had actually bought a piece of pork to boil with the vegetables; somebody had given her a nice little cabbage and some turnips, without a thought of the limitations of her housekeeping. Hetty herself had not a thought. She made the fires as usual that Sunday morning; the meeting-house was very clean; there was not a speck of dust anywhere; the wax cross on the pulpit glistened in a sunbeam slanting through the house. Hetty, sitting in the gallery, thought innocently how nice it looked.

After the meeting, Caleb Gale approached the other deacon. "Somethin's got to be done," said he. And the other deacon nodded. He had not smelt the cabbage until his wife nudged him and mentioned it; neither had Caleb Gale.

In the afternoon of the next Thursday, Caleb and the other two selectmen waited upon Hetty in her tabernacle. They stumped up the gallery stairs, and Hetty emerged from behind the quilt and stood looking at them, scared and defiant. The three men nodded stiffly; there was a pause; Caleb Gale motioned meaningly to one of the others, who shook his head; finally he himself had to speak. "I'm 'fraid you find it pretty cold here, don't you, Hetty?" said he.

"No, thank ye; it's very comfortable," replied Hetty, polite and wary.

"It ain't very convenient for you to do your cookin' here, I guess."

"It's jest as convenient as I want. I don't find no fault."

"I guess it's rayther lonesome here nights, ain't it?"

"I'd 'nough sight ruther be alone than have comp'ny, any day."

"It ain't fit for an old woman like you to be livin' alone here this way."

"Well, I dun' know of anything that's any fitter; mebbe you do."

Caleb looked appealingly at his companions; they stood stiff and irresponsive. Hetty's eyes were sharp and watchful upon them all.

"Well, Hetty," said Caleb, "we've found a nice, comfortable place for you, an' I guess you'd better pack up your things, an' I'll carry you right over there." Caleb stepped back a little closer to the other men. Hetty, small and trembling and helpless before them, looked vicious. She was like a little animal driven from its cover, for whom there is nothing left but desperate warfare and death.

"Where to?" asked Hetty. Her voice shrilled up into a squeak.

Caleb hesitated. He looked again at the other selectmen. There was a solemn, far-away expression upon their faces. "Well," said he, "Mis' Radway wants to git somebody, an'—"

"You ain't goin' to take me to that woman's!"

"You'd be real comfortable—"

"I ain't goin'."

"Now, why not, I'd like to know?"

"I don't like Susan Radway, hain't never liked her, an' I ain't goin' to live with her."

"Mis' Radway's a good Christian woman. You hadn't ought to speak that way about her."

"You know what Susan Radway is, jest as well's I do; an' everybody else does too. I ain't goin' a step, an' you might jest as well make up your mind to it."

Then Hetty seated herself in the corner of the pew nearest her tent, and folded her hands in her lap. She looked over at the pulpit as if she were listening to preaching. She panted, and her eyes glittered, but she had an immovable air.

"Now, Hetty, you've got sense enough to know you can't stay here," said Caleb. "You'd better put on your bonnet, an' come right along before dark. You'll have a nice ride."

Hetty made no response.

The three men stood looking at her. "Come, Hetty," said Caleb, feebly; and another selectman spoke. "Yes, you'd better come," he said, in a mild voice.

Hetty continued to stare at the pulpit.

The three men withdrew a little and conferred. They did not know how to act. This was a new emergency in their simple, even lives. They were not constables; these three steady, sober old men did not want to drag an old woman by main force out of the meeting-house, and thrust her into Caleb Gale's buggy as if it were a police wagon.

Finally Caleb brightened. "I'll go over an' git mother," said he. He started with a brisk air, and went down the gallery stairs; the others followed. They took up their stand in the meeting-house yard, and Caleb got into his buggy and gathered up the reins. The wind blew cold over the hill. "Hadn't you better go inside and wait out of the wind?" said Caleb.

"I guess we'll wait out here," replied one; and the other nodded.

"Well, I sha'n't be gone long," said Caleb. "Mother'll know how to manage her." He drove carefully down the hill; his buggy wings rattled in the wind. The other men pulled up their coat collars and met the blast stubbornly.

"Pretty ticklish piece of business to tackle," said one, in a low grunt.

"That's so," assented the other. Then they were silent and waited for Caleb. Once in a while they stamped their feet and slapped their mittened hands. They did not hear Hetty slip the bolt and turn the key of the meeting-house door, nor see her peeping at them from a gallery window.

Caleb returned in twenty minutes; he had not far to go. His wife, stout and handsome and full of vigor, sat beside him in the buggy. Her face was red with the cold wind; her thick cashmere shawl was pinned tightly over her broad bosom. "Has she come down yet?" she called out in an imperious way.

The two selectmen shook their heads. Caleb kept the horse quiet while his wife got heavily and briskly out of the buggy. She went up the meeting-house steps and reached out confidently to open the door. Then she drew back and looked around. "Why," said she, "the door's locked; she's locked the door. I call this pretty work!"

She turned again quite fiercely and began beating on the door. "Hetty!" she called; "Hetty, Hetty Fifield! Let me in! What have you locked this door for?"

She stopped and turned to her husband.

"Don't you s'pose the barn key would unlock it?" she asked.

"I don't b'lieve 'twould."

"Well, you'd better go home and fetch it."

Caleb again drove down the hill, and the other men searched their pockets for keys. One had the key of his cornhouse, and produced it hopefully; but it would not unlock the meeting-house door.

A crowd seldom gathered in the little village for anything short of a fire; but today in a short time quite a number of people stood on the meeting-house hill, and more kept coming. When Caleb Gale returned with the barn key, his daughter, a tall, pretty young girl, sat beside him, her little face alert and smiling in her red hood. The other selectmen's wives toiled eagerly up the hill, with a young daughter of one of them speeding on ahead. Then the two young girls stood close to each other and watched the proceedings. Key after key was tried; men brought all the large keys they could find, running importantly up the hill, but none would unlock the meeting-house door. After Caleb had tried the last

available key, stooping and screwing it anxiously, he turned around. "There ain't no use in it, any way," said he; "most likely the door's bolted."

"You don't mean there's a bolt on that door?" cried his wife.

"Yes, there is."

"Then you might jest as well have tore 'round for hen's feathers as keys. Of course she's bolted it if she's got any wit, an' I guess she's got most as much as some of you men that have been bringin' keys. Try the windows."

But the windows were fast. Hetty had made her sacred castle impregnable except to violence. Either the door would have to be forced or a window broken to gain an entrance.

The people conferred with one another. Some were for retreating and leaving Hetty in peaceful possession until time drove her to capitulate. "She'll open it tomorrow," they said. Others were for extreme measures, and their impetuosity gave them the lead. The project of forcing the door was urged; one man started for a crowbar.

"They are a parcel of fools to do such a thing," said Caleb Gale's wife to another woman. "Spoil that good door! They'd better leave the poor thing alone till tomorrow. I dun' know what's goin' to be done with her when they git in. I ain't goin' to have father draggin' her over to Mis' Radway's by the hair of her head."

"That's jest what I say," returned the other woman.

Mrs. Gale went up to Caleb and nudged him. "Don't you let them break that door down, father," said she.

"Well, well, we'll see," Caleb replied. He moved away a little; his wife's voice had been drowned out lately by a masculine clamor, and he took advantage of it.

All the people talked at once; the wind was keen, and all their garments fluttered; the two young girls had their arms around each other under their shawls; the man with the crowbar came stalking up the hill.

"Don't you let them break down that door, father," said Mrs. Gale.

"Well, well," grunted Caleb.

Regardless of remonstrances, the man set the crowbar against the door; suddenly there was a cry, "There she is!" Everybody looked up. There was Hetty looking out of a gallery window.

Everybody was still. Hetty began to speak. Her dark old face, peering out of the window, looked ghastly; the wind blew her poor gray locks over it. She extended her little wrinkled hands. "Jest let me say one word," said she; "jest one word." Her voice shook. All her coolness was gone. The magnitude of her last act of defiance had caused it to react upon herself like an overloaded gun.

"Say all you want to, Hetty, an' don't be afraid," Mrs. Gale called out.

"I jest want to say a word," repeated Hetty. "Can't I stay here, nohow? It don't seem as if I could go to Mis' Radway's. I ain't nothin again' her. I s'pose she's a good woman, but she's used to havin' her own way, and I've been livin' all my life with them that was, an' I've had to fight to keep a footin' on the earth, an' now I'm gittin' too old for't. If I can jest stay here in the meetin'-house, I won't ask for nothin' any better. I sha'n't need much to keep me; I wa'n't never a hefty eater; an' I'll keep the meetin'-house jest as clean as I know how. An' I'll make some more of them wool flowers. I'll make a wreath to go the whole length of the gallery, if I can git wool 'nough. Won't you let me stay? I ain't complainin', but I've always had a dretful hard time; seems as if now I might take a little comfort the last of it, if I could stay here. I can't go to Mis' Radway's nohow." Hetty covered her face with her hands; her words ended in a weak wail.

Mrs. Gale's voice rang out clear and strong and irrepressible. "Of course you can stay in the meetin'-house," said she; "I should laugh if you couldn't. Don't you worry another mite about it. You sha'n't go one step to Mis' Radway's; you couldn't live a day with her. You can stay jest where you are; you've kept the meetin'-house enough sight cleaner than I've ever seen it. Don't you worry another mite, Hetty."

Mrs. Gale stood majestically and looked defiantly around; tears were in her eyes. Another woman edged up to her. "Why couldn't she have that little room side of the pulpit, where the minister hangs his hat?" she whispered. "He could hang it somewhere else."

"Course she could," responded Mrs. Gale, with alacrity, "jest as well as not. She can have her stove an' her bed in there, an' be jest as comfortable as can be. I should laugh if she couldn't. Don't you worry, Hetty."

The crowd gradually dispersed, sending out stragglers down the hill until it was all gone. Mrs. Gale waited until the last, sitting in the buggy in state. When her husband gathered up the reins, she called back to Hetty: "Don't you worry one mite more about it, Hetty. I'm comin' up to see you in the mornin'!"

It was almost dusk when Caleb drove down the hill; he was the last of the besiegers, and the feeble garrison was left triumphant.

The next day but one was Christmas, the next night Christmas Eve. On Christmas Eve Hetty had reached what to her was the flood tide of peace and prosperity. Established in that small, lofty room, with her bed and her stove, with gifts of a rocking chair and table, and a goodly store of food, with no one to molest or disturb her, she had nothing to wish for on earth. All her small desires were satisfied. No happy girl could have a merrier Christmas than this old woman with her little measure full of gifts. That Christmas Eve Hetty lay down under her sunflower quilt, and all her old hardships looked dim in the distance, like far away hills, while her new joys came out like stars.

She was a light sleeper; the next morning she was up early. She opened the meeting-house door and stood looking out. The smoke from the village chimneys had not yet begun to rise blue and rosy in the clear frosty air. There was no snow, but over all the hill there was a silver rime of frost; the bare branches of the trees glistened. Hetty stood looking. "Why, it's Christmas mornin'," she said, sud-denly. Christmas had never been a gala-day to this old woman. Christmas had not been kept at all in this New England village when she was young. She was led to think of it now only in connection with the dinner Mrs. Gale had promised to bring her today.

Mrs. Gale had told her she should have some of her Christmas dinner, some turkey and plum pudding. She called it to mind now with a thrill of delight. Her face grew momentarily more radiant. There was a certain beauty in it. A finer morning light than that which lit up the wintry earth seemed to shine over the furrows of her old face. "I'm goin' to have turkey an' plum puddin' today," said she; "it's Christmas." Suddenly she started, and went into the meeting-house, straight up the gallery stairs. There in a clear space hung the bell-rope. Hetty grasped it. Never before had a Christmas bell been rung in this village; Hetty had probably never heard of Christmas bells. She was prompted by pure artless enthusiasm and grateful happiness. Her old arms pulled on the rope with a will; the bell sounded peal on peal. Down in the village, curtains rolled up, letting in the morning light; happy faces looked out of the windows. Hetty had awakened the whole village to Christmas Day.

Study Questions

1. The opening conflict between Hetty and Caleb is resolved when he gives in. Why does Caleb permit her to move into the church? Hetty is also able to talk Sammy into helping her move her belongings. What character trait does she demonstrate in both cases?

2. What happens to disrupt Hetty's three-month stay in the church?

3. Even though the men are quite serious, what is amusing about their attempt to get Hetty out of the church?

4. What is the significance of Hetty's victory being led by Mrs. Gale? Why is Mrs. Gale described as "irrepressible," "majestic," and "defiant"?

5. Why is it appropriate that Hetty's triumph occurs just before Christmas? Why is the story title appropriate?

Composition

1. Write an essay in which you explain how Hetty Fifield demonstrates Emerson's "self-reliance." Discuss the character traits which exemplify Emerson's definition. Tell which of her qualities are less than ideal and why you like or dislike her.

2. Write a character sketch about a person you know who demonstrates persistence and determination similar to Hetty's. Describe a situation in which the person displays that determined persistence.

Vocabulary

A. On a separate sheet of paper, copy the **dictionary definitions** of the following adjectives which appear in "A Church Mouse":

bland	impecunious	imperturbable	inscrutable	sallow
frugal	imperious	impetuous	sacrilegious	sodden

B. Each word above fits the **sentence context** in one (and only one) of the following incomplete sentences. Below the definitions you have written, copy the correct word to complete each statement.

1. Throughout her life, Hetty had been as _____ as the proverbial church mouse.

2. Her thin frame and _____ complexion showed that she had hardly had enough to eat.

3. The family she had been living with expected guests; and for that reason, which seemed somewhat _____ to Hetty, they had asked her to move out.

4. With no place else to go, Hetty made the _____ decision to become church sexton and set up housekeeping in the meeting-house.

5. Unwillingly assisted by a lazy, _____ young man named Sammy, she moved her meager belongings there.

6. She slept in the gallery, and there she cooked her _____ meals.

7. One Sunday the whole meeting-house reeked with the _____ odor of boiled turnips and cabbage.

8. Although Hetty had kept the building spick-and-span, cooking smells in church seemed somehow _____ to the deacons, who decided to put Hetty out of the place.

9. The powerful and _____ Mrs. Gale was assigned the task of persuading Hetty to leave but failed because Hetty melted the woman's heart with an eloquent plea for permission to stay.

10. After that Hetty faced the future optimistically, filled with _____ confidence that she would never again be homeless.

Paul Laurence Dunbar   1872-1906

Paul Laurence Dunbar was the first Black poet in America to gain a national reputation. He was born in Dayton, Ohio, to parents who had been slaves before the Civil War. Dunbar's poetic talent was revealed in high school where he was the only Black student in his class. At age 21, Dunbar was employed by Frederick Douglass, then ambassador to Haiti. Dunbar was Douglass's assistant at the opening of the Haiti Pavilion at the Chicago World's Fair in 1893. Two years later, Dunbar published his first book of poetry, *Majors and Minors.*

In 1896 William Dean Howells reviewed his first book and arranged for publication of the second one, *Lyrics of Lowly Life.* Howell's highest praise was reserved for Dunbar's dialect poetry, which placed some limitation on the acceptance of his other work. Dunbar also wrote numerous short stories and four novels, as well as several volumes of poetry. The poems he preferred are, like "Sympathy," lyrical and expressive of pain and frustration.

Sympathy

PAUL LAURENCE DUNBAR

I know what the caged bird feels, alas!
When the sun is bright on the upland slopes;
When the wind stirs soft through the springing grass
And the river flows like a stream of glass;
When the first bird sings and the first bud opes,   5
And the faint perfume from its chalice steals—
I know what the caged bird feels!

I know why the caged bird beats his wing
Till its blood is red on the cruel bars;
For he must fly back to his perch and cling   10
When he fain would be on the bough a-swing;
And a pain still throbs in the old, old scars
And they pulse again with a keener sting—
I know why he beats his wing!

I know why the caged bird sings, ah me,   15
When his wing is bruised and his bosom sore,
When he beats his bars and would be free;
It is not a carol of joy or glee,
But a prayer that he sends from his heart's deep core,
But a plea, that upward to Heaven he flings—   20
I know why the caged bird sings!

Study Questions

1. Why is the caged bird unhappy?
2. How does the scene depicted in the first stanza contribute to the bird's unhappiness?
3. Even though each of the three stanzas comments on the same situation, there is a progression in the idea. What is this progression? What effect does it have?
4. The title of the poem, "Sympathy," indicates that the poet has some special bond with the bird and that the plight of the bird is a metaphor used to express the poet's own feeling. Explain this relationship between the poet and his subject.

William Edward Burghardt DuBois   1868-1963

"The problem of the twentieth century is the problem of the color-line—the relation of the darker to the lighter races of men in Asia and Africa, in America and the islands of the sea."

This frequently quoted statement was written by William Edward Burghardt DuBois in his book, *The Souls of Black Folk* (1903). During a life which bridged the nineteenth and twentieth centuries, DuBois was able to observe the accuracy of this and other predictions which he made. For some seventy-five years, DuBois actively studied, wrote, and published. He also participated in the struggle of Black Americans for justice and equality. Finally, however, at 93, and in despair, he became a citizen of Ghana. He died there in August, 1963, at the very moment that thousands of Blacks and other Americans were engaged in the historic "March on Washington" (See page 115).

DuBois was foremost a scholar. He received his Ph.D. from Harvard University and studied at the University of Berlin for two years. But he was also a founder of the National Association for the Advancement of Colored People (NAACP), a Pan-Africanist and a major and articulate advocate of Black self-determination. In addition, he wrote novels, poetry, plays, and a set of lyrical essays which makes up *The Souls of Black Folk*. The following essay is taken from that collection. In it he shares with the reader his fascination and love for the Black folk he discovered while a college student in Tennessee. DuBois grew up in Great Barrington, Massachusetts, where there were few other Black families.

Of the Meaning of Progress

W.E.B. DUBOIS

ONCE UPON A TIME I taught school in the hills of Tennessee, where the broad dark vale of the Mississippi begins to roll and crumple to greet the Alleghenies. I was a Fisk[1] student then, and all Fisk men thought that Tennessee—beyond the Veil[2]—was theirs alone, and in vacation time they sallied forth in lusty bands to meet the county school commissioners. Young and happy, I too went, and I shall not soon forget that summer, seventeen years ago.

First, there was a Teachers' Institute at the county seat; and there distinguished guests of the superintendent taught the teachers fractions and spelling and other mysteries,—white teachers in the morning, Negroes at night. A picnic now and then, and a supper, and the rough world was softened by laughter and song. I remember how—But I wander.

There came a day when all the teachers left the Institute and began the hunt for schools. I learn from hearsay (for my mother was mortally afraid of firearms) that the hunting of ducks and bears and men is wonderfully interesting, but I am sure that the man who has never hunted a country school has something to learn of the pleasures of the chase. I see now the white, hot roads lazily rise and fall and wind before me under the burning July sun; I feel the deep weariness of heart and limb as ten, eight, six miles stretch relentlessly ahead; I feel my heart sink heavily as I hear again and again; "Got a teacher? Yes." So I walked on and on—horses were too expensive—until I had wandered beyond railways, beyond stage lines, to a land of "varmints" and rattlesnakes, where the coming of a stranger was an event, and men lived and died in the shadow of one blue hill.

Sprinkled over hill and dale lay cabins and farmhouses, shut out from the world by the forests and the rolling hills toward the east. There I found at last a little school. Josie told me of it; she was a thin, homely girl of twenty, with a dark-brown face and thick, hard hair. I had crossed the stream at Watertown, and rested under the great willows; then I had gone to the little cabin in the lot where Josie was resting on her way to town. The gaunt farmer made me welcome, and Josie, hearing my errand, told me anxiously that they wanted a school over the hill; that but once since the war had a teacher been there; that she herself longed to learn,—and thus she ran on; talking fast and loud, with much earnestness and energy.

Next morning I crossed the tall round hill, lingered to look at the blue and yellow mountains stretching toward the Carolinas, then plunged into the wood, and came out at Josie's home. It was a dull frame cottage with four rooms, perched just below the brow of the hill, amid peach trees. The father was a quiet, simple soul, calmly ignorant, with no touch of vulgarity. The mother was different,—strong, bustling, and energetic, with a quick, restless tongue, and an ambition to live "like folks."[3] There was a crowd of children. Two boys had

1 **Fisk**: private Afro-American university in Nashville, Tennessee.

2 **Veil**: here represents the invisible barrier between blacks and whites.

3 "**like folks**": here, to live decently.

comfortable, and for their knowledge of their own ignorance. There was with them no affectation. The mother would scold the father for being so "easy"; Josie would roundly berate the boys for carelessness; and all knew that it was a hard thing to dig a living out of a rocky side hill.

I secured the school. I remember the day I rode horseback out to the commissioner's house with a pleasant young white fellow who wanted the white school. The road ran down the bed of a stream; the sun laughed and the water jingled, and we rode on. "Come in," said the commissioner,—"come in. Have a seat. Yes, that certificate will do. Stay to dinner. What do you want a month?" "Oh," thought I, "this is lucky"; but even then fell the awful shadow of the Veil, for they ate first, then I—alone.

The schoolhouse was a log hut, where Colonel Wheeler used to shelter his corn. It sat in a lot behind a rail fence and thorn bushes, near the sweetest of springs. There was an entrance where a door once was, and within, a massive rickety fireplace; great chinks between the logs served as windows. Furniture was scarce. A pale blackboard crouched in the corner. My desk was made of three boards, reinforced at critical points, and my chair, borrowed from the landlady, had to be returned every night. Seats for the children—these puzzled me much. I was haunted by a New England vision of neat little desks and chairs, but, alas! the reality was rough plank benches without backs, and at times without legs. They had the one virtue of making naps dangerous,—possibly fatal, for the floor was not to be trusted.

It was a hot morning late in July when the school opened. I trembled when I heard the patter of little feet down the dusty road, and saw the growing row of dark solemn faces and bright eager eyes facing me. First came Josie and her brothers and sisters. The longing to know, to be a student in the great school at Nashville, hovered like a star above this

gone away. There remained two growing girls; a shy midget of eight; John, tall, awkward, and eighteen; Jim, younger, quicker, and better looking; and two babies of indefinite age. Then there was Josie herself. She seemed to be the center of the family: always busy at service, or at home, or berry-picking, a little nervous and inclined to scold, like her mother, yet faithful, too, like her father. She had about her a certain fineness, the shadow of an unconscious moral heroism that would willingly give all of life to make life broader, deeper, and fuller for her and hers. I saw much of this family afterwards, and grew to love them for their honest efforts to be decent and

came,—a midnight beauty, with starry eyes and tapering limbs; and her brother, correspondingly homely. And then the big boys,—the hulking Lawrences; the lazy Neills, unfathered sons of mother and daughter; Hickman, with a stoop in his shoulders; and the rest.

There they sat, nearly thirty of them, on the rough benches, their faces shading from a pale cream to a deep brown, the little feet bare and swinging, the eyes full of expectation, with here and there a twinkle of mischief, and the hands grasping Webster's blue-back spelling-book. I loved my school, and the fine faith the children had in the wisdom of their teacher was truly marvelous. We read and spelled together, wrote a little, picked flowers, sang, and listened to stories of the world beyond the hill. At times the school would dwindle away, and I would start out. I would visit Mun Eddings, who lived in two very dirty rooms, and ask why little Lugene, whose flaming face seemed ever ablaze with the dark-red hair uncombed, was absent all last week, or why I missed so often the inimitable rags of Mack and Ed. Then the father, who worked Colonel Wheeler's farm on shares, would tell me how the crops needed the boys; and the thin, slovenly mother, whose face was pretty when washed, assured me that Lugene must mind the baby. "But we'll start them again next week." When the Lawrences stopped, I knew that the doubts of the old folks about book-learning had conquered again, and so, toiling up the hill, and getting as far into the cabin as possible, I put Cicero "pro Archia Poeta" into the simplest English with local applications, and usually convinced them—for a week or so.

On Friday nights I often went home with some of the children,—sometimes to Doc Burke's farm. He was a great, loud, thin Black, ever working, and trying to buy the seventy-five acres of hill and dale where he lived; but people said that he would surely fail, and the "white folks would get it all." His

child-woman amid her work and worry, and she studied doggedly. There were the Dowells from their farm over toward Alexandria,—Fanny, with her smooth black face and wondering eyes; Martha, brown and dull; the pretty girl-wife of a brother, and the younger brood.

There were the Burkes,—two brown and yellow lads, and a tiny haughty-eyed girl. Fat Reuben's little chubby girl came, with golden face and old-gold hair, faithful and solemn. 'Thenie was on hand early,—a jolly, ugly, good-hearted girl, who slyly dipped snuff and looked after her little bowlegged brother. When her mother could spare her, 'Tildy

wife was a magnificent Amazon, with saffron face and shining hair, uncorseted and barefooted, and the children were strong and beautiful. They lived in a one-and-a-half-room cabin in the hollow of the farm, near the spring. The front room was full of great fat white beds, scrupulously neat; and there were bad chromos on the walls, and a tired center table. In the tiny back kitchen I was often invited to "take out and help" myself to fried chicken and wheat biscuit, "meat" and corn pone, stringbeans and berries. At first I used to be a little alarmed at the approach of bedtime in the one lone bedroom, but embarrassment was very deftly avoided. First, all the children nodded and slept, and were stowed away in one great pile of goose feathers; next, the mother and the father discreetly slipped away to the kitchen while I went to bed; then, blowing out the dim light, they retired in the dark. In the morning all were up and away before I thought of awaking. Across the road, where fat Reuben lived, they all went outdoors while the teacher retired, because they did not boast the luxury of a kitchen.

I liked to stay with the Dowells, for they had four rooms and plenty of good country fare. Uncle Bird had a small, rough farm, all woods and hills, miles from the big road; but he was full of tales,—he preached now and then,—and with his children, berries, horses, and wheat he was happy and prosperous. Often, to keep the peace, I must go where life was less lovely; for instance, 'Tildy's mother was incorrigibly dirty, Reuben's larder was limited seriously, and herds of untamed insects wandered over the Eddingses' beds. Best of all I loved to go to Josie's, and sit on the porch, eating peaches, while the mother bustled and talked: how Josie had bought the sewing machine; how Josie worked at service in winter, but that four dollars a month was "mighty little" wages; how Josie longed to go away to school, but that it "looked like" they never could get far enough ahead to let her; how the crops failed and the well was yet unfinished;

and, finally, how "mean" some of the white folks were.

For two summers I lived in this little world. . . .

I have called my tiny community a world, and so its isolation made it; and yet there was among us but a half-awakened common consciousness, sprung from common joy and grief, at burial, birth, or wedding; from a common hardship in poverty, poor land, and low wages; and, above all, from the sight of the Veil that hung between us and Opportunity. All this caused us to think some thoughts together; but these, when ripe for speech, were spoken in various languages. Those whose eyes twenty-five and more years before had seen "the glory of the coming of the Lord,"[4] saw in every present hindrance or help a dark fatalism bound to bring all things right in His own good time. The mass of those to whom slavery was a dim recollection of childhood found the world a puzzling thing: it asked little of them, and they answered with little, and yet it ridiculed their offering. Such a paradox they could not understand, and therefore sank into listless indifference, or shiftlessness, or reckless bravado. There were, however, some—such as Josie, Jim, and Ben—to whom War, Hell, and Slavery were but childhood tales, whose young appetites had been whetted to an edge by school and story and half-awakened thought. Ill could they be content, born without and beyond the World. And their weak wings beat against their barriers,—barriers of caste, of youth, of life; at last, in dangerous moments, against everything that opposed even a whim.

The ten years that follow youth, the years when first the realization comes that life is leading somewhere,—these were the years that passed after I left my little school. When they were past, I came by chance once more to the walls of Fisk University, to the halls of the

---

4 "the glory . . . Lord": here, referring to the Civil War victory and abolition of slavery.

chapel of melody. As I lingered there in the joy and pain of meeting old school friends, there swept over me a sudden longing to pass again beyond the blue hill, and to see the homes and the school of other days, and to learn how life had gone with my school children; and I went.

Josie was dead, and the gray-haired mother said simply, "We've had a heap of trouble since you've been away." I had feared for Jim. With a cultured parentage and a social caste to uphold him, he might have made a venturesome merchant or a West Point cadet. But here he was, angry with life and reckless; and when Farmer Durham charged him with stealing wheat, the old man had to ride fast to escape the stones which the furious fool hurled after him. They told Jim to run away; but he would not run, and the constable came that afternoon. It grieved Josie, and great awkward John walked nine miles every day to see his little brother through the bars of Lebanon jail. At last the two came back together in the dark night. The mother cooked supper, and Josie emptied her purse, and the boys stole away. Josie grew thin and silent, yet worked the more. The hill became steep for the quiet old father, and with the boys away there was little to do in the valley. Josie helped them to sell the old farm, and they moved nearer town. Brother Dennis, the carpenter, built a new house with six rooms; Josie toiled a year in Nashville, and brought back ninety dollars to furnish the house and change it to a home.

When the spring came, and the birds twittered, and the stream ran proud and full, little sister Lizzie, bold and thoughtless, flushed with the passion of youth, bestowed herself on the tempter, and brought home a nameless child. Josie shivered and worked on, with the vision of schooldays all fled, with a face wan and tired,—worked until, on a summer's day, some one married another; then Josie crept to her mother like a hurt child, and slept—and sleeps.

I paused to scent the breeze as I entered the valley. The Lawrences have gone,—father and son forever,—and the other son lazily digs in the earth to live. A new young widow rents out their cabin to fat Reuben. Reuben is a Baptist preacher now, but I fear as lazy as ever, though his cabin has three rooms; and little Ella has grown into a bouncing woman, and is ploughing corn on the hot hillside. . . .

My log schoolhouse was gone. In its place stood Progress; and Progress, I understand, is necessarily ugly. The crazy foundation stones still marked the former site of my poor little cabin, and not far away, on six weary boulders, perched a jaunty board house, perhaps twenty by thirty feet, with three windows and a door that locked. Some of the window glass was broken, and part of an old iron stove lay mournfully under the house. I peeped through the window half reverently, and found things that were more familiar. The blackboard had grown by about two feet, and the seats were still without backs. The county owns the lot now, I hear, and every year there is a session of school. As I sat by the spring and looked on the Old and the New I felt glad, very glad, and yet—

After two long drinks I started on. There was the great double log house on the corner. I remembered the broken, blighted family that used to live there. . . . I felt sure that Ben and 'Tildy would come to naught from such a home. But this is an odd world; for Ben is a busy farmer in Smith County, "doing well, too," they say, and he had cared for little 'Tildy until last spring, when a lover married her. A hard life the lad had led, toiling for meat, and laughed at because he was homely and crooked. There was Sam Carlon, an impudent old skinflint, who had definite notions about "niggers," and hired Ben a summer and would not pay him. Then the hungry boy gathered his sacks together, and in broad daylight went into Carlon's corn; and when the hard-fisted farmer set upon him, the angry boy flew at him like a beast. Doc Burke saved a murder and a lynching that day.

The story reminded me again of the Burkes, and an impatience seized me to know who won in the battle, Doc or the seventy-five acres. For it is a hard thing to make a farm out of nothing, even in fifteen years. So I hurried on, thinking of the Burkes. They used to have a certain magnificent barbarism about them that I liked. They were never vulgar, never immoral, but rather rough and primitive, with an unconventionality that spent itself in loud guffaws, slaps on the back, and naps in the corner. I hurried by the cottage of the misborn Neill boys. It was empty, and they were grown into fat, lazy farmhands. I saw the home of the Hickmans, but Albert, with his stooping shoulders, had passed from the world. Then I came to the Burkes' gate and peered through; the enclosure looked rough and untrimmed, and yet there were the same fences around the old farm save to the left, where lay twenty-five other acres. And lo! the cabin in the hollow had climbed the hill and swollen to a half-finished six-room cottage.

The Burkes held a hundred acres, but they were still in debt. Indeed, the gaunt father who toiled night and day would scarcely be happy out of debt, being so used to it. Some day he must stop, for his massive frame is showing decline. The mother wore shoes, but the lion like physique of other days was broken. The children had grown up. Rob, the image of his father, was loud and rough with laughter. Birdie, my school baby of six, had grown to a picture of maiden beauty, tall and tawny. "Edgar is gone," said the mother, with head half bowed,—"gone to work in Nashville; he and his father couldn't agree."

Little Doc, the boy born since the time of my school, took me horseback down the creek next morning toward Farmer Dowell's. The road and the stream were battling for mastery, and the stream had the better of it. We splashed and waded, and the merry boy, perched behind

me, chattered and laughed. He showed me where Simon Thompson had bought a bit of ground and a home; but his daughter Lana, a plump, brown, slow girl, was not there. She had married a man and a farm twenty miles away. We wound on down the stream till we came to a gate that I did not recognize, but the boy insisted that it was "Uncle Bird's." The farm was fat with the growing crop. In that little valley was a strange stillness as I rode up; for death and marriage had stolen youth and left age and childhood there. We sat and talked that night after the chores were done. Uncle Bird was grayer, and his eyes did not see so well, but he was still jovial. We talked of the acres bought,—one hundred and twenty five,—of the new guest chamber added, of Martha's marrying. Then we talked of death: Fanny and Fred were gone; a shadow hung over the other daughter, and when it lifted she was to go to Nashville to school. At last we spoke of the neighbors, and as night fell, Uncle Bird told me how, on a night like that, 'Thenie came wandering back to her home over yonder, to escape the blows of her husband. And next morning she died in the home that her little bowlegged brother, working and saving, had bought for their widowed mother.

My journey was done, and behind me lay hill and dale, and Life and Death. How shall man measure Progress there where the dark-faced Josie lies? How many heartfuls of sorrow shall balance a bushel of wheat? How hard a thing is life to the lowly, and yet how human and real! And all this life and love and strife and failure,—is it the twilight of nightfall or the flush of some faint-dawning day?

Thus sadly musing, I rode to Nashville in the Jim Crow[5] car.

---

5 **Jim Crow:** a term used to designate the segregation of blacks and whites.

Study Questions

1. How does DuBois locate his first teaching job?

2. How does DuBois describe Josie's family? What does he say about Josie?

3. How do you know that DuBois loves the school house and his "nearly thirty" students? What details does he give in describing them that reveal his affection?

4. Besides teaching, what other activities did DuBois engage in? How did the weekends with his students' families differ?

5. According to DuBois, what interests and concerns did the people in his school district have in common? What changes had occurred ten years later in the people? in the landscape?

6. In the final paragraph, DuBois says "How many heartfuls of sorrow shall balance a bushel of wheat?" What do you think this means?

Composition

1. In an essay discuss the obstacles to learning encountered by the students in DuBois's rural school around 1885. Tell what factors kept the eager ones from learning and what encouraged the reluctant. Conclude with a statement on whether or not you think these obstacles have been eliminated.

2. DuBois thoroughly describes the area in which he taught. He makes his description vivid by the use of details. For example, "I see now the white, hot roads lazily . . . wind . . . under the burning July sun. . . ." Using this kind of detail, describe a place you know, or can imagine. Tell where the place is, how it looks, and how it makes you feel.

Vocabulary

Below are some words from "Of the Meaning of Progress." Determine the correct **definition** of each word, using a dictionary if necessary. Then write a sentence using each word in its correct **sentence context**.

affectation	bravado	guffaw	saffron
Amazon	fatalism	paradox	wistfulness

Kate O'Flaherty Chopin   1851-1904

Born in St. Louis of Irish and French parents, Kate O'Flaherty grew up bilingual. Thus when she married Oscar Chopin and moved to Louisiana, she was able to understand the French influence in that region. Her writing career began in 1890 with the publication of her first novel, *At Fault.* Her best known work is her second novel, *The*

Awakening (1899). It is a book which explores the life of a troubled woman.

Chopin also wrote nearly a hundred short stories. The story here, though not set in Louisiana, is characteristic of Kate Chopin's fine perception of feminine sensibility. It is from her collection, *The Storm and Other Stories.*

from The Storm and Other Stories

KATE CHOPIN

I

MILDRED ORME, seated in the snuggest corner of the big front porch of the Kraummer farmhouse, was as content as a girl need hope to be.

This was no such farm as one reads about in humorous fiction. Here were swelling acres where the undulating wheat gleamed in the sun like a golden sea. For silver there was the Meramec—or, better, it was pure crystal, for here and there one might look clean through it down to where the pebbles lay like green and yellow gems. Along the river's edge trees were growing to the very water, and in it, sweeping it when they were willows.

The house itself was big and broad, as country houses should be. The master was big and broad, too. The mistress was small and thin, and it was always she who went out at noon to pull the great clanging bell that called the farmhands in to dinner.

From her agreeable corner where she lounged with her Browning or her Ibsen, Mildred watched the woman do this every day. Yet when the clumsy farmhands all came tramping up the steps and crossed the porch in going to their meal that was served within, she never looked at them. Why should she? Farmhands are not so very nice to look at, and she was nothing of an anthropologist. But once when the half dozen men came along, a paper which she had laid carelessly upon the railing was blown across their path. One of them picked it up, and when he had mounted the steps restored it to her. He was young, and brown, of course, as the sun had made him. He had nice blue eyes. His fair hair was dishevelled. His shoulders were broad and square and his limbs strong and clean. A not unpicturesque figure in the rough attire that bared his throat to view and gave perfect freedom to his every motion.

Mildred did not make these several observations in the half second that she looked at him in courteous acknowledgment. It took her as many days to note them all. For she signaled him out each time that he passed her, meaning to give him a condescending little smile, as she knew how. But he never looked at her. To be sure, clever young women of twenty, who are handsome, besides, who have refused their half dozen offers and are settling down to the conviction that life is a tedious affair, are not going to care a straw whether farmhands look at them or not. And Mildred did not care, and the thing would not have occupied her a moment if Satan had not intervened, in offering the employment which natural conditions had failed to supply. It was summer time; she was idle; she was piqued, and that was the beginning of the shameful affair.

"Who are these men, Mrs. Kraummer, that work for you? Where do you pick them up?"

"Oh, ve picks 'em up everyvere. Some is neighbors, some is tramps, and so."

"And that broad-shouldered young fellow—is he a neighbor? The one who handed me my paper the other day—you remember?"

"Gott, no! You might yust as well say he vas a tramp. Aber he vorks like a steam ingine."

"Well, he's an extremely disagreeable-looking man. I should think you'd be afraid to have him about, not knowing him."

"Vat you vant to be 'fraid for?" laughed the little woman. "He don't talk no more un ven he vas deef und dumb. I didn't t'ought you vas sooch a baby."

"But, Mrs. Kraummer, I don't want you to think I'm a baby, as you say—a coward, as you mean. Ask the man if he will drive me to church tomorrow. You see, I'm not so very much afraid of him," she added with a smile.

The answer which this unmannerly farmhand returned to Mildred's request was simply a refusal. He could not drive her to church because he was going fishing.

"Aber," offered good Mrs. Kraummer, "Hans Platzfeldt will drive you to church, oder vereever you vants. He vas a goot boy vat you can trust, dat Hans."

"Oh, thank him very much. But I find I have so many letters to write tomorrow, and it promises to be hot, too. I shan't care to go to church after all."

She could have cried for vexation. Snubbed by a farmhand! a tramp, perhaps. She, Mildred Orme, who ought really to have been with the rest of the family at Narragansett—who had come to seek in this retired spot the repose that would enable her to follow exalted lines of thought. She marvelled at the problematic nature of farmhands.

After sending her the uncivil message already recorded, and as he passed beneath the porch where she sat, he did look at her finally, in a way to make her positively gasp at the sudden effrontery of the man.

But the inexplicable look stayed with her. She could not banish it.

II

It was not so very hot after all, the next day, when Mildred walked down the long narrow footpath that led through the bending wheat to the river. High above her waist reached the yellow grain. Mildred's brown eyes filled with a reflected golden light as they caught the glint of it; as she heard the trill that it answered to the gentle breeze. Anyone who has walked through the wheat in midsummer-time knows that sound.

In the woods it was sweet and solemn and cool. And there beside the river was the wretch who had annoyed her, first, with his indifference, then with the sudden boldness of his glance.

"Are you fishing?" she asked politely and with kindly dignity, which she supposed would define her position toward him. The inquiry lacked not pertinence, seeing that he sat motionless, with a pole in his hand and his eyes fixed on a cork that bobbed aimlessly on the water.

"Yes, madam," was his brief reply.

"It won't disturb you if I stand here a moment, to see what success you will have?"

"No, madam."

She stood very still, holding tight to the book she had brought with her. Her straw hat had slipped disreputably to one side, over the wavy bronze-brown bang that half covered her forehead. Her cheeks were ripe with color that the sun had coaxed there; so were her lips.

All the other farmhands had gone forth in Sunday attire. Perhaps this one had none better than these working clothes that he wore. A feminine commiseration swept her at the thought. He spoke never a word. She wondered how many hours he could sit there, so patiently waiting for fish to come to his hook. For her part, the situation began to pall, and she wanted to change it at last.

"Let me try a moment, please? I have an idea—"

"Yes madam."

"The man is surely an idiot, with his monosyllables," she commented inwardly. But she remembered that monosyllables belong to a boor's equipment.

She laid her book carefully down and took the pole gingerly that he came to place in her hands. Then it was his turn to stand back and look respectfully and silently on at the absorbing performance.

"Oh!" cried the girl, suddenly, seized with excitement upon seeing the line dragged deep in the water.

"Wait, wait! Not yet."

He sprang to her side. With his eyes eagerly fastened on the tense line, he grasped the pole to prevent her drawing it, as her intention seemed to be. That is, he meant to grasp the pole, but instead, his brown hand came down upon Mildred's white one.

He started violently at finding himself so close to a bronze-brown tangle that almost swept his chin—to a hot cheek only a few inches away from his shoulder, to a pair of young, dark eyes that gleamed for an instant unconscious things into his own.

Then, why ever it happened, or how ever it happened, his arms were holding Mildred and he kissed her lips. She did not know if it was ten times or only once.

She looked around—her face milk-white—to see him disappear with rapid strides through the path that had brought her there. Then she was alone.

Only the birds had seen, and she could count on their discretion. She was not wildly indignant, as many would have been. Shame stunned her. But through it she gropingly wondered if she should tell the Kraummers that her chaste lips had been rifled of their innocence. Publish her own confusion? No! Once in her room she would give calm thought to the situation, and determine then how to act. The secret must remain her own: a hateful burden to bear alone until she could forget it.

III

And because she feared not to forget it, Mildred wept that night. All day long a hideous truth had been thrusting itself upon her that made her ask herself if she could be mad. She feared it. Else why was that kiss the most delicious thing she had known in her twenty years of life? The sting of it had never left her lips since it was pressed into them. The sweet trouble of it banished sleep from her pillow.

But Mildred would not bend the outward conditions of her life to serve any shameful whim that chanced to visit her soul, like an ugly dream. She would avoid nothing. She would go and come as always.

In the morning she found in her chair upon the porch the book she had left by the river. A fresh indignity! But she came and went as she intended to, and sat as usual upon the porch amid her familiar surroundings. When the Offender passed her by she knew it, though her eyes were never lifted. Are there only sight and sound to tell such things? She discerned it by a wave that swept her with confusion and she knew not what besides.

She watched him furtively, one day, when he talked with Farmer Kraummer out in the open. When he walked away she remained like one who has drunk much wine. Then unhesitatingly she turned and began her preparations to leave the Kraummer farmhouse.

When the afternoon was far spent they brought letters to her. One of them read like this:

"My Mildred, deary! I am only now at Narragansett, and so broke up not to find you. So you are down at that Kraummer farm, on the Iron Mountain. Well! What do you think of that delicious crank, Fred Evelyn? For a man must be a crank who does such things. Only fancy! Last year he chose to drive an engine back and forth across the plains. This year he tills the soil with laborers. Next year it will be something else as insane—because he likes to live more lives than one kind, and other

Quixotic reasons. We are great chums. He writes me he's grown as strong as an ox. But he hasn't mentioned that you are there. I know you don't get on with him, for he isn't a bit intellectual—detests Ibsen and abuses Tolstoi. He doesn't read 'in books'—says they are spectacles for the short-sighted to look at life through. Don't snub him, dear, or be too hard on him; he has a heart of gold, if he is the first crank in America."

Mildred tried to think—to feel that the intelligence which this letter brought to her would take somewhat of the sting from the shame that tortured her. But it did not. She knew that it could not.

In the gathering twilight she walked again through the wheat that was heavy and fragrant with dew. The path was very long and very narrow. When she was midway she saw the Offender coming toward her. What could she do? Turn and run, as a little child might? Spring into the wheat, as some frightened four-footed creature would? There was nothing but to pass him with the dignity which the occasion clearly demanded.

But he did not let her pass. He stood squarely in the pathway before her, hat in hand, a perturbed look upon his face.

"Miss Orme," he said, "I have wanted to say to you, every hour of the past week, that I am the most consummate hound that walks the earth."

She made no protest. Her whole bearing seemed to indicate that her opinion coincided with his own.

"If you have a father, or brother, or any one, in short, to whom you may say such things—"

"I think you aggravate the offense, sir, by speaking of it. I shall ask you never to mention it again. I want to forget that it ever happened. Will you kindly let me by."

"Oh," he ventured eagerly, "you want to forget it! Then, maybe, since you are willing to forget, you will be generous enough to forgive the offender some day?"

"Some day," she repeated, almost inaudibly, looking seemingly through him, but not at him—"some day—perhaps; when I shall have forgiven myself."

He stood motionless, watching her slim, straight figure lessening by degrees as she walked slowly away from him. He was wondering what she meant. Then a sudden, quick wave came beating into his brown throat and staining it crimson, when he guessed what it might be.

Study Questions

1. What is Mildred Orme's attitude toward the farm hands? What circumstances cause her to take a special interest in one of the men?

2. How does Mildred Orme show her interest in the farmhand? What happens when she discovers that her interest is being ignored?

3. What does Mildred Orme learn from her friend's letter? How does she react to this information?

4. How does the story end? What do you think each of the characters feels?

5 REVIEW

Study Questions

1. The Sense of Place theme is more prominent in some selections than in others. Explain how the New England locale plays an important part in the stories by Mary E. Wilkins Freeman and Henry James. Contrast the New England setting with the Midwestern farm in Chopin's story, the Tennessee backwoods country in the DuBois selection, and Chief Joseph's feeling for the land in his speech. In what ways would the main points of each selection be changed if their locales were changed?

2. The theme of individualism appears explicitly in the selections by Whitman, Dickinson, and Freeman. Explain how each writer follows Thoreau's advice to "explore thyself."

3. Several of these selections comment on death. Compare and contrast the following: Dickinson's poetic treatment, Lincoln's handling of wartime death, Keckley's account of the assassination, and Clemens's joke at the expense of a corpse.

4. Contrast three fictional female characters: Chopin's Mildred Orme, James's Caroline Spencer, and Freeman's Hetty Fifield. In what ways is each admirable? How is each weak? Why is Fifield most likely a forerunner of women's liberation? Which character would most likely have sympathized with Elizabeth Cady Stanton and Sojourner Truth (pages 253 and 258)?

Composition

1. Near the end of the "Gettysburg Address" Lincoln says America shall have "a new birth of freedom." Write an essay in which you explain how this statement applies to the selection by Chief Joseph and the poem by Paul Laurence Dunbar. First explain what you think Lincoln meant. Then use examples from Chief Joseph and Dunbar to show how they would respond to this statement. Conclude with your response to Lincoln's statement.

2. Whitman's introduction of the free verse form opened up new possibilities for writing poetry. Using free verse, write a poem on a topic about which you have deep feelings. Select your topic then decide what type of rhythmical pattern you want to use. Be sure your poem conveys the feeling you have about the topic.

6

Twentieth Century:
The Modern World

I N THE EARLY twentieth century the United States entered the modern world. Internally, the country grew. During the thirty-year period of 1870–1900, the population almost doubled, from thirty-nine million to seventy-six million. In one year alone, 1905, more than a million immigrants entered the country. The last frontiers disappeared with the continual settlement and urbanization of the West. In addition, this growing population provided the country with a new wealth of labor, business, and intellectual talent. Money, innovation, and ideas flourished. It was a time for realizing various aspects of the American Dream. The first successful airplane flight took place in 1903 at about the same time that the cinema became a major medium of entertainment. And in 1905 Albert Einstein published the first formulation of his "Theory of Relativity," an idea that symbolized the emergence of a new, uncharted, unknown modern world.

Thus, by the opening of the twentieth century the United States was sufficiently comfortable in its domestic affairs to have the time, energy, and money to devote to international affairs. In 1906, Theodore Roosevelt became the first President of the United States to travel outside the country while in office. This act symbolized the political and international emergence of the United States. In less than 150 years, an English colony became an expansionist nation. In 1898, the United States acquired Puerto Rico, the Philippines, and Guam as a result of the Spanish-American war. In 1917, it purchased from Denmark what Columbus had named the Virgin Islands. And as the United States expanded its territorial boundaries, it also expanded its international political and diplomatic activities. At

THE STEERAGE *Alfred Steiglitz* 1907

the end of 1917, American troops landed in France to aid the European allies in World War I. This signalled the beginning of United States involvement in twentieth-century international affairs and its full participation in the modern world. During this same period of internal and external growth and expansion, American literature was infused by a wealth of new writers and their literary experimentation. A particularly rich period of creativity occurred in the decade after World War I. Writers like Willa Cather, Edwin Arlington Robinson, Robert Frost, and Carl Sandburg made significant advances in careers already begun. At the same time, a whole new generation of writers appeared on the scene. E. E. Cummings, Claude McKay, F. Scott Fitzgerald, Amy Lowell, Ernest Hemingway, William Faulkner, Thomas Wolfe, and John Steinbeck all published first books between 1919 and 1929. This was also the period of the Harlem Renaissance when Afro-American writers began to celebrate their uniqueness. The Twenties produced Jean Toomer, Countee Cullen, Langston Hughes, Arna Bontemps, Zora Neale Hurston, and many others. In poetry, the drama, prose, American writers had now taken their place among other writers of the world.

THE GLORIOUS VICTORY OF THE SLOOP MARIA *Lyonel Feininger* 1926

Willa Cather   1873-1947

Willa Cather is best known for her novels: *O Pioneers!* (1913), *My Antonia* (1918), and *Death Comes for the Archbishop* (1927). She has been honored with a Pulitzer Prize by the American Academy of Arts and Letters and with honorary degrees from seven major universities. In one of her novels, Willa Cather says, "The history of every country begins in the heart of a man or woman." This quote is also a tribute to her work. As a novelist and writer of short stories Willa Cather examined the country through the "hearts" of people. She particularly wrote of the heroic people who lived in her home state, Nebraska. "A Wagner Matinée," one of her earlier short stories, is a characteristic Cather work.

A Wagner Matinée

WILLA CATHER

I RECEIVED ONE MORNING a letter, written in pale ink on glassy, blue-lined note-paper, and bearing the postmark of a little Nebraska village. This communication, worn and rubbed, looking as though it had been carried for some days in a coat pocket that was none too clean, was from my uncle Howard and informed me that his wife had been left a small legacy by a bachelor relative who had recently died, and that it would be necessary for her to go to Boston to attend to the settling of the estate. He requested me to meet her at the station and render her whatever services might be necessary. On examining the date indicated as that of her arrival, I found it no later than tomorrow. He had characteristically delayed writing until, had I been away from home for a day, I must have missed the good woman altogether.

The name of my Aunt Georgiana called up not alone her own figure, at once pathetic and grotesque, but opened before my feet a gulf of recollection so wide and deep, that, as the letter dropped from my hand, I felt suddenly a stranger to all the present conditions of my existence, wholly ill at ease and out of place amid the familiar surroundings of my study. I became, in short, the gangling farmer-boy my aunt had known, scourged with chilblains[1] and bashfulness, my hands cracked and sore from the corn husking. I felt the knuckles of my thumb tentatively, as though they were raw again. I sat again before her parlour organ, fumbling the scales with my stiff, red hands, while she, beside me, made canvas mittens for the huskers.

The next morning, after preparing my landlady somewhat, I set out for the station. When the train arrived I had some difficulty in finding my aunt. She was the last of the pas-

---

1 chilblains: itching sore caused by exposure to the cold.

sengers to alight, and it was not until I got her into the carriage that she seemed really to recognize me. She had come all the way in a day coach; her linen duster had become black with soot and her black bonnet grey with dust during the journey. When we arrived at my boardinghouse the landlady put her to bed at once and I did not see her again until the next morning.

Whatever shock Mrs. Springer experienced at my aunt's appearance, she considerately concealed. As for myself, I saw my aunt's misshapen figure with that feeling of awe and respect with which we behold explorers who have left their ears and fingers north of Franz-Joseph-Land, or their health somewhere along the Upper Congo. My Aunt Georgiana had been a music teacher at the Boston Conservatory, somewhere back in the latter sixties. One summer, while visiting in the little village among the Green Mountains where her ancestors had dwelt for generations, she had kindled the callow fancy of the most idle and shiftless of all the village lads, and had conceived for this Howard Carpenter one of those extravagant passions which a handsome country boy of twenty-one sometimes inspires in an angular, spectacled woman of thirty. When she returned to her duties in Boston, Howard followed her, and the upshot of this inexplicable infatuation was that she eloped with him, eluding the reproaches of her family and the criticisms of her friends by going with him to the Nebraska frontier. Carpenter, who, of course, had no money, had taken a homestead in Red Willow County, fifty miles from the railroad. There they had measured off their quarter section themselves by driving across the prairie in a wagon, to the wheel of which they had tied a red cotton handkerchief, and counting off its revolutions. They built a dugout in the red hillside, one of those cave dwellings whose inmates so often reverted to primitive conditions. Their water they got from the lagoons where the buffalo drank, and their slender stock of provisions was always at the mercy of bands of roving Indians. For thirty years my aunt had not been further than fifty miles from the homestead.

But Mrs. Springer knew nothing of all this, and must have been considerably shocked at what was left of my kinswoman. Beneath the soiled linen duster which, on her arrival, was the most conspicuous feature of her costume, she wore a black stuff dress, whose ornamentation showed that she had surrendered herself unquestioningly into the hands of a country dressmaker. My poor aunt's figure, however, would have presented astonishing difficulties to any dressmaker. Originally stooped, her shoulders were now almost bent together over her sunken chest. She wore no stays, and her gown, which trailed unevenly behind, rose in a sort of peak over her abdomen. She wore ill-fitting false teeth, and her skin was as yellow as a Mongolian's from constant exposure to a pitiless wind and to the alkaline water which hardens the most transparent cuticle into a sort of flexible leather.

I owed to this woman most of the good that ever came my way in my boyhood, and had a reverential affection for her. During the years when I was riding herd for my uncle, my aunt, after cooking the three meals—the first of which was ready at six o'clock in the morning—and putting the six children to bed, would often stand until midnight at her ironing-board, with me at the kitchen table beside her, hearing me recite Latin declensions and conjugations, gently shaking me when my drowsy head sank down over a page of irregular verbs. It was to her, at her ironing or mending, that I read my first Shakespeare, and her old text-book on mythology was the first that ever came into my empty hands. She taught me my scales and exercises, too—on the little parlour organ, which her husband had bought her after fifteen years, during which she had not so much as seen any instrument, but an accordion that belonged to one of the Norwegian farmhands. She would sit beside me by the hour, darning and counting while I struggled with the "Joyous Farmer," but she seldom talked to me about music, and I understood why. She was a pious woman; she had the consolations of religion and, to her at least, her martyrdom was not wholly sordid. Once when I had been doggedly beating out some easy passages from an old score of *Euryanthe* I had found among her music books, she came up to me and, putting her hands over my eyes, gently drew my head back upon her shoulder, saying tremulously, "Don't love it so well, Clark, or it may be taken from you. Oh! dear boy, pray that whatever your sacrifice may be, it be not that."

When my aunt appeared on the morning after her arrival, she was still in a semi-somnambulant[2] state. She seemed not to realize that she was in the city where she had spent her youth, the place longed for hungrily half a lifetime. She had been so wretchedly train-sick throughout the journey that she had no recollection of anything but her discomfort, and, to all intents and purposes, there were but a few hours of nightmare between the farm in Red Willow County and my study on Newbury Street. I had planned a little pleasure for her that afternoon, to repay her for some of the glorious moments she had given me when we used to milk together in the straw-thatched cowshed and she, because I was more than usually tired, or because her husband had spoken sharply to me, would tell me of the splendid performance of the *Huguenots* she had seen in Paris, in her youth. At two o'clock the Symphony Orchestra was to give a Wagner programme, and I intended to take my aunt; though, as I conversed with her I grew doubtful about her enjoyment of it. Indeed, for her

---

2 **somnambulant**: sleep-walking.

own sake, I could only wish her taste for such things quite dead, and the long struggle mercifully ended at last. I suggested our visiting the Conservatory and the Common before lunch, but she seemed altogether too timid to wish to venture out. She questioned me absently about various changes in the city, but she was chiefly concerned that she had forgotten to leave instructions about feeding half-skimmed milk to a certain weakling calf, "old Maggie's calf, you know, Clark," she explained, evidently having forgotten how long I had been away. She was further troubled because she had neglected to tell her daughter about the freshly-opened kit of mackerel in the cellar, which would spoil if it were not used directly.

I asked her whether she had ever heard any of the Wagnerian operas, and found that she had not, though she was perfectly familiar with their respective situations, and had once possessed the piano score of *The Flying Dutchman.* I began to think it would have been best to get her back to Red Willow County without waking her, and regretted having suggested the concert.

From the time we entered the concert hall, however, she was a trifle less passive and inert, and for the first time seemed to perceive her surroundings. I had felt some trepidation least she might become aware of the absurdities of her attire, or might experience some painful embarrassment at stepping suddenly into the world to which she had been dead for a quarter of a century. But, again, I found how superficially I had judged her. She sat looking about her with eyes as impersonal, almost as stony, as those with which the granite Rameses in a museum watches the froth and fret that ebbs and flows about his pedestal—separated from it by the lonely stretch of centuries. I have seen this same aloofness in old miners who drift into the Brown hotel at Denver, their pockets full of bullion, their linen soiled, their haggard faces unshaven; standing in the thronged corridors as solitary as though they were still in a frozen camp on the Yukon, conscious that certain experiences have isolated them from their fellows by a gulf no haberdasher[3] could bridge.

We sat at the extreme left of the first balcony, facing the arc of our own and the balcony above us, veritable hanging gardens, brilliant as tulip beds. The matinée audience was made up chiefly of women. One lost the contour of faces and figures, indeed any effect of line whatever, and there was only the colour of bodices past counting, the shimmer of fabrics soft and firm, silky and sheer; red, mauve, pink, blue, lilac, purple, ecru, rose, yellow, cream, and white, all the colours that an impressionist finds in a sunlit landscape, with here and there the dead shadow of a frock coat. My Aunt Georgiana regarded them as though they had been so many daubs of tube-paint on a palette.

When the musicians came out and took their places, she gave a little stir of anticipation, and looked with quickening interest down over the rail at that invariable grouping, perhaps the first wholly familiar thing that had greeted her eye since she had left old Maggie and her weakling calf. I could feel how all those details sank into her soul, for I had not forgotten how they had sunk into mine when I came fresh from ploughing forever and forever between green aisles of corn, where, as in a treadmill, one might walk from daybreak to dusk without perceiving a shadow of change. The clean profiles of the musicians, the gloss of their linen, the dull black of their coats, the beloved shapes of the instruments, the patches of yellow light thrown by the green shaded lamps on the smooth, varnished bellies of the 'cellos and the bass viols in the rear, the restless, wind-tossed forest of fiddle necks and bows—I recalled how, in the first orchestra I had ever heard, those long bow strokes seemed to draw the heart out of me, as a conjurer's stick reels out yards of paper ribbon from a hat.

---

3 **haberdasher:** dealer in men's clothing.

The first number was the *Tannhauser* overture. When the horns drew out the first strain of the Pilgrim's chorus, my Aunt Georgiana clutched my coat sleeve. Then it was I first realized that for her this broke a silence of thirty years; the inconceivable silence of the plains. With the battle between the two motives, with the frenzy of the Venusberg theme and its ripping of strings, there came to me an overwhelming sense of the waste and wear we are so powerless to combat; and I saw again the tall, naked house on the prairie, black and grim as a wooden fortress; the black pond where I had learned to swim, its margin pitted with sun-dried cattle tracks; the rain gullied clay banks about the naked house, the four dwarf ash seedlings where the dishcloths were always hung to dry before the kitchen door. The world there was the flat world of the ancients; to the east, a cornfield that stretched to daybreak; to the west, a corral that reached to sunset; between, the conquests of peace, dearer bought than those of war.

The overture closed, my aunt released my coat sleeve, but she said nothing. She sat staring at the orchestra through a dullness of thirty years, through the films made little by little by each of the three hundred and sixty-five days in every one of them. What, I wondered, did she get from it? She had been a good pianist in her day, I knew, and her musical education had been broader than that of most music teachers of a quarter of a century ago. She had often told me of Mozart's operas and Meyerbeer's, and I could remember hearing her sing, years ago, certain melodies of Verdi's. When I had fallen ill with a fever in her house she used to sit by my cot in the evening—when the cool, night wind blew in through the faded mosquito netting tacked over the window and I lay watching a certain bright star that burned red above the cornfield—and sing "Home to our mountains, O, let us return!" in a way fit to break the heart of a Vermont boy near dead of homesickness already.

I watched her closely through the prelude to *Tristan and Isolde,* trying vainly to conjecture what that seething turmoil of strings and winds might mean to her, but she sat mutely staring at the violin bows that drove obliquely downward like the pelting streaks of rain in a summer shower. Had this music any message for her? Had she enough left to at all comprehend this power which had kindled the world since she had left it? I was in a fever of curiosity, but Aunt Georgiana sat silent upon her peak in Darien. She preserved this utter immobility throughout the number from the *Flying Dutchman,* though her fingers worked mechanically upon her black dress, as though, of themselves, they were recalling the piano score they had once played. Poor old hands! They had been stretched and twisted into mere tentacles to hold and lift and knead with; the palm, unduly swollen, the fingers bent and knotted—on one of them a thin, worn band

vailed upon him to join the country church, though his sole fitness for this step, in so far as I could gather, lay in his boyish face and his possession of this divine melody. Shortly afterward he had gone to town on the Fourth of July, been drunk for several days, lost his money at a faro table, ridden a saddled Texan steer on a bet, and disappeared with a fractured collar-bone. All this my aunt told me huskily, wanderingly, as though she were talking in the weak lapses of illness.

"Well, we have come to better things than the old *Trovatore* at any rate, Aunt Georgie?" I queried, with a well meant effort at jocularity.

Her lip quivered and she hastily put her handkerchief up to her mouth. From behind it she murmured, "And you have been hearing this ever since you left me, Clark?" Her question was the gentlest and saddest of reproaches.

The second half of the programme consisted of four numbers from the *Ring,* and closed with Siegfried's funeral march. My aunt wept quietly, but almost continuously, as a shallow vessel overflows in a rain-storm. From time to time her dim eyes looked up at the lights which studded the ceiling, burning softly under their dull glass globes; doubtless they were stars in truth to her. I was still perplexed as to what measure of musical comprehension was left to her, she who had heard nothing but the singing of Gospel Hymns at Methodist services in the square frame schoolhouse on Section Thirteen for so many years. I was wholly unable to gauge how much of it had been dissolved in soapsuds, or worked into bread, or milked into the bottom of a pail.

The deluge of sound poured on and on; I never knew what she found in the shining current of it; I never knew how far it bore her, or past what happy islands. From the trembling of her face I could well believe that before the last numbers she had been carried out where the myriad graves are, into the grey, nameless burying grounds of the sea; or into some world of death vaster yet, where, from the beginning of the world, hope has lain

that had once been a wedding ring. As I pressed and gently quieted one of those groping hands, I remembered with quivering eyelids their services for me in other days.

Soon after the tenor began the "Prize Song," I heard a quick drawn breath and turned to my aunt. Her eyes were closed, but the tears were glistening on her cheeks, and I think, in a moment more, they were in my eyes as well. It never really died, then—the soul that can suffer so excruciatingly and so interminably; it withers to the outward eye only; like that strange moss which can lie on a dusty shelf half a century and yet, if placed in water, grows green again. She wept so throughout the development and elaboration of the melody.

During the intermission before the second half of the concert, I questioned my aunt and found that the "Prize Song" was not new to her. Some years before there had drifted to the farm in Red Willow County a young German, a tramp cow puncher, who had sung the chorus at Beyruth, when he was a boy, along with other peasant boys and girls. Of a Sunday morning he used to sit on his gingham-sheeted bed in the hands' bedroom which opened off the kitchen, cleaning the leather of his boots and saddle, singing the "Prize Song," while my aunt went about her work in the kitchen. She had hovered about him until she had pre-

down with hope and dream with dream and, renouncing, slept.

The concert was over; the people filed out of the hall chattering and laughing, glad to relax and find the living level again, but my kinswoman made no effort to rise. The harpist slipped its green felt cover over his instrument; the flute-players shook the water from their mouthpieces; the men of the orchestra went out one by one, leaving the stage to the chairs and music stands, empty as a winter cornfield.

I spoke to my aunt. She burst into tears and sobbed pleadingly. "I don't want to go, Clark, I don't want to go!"

I understood. For her, just outside the door of the concert hall, lay the black pond with the cattle-tracked bluffs; the tall, unpainted house, with weather-curled boards; naked as a tower, the crook-backed ash seedlings where the dishcloths hung to dry; the gaunt, moulting turkeys picking up refuse about the kitchen door.

AT THE OPERA *Mary Cassatt*

Study Questions

1. What is the history of Aunt Georgiana? How is it revealed?

2. The meaning of the story emerges from the basic contrast between life in Boston and life on a Nebraska farm. What are the values on each side of the contrast as it is presented to us? What details in the story show these values? How does Willa Cather emphasize this contrast? What development does she give it at the end?

3. What is the effect of the story being told by Clark rather than by Georgiana or Howard? What is your final response to the story?

Composition

1. Write an essay in which you explain how The Sense of Place is essential to "A Wagner Matinee." Include the contrast between the two places. Use examples from the story.

2. Write a letter from Georgiana to her husband. In the letter, tell him about the trip and what happens in Boston. Also, make suitable inquiries about home in Nebraska. Conclude with a statement on how Georgiana feels about being in Boston after so long a time.

Zora Neale Hurston   1903-1960

Before Zora Neale Hurston was graduated from Barnard College in 1928, she had had a variety of experiences. At age 17 she moved to Baltimore where she completed high school. Then she enrolled at Howard University in Washington, D.C. At Howard, her writing career began with the short story, "Drenched in Light." Another short story, "Spunk," and a play, *Color Struck,* were awarded prizes in 1925. The renowned anthropologist, Franz Boas, diverted Hurston's interest from English to anthropology while she was a student at Barnard. She combined this new discipline with both her love of writing and her love of Afro-American folk culture. In 1935 she published *Mules and Men,* a collection of folk material gathered in her native Florida. *Tell My Horse* (1938) was published after a trip to Haiti and Jamaica. Another book, *Moses, Man of the Mountain* (1939), combines fiction and folklore. In addition to many other short stories, she also wrote the novels, *Seraph on the Suwanee* (1948) and the memorable *Their Eyes Were Watching God* (1937).

Following is an excerpt from her autobiography, *Dust Tracks on a Road* (1942). It provides a brief look at her early inspiration.

from Dust Tracks on a Road

ZORA NEALE HURSTON

LIKE THE DEAD-SEEMING, cold rocks, I have memories within that came out of the material that went to make me. Time and place have had their say.

So you will have to know something about the time and place where I came from, in order that you may interpret the incidents and directions of my life.

I was born in a Negro town. I do not mean by that the black back-side of an average town. Eatonville, Florida, is, and was at the time of my birth, a pure Negro town—charter, mayor, council, town marshal and all. It was not the first Negro community in America, but it was the first to be incorporated, the first attempt at organized self-government on the part of Negroes in America. . . . White Maitland and Negro Eatonville have lived side by side for fifty-six years without a single instance of enmity. The spirit of the founders has reached beyond the grave.

The whole lake country of Florida sprouted with life—mostly Northerners, and prosperity was everywhere. It was in the late eighties that the stars fell, and many of the original settlers date their coming, "just before, or just after the stars fell."

Into this burly, boiling, hard-hitting, rug-

VICTORIAN INTERIOR *Horace Pippin*

ged-individualistic setting walked one day a tall, heavy-muscled mulatto who resolved to put down roots.

[My father] John Hurston, in his late twenties, had left Macon County, Alabama, because the ordeal of share-cropping on a southern Alabama cotton plantation was crushing to his ambition. There was no rise to the thing. . . .

It was after his marriage that my father began to want things. Plantation life began to irk and bind him. His over-the-creek existence was finished. What else was there for a man like him? He left his wife and three children behind and went out to seek and see.

Months later he pitched into the hurly-burly of South Florida. So he heard about folks building a town all out of colored people. It seemed like a good place to go. Later on, he was to be elected Mayor of Eatonville for three terms, and to write the local laws. The village of Eatonville is still governed by the laws formulated by my father. The town clerk still consults a copy of the original printing which seems to be the only one in existence now. I have tried every way I know how to get this copy for my library, but so far it has not been possible. I had it once, but the town clerk came and took it back.

When my mother joined Papa a year after he had settled in Eatonville, she brought some quilts, her featherbed and bedstead. That was all they had in the house that night. Two burlap bags were stuffed with Spanish moss for the two older children to sleep on. The youngest child was taken into the bed with them.

So these two began their new life. Both of them swore that things were going to get better, and it came to pass as they said. They bought land, built a roomy house, planted their acres and reaped. Children kept coming—more mouths to feed and more feet for shoes. But neither of them seemed to have minded that. In fact, my father not only boasted among other men about "his house full of young'uns" but he boasted that he had never allowed his wife to go out and hit a lick of work for anybody a day in her life. . . .

There were eight children in the family, and our house was noisy from the time school turned out until bedtime. After supper we gathered in Mama's room, and everybody had to get their lessons for the next day. Mama carried us all past long division in arithmetic, and parsing sentences in grammar, by diagrams on the blackboard. That was as far as she had gone. Then the younger ones were turned over to my oldest brother, Bob, and Mama sat and saw to it that we paid attention. You had to keep on going over things until you did know. How I hated the multiplication tables—especially the sevens! . . .

Mama exhorted her children at every opportunity to "jump at de sun." We might not land on the sun, but at least we would get off the ground. Papa did not feel so hopeful. Let well enough alone. It did not do for Negroes to have too much spirit. He was always threatening to break mine or kill me in the attempt. My mother was always standing between us.

She conceded that I was impudent and given to talking back, but she didn't want to "squinch my spirit" too much for fear that I would turn out to be a mealy-mouthed rag doll by the time I got grown. . . .

This is all hear-say. Maybe some of the details of my birth as told me might be a little inaccurate, but it is pretty well established that I really did get born. . . .

They tell me that an old sow-hog taught me how to walk. That is, she didn't instruct me in detail, but she convinced me that I really ought to try.

It was like this. My mother was going to have collard greens for dinner, so she took the dishpan and went down to the spring to wash the greens. She left me sitting on the floor, and gave me a hunk of cornbread to keep me quiet. Everything was going along all right, until the sow with her litter of pigs in convoy came abreast of the door. She must have smelled the cornbread I was messing with and scattering crumbs about the floor. So, she came right on in, and began to nuzzle around.

My mother heard my screams and came running. Her heart must have stood still when she saw the sow in there, because hogs have been known to eat human flesh.

But I was not taking this thing sitting down. I had been placed by a chair, and when my mother got inside the door, I had pulled myself up by that chair and was getting around it right smart.

As for the sow, poor misunderstood lady, she had no interest in me except my bread. I lost that in scrambling to my feet and she was eating it. She had much less intention of eating Mama's baby, than Mama had of eating hers.

With no more suggestions from the sow or anybody else, it seems that I just took to walking and kept the thing a-going. The strangest thing about it was that once I found the use of my feet, they took to wandering. I always wanted to go. I would wander off in the woods all alone, following some inside urge to go places. This alarmed my mother a great deal. She used to say that she believed a woman who was an enemy of hers had sprinkled "travel dust" around the doorstep the day I was born. That was the only explanation she could find. I don't know why it never occurred to her to connect my tendency with my father, who didn't have a thing on his mind but this town and the next one. That should have given her a sort of hint. Some children are just bound to take after their fathers in spite of women's prayers.

Study Questions

1. How is Hurston's hometown of Eatonville described? What makes it unusual?

2. How does Hurston describe her parents? In what ways are they different? similar? What did the mother's advice, "jump at de sun," mean?

3. What is Hurston's tone in writing about herself? about her family?

4. From reading this selection and the biographical information about Hurston, what kind of person do you think she was? a conformist? an innovator? Why?

James Thurber   1894-1961

James Thurber was born in Columbus, Ohio. He attended Ohio State University and served as a code clerk in World War I. In 1927, he joined the staff of *The New Yorker*. He has become possibly the best known of the brilliant humorists who wrote for that magazine. Even the titles of his collections of essays, stories, and sketches are humorous: *My Life and Hard Times* (1933), *The Seal in the Bedroom and Other Predicaments* (1932), and *The Middle-Aged Man on the Flying Trapeze* (1935).

Thurber also wrote a variety of delightful fables and fantasies, such as *Fables for Our Time* (1940), *The Thirteen Clocks* (1950), and *The Wonderful O* (1957).

Thurber's favorite subject, in both stories and cartoons, was what he called "The War between Men and Women." In his version of this combat the women are strong and domineering; the men weak and timid, forced to take refuge in daydreams. As you will see, Walter Mitty is in some ways a reincarnation of Rip Van Winkle.

The Secret Life of Walter Mitty

JAMES THURBER

"WE'RE GOING THROUGH!" The Commander's voice was like thin ice breaking. He wore his full-dress uniform, with the heavily braided white cap pulled down rakishly over one cold gray eye. "We can't make it, sir. It's spoiling for a hurricane, if you ask me." "I'm not asking you, Lieutenant Berg," said the Commander. "Throw on the power lights! Rev her up to 8500! We're going through!" The pounding of the cylinders increased: ta-pocketa-pocketa-pocketa-*pocketa-pocketa*. The Commander stared at the ice forming on the pilot window. He walked over and twisted a row of complicated dials. "Switch on No. 8 auxiliary!" he shouted. "Switch on No. 8 auxiliary!" repeated Lieutenant Berg. "Full strength in No. 3 turret!" shouted the Commander. "Full

strength in No. 3 turret!" The crew, bending to their various tasks in the huge, hurtling eight-engined Navy hydroplane, looked at each other and grinned. "The Old Man'll get us through," they said to one another. "The Old Man ain't afraid of nothing!" . . .

"Not so fast! You're driving too fast!" said Mrs. Mitty. "What are you driving so fast for?"

"Hmm?" said Walter Mitty. He looked at his wife, in the seat beside him, with shocked astonishment. She seemed grossly unfamiliar, like a strange woman who had yelled at him in a crowd. "You were up to fifty-five," she said. "You know I don't like to go more than forty. You were up to fifty-five." Walter Mitty drove on toward Waterbury in silence, the roaring of the SN202 through the worst storm in twenty years of Navy flying fading in the remote, intimate airways of his mind. "You're tensed up again," said Mrs. Mitty. "It's one of your days. I wish you'd let Dr. Renshaw look you over."

Walter Mitty stopped the car in front of the building where his wife went to have her hair done. "Remember to get those overshoes while I'm having my hair done," she said. "I don't need overshoes," said Mitty. She put her mirror back into her bag. "We've been all through that," she said, getting out of the car. "You're not a young man any longer." He raced the engine a little. "Why don't you wear your gloves? Have you lost your gloves?" Walter Mitty reached in a pocket and brought out the gloves. He put them on, but after she had turned and gone into the building and he had driven on to a red light, he took them off again. "Pick it up, brother!" snapped a cop as the light changed, and Mitty hastily pulled on his gloves and lurched ahead. He drove around the streets aimlessly for a time, and then he drove past the hospital on his way to the parking lot.

. . . "It's the millionaire banker, Wellington McMillan," said the pretty nurse. "Yes?" said Walter Mitty, removing his gloves slowly. "Who has the case?" "Dr. Renshaw and Dr. Benbow, but there are two specialists here, Dr. Remington from New York and Mr. Pritchard-Mitford from London. He flew over." A door opened down a long, cool corridor and Dr. Renshaw came out. He looked distraught and haggard. "Hello, Mitty," he said. "We're having the devil's own time with McMillan, the millionaire banker and close personal friend of Roosevelt. Obstreosis of the ductal tract. Tertiary. Wish you'd take a look at him." "Glad to," said Mitty.

In the operating room there were whispered introductions: "Dr. Remington, Dr. Mitty. Mr. Pritchard-Mitford, Dr. Mitty." "I've read your book on streptothricosis," said Pritchard-Mitford, shaking hands. "A brilliant performance, sir." "Thank you," said Walter Mitty. "Didn't know you were in the States, Mitty," grumbled Remington. "Coals to Newcastle, bringing Mitford and me up here for a tertiary." "You are very kind," said Mitty. A huge, complicated machine, connected to the operating table, with many tubes and wires, began at this moment to go pocketa-pocketa- pocketa. "The new anesthetizer is giving way!" shouted an intern. "There is no one in the East who knows how to fix it!" "Quiet, man!" said Mitty, in a low, cool voice. He sprang to the machine, which was now going pocketa-pocketa-queep-pocketa-queep. He began fingering delicately a row of glistening dials. "Give me a fountain pen!" he snapped. Someone handed him a fountain pen. He pulled a faulty piston out of the machine and inserted the pen in its place. "That will hold for ten minutes," he said. "Get on with the operation." A nurse hurried over and whispered to Renshaw, and Mitty saw the man turn pale. "Coreopsis has set in," said Renshaw nervously. "If you would take over, Mitty?" Mitty looked at him and at the craven figure of Benbow, who drank, and at the grave, uncertain faces of the two great specialists. "If you wish," he said. They slipped a white gown on him; he adjusted a mask and drew on thin gloves; nurses handed him shining . . .

"Back it up, Mac! Look out for that Buick!" Walter Mitty jammed on the brakes. "Wrong lane, Mac," said the parking-lot attendant, looking at Mitty closely. "Gee. Yeh," muttered Mitty. He began cautiously to back out of the lane marked "Exit Only." "Leave her sit there," said the attendant. "I'll put her away." Mitty got out of the car. "Hey, better leave the key." "Oh," said Mitty, handing the man the ignition key. The attendant vaulted into the car, backed it up with insolent skill, and put it where it belonged.

They're so darn cocky, thought Walter Mitty, walking along Main Street; they think they know everything. Once he had tried to take his chains off, outside New Milford, and he had got them wound around the axles. A man had had to come out in a wrecking car and unwind them, a young, grinning garageman. Since then Mrs. Mitty always made him drive to a garage to have the chains taken off. The next time, he thought, I'll wear my right arm in a sling; they won't grin at me then. I'll have my right arm in a sling and they'll see I couldn't possibly take the chains off myself. He kicked at the slush on the sidewalk. "Overshoes," he said to himself, and he began looking for a shoe store.

When he came out into the street again, with the overshoes in a box under his arm, Walter Mitty began to wonder what the other thing was his wife had told him to get. She had told him, twice, before they set out from their house for Waterbury. In a way he hated these weekly trips to town—he was always getting something wrong. Kleenex, he thought, Squibb's, razor blades? No. Toothpaste, toothbrush, bicarbonate, carborundum, initiative and referendum? He gave it up. But she would remember it. "Where's the what's-its-name?" she would ask. "Don't tell me you forgot the what's-its-name." A newsboy went by shouting something about the Waterbury trial.

. . . "Perhaps this will refresh your memory." The District Attorney suddenly thrust a heavy automatic at the quiet figure on the witness stand. "Have you ever seen this before?" Walter Mitty took the gun and examined it expertly. "This is my Webley-Vickers 50.80," he said calmly. An excited buzz ran around the courtroom. The Judge rapped for order. "You are a crack shot with any sort of firearms, I believe?" said the District Attorney, insinuatingly. "Objection!" shouted Mitty's attorney. "We have shown that the defendant could not have fired the shot. We have shown that he wore his right arm in a sling on the night of the fourteenth of July." Walter Mitty raised his hand briefly and the bickering attorneys were stilled. "With any known make of gun," he said evenly, "I could have killed Gregory Fitzhurst at three hundred feet *with my left*

hand." Pandemonium broke loose in the courtroom. A woman's scream rose above the bedlam and suddenly a lovely, dark-haired girl was in Walter Mitty's arms. The District Attorney struck at her savagely. Without rising from his chair, Mitty let the man have it on the point of the chin. "You miserable cur!" . . .

"Puppy biscuit," said Walter Mitty. He stopped walking and the buildings of Waterbury rose up out of the misty courtroom and surrounded him again. A woman who was passing laughed. "He said 'Puppy biscuit,'" she said to her companion. "That man said 'Puppy biscuit' to himself." Walter Mitty hurried on. He went into an A. & P., not the first one he came to but a smaller one farther up the street. "I want some biscuit for small, young dogs," he said to the clerk. "Any special brand, sir?" The greatest pistol shot in the world thought a moment. "It says 'Puppies Bark for It' on the box," said Walter Mitty.

His wife would be through at the hairdresser's in fifteen minutes, Mitty saw in looking at his watch, unless they had trouble drying it; sometimes they had trouble drying it. She didn't like to get to the hotel first; she would want him to be there waiting for her as usual. He found a big leather chair in the lobby, facing a window, and he put the overshoes and the puppy biscuit on the floor beside it. He picked up an old copy of *Liberty* and sank down into the chair. "Can Germany Conquer the World Through the Air?" Walter Mitty looked at the pictures of bombing planes and of ruined streets.

. . . "The cannonading has got the wind up in young Raleigh, sir," said the sergeant. Captain Mitty looked up at him through tousled hair. "Get him to bed," he said wearily. "With the others. I'll fly alone." "But you can't, sir," said the sergeant anxiously. "It takes two men to handle that bomber and the Archies are pounding hell out of the air. Von Richtman's circus is between here and Saulier." "Somebody's got to get that ammu-

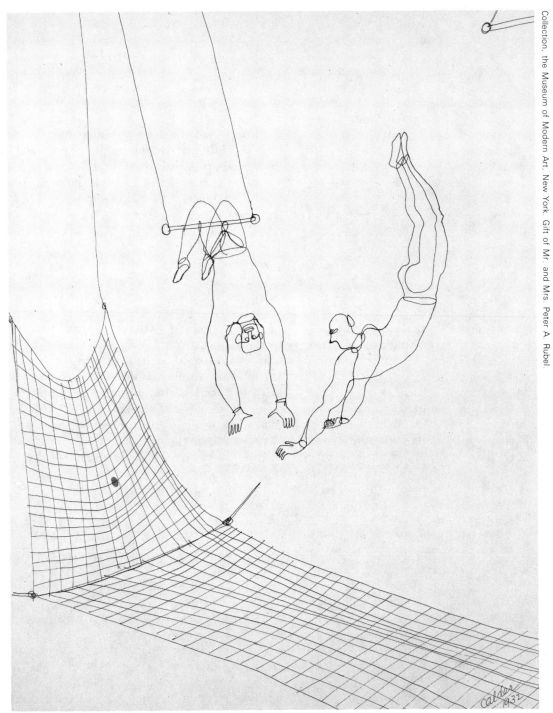

THE CATCH II *Alexander Calder 1932*

434 *Twentieth Century: The Modern World*

nition dump," said Mitty. "I'm going over. Spot of brandy?" He poured a drink for the sergeant and one for himself. War thundered and whined around the dugout and battered at the door. There was a rending of wood and splinters flew through the room. "A bit of a near thing," said Captain Mitty carelessly. "The box barrage is closing in," said the sergeant. "We only live once, Sergeant," said Mitty, with his faint, fleeting smile. "Or do we?" He poured another brandy and tossed it off. "I never see a man could hold his brandy like you, sir," said the sergeant. "Begging your pardon, sir." Captain Mitty stood up and strapped on his huge Webley-Vickers automatic. "It's forty kilometers through hell, sir," said the sergeant. Mitty finished one last brandy. "After all," he said softly, "what isn't?" The pounding of the cannon increased; there was the rat-tat-tatting of machine guns, and from somewhere came the menacing pocketa-pocketa-pocketa of the new flame-throwers. Walter Mitty walked to the door of the dugout humming "Auprès de Ma Blonde." He turned and waved to the sergeant. "Cheerio!" he said. . . .

Something struck his shoulder. "I've been looking all over this hotel for you," said Mrs. Mitty. "Why do you have to hide in this old chair? How did you expect me to find you?" "Things close in," said Walter Mitty vaguely. "What?" Mrs. Mitty said. "Did you get the what's-its-name? The puppy biscuit? What's in that box?" "Overshoes," said Mitty. "Couldn't you have put them on in the store?" "I was thinking," said Walter Mitty. "Does it ever occur to you that I am sometimes thinking?" She looked at him. "I'm going to take your temperature when I get you home," she said.

They went out through the revolving doors that made a faintly derisive whistling sound when you pushed them. It was two blocks to the parking lot. At the drugstore on the corner she said, "Wait here for me. I forgot something. I won't be a minute." She was more than a minute. Walter Mitty lighted a cigarette. It began to rain, rain with sleet in it. He stood up against the wall of the drugstore, smoking. . . . He put his shoulders back and his heels together. "The hell with the handkerchief," said Walter Mitty scornfully. He took one last drag on his cigarette and snapped it away. Then, with that faint, fleeting smile playing about his lips, he faced the firing squad; erect and motionless, proud and disdainful, Walter Mitty the Undefeated, inscrutable to the last.

Study Questions

1. This story consists of five dream sequences and four units of literal reality. What are these segments? How does Thurber signal the changes between them?

2. How would you describe the basic conflict in the story? What is the resolution of the conflict?

3. What is the source of Walter Mitty's dream world? How does Thurber treat this material?

4. The story begins and ends with a dream rather than reality. There are also certain repetitions from dream to dream ("pocketa-pocketa," "Webley-Vickers"). What do these facts indicate about the life of Walter Mitty?

5. How do you interpret the ending of this story?

Vocabulary

Each exciting life that Walter Mitty leads in daydreams is suggested through a different kind of **jargon**. The word *jargon* has two contrasting definitions in this lesson: (1) confused, meaningless, or unintelligible speech or writing; and (2) the technical, or specialized, vocabulary of a specific profession or occupation.

In "The Secret Life of Walter Mitty," the jargon has been purposely chosen for its meaninglessness, to create humorous effects. No actual doctor could cure "streptothricosis" or perform surgery to correct "obstreosis of the ductile tract" because no such medical problems exist. Yet by coupling these made-up ailments with such recognizable hospital terms as *anesthetizer, operating table,* and *intern,* James Thurber gives the illusion that Walter Mitty's imaginary medical world has its own reality—at least in Mitty's mind.

Outside Mitty's mind, the two contrasting definitions of jargon can both apply to the same communication process at the same time. If you visited a medical school and attended a lecture on aneurysms, the professor's jargon would probably be unintelligible to you, fitting the first definition; but to students in the class, the same jargon would be meaningful and important technical language.

The following exercises all deal with jargon in the second sense, as specialized vocabulary.

A. At its simplest level, jargon often includes a number of ordinary English words whose meanings have been narrowed to apply to a particular occupation or profession. The ordinary word *bed,* for instance, has one definition in the jargon of gardening, but quite a different one in the jargon of highway engineering; and neither definition is the one that first comes to most English speakers' minds:

bed: (a) gardening: a piece of land used for planting
(b) highway engineering: the foundation for a roadway

Using a dictionary as needed, define each of the first five terms below as they fit the jargon of the ten occupations or professions, also listed below.

cell	root	military	automotives	anatomy
file	compact	music	penology	linguistics
organ	biology	mathematics	metallurgy	cosmetology

Write your answers on a separate sheet of paper, modeling them after the sample given for *bed.*

B. Some jargon is shared by two or more professions which have overlapping concerns or problems. *Motivation,* for example, is jargon in both advertising and teaching. In each case, even though applied differently, the term has the same meaning:

motivation: the process of stimulating to action: advertising/teaching

Here are five other such terms:

chamber   futures   nuclei   perspective   respiration

Define each word and then think of two or more occupations in whose jargon the term would have the same general meaning. Write your answers as shown above.

C. As you have just seen, it is not always possible to know what profession a single word applies to. But a whole category of jargon can enable a person to identify the field in which they are used. The word *cylinder* by itself may suggest mechanical jargon. However, grouped with the words *determinant, equation, integer,* and *sub- set,* the term *cylinder* is seen as part of a different jargon: mathematics. With the help of a dictionary, figure out and write down the name of the occupation or profession suggested by each group of words.

1. atonality / cadence / conductor / fugue / tympani
2. artifact / cataloguing / excavation / site / stratigraphy
3. behavioralism / data / norm / projection / perception
4. doctrine / dogma / expiation / monasticism / mystic
5. fusion / gravity / mass / oscilloscope / spectrograph

William Faulkner   1897-1962

William Faulkner was born in rural Mississippi and spent most of his life in the small town of Oxford. For more than thirty years he wrote stories about an imaginary Mississippi county called Yoknapatawpha. Taken together these stories make a fictional history of the county from the eighteenth to the twentieth century. The chief novels in this long series are *The Sound and the Fury* (1929), *As I Lay Dying* (1930), *Light in August* (1932), *Absalom, Absalom!* (1936), and *The Hamlet* (1940). Despite the rich local flavor of these works, Faulkner was far more than a regional chronicler. He was a universal poet talking, as he says in "The Bear," about "honor and pride and pity and justice and courage and love." In 1949 his international stature was recognized when he was awarded the Nobel Prize for Literature.

The version of "The Bear" printed here first appeared in *The Saturday Evening Post* in 1942. In the same year Faulkner published a considerably expanded version in a volume of Yoknapatawpha stories entitled *Go Down, Moses.* The story is a straightforward narrative of a boy's growth from childhood to young manhood. The growth coincides with the four years he hunts Old Ben, an enormous and legendary bear.

The Bear

WILLIAM FAULKNER

H E WAS TEN. But it had already begun, long before that day when at last he wrote his age in two figures and he saw for the first time the camp where his father and Major de Spain and old General Compson and the others spent two weeks each November and two weeks again each June. He had already inherited then, without ever having seen it, the tremendous bear with one trap-ruined foot which, in an area almost a hundred miles deep, had earned for itself a name, a definite designation like a living man.

He had listened to it for years: the long legend of corncribs rifled, of shotes and grown pigs and even calves carried bodily into the woods and devoured, of traps and deadfalls[1] overthrown and dogs mangled and slain, and shotgun and even rifle charges delivered at point-blank range and with no more effect than so many peas blown through a tube by a boy—a corridor of wreckage and destruction beginning back before he was born, through which sped, not fast but rather with the ruthless and irresistible deliberation of a locomotive, the shaggy tremendous shape.

It ran in his knowledge before he ever saw it. It looked and towered in his dreams before he even saw the unaxed woods where it left its crooked print, shaggy, huge, red-eyed, not malevolent but just big—too big for the dogs which tried to bay it, for the horses which tried to ride it down, for the men and the bullets they fired into it, too big for the very country which was its constricting scope. He seemed to see it entire with a child's complete divination before he ever laid eyes on either—the doomed wilderness whose edges were being constantly and punily gnawed at by men with axes and plows who feared it because it was wilderness, men myriad and nameless even to one another in the land where the old bear had earned a name, through which ran not even a mortal animal but an anachronism, indomitable and invincible, out of an old dead time, a phantom, epitome and apotheosis of the old wild life at which the puny humans swarmed and hacked in a fury of abhorrence and fear, like pygmies about the ankles of a drowsing elephant; the old bear solitary, indomitable and alone, widowered, childless and absolved of mortality—old Priam[2] reft of his old wife and having outlived all his sons.

Until he was ten, each November he would watch the wagon containing the dogs and the bedding and food and guns and his father and Tennie's Jim, the Negro, and Sam Fathers, the Indian, son of a slave woman and a Chickasaw chief, depart on the road to town, to Jefferson, where Major de Spain and the others would join them. To the boy, at seven and eight and nine, they were not going into the Big Bottom to hunt bear and deer, but to keep yearly rendezvous with the bear which they did not even intend to kill. Two weeks later they would return, with no trophy, no head and skin. He had not expected it. He had not even been afraid it would be in the wagon. He believed that even after he was ten and his father would let him go too, for those two November

---

1 **deadfalls:** traps consisting of a piece of heavy timber which falls on an animal.

2 **Priam:** King of Troy, described in Homer's *Iliad.*

weeks, he would merely make another one, along with his father and Major de Spain and General Compson and the others, the dogs which failed even to bay it and the rifles and shotguns which failed even to bleed it, in the yearly pageant of the old bear's furious immortality.

Then he heard the dogs. It was in the second week of the first time in the camp. He stood with Sam Fathers against a big oak tree beside the faint crossing where they had stood each dawn for nine days now, hearing the dogs. He had heard them once before, one morning last week—a murmur, sourceless, echoing through the wet woods, swelling presently into separate voices which he could recognize and call by name. He had raised and cocked the gun as Sam told him and stood motionless again while the uproar, the invisible course, swept up and past and faded; it seemed to him that he could actually see the deer, the buck, blond, smoke-colored, elongated with speed, fleeing, vanishing, the woods, the gray solitude, still ringing even when the cries of the dogs had died away.

"Now let the hammers down," Sam said.

"You knew they were not coming here too," he said.

"Yes," Sam said. "I want you to learn how to do when you didn't shoot. It's after the chance for the bear or the deer has done already come and gone that men and dogs get killed."

"Anyway," he said, "it was just a deer."

Then on the tenth morning he heard the dogs again. And he readied the too-long, too-heavy gun as Sam had taught him, before Sam even spoke. But this time it was no deer, no ringing chorus of dogs running strong on a free scent, but a moiling yapping an octave too high, with something more than indecision and even abjectness in it, not even moving very fast, taking a long time to pass completely out of hearing, leaving even then somewhere in the air that echo, thin, slightly hysterical, abject, almost grieving, with no sense of a flee-

ing, unseen, smoke-colored, grass-eating shape ahead of it, and Sam, who had taught him first of all to cock the gun and take position where he could see everywhere and then never move again, had himself moved up beside him; he could hear Sam breathing at his shoulder and he could see the arched curve of the old man's inhaling nostrils.

"Hah," Sam said. "Not even running. Walking."

"Old Ben!" the boy said. "But up here!" he cried. "Way up here!"

"He do it every year," Sam said. "Once. Maybe to see who in camp this time, if he can shoot or not. Whether we got the dog yet that can bay and hold him. He'll take them to the river, then he'll send them back home. We may as well go back, too; see how they look when they come back to camp."

When they reached the camp the hounds were already there, ten of them crouching back under the kitchen, the boy and Sam squatting to peer back into the obscurity where they huddled, quiet, the eyes luminous, glowing at them and vanishing, and no sound, only that effluvium of something more than dog, stronger than dog and not just animal, just beast, because still there had been nothing in front of that abject and almost painful yapping save the solitude, the wilderness, so that when the eleventh hound came in at noon and with all the others watching—even old Uncle Ash, who called himself first a cook— Sam daubed the tattered ear and the raked shoulder with turpentine and axle grease, to the boy it was still no living creature, but the wilderness which, leaning for the moment down, had patted lightly once the hound's temerity.

"Just like a man," Sam said. "Just like folks. Put off as long as she could having to be brave, knowing all the time that sooner or later she would have to be brave once to keep on living with herself, and knowing all the time beforehand what was going to happen to her when she done it."

That afternoon, himself on the one-eyed wagon mule which did not mind the smell of blood nor, as they told him, of bear, and with Sam on the other one, they rode for more than three hours through the rapid, shortening winter day. They followed no path, no trail even that he could see; almost at once they were in a country which he had never seen before. Then he knew why Sam had made him ride the mule which would not spook. The sound one stopped short and tried to whirl and bolt even as Sam got down, blowing its breath, jerking and wrenching at the rein while Sam held it, coaxing it forward with his voice, since he could not risk tying it, drawing it forward while the boy got down from the marred one.

Then, standing beside Sam in the gloom of the dying afternoon, he looked down at the rotten overturned log, gutted and scored with claw marks and, in the wet earth beside it, the print of the enormous warped two-toed foot. He knew now what he had smelled when he peered under the kitchen where the dogs huddled. He realized for the first time that the bear which had run in his listening and loomed in his dreams since before he could remember to the contrary, and which, therefore, must have existed in the listening and dreams of his father and Major de Spain and even old General Compson, too, before they began to remember in their turn, was a mortal animal, and that if they had departed for the camp each November without any actual hope of bringing its trophy back, it was not because it could not be slain, but because so far they had had no actual hope to.

"Tomorrow," he said.

"We'll try tomorrow," Sam said. "We ain't got the dog yet."

"We've got eleven. They ran him this morning."

"It won't need but one," Sam said. "He ain't here. Maybe he ain't nowhere. The only other way will be for him to run by accident over somebody that has a gun."

"That wouldn't be me," the boy said. "It will be Walter or Major or ———"

"It might," Sam said. "You watch close in the morning. Because he's smart. That's how come he has lived this long. If he gets hemmed up and has to pick somebody to run over, he will pick out you."

"How?" the boy said. "How will he know ———" He ceased. "You mean he already knows me, that I ain't never been here before, ain't had time to find out yet whether I ———" He ceased again, looking at Sam, the old man whose face revealed nothing until it smiled. He said humbly, not even amazed, "It was me he was watching. I don't reckon he did need to come but once."

The next morning they left the camp three hours before daylight. They rode this time because it was too far to walk, even the dogs in the wagon; again the first gray light found him in a place which he had never seen before, where Sam had placed him and told him to stay and then departed. With the gun which was too big for him, which did not even belong to him, but to Major de Spain, and which he had fired only once—at a stump on the first day, to learn the recoil and how to reload it—he stood against a gum tree beside a little bayou whose black still water crept without movement out of a canebrake and crossed a small clearing and into cane again, where, invisible, a bird—the big woodpecker called Lord-to-God by Negroes—clattered at a dead limb.

It was a stand like any other, dissimilar only in incidentals to the one where he had stood each morning for ten days; a territory new to him, yet no less familiar than that other one which, after almost two weeks, he had come to believe he knew a little—the same solitude, the same loneliness through which human beings had merely passed without altering it, leaving no mark, no scar, which looked exactly as it must have looked when the first ancestor of Sam Fathers' Chickasaw predecessors crept into it and looked about, club or stone ax or bone arrow drawn and poised; different only because, squatting at the edge of the kitchen, he smelled the hounds huddled and cringing beneath it and saw the raked ear and shoulder of the one who, Sam said, had had to be brave once in order to live with herself, and saw yesterday in the earth beside the gutted log the print of the living foot.

He heard no dogs at all. He never did hear them. He only heard the drumming of the woodpecker stop short off and knew that the bear was looking at him. He never saw it. He did not know whether it was in front of him or behind him. He did not move, holding the useless gun, which he had not even had warning to cock and which even now he did not cock, tasting in his saliva that taint as of brass which he knew now because he had smelled it when he peered under the kitchen at the huddled dogs.

Then it was gone. As abruptly as it had ceased, the woodpecker's dry, monotonous clatter set up again, and after a while he even believed he could hear the dogs—a murmur, scarce a sound even, which he had probably been hearing for some time before he even remarked it, drifting into hearing and then out again, dying away. They came nowhere near him. If it was a bear they ran, it was another bear. It was Sam himself who came out of the cane and crossed the bayou, followed by the injured bitch of yesterday. She was almost at heel, like a bird dog, making no sound. She came and crouched against his leg, trembling, staring off into the cane.

"I didn't see him," he said. "I didn't, Sam!"

"I know it," Sam said. "He done the looking. You didn't hear him neither, did you?"

"No," the boy said. "I——"

"He's smart," Sam said. "Too smart." He looked down at the hound, trembling faintly and steadily against the boy's knee. From the raked shoulder a few drops of fresh blood oozed and clung. "Too big. We ain't got the dog yet. But maybe someday. Maybe not next time. But someday."

So I must see him, he thought. *I must look at him.* Otherwise, it seemed to him that it would go on like this forever, as it had gone on with his father and Major de Spain, who was older than his father, and even with old General Compson, who had been old enough to be a brigade commander in 1865. Otherwise, it would go on so forever, next time and next time, after and after and after. It seemed to him that he could see the two of them, himself and the bear, shadowy in the limbo from which time emerged, becoming time; the old bear absolved of mortality and himself partaking, sharing a little of it, enough of it. And he knew now what he had smelled in the huddled dogs and tasted in his saliva. He recognized fear. *So I will have to see him,* he thought, without dread or even hope. *I will have to look at him.*

It was in June of the next year. He was eleven. They were in camp again, celebrating Major de Spain's and General Compson's birthdays. Although the one had been born in September and the other in the depth of winter and in another decade, they had met for two weeks to fish and shoot squirrels and turkey and run coons and wildcats with the dogs at night. That is, he and Boon Hoggenbeck and the Negroes fished and shot squirrels and ran the coons and cats, because the proved hunters, not only Major de Spain and old General Compson, who spent those two weeks sitting in a rocking chair before a tremendous iron pot of Brunswick stew, stirring and tasting, with old Ash to quarrel with about how he was making it and Tennie's Jim to pour whisky from the demijohn into the tin dipper from which he drank it, but even the boy's father and Walter Ewell, who were still young enough, scorned such, other than shooting the wild gobblers with pistols for wagers on their marksmanship.

Or, that is, his father and the others believed he was hunting squirrels. Until the third day he thought that Sam Fathers believed that too. Each morning he would leave the camp right after breakfast. He had his own gun now, a Christmas present. He went back to the tree beside the little bayou where he had stood that morning. Using the compass which old General Compson had given him, he ranged from that point; he was teaching himself to be a better-than-fair woodsman without knowing he was doing it. On the second day he even found the gutted log where he had first seen the crooked print. It was almost completely crumbled now, healing with unbelievable speed, a passionate and almost visible relinquishment, back into the earth from which the tree had grown.

He ranged the summer woods now, green with gloom; if anything, actually dimmer than in November's gray dissolution, where, even at noon, the sun fell only in intermittent dappling upon the earth, which never completely dried out and which crawled with snakes—moccasins and water snakes and rattlers, themselves the color of the dappled gloom, so that he would not always see them until they moved, returning later and later, first day, second day, passing in the twilight of the third evening the little log pen enclosing the log stable where Sam was putting up the horses for the night.

"You ain't looked right yet," Sam said.

He stopped. For a moment he didn't answer. Then he said peacefully, in a peaceful rushing burst as when a boy's miniature dam in a little brook gives way, "All right. But how? I went to the bayou. I even found that log again. I——"

"I reckon that was all right. Likely he's been watching you. You never saw his foot?"

"I," the boy said—"I didn't—I never thought——"

"It's the gun," Sam said. He stood beside the fence, motionless—the old man, the Indian, in the battered faded overalls and the frayed five-cent straw hat which in the Negro's race had been the badge of his enslavement and was now the regalia of his freedom. The camp—the clearing, the house, the barn and its tiny lot with which Major de Spain in his turn had scratched punily and evanescently at the wilderness—faded in the dusk, back into the immemorial darkness of the woods. *The gun,* the boy thought. *The gun.*

"Be scared," Sam said. "You can't help that. But don't be afraid. Ain't nothing in the woods going to hurt you unless you corner it, or it smells that you are afraid. A bear or a deer, too, has got to be scared of a coward the same as a brave man has got to be."

The gun the boy thought.

"You will have to choose," Sam said.

He left the camp before daylight, long before Uncle Ash would wake in his quilts on the kitchen floor and start the fire for breakfast. He had only the compass and a stick for snakes. He could go almost a mile before he would begin to need the compass. He sat on a log, the invisible compass in his invisible hand, while the secret night sounds, fallen still at his movements, scurried again and then ceased for good, and the owls ceased and gave over to the waking of day birds, and he could see the compass. Then he went fast yet still quietly; he was becoming better and better as a woodsman, still without having yet realized it.

He jumped a doe and a fawn at sunrise, walked them out of the bed, close enough to see them—the crash of undergrowth, the white scut,[3] the fawn scudding behind her faster than he had believed it could run. He was hunting right, upwind, as Sam had taught him; not that it mattered now. He had left the gun; of his own will and relinquishment he had accepted not a gambit, not a choice, but a condition in which not only the bear's heretofore inviolable anonymity but all the old rules and balances of hunter and hunted had been abrogated. He would not even be afraid, not even in the moment when the fear would take him completely—blood, skin, bowels, bones, memory from the long time before it became his memory—all save that thin, clear, quench-

---

3 **scut:** short tail.

less, immortal lucidity which alone differed him from this bear and from all the other bear and deer he would ever kill in the humility and pride of his skill and endurance, to which Sam had spoken when he leaned in the twilight on the lot fence yesterday.

By noon he was far beyond the little bayou, farther into the new and alien country than he had ever been. He was traveling now not only by the compass but by the old, heavy, biscuit-thick silver watch which had belonged to his grandfather. When he stopped at last, it was for the first time since he had risen from the log at dawn when he could see the compass. It was far enough. He had left the camp nine hours ago; nine hours from now, dark would have already been an hour old. But he didn't think that. He thought, *All right. Yes. But what?* and stood for a moment, alien and small in the green and topless solitude, answering his own question before it had formed and ceased. It was the watch, the compass, the stick—the three lifeless mechanicals with which for nine hours he had fended the wilderness off; he hung the watch and compass carefully on a bush and leaned the stick beside them and relinquished completely to it.

He had not been going very fast for the last two or three hours. He went no faster now, since distance would not matter even if he could have gone fast. And he was trying to keep a bearing on the tree where he had left the compass, trying to complete a circle which would bring him back to it or at least intersect itself, since direction would not matter now either. But the tree was not there, and he did as Sam had schooled him—made the next circle in the opposite direction, so that the two patterns would bisect somewhere, but crossing no print of his own feet, finding the tree at last, but in the wrong place—no bush, no compass, no watch—and the tree not even the tree, because there was a down log beside it and he did what Sam Fathers had told him was the next thing and the last.

As he sat down on the log he saw the crooked print—the warped, tremendous, two-toed indentation which, even as he watched it, filled with water. As he looked up, the wilderness coalesced, solidified—the glade, the tree he sought, the bush, the watch and the compass glinting where a ray of sunlight touched them. Then he saw the bear. It did not emerge, appear; it was just there, immobile, solid, fixed in the hot dappling of the green and windless noon, not as big as he had dreamed it, but as big as he had expected it, bigger, dimensionless against the dappled obscurity, looking at him where he sat quietly on the log and looked back at it.

Then it moved. It made no sound. It did not hurry. It crossed the glade, walked for an instant into the full glare of the sun; when it reached the other side it stopped again and looked back at him across one shoulder while his quiet breathing inhaled and exhaled three times.

Then it was gone. It didn't walk into the woods, the undergrowth. It faded, sank back into the wilderness as he had watched a fish, a huge old bass, sink and vanish back into the dark depths of its pool without even any movement of its fins.

He thought, *It will be next fall.* But it was not next fall, nor the next nor the next. He was fourteen then. He had killed his buck, and Sam Fathers had marked his face with the hot blood, and in the next year he killed a bear. But even before that accolade he had become as competent in the woods as many grown men with the same experience; by his fourteenth year he was a better woodsman than most grown men with more. There was no territory within thirty miles of the camp that he did not know—bayou, ridge, brake, landmark tree and path. He could have led anyone to any point in it without deviation, and brought them out again. He knew game trails that even Sam Fathers did not know; in his thirteenth year he found a buck's bedding place, and unbeknown to his father he borrowed Walter Ewell's rifle and lay in wait at dawn and killed the buck when it walked back to the bed, as Sam had told him how the old Chickasaw fathers did.

But not the old bear, although by now he knew its footprint better than he did his own, and not only the crooked one. He could see any one of the three sound ones and distinguish it from any other, and not only by its size. There were other bears within those thirty miles which left tracks almost as large, but this was more than that. If Sam Fathers had been his mentor and the back-yard rabbits and squirrels at home his kindergarten, then the wilderness the old bear ran was his college, the old male bear itself, so long unwifed and childless as to have become its own ungendered progenitor, was his alma mater. But he never saw it.

He could find the crooked print now almost whenever he liked, fifteen or ten or five miles, or sometimes nearer the camp than that. Twice while on stand during the three years he heard the dogs strike its trail by accident; on the second time they jumped it seemingly, the voices high, abject, almost human in hysteria, as on that first morning two years ago. But not the bear itself. He would remember that noon three years ago, the glade, himself and the bear fixed during that moment in the windless and dappled blaze, and it would seem to him that it had never happened, that he had dreamed that too. But it had happened. They had looked at each other, they had emerged from the wilderness old as earth, synchronized to that instant by something more than the blood that moved the flesh and bones which bore them, and touched, pledged something, affirmed something more lasting than the frail web of bones and flesh which any accident could obliterate.

Then he saw it again. Because of the very fact that he thought of nothing else, he had forgotten to look for it. He was still-hunting with Walter Ewell's rifle. He saw it cross the end of a long blow-down, a corridor where a tornado had swept, rushing through rather than over the tangle of trunks and branches as a locomotive would have, faster than he had ever believed it could move, almost as fast as a deer even, because a deer would have spent most of that time in the air, faster than he could bring the rifle sights up to it, so that he believed the reason he never let off the shot was that he was still behind it, had never caught up with it. And now he knew what had been wrong during all the three years. He sat on a log, shaking and trembling as if he had never seen the woods before nor anything that ran them, wondering with incredulous amazement how he could have forgotten the very thing which Sam Fathers had told him and which the bear itself had proved the next day and had now returned after three years to reaffirm.

And he now knew what Sam Fathers had meant about the right dog, a dog in which size would mean less than nothing. So when he returned alone in April—school was out then, so that the sons of farmers could help with the land's planting, and at last his father had granted him permission, on his promise to be back in four days—he had the dog. It was his own, a mongrel of the sort called by Negroes a fyce,[4] a ratter, itself not much bigger than a rat and possessing that bravery which had long since stopped being courage and had become foolhardiness.

It did not take four days. Alone again, he found the trail on the first morning. It was not a stalk; it was an ambush. He timed the meeting almost as if it were an appointment with a human being. Himself holding the fyce muffled in a feed sack and Sam Fathers with two of the hounds on a piece of plowline rope, they lay down wind of the trail at dawn of the second morning. They were so close that the bear turned without even running, as if in surprised amazement at the shrill and frantic uproar of the released fyce, turning at bay against the trunk of a tree, on its hind feet; it seemed to the boy that it would never stop rising, taller and taller, and even the two hounds seemed to take a sort of desperate and despair-

---

4 **fyce:** for feist, a small dog of mixed breed.

ing courage from the fyce, following it as it went in.

Then he realized that the fyce was actually not going to stop. He flung, threw the gun away, and ran; when he overtook and grasped the frantically pinwheeling little dog, it seemed to him that he was directly under the bear.

He could smell it, strong and hot and rank. Sprawling, he looked up to where it loomed and towered over him like a cloudburst and colored like a thunderclap, quite familiar, peacefully and even lucidly familiar, until he remembered: This was the way he had used to dream about it. Then it was gone. He didn't see it go. He knelt, holding the frantic fyce with both hands, hearing the abased wailing of the hounds drawing farther and farther away, until Sam came up. He carried the gun. He laid it down quietly beside the boy and stood looking down at him.

"You've done seed him twice now with a gun in your hands," he said. "This time you couldn't have missed him."

The boy rose. He still held the fyce. Even in his arms and clear of the ground, it yapped frantically, straining and surging after the fading uproar of the two hounds like a tangle of wire springs. He was panting a little, but he was neither shaking nor trembling now.

"Neither could you!" he said. "You had the gun! Neither did you!"

"And you didn't shoot," his father said. "How close were you?"

"I don't know, sir," he said. "There was a big wood tick inside his right hind leg. I saw that. But I didn't have the gun then."

"But you didn't shoot when you had the gun," his father said. "Why?"

But he didn't answer, and his father didn't wait for him to, rising and crossing the room, across the pelt of the bear which the boy had killed two years ago and the larger one which his father had killed before he was born, to the bookcase beneath the mounted head of the boy's first buck. It was the room which his father called the office, from which all the plantation business was transacted; in it for the fourteen years of his life he had heard the best of all talking. Major de Spain would be there and sometimes old General Compson, and Walter Ewell and Boon Hoggenbeck and Sam Fathers and Tennie's Jim, too, because they, too, were hunters, knew the woods and what ran them.

He would hear it, not talking himself but listening—the wilderness, the big woods, bigger and older than any recorded document of white man fatuous enough to believe he had bought any fragment of it or Indian ruthless enough to pretend that any fragment of it had been his to convey. It was of the men, not white nor black nor red, but men, hunters with the will and hardihood to endure and the humility and skill to survive, and the dogs and the bear and deer juxtaposed and reliefed against it, ordered and compelled by and within the wilderness in the ancient and unremitting contest by the ancient and immitigable rules which voided all regrets and brooked no quarter, the voices quiet and weighty and deliberate for retrospection and recollection and exact remembering, while he squatted in the blazing firelight as Tennie's Jim squatted, who stirred only to put more wood on the fire and to pass the bottle from one glass to another. Because the bottle was always present, so that after a while it seemed to him that those fierce instants of heart and brain and courage and wiliness and speed were concentrated and distilled into that brown liquor which not women, not boys and children, but only hunters drank, drinking not of the blood they had spilled but some condensation of the wild immortal spirit, drinking it moderately, humbly even, not with the pagan's base hope of acquiring thereby the virtues of cunning and strength and speed, but in salute to them.

His father returned with the book and sat down again and opened it. "Listen," he said. He read the five stanzas aloud, his voice quiet and deliberate in the room where there was no fire now because it was already spring. Then he looked up. The boy watched him. "All right," his father said. "Listen." He read again, but only the second stanza this time, to the end of it, the last two lines, and closed the book and put it on the table beside him. "'She cannot fade, though thou hast not thy bliss, for ever wilt thou love, and she be fair,'"[5] he said.

"He's talking about a girl," the boy said.

"He had to talk about something," his father said. Then he said, "He was talking about truth. Truth doesn't change. Truth is one thing. It covers all things which touch the heart—honor and pride and pity and justice and courage and love. Do you see now?"

He didn't know. Somehow it was simpler than that. There was an old bear, fierce and ruthless, not merely just to stay alive, but with the fierce pride of liberty and freedom, proud enough of that liberty and freedom to see it threatened without fear or even alarm; nay, who at times even seemed deliberately to put that freedom and liberty in jeopardy in order to savor them, to remind his old strong bones and flesh to keep supple and quick to defend and preserve them. There was an old man, son of a Negro slave and an Indian king, inheritor on the one side of the long chronicle of a people who had learned humility through suffering, and pride through the endurance which survived the suffering and injustice, and on the other side, the chronicle of a people even longer in the land than the first, yet who no longer existed in the land at all save in the solitary brotherhood of an old Negro's alien blood and the wild and invincible spirit of an old bear. There was a boy who wished to learn humility and pride in order to become skillful and worthy in the woods, who suddenly found himself becoming so skillful so rapidly that he feared he would never become worthy because he had not learned humility and pride, although he had tried to, until one day and as suddenly he discovered that an old man who could not have defined either had led him, as

though by the hand, to that point where an old bear and a little mongrel dog showed him that, by possessing one thing other, he would possess them both.

And a little dog, nameless and mongrel and many-fathered, grown, yet weighing less than six pounds, saying as if to itself, "I can't be dangerous, because there's nothing much smaller than I am; I can't be fierce, because they would call it just noise; I can't be humble, because I'm already too close to the ground to genuflect; I can't be proud, because I wouldn't be near enough to it for anyone to know who was casting that shadow, and I don't even know that I'm not going to heaven, because they have already decided that I don't possess an immortal soul. So all I can be is brave. But it's all right. I can be that, even if they still call it just noise."

That was all. It was simple, much simpler than somebody talking in a book about a youth and a girl he would never need to grieve over, because he could never approach any nearer her and would never have to get any farther away. He had heard about a bear, and finally got big enough to trail it, and he trailed it four years and at last met it with a gun in his hands and he didn't shoot. Because a little dog—— But he could have shot long before the little dog covered the twenty yards to where the bear waited, and Sam Fathers could have shot at any time during that interminable minute while Old Ben stood on his hind feet over them. He stopped. His father was watching him gravely across the spring-rife twilight of the room; when he spoke, his words were as quiet as the twilight, too, not loud, because they did not need to be because they would last, "Courage, and honor, and pride," his father said, "and pity, and love of justice and of liberty. They all touch the heart, and what the heart holds to becomes truth, as far as we know truth. Do you see now?"

Sam and Old Ben, and Nip, he thought. And himself too. He had been all right too. His father had said so. "Yes, sir," he said.

---

5 'She cannot fade . . . she be fair': The quotation is from Keats's "Ode on a Grecian Urn."

Study Questions

1. During the first bear hunt why, according to Sam Fathers, is the boy likely to see Old Ben?
2. What does the boy smell when he looks at the dogs under the porch? How does his recognition of this smell determine his conduct?
3. What does Sam Fathers tell the boy about seeking an encounter with the bear? Explain this advice.
4. Describe the circumstances of the boy's three face-to-face encounters with Old Ben. What is significant about each meeting?
5. What details in the story show that Old Ben is more than just a bear? What does he symbolize?
6. What familiar pattern in human life do you think the boy's experiences with the bear represent? How does the boy's character change in the course of the story? What knowledge is implied in his final "Yes, sir"?
7. The father interprets the boy's failure to shoot Old Ben by reading aloud Keats's "Ode on a Grecian Urn." The second stanza, which the father reads twice, is printed here:

> Heard melodies are sweet, but those unheard
>   Are sweeter; therefore, ye soft pipes, play on;
> Not to the sensual ear, but, more endeared,
>   Pipe to the spirit ditties of no tone:
> Fair youth, beneath the trees, thou canst not leave
>   Thy song nor ever can those trees be bare;
>   Bold Lover, never, never canst thou kiss,
> Though winning near the goal—yet, do not grieve;
>   She cannot fade, though thou has not thy bliss,
>   Forever wilt thou love, and she be fair!

What is the common meaning of this stanza and the boy's failure to shoot the bear? What is the fundamental principle of imaginative literature the father refers to when he says, "He had to talk about something"?

Vocabulary

Context clues are the hints which recognizable terms and ideas in a piece of writing give about the meanings of unfamiliar words that the writing contains. For example, context clues in the following sentence should give a person who had never previously seen the word *shoat* the correct impression that this word means "a young pig":

For years the boy had heard that the bear carried off *shoats* and grown pigs, and even calves, to devour bodily in the woods.

As the exercise below will demonstrate, however, context clues are not always so easy to recognize as this. Moreover, they can sometimes actually be misleading.

Each of the following ten sentences based upon William Faulkner's "The Bear" contains an *italicized* word. With each sentence, take three steps, writing all your answers on a separate sheet of paper: (a) Give the best guess you can about the definition of the *italicized* word, realizing that there is no penalty for error. (b) Look up the word in a dictionary. (c) If your guess was accurate, write *correct* after it; but if your guess was wrong, copy the appropriate definition instead.

1. The bear was too big for the dogs which tried to bay it, for the horses which tried to ride it down, for the men and the bullets they fired into it, too big for the very country which was its *constricting* scope.

2. The edges of the wilderness were being constantly gnawed at by *myriad* men who were nameless, even to one another.

3. The old bear had earned a reputation as the *epitome* of the old wild life at which humans swarmed and hacked in a fury of dread and fear.

4. To the boy, the bear was not a living creature, but the whole wilderness which, leaning for the moment down, had patted once the hound's *temerity*.

5. Major de Spain in his turn had scratched punily and *evanescently* at the wilderness.

6. Since all the old rules and balances of hunter and hunted seemed to have been *abrogated,* the boy believed he would not be afraid.

7. Only a thin, clear, quenchless, immortal *lucidity* made the boy different from this bear and all the other bear and deer he would ever kill.

8. Sam Fathers had marked the boy's face with the hot blood of the buck and in the next year, the boy killed a bear; but even before that *accolade* the boy had become competent in the woods.

9. The old male bear, so long unwifed and childless, seemed to have become its own *progenitor*.

10. The boy knelt, holding the frantic fyce, hearing the *abased* wailing of the hounds drawing farther and farther away.

Ernest Hemingway   1899-1961

It is almost impossible to separate the legendary Ernest Hemingway from the books he wrote. The bearded adventurer who hunted and fished all over the world, who was fascinated by wars and bullfights, and who committed suicide is still more vivid than any of his fictional characters.

Hemingway was born in Oak Park, Illinois, the son of a doctor who took him on hunting and fishing trips. The trips were to northern Michigan, the locale of many of his stories, including "Big Two-Hearted River." After working as a reporter on the *Kansas City Star,* Hemingway joined a Red Cross ambulance unit during World War I. He served for a brief time on the front lines in Italy before he was seriously wounded. After the war Hemingway lived in Paris, where he began writing. There he became friends with other expatriate Americans who influenced his writing style. The books, *In Our Time* (1924) and *The Sun Also Rises* (1926), established him as an important writer. The novels, *A Farewell to Arms* (1929) and *For Whom the Bell Tolls* (1940), assured his fame. In 1953 he received a Pulitzer Prize for *The Old Man and the Sea* and in 1954, the Nobel Prize for Literature.

In Part I of "Big Two-Hearted River" the hero, Nick Adams, goes on a fishing trip alone. He finds a pleasant campsite, sets up his tent, checks out the stream he is to fish the next day, and goes to bed. As Part II begins, Nick crawls out of his tent in the morning and prepares for fishing.

"Big Two-Hearted River" can be read simply as a story of a fishing trip. More meaning comes, however, from the realization that Nick has been wounded in the war and has just recently returned from Europe. He has recovered physically, but he is still carrying mental and spiritual wounds which the horror and violence of war have inflicted.

Ernest Hemingway in the 1940s.

Big Two-Hearted River: Part II

ERNEST HEMINGWAY

IN THE MORNING the sun was up and the tent was starting to get hot. Nick crawled out under the mosquito netting stretched across the mouth of the tent, to look at the morning. The grass was wet on his hands as he came out. He held his trousers and his shoes in his hands. The sun was just up over the hill. There was the meadow, the river and the swamp. There were birch trees in the green of the swamp on the other side of the river.

The river was clear and smoothly fast in the early morning. Down about two hundred yards were three logs all the way across the stream. They made the water smooth and deep above them. As Nick watched, a mink crossed the river on the logs and went into the swamp. Nick was excited. He was excited by the early morning and the river. He was really too hurried to eat breakfast, but he knew he must. He built a little fire and put on the coffee pot. While the water was heating in the pot he took an empty bottle and went down over the edge of the high ground to the meadow. The meadow was wet with dew and Nick wanted to catch grasshoppers for bait before the sun dried the grass. He found plenty of good grasshoppers. They were at the base of the grass stems. Sometimes they clung to a grass stem. They were cold and wet with the dew, and could not jump until the sun warmed them. Nick picked them up, taking only the medium sized brown ones, and put them into the bottle. He turned over a log and just under the shelter of the edge were several hundred hoppers. It was a grasshopper lodging house. Nick put about fifty of the medium browns into the bottle. While he was picking up the hoppers the others warmed in the sun and commenced to hop away. They flew when they hopped. At first they made one flight and stayed stiff when they landed, as though they were dead.

Nick knew that by the time he was through with breakfast they would be as lively as ever. Without dew in the grass it would take him all day to catch a bottle full of good grasshoppers and he would have to crush many of them, slamming at them with his hat. He washed his hands at the stream. He was excited to be near it. Then he walked up to the tent. The hoppers were already jumping stiffly in the grass. In the bottle, warmed by the sun, they were jumping in a mass. Nick put in a pine stick as a cork. It plugged the mouth of the bottle enough, so the hoppers could not get out and left plenty of air passage.

He had rolled the log back and knew he could get grasshoppers there every morning.

Nick laid the bottle full of jumping grasshoppers against a pine trunk. Rapidly he mixed some buckwheat flour with water and stirred it smooth, one cup of flour, one cup of water. He put a handful of coffee in the pot and dipped a lump of grease out of a can and slid it sputtering across the hot skillet. On the smoking skillet he poured smoothly the buckwheat batter. It spread like lava, the grease spitting sharply. Around the edges the buckwheat cake began to firm, then brown, then crisp. The surface was bubbling slowly to porousness. Nick pushed under the browned under surface with a fresh pine chip. He shook the skillet sideways and the cake was loose on the surface. I won't try and flop it, he thought. He slid the chip of clean wood all the way under the cake, and flopped it over onto its face. It sputtered in the pan.

When it was cooked Nick regreased the skillet. He used all the batter. It made another big flapjack and one smaller one.

Nick ate a big flapjack and a smaller one, covered with apple butter. He put apple butter on the third cake, folded it over twice, wrapped it in oiled paper and put it in his shirt pocket. He put the apple butter jar back in the pack and cut bread for two sandwiches.

In the pack he found a big onion. He sliced it in two and peeled the silky outer skin. Then he cut one half into slices and made onion sandwiches. He wrapped them in oiled paper and buttoned them in the other pocket of his khaki shirt. He turned the skillet upside down on the grill, drank the coffee, sweetened and yellow brown with the condensed milk in it, and tidied up the camp. It was a nice little camp.

Nick took his fly rod out of the leather rod-case, jointed it, and shoved the rod-case back into the tent. He put on the reel and threaded the line through the guides. He had to hold it from hand to hand, as he threaded it, or it would slip back through its own weight. It was a heavy, double tapered fly line. Nick had paid eight dollars for it a long time ago. It was made heavy to lift back in the air and come forward flat and heavy and straight to make it possible to cast a fly which has no weight. Nick opened the aluminum leader box. The leaders were coiled between the damp flannel pads. Nick had wet the pads at the water cooler on the train up to St. Ignace. In the damp pads the gut leaders had softened and Nick unrolled one and tied it by a loop at the end to the heavy fly line. He fastened a hook on the end of the leader. It was a small hook; very thin and springy.

Nick took it from his hook book, sitting with the rod across his lap. He tested the knot and spring of the rod by pulling the line taut. It was a good feeling. He was careful not to let the hook bite into his finger.

He started down to the stream, holding his rod, the bottle of grasshoppers hung from his neck by a thong tied in half hitches around the neck of the bottle. His landing net hung by a hook from his belt. Over his shoulder was a long flour sack tied at each corner into an ear. The cord went over his shoulder. The sack flapped against his legs.

Nick felt awkward and professionally happy with all his equipment hanging from him. The grasshopper bottle swung against his chest. In his shirt the breast pockets bulged against him with the lunch and his fly book.

He stepped into the stream. It was a shock. His trousers clung tight to his legs. His shoes felt the gravel. The water was a rising cold shock.

Rushing, the current sucked against his legs. Where he stepped in, the water was over his knees. He waded with the current. The gravel slid under his shoes. He looked down at the swirl of water below each leg and tipped up the bottle to get a grasshopper.

The first grasshopper gave a jump in the neck of the bottle and went out into the water. He was sucked under in the whirl by Nick's right leg and came to the surface a little way down stream. He floated rapidly, kicking. In a quick circle, breaking the smooth surface of the water, he disappeared. A trout had taken him.

Another hopper poked his head out of the bottle. His antennae wavered. He was getting his front legs out of the bottle to jump. Nick took him by the head and held him while he threaded the slim hook under his chin, down through his thorax and into the last segments of his abdomen. The grasshopper took hold of the hook with his front feet, spitting tobacco juice on it. Nick dropped him into the water.

Holding the rod in his right hand he let out line against the pull of the grasshopper in the current. He stripped off line from the reel with his left hand and let it run free. He could see the hopper in the little waves of the current. It went out of sight.

There was a tug on the line. Nick pulled against the taut line. It was his first strike.

Holding the now living rod across the current, he brought in the line with his left hand. The rod bent in jerks, the trout pumping against the current. Nick knew it was a small one. He lifted the rod straight up in the air. It bowed with the pull.

He saw the trout in the water jerking with his head and body against the shifting tangent of the line in the stream.

Nick took the line in his left hand and pulled the trout, thumping tiredly against the current, to the surface. His back was mottled the clear, water-over-gravel color, his side flashing in the sun. The rod under his right arm, Nick stooped, dipping his right hand into the current. He held the trout, never still, with his moist right hand, while he unhooked the barb from his mouth, then dropped him back into the stream.

He hung unsteadily in the current, then settled to the bottom beside a stone. Nick reached down his hand to touch him, his arm to the elbow under water. The trout was steady in the moving stream, resting on the gravel, beside a stone. As Nick's fingers touched him, touched his smooth, cool, underwater feeling he was gone, gone in a shadow across the bottom of the stream.

He's all right, Nick thought. He was only tired.

He had wet his hand before he touched the trout, so he would not disturb the delicate mucus that covered him. If a trout was touched with a dry hand, a white fungus attacked the unprotected spot. Years before when he had fished crowded streams, with fly fishermen ahead of him and behind him, Nick had again and again come on a dead trout, furry with white fungus, drifting against a rock, or floating belly up in some pool. Nick did not like to fish with other men on the river. Unless they were of your party, they spoiled it.

He wallowed down the stream, above his knees in the current, through the fifty yards of shallow water above the pile of logs that crossed the stream. He did not rebait his hook and held it in his hands as he waded. He was certain he could catch small trout in the shallows, but he did not want them. There would be no big trout in the shallows this time of day.

Now the water deepened up his thighs sharply and coldly. Ahead was the smooth dammed-back flood of water above the logs. The water was smooth and dark; on the left, the lower edge of the meadow; on the right the swamp.

Nick leaned back against the current and took a hopper from the bottle. He threaded the hopper on the hook and spat on him for good luck. Then he pulled several yards of line from the reel and tossed the hopper out ahead onto the fast, dark water. It floated down towards the logs, then the weight of the line pulled the bait under the surface. Nick held the rod in his right hand, letting the line run out through his fingers.

There was a long tug. Nick struck and the rod came alive and dangerous, bent double, the line tightening, coming out of water, tightening, all in a heavy, dangerous, steady pull. Nick felt the moment when the leader would break if the strain increased and let the line go.

The reel ratcheted into a mechanical shriek as the line went out in a rush. Too fast. Nick could not check it, the line rushing out, the reel note rising as the line ran out.

With the core of the reel showing, his heart feeling stopped with the excitement, leaning back against the current that mounted icily his thighs, Nick thumbed the reel hard with his left hand. It was awkward getting his thumb inside the fly reel frame.

As he put on pressure the line tightened into sudden hardness and beyond the logs a huge trout went high out of water. As he jumped, Nicked lowered the tip of the rod. But he felt, as he dropped the tip to ease the strain, the moment when the strain was too great; the hardness too tight. Of course, the leader had broken. There was no mistaking the feeling when all spring left the line and it became dry and hard. Then it went slack.

His mouth dry, his heart down, Nick reeled in. He had never seen so big a trout. There was a heaviness, a power not to be held, and then the bulk of him, as he jumped. He looked as broad as a salmon.

Nick's hand was shaky. He reeled in slowly. The thrill had been too much. He felt, vaguely, a little sick, as though it would be better to sit down.

The leader had broken where the hook was tied to it. Nick took it in his hand. He thought of the trout somewhere on the bottom, holding himself steady over the gravel, far down below the light, under the logs, with the hook in his jaw. Nick knew the trout's teeth would cut through the snell of the hook. The hook would imbed itself in his jaw. He'd bet the trout was angry. Anything that size would be angry. That was a trout. He had been solidly hooked. Solid as a rock. He felt like a rock, too, before he started off. By God, he was a big one. By God, he was the biggest one I ever heard of.

Nick climbed out onto the meadow and stood, water running down his trousers and out of his shoes, his shoes squlchy. He went over and sat on the logs. He did not want to rush his sensations any.

He wriggled his toes in the water, in his shoes, and got out a cigarette from his breast pocket. He lit it and tossed the match into the fast water below the logs. A tiny trout rose at the match, as it swung around in the fast current. Nick laughed. He would finish the cigarette.

He sat on the logs, smoking, drying in the sun, the sun warm on his back, the river shallow ahead entering the woods, curving into the woods, shallows, light glittering, big water-smooth rocks, cedars along the bank and white birches, the logs warm in the sun, smooth to sit on, without bark, gray to the touch; slowly the feeling of disappointment left him. It went away slowly, the feeling of disappointment that came sharply after the thrill that made his shoulders ache. It was all right now. His rod lying out on the logs, Nick tied a new hook on the leader, pulling the gut tight until it grimped into itself in a hard knot.

He baited up, then picked up the rod and walked to the far end of the logs to get into the water, where it was not too deep. Under and beyond the logs was a deep pool. Nick walked around the shallow shelf near the swamp shore until he came out on the shallow bed of the stream.

On the left, where the meadow ended and the woods began, a great elm tree was uprooted. Gone over in a storm, it lay back into the woods, its roots clotted with dirt, grass growing in them, rising a solid bank beside the stream. The river cut to the edge of the uprooted tree. From where Nick stood he could see deep channels, like ruts, cut in the shallow bed of the stream by the flow of the current. Pebbly where he stood and pebbly and full of boulders beyond; where it curved near the tree roots, the bed of the stream was marly[1] and between the ruts of deep water green weed fronds swung in the current.

Nick swung the rod back over his shoulder and forward, and the line, curving forward, laid the grasshopper down on one of the deep channels in the weeds. A trout struck and Nick hooked him.

Holding the rod far out toward the uprooted tree and sloshing backward in the current, Nick worked the trout, plunging, the rod bending alive, out of the danger of the weeds into the open river. Holding the rod, pumping alive against the current, Nick brought the trout in. He rushed, but always came, the spring of the rod yielding to the rushes, sometimes jerking under water, but always bringing him in. Nick eased downstream with the rushes. The rod above his head he led the trout over the net, then lifted.

The trout hung heavy in the net, mottled

---

1 **marly:** full of marl, a kind of crumbling clay.

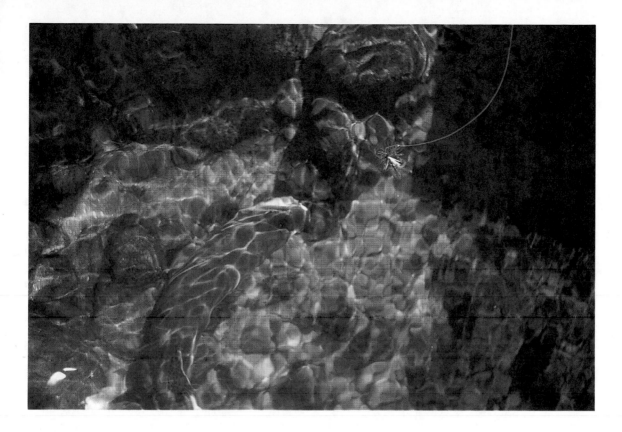

trout back and silver sides in the meshes. Nick unhooked him; heavy sides, good to hold, big undershot jaw, and slipped him, heaving and big sliding, into the long sack that hung from his shoulders in the water.

Nick spread the mouth of the sack against the current and it filled, heavy with water. He held it up, the bottom in the stream, and the water poured out through the sides. Inside at the bottom was the big trout, alive in the water.

Nick moved downstream. The sack out ahead of him sunk, heavy in the water, pulling from his shoulders.

It was getting hot, the sun hot on the back of his neck.

Nick had one good trout. He did not care about getting many trout. Now the stream was shallow and wide. There were trees along both banks. The trees of the left bank made short shadows on the current in the forenoon sun. Nick knew there were trout in each shadow. In the afternoon, after the sun had crossed toward the hills, the trout would be in the cool shadows on the other side of the stream.

The very biggest ones would lie up close to the bank. You could always pick them up there on the Black. When the sun was down they all moved out into the current. Just when the sun made the water blinding in the glare before it went down, you were liable to strike a big trout anywhere in the current. It was almost impossible to fish then, the surface of the water was blinding as a mirror in the sun. Of course, you could fish upstream, but in a stream like the Black, or this, you had to wallow against the current and in a deep place, the water piled up on you. It was no fun to fish upstream with this much current.

Nick moved along through the shallow

stretch watching the banks for deep holes. A beech tree grew close beside the river, so that the branches hung down into the water. The stream went back in under the leaves. There were always trout in a place like that.

Nick did not care about fishing that hole. He was sure he would get hooked in the branches.

It looked deep though. He dropped the grasshopper so the current took it under water, back in under the overhanging branch. The line pulled hard and Nick struck. The trout threshed heavily, half out of water in the leaves and branches. The line was caught. Nick pulled hard and the trout was off. He reeled in and holding the hook in his hand, walked down the stream.

Ahead, close to the left bank, was a big log. Nick saw it was hollow; pointing up river the current entered it smoothly, only a little ripple spread each side of the log. The water was deepening. The top of the hollow log was gray and dry. It was partly in the shadow.

Nick took the cork out of the grasshopper bottle and a hopper clung to it. He picked him off, hooked him and tossed him out. He held the rod far out so that the hopper on the water moved into the current flowing into the hollow log. Nick lowered the rod and the hopper floated in. There was a heavy strike. Nick swung the rod against the pull. It felt as though he were hooked into the log itself, except for the live feeling.

He tried to force the fish out into the current. It came, heavily.

The line went slack and Nick thought the trout was gone. Then he saw him, very near, in the current, shaking his head, trying to get the hook out. His mouth was clamped shut. He was fighting the hook in the clear flowing current.

Looping in the line with his left hand, Nick swung the rod to make the line taut and tried to lead the trout toward the net, but he was gone, out of sight, the line pumping. Nick fought him against the current, letting him

thump in the water against the spring of the rod. He shifted the rod to his left hand, worked the trout upstream, holding his weight, fighting on the rod, and then let him down into the net. He lifted him clear of the water, a heavy half circle in the net, the net dripping, unhooked him and slid him into the sack.

He spread the mouth of the sack and looked down in at the two big trout alive in the water.

Through the deepening water, Nick waded over to the hollow log. He took the sack off, over his head, the trout flopping as it came out of water, and hung it so the trout were deep in the water. Then he pulled himself up on the log and sat, the water from his trousers and boots running down into the stream. He laid his rod down, moved along the shady end of the log and took the sandwiches out of his pocket. He dipped the sandwiches in the cold water. The current carried away the crumbs. He ate the sandwiches and dipped his hat full of water to drink, the water running out through his hat just ahead of his drinking.

It was cool in the shade, sitting on the log. He took a cigarette out and struck a match to light it. The match sunk into the gray wood, making a tiny furrow. Nick leaned over the side of the log, found a hard place and lit the match. He sat smoking and watching the river.

Ahead the river narrowed and went into a swamp. The river became smooth and deep and the swamp looked solid with cedar trees, their trunks close together, their branches solid. It would not be possible to walk through a swamp, like that. The branches grew so low. You would have to keep almost level with the ground to move at all. You could not crash through the branches. That must be why the animals that lived in swamps were built the way they were, Nick thought.

He wished he had brought something to read. He felt like reading. He did not feel like going on into the swamp. He looked down the river. A big cedar slanted all the way across the stream. Beyond that the river went in to the swamp.

Nick did not want to go in there now. He felt a reaction against deep wading with the water deepening up under his armpits, to hook big trout in places impossible to land them. In the swamp the banks were bare, the big cedars came together overhead, the sun did not come through, except in patches; in the fast deep water, in the half light, the fishing would be tragic. In the swamp fishing was a tragic adventure. Nick did not want it. He did not want to go down the stream any further today.

He took out his knife, opened it and stuck it in the log. Then he pulled up the sack, reached into it and brought out one of the trout. Holding him near the tail, hard to hold, alive, in his hand, he whacked him against the log. The trout quivered, rigid. Nick laid him on the log in the shade and broke the neck of the other fish the same way. He laid them side by side on the log. They were fine trout.

Nick cleaned them, slitting them from the vent to the tip of the jaw. All the insides and the gills and tongue came out in one piece. They were both males; long gray-white strips of milt, smooth and clean. All the insides clean and compact, coming out all together. Nick tossed the offal ashore for the minks to find.

He washed the trout in the stream. When he held them back up in the water they looked like live fish. Their color was not gone yet. He washed his hands and dried them on the log. Then he laid the trout on the sack spread out on the log, rolled them up in it, tied the bundle and put it in the landing net. His knife was still standing, blade stuck in the log. He cleaned it on the wood and put it in his pocket.

Nick stood up on the log, holding his rod, the landing net hanging heavy, then stepped into the water and splashed ashore. He climbed the bank and cut up into the woods, toward the high ground. He was going back to camp. He looked back. The river just showed through the trees. There were plenty of days coming when he could fish the swamp.

Study Questions

1. Most of the story is concerned with physical activities: catching grasshoppers, making breakfast, packing lunch, and fishing. By such careful attention to these concrete details what might Nick be avoiding? What other details reveal the tension Nick controls?

2. Nick is using grasshoppers to catch fish, but how does he show compassion for both the grasshoppers and the fish?

3. How can Nick's outright violence, whacking the trout against the log to break their necks, be justified?

4. Toward the end of the story Nick repeatedly mentions the swamp. Why does he avoid it? What, possibly, does the swamp symbolize?

5. How does Hemingway's precise language reflect Nick's determination to act, not to think? What is the effect of the repetition? of the conjunctions? of the declarative sentences?

6. In this story nature is beautiful, undefiled, and timeless. Why does Nick return to nature? What does the last sentence suggest about Nick and his future?

Composition

1. In a short composition explain why the title, "Big Two-Hearted River," is, or is not, appropriate. Then cite relevant details from the story to support your position.

2. In a short story describe someone's participation in a sport (for example, bowling, tennis, sailing, basketball, scuba diving, skiing). Tell everything from that person's point of view. Include a description of the technique involved and of the personal satisfaction derived from the sport. Use details, simple vocabulary, short sentences, and action verbs to convey the person's enthusiasm.

Vocabulary

The following list contains ten terms taken from the jargon, or specialized vocabulary, of fishing:

bait	barb	current	reel	slack
bank	catch	leader	rod	strike

Each term is a **multiple-meaning word** and has at least one additional definition which has nothing whatever to do with fishing. One such additional definition for each term is given below. On a separate sheet of paper, write the fishing definition for each term, and then match each term to its second definition below.

a. to participate in a work stoppage
b. to pester or harass
c. a horse that is placed at the front of a team
d. a unit of measurement ($16\frac{1}{2}$ feet)
e. contemporary; belonging to the present time
f. a lively folk dance
g. a break in the voice that results from emotional strain
h. a sharp, stinging remark
i. small bits of coal that remain after larger ones have been removed by screening
j. a lateral inclination of an airplane

John Steinbeck   1902-1968

John Steinbeck specialized in fiction set in his native California. His knowledge of the Salinas River Valley farms and farm people was gained at first hand. He was a versatile writer, moving easily from the gentle sadness of *Of Mice and Men* (1937) to the social protest of *The Grapes of Wrath* to the moral symbolism of *East of Eden* (1952). His novella *The Pearl* (1947) is regarded by many as a classic in the genre. His short stories, especially those in a collection entitled *The Long Valley* (1938), show the sure hand of a craftsman. When Steinbeck won the Nobel Prize for Literature in 1962, the citation from the Swedish Literary Academy announcing the award read, in part:

Among the masters of modern American literature who have already been awarded this prize—from Sinclair Lewis to Ernest Hemingway—Steinbeck more than holds his own, independent in position and achievement. His sympathies always go out to the oppressed, the misfits, and the distressed. He likes to contrast the simple joy of life with the brutal and cynical craving for money. But in him we find the American temperament also expressed in his great feeling for nature, for the tilled soil, the wasteland, the mountains and the ocean coasts, all an inexhaustible source of inspiration to Steinbeck in the midst of, and beyond, the world of human beings.

Steinbeck is particularly skillful in focusing on a revelation of character rather than upon physical action or plot. In "The Chrysanthemums" a good deal is quietly happening to the main character, Elisa Allen.

The Chrysanthemums

JOHN STEINBECK

THE HIGH GRAY-FLANNEL FOG of winter closed off the Salinas Valley[1] from the sky and from all the rest of the world. On every side it sat like a lid on the mountains and made of the great valley a closed pot. On the broad, level land floor the gang plows[2] bit deep and left the black earth shining like metal where the shares had cut.

On the foothill ranches across the Salinas River, the yellow stubble fields seemed to be bathed in pale cold sunshine, but there was no sunshine in the valley now in December. The thick willow scrub along the river flamed with sharp and positive yellow leaves.

It was a time of quiet and of waiting. The air was cold and tender. A light wind blew up from the southwest so that the farmers were mildly hopeful of a good rain before long; but fog and rain do not go together.

---

1 **Salinas Valley:** in California near Monterey Bay.
2 **gang plows:** several plows operating in a single unit.

Across the river, on Henry Allen's foothill ranch there was little work to be done, for the hay was cut and stored and the orchards were plowed up to receive the rain deeply when it should come. The cattle on the higher slopes were becoming shaggy and rough-coated.

Elisa Allen, working in her flower garden, looked down across the yard and saw Henry, her husband, talking to two men in business suits. The three of them stood by the tractor shed, each man with one foot on the side of the little Fordson. They smoked cigarettes and studied the machine as they talked.

Elisa watched them for a moment and then went back to her work. She was thirty-five. Her face was lean and strong and her eyes were as clear as water. Her figure looked blocked and heavy in her gardening costume, a man's black hat pulled low down over her eyes, clod-hopper shoes, a figured print dress almost completely covered by a big corduroy apron with four big pockets to hold the snips, the trowel and scratcher, the seeds and the knife she worked with. She wore heavy leather gloves to protect her hands while she worked.

She was cutting down the old year's chrysanthemum stalks with a pair of short and powerful scissors. She looked down toward the men by the tractor shed now and then. Her face was eager and mature and handsome; even her work with the scissors was overeager, overpowerful. The chrysanthemum stems seemed too small and easy for her energy.

She brushed a cloud of hair out of her eyes with the back of her glove, and left a smudge of earth on her cheek in doing it. Behind her stood the neat white farmhouse with red geraniums close-banked around it as high as the windows. It was a hard-swept looking little house, with hard-polished windows, and a clean mud-mat on the front steps.

Elisa cast another glance toward the tractor shed. The strangers were getting into their Ford coupe. She took off a glove and put her strong fingers down into the forest of new green chrysanthemum sprouts that were growing around the old roots. She spread the leaves and looked down among the close-growing stems. No aphids were there, no sow-bugs or snails or cutworms. Her terrier fingers destroyed such pests before they could get started.

Elisa started at the sound of her husband's voice. He had come near quietly, and he leaned over the wire fence that protected her flower garden from cattle and dogs and chickens.

"At it again," he said. "You've got a strong new crop coming."

Elisa straightened her back and pulled on the gardening glove again. "Yes. They'll be strong this coming year." In her tone and on her face there was a little smugness.

"You've got a gift with things," Henry observed. "Some of those yellow chrysanthemums you had this year were ten inches across. I wish you'd work out in the orchard and raise some apples that big."

Her eyes sharpened. "Maybe I could do it, too. I've a gift with things, all right. My mother had it. She could stick anything in the ground and make it grow. She said it was having planter's hands that knew how to do it."

"Well, it sure works with flowers," he said.

"Henry, who were those men you were talking to?"

"Why, sure, that's what I came to tell you. They were from the Western Meat Company. I sold those thirty head of three-year-old steers. Got nearly my own price, too."

"Good," she said. "Good for you."

"And I thought," he continued, "I thought how it's Saturday afternoon, and we might go into Salinas for dinner at a restaurant, and then to a picture show—to celebrate, you see."

"Good," she repeated. "Oh, yes. That will be good."

Henry put on his joking tone. "There's fights tonight. How'd you like to go to the fights?"

"Oh, no," she said breathlessly. "No, I wouldn't like fights."

"Just fooling, Elisa. We'll go to a movie. Let's see. It's two now. I'm going to take Scotty and bring down those steers from the hill. It'll take us maybe two hours. We'll go in town about five and have dinner at the Cominos Hotel. Like that?"

"Of course I'll like it. It's good to eat away from home."

"All right, then. I'll go get up a couple of horses."

She said, "I'll have plenty of time to transplant some of these sets, I guess."

She heard her husband calling Scotty down by the barn. And a little later she saw the two men ride up the pale yellow hillside in search of the steers.

There was a little square sandy bed kept for rooting the chrysanthemums. With her trowel she turned the soil over and over, and smoothed it and patted it firm. Then she dug ten parallel trenches to receive the sets. Back at the chrysanthemum bed she pulled out the little crisp shoots, trimmed off the leaves of each one with her scissors and laid it on a small orderly pile.

A squeak of wheels and plod of hoofs came from the road. Elisa looked up. The country road ran along the dense bank of willows and cottonwoods that bordered the river, and up this road came a curious vehicle, curiously drawn. It was an old spring-wagon, with a round canvas top on it like the cover of a prairie schooner.[3] It was drawn by an old bay horse and a little gray-and-white burro. A big stubble-bearded man sat between the cover flaps and drove the crawling team. Underneath the wagon, between the hind wheels, a lean and rangy mongrel dog walked sedately. Words were painted on the canvas, in clumsy, crooked letters. "Pots, pans, knives, sisors, lawn mores, Fixed." Two rows of articles, and the triumphantly definitive "Fixed" below. The black paint had run down in little sharp points beneath each letter.

Elisa, squatting on the ground, watched to see the crazy, loose-jointed wagon pass by. But it didn't pass. It turned into the farm road in front of her house, crooked old wheels skirling[4] and squeaking. The rangy dog darted from between the wheels and ran ahead. Instantly the two ranch shepherds flew out at him. Then all three stopped and with stiff and quivering tails, with taut straight legs, with ambassadorial dignity, they slowly circled, sniffing daintily. The caravan pulled up to Elisa's wire fence and stopped. Now the newcomer dog, feeling outnumbered, lowered his tail and retired under the wagon with raised hackles and bared teeth.

The man on the wagon seat called out, "That's a bad dog in a fight when he gets started."

Elisa laughed. "I see he is. How soon does he generally get started?"

The man caught up her laughter and echoed it heartily. "Sometimes not for weeks and weeks," he said. He climbed stiffly down, over the wheel. The horse and the donkey drooped like unwatered flowers.

Elisa saw that he was a very big man. Although his hair and beard were graying, he did not look old. His worn black suit was wrinkled and spotted with grease. The laughter had disappeared from his face and eyes the moment his laughing voice ceased. His eyes were dark, and they were full of the brooding that gets in the eyes of teamsters and of sailors. The calloused hands he rested on the wire fence were cracked, and every crack was a black line. He took off his battered hat.

"I'm off my general road, ma'am," he said. "Does this dirt road cut over across the river to the Los Angeles highway?"

Elisa stood up and shoved the thick scissors in her apron pocket. "Well, yes, it does, but it winds around and then fords the river. I don't think your team could pull through the sand."

He replied with some asperity. "It might

3 **prairie schooner:** small covered wagon used by pioneers.

4 **skirling:** shrieking.

surprise you what them beasts can pull through."

"When they get started?" she asked.

He smiled for a second. "Yes. When they get started."

"Well," said Elisa, "I think you'll save time if you go back to the Salinas road and pick up the highway there."

He drew a big finger down the chicken wire and made it sing. "I ain't in any hurry, ma'am. I go from Seattle to San Diego and back every year. Takes all my time. About six months each way. I aim to follow nice weather."

Elisa took off her gloves and stuffed them in the apron pocket with the scissors. She touched the under edge of her man's hat, searching for fugitive hairs. "That sounds like a nice kind of a way to live," she said.

He leaned confidentially over the fence. "Maybe you noticed the writing on my wagon. I mend pots and sharpen knives and scissors. You got any of them things to do?"

"Oh, no," she said quickly. "Nothing like that." Her eyes hardened with resistance.

"Scissors is the worst thing," he explained. "Most people just ruin scissors trying to sharpen 'em, but I know how. I got a special tool. It's a little bobbit kind of thing, and patented. But it sure does the trick."

"No. My scissors are all sharp."

"All right, then. Take a pot," he continued earnestly, "a bent pot, or a pot with a hole. I can make it like new so you don't have to buy no new ones. That's a saving for you."

"No," she said shortly. "I tell you I have nothing like that for you to do."

His face fell to an exaggerated sadness. His voice took on a whining undertone. "I ain't had a thing to do today. Maybe I won't have no supper tonight. You see I'm off my regular road. I know folks on the highway clear from Seattle to San Diego. They save their things for me to sharpen up because they know I do it so good and save them money."

"I'm sorry," Elisa said irritably. "I haven't anything for you to do."

His eyes left her face and fell to searching the ground. They roamed about until they came to the chrysanthemum bed where she had been working. "What's them plants, ma'am?"

The irritation and resistance melted from Elisa's face. "Oh, those are chrysanthemums, giant whites and yellows. I raise them every year, bigger than anybody around here."

"Kind of a long-stemmed flower? Looks like a quick puff of colored smoke?" he asked.

"That's it. What a nice way to describe them."

"They smell kind of nasty till you get used to them," he said.

"It's a good bitter smell," she retorted, "not nasty at all."

He changed his tone quickly. "I like the smell myself."

"I had ten-inch blooms this year," she said.

The man leaned farther over the fence. "Look. I know a lady down the road a piece, has got the nicest garden you ever seen. Got nearly every kind of flower but no chrysantheums. Last time I was mending a copper-bottom washtub for her (that's a hard job but I do it good), she said to me, 'If you ever run acrost some nice chrysantheums I wish you'd try to get me a few seeds.' That's what she told me."

Elisa's eyes grew alert and eager. "She couldn't have known much about chrysanthemums. You *can* raise them from seed, but it's much easier to root the little sprouts you see there."

"Oh," he said. "I s'pose I can't take none to her, then."

"Why yes you can," Elisa cried. "I can put some in damp sand, and you can carry them right along with you. They'll take root in the pot if you keep them damp. And then she can transplant them."

"She'd sure like to have some, ma'am. You say they're nice ones?"

"Beautiful," she said. "Oh, beautiful." Her eyes shone. She tore off the battered hat and

shook out her dark, pretty hair. "I'll put them in a flower-pot, and you can take them right with you. Come into the yard."

While the man came through the picket gate Elisa ran excitedly along the geranium-bordered path to the back of the house. And she returned carrying a big red flower-pot. The gloves were forgotten now. She kneeled on the ground by the starting bed and dug up the sandy soil with her fingers and scooped it into the bright new flower-pot. Then she picked up the little pile of shoots she had prepared. With her strong fingers she pressed them into the sand and tamped around them with her knuckles. The man stood over her. "I'll tell you what to do," she said. "You remember so you can tell the lady."

"Yes, I'll try to remember."

"Well, look. These will take root in about a month. Then she must set them out, about a foot apart in good rich earth like this, see?" She lifted a handful of dark soil for him to look at. "They'll grow fast and tall. Now remember this: In July tell her to cut them down, about eight inches from the ground."

"Before they bloom?" he asked.

"Yes, before they bloom." Her face was tight with eagerness. "They'll grow right up again. About the last of September the buds will start."

She stopped and seemed perplexed. "It's the budding that takes the most care," she said hesitantly. "I don't know how to tell you." She looked deep into his eyes, searchingly. Her mouth opened a little, and she seemed to be listening. "I'll try to tell you," she said. "Did you ever hear of planting hands?"

"Can't say I have, ma'am."

"Well, I can only tell you what it feels like. It's when you're picking off the buds you don't want. Everything goes right down into your finger tips. You watch your fingers work. They do it themselves. You can feel how it is. They pick and pick the buds. They never make

The Chrysanthemums 465

a mistake. They're with the plant. Do you see? Your fingers and the plant. You can feel that, right up your arm. They know. They never make a mistake. You can feel it. When you're like that you can't do anything wrong. Do you see that? Can you understand that?"

She was kneeling on the ground looking up at him. Her breast swelled passionately.

The man's eyes narrowed. He looked away self-consciously. "Maybe I know," he said. "Sometimes in the night in the wagon there—"

Elisa's voice grew husky. She broke in on him. "I've never lived as you do, but I know what you mean. When the night is dark—why, the stars are sharp-pointed, and there's quiet. Why, you rise up and up! Every pointed star gets driven into your body. It's like that. Hot and sharp and—lovely."

Kneeling there, her hand went out toward his legs in the greasy black trousers. Her hesitant fingers almost touched the cloth. Then her hand dropped to the ground. She crouched low like a fawning dog.

He said, "It's nice, just like you say. Only when you don't have no dinner, it ain't."

She stood up then, very straight, and her face was ashamed. She held the flower-pot out to him and placed it gently in his arms. "Here. Put it in your wagon, on the seat, where you can watch it. Maybe I can find something for you to do."

At the back of the house she dug in the can pile and found two old and battered aluminum saucepans. She carried them back and gave them to him. "Here, maybe you can fix these."

His manner changed. He became professional. "Good as new I can fix them." At the back of his wagon he set a little anvil, and out of an oily tool-box dug a small machine hammer. Elisa came through the gate to watch him while he pounded out the dents in the kettles. His mouth grew sure and knowing. At a difficult part of the work he sucked his underlip.

"You sleep right in the wagon?" Elisa asked.

"Right in the wagon, ma'am. Rain or shine I'm dry as a cow in there."

"It must be nice," she said. "It must be very nice. I wish women could do such things."

"It ain't the right kind of a life for a woman."

Her upper lip raised a little, showing her teeth. "How do you know? How can you tell?" she said.

"I don't know, ma'am," he protested. "Of course I don't know. Now here's your kettles, done. You don't have to buy no new ones."

"How much?"

"Oh, fifty cents'll do. I keep my prices down and my work good. That's why I have all them satisfied customers up and down the highway."

Elisa brought him a fifty-cent piece from the house and dropped it in his hand. "You might be surprised to have a rival some time. I can sharpen scissors, too. And I can beat the dents out of little pots. I could show you what a woman might do."

He put his hammer back in the oily box and shoved the little anvil out of sight. "It would be a lonely life for a woman, ma'am, and a scarey life, too, with animals creeping under the wagon all night." He climbed over the singletree,[5] steadying himself with a hand on the burro's white rump. He settled himself in the seat, picked up the lines. "Thank you kindly, ma'am," he said. "I'll do like you told me; I'll go back and catch the Salinas road."

"Mind," she called, "if you're long in getting there, keep the sand damp."

"Sand, ma'am? . . . Sand? Oh, sure. You mean around the chrysantheums. Sure I will." He clucked his tongue. The beasts leaned luxuriously into their collars. The mongrel dog took his place between the back wheels. The wagon turned and crawled out the entrance road and back the way it had come, along the river.

---

5 **singletree:** a crossbar between an animal and the wagon or plow it pulls.

Elisa stood in front of her wire fence watching the slow progress of the caravan. Her shoulders were straight, her head thrown back, her eyes half-closed, so that the scene came vaguely into them. Her lips moved silently, forming the words "Good-by—good-by." Then she whispered, "That's a bright direction. There's a glowing there." The sound of her whisper startled her. She shook herself free and looked about to see whether anyone had been listening. Only the dogs had heard. They lifted their heads toward her from their sleeping in the dust, and then stretched out their chins and settled asleep again. Elisa turned and ran hurriedly into the house.

In the kitchen she reached behind the stove and felt the water tank. It was full of hot water from the noonday cooking. In the bathroom she tore off her soiled clothes and flung them into the corner. And then she scrubbed herself with a little block of pumice, legs and thighs, loins and chest and arms, until her skin was scratched and red. When she had dried herself she stood in front of a mirror in her bedroom and looked at her body. She tightened her stomach and threw out her chest. She turned and looked over her shoulder at her back.

After a while she began to dress, slowly. She put on her newest underclothing and her nicest stockings and the dress which was the symbol of her prettiness. She worked carefully on her hair, penciled her eyebrows and rouged her lips.

Before she was finished she heard the little thunder of hoofs and the shouts of Henry and his helper as they drove the red steers into the corral. She heard the gate bang shut and set herself for Henry's arrival.

His step sounded on the porch. He entered the house calling, "Elisa, where are you?"

"In my room, dressing. I'm not ready. There's hot water for your bath. Hurry up. It's getting late."

When she heard him splashing in the tub, Elisa laid his dark suit on the bed, and shirt and socks and tie beside it. She stood his polished shoes on the floor beside the bed. Then she went to the porch and sat primly and stiffly down. She looked toward the river road where the willow line was still yellow with frosted leaves so that under the high gray fog they seemed a thin band of sunshine. This was the only color in the gray afternoon. She sat unmoving for a long time. Her eyes blinked rarely.

Henry came banging out of the door, shoving his tie inside his vest as he came. Elisa stiffened and her face grew tight. Henry stopped short and looked at her. "Why—why, Elisa. You look so nice!"

"Nice? You think I look nice? What do you mean by 'nice'?"

Henry blundered on. "I don't know. I mean you look different, strong and happy."

"I am strong? Yes, strong. What do you mean 'strong'?"

He looked bewildered. "You're playing some kind of a game," he said helplessly. "It's a kind of a play. You look strong enough to break a calf over your knee, happy enough to eat it like a watermelon."

For a second she lost her rigidity. "Henry! Don't talk like that. You didn't know what you said." She grew complete again. "I'm strong," she boasted. "I never knew before how strong."

Henry looked down toward the tractor shed, and when he brought his eyes back to her, they were his own again. "I'll get out the car. You can put on your coat while I'm starting."

Elisa went into the house. She heard him drive to the gate and idle down his motor, and then she took a long time to put on her hat. She pulled it here and pressed it there. When Henry turned the motor off she slipped into her coat and went out.

The little roadster bounced along on the dirt road by the river, raising the birds and driving the rabbits into the brush. Two cranes flapped heavily over the willow line and dropped into the river bed.

Far ahead on the road Elisa saw a dark speck. She knew.

She tried not to look as they passed it, but her eyes would not obey. She whispered to herself sadly. "He might have thrown them off the road. That wouldn't have been much trouble, not very much. But he kept the pot," she explained. "He had to keep the pot. That's why he couldn't get them off the road."

The roadster turned a bend and she saw the caravan ahead. She swung full around toward her husband so she could not see the little covered wagon and the mismatched team as the car passed them.

In a moment it was over. The thing was done. She did not look back.

She said loudly, to be heard above the motor, "It will be good, tonight, a good dinner."

"Now you're changed again," Henry complained. He took one hand from the wheel and patted her knee. "I ought to take you in to dinner oftener. It would be good for both of us. We get so heavy out on the ranch."

"Henry," she asked, "could we have wine at dinner?"

"Sure we could. Say! That will be fine."

She was silent for a while; then she said, "Henry, at those prize fights, do the men hurt each other very much?"

"Sometimes a little, not often. Why?"

"Well, I've read how they break noses, and blood runs down their chests. I've read how the fighting gloves get heavy and soggy with blood."

He looked around at her. "What's the matter, Elisa? I didn't know you read things like that." He brought the car to a stop, then turned to the right over the Salinas River bridge.

"Do any women ever go to the fights?" she asked.

"Oh, sure, some. What's the matter, Elisa? Do you want to go? I don't think you'd like it, but I'll take you if you really want to go."

She relaxed limply in the seat. "Oh, no. No. I don't want to go. I'm sure I don't." Her face was turned away from him. "It will be enough if we can have wine. It will be plenty." She turned up her coat collar so he could not see that she was crying weakly—like an old woman.

Study Questions

1. In the beginning of the story how is Elisa Allen characterized? How is her close connection with nature established? Describe her husband. What details suggest there is something lacking in their relationship?

2. The arrival of the repairman reveals another side of Elisa. How do her actions and remarks differ from those with her husband earlier?

3. How is Elisa affected by the repairman's visit? What does he represent to her? What emotions has his visit aroused in her?

4. After seeing the discarded plant shoots, Elisa realizes the repairman has exploited her dreams. Why does she ask detailed questions about the fights in which she had earlier shown no interest?

5. What do Elisa's tears mean? What does the final phrase, "like an old woman," mean?

Richard Wright   1908-1960

Richard Wright was born in Mississippi, where he suffered from oppression, poverty, and an unsettled family life. His education stopped at junior high school. Wright moved to Memphis in 1925 and there he began to read. From there he moved on to Chicago where he began his distinguished literary career. His novel, *Native Son* (1940), was the first by a Black writer to be selected as Book-of-the-Month. This gave Wright a kind of exposure previously denied to Black writers. The national attention also established him as a major influence on subsequent Afro-American writers. His other novels are: *The Outsider* (1953), *Savage Holiday* (1954), *The Long Dream* (1958), and *Lawd Today* (1963). Wright also wrote poetry, travel books, essays, and short stories. *Black Boy* (1945), an autobiography, is considered by some to be his best work. After 1947 he, like so many American writers before him, found an artistic and intellectual home in Paris.

"The Man Who Saw the Flood" was first published in 1937. It later appeared in Wright's collection of stories, *Eight Men* (1961). The short stories in that collection depict the harsh life with which Wright was so familiar. His restrained artistic portrayal of such bitter things shows why he became such a powerful writer.

The Man Who Saw the Flood

RICHARD WRIGHT

When the flood waters recede, the poor folk along the river start from scratch.

AT LAST the flood waters had receded. A black father, a black mother, and a black child tramped through muddy fields, leading a tired cow by a thin bit of rope. They stopped on a hilltop and shifted the bundles on their shoulders. As far as they could see the ground was covered with flood silt. The little girl lifted a skinny finger and pointed to a mud-caked cabin.

"Look, Pa! Ain tha our home?"

The man, round-shouldered, clad in blue, ragged overalls, looked with bewildered eyes.

Without moving a muscle, scarcely moving his lips, he said: "Yeah."

For five minutes they did not speak or move. The flood waters had been more than eight feet high here. Every tree, blade of grass, and stray stick had its flood mark; caky, yellow mud. It clung to the ground, cracking thinly here and there in spider web fashion. Over the stark fields came a gusty spring wind. The sky was high, blue, full of white clouds and sunshine. Over all hung a first-day strangeness.

"The henhouse is gone," sighed the woman.

"N the pigpen," sighed the man.

They spoke without bitterness.

"Ah reckon them chickens is all done drowned."

"Yeah."

"Miz Flora's house is gone, too," said the little girl.

They looked at a clump of trees where their neighbor's house had stood.

"Lawd!"

"Yuh reckon anybody knows where they is?"

"Hard t tell."

The man walked down the slope and stood uncertainly.

"There wuz a road erlong here somewheres," he said.

But there was no road now. Just a wide sweep of yellow, scalloped silt.

"Look, Tom!" called the woman. "Here's a piece of our gate!"

The gatepost was half buried in the ground. A rusty hinge stood stiff, like a lonely finger. Tom pried it loose and caught it firmly in his hand. There was nothing particular he wanted to do with it; he just stood holding it firmly. Finally he dropped it, looked up, and said:

"C mon. Les go down n see whut we kin do."

Because it sat in a slight depression, the ground about the cabin was soft and slimy.

"Gimme tha bag o lime, May," he said.

With his shoes sucking in mud, he went slowly around the cabin, spreading the white lime with thick fingers. When he reached the front again he had a little left; he shook the bag out on the porch. The fine grains of floating lime flickered in the sunlight.

"Tha oughta hep some," he said.

"Now, yuh be careful, Sal!" said May. "Don yuh go n fall down in all this mud, yuh hear?"

"Yessum."

The steps were gone. Tom lifted May and Sally to the porch. They stood a moment looking at the half-opened door. He had shut it when he left, but somehow it seemed natural that he should find it open. The planks in the porch floor were swollen and warped. The cabin had two colors; near the bottom it was a solid yellow; at the top it was the familiar gray. It looked weird, as though its ghost were standing beside it.

The cow lowed.

"Tie Pat t the pos on the en of the porch, May."

May tied the rope slowly, listlessly. When they attempted to open the front door, it would not budge. It was not until Tom placed his shoulder against it and gave it a stout shove that it scraped back jerkily. The front room was dark and silent. The damp smell of flood silt came fresh and sharp to their nostrils. Only one-half of the upper window was clear, and through it fell a rectangle of dingy light. The floors swam in ooze. Like a mute warning, a wavering flood mark went high around the walls of the room. A dresser sat cater-cornered, its drawers and sides bulging like a bloated corpse. The bed, with the mattress still on it, was like a giant casket forged of mud. Two smashed chairs lay in a corner, as though huddled together for protection.

"Les see the kitchen," said Tom.

The stovepipe was gone. But the stove stood in the same place.

"The stove's still good. We kin clean it."

"Yeah."

"But where's the table?"

"Lawd knows."

"It must've washed erway wid the rest of the stuff, Ah reckon."

They opened the back door and looked out. They missed the barn, the henhouse, and the pigpen.

"Tom, yuh bettah try tha ol pump n see ef eny watah's there."

The pump was stiff. Tom threw his weight on the handle and carried it up and down. No water came. He pumped on. There was a dry, hollow cough. The yellow water trickled. He caught his breath and kept pumping. The water flowed white.

"Thank Gawd! We's got some watah."

"Yuh bettah boil it fo yuh use it," he said.

"Yeah. Ah know."

"Look, Pa! Here's yo ax," called Sally.

Tom took the ax from her. "Yeah. Ah'll need this."

"N here's somethin else," called Sally, digging spoons out of the mud.

"Waal, Ahma git a bucket n start cleanin," said May. "Ain no use in waitin, cause we's gotta sleep on them floors tonight."

When she was filling the bucket from the pump, Tom called from around the cabin. "May, look! Ah done foun mah plow!" Proudly he dragged the silt-caked plow to the pump. "Ah'll wash it n it'll be awright."

"Ahm hongry," said Sally.

"Now, yuh jus wait! Yuh et this mawnin," said May. She turned to Tom. "Now, whutcha gonna do, Tom?"

He stood looking at the mud-filled fields.

"Yuh goin back t Burgess?"

"Ah reckon Ah have to."

"What else kin yuh do?"

"Nothin," he said. "Lawd, but Ah sho hate t start all over wid tha white man. Ah'd leave here ef Ah could. Ah owes im nigh eight hundred dollahs. N we needs a hoss, grub, seed, n a lot mo other things. Ef we keeps on like this tha white man'll own us body n soul."

"But there ain nothin else to do," she said.

"Ef we try t run erway they'll put us in jail."

"It coulda been worse," she said.

Sally came running from the kitchen. "Pa!"

"Hunh?"

"There's a shelf in the kitchen the flood didn git!"

"Where?"

"Right up over the stove."

"But, chile, ain nothin up there," said May.

"But there's somethin on it," said Sally.

"C mon. Les see."

High and dry, untouched by the flood-water, was a box of matches. And beside it a half-full sack of Bull Durham tobacco. He took a match from the box and scratched it on his overalls. It burned to his fingers before he dropped it.

"May!"

"Hunh?"

"Look! Here's ma bacco n some matches!"

She stared unbelievingly. "Lawd!" she breathed.

Tom rolled a cigarette clumsily.

May washed the stove, gathered some sticks, and after some difficulty, made a fire. The kitchen stove smoked, and their eyes smarted. May put water on to heat and went into the front room. It was getting dark. From the bundles they took a kerosene lamp and lit it. Outside Pat lowed longingly into the thickening gloam and tinkled her cowbell.

"Tha old cow's hongry," said May.

"Ah reckon Ah'll have t be gittin erlong t Burgess."

They stood on the front porch.

"Yuh bettah git on, Tom, fo its gits too dark."

"Yeah."

The wind had stopped blowing. In the east a cluster of stars hung.

"Yuh goin, Tom?"

"Ah reckon Ah have t."

"Ma, Ah'm hongry," said Sally.

"Wait erwhile, honey. Ma knows yuh's hongry."

Tom threw his cigarette away and sighed.

"Look! Here comes somebody!"

"Thas Mistah Burgess now!"

A mud-caked buggy rolled up. The shaggy horse was splattered all over. Burgess leaned his white face out of the buggy and spat.

"Well, I see you're back."

"Yessuh."

"How things look?"

"They don look so good, Mistah."

"What seems to be the trouble?"

"Waal. Ah ain got no hoss, no grub, nothing. The only thing Ah got is tha ol cow there . . ."

"You owe eight hundred dollahs down at the store, Tom."

"Yessuh, Ah know. But, Mistah Burgess, can't yuh knock somethin off of tha, seein as how Ahm down n out now?"

"You ate that grub, and I got to pay for it, Tom."

"Yessuh, Ah know."

"It's going to be a little tough, Tom. But you got to go through with it. Two of the boys tried to run away this morning and dodge their debts, and I had to have the sheriff pick em up. I wasn't looking for no trouble out of you, Tom . . . The rest of the families are going back."

Leaning out of the buggy, Burgess waited. In the surrounding stillness the cowbell tinkled again. Tom stood with his back against a post.

"Yuh got t go on, Tom. We ain't got nothin here," said May.

Tom looked at Burgess.

"Mistah Burgess, Ah don wanna make no trouble. But this is jus *too* hard. Ahm worse off now than befo. Ah got to start from scratch."

"Get in the buggy and come with me. I'll stake you with grub. We can talk over how you can pay it back." Tom said nothing. He rested his back against the post and looked at the mud-filled fields.

"Well," asked Burgess. "You coming?" Tom said nothing. He got slowly to the ground and pulled himself into the buggy. May watched them drive off.

"Hurry back, Tom!"

"Awright."

"Ma, tell Pa t bring me some 'lasses," begged Sally.

"Oh, Tom!"

Tom's head came out of the side of the buggy.

"Hunh?"

"Bring some 'lasses!"

"Hunh?"

"Bring some 'lasses for Sal!"

"Awright!"

She watched the buggy disappear over the crest of the muddy hill. Then she sighed, caught Sally's hand, and turned back into the cabin.

Study Questions

1. Why must the family move back into their ruined house?

2. Inside the house Wright compares the flood mark to "a mute warning," the dresser to "a bloated corpse," the bed to "a giant casket," and says the chairs seem to be "huddled together for protection." Why are these comparisons effective?

3. In what way is the mood at the end of the story different from the mood at the beginning? What details reveal this change?

4. His narrative is a flat statement of fact. The author offers a minimum of descriptive detail, and indulges in no editorial comment. Why do you think the author uses this method of telling the story?

Katherine Anne Porter   1890-1980

Katherine Anne Porter was born in Texas, but traveled extensively, particularly in Mexico and Germany. Both places provided settings for her fiction. Porter demanded a lot of herself as a writer. She destroyed or refused to publish much of what she produced because it failed to meet her standards. Over the years, however, she achieved an excellent reputation. She was awarded both the National Book Award and the Pulitzer Prize. Her work included *Flowering Judas* (1930) and *The Leaning Tower* (1944), both short-story collections. Other publications are *Pale Horse, Pale Rider* (1939) and *Noon Wine* (1937), containing novelettes; and the novel, *Ship of Fools* (1962). Porter's writing makes us feel more than she actually states. She creates by suggestion. This device apparently is achieved only through careful design and control of the right word in the right place. In the following story, for example, a dying woman recalls a lifetime which is confused by her half-conscious state.

The Jilting of Granny Weatherall

KATHERINE ANNE PORTER

SHE FLICKED HER WRIST neatly out of Doctor Harry's pudgy careful fingers and pulled the sheet up to her chin. The brat ought to be in knee breeches. Doctoring around the country with spectacles on his nose! "Get along now, take your schoolbooks and go. There's nothing wrong with me."

Doctor Harry spread a warm paw like a cushion on her forehead where the forked green vein danced and made her eyelids twitch. "Now, now, be a good girl, and we'll have you up in no time."

"That's no way to speak to a woman nearly eighty years old just because she's down. I'd have you respect your elders, young man."

"Well, Missy, excuse me." Doctor Harry patted her cheek. "But I've got to warn you, haven't I? You're a marvel, but you must be careful or you're going to be good and sorry."

"Don't tell me what I'm going to be. I'm on my feet now, morally speaking. It's Cornelia. I had to go to bed to get rid of her."

Her bones felt loose, and floated around in her skin, and Doctor Harry floated like a balloon around the foot of the bed. He floated and pulled down his waistcoat and swung his glasses on a cord. "Well, stay where you are, it certainly can't hurt you."

"Get along and doctor your sick," said Granny Weatherall. "Leave a well woman alone. I'll call for you when I want you. . . . Where were you forty years ago when I pulled through milk-leg[1] and double pneumonia? You weren't even born. Don't let Cornelia

---

1 milk-leg: swelling of the legs after childbirth.

lead you on," she shouted, because Doctor Harry appeared to float up to the ceiling and out. "I pay my own bills, and I don't throw my money away on nonsense!"

She meant to wave good-by, but it was too much trouble. Her eyes closed of themselves, it was like a dark curtain drawn around the bed. The pillow rose and floated under her, pleasant as a hammock in a light wind. She listened to the leaves rustling outside the window. No, somebody was swishing newspapers: no, Cornelia and Doctor Harry were whispering together. She leaped broad awake, thinking they whispered in her ear.

"She was never like this, *never* like this!" "Well, what can we expect?" "Yes, eighty years old. . . ."

Well, and what if she was? She still had ears. It was like Cornelia to whisper around doors. She always kept things secret in such a public way. She was always being tactful and kind. Cornelia was dutiful; that was the trouble with her. Dutiful and good: "So good and dutiful," said Granny, "that I'd like to spank her." She saw herself spanking Cornelia and making a fine job of it.

"What'd you say, Mother?"

Granny felt her face tying up in hard knots.

"Can't a body think, I'd like to know?"

"I thought you might want something."

"I do. I want a lot of things. First off, go away and don't whisper."

She lay and drowsed, hoping in her sleep that the children would keep out and let her rest a minute. It had been a long day. Not that she was tired. It was always pleasant to snatch a minute now and then. There was always so much to be done, let me see: tomorrow.

Tomorrow was far away and there was nothing to trouble about. Things were finished somehow when the time came; thank God there was always a little margin over for peace: then a person could spread out the plan of life and tuck in the edges orderly. It was good to have everything clean and folded away, with the hair brushes and tonic bottles sitting straight on the white embroidered linen: the day started without fuss and the pantry shelves laid out with rows of jelly glasses and brown jugs and white stone-china jars with blue whirligigs and words painted on them: coffee, tea, sugar, ginger, cinnamon, allspice: and the bronze clock with the lion on top nicely dusted off. The dust that lion could collect in twenty-four hours! The box in the attic with all those letters tied up, well, she'd have to go through that tomorrow. All those letters—George's letters and John's letters and her letters to them both—lying around for the children to find afterwards made her uneasy. Yes, that would be tomorrow's business. No use to let them know how silly she had been once.

While she was rummaging around she found death in her mind and it felt clammy and unfamiliar. She had spent so much time preparing for death there was no need for bringing it up again. Let it take care of itself now. When she was sixty she had felt very old, finished, and went around making farewell trips to see her children and grandchildren, with a secret in her mind: This is the very last of your mother, children! Then she made her will and came down with a long fever. That was all just a notion like a lot of other things, but it was lucky too, for she had once for all got over the idea of dying for a long time. Now she couldn't be worried. She hoped she had better sense now. Her father had lived to be one hundred and two years old and had drunk a noggin of strong hot toddy on his last birthday. He told the reporters it was his daily habit, and he owed his long life to that. He had made quite a scandal and was very pleased about it. She believed she'd just plague Cornelia a little.

"Cornelia! Cornelia!" No footsteps, but a sudden hand on her cheek. "Bless you, where have you been?"

"Here, Mother."

"Well, Cornelia, I want a noggin of hot toddy."

"Are you cold, darling?"

"I'm chilly, Cornelia. Lying in bed stops the circulation. I must have told you that a thousand times."

Well, she could just hear Cornelia telling her husband that Mother was getting a little childish and they'd have to humor her. The thing that most annoyed her was that Cornelia thought she was deaf, dumb, and blind. Little hasty glances and tiny gestures tossed around her and over her head saying, "Don't cross her, let her have her way, she's eighty years old," and she sitting there as if she lived in a thin glass cage. Sometimes Granny almost made up her mind to pack up and move back to her own house where nobody could remind her every minute that she was old. Wait, wait, Cornelia, till your own children whisper behind your back!

In her day she had kept a better house and had got more work done. She wasn't too old yet for Lydia to be driving eighty miles for advice when one of the children jumped the track, and Jimmy still dropped in and talked things over: "Now, Mammy, you've a good business head, I want to know what you think of this? . . ." Old. Cornelia couldn't change the furniture around without asking. Little things, little things! They had been so sweet when they were little. Granny wished the old days were back again with the children young and everything to be done over. It had been a hard pull, but not too much for her. When she thought of all the food she had cooked, and all the clothes she had cut and sewed, and all the gardens she had made—well, the children showed it. There they were, made out of her, and they couldn't get away from that. Sometimes she wanted to see John again and point to them and say, Well, I didn't do so badly, did I? But that would have to wait. That was for tomorrow. She used to think of him as a man, but now all the children were older than their father, and he would be a child beside her if she saw him now. It seemed strange and there was something wrong in the idea. Why, he couldn't possibly recognize her. She had fenced in a hundred acres once, digging the post holes herself and clamping the wires with just a Negro boy to help. That changed a woman. John would be looking for a young woman with the peaked Spanish comb in her hair and the painted fan. Digging post holes changed a woman. Riding country roads in the winter when women had their babies was another thing: sitting up nights with sick horses and sick Negroes and sick children and hardly ever losing one. John, I hardly ever lost one of them! John would see that in a minute, that would be something he could understand, she wouldn't have to explain anything!

It made her feel like rolling up her sleeves and putting the whole place to rights again. No matter if Cornelia was determined to be everywhere at once, there were a great many things left undone on this place. She would start tomorrow and do them. It was good to be strong enough for everything, even if all you made melted and changed and slipped under your hands, so that by the time you were finished you almost forgot what you were working for. What was it I set out to do? she asked herself intently, but she could not remember. A fog rose over the valley, she saw it marching across the creek swallowing the trees and moving up the hill like an army of ghosts. Soon it would be at the near edge of the orchard, and then it was time to go in and light the lamps. Come in, children, don't stay out in the night air.

Lighting the lamps had been beautiful. The children huddled up to her and breathed like little calves waiting at the bars in the twilight. Their eyes followed the match and watched the flame rise and settle in a blue curve, then they moved away from her. The lamp was lit, they didn't have to be scared and hang on to mother any more. God, for all my life I thank Thee. Without Thee, my God, I could never have done it. Hail, Mary, full of grace.

I want you to pick all the fruit this year and see that nothing is wasted. There's always someone who can use it. Don't let good things rot for want of using. You waste life when you waste good food. Don't let things get lost. It's bitter to lose things. Now, don't let me get to thinking, not when I am tired and taking a little nap before supper. . . .

The pillow rose about her shoulders and pressed against her heart and the memory was being squeezed out of it: oh, push down the pillow, somebody: it would smother her if she tried to hold it. Such a fresh breeze blowing and such a green day with no threats in it. But he had not come, just the same. What does a woman do when she has put on the white veil and set out the white cake for a man and he doesn't come? She tried to remember. No, I swear he never harmed me but in that. He never harmed me but in that . . . and what if

he did? There was the day, the day, but a whirl of dark smoke rose and covered it, crept up and over into the bright field where everything was planted so carefully in orderly rows. That was hell, she knew hell when she saw it. For sixty years she had prayed against remembering him and against losing her soul in the deep pit of hell, and now the two things were mingled in one and the thought of him was a smoky cloud from hell that moved and crept in her head when she had just got rid of Doctor Harry and was trying to rest a minute. Wounded vanity, Ellen, said a sharp voice in the top of her mind. Don't let your wounded vanity get the upper hand of you. Plenty of girls get jilted. You were jilted, weren't you? Then stand up to it. Her eyelids wavered and let in streamers of blue-gray light like tissue

paper over her eyes. She must get up and pull the shades down or she'd never sleep. She was in bed again and the shades were not down. How could that happen? Better turn over, hide from the light, sleeping in the light gave you nightmares. "Mother, how do you feel now?" and a stinging wetness on her forehead. But I don't like having my face washed in cold water!

Hapsy? George? Lydia? Jimmy? No, Cornelia, and her features were swollen and full of little puddles. "They're coming, darling, they'll all be here soon." Go wash your face, child, you look funny.

Instead of obeying, Cornelia knelt down and put her head on the pillow. She seemed to be talking but there was no sound. "Well, are you tongue-tied? Whose birthday is it? Are you going to give a party?"

Cornelia's mouth moved urgently in strange shapes. "Don't do that, you bother me, daughter."

"Oh, no, Mother. Oh, no. . . ."

Nonsense. It was strange about children. They disputed your every word. "No what, Cornelia?"

"Here's Doctor Harry."

"I won't see that boy again. He just left five minutes ago."

"That was this morning, Mother. It's night now. Here's the nurse."

"This is Doctor Harry, Mrs. Weatherall. I never saw you look so young and happy!"

"Ah, I'll never be young again—but I'd be happy if they'd let me lie in peace and get rested."

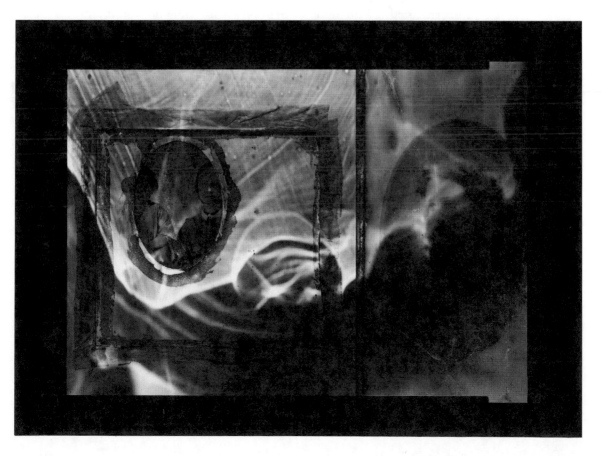

She thought she spoke up loudly, but no one answered. A warm weight on her forehead, a warm bracelet on her wrist, and a breeze went on whispering, trying to tell her something. A shuffle of leaves in the everlasting hand of God, He blew on them and they danced and rattled. "Mother, don't mind, we're going to give you a little hypodermic." "Look here, daughter, how do ants get in this bed? I saw sugar ants yesterday." Did you send for Hapsy too?

It was Hapsy she really wanted. She had to go a long way back through a great many rooms to find Hapsy standing with a baby on her arm. She seemed to herself to be Hapsy also, and the baby on Hapsy's arm was Hapsy and himself and herself, all at once, and there was no surprise in the meeting. Then Hapsy melted from within and turned flimsy as gray gauze and the baby was a gauzy shadow, and Hapsy came up close and said, "I thought you'd never come," and looked at her very searchingly and said, "You haven't changed a bit!" They leaned forward to kiss, when Cornelia began whispering from a long way off, "Oh, is there anything you want to tell me? Is there anything I can do for you?"

Yes, she had changed her mind after sixty years and she would like to see George. I want you to find George. Find him and be sure to tell him I forgot him. I want him to know I had my husband just the same and my children and my house like any other woman. A good house too and a good husband that I loved and fine children out of him. Better than I hoped for even. Tell him I was given back everything he took away and more. Oh, no, oh, God, no, there was something else besides the house and the man and the children. Oh, surely they were not all? What was it? Something not given back. . . . Her breath crowded down under her ribs and grew into a monstrous frightening shape with cutting edges; it bored up into her head, and the agony was unbelievable: Yes, John, get the Doctor now, no more talk, my time has come.

When this one was born it should be the

last. The last. It should have been born first, for it was the one she had truly wanted. Everything came in good time. Nothing left out, left over. She was strong, in three days she would be as well as ever. Better. A woman needed milk in her to have her full health.

"Mother, do you hear me?"

"I've been telling you—"

"Mother, Father Connolly's here."

"I went to Holy Communion only last week. Tell him I'm not so sinful as all that."

"Father just wants to speak to you."

He could speak as much as he pleased. It was like him to drop in and inquire about her soul as if it were a teething baby, and then stay on for a cup of tea and a round of cards and gossip. He always had a funny story of some sort, usually about an Irishman who made his little mistakes and confessed them, and the point lay in some absurd thing he would blurt out in his confessional showing his struggles between native piety and original sin. Granny felt easy about her soul. Cornelia, where are your manners? Give Father Connolly a chair. She had her secret comfortable understanding with a few favorite saints who cleared a straight road to God for her. All as surely signed and sealed as the papers for the new Forty Acres. Forever . . . heirs and assigns forever. Since the day the wedding cake was not cut, but thrown out and wasted. The whole bottom dropped out of the world, and there she was blind and sweating with nothing under her feet and the walls falling away. His hand had caught her under the breast, she had not fallen, there was the freshly polished floor with the green rug on it, just as before. He had cursed like a sailor's parrot and said, "I'll kill him for you." Don't lay a hand on him, for my sake leave something to God. "Now, Ellen, you must believe what I tell you. . . ."

So there was nothing to worry about anymore, except sometimes in the night one of the children screamed in a nightmare, and they both hustled out shaking and hunting for the matches and calling, "There, wait a minute, here we are!" John, get the doctor now, Hapsy's time has come. But there was Hapsy standing by the bed in a white cap. "Cornelia, tell Hapsy to take off her cap. I can't see her plain."

Her eyes opened very wide and the room stood out like a picture she had seen somewhere. Dark colors with the shadows rising towards the ceiling in long angles. The tall black dresser gleamed with nothing on it but John's picture, enlarged from a little one, with John's eyes very black when they should have been blue. You never saw him, so how do you know how he looked? But the man insisted the copy was perfect, it was very rich and handsome. For a picture, yes, but it's not my husband. The table by the bed had a linen cover and a candle and a crucifix. The light was blue from Cornelia's silk lampshades. No sort of light at all, just frippery. You had to live forty years with kerosene lamps to appreciate honest electricity. She felt very strong and she saw Doctor Harry with a rosy nimbus around him.

"You look like a saint, Doctor Harry, and I vow that's as near as you'll ever come to it."

"She's saying something."

"I heard you, Cornelia. What's all this carrying-on?"

"Father Connolly's saying—"

Cornelia's voice staggered and bumped like a cart in a bad road. It rounded corners and turned back again and arrived nowhere. Granny stepped up in the cart very lightly and reached for the reins, but a man sat beside her and she knew him by his hands, driving the cart. She did not look in his face, for she knew without seeing, but looked instead down the road where the trees leaned over and bowed to each other and a thousand birds were singing a Mass. She felt like singing too, but she put her hand in the bosom of her dress and pulled out a rosary, and Father Connolly murmered Latin in a very solemn voice and tickled her feet. My God, will you stop that nonsense? I'm a married woman. What if he did run away and leave me to face the priest by myself? I found

another a whole world better. I wouldn't have exchanged my husband for anybody except St. Michael himself, and you may tell him that for me with a thank you in the bargain.

Light flashed on her closed eyelids, and a deep roaring shook her. Cornelia, is that lightning? I hear thunder. There's going to be a storm. Close all the windows. Call the children in. . . . "Mother, here we are, all of us." "Is that you, Hapsy?" "Oh, no, I'm Lydia. We drove as fast as we could." Their faces drifted above her, drifted away. The rosary fell out of her hands and Lydia put it back. Jimmy tried to help, their hands fumbled together, and Granny closed two fingers around Jimmy's thumb. Beads wouldn't do, it must be something alive. She was so amazed her thoughts ran round and round. So, my dear Lord, this is my death and I wasn't even thinking about it. My children have come to see me die. But I can't, it's not time. Oh, I always hated surprises. I wanted to give Cornelia the amethyst set—Cornelia, you're to have the amethyst set, but Hapsy's to wear it when she wants, and, Doctor Harry, do shut up. Nobody sent for you. Oh, my dear Lord, do wait a minute. I meant to do something about the Forty Acres, Jimmy doesn't need it and Lydia will later on, with that worthless husband of hers. I meant to finish the altar cloth and send six bottles of wine to Sister Borgia for her dyspepsia. I want to send six bottles of wine to Sister Borgia, Father Connolly, now don't let me forget.

Cornelia's voice made short turns and tilted over and crashed. "Oh, Mother, oh, Mother, oh, Mother. . . ."

"I'm not going, Cornelia. I'm taken by surprise. I can't go."

You'll see Hapsy again. What about her? "I thought you'd never come." Granny made a long journey outward, looking for Hapsy. What if I don't find her? What then? Her heart sank down and down, there was no bottom to death, she couldn't come to the end of it. The blue light from Cornelia's lampshade drew into a tiny point in the center of her brain, it flickered and winked like an eye, quietly it fluttered and dwindled. Granny lay curled down within herself, amazed and watchful, staring at the point of light that was herself; her body was now only a deeper mass of shadow in an endless darkness and this darkness would curl around the light and swallow it up. God, give a sign!

For the second time there was no sign. Again no bridegroom and the priest in the house. She could not remember any other sorrow because this grief wiped them all away. Oh, no, there's nothing more cruel than this—I'll never forgive it. She stretched herself with a deep breath and blew out the light.

Study Questions

1. On the day of her death Granny Weatherall remembers, in jumbled fashion, the principal events of her eighty years of life. What are these events? Summarize them in chronological order.

2. What event overshadows all others in her memory? When did it occur? How does this event justify the title?

3. The story contains repeated references to darkness and to light. What do these references symbolize? What is the eerie light which Granny blows out at the end?

4. Granny's sense of time is different from Cornelia's. Find passages in which we become especially aware of the difference between the two. How is Granny's sense of time particularly effective in conveying the underlying meaning of her life?

Vocabulary

A **derivative** is a word formed on the basis of some other word. For example, *basic* and *basis* are derivatives of the word *base,* while *derivative* is based on the word *derive,* meaning "to get or to obtain." The following words are among the many English derivatives of the Latin word *specere,* which means "to look at":

circumspection	perspective	retrospect	spectator
disrespect	prospective	self-respect	spectral
inspection	respect	spectacles	suspect
introspection	respective	spectacular	unsuspecting

On a separate sheet of paper, name one word from this list that could replace the *italicized* phrase contained in each of the following sentences. If you are in doubt about the meaning of any word, consult a dictionary.

1. Katherine Anne Porter's story is written from Granny Weatherall's *way of looking at things* during the time the old woman lies on her deathbed.

2. Granny Weatherall's thoughts reflect the widespread belief that at such a time people review their lives in *a backward look.*

3. By far the most memorable highlight has been the cruel neglect of George, Granny Weatherall's once *looked-forward-to* bridegroom, to join her at the altar when their marriage was scheduled.

4. With neither *failure to look up* to John, the man she actually married, nor lack of appreciation for their children, Granny Weatherall has never been able to forget or forgive George.

5. As her mind grows more and more blurred, Granny yearns for solitude, feeling that rest and *the process of looking inward* will enable her to sort out her thoughts once more.

6. She resents such well-intentioned intrusions as Cornelia's whispering, Father Connoly's gossiping, and Dr. Harry's swinging his *eye-glasses* idly on their cord.

7. The one person Granny Weatherall really longs to see is her daughter Hapsy, who is already dead, but whose *ghostly looking* form seems to materialize at the bedside.

8. Granny Weatherall gradually begins to *look about with the distrustful thought* that death will claim her before she has announced who is to inherit her Forty Acres and who is to wear her amethyst set.

9. *Looking at such matters with caution* has already made Granny decide to destroy her collection of letters from John and George so that the children can never read them; but it is too late to do that.

10. During her final moments, Granny Weatherall feels the last sharp pangs of grief and humiliation about the jilting, which has so deeply affected her *way of looking at herself* ever since it happened.

E. B. White   1899-

E. B. (Elwyn Brooks) White was born in Mount Vernon, New York, and educated at Cornell University. After serving as a private in World War I, he began his writing career as a reporter for *The Seattle Times.* He returned to New York City in the 1920s and became a staff writer for *The New Yorker* magazine. His wise and funny capsule essays distinguished the "Talk of the Town" section of that magazine for many years.

White's variety of books includes—besides collections of his essays such as *One Man's Meat* (1942) and *The Points of My Compass* (1962)—two fantasies enjoyed by adults as well as children, *Charlotte's Web* (1952) and *Stuart Little* (1945).

In the essay included here White looks closely at the kinds of attitudes that allowed the ideals of the Nazi party and Hitler to flourish in the 1940s.

Freedom——July, 1940

E. B. WHITE

I HAVE OFTEN NOTICED on my trips up to the city that people have recut their clothes to follow the fashion. On my last trip, however, it seemed to me that people had remodeled their ideas too—taken in their convictions a little at the waist, shortened the sleeves of their resolve, and fitted themselves out in a new intellectual ensemble copied from a smart design out of the very latest page of history. It seemed to me they had strung along with Paris a little too long.

I confess to a disturbed stomach. I feel sick when I find anyone adjusting his mind to the new tyranny which is succeeding abroad. Because of its fundamental strictures, fascism does not seem to me to admit of any compromise or any rationalization, and I resent the patronizing air of persons who find in my plain belief in freedom a sign of immaturity. If it is boyish to believe that a human being should live free, then I'll gladly arrest my development and let the rest of the world grow up.

I shall report some of the strange remarks I heard in New York. One man told me that he thought perhaps the Nazi ideal was a sounder ideal than our constitutional system "because have you ever noticed what fine alert young faces the young German soldiers have in the news-reel?" He added: "Our American youngsters spend all their time at the movies—they're a mess." That was his summation of the case, his interpretation of the new Europe. Such a remark leaves me pale and shaken. If it represents the peak of our intelligence, then the steady march of despotism will not receive any considerable setback at our shores.

Another man informed me that our democratic notion of popular government was decadent and not worth bothering about—"because England is really rotten and the industrial towns there are a disgrace." That was the only reason he gave for the hopelessness of democracy; and he seemed mightily pleased with himself, as though he were more familiar than most with the anatomy of decadence, and had detected subtler aspects of the situation than were discernible to the rest of us.

Another man assured me that anyone who took *any* kind of government seriously was a gullible fool. You could be sure, he said, that there is nothing but corruption "because of the way Clemenceau acted at Versailles."[1] He said it didn't make any difference really about this war. It was just another war. Having relieved himself of this majestic bit of reasoning, he subsided.

Another individual, discovering signs of zeal creeping into my blood, berated me for having lost my detachment, my pure skeptical point of view. He announced that he wasn't going to be swept away by all this nonsense, but would prefer to remain in the role of innocent bystander, which he said was the duty of any intelligent person. (I noticed, however, that he phoned later to qualify his remark, as though he had lost some of his innocence in the cab on the way home.)

Those are just a few samples of the sort of talk that seemed to be going round—talk which was full of defeatism and disillusion and sometimes of a too studied innocence. Men are not merely annihilating themselves at a great rate these days, but they are telling one another enormous lies, grandiose fibs. Such remarks as I heard are fearfully disturbing in their cumulative effect. They are more destructive than dive bombers and mine fields, for they challenge not merely one's immediate position but one's main defenses. They seemed to me to issue either from persons who could never have really come to grips with freedom, so as to understand her, or from renegades. Where I expected to find indignation, I found paralysis, or a sort of dim acquiescence, as in a child who is dully swallowing a distasteful pill. I was advised of the growing anti-Jewish sentiment by a man who seemed to be watching the phenomenon of intolerance not through tears of shame but with a clear intellectual gaze, as through a well-ground lens.

The least a man can do at such a time is to declare himself and tell where he stands. I believe in freedom with the same burning delight, the same faith, the same intense abandon which attended its birth on this continent more than a century and a half ago. I am writing my declaration rapidly, much as though I were shaving to catch a train. Events abroad give a man a feeling of being pressed for time. Actually I do not believe I am pressed for time, and I apologize to the reader for a false impression that may be created. I just want to tell, before I get slowed down, that I am in love with freedom and that it is an affair of long standing and that it is a fine state to be in, and that I am deeply suspicious of people who are beginning to adjust to fascism and dictators merely because they are succeeding in war. From such adaptable natures a smell rises. I pinch my nose.

For as long as I can remember I have had a sense of living somewhat freely in a natural world. I don't mean I enjoyed freedom of action, but my existence seemed to have the quality of free-ness. I traveled with secret papers pertaining to a divine conspiracy. Intuitively I've always been aware of the vitally important pact which a man has with himself, to be all things to himself, and to be identified with all things, to stand self-reliant, taking advantage of his haphazard connection with a planet, riding his luck, and following his bent with the tenacity of a hound. My first and

---

1 **Clemenceau . . . Versailles** (klem′ ən sō)(ver sī′): Georges Clemenceau (1841–1929), Premier of France when treaty was signed at end of World War I in Versailles, France.

greatest love affair was with this thing we call freedom, this lady of infinite allure, this dangerous and beautiful sublime being who restores and supplies us all.

It began with the haunting intimation (which I presume every child receives) of his mystical inner life; of God in man; of nature publishing herself through the "I." This elusive sensation is moving and memorable. It comes early in life: a boy, we'll say, sitting on the front steps on a summer night, thinking of nothing in particular, suddenly hearing as with a new perception and as though for the first time the pulsing sound of crickets, overwhelmed with the novel sense of identification with the natural company of insects and grass and night, conscious of a faint answering cry to the universal perplexing question: "What is 'I'?" Or a little girl, returning from the grave of a pet bird leaning with her elbows on the windowsill, inhaling the unfamiliar draught of death, suddenly seeing herself as part of the complete story. Or to an older youth, encountering for the first time a great teacher who by some chance word or mood awakens something and the youth beginning to breathe as an individual and conscious of strength in his vitals. I think the sensation must develop in many men as a feeling of identity with God—an eruption of the spirit caused by allergies and the sense of divine existence as distinct from mere animal existence. This is the beginning of the affair with freedom.

But a man's free condition is of two parts: the instinctive freeness he experiences as an animal dweller on a planet, and the practical liberties he enjoys as a privileged member of human society. The latter is, of the two, more generally understood, more widely admired, more violently challenged and discussed. It is the practical and apparent side of freedom. The United States, almost alone today, offers the liberties and the privileges and the tools of freedom. In this land the citizens are still invited to write their plays and books, to paint their pictures, to meet for discussion, to dissent as well as to agree, to mount soapboxes in the public square, to enjoy education in all subjects without censorship, to hold court and judge one another, to compose music, to talk politics with their neighbors without wondering whether the secret police are listening, to exchange ideas as well as goods, to kid the government when it needs kidding, and to read real news of real events instead of phony news manufactured by a paid agent of the state. This is a fact and should give every person pause.

To be free, in a planetary sense, is to feel that you belong to earth. To be free, in a social sense, is to feel at home in a democratic framework. In Adolf Hitler, although he is a freely flowering individual, we do not detect either type of sensibility. From reading his book I gather that his feeling for earth is not a sense of communion but a driving urge to prevail. His feeling for men is not that they co-exist, but that they are capable of being arranged and standardized by a superior intellect—that their existence suggests not a fulfillment of their personalities but a submersion of the personalities in the common racial destiny. His very great absorption in the destiny of the German people somehow loses some of its effect when you discover, from his writings, in what vast contempt he holds all people. "I learned," he wrote, ". . . to gain an insight into the unbelievably primitive opinions and arguments of the people." To him the ordinary man is a primitive, capable only of being used and led. He speaks continually of people as sheep, halfwits, and impudent fools—the same people from whom he asks the utmost in loyalty, and to whom he promises the ultimate in prizes.

Here in America, where our society is based on belief in the individual, not contempt for him, the free principle of life has a chance of surviving. I believe that it must and will survive. To understand freedom is an accomplishment which all men may acquire who set their minds in that direction; and to love freedom is a tendency which many Americans are born with. To live in the same room with freedom, or in the same hemisphere, is still a profoundly shaking experience for me.

One of the earliest truths (and to him most valuable) that the author of *Mein Kampf*[2] discovered was that it is not the written word, but the spoken word, which in heated moments moves great masses of people to noble or ignoble action. The written word, unlike the spoken word, is something which every person examines privately and judges calmly by his own intellectual standards, not by what the man standing next to him thinks. "I know," wrote Hitler, "that one is able to win people far more by the spoken than by the written word. . . ." Later he adds contemptuously: "For let it be said to all knights of the pen and to all the political dandies, especially of today: the greatest changes in this world have never yet been brought about by a goose quill![3] No, the pen has always been reserved to motivate these changes theoretically."

Luckily I am not out to change the world—that's being done for me, and at a great clip. But I know that the free spirit of man is persistent in nature; it recurs, and has never successfully been wiped out, by fire or flood. I set down the above remarks merely (in the words of Mr. Hitler) to motivate that spirit, theoretically. Being myself a knight of the goose quill, I am under no misapprehension about "winning people"; but I am inordinately proud these days of the quill, for it has shown itself, historically, to be the hypodermic which inoculates men and keeps the germ of freedom always in circulation, so that there are individuals in every time in every land who are the carriers, the Typhoid Mary's, capable of infecting others by mere contact and example. These persons are feared by every tyrant—who shows his fear by burning the books and destroying the individuals. A writer goes about his task today with the extra satisfaction which comes from knowing that he will be the first to have his head lopped off—even before the political dandies. In my own case this is a double satisfaction, for if freedom were denied me by force of earthly circumstance, I am the same as dead and would infinitely prefer to go into fascism without my head than with it, having no use for it any more and not wishing to be saddled with so heavy an encumbrance.

---

2 *Mein Kampf* (mīn kä mf): book by Hitler setting forth his doctrine and program; it was regarded by some people as the "Bible" of the Nazi Party.
3 goose quill: a writing pen made from a hollow feather of a goose.

Study Questions

1. What is "the new tyranny" about which White is so concerned?
2. What four arguments for the new tyranny does White encounter?
3. After discussing the ways people find to excuse tyranny, White says scornfully, "From such adaptable natures a smell arises." What do you think he means?
4. Explain the distinction White makes between "planetary" and "social" freedom. How does this distinction relate to the essential form of American society?
5. How, according to White, does Hitler misunderstand the role of the writer? What is White's special satisfaction as a writer?

6. As an indicator of how the written word persists through the years, this essay contains allusions to both Thomas Jefferson and Ralph Waldo Emerson. What are these allusions?

7. In what ways does this essay reinforce the themes of The Individual and The American Dream?

Vocabulary

A. By the time American students are graduated from high school, most of them are able to define the **suffix** -ism as a "a belief, a theory, a system, or a principle." With whatever assistance you may need from a dictionary, give a clear definition of the specific *type* of belief, theory, system, or principle denoted by each of these words:

capitalism   communism   fascism   socialism

Write your answers on a separate sheet of paper. In each definition, underline the word *belief, theory, system,* or *principle*—or any other word(s) used to substitute for one of these terms.

B. Besides (1) "belief, theory, system, or principle," *The American Heritage Dictionary* gives four more definitions for the suffix -ism:
(2) action, practice, or process *(favoritism, terrorism)*
(3) state or condition of being *(parallelism, pauperism)*
(4) characteristic behavior or quality *(heroism, individualism)*
(5) distinctive usage, especially of language *(malapropism, Latinism)*

On a separate sheet of paper, copy the following words:

Americanism	despotism	rationalism
defeatism	primitivism	skepticism

After each word, write the number(s) of any definition(s) listed above for the suffix -ism that apply to the term. In most cases, more than one definition will apply. Consult a dictionary to make sure that you include all the definitions.

Edwin Arlington Robinson   1869-1935

Edwin Arlington Robinson grew up in Gardiner, Maine. His father's death cut short his education. For a number of years after this he wrote poetry while barely supporting himself in various jobs. In 1905 President Theodore Roosevelt gave him an appointment in the New York Custom House. Robinson resigned this position after four years and from then on writing was his occupation. He won three Pulitzer Prizes.

Today Robinson is best known for his series of short poems depicting the inner lives of the people in Tilbury Town. This imaginary place is patterned on his own home town. In each poem Robinson creates a character portrait that combines psychological insight with striking poetic images. Richard Cory is one of the more memorable inhabitants of Tilbury Town. He is a man who has everything—or so it's thought.

Richard Cory

EDWIN ARLINGTON ROBINSON

Whenever Richard Cory went down town,
We people on the pavement looked at him:
He was a gentleman from sole to crown,
Clean favored, and imperially slim.

And he was always quietly arrayed,   5
And he was always human when he talked;
But still he fluttered pulses when he said,
"Good-morning," and he glittered when he walked.

And he was rich—yes, richer than a king—
And admirably schooled in every grace: 10
In fine, we thought that he was everything
To make us wish that we were in his place.

So on we worked, and waited for the light,
And went without the meat, and cursed the bread;
And Richard Cory, one calm summer night,   15
Went home and put a bullet through his head.

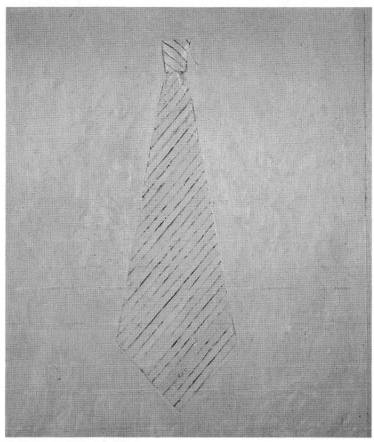

FLESH STRIPED TIE *Jim Dine*

Study Questions

1. In the first three stanzas from what point of view is Richard Cory seen? Why does Robinson use "we" instead of "I"?

2. What do each of the following phrases tell you about Richard Cory: "quietly arrayed," "human when he talked," "fluttered pulses," "glittered when he walked," "admirably schooled in every grace"?

3. In lines 13 and 14 what kind of life do the townspeople lead? What is the nature of their goals? "the light" for which they wait? Do they think Richard Cory is waiting for "the light" too?

4. What is the tone of the final two lines? What do these two lines and the poem as a whole say about appearance and reality? What was missing in Richard Cory's life?

Amy Lowell 1874-1925

Amy Lowell, born in a Boston suburb, belonged to a wealthy and distinguished old Massachusetts family. Her Brookline home was called Sevenels (seven "Ls") for the seven Lowells who had owned it. But beyond her social standing, she was a formidable poet. Her career began when she met Ezra Pound, the originator of a poetic movement known as Imagism. The Imagist creed called for "poetry that is hard and clear," emphasizing the language of common speech, the exact word, and the exact image. Amy Lowell published eleven volumes of poetry in thirteen years (1912–1925). She became the leader of the Imagists in America. In her dramatic poems such as "Patterns" (below), images are used to reflect the emotions of a character. Although she has selected the images carefully, she makes them appear to be the result of free association on the part of the poem's character—one image suggesting and sliding into another as it would in a person's mind.

THE JACKET *Bernard Perlin* 1951

Patterns

AMY LOWELL

I walk down the garden paths,
And all the daffodils
Are blowing, and the bright blue squills.[1]
I walk down the patterned garden paths
In my stiff, brocaded gown.   5
With my powdered hair and jeweled fan,
I too am a rare
Pattern. As I wander down
The garden paths.

1 **squills:** lily-like flowers.

My dress is richly figured,   10
And the train
Makes a pink and silver stain
On the gravel, and the thrift[2]
Of the borders.
Just a plate of current fashion,   15
Tripping by in high-heeled, ribboned shoes.
Not a softness anywhere about me,
Only whalebone[3] and brocade.
And I sink on a seat in the shade
Of a lime tree. For my passion   20
Wars against the stiff brocade.
The daffodils and squills
Flutter in the breeze
As they please.
And I weep;   25
For the lime tree is in blossom
And one small flower has dropped upon my bosom.

And the plashing of waterdrops
In the marble fountain
Comes down the garden paths.   30
The dripping never stops.
Underneath my stiffened gown
Is the softness of a woman bathing in a marble basin,
A basin in the midst of hedges grown
So thick, she cannot see her lover hiding,   35
But she guesses he is near,
And the sliding of the water
Seems the stroking of a dear
Hand upon her.
What is Summer in a fine brocaded gown!   40
I should like to see it lying in a heap upon the ground.
All the pink and silver crumpled up on the ground.

I would be the pink and silver as I ran along the paths,
And he would stumble after,
Bewildered by my laughter.   45
I should see the sun flashing from his sword hilt and the
    buckles on his shoes.
I would choose
To lead him in a maze along the patterned paths,
A bright and laughing maze for my heavy-booted lover.

---

2 **thrift**: pink or white flowers.
3 **whalebone**: corset stiffening.

Till he caught me in the shade,   50
And the buttons of his waistcoat bruised my body as he clasped me,
Aching, melting, unafraid.
With the shadows of the leaves and the sundrops,
And the plopping of the waterdrops,
All about us in the open afternoon—   55
I am very like to swoon
With the weight of this brocade,
For the sun sifts through the shade.

Underneath the fallen blossom
In my bosom,   60
Is a letter I have hid.
It was brought to me this morning by a rider from the Duke.
"Madam, we regret to inform you that Lord Hartwell
Died in action Thursday se'nnight."
As I read it in the white, morning sunlight,   65
The letters squirmed like snakes.
"Any answer, Madam," said my footman.
"No," I told him.
"See that the messenger takes some refreshment.
No, no answer."   70
And I walked into the garden,
Up and down the patterned paths,
In my stiff, correct brocade.
The blue and yellow flowers stood up proudly in the sun,
Each one.   75
I stood upright too,
Held rigid to the pattern
By the stiffness of my gown.
Up and down I walked,
Up and down.   80

In a month he would have been my husband.
In a month, here, underneath this lime,
We would have broke the pattern;
He for me, and I for him,
He as Colonel, I as Lady,   85
On this shady seat.
He had a whim
That sunlight carried blessing.
And I answered, "It shall be as you have said."
Now he is dead.   90

In Summer and in Winter I shall walk
Up and down
The patterned garden paths
In my stiff, brocaded gown.
The squills and daffodils   95
Will give place to pillared roses, and to asters, and to snow.
I shall go
Up and down
In my gown.
Gorgeously arrayed,   100
Boned and stayed.
And the softness of my body will be guarded from embrace
By each button, hook, and lace.
For the man who should loose me is dead,
Fighting with the Duke in Flanders,   105
In a pattern called a war.
Christ! What are patterns for?

Study Questions

1. More than half way through the poem we discover why the speaker is upset. What is the news she has received?

2. The theme, "patterns," is repeated throughout the poem. In the first two stanzas the speaker is aware of what two visual patterns? What kind of pattern is referred to in lines 76–78? What pattern would have been broken in line 83? How is war also a pattern (line 106)?

3. How does the question in the last line sum up the speaker's feelings?

Carl Sandburg   1878-1967

Of the many contemporary poets who have sounded, as Whitman said, their "barbaric yawp over the roofs of the world," few secured a larger audience than Carl Sandburg. The child of Swedish immigrant parents in Galesburg, Illinois, he began at the age of thirteen to work at a variety of jobs. He worked as a milk wagon driver, barbershop porter, field hand, dishwasher, theatrical scene-shifter, brickyard trucker, soldier— occupations which enabled him to write authentically about the American worker. His first acclaim as a poet came in 1914 with the publication of "Chicago." From then on his fame increased rapidly as a poet, novelist, biographer of Lincoln, singer and collector of folk songs, and movie scenarist. His *Complete Poems* was awarded the Pulitzer Prize in 1951. His poetry is full of robust, throbbing praise for the vital city life and of American democracy, as evidenced in the following poems.

Chicago

CARL SANDBURG

Hog Butcher for the World,
Tool Maker, Stacker of Wheat,
Player with Railroads and the Nation's Freight Handler;
Stormy, husky, brawling,
City of the Big Shoulders: 5
They tell me you are wicked and I believe them, for I have seen
    your painted women under the gas lamps luring the farm boys.
And they tell me you are crooked and I answer: Yes, it is true I
    have seen the gunman kill and go free to kill again.
And they tell me you are brutal and my reply is: On the faces of
    women and children I have seen the marks of wanton hunger.
And having answered so I turn once more to those who sneer at this
    my city, and I give them back the sneer and say to them:
Come and show me another city with lifted head singing so proud to
    be alive and coarse and strong and cunning.   10

Flinging magnetic curses amid the toil of piling job on job, here is
    a tall bold slugger set vivid against the little soft cities;
Fierce as a dog with tongue lapping for action, cunning as a savage
    pitted against the wilderness,
        Bareheaded,
        Shoveling,
        Wrecking,   15
        Planning,
        Building, breaking, rebuilding,
Under the smoke, dust all over his mouth, laughing with white teeth,
Under the terrible burden of destiny laughing as a young man laughs,
Laughing even as an ignorant fighter laughs who has never lost a battle,   20
Bragging and laughing that under his wrist is the pulse, and under
    his ribs the heart of the people,
          Laughing!
Laughing the stormy, husky, brawling laughter of Youth, half-naked,
    sweating, proud to be Hog Butcher, Tool Maker, Stacker of
    Wheat, Player with Railroads and Freight Handler to the Nation.

"The people will live on"

CARL SANDBURG

    The people will live on.
The learning and blundering people will live on.
    They will be tricked and sold and again sold
And go back to the nourishing earth for rootholds,
    The people so peculiar in renewal and comeback,   5
    You can't laugh off their capacity to take it.
The mammoth rests between his cyclonic dramas.

The people so often sleepy, weary, enigmatic,
is a vast huddle with many units saying:
    "I earn my living.   10
    I make enough to get by
    and it takes all my time.
    If I had more time
    I could do more for myself
    and maybe for others.   15

I could read and study
and talk things over
and find out about things.
It takes time.
I wish I had the time."   20

The people is a tragic and comic two-face:
hero and hoodlum: phantom and gorilla twisting to moan with a gargoyle mouth: "They
buy me and sell me . . . it's a game . . .
sometime I'll break loose . . ."   25

    Once having marched
Over the margins of animal necessity,
Over the grim line of sheer subsistence
    Then man came
To the deeper rituals of his bones,   30
To the lights lighter than any bones,
To the time for thinking things over,
To the dance, the song, the story,
Or the hours given over to dreaming,
    Once having so marched.   35

Between the finite limitations of the five senses
and the endless yearnings of man for the beyond
the people hold to the humdrum bidding of work and food
while reaching out when it comes their way
for lights beyond the prism of the five senses,   40
for keepsakes lasting beyond any hunger or death.
    This reaching is alive.
The panderers and liars have violated and smutted it.
    Yet this reaching is alive yet
    for lights and keepsakes.   45

    The people know the salt of the sea
    and the strength of the winds
    lashing the corners of the earth.
    The people take the earth
    as a tomb of rest and a cradle of hope.   50
    Who else speaks for the Family of Man?[1]

They are in tune and step
with constellations of universal law.

The people is a polychrome,[2]   55
a spectrum and a prism

---

1 **Family of Man:** a book of photographs edited by
Sandburg's brother-in-law, Edward Steichen.
2 **polychrome:** something multicolored.

held in a moving monolith,
a console organ of changing themes,
a clavilux[3] of color poems
wherein the sea offers fog
and the fog moves off in rain   60
and the labrador sunset shortens
to a nocturne of clear stars
serene over the shot spray
of northern lights.

The steel mill sky is alive.   65
The fire breaks white and zigzag
shot on a gun-metal gloaming.

3 clavilux: a device for showing patterns of color on a
screen.

Man is a long time coming.
Man will yet win.
Brother may yet line up with brother: 70

This old anvil laughs at many broken hammers.
There are men who can't be bought.
The fireborn are at home in fire.
The stars make no noise.
You can't hinder the wind from blowing.   75
Time is a great teacher.
Who can live without hope?

In the darkness with a great bundle of grief
    the people march.
In the night, and overhead a shovel of stars for   80
    keeps, the people march:
        "Where to? what next?"

Study Questions

Chicago

1. Identify the "you" in line 6.
2. Why is the city "wicked," "crooked," and "brutal"?
3. Beginning with line 10, to whom is the poem addressed?
4. What are the good qualities of the city which offset the bad ones?

"The people will live on"

1. When do you first know that "people" means working people who struggle for existence?
2. What evidence is there in the poem that the people have dreams which help them endure present hardships?
3. Explain the "lights" and "keepsakes" in lines 36–45.
4. Is the poem optimistic or pessimistic about the future of ordinary people?

Composition

1. Write an essay in which you compare Richard Cory with the people described in "The people will live on." Tell how they are similar and how they differ. Use examples from the poems to support your points. End by telling whom you most or least admire.
2. The poems by Robinson, Lowell and Sandburg all deal with people. Write a description of someone you know who resembles one of the persons being described in the poems. Tell which character your subject resembles. Describe your subject in enough detail so that the reader recognizes the similarity.

Robert Frost   1874-1963

Though Robert Frost was born in San Francisco, he returned to his ancestral New England at an early age. He has always been popularly associated with New England. During his long career he was both a farmer and a teacher but always chiefly a poet. In the last thirty years of his life Frost became unofficial poet laureate of the United States. This position almost became formal when he was invited to read at the Presidential inauguration in 1961 (see page 8). Such recognition was long in coming, however. Only after he had published his first book, *A*

Boy's Will, in England did Frost begin to have a reputation in his own country.

Frost wrote in a conversational style which made him seem more accessible than many modern poets. This apparently artless simplicity can be deceiving. His mind was both tough and subtle, and his view of life was not naively cheerful. Beneath the quiet surface of a poem like "Stopping by Woods," for example, can be glimpsed hidden depths and tensions. Likewise, this first poem "Departmental," is no mere comment on ants.

Departmental or, *My Ant Jerry*

ROBERT FROST

An ant on the table-cloth
Ran into a dormant moth
Of many times her size.
He showed not the least surprise.
His business wasn't with such.   5
He gave it scarcely a touch,
And was off on his duty run.
Yet if he encountered one
Of the hive's enquiry squad
Whose work is to find out God   10
And the nature of time and space,
He would put him onto the case.
Ants are a curious race;
One crossing with hurried tread
The body of one of their dead   15
Isn't given a moment's arrest—
Seems not even impressed.

But he no doubt reports to any
With whom he crosses antennae,
And they no doubt report   20
To the higher up at court.
Then word goes forth in Formic:
"Death's come to Jerry McCormic,
Our selfless forager Jerry.
Will the special Janizary   25
Whose office it is to bury
The dead of the commissary
Go bring him home to his people
Lay him in state on a sepal.[1]
Wrap him for shroud in a petal.   30
Embalm him with ichor of nettle.[2]
This is the word of your Queen."
And presently on the scene
Appears a solemn mortician;
And taking formal position   35
With feelers calmly atwiddle,
Seizes the dead by the middle,
And heaving him high in air,
Carries him out of there.
No one stands round to stare.   40
It is nobody else's affair.
It couldn't be called ungentle.
But how thoroughly departmental.

---

1 **sepal** (sē′pǝl): one of the leaf-like parts of a flower.
2 **ichor of nettle** (ī′kôr): fluid made of prickly leafed plant.
Ichor flowed in the veins of the gods in Greek mythology.

Study Questions

1. In line 13 Frost says, "Ants are a curious race," and then gives examples of ants in action. What do these examples tell you about the meaning of the word "curious"?

2. As a fable, this poem is intended to apply to people as well as ants. How does the behavior of the ants resemble that of people?

3. Some of the rhymes have an element of witty surprise in them: for example, squad/God, any/antennae, people/sepal. Find other examples of language which add to the satire. How does the rhythm of the poem also contribute to the tone?

Birches

ROBERT FROST

When I see birches bend to left and right
Across the lines of straighter darker trees,
I like to think some boy's been swinging them.
But swinging doesn't bend them down to stay
As ice storms do. Often you must have seen them   5
Loaded with ice a sunny winter morning
After a rain. They click upon themselves
As the breeze rises, and turn many-colored
As the stir cracks and crazes their enamel.
Soon the sun's warmth makes them shed crystal shells   10
Shattering and avalanching on the snow crust—
Such heaps of broken glass to sweep away
You'd think the inner dome of heaven had fallen.
They are dragged to the withered bracken by the load,
And they seem not to break; though once they are bowed   15
So low for long, they never right themselves:
You may see their trunks arching in the woods
Years afterwards, trailing their leaves on the ground
Like girls on hands and knees that throw their hair
Before them over their heads to dry in the sun.   20
But I was going to say when Truth broke in
With all her matter of fact about the ice storm,
I should prefer to have some boy bend them
As he went out and in to fetch the cows—
Some boy too far from town to learn baseball,   25
Whose only play was what he found himself,
Summer or winter, and could play alone.
One by one he subdued his father's trees
By riding them down over and over again
Until he took the stiffness out of them,   30
And not one but hung limp, not one was left
For him to conquer. He learned all there was
To learn about not launching out too soon
And so not carrying the tree away
Clear to the ground. He always kept his poise   35
To the top branches, climbing carefully
With the same pains you use to fill a cup

Up to the brim, and even above the brim.
Then he flung outward, feet first, with a swish,
Kicking his way down through the air to the ground.   40
So was I once myself a swinger of birches.
And so I dream of going back to be.
It's when I'm weary of considerations,
And life is too much like a pathless wood
Where your face burns and tickles with the cobwebs   45
Broken across it, and one eye is weeping
From a twig's having lashed across it open.
I'd like to get away from earth awhile
And then come back to it and begin over.
May no fate willfully misunderstand me   50
And half grant what I wish and snatch me away
Not to return. Earth's the right place for love:
I don't know where it's likely to go better.
I'd like to go by climbing a birch tree,
And climb black branches up a snow-white trunk   55
Toward heaven, till the tree could bear no more,
But dipped its top and set me down again.
That would be good both going and coming back.
One could do worse than be a swinger of birches.

Study Questions

1. The poet says that birch trees are bent by ice storms, which weigh them down, or by boys swinging on them. Which kind of bending does he prefer? Why?

2. After four introductory lines, the poem is divided into three sections— first, a word picture of birches after an ice storm; second, a description of how a boy swings on birches; and third, the poet's metaphorical interpretation. Identify each of these three sections, and point out which lines serve as transitions between the sections.

3. In the last section of the poem, what is the poet's comparison for life? What do you think he means by "considerations," "pathless," and "cobwebs"?

4. What does the poet say he would like to do when life becomes too complicated?

5. What is the significance of lines 50–52? Why do you think he italicizes "Toward" in line 56?

6. Why is the climbing of birch trees a suitable metaphor for what the poet wants to do?

Stopping by Woods on a Snowy Evening

ROBERT FROST

Whose woods these are I think I know
His house is in the village, though;
He will not see me stopping here
To watch his woods fill up with snow.

My little horse must think it queer   5
To stop without a farmhouse near
Between the woods and frozen lake
The darkest evening of the year.

He gives his harness bells a shake
To ask if there is some mistake.   10
The only other sound's the sweep
Of easy wind and downy flake.

The woods are lovely, dark and deep.
But I have promises to keep,
And miles to go before I sleep,   15
And miles to go before I sleep.

Study Questions

1. What is happening in this poem?
2. What is the contrast in the poem between the speaker and the horse?
3. The woods seem to have some special meaning for the speaker. What do you think it is?
4. What is the difference between the rhythm of the first two lines and the last two lines in the third stanza? How is the sound related to the meaning?
5. What is the effect of the repetition in the last two lines? Do you think "sleep" has the same meaning in each line?

Vocabulary

Each item below starts with two *italicized* words. Try to establish a relationship between those words. Then, from the five word-pairs which follow, choose the one which has the most similar relationship to that of the italicized words. You will be completing **verbal analogies**. Copy your answers on a separate sheet of paper.

1. *slim : thin* ::
   (a) earn : spend   (b) marble : fountain   (c) bow : low
   (d) rigid : stiff   (e) king : queen

2. *garden : flower* ::
   (a) heel : shoe   (b) union : laborer   (c) left : right
   (d) hammer : anvil   (e) dance : marsh

3. *rich : poor* ::
   (a) bee : moth   (b) mortician : undertaker
   (c) sleepy : weary   (d) smoke : dust   (e) up : down

4. *weeping : tear* ::
   (a) earth : heaven   (b) pork : butcher
   (c) spider : cobweb   (d) study : read   (e) shroud : embalm

5. *conquer : conquest* ::
   (a) pattern : patterned   (b) shovelfuls : shovel
   (c) subsist : subsistence   (d) ignorance : ignore
   (e) department : departmental

6. *build : wreck* ::
   (a) crooked : straight   (b) prism : spectrum
   (c) shatter : break   (d) star : noise   (e) stop : pause

7. *button : dress* ::
   (a) animal : horse   (b) summer : spring
   (c) dark : deep   (d) cup : brim   (e) freight car : railroad

8. *despair : suicide* ::
   (a) breeze : wind   (b) cloth : brocade   (c) afternoon : day
   (d) cold : snow   (e) lime : birch

9. *educated : schooled* ::
   (a) coarse : cunning   (b) tragic : comic
   (c) buy : sell   (d) bread : hunger   (e) destiny : fate

10. *tree : woods* ::
    (a) wish : grants   (b) ant : insects   (c) army : colonels
    (d) sit : walks   (e) gunman : bullets

William Carlos Williams   1883-1963

William Carlos Williams was the son of an English father and a Puerto Rican mother. He attended schools in New York and Geneva, Switzerland, and received a medical degree at the University of Pennsylvania. Then he returned to his home town of Rutherford, New Jersey, where he practiced medicine for the rest of his life. In addition to a thriving medical practice, he published over forty separate volumes of poetry, short stories, novels, and plays. Though originally his poetry was influenced by the Imagists (see p. 519), he later formed his own style. He experimented with varying kinds of internal verse structures. *Paterson,* his long verse masterpiece, envisions the epic development of that New Jersey town and its inhabitants as representative of modern times. *Paterson* also emphasizes the importance for Williams of particulars, the theme of "no ideas but in *things.*" The poem on the next page shows his concern for tangible objects, the sheer joy of things, the vivid awareness of sense impressions.

Spring and All: I

WILLIAM CARLOS WILLIAMS

By the road to the contagious-hospital
under the surge of the blue
mottled clouds driven from the
northeast—a cold wind. Beyond, the
waste of broad, muddy fields   5
brown with dried weeds, standing and fallen

patches of standing water
the scattering of tall trees

All along the road the reddish
purplish, forked, upstanding, twiggy   10
stuff of bushes and small trees
with dead, brown leaves under them
leafless vines—

Lifeless in appearance, sluggish
dazed spring approaches—   15

They enter the new world naked,
cold, uncertain of all
save that they enter. All about them
the cold, familiar wind—

Now the grass, tomorrow   20
the stiff curl of wildcarrot leaf

One by one objects are defined—
It quickens: clarity, outline of leaf

But now the stark dignity of
entrance—Still, the profound change   25
has come upon them: rooted they
grip down and begin to awaken

Study Questions

1. The first fifteen lines describe a spring landscape which the speaker calls "dazed" (line 15). Why is spring "dazed" or "lifeless"?

2. What does the pronoun "they" refer to in lines 16 and 26?

3. What is the change in spring described in lines 16–27?

4. The first section (ending with line 15) of the poem has no explicit verbs, while the second section does. How does this arrangement fit the subject matter of the two sections?

5. What else, besides nature, do you think the speaker might be thinking of as "awakening"?

Edna St. Vincent Millay   1892-1950

Edna St. Vincent Millay spent her childhood on the Maine coast and her college years at Vassar. She lived for five years in Greenwich Village in New York City during the 1920s. She supported herself by writing poems and stories and by acting. She spent the latter part of her life on a farm in New York state and continued to write poetry. In 1981, the U. S. Postal Service issued a commemorative stamp in Millay's honor. The following sonnet, with its bitter-sweet note of romance, is characteristic of her work.

"Pity me not because the light of day"

EDNA ST. VINCENT MILLAY

Pity me not because the light of day
At close of day no longer walks the sky;
Pity me not for beauties passed away
From field and thicket as the year goes by;
Pity me not the waning of the moon,   5
Nor that the ebbing tide goes out to sea,
Nor that a man's desire is hushed so soon,
And you no longer look with love on me.
This have I known always: Love is no more
Than the wide blossom which the wind assails,   10
Than the great tide that treads the shifting shore,
Strewing fresh wreckage gathered in the gales:
Pity me that the heart is slow to learn
What the swift mind beholds at every turn.

Study Questions

1. What are the things for which the speaker wants no pity?
2. According to lines 9–12, what is the nature of love?
3. In the concluding couplet we learn that, although the speaker rejects one kind of pity, she asks for another kind. What is the distinction?
4. How does the phrase "at every turn" contribute to the unity of the poem?

e. e. cummings 1894-1962

Edward Estlin Cummings (or e. e. cummings, as he preferred to sign his name) made poetic history by experimenting with typographical arrangements. What seemed unorthodox in his first poetry in the 1920s is less shocking today. As we have become accustomed to the lower-case letters, unusual punctuation, and coined words, we have become more aware of his old-fashioned lyricism. Repeatedly, he celebrates traditional themes—love and death, springtime and childhood. Also he frequently satirizes the hypocrisy and self-deception in our materialistic culture.

Cummings was born in Cambridge, Massachusetts where he attended Harvard and studied Greek, Latin, and French. From these languages he drew some observations which he applied to his own writing. Classical texts, he pointed out, never begin a sentence with a capital. Only in English is the pronoun "I" capitalized. Old French texts have no spaces around commas since commas make their own space. In New York City's Greenwich Village, Cummings gradually established a reputation as an avant-garde poet, painter, lecturer, and playwright.

His poetry appeared in volumes with intriguing titles such as: *Tulips and Chimneys, ViVa.* The title of *1 X 1,* love poems dedicated to his wife, suggests two people who become one. For a collection of his art work containing charcoal, ink, oil, pencil, and watercolor, the title is *CIOPW.* A group of lectures about poetry and his own life is titled *i. Six Nonlectures.* With such a substantial body of work, Cummings is no longer considered an upstart innovator but an authentic voice of our times.

THE BEACH *William Baziotes* 1955

"l(a"

e. e. cummings

---

l(a

le
af
fa

ll

s)
one
l

iness

"maggie and milly and molly and may"

e. e. cummings

---

maggie and milly and molly and may
went down to the beach(to play one day)

and maggie discovered a shell that sang
so sweetly she couldn't remember her troubles,and

milly befriended a stranded star   5
whose rays five languid fingers were;

and molly was chased by a horrible thing
which raced sideways while blowing bubbles:and

may came home with a smooth round stone
as small as a world and as large as alone.   10

For whatever we lose(like a you or a me)
it's always ourselves we find in the sea

"!"

e. e. cummings

!

o(rounD)moon,how
do
you(rouNd
er
than roUnd)float;
who
lly &(rOunder than)
go
:ldenly(Round
est)

?

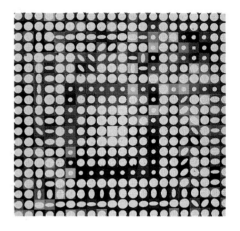

Study Questions

"1(a"

1. What relationship do you see between the concrete image inside the parentheses and the abstract word outside?
2. By printing the poem in a narrow vertical line, both the concrete image and the image of "oneness" is reinforced. What other aspects of the visual arrangement reinforce the main idea of the poem?

"maggie and milly and molly and may"

1. How is each of the four people described in the poem?
2. How do the discoveries made by the four girls exemplify the final statement in the poem?
3. What unusual rhythms and words does Cummings use here?

"!"

1. What do the words outside the parentheses say? What do those inside say? Why do you think Cummings used this arrangement?
2. The repeated vowel sounds and crescent-shapes (like the moon) help the reader to "feel" as well as see the moon. Which other devices force the reader into a new awareness of language? into a fresh awareness of the emotional experience produced by looking at the moon?

Arna Bontemps 1902-1973

Langston Hughes (see p. 89) described Arna Bontemps as looking like "a young edition of Dr. DuBois" (see p. 401). Hughes was referring not only to Bontemps' physical attributes but also to his scholarly brilliance and stable family life. Bontemps began his literary career during the Harlem Renaissance. He was awarded prizes for his poetry, but soon turned to prose and fiction. One of his novels, *Black Thunder* (1936), was the first fictional account of slavery written by a descendant of slaves.

In his later years, Bontemps made invaluable contributions to the conservation of Afro-American literature. He edited a number of books including *Golden Slippers, An Anthology of Poetry for Children* (1941); *American Negro Poetry* (1963); and *Great Slave Narratives* (1969). He and Hughes collaborated on *The Book of Negro Folklore* (1958).

A Black Man Talks of Reaping

ARNA BONTEMPS

I have sown beside all waters in my day.
I planted deep, within my heart the fear
That wind or fowl would take the grain away.
I planted safe against this stark, lean year.

I scattered seed enough to plant the land   5
In rows from Canada to Mexico,
But for my reaping only what the hand
Can hold at once is all that I can show.

Yet what I sowed and what the orchard yields
My brother's sons are gathering stalk and root,   10
Small wonder then my children glean in fields
They have not sown, and feed on bitter fruit.

Study Questions

1. What extended metaphor is used to indicate that the speaker is not in control of his life?
2. Which images suggest that the condition has lasted for a long time?
3. What are the implications of the last two lines?

Collection, the Museum of Modern Art, New York Gift of Albert M. Bender

Claude McKay   1891-1948

The details of Claude McKay's life form a series of paradoxes. He was born a peasant, but became an internationally acclaimed writer. Though he was born in Jamaica, he is often hailed as the "father" of the Harlem (New York) Renaissance. This celebrated renaissance of Afro-American literature occurred while McKay was traveling throughout Europe and North Africa.

As a child in Jamaica, McKay read books by writers from all over the world. After the publication of his first two poetry collections in 1912, he came to the United States. These two books, *Constab Ballads* and *Songs of Jamaica,* were both written in the Jamaican dialect or *patois.* With the publication of *Harlem Shadows* in 1922, his reputation as a poet was secured. McKay also published three novels, *Home to Harlem* (1928), *Banjo* (1929), and *Banana Bottom* (1933). He also wrote a controversial autobiography, *A Long Way from Home,* in 1937.

Harlem Shadows has been termed the first great literary achievement of the Harlem Renaissance. In it, McKay favored the sonnet form for his "most lawless and revolutionary passions and moods." "America" is a prime example of this.

America

CLAUDE McKAY

Although she feeds me bread of bitterness,
And sinks into my throat her tiger's tooth,
Stealing my breath of life, I will confess
I love this cultured hell that tests my youth!
Her vigor flows like tides into my blood,   5
Giving me strength erect against her hate.
Her bigness sweeps my being like a flood.
Yet as a rebel fronts a king in state,
I stand within her walls with not a shred
Of terror, malice, not a word of jeer.   10
Darkly I gaze into the days ahead,
And see her might and granite wonders there,
Beneath the touch of Time's unerring hand,
Like priceless treasures sinking in the sand.

Jean Toomer   1894-1967

In 1922, Jean Toomer sent some of his work to the *Liberator,* a journal edited by Max Eastman and Claude McKay (see p. 513). They accepted his material enthusiastically and asked for some biographical information. In part, this was Toomer's response:

Whenever the desire to know something about myself comes from a sincere source, I am always glad to meet it. For in telling other folks I invariably tell my own self something. My family is from the South. My mother's father, P.B.S. Pinchback, was born in Macon, Georgia. . . . He organized and was commissioned captain of a Negro company in New Orleans [during the Civil War]. Later, in the days of Reconstruction, he utilized the Negro's vote and won offices for himself, the highest being that of lieutenant, and then acting governor of Louisiana. When his heyday was over, he . . . came to Washington, [D.C.]. Here I was born. My own father likewise came from Middle Georgia. Racially, I seem to have (who knows for sure) seven blood mixtures: French, Dutch, Welsh, Negro, German, Jewish, and Indian. Because of these, my position in America has been a curious one. I have lived equally amid the two race groups. Now white, now colored. From my own point of view I am naturally and inevitably an American. I have strived for a spiritual fusion analagous to the fact of racial intermingling. Without denying a single element in me, with no desire to subdue one to the other, I have sought to let them function as complements. I have tried to let them live in harmony. Within the last two or three years, however, my growing need for artistic expression has pulled me deeper and deeper into the Negro group. And as my powers of receptivity increased, I found myself loving it in a way that I could never love the other. It has stimulated and fertilized whatever creative talent I may contain within me. A visit to Georgia last fall was the starting point of almost everything of worth that I have done. . . .

Cane (1923), a collection of intricately related stories, sketches, and poems, was a result of that visit. "Song of the Son" is from that book.

Song of the Son

JEAN TOOMER

Pour O pour that parting soul in song,
O pour it in the sawdust glow of night,
Into the velvet pine-smoke air to-night,
And let the valley carry it along.
And let the valley carry it along.   5

O land and soil, red soil and sweet-gum tree,
So scant of grass, so profligate[1] of pines,
Now just before an epoch's sun declines
Thy son, in time, I have returned to thee,
Thy son, I have in time returned to thee.   10

In time, for though the sun is setting on
A song-lit race of slaves, it has not set;
Though late, O soil, it is not too late yet
To catch thy plaintive soul, leaving, soon gone,
Leaving, to catch thy plaintive soul soon gone.   15

O Negro slaves, dark purple ripened plums,
Squeezed, and bursting in the pine-wood air,
Passing, before they stripped the old tree bare
One plum was saved for me, one seed becomes

An everlasting song, a singing tree,   20
Caroling softly souls of slavery,
What they were, and what they are to me,
Caroling softly souls of slavery.

---

1 **profligate** (prof' lə git): recklessly extravagant.

Study Questions

America

1. What types of images are used to describe America? Find examples of cacophony.

2. What effect does America have on the speaker?

3. What is the tone of the first ten lines? of the last four lines?

4. How is the sonnet form appropriate or inappropriate for this subject?

Song of the Son

1. What actions are described in the first two stanzas? How is the action of the second stanza foreshadowed in the first stanza?

2. In stanza three the pull of the land is associated with the racial memory of slavery. How does the speaker merge these twin themes in the last two stanzas?

3. In lines 18–19, how does the speaker indicate that it is not too late to return?

4. Discuss the meaning of the poem's title.

5. There are several poetic devices in this poem. What aspects of a ballad does it have? Find examples of alliteration.

Louise Bogan   1897-1970

Poet, editor, critic, Louise Bogan was born in Maine but pursued her literary career primarily in New York City. In her book, *Achievement in American Poetry* (1951), Bogan said that "warmth of feeling (in poetry) was accomplished almost entirely by women poets." As "Musician" shows, she wrote carefully crafted verses marked by restrained but sharply perceived emotions and by subtle verbal effects. In 1954 she won the Bollingen Prize for her *Collected Poems*.

Musician

LOUISE BOGAN

Where have these hands been,
By what delayed,
That so long stayed
Apart from the thin

Strings which they now grace   5
With their lonely skill?
Music and their cool will
At last interlace.

Now with great ease, and slow,
The thumb, the finger, the strong   10
Delicate hand plucks the long
String it was born to know.

And, under the palm, the string
Sings as it wished to sing.

Study Questions

1. The poem begins with a question. What does the poet want to know?

2. The remainder of the poem explains the reason for the question. What phrases show why the question is asked?

3. There is a tonal and rhythmic contrast between the energy of the question, which speaks rather quickly, and the relaxed, deliberate movement of the answer. How does Bogan achieve this effect?

STILL MUSIC *(detail)* Ben Shahn

Karl Shapiro   1913—

Born in Baltimore, Karl Shapiro was awarded a Pulitzer Prize in 1945 for his book *V-Letter and Other Poems.* The Bollingen Prize was awarded in 1968 for his *Selected Poems.* In addition to editing *Poetry* magazine, he has taught at several universities and served as consultant on poetry to the Library of Congress. Most often his work is praised for the accuracy of his concrete images. The titles of many of his poems—for example, "Buick," "Hollywood," "Drug Store," "Auto Wreck"—indicate his concern with modern experience. The poem below deals with manhole covers—what some might consider an unlikely subject for a poem.

Manhole Covers

KARL SHAPIRO

The beauty of manhole covers—what of that?
Like medals struck by a great savage khan,
Like Mayan calendar stones, unliftable, indecipherable,
Not like the old electrum, chased and scored,
Mottoed and sculptured to a turn,   5
But notched and whelked and pocked and smashed
With the great company names
(Gentle Bethlehem, smiling United States).
This rustproof artifact of my street,
Long after roads are melted away will lie   10
Sidewise in the grave of the iron-old world,
Bitten at the edges,
Strong with its cryptic American,
Its dated beauty.

Study Questions

1. Why are the manhole covers like medals of the khans and calendar stones of the Mayans? What is the irony in the speaker's use of history to describe the manhole covers?

2. Why will the manhole covers remain for future generations as relics of our civilization? How might they be interpreted?

Hilda Doolittle   1886-1961

Hilda Doolittle was known in literary circles as H.D. She was one of the many expatriate American writers who gathered chiefly in London and Paris during the early years of the twentieth century. In particular she belonged to the little group of Imagists, which also included Amy Lowell (see page 490). H.D.'s Imagist poems were characteristically short, pointed observations rendered by means of clear and precise imagery. The emphasis was all on light and color and physical surfaces. The lines were free patterns of musical phrase. "Song" is a good illustration of these principles.

Song

H. D.

You are as gold
as the half-ripe grain
that merges to gold again,
as white as the white rain
that beats through   5
the half-opened flowers
of the great flower tufts
thick on the black limbs
of an Illyrian[1] apple bough.

Can honey distill such fragrance   10
as your bright hair—
for your face is as fair as rain,
yet as rain that lies clear
on white honey-comb,
lends radiance to the white wax,   15
so your hair on your brow
casts light for a shadow.

---

1 **Illyrian:** Illyria was a part of ancient Greece.

Study Questions

1. How does the speaker convey the beauty of the person being described?

2. How does the imagery of the second stanza differ from the imagery of the first stanza?

3. How is the growing intensity of emotion developed from the first stanza to the second stanza?

Marianne Moore   1887-1972

T. S. Eliot said that the poems of Marianne Moore "form part of the small body of durable poetry written in our time." She was born in St. Louis and educated at Bryn Mawr College. For many years she taught school in Pennsylvania, worked as a public librarian in New York City, and edited *Dial,* a poetry magazine. In fifty years of writing, she published a half dozen thin books of verse, along with a book of essays and translations of La Fontaine's fables. She won every major poetry award. Moore said that the poet's job is to present "imaginary gardens with real toads in them." The wide variety of subjects which she meticulously describes—from pelicans to the Brooklyn (not Los Angeles) Dodgers—are quite real, but in the garden of her mind they assume a new and fascinating appearance.

MIST *Adolph Gottlieb* 1961

What Are Years?

MARIANNE MOORE

What is our innocence,
what is our guilt? All are
    naked, none is safe. And whence
is courage: the unanswered question,
the resolute doubt—   5
dumbly calling, deafly listening—that
in misfortune, even death,
    encourages others
    and in its defeat, stirs

    the soul to be strong? He   10
sees deep and is glad, who
    accedes to mortality
and in his imprisonment, rises
upon himself as
the sea in a chasm, struggling to be   15
free and unable to be,
    in its surrendering
    finds its continuing.

So he who strongly feels,
behaves. The very bird,   20
    grown taller as he sings, steels
his form straight up. Though he is captive,
his mighty singing
says, satisfaction is a lowly
thing, how pure a thing is joy.   25
    This is mortality,
    this is eternity.

Study Questions

1. What are the three questions asked in the first ten lines? How is each answered?
2. What does the person see or realize who "sees deep and is glad"?
3. Explain how the metaphor of the bird in the third stanza applies to the courageous person.
4. What is the answer to the title of the poem?
5. Find examples of the poem's structure: for example alliteration, end rhyme, and rhythm.

Silence

MARIANNE MOORE

My father used to say,
'Superior people never make long visits,
have to be shown Longfellow's grave
or the glass flowers at Harvard.[1]
Self-reliant like the cat—   5
that takes its prey to privacy,
the mouse's limp tail hanging like a shoelace from its mouth—
they sometimes enjoy solitude,
and can be robbed of speech
by speech which has delighted them.   10
The deepest feeling always shows itself in silence;
not in silence, but restraint.'
Nor was he insincere in saying, 'Make my house your inn'.
Inns are not residences.

---

1 **glass** . . . **Harvard:** a collection of glass flowers in a
museum at Harvard University.

Study Questions

1. What makes certain visitors "superior," according to the father?

2. Which lines are not in quotation marks? These lines are attributed directly to the speaker of the poem. How does the last line reveal that the speaker agrees with the sentiments expressed by the father?

3. Marianne Moore often supplied notes to her poems acknowledging the source of any phrases she had adapted to her poetry. For example, a note for "Silence" reads: "Edmund Burke, in *Burke's Life* by Prior: 'Throw yourself into a coach,' said he. 'Come down and make my house your inn.'" Point out which part of the source Moore used and how she elaborated and enriched its meaning in the new context of her poem.

Elizabeth Bishop   1911-1979

Elizabeth Bishop's total output of poems is contained in a volume of about 200 pages. However this is no indication of her stature as a poet. Born in Worcester, Massachusetts, she had a tragic childhood. Her father died before she was one, and her mother soon entered an insane asylum. Following graduation from Vassar, Bishop began a lifelong passion for travel. This eventually included periods spent in Mexico, Europe, and Brazil, her home for eighteen years. Her lean, immaculately wrought poetry won her a Pulitzer Prize, a National Book Award, and a Guggenheim Fellowship. She was also elected to the American Academy of Arts and Letters, and consultant for poetry to the Library of Congress. During the last ten years of her life she taught writing classes at Harvard and the Massachusetts Institute of Technology. The poem below demonstrates

Bishop's ability to combine haunting descriptive details with an imaginative leap to a solemn question about the nature of knowledge.

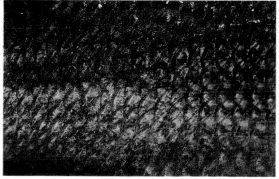

At the Fishhouses

ELIZABETH BISHOP

Although it is a cold evening,
down by one of the fishhouses
an old man sits netting,
his net, in the gloaming almost invisible
a dark purple-brown,   5
and his shuttle worn and polished.
The air smells so strong of codfish
it makes one's nose run and one's eyes water.
The five fishhouses have steeply peaked roofs
and narrow, cleated gangplanks slant up   10

to storerooms in the gables
for the wheelbarrows to be pushed up and down on.
All is silver: the heavy surface of the sea,
swelling slowly as if considering spilling over,
is opaque, but the silver of the benches,   15
the lobster pots, and masts, scattered
among the wild jagged rocks,
is of an apparent translucence
like the small old buildings with an emerald moss
growing on their shoreward walls.   20
The big fish tubs are completely lined
with layers of beautiful herring scales
and the wheelbarrows are similarly plastered
with creamy iridescent coats of mail,
with small iridescent flies crawling on them.   25
Up on the little slope behind the houses,
set in the sparse bright sprinkle of grass,
is an ancient wooden capstan,
cracked, with two long bleached handles
and some melancholy stains, like dried blood,   30
where the ironwork has rusted.

The old man accepts a Lucky Strike.
He was a friend of my grandfather.
We talk of the decline in the population
and of codfish and herring   35
while he waits for a herring boat to come in.
There are sequins on his vest and on his thumb.
He has scraped the scales, the principal beauty,
from unnumbered fish with that black old knife,
the blade of which is almost worn away.   40
Down at the water's edge, at the place
where they haul up the boats, up the long ramp
descending into the water, thin silver
tree trunks are laid horizontally
across the gray stones, down and down   45
at intervals of four or five feet.

Cold dark deep and absolutely clear,
element bearable to no mortal,
to fish and to seals . . . One seal particularly
I have seen here evening after evening.   50
He was curious about me. He was interested in music;
like me a believer in total immersion,
so I used to sing him Baptist hymns.
I also sang "A Mighty Fortress Is Our God."
He stood up in the water and regarded me   55

steadily, moving his head a little.
Then he would disappear, then suddenly emerge
almost in the same spot, with a sort of shrug
as if it were against his better judgment.
Cold dark deep and absolutely clear,   60
the clear gray icy water . . . Back, behind us,
the dignified tall firs begin.
Bluish, associating with their shadows,
a million Christmas trees stand
waiting for Christmas. The water seems suspended   65
above the rounded gray and blue-gray stones.
I have seen it over and over, the same sea, the same,
slightly, indifferently swinging above the stones,
icily free above the stones,
above the stones and then the world.   70
If you should dip your hand in,
your wrist would ache immediately,
your bones would begin to ache and your hand would burn
as if the water were a transmutation of fire
that feeds on stones and burns with a dark gray flame.   75
If you tasted it, it would first taste bitter,
then briny, then surely burn your tongue.
It is like what we imagine knowledge to be:
dark, salt, clear, moving, utterly free,
drawn from the cold hard mouth   80
of the world, derived from the rocky breasts
forever, flowing and drawn, and since
our knowledge is historical, flowing, and flown.

Study Questions

1. In the first section the speaker describes a fisherman and his surroundings. What colors predominate? Which visual details contribute to
   the aged, weather-beaten atmosphere?

2. How does the speaker communicate with the old fisherman in lines 32–
   46? What images in these lines echo the previous lines?

3. In the third section the speaker recounts another sort of communication,
   with a seal. Explain the humor in "total immersion."

4. Visual images are emphasized throughout the poem. In lines 7 and 8
   the sense of smell is included. In lines 71–77 the touch and taste of sea
   water are made vivid. How is this accomplished?

5. How is knowledge like the sea?

Countee Cullen   1903-1946

Countee Cullen was one of the few Harlem Renaissance writers who was a native New Yorker. Cullen was reared in New York City and earned a Phi Beta Kappa key at New York University. He went on to Harvard University to do graduate study. Cullen has sometimes been called the "Black Keats" because of his concern for the transience of truth and beauty. He was also very much aware of his African heritage. The titles of some of his volumes of poetry are *Color, Copper Sun,* and *Ballad of a Brown Girl.* Cullen also wrote poetry for children and a novel, *One Way to Heaven.*

In "From the Dark Tower," Cullen addresses a subject similar to Bontemps's "A Black Man Talks of Reaping" but with a completely different tone.

From the Dark Tower

COUNTEE CULLEN

We shall not always plant while others reap
The golden increment of bursting fruit,
Not always countenance, abject and mute,
That lesser men should hold their brothers cheap;
Not everlastingly while others sleep   5
Shall we beguile their limbs with mellow flute,
Not always bend to some more subtle brute;
We were not made eternally to weep.

The night whose sable breast relieves the stark,
White stars is no less lovely being dark,   10
And there are buds that cannot bloom at all
In light, but crumple, piteous, and fall;
So in the dark we hide the heart that bleeds,
And wait, and tend our agonizing seeds.

Study Questions

1. What are the four declarations the speaker makes in the first eight lines? How does line 8 finish the statements of the octave?

2. In the sestet the first four lines contain two striking and unconventional comments on darkness. What are they?

3. The sestet concludes with a couplet. How do these two lines reaffirm and extend the assertion in line 8?

6 REVIEW

Study Questions

1. Many of the writers in this unit demonstrate that the theme "Sense of Place" endures in the twentieth century. Which selections best exemplify this by the inclusion of nature?

2. Bontemps, Toomer, and Cullen all use land as the metaphor by which they express their anguish. What are the similarities and differences in their tones? What progression is there in the three poems? Why is it appropriate to the theme of the American Dream that Cullen's poem be the final one?

3. Compare the images of women in the stories by Cather, Porter, and Steinbeck.

4. Contrast Hemingway's writing style in "Big Two-Hearted River" with Faulkner's in "The Bear." Analyze both writers' use of language, time-sequence, action, and characterization. Cite specific examples. Compare the similarities. For example, which of Nick's traits resemble those of characters in "The Bear"?

5. Which poems best exemplify for you the theme of The Individual? Why?

Composition

1. In a two-page composition discuss the author's handling of the relationship between people and nature in the following selections: "The Bear," "Big Two-Hearted River," and "The Chrysanthemums." State the points you want to make about each story. Look for similarities and contrasts. Use examples from the stories to support your points.

2. Create an imaginary dramatic scene using two or more characters from the stories in this unit. For example, imagine the boy in "The Bear" meeting Granny Weatherall and Nick Adams. Think of a situation where the three characters might meet. Say, a year before Granny's death she goes to the airport to take a plane to the Bahamas. At the air terminal she encounters Nick Adams and the boy. Imagine what they might say to one another and create appropriate dialogue. The scene might end as their flights are called over the public address system.

7

Twentieth Century:
American Drama

THE first American drama, imported from England about 1790, faced strong political and religious opposition. Called "the house of the devil" by the Puritans, the theater was restricted by legislators because they argued it was "contrary to the public good." In spite of this rocky beginning, the theater was fairly well established by the end of the century.

During the nineteenth century, the American theater finally broke with English theatrical traditions and established its own concerns and themes. For example, many plays during this period portrayed American honesty and ingenuity overcoming foreign deception. By midcentury, theater began to spread across the country with the introduction of the showboats. Throughout the nineteenth century, however, American drama was limited to melodrama and farce.

It was not until the early twentieth century that the American theater turned to realism. In the summer of 1916, a small group of actors, called the Provincetown Players, performed *Bound East for Cardiff,* which was written by an unknown playwright named Eugene O'Neill. A few years later, O'Neill received worldwide recognition for his play *Beyond the Horizon* (1920), and eventually became known as America's first great dramatist. In fact, O'Neill affected the development of American Drama more than any other twentieth-century playwright. He wrote a wide range of realistic, naturalistic, and expressionistic plays. *Anna Christie* (1921), *Desire Under the Elms* (1924), *Strange Interlude* (1928), *Mourning Becomes Electra* (1931), *The Iceman Cometh* (1946), *Long Day's Journey into Night* (1956), and *A Touch of the Poet* (1957) are but a few of his

highly successful and experimental plays. He elevated American theater from its conventional presentation of sentimental melodrama and farce to an experimental tragic drama exploring the universal themes of loss, belonging, and searching. In 1936 he was awarded the Nobel Prize for Literature.

During and following World War II, American theater flourished with new voices. Among these were Arthur Miller, Tennessee Williams, and Lillian Hellman. Miller's *Death of a Salesman* (1949) portrayed an ordinary man, Willy Loman, who destroyed himself in his pursuit of the American Dream. Williams's *The Glass Menagerie* (1945) and *A Streetcar Named Desire* (1947) also focused on characters who were unable to cope with the harsh realities of life. Hellman's *The Little Foxes* (1939) treated the theme of a Southern family's struggle to maintain its identity in a changing modern society.

Black dramatists also emerged between the 1930s and 1950s. Langston Hughes and Lorraine Hansberry successfully brought Black culture to the American dramatic stage for the first time. Hansberry's *A Raisin in the Sun* (1959) explored the American Dream from another perspective. In the 1960s and 1970s, the plays of Alice Childress, Amiri Baraka, and Ed Bullins continued the tradition established by Hughes and Hansberry.

Today, American Drama is involved in an experimental presentation of modern themes and concerns. Among the many contemporary playwrights are Edward Albee, David Rabe, Sam Shepard, Elizabeth Swados, Lonne Elder, David Mamet, and Arthur Kopit.

In less than two centuries of literary development, American theater has become a seri-

WEST CHESTER COURT HOUSE
Horace Pippin 1946

ous and respected art form. Probably the most significant period of development occurred in the early twentieth century with the plays of Eugene O'Neill. Another playwright involved in the reaction against farce and melodrama and the development of an innovative, realistic drama was Thorton Wilder. In his preface to *Our Town* (1938), Wilder wrote, "Toward the end of the twenties I began to lose pleasure in going to the theater. I ceased to believe in the stories I saw presented there." He went on to write, "The trouble began in the nineteenth century and was connected with the rise of the middle classes—they wanted their theater soothing." But Wilder, along with other twentieth-century playwrights, was determined to exact a greater potential from the American theater. Commenting specifically on *Our Town,* Wilder wrote that the play "is not offered as a picture of life in a New Hampshire village; or as a speculation about the con-

ditions of life after death. . . . It is an attempt to find a value above all price for the smallest events in our daily life." He added that he had set the village against "the largest dimensions of time and place." He attempted, in *Our Town,* to give universal meaning to specific incidents, actions, and characters.

Wilder also brought to the American theater innovative stage techniques. He eliminated the traditional box set with its three walls and curtain and substituted an almost bare stage, forcing members of the audience to participate more actively by using their imaginations. In *Our Town,* he also invented the role of stage manager, a character who acts as interpreter and scene changer and who plays several of the minor roles in the play. Although Wilder's new stage conventions were not instantly praised by the critics, they later set the framework for further experimentation in the American theater.

Thornton Wilder   1897-1975

Thornton Wilder's novels and plays are highly original works which broke with the traditions of his time. His creative techniques were recognized by his contemporaries, and his works are equally respected and enjoyed by subsequent readers and viewers.

Born in Madison, Wisconsin, Wilder spent most of his childhood in China where his father was American Consul General. Upon his return to this country, Wilder continued his education in California and received degrees from Oberlin College, Yale, and Princeton. His first novel, *The Cabala,* appeared in 1926 while he was teaching French at Lawrenceville School in New Jersey. The following year he published his Pulitzer Prize winning novel, *The Bridge of San Luis Rey.*

As a playwright, Wilder equaled his success as a novelist. He received Pulitzer Prizes for *The Skin of Our Teeth* (1942) and *Our Town* (1938). Originally ignored by the critics, *Our Town* closed after only one week when it first opened in Boston in 1938. However, that same year it reopened in New York and went on to be one of the most widely produced American plays. Wilder is also the author of *The Matchmaker* and two one-act plays, *The Happy Journey to Trenton and Camden* and *The Long Christmas Dinner.* In 1963 Wilder was cited in the President's first Medal of Freedom list, and in 1965 he received the first National Medal for Literature.

Our Town

THORNTON WILDER

Characters (*in the order of their appearance*)

Stage Manager	**Wally Webb**	**Mrs. Soames**
Dr. Gibbs	**Emily Webb**	**Constable Warren**
Joe Crowell, Jr.	**Professor Willard**	**Si Crowell**
Howie Newsome	**Mr. Webb**	**Three Baseball Players**
Mrs. Gibbs	**Woman in the Balcony**	**Sam Craig**
Mrs. Webb	**Man in the Auditorium**	**Joe Stoddard**
George Gibbs	**Lady in the Box**	
Rebecca Gibbs	**Simon Stimson**	

The entire play takes place in Grover's Corners, New Hampshire.[1]

ACT I

[*No curtain. No scenery.*

The audience, arriving, sees an empty stage in half-light. Presently the Stage Manager, *hat on and pipe in mouth, enters and begins placing a table and three chairs downstage left, and a table and three chairs downstage right. He also places a low bench at the corner of what will be the Webb house, left.*

"Left" and "right" are from the point of view of the actor facing the audience. "Up" is toward the back wall.

As the house lights go down he has finished setting the stage and leaning against the right proscenium pillar watches the late arrivals in the audience. When the auditorium is in complete darkness he speaks.]

Stage Manager. This play is called "Our Town." It was written by Thornton Wilder; produced and directed by A. . . . (or: produced by A. . . .; directed by B. . . .). In it you will see Miss C. . . .; Miss D. . . .; Miss E. . . .; and Mr. F. . . .; Mr. G. . . .; Mr. H. . . .; and many others. The name of the town is Grover's Corners, New Hampshire—just across the Massachusetts line: latitude 42 degrees 40 minutes; longitude 70 degrees 37 minutes. The First Act shows a day in our town. The day is May 7, 1901. The time is just before dawn.

(*A rooster crows.*)

The sky is beginning to show some streaks of light over in the East there, behind our mount'in.

The morning star always gets wonderful

---

1 Grover's Corners, New Hampshire: an imaginary town.

bright the minute before it has to go,—doesn't it?

(*He stares at it for a moment, then goes upstage.*)

Well, I'd better show you how our town lies. Up here—

(*That is, parallel with the back wall.*)

is Main Street. Way back there is the railway station; tracks go that way. Polish Town's across the tracks, and some Canuck[2] families.

(*Toward the left.*)

Over there is the Congregational Church; across the street's the Presbyterian.

Methodist and Unitarian are over there.

Baptist is down in the holla' by the river.

Catholic Church is over beyond the tracks.

Here's the Town Hall and Post Office combined; jail's in the basement.

Bryan[3] once made a speech from these very steps here.

Along here's a row of stores. Hitching posts and horse blocks in front of them. First automobile's going to come along in about five years—belonged to Banker Cartwright, our richest citizen . . . lives in the big white house up on the hill.

Here's the grocery store and here's Mr. Morgan's drugstore. Most everybody in town manages to look into those two stores once a day.

Public School's over yonder. High School's still farther over. Quarter of nine mornings, noontimes, and three o'clock afternoons, the hull town can hear the yelling and screaming from those school yards.

(*He approaches the table and chairs downstage right.*)

This is our doctor's house,—Doc Gibbs'. This is the back door.

(*Two arched trellises, covered with vines and flowers, are pushed out, one by each proscenium pillar.*)

There's some scenery for those who think they have to have scenery.

This is Mrs. Gibbs' garden. Corn . . . peas . . . beans . . . hollyhocks . . . heliotrope . . . and a lot of burdock.

(*Crosses the stage.*)

In those days our newspaper come out twice a week—the Grover's Corners *Sentinel*—and this is Editor Webb's house.

And this is Mrs. Webb's garden.

Just like Mrs. Gibbs', only it's got a lot of sunflowers, too.

(*He looks upward, center stage.*)

Right here . . . 's a big butternut tree.

(*He returns to his place by the right proscenium pillar and looks at the audience for a minute.*)

Nice town, y'know what I mean?

Nobody very remarkable ever come out of it, s'far as we know.

The earliest tombstones in the cemetery up there on the mountain say 1670–1680— they're Grovers and Cartwrights and Gibbses and Herseys—same names as are around here now.

Well, as I said: it's about dawn.

The only lights on in town are in a cottage over by the tracks where a Polish mother's just had twins. And in the Joe Crowell house, where Joe Junior's getting up so as to deliver the paper. And in the depot, where Shorty Hawkins is gettin' ready to flag the 5:45 for Boston.

(*A train whistle is heard. The* Stage Manager *takes out his watch and nods.*)

Naturally, out in the country—all around—there've been lights on for some time, what with milkin's and so on. But town people sleep late.

So—another day's begun.

There's Doc Gibbs comin' down Main Street now, comin' back from that baby case. And here's his wife comin' downstairs to get breakfast.

(Mrs. Gibbs, *a plump, pleasant woman in the middle thirties, comes "downstairs" right. She pulls*

---

2 **Canuck**: slang for French-Canadian.
3 **Bryan**: William Jennings Bryan (1860–1925), lawyer, orator and politician.

up an imaginary window shade in her kitchen and starts to make a fire in her stove.)

Doc Gibbs died in 1930. The new hospital's named after him.

Mrs. Gibbs died first—long time ago, in fact. She went out to visit her daughter, Rebecca, who married an insurance man in Canton, Ohio, and died there—pneumonia—but her body was brought back here. She's up in the cemetery there now—in with a whole mess of Gibbses and Herseys—she was Julia Hersey 'fore she married Doc Gibbs in the Congregational Church over there.

In our town we like to know the facts about everybody.

There's Mrs. Webb, coming downstairs to get her breakfast, too.

—That's Doc Gibbs. Got that call at half past one this morning.

And there comes Joe Crowell, Jr., delivering Mr. Webb's *Sentinel*.

[Dr. Gibbs *has been coming along Main Street from the left. At the point where he would turn to approach his house he stops, sets down his— imaginary—black bag, takes off his hat, and rubs his face with fatigue, using an enormous handkerchief.* Mrs. Webb, *a thin, serious, crisp woman, has entered her kitchen, left, tying on an apron. She goes through the motions of putting wood into a stove, lighting it, and preparing breakfast. Suddenly,* Joe Crowell, Jr., *eleven, starts down Main Street from the right, hurling imaginary newspapers into doorways.*]

Joe Crowell, Jr. Morning, Doc Gibbs.

Dr. Gibbs. Morning, Joe.

Joe Crowell, Jr. Somebody been sick, Doc?

Dr. Gibbs. No. Just some twins born over in Polish Town.

Joe Crowell, Jr. Do you want your paper now?

Dr. Gibbs. Yes, I'll take it.—Anything serious goin' on in the world since Wednesday?

Joe Crowell, Jr. Yessir. My schoolteacher, Miss Foster, 's getting married to a fella over in Concord.

Dr. Gibbs. I declare.—How do you boys feel about that?

Joe Crowell, Jr. Well, of course, it's none of my business—but I think if a person starts out to be a teacher, she ought to stay one.

Dr. Gibbs. How's your knee, Joe?

Joe Crowell, Jr. Fine, Doc, I never think about it at all. Only like you said, it always tells me when it's going to rain.

Dr. Gibbs. What's it telling you today? Goin' to rain?

Joe Crowell, Jr. No, sir.

Dr. Gibbs. Sure?

Joe Crowell, Jr. Yessir.

Dr. Gibbs. Knee ever make a mistake?

Joe Crowell, Jr. No, sir.

[Joe *goes off.* Dr. Gibbs *stands reading his paper.*]

Stage Manager. Want to tell you something about that boy Joe Crowell there. Joe was awful bright—graduated from high school here, head of his class. So he got a scholarship to Massachusetts Tech. Graduated head of his class there, too. It was all wrote up in the Boston paper at the time. Goin' to be a great engineer, Joe was. But the war broke out and he died in France.—All that education for nothing.

Howie Newsome (*off left*). Giddap, Bessie! What's the matter with you today?

Stage Manager. Here comes Howie Newsome, deliverin' the milk.

[Howie Newsome, *about thirty, in overalls, comes along Main Street from the left, walking beside an invisible horse and wagon and carrying an imaginary rack with milk bottles. The sound of clinking milk bottles is heard. He leaves some bottles at* Mrs. Webb's *trellis, then, crossing the stage to* Mrs. Gibbs', *he stops center to talk to* Dr. Gibbs.]

Howie Newsome. Morning, Doc.

Dr. Gibbs. Morning, Howie.

Howie Newsome. Somebody sick?

Dr. Gibbs. Pair of twins over to Mrs. Goruslawski's.

Howie Newsome. Twins, eh? This town's gettin' bigger every year.

Dr. Gibbs. Goin' to rain, Howie?

Howie Newsome. No, no. Fine day—that'll burn through. Come on, Bessie.

Dr. Gibbs. Hello Bessie. (*He strokes the horse, which has remained up center.*) How old is she, Howie?

Howie Newsome. Going on seventeen. Bessie's all mixed up about the route ever since the Lockharts stopped takin' their quart of milk every day. She wants to leave 'em a quart just the same—keeps scolding me the hull trip.

[*He reaches* Mrs. Gibbs' *back door. She is waiting for him.*]

Mrs. Gibbs. Good morning, Howie.

Howie Newsome. Morning, Mrs. Gibbs. Doc's just comin' down the street.

Mrs. Gibbs. Is he? Seems like you're late today.

Howie Newsome. Yes. Somep'n went wrong with the separator. Don't know what 'twas. (*He passes* Dr. Gibbs *up center.*) Doc!

Dr. Gibbs. Howie!

Mrs. Gibbs (*calling upstairs*). Children! Children! Time to get up.

Howie Newsome. Come on, Bessie! (*He goes off right.*)

Mrs. Gibbs. George! Rebecca!

[Dr. Gibbs *arrives at his back door and passes through the trellis into his house.*]

Mrs. Gibbs. Everything all right, Frank?

Dr. Gibbs. Yes. I declare—easy as kittens.

Mrs. Gibbs. Bacon'll be ready in a minute. Set down and drink your coffee. You can catch a couple hours' sleep this morning, can't you?

Dr. Gibbs. Hm! . . . Mrs. Wentworth's coming at eleven. Guess I know what it's about, too. Her stummick ain't what it ought to be.

Mrs. Gibbs. All told, you won't get more'n three hours' sleep. Frank Gibbs, I don't know what's goin' to become of you. I do wish I could get you to go away someplace and take a rest. I think it would do you good.

Mrs. Webb. Emileeee! Time to get up! Wally! Seven o'clock!

Mrs. Gibbs. I declare, you got to speak to George. Seems like something's come over him lately. He's no help to me at all. I can't even get him to cut me some wood.

Dr. Gibbs (*washing and drying his hands at the sink;* Mrs. Gibbs *is busy at the stove*). Is he sassy to you?

Mrs. Gibbs. No. He just whines! All he thinks about is that baseball—George! Rebecca! You'll be late for school.

Dr. Gibbs. M-m-m . . .

Mrs. Gibbs. George!

Dr. Gibbs. George, look sharp!

George's Voice. Yes, Pa!

Dr. Gibbs (*as he goes off the stage*). Don't you hear your mother calling you? I guess I'll go upstairs and get forty winks.

Mrs. Webb. Walleee! Emileee! You'll be late for school! Walleee! You wash yourself good or I'll come up and do it myself.

Rebecca Gibbs' Voice. Ma! What dress shall I wear?

Mrs. Gibbs. Don't make a noise. Your father's been out all night and needs his sleep. I washed and ironed the blue gingham for you special.

Rebecca. Ma, I hate that dress.

Mrs. Gibbs. Oh, hush-up-with-you.

Rebecca. Every day I go to school dressed like a sick turkey.

Mrs. Gibbs. Now, Rebecca, you always look *very* nice.

Rebecca. Mama, George's throwing soap at me.

Mrs. Gibbs. I'll come and slap the both of you,—that's what I'll do.

[*A factory whistle sounds. The* Children *dash in and take their places at the tables. Right,* George, *about sixteen, and* Rebecca, *eleven. Left,* Emily *and* Wally, *same ages. They carry strapped schoolbooks.*]

Stage Manager. We've got a factory in our town too—hear it? Makes blankets. Cartwrights own it and it brung 'em a fortune.

Mrs. Webb. Children! Now I won't have it. Breakfast is just as good as any other meal and I won't have you gobbling like wolves. It'll stunt your growth,—that's a fact. Put away your book, Wally.

Wally. Aw, Ma! By ten o'clock I got to know all about Canada.

Mrs. Webb. You know the rule's well as I do—no books at table. As for me, I'd rather have my children healthy than bright.

Emily. I'm both, Mama, you know I am. I'm the brightest girl in school for my age. I have a wonderful memory.

Mrs. Webb. Eat your breakfast.

Wally. I'm bright, too, when I'm looking at my stamp collection.

Mrs. Gibbs. I'll speak to your father about it when he's rested. Seems to me twenty-five cents a week's enough for a boy your age. I declare I don't know how you spend it all.

George. Aw, Ma,—I gotta lotta things to buy.

Mrs. Gibbs. Strawberry phosphates—that's what you spend it on.

George. I don't see how Rebecca comes to have so much money. She has more'n a dollar.

Rebecca (*spoon in mouth, dreamily*). I've been saving it up gradual.

Mrs. Gibbs. Well, dear, I think it's a good thing to spend some every now and then.

Rebecca. Mama, do you know what I love most in the world—do you?—Money.

Mrs. Gibbs. Eat your breakfast.

The Children. Mama, there's first bell.—I gotta hurry.—I don't want any more.—I gotta hurry.

[*The* Children *rise, seize their books and dash out through the trellises. They meet, down center, and chattering, walk to Main Street, then turn left. The* Stage Manager *goes off, unobtrusively, right.*]

Mrs. Webb. Walk fast, but you don't have to run. Wally, pull up your pants at the knee. Stand up straight, Emily.

Mrs. Gibbs. Tell Miss Foster I send her my best congratulations—can you remember that?

Rebecca. Yes, Ma.

Mrs. Gibbs. You look real nice, Rebecca. Pick up your feet.

All. Good-by.

[Mrs. Gibbs *fills her apron with food for the chickens and comes down to the footlights.*]

Mrs. Gibbs. Here, chick, chick, chick.
No, go away, you. Go away.

Here, chick, chick, chick.

What's the matter with *you?* Fight, fight, fight,—that's all you do.

Hm . . . *you* don't belong to me. Where'd you come from?

(*She shakes her apron.*)

Oh, don't be so scared. Nobody's going to hurt you.

[Mrs. Webb *is sitting on the bench by her trellis, stringing beans.*]

Good morning, Myrtle. How's your cold?

Mrs. Webb. Well, I still get that tickling feeling in my throat. I told Charles I didn't know as I'd go to choir practice tonight. Wouldn't be any use.

Mrs. Gibbs. Have you tried singing over your voice?

Mrs. Webb. Yes, but somehow I can't do that and stay on key. While I'm resting myself I thought I'd string some of these beans.

Mrs. Gibbs (*rolling up her sleeves as she crosses the stage for a chat*). Let me help you. Beans have been good this year.

Mrs. Webb. I've decided to put up forty quarts if it kills me. The children say they hate 'em, but I notice they're able to get 'em down all winter. (*Pause. Brief sound of chickens cackling.*)

Mrs. Gibbs. Now, Myrtle. I've got to tell you something, because if I don't tell somebody I'll burst.

Mrs. Webb. Why, Julia Gibbs!

Mrs. Gibbs. Here, give me some more of those beans. Myrtle, did one of those second-hand-furniture men from Boston come to see you last Friday?

Mrs. Webb. No-o.

Mrs. Gibbs. Well, he called on me. First I thought he was a patient wantin' to see Dr. Gibbs. 'N he wormed his way into my parlor, and, Myrtle Webb, he offered me three hundred and fifty dollars for Grandmother Wentworth's highboy, as I'm sitting here!

Mrs. Webb. Why, Julia Gibbs!

Mrs. Gibbs. He did! That old thing! Why, it was so big I didn't know where to put it and I almost give it to Cousin Hester Wilcox.

Mrs. Webb. Well, you're going to take it, aren't you?

Mrs. Gibbs. I don't know.

Mrs. Webb. You don't know—three hundred and fifty dollars! What's come over you?

Mrs. Gibbs. Well, if I could get the Doctor to take the money and go away someplace on a real trip, I'd sell it like that.—Y'know, Myrtle, it's been the dream of my life to see Paris, France.—Oh, I don't know. It sounds crazy, I suppose, but for years I've been promising myself that if we ever had the chance—

Mrs. Webb. How does the Doctor feel about it?

Mrs. Gibbs. Well, I did beat about the bush a little and said that if I got a legacy—that's the way I put it—I'd make him take me somewhere.

Mrs. Webb. M-m-m . . . What did he say?

Mrs. Gibbs. You know how he is. I haven't heard a serious word out of him since I've known him. No, he said, it might make him discontented with Grover's Corners to go traipsin' about Europe; better let well enough alone, he says. Every two years he makes a trip to the battlefields of the Civil War and that's enough treat for anybody, he says.

Mrs. Webb. Well, Mr. Webb just *admires* the way Dr. Gibbs knows everything about the Civil War. Mr. Webb's a good mind to give up Napoleon and move over to the Civil War, only Dr. Gibbs being one of the greatest experts in the country just makes him despair.

Mrs. Gibbs. It's a fact! Dr. Gibbs is never so happy as when he's at Antietam or Gettysburg. Three times I've walked over those hills, Myrtle, stopping at every bush and pacing it all out, like we were going to buy it.

Mrs. Webb. Well, if that secondhand man's really serious about buyin' it, Julia, you sell it. And then you'll get to see Paris, all right. Just keep droppin' hints from time to time—that's how I got to see the Atlantic Ocean, y'know.

Mrs. Gibbs. Oh, I'm sorry I mentioned it. Only it seems to me that once in your life before you die you ought to see a country where they don't talk in English and don't even want to.

[*The Stage Manager enters briskly from the right. He tips his hat to the ladies, who nod their heads.*]

Stage Manager. Thank you, ladies. Thank you very much.

[Mrs. Gibbs *and* Mrs. Webb *gather up their things, return into their homes and disappear.*]

Now we're going to skip a few hours.

But first we want a little more information about the town, kind of a scientific account, you might say.

So I've asked Professor Willard of our State University to sketch in a few details of our past history here.

Is Professor Willard here?

[Professor Willard, *a rural savant,*[4] *pince-nez on a wide satin ribbon, enters from the right with some notes in his hand.*]

May I introduce Professor Willard of our State University.

A few brief notes, thank you, Professor,—unfortunately our time is limited.

Professor Willard. Grover's Corners . . . let me see . . . Grover's Corners lies on the old Pleistocene granite of the Appalachian range. I may say it's some of the oldest land in the world. We're very proud of that. A shelf of Devonian basalt crosses it with vestiges of Mesozoic shale, and some sandstone outcroppings; but that's all more recent: two hundred, three hundred million years old.

Some highly interesting fossils have been found . . . I may say: unique fossils . . . two miles out of town, in Silas Peckham's cow pasture. They can be seen at the museum in our University at any time—that is, at any reasonable time. Shall I read some of Professor Gruber's notes on the meteorological situation—mean precipitation, et cetera?

Stage Manager. Afraid we won't have time for that, Professor. We might have a few words on the history of man here.

Professor Willard. Yes . . . anthropological data: Early Amerindian stock. Cotahatchee tribes . . . no evidence before the tenth century of this era . . . hm . . . now entirely disappeared . . . possible traces in three families. Migration toward the end of the seventeenth century of English brachiocephalic[5] blue-eyed stock . . . for the most part. Since then some Slav and Mediterranean—

Stage Manager. And the population, Professor Willard?

Professor Willard. Within the town limits: 2,640.

Stage Manager. Just a moment, Professor. (*He whispers into the professor's ear.*)

Professor Willard. Oh, yes, indeed?—The population, *at the moment,* is 2,642. The Postal District brings in 507 more, making a total of 3,149.—Mortality and birth rates: constant.—By MacPherson's gauge: 6.032.

---

4 **savant** (sé vant): person of learning, a scholar.

5 **brachiocephalic**: usually brachycephalic (brak′ ē se fal′ ik), having a short, broad skull.

Stage Manager. Thank you very much, Professor. We're all very much obliged to you, I'm sure.

Professor Willard. Not at all, sir; not at all.

Stage Manager. This way, Professor, and thank you again. (*Exit* Professor Willard.) Now the political and social report: Editor Webb.—Oh, Mr. Webb?

[Mrs. Webb *appears at her back door.*]

Mrs. Webb. He'll be here in a minute. . . . He just cut his hand while he was eatin' an apple.

Stage Manager. Thank you, Mrs. Webb.

Mrs. Webb. Charles! Everybody's waitin'. (*Exit* Mrs. Webb.)

Stage Manager. Mr. Webb is Publisher and Editor of the Grover's Corners *Sentinel.* That's our local paper, y'know.

[Mr. Webb *enters from his house, pulling on his coat. His finger is bound in a handkerchief.*]

Mr. Webb. Well . . . I don't have to tell you that we're run here by a Board of Selectmen.—All males vote at the age of twenty-one. Women vote indirect. We're lower middle class: sprinkling of professional men . . . ten per cent illiterate laborers. Politically, we're eighty-six per cent Republicans; six per cent Democrats; four per cent Socialists; rest, indifferent.

Religiously, we're eighty-five per cent Protestants; twelve per cent Catholics; rest, indifferent.

Stage Manager. Have you any comments, Mr. Webb?

Mr. Webb. Very ordinary town, if you ask me. Little better behaved than most. Probably a lot duller.

But our young people here seem to like it well enough. Ninety per cent of 'em graduating from high school settle down right here to live—even when they've been away to college.

Stage Manager. Now, is there anyone in the audience who would like to ask Editor Webb anything about the town?

Woman in the Balcony. Is there much drinking in Grover's Corners?

Mr. Webb. Well, ma'am, I wouldn't know what you'd call *much.* Satiddy nights the farm-hands meet down in Ellery Greenough's stable and holler some. We've got one or two town drunks, but they're always having remorses every time an evangelist comes to town. No, ma'am, I'd say likker ain't a regular thing in the home here, except in the medicine chest. Right good for snake bite, y'know—always was.

Belligerent Man at Back of Auditorium. Is there no one in town aware of—

Stage Manager. Come forward, will you, where we can all hear you—What were you saying?

Belligerent Man. Is there no one in town aware of social injustice and industrial inequality?

Mr. Webb. Oh, yes, everybody is—somethin' terrible. Seems like they spend most of their time talking about who's rich and who's poor.

Belligerent Man. Then why don't they do something about it?

[*He withdraws without waiting for an answer.*]

Mr. Webb. Well, I dunno. . . . I guess we're all hunting like everybody else for a way the diligent and sensible can rise to the top and the lazy and quarrelsome can sink to the bottom. But it ain't easy to find. Meanwhile, we do all we can to help those that can't help themselves and those that can we leave alone.—Are there any other questions?

Lady in a Box. Oh, Mr. Webb? Mr. Webb, is there any culture or love of beauty in Grover's Corners?

Mr. Webb. Well, ma'am, there ain't much—not in the sense you mean. Come to think of it, there's some girls that play the piano at High School Commencement; but they ain't happy about it. No, ma'am, there isn't much culture; but maybe this is the place to tell you that we've got a lot of pleasures of a kind here: we like the sun comin' up over the mountain in the morning, and we all notice a good deal about the birds. We pay a lot of attention to them. And we watch the change of the seasons; yes, everybody knows about them. But those other things—you're right, ma'am,—there ain't much—*Robinson Crusoe* and the *Bible;* and Handel's "Largo," we all know that; and Whistler's "Mother"—those are just about as far as we go.

Lady in a Box. So I thought. Thank you, Mr. Webb.

Stage Manager. Thank you, Mr. Webb. (Mr. Webb *retires.*) Now, we'll go back to the town. It's early afternoon. All 2,642 have had their dinners and all the dishes have been washed. (Mr. Webb, *having removed his coat, returns and starts pushing a lawn mower to and fro beside his house.*) There's an early-afternoon calm in our town: a buzzin' and a hummin' from the school buildings; only a few buggies on Main Street—the horses dozing at the hitching posts; you all remember what it's like. Doc Gibbs is in his office, tapping people and making them say "ah." Mr. Webb's cuttin' his lawn over there; one man in ten thinks it's a privilege to push his own lawn mower. No, sir. It's later than I thought. There are the children coming home from school already.

[*Shrill girls' voices are heard, off left. Emily comes along Main Street, carrying some books. There are some signs that she is imagining herself to be a lady of startling elegance.*]

Emily. I *can't,* Lois. I've got to go home and help my mother. I *promised.*

Mr. Webb. Emily, walk simply. Who do you think you are today?

Emily. Papa, you're terrible. One minute you tell me to stand up straight and the next minute you call me names. I just don't listen to you. (*She gives him an abrupt kiss.*)

Mr. Webb. Golly, I never got a kiss from such a great lady before.

[*He goes out of sight. Emily leans over and picks some flowers by the gate of her house.*

George Gibbs comes careening down Main Street. He is throwing a ball up to dizzying heights, and waiting to catch it again. This sometimes requires his taking six steps backward. He bumps into an Old Lady *invisible to us.*]

George. Excuse me, Mrs. Forrest.

Stage Manager (*as Mrs. Forrest*). Go out and play in the fields, young man. You got no business playing baseball on Main Street.

George. Awfully sorry, Mrs. Forrest.—Hello, Emily.

Emily. H'lo.

George. You made a fine speech in class.

Emily. Well . . . I was really ready to make a speech about the Monroe Doctrine, but at the last minute Miss Corcoran made me talk about the Louisiana Purchase instead. I worked an awful long time on both of them.

George. Gee, it's funny, Emily. From my window up there I can just see your head nights when you're doing your homework over in your room.

Emily. Why, can you?

George. You certainly do stick to it, Emily. I don't see how you can sit still that long. I guess you like school.

Emily. Well, I always feel it's something you have to go through.

George. Yeah.

Emily. I don't mind it really. It passes the time.

George. Yeah.—Emily, what do you think? We might work out a kinda telegraph from your window to mine; and once in a while you could give me a kinda hint or two about one of those algebra problems. I don't mean the answers, Emily, of course not . . . just some little hint. . . .

Emily. Oh, I think *hints* are allowed.—So—ah—if you get stuck, George, you whistle to me; and I'll give you some hints.

George. Emily, you're just naturally bright, I guess.

Emily. I figure that it's just the way a person's born.

George. Yeah. But, you see, I want to be a farmer, and my Uncle Luke says whenever I'm ready I can come over and work on his farm and if I'm any good I can just gradually have it.

Emily. You mean the house and everything?

[*Enter Mrs. Webb with a large bowl and sits on the bench by her trellis.*]

George. Yeah. Well, thanks . . . I better be getting out to the baseball field. Thanks for the talk, Emily.—Good afternoon, Mrs. Webb.

Mrs. Webb. Good afternoon, George.

George. So long, Emily.

Emily. So long, George.

Mrs. Webb. Emily, come and help me string these beans for the winter. George Gibbs let himself have a real conversation, didn't he? Why, he's growing up. How old would George be?

Emily. I don't know.

Mrs. Webb. Let's see. He must be almost sixteen.

Emily. Mama, I made a speech in class today and I was very good.

Mrs. Webb. You must recite it to your father at supper. What was it about?

Emily. The Louisiana Purchase. It was like silk off a spool. I'm going to make speeches all my life.—Mama, are these big enough?

Mrs. Webb. Try and get them a little bigger if you can.

Emily. Mama, will you answer me a question, serious?

Mrs. Webb. Seriously, dear—not serious.

Emily. Seriously,—will you?

Mrs. Webb. Of course, I will.

Emily. Mama, am I good-looking?

Mrs. Webb. Yes, of course you are. All my children have got good features; I'd be ashamed if they hadn't.

Emily. Oh, Mama, that's not what I mean. What I mean is: am I *pretty?*

Mrs. Webb. I've already told you, yes. Now that's enough of that. You have a nice young pretty face. I never heard of such foolishness.

Emily. Oh, Mama, you never tell us the truth about anything.

Mrs. Webb. I *am* telling you the truth.

Emily. Mama, were *you* pretty?

Mrs. Webb. Yes, I was, if I do say it. I was the prettiest girl in town next to Mamie Cartwright.

Emily. But, Mama, you've got to say *some*thing about me. Am I pretty enough . . . to get anybody . . . to get people interested in me?

Mrs. Webb. Emily, you make me tired. Now stop it. You're pretty enough for all normal purposes.—Come along now and bring that bowl with you.

Emily. Oh, Mama, you're no help at all.

Stage Manager. Thank you. Thank you! That'll do. We'll have to interrupt again here. Thank you, Mrs. Webb; thank you, Emily.

(Mrs. Webb *and* Emily *withdraw.*)

There are some more things we want to explore about this town.

(*He comes to the center of the stage. During the following speech the lights gradually dim to darkness, leaving only a spot on him.*)

I think this is a good time to tell you that the Cartwright interests have just begun building a new bank in Grover's Corners—had to go to Vermont for the marble, sorry to say. And they've asked a friend of mine what they should put in the cornerstone for people to dig up . . . a thousand years from now. . . . Of course, they put in a copy of the *New York Times* and a copy of Mr. Webb's *Sentinel*. . . . We're kind of interested in this because some scientific fellas have found a way of painting all that reading matter with a glue—a silicate glue—that'll make it keep a thousand—two thousand years.

We're putting in a Bible . . . and the Constitution of the United States—and a copy of William Shakespeare's plays. What do you say, folks? What do you think?

Y'know—Babylon once had two million people in it, and all we know about 'em is the names of the kings and some copies of wheat contracts . . . and contracts for the sale of slaves. Yet every night all those families sat down to supper, and the father came home from his work, and the smoke went up the chimney,—same as here. And even in Greece and Rome, all we know about the *real* life of the people is what we can piece together out of the joking poems and the comedies they wrote for the theater back then.

So I'm going to have a copy of this play put in the cornerstone and the people a thousand years from now'll know a few simple facts about us—more than the Treaty of Versailles and the Lindbergh flight.

See what I mean?

So—people a thousand years from now—this is the way we were in the provinces north of New York at the beginning of the twentieth century.—This is the way we were: in our growing up and in our marrying and in our living and in our dying.

(*A choir partially concealed in the orchestra pit has begun singing "Blessed Be the Tie That Binds."*

Simon Stimson *stands directing them. Two ladders have been pushed onto the stage; they serve as indication of the second story in the* Gibbs *and* Webb *houses.* George *and* Emily *mount them, and apply themselves to their schoolwork.*

Dr. Gibbs *has entered and is seated in his kitchen reading.*)

Well!—good deal of time's gone by. It's evening.

You can hear choir practice going on in the Congregational Church.

The children are at home doing their schoolwork.

The day's running down like a tired clock.

Simon Stimson. Now look here, everybody. Music come into the world to give pleasure.—Softer! Softer! Get it out of your heads that music's only good when it's loud. You leave loudness to the Methodists. You couldn't beat 'em, even if you wanted to. Now again. Tenors!

George. Hssst! Emily!

Emily. Hello.

George. Hello!

Emily. I can't work at all. The moonlight's so *terrible.*

George. Emily, did you get the third problem?

Emily. Which?

George. The *third?*

Emily. Why, yes, George—that's the easiest of them all.

George. I don't see it. Emily, can you give me a hint?

Emily. I'll tell you one thing: the answer's in yards.

George. ! ! ! In yards? How do you mean?

Emily. In *square* yards.

George. Oh . . . in square yards.

Emily. Yes, George, don't you see?

George. Yeah.

Emily. In square yards of *wallpaper.*

George. Wallpaper,—oh, I see. Thanks a lot, Emily.

Emily. You're welcome. My, isn't the moonlight *terrible?* And choir practice going on.—I think if you hold your breath you can hear the train all the way to Contoocook. Hear it?

George. M-m-m—What do you know!

Emily. Well, I guess I better go back and try to work.

George. Good night, Emily. And thanks.

Emily. Good night, George.

Simon Stimson. Before I forget it: how many of you will be able to come in Tuesday afternoon and sing at Fred Hersey's wedding?—show your hands. That'll be fine; that'll be right nice. We'll do the same music we did for Jane Trowbridge's last month.

—Now we'll do: "Art Thou Weary; Art Thou Languid?" It's a question, ladies and gentlemen, make it talk. Ready.

Dr. Gibbs. Oh, George, can you come down a minute?

George. Yes, pa. (*He descends the ladder.*)

Dr. Gibbs. Make yourself comfortable, George; I'll only keep you a minute. George, how old are you?

George. I? I'm sixteen, almost seventeen.

Dr. Gibbs. What do you want to do after school's over?

George. Why, you know, Pa. I want to be a farmer on Uncle Luke's farm.

Dr. Gibbs. You'll be willing, will you, to get up early and milk and feed the stock . . . and you'll be able to hoe and hay all day?

George. Sure, I will. What are you . . . what do you mean, Pa?

Dr. Gibbs. Well, George, while I was in my office today I heard a funny sound . . . and what do you think it was? It was your mother chopping wood. There you see your mother—getting up early; cooking meals all day long; washing and ironing;—and still she has to go out in the back yard and chop wood. I suppose she just got tired of asking you. She just gave up and decided it was easier to do it herself. And you eat her meals, and put on the clothes she keeps nice for you, and you run off and play baseball,—like she's some hired girl we keep around the house but that we don't like very much. Well, I knew all I had to do was call your attention to it. Here's a handkerchief, son. George, I've decided to raise your spending money twenty-five cents a week. Not, of course, for chopping wood for your mother, because that's a present you give her, but because you're getting older—and I imagine there are lots of things you must find to do with it.

George. Thanks, Pa.

Dr. Gibbs. Let's see—tomorrow's your pay-day. You can count on it—Hmm. Probably Rebecca'll feel she ought to have some more too. Wonder what could have happened to your mother. Choir practice never was as late as this before.

George. It's only half past eight, Pa.

Dr. Gibbs. I don't know why she's in that old choir. She hasn't any more voice than an old crow. . . . Traipsin' around the streets at this hour of the night. . . . Just about time you retired, don't you think?

George. Yes, Pa.

[George *mounts to his place on the ladder. Laughter and good nights can be heard on stage left and presently* Mrs. Gibbs, Mrs. Soames, *and* Mrs. Webb *come down Main Street. When they arrive at the corner of the stage they stop.*]

Mrs. Soames. Good night, Martha. Good night, Mr. Foster.

Mrs. Webb. I'll tell Mr. Webb; I *know* he'll want to put it in the paper.

Mrs. Gibbs. My, it's late!

Mrs. Soames. Good night, Irma.

Mrs. Gibbs. Real nice choir practice, wa'n't it? Myrtle Webb! Look at that moon, will you! Tsk-tsk-tsk. Potato weather, for sure.

[*They are silent a moment, gazing up at the moon.*]

Mrs. Soames. Naturally I didn't want to say a word about it in front of those others, but now we're alone—really, it's the worst scandal that ever was in this town!

Mrs. Gibbs. What?

Mrs. Soames. Simon Stimson!

Mrs. Gibbs. Now, Louella!

Mrs. Soames. But, Julia. To have the organist of a church *drink* and *drunk* year after year. You know he was drunk tonight.

Mrs. Gibbs. Now, Louella! We all know about Mr. Stimson, and we all know about the troubles he's been through, and Dr. Ferguson knows too, and if Dr. Ferguson keeps him on there in his job the only thing the rest of us can do is just not to notice it.

Mrs. Soames. *Not to notice it!* But it's getting worse.

Mrs. Webb. No, it isn't, Louella. It's getting better. I've been in that choir twice as long as you have. It doesn't happen anywhere near so often. . . . My, I hate to go to bed on a night like this.—I better hurry. Those children'll be sitting up till all hours. Good night, Louella.

[*They all exchange good nights. She hurries downstage, enters her house and disappears.*]

Mrs. Gibbs. Can you get home safe, Louella?

Mrs. Soames. It's as bright as day. I can see Mr. Soames scowling at the window now. You'd think we'd been to a dance the way the menfolk carry on.

[*More good nights. Mrs. Gibbs arrives at her home and passes through the trellis into the kitchen.*]

Mrs. Gibbs. Well, we had a real good time.

Dr. Gibbs. You're late enough.

Mrs. Gibbs. Why, Frank, it ain't any later 'n usual.

Dr. Gibbs. And you stopping at the corner to gossip with a lot of hens.

Mrs. Gibbs. Now, Frank, don't be grouchy. Come out and smell the heliotrope in the moonlight. (*They stroll out arm in arm along the footlights.*) Isn't that wonderful? What did you do all the time I was away?

Dr. Gibbs. I read—as usual. What were the girls gossiping about tonight?

Mrs. Gibbs. Well, believe me, Frank—there is something to gossip about.

Dr. Gibbs. Hmm! Simon Stimson far gone, was he?

Mrs. Gibbs. Worst I've ever seen him. How'll that end, Frank? Dr. Ferguson can't forgive him forever.

Dr. Gibbs. I guess I know more about Simon Stimson's affairs than anybody in this town. Some people ain't made for small-town life. I

don't know how that'll end; but there's nothing we can do but just leave it alone. Come, get in.

Mrs. Gibbs. No, not yet . . . Frank, I'm worried about you.

Dr. Gibbs. What are you worried about?

Mrs. Gibbs. I think it's my duty to make plans for you to get a real rest and change. And if I get that legacy, well, I'm going to insist on it.

Dr. Gibbs. Now, Julia, there's no sense in going over that again.

Mrs. Gibbs. Frank, you're just *unreasonable!*

Dr. Gibbs (*starting into the house*). Come on, Julia, it's getting late. First thing you know you'll catch cold. I gave George a piece of my mind tonight. I reckon you'll have your wood chopped for a while anyway. No, no, start getting upstairs.

Mrs. Gibbs. Oh, dear. There's always so many things to pick up, seems like. You know, Frank, Mrs. Fairchild always locks her front door every night. All those people up that part of town do.

Dr. Gibbs (*blowing out the lamp*). They're all getting citified, that's the trouble with them. They haven't got nothing fit to burgle and everybody knows it. (*They disappear.*)

[Rebecca *climbs up the ladder beside* George.]

George. Get out, Rebecca. There's only room for one at this window. You're always spoiling everything.

Rebecca. Well, let me look just a minute.

George. Use your own window.

Rebecca. I did, but there's no moon there. . . George, do you know what I think, do you? I think maybe the moon's getting nearer and nearer and there'll be a big 'splosion.

George. Rebecca, you don't know anything.

If the moon were getting nearer, the guys that sit up all night with telescopes would see it first and they'd tell about it, and it'd be in all the newspapers.

Rebecca. George, is the moon shining on South America, Canada and half the whole world?

George. Well—prob'ly is.

[*The* Stage Manager *strolls on. Pause. The sound of crickets is heard.*]

Stage Manager. Nine thirty. Most of the lights are out. No, there's Constable Warren trying a few doors on Main Street. And here comes Editor Webb, after putting his newspaper to bed.

[*Mr. Warren, an elderly policeman, comes along Main Street from the right,* Mr. Webb *from the left.*]

Mr. Webb. Good evening, Bill.

Constable Warren. Evenin', Mr. Webb.

Mr. Webb. Quite a moon!

Constable Warren. Yepp.

Mr. Webb. All quiet tonight?

Constable Warren. Simon Stimson is rollin' around a little. Just saw his wife movin' out to hunt for him so I looked the other way—there he is now.

[Simon Stimson *comes down Main Street from the left, only a trace of unsteadiness in his walk.*]

Mr. Webb. Good evening, Simon. . . . Town seems to have settled down for the night pretty well. . . . (Simon Stimson *comes up to him and pauses a moment and stares at him, swaying slightly.*) Good evening . . . Yes, most of the town's settled down for the night, Simon. . . . I guess we better do the same. Can I walk along a ways with you? (Simon Stimson *continues on his way without a word and disappears at the right.*) Good night.

Constable Warren. I don't know how that's goin' to end, Mr. Webb.

Mr. Webb. Well, he's seen a peck of trouble, one thing after another . . . . Oh, Bill . . . if you see my boy smoking cigarettes, just give him a word, will you? He thinks a lot of you, Bill.

Constable Warren. I don't think he smokes no cigarettes, Mr. Webb. Leastways, not more'n two or three a year.

Mr. Webb. Hm . . . I hope not.—Well, good night, Bill.

Constable Warren. Good night, Mr. Webb. (*Exit.*)

Mr. Webb. Who's that up there? Is that you, Myrtle?

Emily. No, it's me, Papa.

Mr. Webb. Why aren't you in bed?

Emily. I don't know. I just can't sleep yet, Papa. The moonlight's so *won-*derful. And the smell of Mrs. Gibbs' heliotrope. Can you smell it?

Mr. Webb. Hm . . . Yes. Haven't any troubles on your mind, have you, Emily?

Emily. *Troubles,* Papa? *No.*

Mr. Webb. Well, enjoy yourself, but don't let your mother catch you. Good night, Emily.

Emily. Good night, Papa.

[Mr. Webb *crosses into the house, whistling "Blessed Be the Tie That Binds" and disappears.*]

Rebecca. I never told you about that letter Jane Crofut got from her minister when she was sick. He wrote Jane a letter and on the envelope the address was like this: It said: Jane Crofut; the Crofut Farm; Grover's Corners; Sutton County; New Hampshire; United States of America.

George. What's funny about that?

Rebecca. But listen, it's not finished: the United States of America; Continent of North America; Western Hemisphere; the Earth; the Solar System; the Universe; the Mind of God—that's what it said on the envelope.

George. What do you know!

Rebecca. And the postman brought it just the same.

George. What do you know!

Stage Manager. That's the end of the First Act, friends. You can go and smoke now, those that smoke.

Study Questions

1. What unusual stage techniques does Wilder use to make the audience feel closer to the action in the play?

2. The first act shows a single day in the lives of the people in Grover's Corners, New Hampshire. How is the complete day indicated by the playwright? What events occur during this day? What interrupts the action of the play?

3. How does the Stage Manager seem to control the action of the play?

4. What questions do the following characters ask: the woman in the balcony? the belligerent man? the lady in the box? How does Mr. Webb answer each of these questions? What do you think the questions and answers indicate about the nature or makeup of the whole community?

5. What questions are raised in Act I that the audience would hope to find answered in the rest of the play? What conflict is established?

6. What elements contribute to the general mood of serenity in this act?

7. What do you think is the significance of Rebecca's final speech in Act I?

Composition

1. Since so little scenery is used in a production of *Our Town,* members of the audience must use their imaginations to visualize Grover's Corners, New Hampshire. How did you see the town as you read the first act? Write a description of the town including the information the Stage Manager gives at the beginning. Fill in any details which your own imagination created. End by stating any advantages or disadvantages you see in living in a small town like Grover's Corners.

2. Although the scenes of daily life in the first act of *Our Town* occurred in 1901, many of the elements still exist in contemporary American life. Choose one of the scenes that occurs in Act I, and compare it to an experience in your own life. You may want to choose the breakfast scene, the father/son or the mother/daughter talk. First describe the scene as it occurred in the play. Then describe the similar scene you have experienced. Conclude with a statement that reflects the idea that time makes little change in human nature.

Vocabulary

Like other words, the name of a town often has an **etymology**, or word history. Although the exact origins of many American place names have been lost through time, it still is possible to determine general categories to which some place names can be assigned. Here are six such categories, described by H.L. Menckens and Albert H. Marckwardt.[2]

1. Native American words, either (1) remaining in their original languages (e.g., *Chicago, Manhattan, Wichita, Mississippi*) or (2) translated into English (e.g., *Blue Ridge, Four Horns, Stinking Water*). •

2. Names transferred to America from older lands *(New England, New Orleans, Athens, Memphis, Moscow).*

3. People's names, including (1) those of persons who took part in or who sponsored exploration or colonization *(Columbus, Williamsburg, Baltimore);* (2) those of American leaders *(Jefferson, Franklin);* and (3) those of pioneer settlers and outstanding citizens of particular localities *(Conway, Jaffrey).*

4. Regional features of topography, plant and animal life, and the like *(Hot Springs, Lake Forest, Palm Desert, Elk City).*

5. Ideals or goals that pioneers strove for in establishing settlements *(Union, Independence, New Harmony).*

6. Combinations of words from more than one of the preceding categories *(Sioux Falls, Lincoln Heights).*

By examining these sources thoughtfully, you should be able to assign each of the following place names mentioned in *Our Town* to one of the six categories. On a separate sheet of paper, copy the names. After each one, write the category number(s) that indicates the place name's source.

Buffalo	Crawford Notch	Mount Washington
Concord	Dublin	New Hampshire
Contoocook	Grover's Corners	Winnipesaukee

---

1 *The American Language* 4th ed. (New York: Alfred A. Knopf, 1963), pp. 642–66.
2 *American English* (New York: Oxford University Press, 1958), pp. 151–62.

ACT II

[The tables and chairs of the two kitchens are still on the stage.

The ladders and the small bench have been withdrawn.

The Stage Manager *has been at his accustomed place watching the audience return to its seats.]*

Stage Manager. Three years have gone by.

Yes, the sun's come up over a thousand times.

Summers and winters have cracked the mountains a little bit more and the rains have brought down some of the dirt.

Some babies that weren't even born before have begun talking regular sentences already; and a number of people who thought they were right young and spry have noticed that they can't bound up a flight of stairs like they used to, without their heart fluttering a little.

All that can happen in a thousand days.

Nature's been pushing and contriving in other ways, too: a number of young people fell in love and got married.

Yes, the mountain got bit away a few fractions of an inch; millions of gallons of water went by the mill; and here and there a new home was set up under a roof.

Almost everybody in the world gets married,—you know what I mean? In our town there aren't hardly any exceptions. Most everybody in the world climbs into their graves married.

The First Act was called the Daily Life. This act is called Love and Marriage. There's another act coming after this: I reckon you can guess what that's about.

So:

It's three years later. It's 1904.

It's July 7th, just after High School Commencement.

That's the time most of our young people jump up and get married.

Soon as they've passed their last examinations in solid geometry and Cicero's Orations, looks like they suddenly feel themselves fit to be married.

It's early morning. Only this time it's been raining. It's been pouring and thundering.

Mrs. Gibbs' garden, and Mrs. Webb's here: drenched.

All those bean poles and pea vines: drenched.

All yesterday over there on Main Street, the rain looked like curtains being blown along.

Hm . . . it may begin again any minute.

There! You can hear the 5:45 for Boston.

(Mrs. Gibbs *and* Mrs. Webb *enter their kitchens and start the day as in the First Act.*)

And there's Mrs. Gibbs and Mrs. Webb come down to make breakfast, just as though it were an ordinary day. I don't have to point out to the women in my audience that those ladies they see before them, both of those ladies cooked three meals a day—one of 'em for twenty years, the other for forty—and no summer vacation. They brought up two children apiece, washed, cleaned the house,—and never a nervous breakdown.

It's like what one of those Middle West poets[6] said: You've got to love life to have life, and you've got to have life to love life. . . . It's what they call a vicious circle.

Howie Newsome (*off stage left*). Giddap, Bessie!

Stage Manager. Here comes Howie Newsome delivering the milk. And there's Si Crowell delivering the papers like his brother before him.

[Si Crowell has entered hurling imaginary newspapers into doorways; Howie Newsome has come along Main Street with Bessie.]

---

6 one . . . poets: "It takes life to love life." from *Spoon River Anthology* by Edgar Lee Masters.

Si Crowell. Morning, Howie.

Howie Newsome. Morning, Si.—Anything in the papers I ought to know?

Si Crowell. Nothing much, except we're losing about the best baseball pitcher Grover's Corners ever had—George Gibbs.

Howie Newsome. Reckon he is.

Si Crowell. He could hit and run bases, too.

Howie Newsome. Yep. Mighty fine ball player.—Whoa! Bessie! I guess I can stop and talk if I've a mind to!

Si Crowell. I don't see how he could give up a thing like that just to get married. Would you, Howie?

Howie Newsome. Can't tell, Si. Never had no talent that way. (Constable Warren *enters. They exchange good mornings.*) You're up early, Bill.

Constable Warren. Seein' if there's anything I can do to prevent a flood. River's been risin' all night.

Howie Newsome. Si Crowell's all worked up here about George Gibbs' retiring from baseball.

Constable Warren. Yes, sir; that's the way it goes. Back in '84 we had a player, Si—even George Gibbs couldn't touch him. Name of Hank Todd. Went down to Maine and became a parson. Wonderful ball player.—Howie, how does the weather look to you?

Howie Newsome. Oh, 'tain't bad. Think maybe it'll clear up for good.

[Constable Warren *and* Si Crowell *continue on their way.* Howie Newsome *brings the milk first to* Mrs. Gibbs' *house. She meets him by the trellis.*]

Mrs. Gibbs. Good morning, Howie. Do you think it's going to rain again?

Howie Newsome. Morning, Mrs. Gibbs. It rained so heavy, I think maybe it'll clear up.

Mrs. Gibbs. Certainly hope it will.

Howie Newsome. How much did you want today?

Mrs. Gibbs. I'm going to have a houseful of relations, Howie. Looks to me like I'll need three-a-milk and two-a-cream.

Howie Newsome. My wife says to tell you we both hope they'll be very happy, Mrs. Gibbs. Know they *will*.

Mrs. Gibbs. Thanks a lot, Howie. Tell your wife I hope she gits there to the wedding.

Howie Newsome. Yes, she'll be there; she'll be there if she kin. (Howie Newsome *crosses to* Mrs. Webb's *house.*) Morning, Mrs. Webb.

Mrs. Webb. Oh, good morning, Mr. Newsome. I told you four quarts of milk, but I hope you can spare me another.

Howie Newsome. Yes'm . . . and the two of cream.

Mrs. Webb. Will it start raining again, Mr. Newsome?

Howie Newsome. Well. Just sayin' to Mrs. Gibbs as how it may lighten up. Mrs. Newsome told me to tell you as how we hope they'll both be very happy, Mrs. Webb. Know they *will*.

Mrs. Webb. Thank you, and thank Mrs. Newsome and we're counting on seeing you at the wedding.

Howie Newsome. Yes, Mrs. Webb. We hope to git there. Couldn't miss that. Come on, Bessie.

[*Exit* Howie Newsome. Dr. Gibbs *descends in shirt sleeves, and sits down at his breakfast table.*]

Dr. Gibbs. Well, Ma, the day has come. You're losin' one of your chicks.

Mrs. Gibbs. Frank Gibbs, don't you say another word. I feel like crying every minute. Sit down and drink your coffee.

Dr. Gibbs. The groom's up shaving himself—only there ain't an awful lot to shave. Whistling and singing, like he's glad to leave us.—Every now and then he says "I do" to the mirror, but it don't sound convincing to me.

Mrs. Gibbs. I declare, Frank, I don't know how he'll get along. I've arranged his clothes and seen to it he's put warm things on,—Frank! they're too *young.* Emily won't think of such things. He'll catch his death of cold within a week.

Dr. Gibbs. I was remembering my wedding morning, Julia.

Mrs. Gibbs. Now don't start that, Frank Gibbs.

Dr. Gibbs. I was the scaredest young fella in the State of New Hampshire. I thought I'd make a mistake for sure. And when I saw you comin' down the aisle I thought you were the prettiest girl I'd ever seen, but the only trouble was that I'd never seen you before. There I was in the Congregational Church marryin' a total stranger.

Mrs. Gibbs. And how do you think I felt!—Frank, weddings are perfectly awful things. Farces,—that's what they are! (*She puts a plate before him.*) Here, I've made something for you.

Dr. Gibbs. Why, Julia Hersey—French toast!

Mrs. Gibbs. 'Tain't hard to make and I had to do something.

[*Pause.* Dr. Gibbs *pours on the syrup.*]

Dr. Gibbs. How'd you sleep last night, Julia?

Mrs. Gibbs. Well, I heard a lot of the hours struck off.

Dr. Gibbs. Ye-e-s! I get a shock every time I think of George setting out to be a family man—that great gangling thing!—I tell you Julia, there's nothing so terrifying in the world as a *son*. The relation of father and son is the darndest, awkwardest—

Mrs. Gibbs. Well, mother and daughter's no picnic, let me tell you.

Dr. Gibbs. They'll have a lot of troubles, I suppose, but that's none of our business. Everybody has a right to their own troubles.

Mrs. Gibbs (*at the table, drinking her coffee, meditatively*). Yes . . . people are meant to go through life two by two. 'Tain't natural to be lonesome.

[*Pause.* Dr. Gibbs *starts laughing.*]

Dr. Gibbs. Julia, do you know one of the things I was scared of when I married you?

Mrs. Gibbs. Oh, go along with you!

Dr. Gibbs. I was afraid we wouldn't have material for conversation more'n'd last us a few weeks. (*Both laugh.*) I was afraid we'd run out and eat our meals in silence, that's a fact.—Well, you and I been conversing for twenty years now without any noticeable barren spells.

Mrs. Gibbs. Well,—good weather, bad weather—'tain't very choice, but I always find something to say. (*She goes to the foot of the stairs.*) Did you hear Rebecca stirring around upstairs?

Dr. Gibbs. No. Only day of the year Rebecca hasn't been managing everybody's business up there. She's hiding in her room.—I got the impression she's crying.

Mrs. Gibbs. Lord's sakes!—This has got to stop.—Rebecca! Rebecca! Come and get your breakfast.

[George *comes rattling down the stairs, very brisk.*]

George. Good morning, everybody. Only five more hours to live.

[*Makes the gesture of cutting his throat, and a loud "k-k-k," and starts through the trellis.*]

Mrs. Gibbs. George Gibbs, where are you going?

George. Just stepping across the grass to see my girl.

Mrs. Gibbs. Now, George! You put on your overshoes. It's raining torrents. You don't go out of this house without you're prepared for it.

George. Aw, Ma. It's just a *step!*

Mrs. Gibbs. George! You'll catch your death of cold and cough all through the service.

Dr. Gibbs. George, do as your mother tells you!

[Dr. Gibbs *goes upstairs.* George *returns reluctantly to the kitchen and pantomimes putting on overshoes.*]

Mrs. Gibbs. From tomorrow on you can kill yourself in all weathers, but while you're in my house you'll live wisely, thank you.—Maybe Mrs. Webb isn't used to callers at seven in the morning.—Here, take a cup of coffee first.

George. Be back in a minute. (*He crosses the stage, leaping over the puddles.*) Good morning, Mother Webb.

Mrs. Webb. Goodness! You frightened me!—Now, George, you can come in a minute out of the wet, but you know I can't ask you in.

George. Why not—?

Mrs. Webb. George, you know's well as I do: the groom can't see his bride on his wedding day, not until he sees her in church.

George. Aw!—that's just a superstition.— Good morning, Mr. Webb.

[*Enter* Mr. Webb.]

Mr. Webb. Good morning, George.

George. Mr. Webb, you don't believe in that superstition, do you?

Mr. Webb. There's a lot of common sense in some superstitions, George. (*He sits at the table, facing right.*)

Mrs. Webb. Millions have folla'd it, George, and you don't want to be the first to fly in the face of custom.

George. How is Emily?

Mrs. Webb. She hasn't waked up yet. I haven't heard a sound out of her.

George. Emily's *asleep!!!*

Mrs. Webb. No wonder! We were up 'til all hours, sewing and packing. Now I'll tell you what I'll do; you set down here a minute with Mr. Webb and drink this cup of coffee; and I'll go upstairs and see she doesn't come down and surprise you. There's some bacon, too; but don't be long about it.

[*Exit* Mrs. Webb. *Embarrassed silence.* Mr. Webb *dunks doughnuts in his coffee. More silence.*]

Mr. Webb (*suddenly and loudly*). Well, George, how are you?

George (*startled, choking over his coffee*). Oh, fine, I'm fine. (*Pause.*) Mr. Webb, what sense could there be in a superstition like that?

Mr. Webb. Well, you see,—on her wedding morning a girl's head's apt to be full of . . . clothes and one thing and another. Don't you think that's probably it?

George. Ye-e-s. I never thought of that.

Mr. Webb. A girl's apt to be a mite nervous on her wedding day.

[*Pause.*]

George. I wish a fellow could get married without all that marching up and down.

Mr. Webb. Every man that's ever lived has felt that way about it, George; but it hasn't been any use. It's the womenfolk who've built up weddings, my boy. For a while now the women have it all their own. A man looks pretty small at a wedding, George. All those good women standing shoulder to shoulder making sure that the knot's tied in a mighty public way.

George. But . . . you *believe* in it, don't you, Mr. Webb?

Mr. Webb (*with alacrity*). Oh, yes; *oh, yes.* Don't you misunderstand me, my boy. Marriage is a wonderful thing—wonderful thing. And don't you forget that, George.

George. No, sir.—Mr. Webb, how old were you when you got married?

Mr. Webb. Well, you see: I'd been to college and I'd taken a little time to get settled. But Mrs. Webb—she wasn't much older than what Emily is. Oh, age hasn't much to do with it, George,—not compared with . . . uh . . . other things.

George. What were you going to say, Mr. Webb?

Mr. Webb. Oh, I don't know.—Was I going to say something? (*Pause.*) George, I was thinking the other night of some advice my father gave me when I got married. Charles, he said, Charles, start out early showing who's boss, he said. Best thing to do is to give an order, even if it don't make sense; just so she'll learn to obey. And he said: if anything about your wife irritates you—her conversation, or anything—just get up and leave the house. That'll make it clear to her, he said. And, oh, yes! he said never, *never* let your wife know how much money you have, never.

George. Well, Mr. Webb . . . I don't think I could . . . .

Mr. Webb. So I took the opposite of my father's advice and I've been happy ever since.

And let that be a lesson to you, George, never to ask advice on personal matters.—George, are you going to raise chickens on your farm?

George. What?

Mr. Webb. Are you going to raise chickens on your farm?

George. Uncle Luke's never been much interested, but I thought—

Mr. Webb. A book came into my office the other day, George, on the Philo System of raising chickens. I want you to read it. I'm thinking of beginning in a small way in the back yard, and I'm going to put an incubator in the cellar—

[*Enter* Mrs. Webb.]

Mrs. Webb. Charles, are you talking about that old incubator again? I thought you two'd be talking about things worth while.

Mr. Webb (*bitingly*). Well, Myrtle, if you want to give the boy some good advice, I'll go upstairs and leave you alone with him.

Mrs. Webb (*pulling* George *up*). George, Emily's got to come downstairs and eat her breakfast. She sends you her love but she doesn't want to lay eyes on you. Good-by.

George. Good-by.

[George *crosses the stage to his own home, bewildered and crestfallen. He slowly dodges a puddle and disappears into his house.*]

Mr. Webb. Myrtle, I guess you don't know about that older superstition.

Mrs. Webb. What do you mean, Charles?

Mr. Webb. Since the cave men: no bridegroom should see his father-in-law on the day of the wedding, or near it. Now remember that.

[*Both leave the stage.*]

Stage Manager. Thank you very much, Mr. and Mrs. Webb.—Now I have to interrupt again here. You see, we want to know how all this began—this wedding, this plan to spend a lifetime together. I'm awfully interested in how big things like that begin.

You know how it is: you're twenty-one or twenty-two and you make some decisions; then whisssh! you're seventy: you've been a lawyer for fifty years, and that white-haired lady at your side has eaten over fifty thousand meals with you.

How do such things begin?

George and Emily are going to show you now the conversation they had when they first knew that . . . that . . . as the saying goes . . . they were meant for one another.

But before they do it I want you to try and remember what it was like to have been very young.

And particularly the days when you were first in love; when you were like a person sleepwalking, and you didn't quite see the street you were in, and didn't quite hear everything that was said to you.

You're just a little bit crazy. Will you remember that, please?

Now they'll be coming out of high school at three o'clock. George has just been elected President of the Junior Class, and as it's June, that means he'll be President of the Senior Class all next year. And Emily's just been elected Secretary and Treasurer.

I don't have to tell you how important that is.

[*He places a board across the backs of two chairs, which he takes from those at the Gibbs family's table. He brings two high stools from the wings and places them behind the board. Persons sitting on the stools will be facing the audience. This is the counter of Mr. Morgan's drugstore. The sounds of young people's voices are heard off left.*]

Yepp,—there they are coming down Main Street now.

[Emily, *carrying an armful of—imaginary— schoolbooks, comes along Main Street from the left.*]

Emily. I can't, Louise. I've got to go home. Good-by. Oh, Ernestine! Ernestine! Can you come over tonight and do Latin? Isn't that Cicero the worst thing—! Tell your mother you *have* to. G'by. G'by, Helen. G'by, Fred.

[George, *also carrying books, catches up with her.*]

George. Can I carry your books home for you, Emily?

Emily (*coolly*). Why . . . uh . . . Thank you. It isn't far. (*She gives them to him.*)

George. Excuse me a minute, Emily.—Say, Bob, if I'm a little late, start practice anyway. And give Herb some long high ones.

Emily. Good-by, Lizzy.

George. Good-by, Lizzy.—I'm awfully glad you were elected, too, Emily.

Emily. Thank you.

[*They have been standing on Main Street, almost against the back wall. They take the first steps toward the audience when* George *stops and says:*]

George. Emily, why are you mad at me?

Emily. I'm not mad at you.

George. You've been treating me so funny lately.

Emily. Well, since you ask me, I might as well say it right out, George,—(*She catches sight of a teacher passing.*) Good-by, Miss Corcoran.

George. Good-by, Miss Corcoran.—Wha—what is it?

Emily (*not scoldingly; finding it difficult to say*). I don't like the whole change that's come over you in the last year. I'm sorry if that hurts your feelings, but I've got to—tell the truth and shame the devil.

George. A *change?*—Wha—what do you mean?

Emily. Well, up to a year ago I used to like you a lot. And I used to watch you as you did everything . . . because we'd been friends so long . . . and then you began spending all your time at *baseball* . . . and you never stopped to speak to anybody any more. Not even to your own family you didn't . . . and, George, it's a fact, you've got awful conceited and stuck-up, and all the girls say so. They may not say so to your face, but that's what they say about you behind your back, and it hurts me to hear them say it, but I've got to agree with them a little. I'm sorry if it hurts your feelings . . . but I can't be sorry I said it.

George. I . . . I'm glad you said it, Emily. I never thought that such a thing was happening to me. I guess it's hard for a fella not to have faults creep into his character.

[*They take a step or two in silence, then stand still in misery.*]

Emily. I always expect a man to be perfect and I think he should be.

George. Oh . . . I don't think it's possible to be perfect, Emily.

Emily. Well, my *father* is, and as far as I can see *your* father is. There's no reason on earth why you shouldn't be, too.

George. Well, I feel it's the other way around. That men aren't naturally good; but girls are.

Emily. Well, you might as well know right now that I'm not perfect. It's not as easy for a girl to be perfect as a man, because we girls are more—more—nervous.—Now I'm sorry I said all that about you. I don't know what made me say it.

George. Emily,—

Emily. Now I can see it's not the truth at all. And I suddenly feel that it isn't important, anyway.

George. Emily . . . would you like an ice-cream soda, or something, before you go home?

Emily. Well, thank you . . . I would.

[*They advance toward the audience and make an abrupt right turn, opening the door of Morgan's drugstore. Under strong emotion, Emily keeps her face down. George speaks to some passers-by.*]

George. Hello, Stew,—how are you?—Good afternoon, Mrs. Slocum.

[*The* Stage Manager, *wearing spectacles and assuming the role of* Mr. Morgan, *enters abruptly from the right and stands between the audience and the counter of his soda fountain.*]

Stage Manager. Hello, George. Hello, Emily.—What'll you have?—Why, Emily Webb—what you been crying about?

George (*he gropes for an explanation*). She . . . she just got an awful scare, Mr. Morgan. She almost got run over by that hardware-store wagon. Everybody says that Tom Huckins drives like a crazy man.

Stage Manager (*drawing a drink of water*). Well, now! You take a drink of water, Emily. You look all shook up. I tell you, you've got to look both ways before you cross Main Street these days. Gets worse every year.—What'll you have?

Emily. I'll have a strawberry phosphate, thank you, Mr. Morgan.

George. No, no, Emily. Have an ice-cream soda with me. Two strawberry ice-cream sodas, Mr. Morgan.

Stage Manager (*working the faucets*). Two strawberry ice-cream sodas, yes sir. Yes, sir. There are a hundred and twenty-five horses in Grover's Corners this minute I'm talking to you. State Inspector was in here yesterday. And now they're bringing in these auto–mobiles, the best thing to do is to just stay home. Why, I can remember when a dog could go to

sleep all day in the middle of Main Street and nothing come along to disturb him. (*He sets the imaginary glasses before them.*) There they are. Enjoy 'em. (*He sees a customer, right.*) Yes, Mrs. Ellis. What can I do for you? (*He goes out right.*)

Emily. They're so expensive.

George. No, no,—don't think of that. We're celebrating our election. And then do you know what else I'm celebrating?

Emily. N-no.

George. I'm celebrating because I've got a friend who tells me all the things that ought to be told me.

Emily. George, *please* don't think of that. I don't know why I said it. It's not true. You're—

George. No, Emily, you stick to it. I'm glad you spoke to me like you did. But you'll *see:* I'm going to change so quick—you bet I'm going to change. And, Emily, I want to ask you a favor.

Emily. What?

George. Emily, if I go away to State Agriculture College next year, will you write me a letter once in a while?

Emily. I certainly will. I certainly will, George. . . . (*Pause. They start sipping the sodas through the straws.*) It certainly seems like being away three years you'd get out of touch with things. Maybe letters from Grover's Corners wouldn't be so interesting after a while. Grover's Corners isn't a very important place when you think of all—New Hampshire; but I think it's a very nice town.

George. The day wouldn't come when I wouldn't want to know everything that's happening here. I know *that's* true, Emily.

Emily. Well, I'll try to make my letters interesting.

[*Pause.*]

George. Y'know. Emily, whenever I meet a farmer I ask him if he thinks it's important to go to Agriculture School to be a good farmer.

Emily. Why, George—

George. Yeah, and some of them say that it's even a waste of time. You can get all those things, anyway, out of the pamphlets the government sends out. And Uncle Luke's getting old,—he's about ready for me to start in taking over his farm tomorrow, if I could.

Emily. My!

George. And, like you say, being gone all that time . . . in other places and meeting other people . . . Gosh, if anything like that can happen I don't want to go away. I guess new people aren't any better than old ones. I'll bet they almost never are. Emily . . . I feel that you're as good a friend as I've got. I don't need to go and meet the people in other towns.

Emily. But, George, maybe it's very important for you to go and learn all that about— cattle judging and soils and those things. . . . Of course, I don't know.

George (*after a pause, very seriously*). Emily, I'm going to make up my mind right now. I won't go. I'll tell Pa about it tonight.

Emily. Why, George, I don't see why you have to decide right now. It's a whole year away.

George. Emily, I'm glad you spoke to me about that . . . that fault in my character. What you said was right; but there was one thing wrong in it, and that was when you said that for a year I wasn't noticing people, and . . . you, for instance. Why, you say you were watching me when I did everything . . . I was doing the same about you all the time. Why, sure,—I always thought about you as one of the chief people I thought about. I always made sure where you were sitting on the bleachers, and who you were with, and for three days now I've been trying to walk home

with you; but something's always got in the way. Yesterday I was standing over against the wall waiting for you, and you walked home with *Miss Corcoran.*

Emily. George! . . . Life's awful funny! How could I have known that? Why, I thought—

George. Listen, Emily, I'm going to tell you why I'm not going to Agriculture School. I think that once you've found a person that you're very fond of . . . I mean a person who's fond of you, too, and likes you enough to be interested in your character . . . Well, I think that's just as important as college is, and even more so. That's what I think.

Emily. I think it's awfully important, too.

George. Emily.

Emily. Y-yes, George.

George. Emily, if I *do* improve and make a big change . . . would you be . . . I mean: *could* you be . . .

Emily. I . . . I am now; I always have been.

George (*pause*). So I guess this is an important talk we've been having.

Emily. Yes . . . yes.

George (*takes a deep breath and straightens his back*). Wait just a minute and I'll walk you home. (*With mounting alarm he digs into his pockets for the money. The Stage Manager enters, right.* George, *deeply embarrassed, but direct, says to him:*) Mr. Morgan, I'll have to go home and get the money to pay you for this. It'll only take me a minute.

Stage Manager (*pretending to be affronted*). What's that? George Gibbs, do you mean to tell me—!

George. Yes, but I had reasons, Mr. Morgan.—Look, here's my gold watch to keep until I come back with the money.

Stage Manager. That's all right. Keep your watch. I'll trust you.

George. I'll be back in five minutes.

Stage Manager. I'll trust you ten years, George,—not a day over.—Got all over your shock, Emily?

Emily. Yes, thank you, Mr. Morgan. It was nothing.

George (*taking up the books from the counter*). I'm ready.

[*They walk in grave silence across the stage and pass through the trellis at the Webbs' back door and disappear. The* Stage Manager *watches them go out, then turns to the audience, removing his spectacles.*]

Stage Manager. Well,—(*He claps his hands as a signal.*) Now we're ready to get on with the wedding.

(*He stands waiting while the set is prepared for the next scene.*

Stagehands *remove the chairs, tables, and trellises from the* Gibbs *and* Webb *houses.*

They arrange the pews for the church in the center of the stage. The congregation will sit facing the back wall. The aisle of the church starts at the center of the back wall and comes toward the audience. A small platform is placed against the back wall on which the Stage Manager *will stand later, playing the minister. The image of a stained-glass window is cast from a lantern slide upon the back wall.*

When all is ready the Stage Manager *strolls to the center of the stage, down front, and, musingly, addresses the audience.*)

There are a lot of things to be said about a wedding; there are a lot of thoughts that go on during a wedding.

We can't get them all into one wedding, naturally, and especially not into a wedding at Grover's Corners, where they're awfully plain and short.

In this wedding I play the minister. That gives me the right to say a few more things about it.

For a while now, the play gets pretty serious.

Y'see, some churches say that marriage is a sacrament. I don't quite know what that means, but I can guess. Like Mrs. Gibbs said a few minutes ago: People were made to live two-by-two.

This is a good wedding, but people are so put together that even at a good wedding there's a lot of confusion way down deep in people's minds and we thought that that ought to be in our play, too.

The real hero of this scene isn't on the stage at all, and you know who that is. It's like what one of those European fellas said: every child born into the world is nature's attempt to make a perfect human being. Well, we've seen nature pushing and contriving for some time now. We all know that nature's interested in quantity; but I think she's interested in quality, too,—that's why I'm in the ministry.

And don't forget all the other witnesses at this wedding,—the ancestors. Millions of them. Most of them set out to live two-by-two, also. Millions of them.

Well, that's all my sermon. 'Twan't very long, anyway.

[*The organ starts playing Handel's "Largo." The congregation streams into the church and sits in silence. Church bells are heard.* Mrs. Gibbs *sits in the front row, the first seat on the aisle, the right section; next to her are* Rebecca *and* Dr. Gibbs. *Across the aisle* Mrs. Webb, Wally, *and* Mr. Webb. *A small choir takes its place, facing the audience under the stained-glass window.* Mrs. Webb, *on the way to her place, turns back and speaks to the audience.*]

Mrs. Webb. I don't know why on earth I should be crying. I suppose there's nothing to cry about. It came over me at breakfast this morning; there was Emily eating her breakfast as she's done for seventeen years and now she's going off to eat it in someone else's house. I suppose that's it.

And Emily! She suddenly said: I can't eat another mouthful, and she put her head down on the table and *she* cried. (*She starts toward her seat in the church, but turns back and adds:*)

Oh, I've got to say it: you know, there's something downright cruel about sending our girls out into marriage this way.

I hope some of her girl friends have told her a thing or two. It's cruel, I know, but I couldn't bring myself to say anything. I went into it blind as a bat myself. (*In half-amused exasperation.*) The whole world's wrong, that's what's the matter.

There they come.

[*She hurries to her place in the pew. George starts to come down the right aisle of the theater, through the audience. Suddenly Three Members of his baseball team appear by the right proscenium pillar and start whistling and catcalling to him. They are dressed for the ball field.*]

The Baseball Players. Eh, George, George! Hast-yaow! Look at him, fellas—he looks scared to death. Yaow! George, don't look so innocent, you old geezer. We know what you're thinking. Don't disgrace the team, big boy. Whoo-oo-oo.

Stage Manager. All right! All right! That'll do. That's enough of that. (*Smiling, he pushes them off the stage. They lean back to shout a few more catcalls.*) There used to be an awful lot of that kind of thing at weddings in the old days,—Rome, and later. We're more civilized now,—so they say.

[*The choir starts singing "Love Divine, All Love Excelling—." George has reached the stage. He stares at the congregation a moment, then takes a few steps of withdrawal, toward the right proscenium pillar. His mother, from the front row, seems to have felt his confusion. She leaves her seat and comes down the aisle quickly to him.*]

Mrs. Gibbs. George! George! What's the matter?

George. Ma, I don't want to grow old. Why's everybody pushing me so?

Mrs. Gibbs. Why, George . . . you wanted it.

George. No, Ma, listen to me—

Mrs. Gibbs. No, no, George,—you're a man now.

George. Listen, Ma,—for the last time I ask you. . . . All I want to do is to be a fella—

Mrs. Gibbs. George! If anyone should hear you! Now stop. Why, I'm ashamed of you!

George (*he comes to himself and looks over the scene*). What? Where's Emily?

Mrs. Gibbs (*relieved*). George! You gave me such a turn.

George. Cheer up. Ma. I'm getting married.

Mrs. Gibbs. Let me catch my breath a minute.

George (*comforting her*). Now, Ma, you save Thursday nights. Emily and I are coming over to dinner every Thursday night . . . you'll see. Ma, what are you crying for? Come on; we've got to get ready for this.

[*Mrs. Gibbs, mastering her emotion, fixes his tie and whispers to him. In the meantime, Emily, in white and wearing her wedding veil, has come through the audience and mounted onto the stage. She too draws back, frightened, when she sees the congregation in the church. The choir begins: "Blessed Be the Tie That Binds."*]

Emily. I never felt so alone in my whole life. And George over there, looking so . . . ! I hate him. I wish I were dead. Papa! Papa!

Mr. Webb (*leaves his seat in the pews and comes toward her anxiously*). Emily! Emily! Now don't get upset. . . .

Emily. But, Papa,—I don't want to get married. . . .

Mr. Webb. Sh—sh—Emily. Everything's all right.

Emily. Why can't I stay for a while just as I am? Let's go away,—

Mr. Webb. No, no, Emily. Now stop and think a minute.

Emily. Don't you remember that you used to say,—all the time you used to say—all the time: that I was *your* girl! There must be lots of places we can go to. I'll work for you. I could keep house.

Mr. Webb. Sh . . . You mustn't think of such things. You're just nervous, Emily. (*He turns and calls:*) George! George! Will you come here a minute? (*He leads her toward* George.) Why you're marrying the best young fellow in the world. George is a fine fellow.

Emily. But Papa,—

[Mrs. Gibbs *returns unobtrusively to her seat.* Mr. Webb *has one arm around his daughter. He places his hand on* George's *shoulder.*]

Mr. Webb. I'm giving away my daughter, George. Do you think you can take care of her?

George. Mr. Webb, I want to . . . I want to try. Emily, I'm going to do my best. I love you, Emily. I need you.

Emily. Well, if you love me, help me. All I want is someone to love me.

George. I will, Emily. Emily, I'll try.

Emily. And I mean for *ever.* Do you hear? For ever and ever.

[*They fall into each other's arms. The March from Lohengrin is heard. The* Stage Manager, *as* Clergyman, *stands on the box, up center.*]

Mr. Webb. Come, they're waiting for us. Now you know it'll be all right. Come, quick.

[George *slips away and takes his place beside the* Stage Manager-Clergyman. Emily *proceeds up the aisle on her father's arm.*]

Stage Manager. Do you, George, take this woman, Emily, to be your wedded wife, to have. . . .

[Mrs. Soames *has been sitting in the last row of the congregation. She now turns to her neighbors and speaks in a shrill voice. Her chatter drowns out the rest of the clergyman's words.*]

Mrs. Soames. Perfectly lovely wedding! Loveliest wedding I ever saw. Oh, I do love a good wedding, don't you? Doesn't she make a lovely bride?

George. I do.

Stage Manager. Do you, Emily, take this man, George, to be your wedded husband,—

[*Again his further words are covered by those of* Mrs. Soames.]

Mrs. Soames. Don't know *when* I've seen such a lovely wedding. But I always cry. Don't know why it is, but I always cry. I just like to see young people happy, don't you? Oh, I think it's lovely.

[*The ring. The kiss. The stage is suddenly arrested into silent tableau. The* Stage Manager, *his eyes on the distance, as though to himself:*]

Stage Manager. I've married over two hundred couples in my day.
Do I believe in it?
I don't know.
M . . . marries N . . . millions of them.
The cottage, the go-cart, the Sunday-afternoon drives in the Ford, the first rheumatism, the grandchildren, the second rheumatism, the deathbed, the reading of the will,— (*He now looks at the audience for the first time, with a warm smile that removes any sense of cynicism from the next line.*) Once in a thousand times it's interesting.
—Well, let's have Mendelssohn's "Wedding March"!

[*The organ picks up the March. The* Bride *and* Groom *come down the aisle, radiant, but trying to be very dignified.*]

Mrs. Soames. Aren't they a lovely couple? Oh, I've never been to such a nice wedding.

I'm sure they'll be happy. I always say: *happiness,* that's the great thing! The important thing is to be happy.

[*The* Bride *and* Groom *reach the steps leading into the audience. A bright light is thrown upon them. They descend into the auditorium and run up the aisle joyously.*]

Stage Manager. That's all the Second Act, folks. Ten minutes' intermission.

Curtain

Study Questions

1. What details in the opening speech by the Stage Manager and in the street scene recall the beginning of Act I?

2. What general statements are made throughout Act II by the Stage Manager on love and marriage? What specific example of proven love does the Stage Manager give in his opening speech?

3. Where does the flashback begin? What incident triggers the flashback? How does the Stage Manager prepare the audience for the scene in the drugstore? Why do you think this scene is punctuated with frequent pauses and silences?

4. Several pieces of evidence in Act II show that Wilder is broadening the scope of the play from Act I. The theme is much larger than the portrayal of a complete day in an ordinary town. As the Stage Manager introduces the wedding, what parallel does he draw between physical nature and human nature? Why do you think Mrs. Soames's voice drowns out most of the wedding ceremony? What do you think is the meaning of the Stage Manager's last long speech in Act II? What do you think the wedding symbolizes?

Composition

1. At the beginning of the wedding scene, the Stage Manager says that "even at a good wedding there's a lot of confusion way down deep in people's minds." Describe the confusion experienced by both George and Emily, and tell how the situation is resolved. End by explaining why you think George and Emily react as they do.

2. When George and Emily are walking down the street, Emily criticizes his recent behavior. Describe a situation in which you have given or received criticism from a friend. Tell how both of you reacted to the situation. You may want to include the change or lack of change that resulted from the conversation.

Vocabulary

Even though most words have many synonyms, usually only one word is exactly right for a particular context. That's why an author's particular **word choice** is very important to the overall meaning of a work. It is often the case, too, that the biggest, most impressive words are not always the best ones to use.

A. The meanings of all the following words relate in some way to the dialogue and action of Act II of *Our Town:*

apprehensiveness	felicitations	lugubriousness	nuptials
connubiality	inarticulateness	nostalgia	solicitude
somnambulist	tribulations		

On a separate sheet of paper, write a definition for each of the above words. Consult a dictionary if necessary.

B. Thornton Wilder no doubt knew all of the above words, and he could easily have incorporated them into his play. Tell which word he could have substituted for each *italicized* word or phrase in the following segments of dialogue based on Act II.

1. **Stage Manager.** The First Act was called Daily Life. This act is called Love and *Marriage.*

2. **Mrs. Gibbs.** Thanks for the extra milk and cream, Howie. Tell your wife I hope she gits there to the *wedding.*

3. **Howie Newsome.** Mrs. Newsome said ask you to give George and Emily our *best wishes.* We hope they'll both be very happy.

4. **Dr. Gibbs.** Today I woke up full of *yearning for the past,* Julia. Do you remember our wedding day?

5. **Mrs. Gibbs.** I declare, I don't know how you can act so calm, Frank—as if there wasn't a reason in the world for *anxiety!* Frank, they're too young!

6. **Dr. Gibbs.** They'll have a lot of *troubles* I suppose. But that's none of our business.

7. **Stage Manager.** I want you to remember when you were first in love; when you were like a *person sleepwalking,* and you didn't quite see the street you were in, and didn't quite hear everything that was said to you.

8. **George.** Can I carry your books home for you, Emily?
   Emily. Why, uh, thank you for your *attention,* George.

9. **George.** So. I guess in spite of my *being tongue-tied* this is an important talk we've been having.

10. **Mrs. Webb.** I don't know why I'm crying. At breakfast, Emily was crying, too. This is supposed to be a day for joy, not *silly tears!*

C. In a sentence or two, explain why the words Thornton Wilder actually chose for *Our Town* are more suitable to the play than the synonyms you have substituted for them. Name two or more types of writing in which it might be especially appropriate to use words such as the ones you defined in Exercise A.

ACT III

[*During the intermission the audience has seen the* Stage Hands *arranging the stage. On the right-hand side, a little right of the center, ten or twelve ordinary chairs have been placed in three openly spaced rows facing the audience. These are graves in the cemetery.*

Toward the end of the intermission the Actors *enter and take their places. The front row contains: toward the center of the stage, an empty chair; then* Mrs. Gibbs; Simon Stimson. *The second row contains, among others,* Mrs. Soames. *The third row has* Wally Webb. *The dead do not turn their heads or their eyes to right or left, but they sit quietly without stiffness. When they speak their tone is matter-of-fact, without sentimentality and, above all, without lugubriousness. The* Stage Manager *takes his accustomed place and waits for the house lights to go down.*]

Stage Manager. This time nine years have gone by, friends—summer, 1913.

Gradual changes in Grover's Corners. Horses are getting rarer.

Farmers coming into town in Fords.

Everybody locks their house doors now at night. Ain't been any burglars in town yet, but everybody's heard about 'em.

You'd be surprised, though—on the whole, things don't change much around here.

This is certainly an important part of Grover's Corners. It's on a hilltop—a windy hilltop—lots of sky, lots of clouds,—often lots of sun and moon and stars.

You come up here, on a fine afternoon and you can see range on range of hills—awful blue they are—up there by Lake Sunapee and Lake Winnipesaukee . . . and way up, if you've got a glass, you can see the White Mountains and Mt. Washington—where North Conway and Conway is. And, of course, our favorite mountain, Mt. Monadnock, 's right here—and all these towns that lie around it: Jaffrey, 'n East Jaffrey, 'n Peterborough, 'n Dublin; and (*then pointing down in the audience*) there, quite a ways down, is Grover's Corners.

Yes, beautiful spot up here. Mountain laurel and li-lacks. I often wonder why people like to be buried in Woodlawn and Brooklyn when they might pass the same time up here in New Hampshire.

Over there—(*pointing to stage left*) are the old stones,—1670, 1680. Strong-minded people that come a long way to be independent. Summer people walk around there laughing at the funny words on the tombstones . . . it don't do any harm. And genealogists come up from Boston—get paid by city people for looking up their ancestors. They want to make sure they're Daughters of the American Revolution and of the *Mayflower*. . . . Well, I guess that don't do any harm, either. Wherever you come near the human race, there's layers and layers of nonsense. . . .

Over there are some Civil War veterans. Iron flags on their graves . . . New Hampshire boys . . . had a notion that the Union ought to be kept together, though they'd never seen more than fifty miles of it themselves. All they knew was the name, friends—the United States of America. The United States of America. And they went and died about it.

This here is the new part of the cemetery. Here's your friend Mrs. Gibbs. 'N let me see—Here's Mr. Stimson, organist at the Congregational Church. And Mrs. Soames who enjoyed the wedding so—you remember? Oh, and a lot of others. And Editor Webb's boy, Wallace, whose appendix burst while he was on a Boy Scout trip to Crawford Notch.

Yes, an awful lot of sorrow has sort of quieted down up here. People just wild with grief have brought their relatives up to this hill. We all know how it is . . . and then time . . . and sunny days . . . and rainy days . . . 'n snow. . . .We're all glad they're in a beautiful place and we're coming up here ourselves when our fit's over.

Now there are some things we all know, but we don't take'm out and look at'm very often. We all know that *something* is eternal. And it ain't houses and it ain't names, and it ain't earth, and it ain't even the stars . . . everybody knows in their bones that *something* is eternal, and that something has to do with human beings. All the greatest people ever lived have been telling us that for five thousand years and yet you'd be surprised how people are always losing hold of it. There's something way down deep that's eternal about every human being.

(*Pause.*)

You know as well as I do that the dead don't stay interested in us living people for very long. Gradually, gradually, they lose hold of the earth . . . and the ambitions they had . . . and the pleasures they had . . . and the things they suffered . . . and the people they loved.

They get weaned away from earth—that's the way I put it,—weaned away.

And they stay here while the earth part of 'em burns away, burns out; and all that time they slowly get indifferent to what's goin' on in Grover's Corners.

They're waitin'. They're waitin' for something that they feel is comin'. Something important, and great. Aren't they waitin' for the eternal part in them to come out clear?

Some of the things they're going to say maybe'll hurt your feelings—but that's the way it is: mother'n daughter . . . husband 'n wife . . . enemy 'n enemy . . . money 'n miser . . . all those terribly important things kind of grow pale around here. And what's left when memory's gone, and your identity, Mrs. Smith?

(*He looks at the audience a minute, then turns to the stage.*)

Well! There are some *living* people. There's Joe Stoddard, our undertaker, supervising a new-made grave. And here comes a Grover's Corners boy, that left town to go out West.

[Joe Stoddard *has hovered about in the background.* Sam Craig *enters left, wiping his forehead from the exertion. He carries an umbrella and strolls front.*]

Sam Craig. Good afternoon, Joe Stoddard.

Joe Stoddard. Good afternoon, good afternoon. Let me see now: do I know you?

Sam Craig. I'm Sam Craig.

Joe Stoddard. Gracious sakes' alive! Of all people! I should'a knowed you'd be back for the funeral. You've been away a long time, Sam.

Sam Craig. Yes, I've been away over twelve years. I'm in business out in Buffalo now, Joe. But I was in the East when I got news of my cousin's death, so I thought I'd combine things a little and come and see the old home. You look well.

Joe Stoddard. Yes, yes, can't complain. Very sad, our journey today, Samuel.

Sam Craig. Yes.

Joe Stoddard. Yes, yes. I always say I hate to supervise when a young person is taken. They'll be here in a few minutes now. I had to come here early today—my son's supervisin' at the home.

Sam Craig (*reading stones*). Old Farmer McCarty, I used to do chores for him—after school. He had the lumbago.

Joe Stoddard. Yes, we brought Farmer McCarty here a number of years ago now.

Sam Craig (*staring at* Mrs. Gibbs' *knees*). Why, this is my Aunt Julia . . . I'd forgotten that she'd . . . of course, of course.

Joe Stoddard. Yes, Doc Gibbs lost his wife two-three years ago . . . about this time. And today's another pretty bad blow for him, too.

Mrs. Gibbs (*to Simon Stimson: in an even voice*). That's my sister Carey's boy, Sam . . . Sam Craig.

Simon Stimson. I'm always uncomfortable when *they're* around.

Mrs. Gibbs. Simon.

Sam Craig. Do they choose their own verses much, Joe?

Joe Stoddard. No . . . not usual. Mostly the bereaved pick a verse.

Sam Craig. Doesn't sound like Aunt Julia. There aren't many of those Hersey sisters left now. Let me see: where are . . . I wanted to look at my father's and mother's . . .

Joe Stoddard. Over there with the Craigs . . . Avenue F.

Sam Craig (*reading* Simon Stimson's *epitaph*). He was organist at church, wasn't he?—Hm, drank a lot, we used to say.

Joe Stoddard. Nobody was supposed to know about it. He'd seen a peck of trouble. (*Behind his hand.*) Took his own life, y' know?

Sam Craig. Oh, did he?

Joe Stoddard. Hung himself in the attic. They tried to hush it up, but of course it got around. He chose his own epy-taph. You can see it there. It ain't a verse exactly.

Sam Craig. Why, it's just some notes of music—what is it?

Joe Stoddard. Oh, I wouldn't know. It was wrote up in the Boston papers at the time.

Sam Craig. Joe, what did she die of?

Joe Stoddard. Who?

Sam Craig. My cousin.

Joe Stoddard. Oh, didn't you know? Had some trouble bringing a baby into the world. 'Twas her second, though. There's a little boy 'bout four years old.

Sam Craig (*opening his umbrella*). The grave's going to be over there?

Joe Stoddard. Yes, there ain't much more room over here among the Gibbses, so they're opening up a whole new Gibbs section over by Avenue B. You'll excuse me now. I see they're comin'.

[*From left to center, at the back of the stage, comes a procession. Four Men carry a casket, invisible to us. All the rest are under umbrellas. One can vaguely see:* Dr. Gibbs, George, *the* Webbs, *etc. They gather about a grave in the back center of the stage, a little to the left of center.*]

Mrs. Soames. Who is it, Julia?

Mrs. Gibbs (*without raising her eyes*). My daughter-in-law, Emily Webb.

Mrs. Soames (*a little surprised, but no emotion*). Well, I declare! The road up here must have been awful muddy. What did she die of, Julia?

Mrs. Gibbs. In childbirth.

Mrs. Soames. Childbirth. (*Almost with a laugh.*) I'd forgotten all about that. My, wasn't life awful—(*with a sigh*) and wonderful.

Simon Stimson (*with a sideways glance*). Wonderful, was it?

Mrs. Gibbs. Simon! Now, remember!

Mrs. Soames. I remember Emily's wedding. Wasn't it a lovely wedding! And I remember her reading the class poem at Graduation Exercises. Emily was one of the brightest girls ever graduated from High School. I've heard Principal Wilkins say so time after time. I called on them at their new farm, just before I died. Perfectly beautiful farm.

A Woman from among the Dead. It's on the same road we lived on.

A Man among the Dead. Yepp, right smart farm.

[*They subside. The group by the grave starts singing "Blessed Be the Tie That Binds."*]

A Woman among the Dead. I always liked that hymn. I was hopin' they'd sing a hymn.

[*Pause. Suddenly* Emily *appears from among the umbrellas. She is wearing a white dress. Her hair is down her back and tied by a white ribbon like a little girl. She comes slowly, gazing wonderingly at the dead, a little dazed. She stops halfway and smiles faintly. After looking at the mourners for a moment, she walks slowly to the vacant chair beside* Mrs. Gibbs *and sits down.*]

Emily (*to them all, quietly, smiling*). Hello.

Mrs. Soames. Hello, Emily.

A Man among the Dead. Hello, M's Gibbs.

Emily (*warmly*). Hello, Mother Gibbs.

Mrs. Gibbs. Emily.

Emily. Hello. (*With surprise.*) It's raining. (*Her eyes drift back to the funeral company.*)

Mrs. Gibbs. Yes . . . They'll be gone soon, dear. Just rest yourself.

Emily. It seems thousands and thousands of years since I . . . Papa remembered that that was my favorite hymn.

Oh, I wish I'd been here a long time. I don't like being new here.—How do you do, Mr. Stimson?

Simon Stimson. How do you do, Emily.

[Emily *continues to look about her with a wondering smile; as though to shut out from her mind the thought of the funeral company she starts speaking to* Mrs. Gibbs *with a touch of nervousness.*]

Emily. Mother Gibbs, George and I have made that farm into just the best place you ever saw. We thought of you all the time. We wanted to show you the new barn and a great long ce-ment drinking fountain for the stock. We bought that out of the money you left us.

Mrs. Gibbs. I did?

Emily. Don't you remember, Mother Gibbs—the legacy you left us? Why, it was over three hundred and fifty dollars.

Mrs. Gibbs. Yes, yes, Emily.

Emily. Well, there's a patent device on the drinking fountain so that it never overflows, Mother Gibbs, and it never sinks below a certain mark they have there. It's fine. (*Her voice trails off and her eyes return to the funeral group.*) It won't be the same to George without me, but it's a lovely farm. (*Suddenly she looks directly at* Mrs. Gibbs.) Live people don't understand, do they?

Mrs. Gibbs. No, dear—not very much.

Emily. They're sort of shut up in little boxes, aren't they? I feel as though I knew them last a thousand years ago . . . My boy is spending the day at Mrs. Carter's. (*She sees* Mr. Carter *among the dead.*) Oh, Mr. Carter, my little boy is spending the day at your house.

Mr. Carter. Is he?

Emily. Yes, he loves it there.—Mother Gibbs, we have a Ford, too. Never gives any trouble. I don't drive, though. Mother Gibbs, when does this feeling go away?—Of being . . . one of *them*? How long does it . . . ?

Mrs. Gibbs. Sh! dear. Just wait and be patient.

Emily (*with a sigh*). I know.—Look, they're finished. They're going.

Mrs. Gibbs. Sh—.

[*The umbrellas leave the stage.* Dr. Gibbs *has come over to his wife's grave and stands before it a moment.* Emily *looks up at his face.* Mrs. Gibbs *does not raise her eyes.*]

Emily. Look. Father Gibbs is bringing some of my flowers to you. He looks just like George, doesn't he? Oh, Mother Gibbs, I never realized before how troubled and how . . . how in the dark live persons are. Look at him. I loved him so. From morning till night, that's all they are—troubled.

[Dr. Gibbs *goes off.*]

The Dead. Little cooler than it was.—Yes, that rain's cooled it off a little. Those northeast winds always do the same thing, don't they? If it isn't a rain, it's a three-day blow.—

[*A patient calm falls on the stage. The* Stage Manager *appears at his proscenium pillar, smoking.* Emily *sits up abruptly with an idea.*]

Emily. But, Mother Gibbs, one can go back; one can go back there again . . . into living. I feel it. I know it. Why just then for a moment I was thinking about . . . about the farm . . . and for a moment I *was* there, and my baby was on my lap as plain as day.

Mrs. Gibbs. Yes, of course you can.

Emily. I can go back there and live all those days over again . . . why not?

Mrs. Gibbs. All I can say is, Emily, don't.

Emily (*she appeals urgently to the* Stage Manager). But it's true, isn't it? I can go and live . . . back there . . . again.

Stage Manager. Yes, some have tried—but they soon come back here.

Mrs. Gibbs. Don't do it, Emily.

Mrs. Soames. Emily, don't. It's not what you think it'd be.

Emily. But I won't live over a sad day. I'll choose a happy one—I'll choose the day I first knew that I loved George. Why should that be painful?

[*They are silent. Her question turns to the* Stage Manager.]

Stage Manager. You not only live it; but you watch yourself living it.

Emily. Yes?

Stage Manager. And as you watch it, you see the thing that they—down there—never know. You see the future. You know what's going to happen afterwards.

Emily. But is that—painful? Why?

Mrs. Gibbs. That's not the only reason why you shouldn't do it, Emily. When you've been here longer you'll see that our life here is to forget all that, and think only of what's ahead, and be ready for what's ahead. When you've been here longer you'll understand.

Emily (*softly*). But, Mother Gibbs, how can I ever forget that life? It's all I know. It's all I had.

Mrs. Soames. Oh, Emily. It isn't wise. Really, it isn't.

Emily. But it's a thing I must know for myself. I'll choose a happy day, anyway.

Mrs. Gibbs. *No!*—At least, choose an unimportant day. Choose the least important day in your life. It will be important enough.

Emily (*to herself*). Then it can't be since I was married; or since the baby was born. (*To the Stage Manager, eagerly.*) I can choose a birthday at least, can't I?—I choose my twelfth birthday.

Stage Manager. All right. February 11th, 1899. A Tuesday.—Do you want any special time of day?

Emily. Oh, I want the whole day.

Stage Manager. We'll begin at dawn. You remember it had been snowing for several days; but it had stopped the night before, and they had begun clearing the roads. The sun's coming up.

Emily (*with a cry; rising*). There's Main Street . . . why, that's Mr. Morgan's drugstore before he changed it! . . . And there's the livery stable.

[*The stage at no time in this act has been very dark; but now the left half of the stage gradually becomes very bright—the brightness of a crisp winter morning. Emily walks toward Main Street.*]

Stage Manager. Yes, it's 1899. This is fourteen years ago.

Emily. Oh, that's the town I knew as a little girl. And, *look,* there's the old white fence that used to be around our house. Oh, I'd forgotten that! Oh, I love it so! Are they inside?

Stage Manager. Yes, your mother'll be coming downstairs in a minute to make breakfast.

Emily (*softly*). Will she?

Stage Manager. And you remember: your father had been away for several days; he came back on the early-morning train.

Emily. No . . . ?

Stage Manager. He'd been back to his college to make a speech—in western New York, at Clinton.

Emily. Look! There's Howie Newsome. There's our policeman. But he's *dead;* he *died.*

[*The voices of* Howie Newsome, Constable Warren *and* Joe Crowell, Jr., *are heard at the left of the stage. Emily* listens in delight.]

Howie Newsome. Whoa, Bessie!—Bessie! 'Morning, Bill.

Constable Warren. Morning, Howie.

Howie Newsome. You're up early.

Constable Warren. Been rescuin' a party; darn near froze to death, down by Polish Town thar. Got drunk and lay out in the snowdrifts. Thought he was in bed when I shook'm.

Emily. Why, there's Joe Crowell. . . .

Joe Crowell. Good morning, Mr. Warren. 'Morning, Howie.

[Mrs. Webb *has appeared in her kitchen, but* Emily *does not see her until she calls.*]

Mrs. Webb. Chil-*dren!* Wally! Emily! . . . Time to get up.

Emily. Mama, I'm here! Oh! how young Mama looks! I didn't know Mama was ever that young.

Mrs. Webb. You can come and dress by the kitchen fire, if you like; but hurry. (*Howie Newsome has entered along Main Street and brings the milk to* Mrs. Webb's *door.*) Good Morning, Mr. Newsome, Whhhh—it's cold.

Howie Newsome. Ten below by my barn, Mrs. Webb.

[*She takes her bottles in, shuddering.*]

Emily (*with an effort*). Mama, I can't find my blue hair ribbon anywhere.

Mrs. Webb. Just open your eyes, dear, that's all. I laid it out for you special—on the dresser, there. If it were a snake it would bite you.

Emily. Yes, yes. . . .

[*She puts her hand on her heart.* Mr. Webb *comes along Main Street, where he meets* Constable Warren. *Their movements and voices are increasingly lively in the sharp air.*]

Mr. Webb. Good morning, Bill.

Constable Warren. Good morning, Mr. Webb. You're up early.

Mr. Webb. Yes, just been back to my old college in New York State. Been any trouble here?

Constable Warren. Well, I was called up this mornin' to rescue a Polish fella—darn near froze to death he was.

Mr. Webb. We must get it in the paper.

Constable Warren. 'Twan't much.

Emily (*whispers*). Papa.

[Mr. Webb *shakes the snow off his feet and enters his house.* Constable Warren *goes off, right.*]

Mr. Webb. Good morning, Mother.

Mrs. Webb. How did it go, Charles?

Mr. Webb. Oh, fine, I guess. I told'm a few things.—Everything all right here?

Mrs. Webb. Yes—can't think of anything that's happened, special. Been right cold. Howie Newsome says it's ten below over to his barn.

Mr. Webb. Yes, well, it's colder than that at Hamilton College. Students' ears are falling off. It ain't Christian.—Paper have any mistakes in it?

Mrs. Webb. None that I noticed. Coffee's ready when you want it. (*He starts upstairs.*) Charles! Don't forget; it's Emily's birthday. Did you remember to get her something?

Mr. Webb (*patting his pocket*). Yes, I've got something here. (*Calling up the stairs.*) Where's my girl? Where's my birthday girl? (*He goes off left.*)

Mrs. Webb. Don't interrupt her now, Charles. You can see her at breakfast. She's slow enough as it is. Hurry up, children! It's seven o'clock. Now, I don't want to call you again.

Emily (*softly, more in wonder than in grief*). I can't bear it. They're so young and beautiful. Why did they ever have to get old? Mama, I'm here. I'm grown up. I love you all, everything.—I can't look at everything hard enough. (*She looks questioningly at the* Stage Manager, *saying or suggesting: "Can I go in?" He nods briefly.* She crosses to the inner door to the kitchen, left of her mother, and as though entering the room, says, suggesting the voice of a girl of twelve:) Good morning, Mama.

Mrs. Webb (*crossing to embrace and kiss her; in her characteristic matter-of-fact manner*). Well, now, dear, a very happy birthday to my girl and many happy returns. There are some surprises waiting for you on the kitchen table.

Emily. Oh, Mama, you *shouldn't* have. (*She throws an anguished glance at the* Stage Manager.) I can't—I can't.

Mrs. Webb (*facing the audience, over her stove*). But birthday or no birthday, I want you to eat your breakfast good and slow. I want you to grow up and be a good strong girl.

That in the blue paper is from your Aunt Carrie; and I reckon you can guess who brought the post-card album. I found it on the doorstep when I brought in the milk—George Gibbs . . . must have come over in the cold pretty early . . . right nice of him.

Emily (*to herself*). Oh, George! I'd forgotten that. . . .

Mrs. Webb. Chew that bacon good and slow. It'll help keep you warm on a cold day.

Emily (*with mounting urgency*). Oh, Mama, just look at me one minute as though you really saw me. Mama, fourteen years have gone by. I'm dead. You're a grandmother, Mama. I married George Gibbs, Mama. Wally's dead, too. Mama, his appendix burst on a camping trip to North Conway. We just felt terrible about it—don't you remember? But, just for a moment now we're all together. Mama, just for a moment we're happy. *Let's look at one another.*

Mrs. Webb. That in the yellow paper is something I found in the attic among your grandmother's things. You're old enough to wear it now, and I thought you'd like it.

Emily. And this is from you. Why, Mama, it's just lovely and it's just what I wanted. It's beautiful!

[*She flings her arms around her mother's neck. Her Mother goes on with her cooking, but is pleased.*]

Mrs. Webb. Well, I hoped you'd like it. Hunted all over. Your Aunt Norah couldn't find one in Concord, so I had to send all the way to Boston. (*Laughing.*) Wally has something for you, too. He made it at manual-training class and he's very proud of it. Be sure you make a big fuss about it.—Your father has

a surprise for you, too; don't know what it is myself. Sh—here he comes.

Mr. Webb (*off stage*). Where's my girl? Where's my birthday girl?

Emily (*in a loud voice to the* Stage Manager). I can't. I can't go on. It goes so fast. We don't have time to look at one another. (*She breaks down sobbing.*)

[*The lights dim on the left half of the stage.* Mrs. Webb *disappears.*]

I didn't realize. So all that was going on and we never noticed. Take me back—up the hill—to my grave. But first: Wait! One more look.

Good-by, Good-by, world. Good-by, Grover's Corners . . . Mama and Papa. Good-by to clocks ticking . . . and Mama's sunflowers. And food and coffee. And new-ironed dresses and hot baths . . . and sleeping and waking up. Oh, earth, you're too wonderful for anybody to realize you. (*She looks toward the* Stage Manager *and asks abruptly, through her tears:*) Do any human beings ever realize life while they live it?—every, every minute?

Stage Manager. No. (*Pause.*) The saints and poets, maybe—they do some.

Emily. I'm ready to go back. (*She returns to her chair beside* Mrs. Gibbs. *Pause.*)

Mrs. Gibbs. Were you happy?

Emily. No . . . I should have listened to you. That's all human beings are! Just blind people.

Mrs. Gibbs. Look, it's clearing up. The stars are coming out.

Emily. Oh, Mr. Stimson, I should have listened to them.

Simon Stimson (*with mounting violence; bitingly*). Yes, now you know. Now you know! That's what it was to be alive. To move about in a cloud of ignorance; to go up and down trampling on the feelings of those . . . of those

about you. To spend and waste time as though you had a million years. To be always at the mercy of one self-centered passion, or another. Now you know—that's the happy existence you wanted to go back to. Ignorance and blindness.

Mrs. Gibbs (*spiritedly*). Simon Stimson, that ain't the whole truth and you know it. Emily, look at that star. I forget its name.

A Man among the Dead. My boy Joel was a sailor—knew 'em all. He'd set on the porch evenings and tell 'em all by name. Yes, sir, wonderful!

Another Man among the Dead. A star's mighty good company.

A Woman among the Dead. Yes. Yes, 'tis.

Simon Stimson. Here's one of *them* coming.

The Dead. That's funny. 'Tain't no time for one of them to be here.—Goodness sakes.

Emily. Mother Gibbs, it's George.

Mrs. Gibbs. Sh, dear. Just rest yourself.

Emily. It's George. (George *enters from the left, and slowly comes toward them.*)

A Man from among the Dead. And my boy, Joel, who knew the stars—he used to say it took millions of years for that speck o' light to git to the earth. Don't seem like a body could believe it, but that's what he used to say—millions of years.

[George *sinks to his knees, then falls full length at* Emily's *feet.*]

A Woman among the Dead. Goodness! That ain't no way to behave!

Mrs. Soames. He ought to be home.

Emily. Mother Gibbs?

Mrs. Gibbs. Yes, Emily?

Emily. They don't understand, do they?

Mrs. Gibbs. No dear. They don't understand.

[*The* Stage Manager *appears at the right, one hand on a dark curtain which he slowly draws across the scene. In the distance a clock is heard striking the hour very faintly.*]

Stage Manager. Most everybody's asleep in Grover's Corners. There are a few lights on: Shorty Hawkins, down at the depot, has just watched the Albany train go by. And at the livery stable somebody's setting up late and talking.—Yes, it's clearing up. There are the stars—doing their old, old crisscross journeys in the sky. Scholars haven't settled the matter yet, but they seem to think there are no living beings up there. Just chalk . . . or fire. Only this one is straining away, straining away all the time to make something of itself. The strain's so bad that every sixteen hours everybody lies down and gets a rest.

(*He winds his watch.*)

Hm . . . Eleven o'clock in Grover's Corners.—You get a good rest, too. Good night.

The End

Study Questions

1. Act III of *Our Town* is concerned with death. In the second act, Wilder prepared the audience for Emily's death by the use of foreshadowing. Where is death mentioned at the beginning and end of Act II? How does Emily die? What impact does her death have on the life of the town?

2. What does the Stage Manager say the dead are waiting for?

3. Why does Mrs. Gibbs suggest that Emily relive her least important day? What does Emily discover about that day? Why does she want to go back to the dead? What moral or lesson could you draw from Emily's return to Grover's Corners?

4. At what time of day does the play end? Why is this time appropriate? What do you think the stars symbolize?

5. The Stage Manager says that scholars do not seem to think there are any living beings other than those on earth. Earth, he says, "straining away all the time to make something of itself. The strain's so bad that every sixteen hours everybody lies down and gets a rest." How do you think this statement summarizes the theme and action of *Our Town*?

Vocabulary

Using almost no scenery, *Our Town* creates a vivid image of an American community. No such picture could have been drawn in vague, generalized terms. The playwright had to focus upon precise details and then find **concrete language** which would convey each detail to the audience.

For example, the play does not begin "just before dawn on a spring morning early in the twentieth century." Rather, it starts at exactly "5:45 a.m. on May 7, 1901." In a similar way, instead of calling Mr. Webb "the local newspaper owner," Wilder describes him as the "editor of the Grover's Corners *Sentinel.*" Instead of Bessie being described as "an old horse" that "pulls the dairy wagon slowly," the playwright says Bessie is "going on seventeen" and is "all mixed up about the route ever since the Lockharts stopped takin' their quart of milk every day."

Below you will find ten lines based on the dialogue of the play. Each line contains one or more *italicized* words or phrases that generally describe people, places, or actions in the play. On a separate sheet of paper, copy each *italicized* word or phrase. After each one, go back to the text and copy the concrete language Wilder used to say the same thing. To help you find Wilder's original words and phrases, the page numbers on which they appear are given in parentheses. Write your answers this way:

just before dawn on a spring morning early in the twentieth century:
  5:45 a.m. on May 7, 1901

1. **Mrs. Gibbs.** One of those secondhand-furniture men from *the city* offered me a *lot of money* for *one old piece of furniture.* (538)

2. **Mr. Webb.** Politically, we're *mostly* Republicans; *a few* Democrats; *even fewer* Socialists; rest, indifferent. (540)

3. **Mrs. Webb.** If I do say it, I was *a pretty girl.* (543)

4. **Simon Stimson.** Softer! Get it out of your head that music's only good when it's loud. You leave loudness to *some other church choir.* (544)

5. **Mrs. Gibbs.** Now, Frank, don't be grouchy. Come out and smell the *flowers* in the moonlight. (546)

6. **Stage Manager.** I often wonder why people like to be buried in *city cemeteries* when they might pass the same time up here. (564)

7. **Emily.** There's Main Street. Why, that's *the drugstore!* . . . And there's the livery stable. . . . And, look, there's *our fence.* (569)

8. **Mrs. Webb.** I reckon you can guess who brought *that present.* I found it *outside.* George Gibbs must have come over in the cold mighty early. (571)

9. **Emily.** Wally's dead, too. Mama, *he died* on a *trip.* (571)

10. **Stage Manager.** Only this planet is straining away to make something of itself. The strain's so bad that every *night* everybody lies down and gets a rest. Hm. *It's late in our town.* You get a good rest too. Good night. (573)

7 REVIEW

Study Questions

1. *Our Town* is considered one of the most technically innovative plays in American drama. One of the factors which contributes to its uniqueness is the intimacy created by the audience's involvement. Find examples of how Wilder includes the audience in the play.

2. Each of the three acts contains a breakfast scene. How is each scene presented differently?

3. Time is a very important aspect in *Our Town*. In what instances throughout the play is the chronological time sequence interrupted? In each case, explain why you think Wilder manipulated the time sequence. What do you think the play gains by this use of distorted time sequences?

4. Throughout *Our Town,* there is a movement from the small to the infinite, from the temporal to the eternal, from the individual to the universal. How do the following incidents relate to these movements?
   a. Rebecca's speech at the end of Act I.
   b. the Stage Manager's description at the beginning of Act II about what has happened to Grover's Corners during the three years since Act I.
   c. the wedding.
   d. the Stage Manager's final speech at the end of Act III.

5. Why is the Stage Manager's role the most important one in the play? How does he unify the whole play?

Composition

1. At the end of Act III, Simon Stimson makes a statement to Emily which begins, "Yes, now you know. . . . That's what it was to be alive." Reread what Stimson says (page 572). In a short essay, either defend or refute his statement by using examples from the play and from your own life. Present sufficient arguments to persuade someone else to believe as you do.

2. Write a brief scene for a play. Follow Wilder's example and use very little scenery. Make sure that the dialogue of your characters provides the scenery. Use precise details in their lines and concrete images to accomplish this.

8

Twentieth Century:
Our Time

TWENTIETH CENTURY: OUR TIME

THE KEYNOTE of American literature in our time is variety. The most obvious development of our literature since its beginnings has been from uniformity to diversity. In this unit that diversity is reflected in the number of female writers and writers of different ethnic groups. All make up the rich variety which is American Literature.

A second distinction between the early writers and those of our own day is one of tone or mood. The religious tone of John Winthrop and Mary Rowlandson gave way to Patrick Henry and Thomas Paine and their desperation concerning life and independence. However, these earlier writers also had an essential, underlying faith that their destiny was somehow favorable. They felt that right would prevail, that people of courage and good will would prosper.

After 300 years of a frequently troubled history—including a Civil War, two world wars, an economic depression, and social unrest for

CHIEF *Franz Kline* 1950

numerous reasons—today's writers are not as certain of a favorable destiny. Thus, Bernard Malamud writes of a young man trapped in a world of alternate boredom and antagonism. Tillie Olsen shows us a working mother uncertain of her relationship with her daughter. Raymond Barrio writes of trapped workers.

This is not to say that contemporary literature is a record of despair. If the Black characters in Ralph Ellison's "Did You Ever Dream Lucky?" feel excluded from the American Dream, they nonetheless view themselves with irrepressible humor. Annie Dillard discovers miracles in nature. Even Roberta Hill, despite the bitterness of Native American life, offers a vision of restoration and hope.

Bernard Malamud   1914—

Born in Brooklyn, Bernard Malamud has been compared to such great Yiddish writers as Sholem Aleichem and I.B. Singer. For many years he has been a teacher, first at Bennington College and then at Oregon State University. Malamud has published seven novels including *The Natural* (1952) *The Assistant* (1957), *Dubin's Lives* (1979), and *God's Grace* (1982). His three short-story collections include *The Magic Barrel* (1958). Malamud was presented the National Book Award twice and has also received a Pulitzer Prize. One of the recurring themes in his work is a person's inability to make a choice, as seen in the following story from *The Magic Barrel.*

The Prison

BERNARD MALAMUD

THOUGH HE TRIED not to think of it, at twenty-nine Tommy Castelli's life was a screaming bore. It wasn't just Rosa or the store they tended for profits counted in pennies, or the unendurably slow hours and endless drivel that went with selling candy, cigarettes, and soda water; it was this sick-in-the-stomach feeling of being trapped in old mistakes, even some he had made before Rosa changed Tony into Tommy. He had been as Tony a kid of many dreams and schemes, especially getting out of this tenement-crowded, kid-squawking neighborhood, with its lousy poverty, but everything had fouled up against him before he could. When he was sixteen he quit the vocational school where they were making him into a shoemaker, and began to hang out with the gray-hatted, thick-soled-shoe boys, who had the spare time and the mazuma and showed it in fat wonderful rolls down in the cellar clubs to all who would look, and everybody did, popeyed. They were the ones who had bought the silver caffe espresso urn and later the television, and they arranged the pizza parties and had the girls down; but it was getting in with them and their cars, leading to the holdup of a liquor store, that had started all the present trouble. Lucky for him the coal-and-ice man who was their landlord knew the leader in the district, and they arranged something so nobody bothered him after that. Then before he knew what was going on—he had been frightened sick by the whole mess—there was his father cooking up a deal with Rosa Agnello's old man that Tony would marry her and the father-in-law would, out of his savings, open a candy store for him to make an honest living. He wouldn't spit on a candy store, and Rosa was too plain and lank a chick for his personal taste, so he beat it off to Texas and bummed around in too much space, and when he came back everybody said it was for Rosa and the candy store, and it was all arranged again and he, without saying no, was in it.

That was how he had landed on Prince Street in the Village, working from eight in the morning to almost midnight every day, except for an hour off each afternoon when he went upstairs to sleep, and on Tuesdays, when the store was closed and he slept some more and went at night alone to the movies. He was too tired always for schemes now, but once he tried to make a little cash on the side by secretly taking in punchboards some syndicate was distributing in the neighborhood, on which he collected a nice cut and in this way saved fifty-five bucks that Rosa didn't know about; but then the syndicate was written up by a newspaper, and the punchboards all disappeared. Another time, when Rosa was at her mother's house, he took a chance and let them put in a slot machine that could guarantee a nice piece of change if he kept it long enough. He knew of course he couldn't hide it from her, so when she came and screamed when she saw it, he was ready and patient, for once not yelling back when she yelled, and he explained

it was not the same as gambling because anybody who played it got a roll of mints every time he put in a nickel. Also the machine would supply them a few extra dollars cash they could use to buy television so he could see the fights without going to a bar; but Rosa wouldn't let up screaming, and later her father came in shouting that he was a criminal and chopped the machine apart with a plumber's hammer. The next day the cops raided for slot machines and gave out summonses wherever they found them, and though Tommy's place was practically the only candy store in the neighborhood that didn't have one, he felt bad about the machine for a long time.

Mornings had been his best time of day because Rosa stayed upstairs cleaning, and since few people came into the store till noon, he could sit around alone, a toothpick in his teeth, looking over the *News* and *Mirror* on the fountain counter, or maybe gab with one of the old cellar-club guys who had happened to come by for a pack of butts, about a horse that was running that day or how the numbers were paying lately; or just sit there, drinking coffee and thinking how far away he could get on the fifty-five he had stashed away in the cellar. Generally the mornings were this way, but after the slot machine, usually the whole day stank and he along with it. Time rotted in him, and all he could think of the whole morning, was going to sleep in the afternoon, and he would wake up with the sour remembrance of the long night in the store ahead of him, while everybody else was doing as he damn pleased. He cursed the candy store and Rosa, and cursed, from its beginning, his unhappy life.

It was on one of these bad mornings that a ten-year-old girl from around the block came in and asked for two rolls of colored tissue paper, one red and one yellow. He wanted to tell her to go to hell and stop bothering, but instead went with bad grace to the rear, where Rosa, whose bright idea it was to keep the stuff, had put it. He went from force of habit,

for the girl had been coming in every Monday since the summer for the same thing, because her rockfaced mother, who looked as if she arranged her own widowhood, took care of some small kids after school and gave them the paper to cut out dolls and such things. The girl, whose name he didn't know, resembled her mother, except her features were not quite so sharp and she had very light skin with dark eyes; but she was a plain kid and would be more so at twenty. He had noticed, when he went to get the paper, that she always hung back as if afraid to go where it was dark, though he kept the comics there and most of the other kids had to be slapped away from them; and that when he brought her the tissue paper her skin seemed to grow whiter and her eyes shone. She always handed him two hot dimes and went out without glancing back.

It happened that Rosa, who trusted nobody, had just hung a mirror on the back wall, and as Tommy opened the drawer to get the girl her paper this Monday morning that he felt so bad, he looked up and saw in the glass something that made it seem as if he were dreaming. The girl had disappeared, but he saw a white hand reach into the candy case for a chocolate bar and for another, then she came forth from behind the counter and stood there, innocently waiting for him. He felt at first like grabbing her by the neck and socking till she threw up, but he had been caught, as he sometimes was, by this thought of how his Uncle Dom, years ago before he went away, used to take with him Tony alone of all the kids, when he went crabbing to Sheepshead Bay. Once they went at night and threw the baited wire traps into the water and after a while pulled them up and they had this green lobster in one, and just then this fat-faced cop came along and said they had to throw it back unless it was nine inches. Dom said it was nine inches, but the cop said not to be a wise guy so Dom measured it and it was ten, and they laughed about that lobster all night. Then he remembered how he had felt after Dom was gone, and tears filled

his eyes. He found himself thinking about the way his life had turned out, and then about this girl, moved that she was so young and a thief. He felt he ought to do something for her, warn her to cut it out before she got trapped and fouled up her life before it got started. His urge to do this was strong, but when he went forward she looked up frightened because he had taken so long. The fear in her eyes bothered him and he didn't say anything. She thrust out the dimes, grabbed at the tissue rolls and ran out of the store.

He had to sit down. He kept trying to make the desire to speak to her go away, but it came back stronger than ever. He asked himself what difference does it make if she swipes candy—so she swipes it; and the role of reformer was strange and distasteful to him, yet he could not convince himself that what he felt he must do was unimportant. But he worried he would not know what to say to her. Always he had trouble speaking right, stumbled over words, especially in new situations. He was afraid he would sound like a jerk and she would not take him seriously. He had to tell her in a sure way so that even if it scared her, she would understand he had done it to set her straight. He mentioned her to no one but often thought about her, always looking around whenever he went outside to raise the awning or wash the window, to see if any of the girls playing in the street was her, but they never were. The following Monday, an hour after opening the store he had smoked a full pack of butts. He thought he had found what he wanted to say but was afraid for some reason she wouldn't come in, or if she did, this time she would be afraid to take the candy. He wasn't sure he wanted that to happen until he had said what he had to say. But at about eleven, while he was reading the *News,* she appeared, asking for the tissue paper, her eyes shining so he had to look away. He knew she meant to steal. Going to the rear he slowly opened the drawer, keeping his head lowered as he sneaked a look into the glass and saw her

took two candy bars from the next plate and dropped them into the black patent leather purse she always had with her. The time after that he cleaned out the whole top shelf, and still she was not suspicious, and reached down to the next and took something different. One Monday he put some loose change, nickles and dimes, on the candy plate, but she left them there, only taking the candy, which bothered him a little. Rosa asked him what he was mooning about so much and why was he eating chocolate lately. He didn't answer her, and she began to look suspiciously at the women who came in, not excluding the little girls; and he would have been glad to rap her in the teeth, but it didn't matter as long as she didn't know what he had on his mind. At the same time he figured he would have to do something sure soon, or it would get harder for the girl to stop her stealing. He had to be strong about it. Then he thought of a plan that satisfied him. He would leave two bars on the plate and put in the wrapper of one a note she could read when she was alone. He tried out on paper many messages to her, and the one that seemed best he cleanly printed on a strip of cardboard and slipped it under the wrapper of one chocolate bar. It said, "Don't do this any more or you will suffer your whole life." He puzzled whether to sign it A Friend or Your Friend and finally chose Your Friend.

This was Friday, and he could not hold his impatience for Monday. But on Monday she did not appear. He waited for a long time, until Rosa came down, then he had to go up and the girl still hadn't come. He was greatly disappointed because she had never failed to come before. He lay on the bed, his shoes on, staring at the ceiling. He felt hurt, the sucker she had played him for and was now finished with because she probably had another on her hook. The more he thought about it the worse he felt. He worked up a splitting headache that kept him from sleeping, then he suddenly slept and woke without it. But he had awaked depressed, saddened. He thought about Dom get-

slide behind the counter. His heart beat hard and his feet felt nailed to the floor. He tried to remember what he had intended to do, but his mind was like a dark, empty room so he let her, in the end, slip away and stood tongue-tied, the dimes burning his palm.

Afterwards, he told himself that he hadn't spoken to her because it was while she still had the candy on her, and she would have been scared worse than he wanted. When he went upstairs, instead of sleeping, he sat at the kitchen window, looking out into the back yard. He blamed himself for being too soft, too chicken, but then he thought, no there was a better way to do it. He would do it indirectly, slip her a hint he knew, and he was pretty sure that would stop her. Sometime after, he would explain her why it was good she had stopped. So next time he cleaned out this candy platter she helped herself from, thinking she might get wise he was on to her, but she seemed not to, only hesitated with her hand before she

ting out of jail and going away God knows where. He wondered whether he would ever meet up with him somewhere, if he took the fifty-five bucks and left. Then he remembered Dom was a pretty old guy now, and he might not know him if they did meet. He thought about life. You never really got what you wanted. No matter how hard you tried you made mistakes and couldn't get past them. You could never see the sky outside or the ocean because you were in a prison, except nobody called it a prison, and if you did they didn't know what you were talking about, or they said they didn't. A pall settled on him. He lay motionless, without thought or sympathy for himself or anybody.

But when he finally went downstairs, ironically amused that Rosa had allowed him so long a time off without bitching, there were people in the store and he could hear her screeching. Shoving his way through the crowd he saw in one sickening look that she had caught the girl with the candy bars and was shaking her so hard the kid's head bounced back and forth like a balloon on a stick. With a curse he tore her away from the girl, whose sickly face showed the depth of her fright.

"Whatsamatter," he shouted at Rosa, "you want her blood?"

"She's a thief," cried Rosa.

"Shut your face."

To stop her yowling he slapped her across her mouth, but it was a harder crack than he had intended. Rosa fell back with a gasp. She did not cry but looked around dazedly at everybody, and tried to smile, and everybody there could see her teeth were flecked with blood.

"Go home," Tommy ordered the girl, but then there was a movement near the door and her mother came into the store.

"What happened?" she said.

"She stole my candy," Rosa cried.

"I let her take it," said Tommy.

Rosa stared at him as if she had been hit again, then with mouth distorted began to sob.

"One was for you, Mother," said the girl.

Her mother socked her hard across the face. "You little thief, this time you'll get your hands burned good."

She pawed at the girl, grabbed her arm and yanked it. The girl, like a grotesque dancer, half ran, half fell forward, but at the door she managed to turn her white face and thrust out at him her red tongue.

Study Questions

1. The first three paragraphs of the story establish the character of Tommy Castelli. From his point of view how is his life in the candy store both a prison and a refuge?

2. Tommy wants to stop a ten-year-old girl from stealing before she is "trapped" and her life is "fouled up." Why doesn't he stop her?

3. What does Uncle Dom represent to Tommy? Why does he associate the memory of his uncle with the little girl?

4. What is the irony of the ending when the little girl sticks out her tongue at Tommy? Why does she do it? How does Tommy feel?

5. What do you think causes Tommy's indecisiveness? Is it the result of his inability to communicate with others? Why or why not?

"The Prison" contains a variety of both informal expressions and slang words. **Informal expressions** are appropriate nearly everywhere—in conversations, friendly letters, and almost any situation in which *cops* and *foul-up* are acceptable substitutes for the standard terms *police* and *mistake*. This, of course, is not to say that informal expressions are suited for use in church sermons, legal documents, term papers, or other such formal and dignified forms of communication.

Dictionaries sometimes disagree about where informal expressions end and slang begins; but **slang** generally means terms that are informal in the extreme. Many "folksy" slang terms (e.g., *buck* for "dollar") are known by almost everyone who speaks the language. These words gradually achieve permanent, though not "standard," status. Other types of slang (e.g., *heist* for "robbery") may be coined as jargon or code words among small groups. These words are sometimes used only for short intervals before being forgotten.

Many people imagine that informal and slang expressions give communication an up-to-date ring. Such people are surprised to learn how ancient many of these expressions actually are. The informal term *O.K.,* for example, dates back at least as far as 1828. Two of the slang meanings of *kid* are even older: defined "to make someone believe false information," *kid* was in use as early as 1811; defined as "a child," *kid* dates from 1690.[1]

A. The ten words below, selected from "The Prison," are labeled by most dictionaries as either informal or slang. After each word and its parenthesized definition, a date indicates the earliest recorded printing of this word in the informal or slang sense.

chicken (coward) 1610
cut (share) 1805
deal (agreement) 1588
lousy (disgusting) 1830
sock (strike) 1700
figure (decide) 17th C.
gab (chatter) 1681
guy (man) 1896
swipe (steal) 1890
yank (jerk) 1822

On a separate sheet of paper, copy each term with its definition and date. Then, with the help of a dictionary, classify each expression as either *informal* or *slang*.

B. Some words which sound like informal or slang expressions are neither. Some words of this kind are *italicized* in the following sentences. Copy

---

1 *The Oxford Universal Dictionary on Historical Principles* (3d ed., London: Oxford University Press, 1955), pp. 1083–84.

each word. Then, consulting a dictionary, (1) define the word as it is used in the sentence below, and (2) tell whether the word is classified as *informal, slang,* or *standard. (Note:* Any word not classified otherwise in a dictionary is considered *standard*—appropriate for use in formal as well as informal speech and writing.)

1. His objection was not limited to the endless *drivel* that went with selling candy, cigarettes, and soda water.
2. He wanted to get out of this tenement-crowded, kid-*squawking* neighborhood.
3. He could gab with some old cellar-club guy who came by for a pack of *butts.*
4. To stop Rosa's *yowling,* he slapped her across the mouth.
5. She *pawed* at the girl, grabbed her arm, and yanked it.

C. In each sentence below, a standard word or phrase replaces an expression that appears in "The Prison." This replacement is *italicized.* Copy the *italicized* word(s), and then copy the word(s) the author originally used in the story. Finally, tell how the dictionary classifies the original word(s): *informal, slang,* or *standard.*

1. Rosa was too plain and lank a *girl* for his taste.
2. He *went away fast* to Texas and bummed around in too much space.
3. He could sit there thinking how far away he could get on the fifty-five he had *hidden* away in the cellar.
4. He was afraid he would sound like a *numskull* and she would not take him seriously.
5. He felt hurt, the *fool* she had played him for and was now finished because she had another on her hook.

Flannery O'Connor   1925-1964

Except for her attendance at a creative writing workshop at the University of Iowa, Flannery O'Connor spent most of her life on a dairy farm in her native Georgia. She published two short story collections, *A Good Man Is Hard To Find* (1955) and *Everything That Rises Must Converge* (published posthumously in 1965). Her two novels are *Wise Blood* (1952) and *The Violent Bear It Away* (1960). All of her work is set in either Georgia or Tennessee, and often in rural areas. A rare disease, *lupus erythematosus,* cut short her life, but she was already recognized as one of our best writers. O'Connor claimed that fiction is "about everything human and we are made of dust, and if you scorn getting yourself dusty, then you shouldn't try to write fiction." In the story which follows, taken from her 1955 collection, you will see some very human characters, who are odd, flawed, and "dusty."

The Life You Save May Be Your Own

FLANNERY O'CONNOR

THE OLD WOMAN and her daughter were sitting on their porch when Mr. Shiftlet came up their road for the first time. The old woman slid to the edge of her chair and leaned forward, shading her eyes from the piercing sunset with her hand. The daughter could not see far in front of her and continued to play with her fingers. Although the old woman lived in this desolate spot with only her daughter and she had never seen Mr. Shiftlet before, she could tell, even from a distance, that he was a tramp and no one to be afraid of. His left coat sleeve was folded up to show there was only half an arm in it and his gaunt figure listed slightly to the side as if the breeze were pushing him. He had on a black town suit and a brown felt hat that was turned up in the front and down in the back and he carried a tin tool box by a handle. He came on, at an amble, up her road, his face turned toward the sun which appeared to be balancing itself on a small mountain.

The old woman didn't change her position until he was almost into her yard; then she rose with one hand fisted on her hip. The daughter, a large girl in a short blue organdy dress, saw him all at once and jumped up and began to stamp and point and make excited speechless sounds.

Mr. Shiftlet stopped just inside the yard and set his box on the ground and tipped his hat at her as if she were not in the least afflicted; then he turned toward the old woman and swung the hat all the way off. He had long black slick hair that hung flat from a part in the middle to beyond the tips of his ears on either side. His face descended in forehead for more than half its length and ended suddenly with his features just balanced over a jutting steel-trap jaw. He seemed to be a young man but he had a look of composed dissatisfaction as if he understood life thoroughly.

"Good evening," the old woman said. She was about the size of a cedar fence post and she had a man's gray hat pulled down low over her head.

The tramp stood looking at her and didn't answer. He turned his back and faced the sunset. He swung both his whole and his short arm up slowly so that they indicated an expanse of sky and his figure formed a crooked cross. The old woman watched him with her arms folded across her chest as if she were the owner of the sun, and the daughter watched, her head thrust forward and her fat helpless hands hanging at the wrists. She had long pink-gold hair and eyes as blue as a peacock's neck.

He held the pose for almost fifty seconds and then he picked up his box and came on to the porch and dropped down on the bottom step. "Lady," he said in a firm nasal voice, "I'd give a fortune to live where I could see me a sun do that every evening."

"Does it every evening," the old woman said and sat back down. The daughter sat down too and watched him with a cautious sly look as if he were a bird that had come up very close. He leaned to one side, rooting in his pants pocket, and in a second he brought out a package of chewing gum and offered her a piece. She took it and unpeeled it and began to chew without taking her eyes off him. He offered the old woman a piece but she only raised her upper lip to indicate she had no teeth.

Mr. Shiftlet's pale sharp glance had already passed over everything in the yard—the pump near the corner of the house and the big fig tree that three or four chickens were preparing to roost in—and had moved to a shed where he saw the square rusted back of an automobile. "You ladies drive?" he asked.

"That car ain't run in fifteen years," the old woman said. "The day my husband died, it quit running."

"Nothing is like it used to be, lady," he said. "The world is almost rotten."

"That's right," the old woman said. "You from around here?"

"Name Tom T. Shiftlet," he murmured, looking at the tires.

"I'm pleased to meet you," the old woman said. "Name Lucynell Crater and daughter Lucynell Crater. What you doing around here, Mr. Shiftlet?"

He judged the car to be about a 1928 or '29 Ford. "Lady," he said, and turned and gave her his full attention, "lemme tell you something. There's one of these doctors in Atlanta that's taken a knife and cut the human heart—the human heart," he repeated, leaning forward, "out of a man's chest and held it in his hand," and he held his hand out, palm up, as if it were slightly weighted with the human heart, "and studied it like it was a day-old chicken, and lady," he said, allowing a long significant pause in which his head slid forward and his clay-colored eyes brightened, "he don't know no more about it than you or me."

"That's right," the old woman said.

"Why, if he was to take that knife and cut into every corner of it, he still wouldn't know no more than you or me. What you want to bet?"

"Nothing," the old woman said wisely. "Where you come from, Mr. Shiftlet?"

He didn't answer. He reached into his pocket and brought out a sack of tobacco and a package of cigarette papers and rolled himself a cigarette, expertly with one hand, and attached it in a hanging position to his upper lip. Then he took a box of wooden matches from his pocket and struck one on his shoe. He held the burning match as if he were studying the mystery of flame while it traveled dangerously toward his skin. The daughter began to make loud noises and to point to his hand and shake her finger at him, but when the flame was just before touching him, he leaned down with his hand cupped over it as if he were going to set fire to his nose and lit the cigarette.

He flipped away the dead match and blew a stream of gray into the evening. A sly look came over his face. "Lady," he said, "nowadays, people'll do anything anyways. I can tell you my name is Tom T. Shiftlet and I come from Tarwater, Tennessee, but you never have seen me before: how you know I ain't lying? How you know my name ain't Aaron Sparks, lady, and I come from Singleberry, Georgia, or how you know it's not George Speeds and I come from Lucy, Alabama, or how you know I ain't Thompson Bright from Toolafalls, Mississippi?"

"I don't know nothing about you," the old woman muttered, irked.

"Lady," he said, "people don't care how they lie. Maybe the best I can tell you is, I'm a man, but listen lady," he said and paused and made his tone more ominous still, "what is a man?"

The old woman began to gum a seed. "What you carry in that tin box, Mr. Shiftlet?" she asked.

"Tools," he said, put back. "I'm a carpenter."

"Well, if you come out here to work, I'll be able to feed you and give you a place to sleep but I can't pay. I'll tell you that before you begin," she said.

There was no answer at once and no particular expression on his face. He leaned back against the two-by-four that helped support the porch roof. "Lady," he said slowly, "there's some men that some things mean more to them than money." The old woman rocked without comment and the daughter watched the trigger that moved up and down in his neck. He told the old woman then that all most people were interested in was money, but he asked what a man was made for. He asked her if a man was made for money, or what. He asked her what she thought she was made for but she didn't answer, she only sat rocking and wondered if a one-armed man could put a new roof on her garden house. He asked a lot of questions that she didn't answer. He told her that he was twenty-eight years old and had lived a varied life. He had been a gospel singer, a foreman on the railroad, an assistant in an undertaking parlor, and he had come over the radio for three months with Uncle Roy and his Red Creek Wranglers. He said he had fought and bled in the Arm Service of his country and visited every foreign land and that everywhere he had seen people that didn't care if they did a thing one way or another. He said he hadn't been raised thataway.

A fat yellow moon appeared in the branches of the fig tree as if it were going to roost there with the chickens. He said that a man had to escape to the country to see the world whole and that he wished he lived in a desolate place like this where he could see the sun go down every evening like God made it to do.

"Are you married or are you single?" the old woman asked.

There was a long silence. "Lady," he asked finally, "where would you find you an innocent woman today? I wouldn't have any of this trash I could just pick up."

The daughter was leaning very far down, hanging her head almost between her knees, watching him through a triangular door she had made in her overturned hair; and she suddenly fell in a heap on the floor and began to whimper. Mr. Shiftlet straightened her out and helped her get back in the chair.

"Is she your baby girl?" he asked.

"My only," the old woman said, "and she's the sweetest girl in the world. I wouldn't give her up for nothing on earth. She's smart too. She can sweep the floor, cook, wash, feed the chickens, and hoe. I wouldn't give her up for a casket of jewels."

"No," he said kindly, "don't ever let any man take her away from you."

"Any man come after her," the old woman said, "I'll have to stay around the place."

Mr. Shiftlet's eye in the darkness was focused on a part of the automobile bumper that glittered in the distance. "Lady," he said, jerking his short arm up as if he could point with it to her house and yard and pump, "there ain't a broken thing on this plantation that I couldn't fix for you, one-arm jackleg or not. I'm a man," he said with a sullen dignity, "even if I ain't a whole one. I got," he said, tapping his knuckles on the door to emphasize the immensity of what he was going to say "a moral intelligence!" and his face pierced out of the darkness into a shaft of doorlight and he stared at her as if he were astonished himself at this impossible truth.

The old woman was not impressed with the phrase. "I told you you could hang around and work for food," she said, "if you don't mind sleeping in that car yonder."

"Why listen, Lady," he said with a grin of delight, "the monks of old slept in their coffins!"

"They wasn't as advanced as we are," the old woman said.

The next morning he began on the roof of the garden house while Lucynell, the daughter, sat on a rock and watched him work. He had not been around a week before the change he had made in the place was apparent. He had patched the front and back steps, built a new hog pen, restored a fence, and taught Lucynell, who was completely deaf and had never said a word in her life, to say the word "bird." The big rosy-faced girl followed him everywhere, saying "Burrttddt ddbirrttdt," and clapping her hands. The old woman watched from a distance, secretly pleased. She was ravenous for a son-in-law.

Mr. Shiftlet slept on the hard narrow back seat of the car with his feet out the side window. He had his razor and a can of water on a crate that served him as a bedside table and he put up a piece of mirror against the back glass and kept his coat neatly on a hanger that he hung over one of the windows.

In the evenings he sat on the steps and talked while the old woman and Lucynell rocked violently in their chairs on either side of him. The old woman's three mountains were black against the dark blue sky and were visited off and on by various planets and by the moon after it had left the chickens. Mr. Shiftlet pointed out that the reason he had improved this plantation was because he had taken a personal interest in it. He said he was even going to make the automobile run.

He had raised the hood and studied the mechanism and he said he could tell that the car had been built in the days when cars were really built. You take now, he said, one man puts in one bolt and another man puts in another bolt and another man puts in another bolt so that it's a man for a bolt. That's why you have to pay so much for a car: you're paying all those men. Now if you didn't have to pay but one man, you could get you a cheaper car and one that had had a personal interest taken in it, and it would be a better car. The old woman agreed with him that this was so.

Mr. Shiftlet said that the trouble with the world was that nobody cared, or stopped and took any trouble. He said he never would have been able to teach Lucynell to say a word if he hadn't cared and stopped long enough.

"Teach her to say something else," the old woman said.

"What you want her to say next?" Mr. Shiftlet asked.

The old woman's smile was broad and toothless and suggestive. "Teach her to say 'sugarpie,'" she said.

Mr. Shiftlet already knew what was on her mind.

The next day he began to tinker with the automobile and that evening he told her that if she would buy a fan belt, he would be able to make the car run.

The old woman said she would give him the

money. "You see that girl yonder?" she asked, pointing to Lucynell who was sitting on the floor a foot away, watching him, her eyes blue even in the dark. "If it was ever a man wanted to take her away, I would say, 'No man on earth is going to take that sweet girl of mine away from me!' but if he was to say, 'Lady, I don't want to take her away, I want her right here,' I would say, 'Mister, I don't blame you none. I wouldn't pass up a chance to live in a permanent place and get the sweetest girl in the world myself. You ain't no fool.' I would say."

"How old is she?" Mr. Shiftlet asked casually.

"Fifteen, sixteen," the old woman said. The girl was nearly thirty but because of her innocence it was impossible to guess.

"It would be a good idea to paint it too," Mr. Shiftlet remarked. "You don't want it to rust out."

"We'll see about that later," the old woman said.

The next day he walked into town and returned with the parts he needed and a can of gasoline. Late in the afternoon, terrible noises issued from the shed and the old woman rushed out of the house, thinking Lucynell was somewhere having a fit. Lucynell was sitting on a chicken crate, stamping her feet and screaming, "Burrddttt! bddurrddtttt!" but her fuss was drowned out by the car. With a volley of blasts it emerged from the shed, moving in a fierce and stately way. Mr. Shiftlet was in the driver's seat, sitting very erect. He had an expression of serious modesty on his face as if he had just raised the dead.

That night, rocking on the porch, the old woman began her business at once. "You want you an innocent woman, don't you?" she asked sympathetically. "You don't want none of this trash."

"No'm, I don't," Mr. Shiftlet said.

"One that can't talk," she continued, "can't sass you back or use foul language. That's the kind for you to have. Right there," and she pointed to Lucynell sitting cross-legged in her chair, holding both feet in her hands.

"That's right," he admitted. "She wouldn't give me any trouble."

"Saturday," the old woman said, "you and her and me can drive into town and get married."

Mr. Shiftlet eased his position on the steps.

"I can't get married right now," he said. "Everything you want to do takes money and I ain't got any."

"What you need with money?" she asked.

"It takes money," he said. "Some people'll do anything anyhow these days, but the way I think, I wouldn't marry no woman that I couldn't take on a trip like she was somebody. I mean take her to a hotel and treat her. I wouldn't marry the Duchesser Windsor," he said firmly, "unless I could take her to a hotel and give her something good to eat.

"I was raised thataway and there ain't a thing I can do about it. My old mother taught me how to do."

"Lucynell don't even know what a hotel is," the old woman muttered. "Listen here, Mr. Shiftlet," she said, sliding forward in her chair, "you'd be getting a permanent house and a deep well and the most innocent girl in the world. You don't need no money. Lemme tell you something: there ain't any place in the world for a poor disabled friendless drifting man."

The ugly words settled in Mr. Shiftlet's head like a group of buzzards in the top of a tree. He didn't answer at once. He rolled himself a cigarette and lit it and then he said in an even voice, "Lady, a man is divided into two parts, body and spirit."

The old woman clamped her gums together.

"A body and a spirit," he repeated. "The body, lady, is like a house: it don't go anywhere; but the spirit, lady, is like a automobile: always on the move, always. . ."

"Listen, Mr. Shiftlet," she said, "my well never goes dry and my house is always warm in the winter and there's no mortgage on a thing about this place. You can go to the courthouse and see for yourself. And yonder under that shed is a fine automobile." She laid the bait carefully. "You can have it painted by Saturday. I'll pay for the paint."

In the darkness, Mr. Shiftlet's smile stretched like a weary snake waking up by a fire. After a second he recalled himself and said, "I'm only saying a man's spirit means more to him than anything else. I would have to take my wife off for the weekend without no regards at all for cost. I got to follow where my spirit says to go."

"I'll give you fifteen dollars for a weekend trip," the old woman said in a crabbed voice. "That's the best I can do."

"That wouldn't hardly pay for more than the gas and the hotel," he said. "It wouldn't feed her."

"Seventeen-fifty," the old woman said. "That's all I got so it isn't any use you trying to milk me. You can take a lunch."

Mr. Shiftlet was deeply hurt by the word "milk." He didn't doubt that she had more money sewed up in her mattress but he had already told her he was not interested in her money. "I'll make that do," he said and rose and walked off without treating with her further.

On Saturday the three of them drove into town in the car that the paint had barely dried on and Mr. Shiftlet and Lucynell were married in the Ordinary's office while the old woman witnessed. As they came out of the courthouse, Mr. Shiftlet began twisting his neck in his collar. He looked morose and bitter as if he had been insulted while someone held him. "That didn't satisfy me none," he said. "That was just something a woman in an office did, nothing but paper work and blood tests. What do they know about my blood? If they was to take my heart and cut it out," he said, "they wouldn't know a thing about me. It didn't satisfy me at all."

"It satisfied the law," the old woman said sharply.

"The law," Mr. Shiftlet said and spit. "It's the law that don't satisfy me."

He had painted the car dark green with a yellow band around it just under the windows. The three of them climbed in the front seat and the old woman said, "Don't Lucynell look pretty? Looks like a baby doll." Lucynell was dressed up in a white dress that her mother had uprooted from a trunk and there was a Panama hat on her head with a bunch of red wooden cherries on the brim. Every now and then her placid expression was changed by a sly isolated little thought like a shoot of green in the desert. "You got a prize!" the old woman said.

Mr. Shiftlet didn't even look at her.

They drove back to the house to let the old woman off and pick up the lunch. When they were ready to leave, she stood staring in the window of the car, with her fingers clenched around the glass. Tears began to seep sideways out of her eyes and run along the dirty creases in her face. "I ain't ever been parted with her for two days before," she said.

Mr. Shiftlet started the motor.

"And I wouldn't let no man have her but you because I seen you would do right. Good-by, Sugarbaby," she said, clutching at the sleeve of the white dress. Lucynell looked straight at her and didn't seem to see her there at all. Mr. Shiftlet eased the car forward so that she had to move her hands.

The early afternoon was clear and open and surrounded by pale blue sky. Although the car would go only thirty miles an hour, Mr. Shiftlet imagined a terrific climb and dip and swerve that went entirely to his head so that he forgot his morning bitterness. He had always wanted an automobile but he had never been able to afford one before. He drove very fast because he wanted to make Mobile by nightfall.

Occasionally he stopped his thought long enough to look at Lucynell in the seat beside him. She had eaten the lunch as soon as they were out of the yard and now she was pulling the cherries off the hat one by one and throwing them out the window. He became depressed in spite of the car. He had driven about a hundred miles when he decided that she must be hungry again and at the next small town they came to, he stopped in front of an aluminum-painted eating place called The Hot Spot and took her in and ordered her a plate of ham and grits. The ride had made her sleepy and as soon as she got up on the stool, she rested her head on the counter and shut her eyes. There was no one in The Hot Spot but Mr. Shiftlet and the boy behind the counter, a pale youth with a greasy rag hung over his shoulder. Before he could dish up the food, she was snoring gently.

"Give it to her when she wakes up," Mr. Shiftlet said. "I'll pay for it now."

The boy bent over her and stared at the long pink-gold hair and the half-shut sleeping eyes. Then he looked up and stared at Mr. Shiftlet. "She looks like an angel of Gawd," he murmured.

"Hitchhiker," Mr. Shiftlet explained. "I can't wait. I got to make Tuscaloosa."

The boy bent over again and very carefully touched his finger to a strand of the golden hair and Mr. Shiftlet left.

He was more depressed than ever as he drove on by himself. The late afternoon had grown hot and sultry and the country had flattened out. Deep in the sky a storm was preparing very slowly and without thunder as if it meant to drain every drop of air from the earth before it broke. There were times when Mr. Shiftlet preferred not to be alone. He felt too that a man with a car had a responsibility to others and he kept his eye out for a hitchhiker. Occasionally he saw a sign that warned: "Drive carefully. The life you save may be your own."

The narrow road dropped off on either side into dry fields and here and there a shack or a filling station stood in a clearing. The sun began to set directly in front of the automobile. It was a reddening ball that through his windshield was slightly flat on the bottom and top. He saw a boy in overalls and a gray hat standing on the edge of the road and he slowed the car down and stopped in front of him. The boy didn't have his hand raised to thumb the ride, he was only standing there, but he had a small cardboard suitcase and his hat was set on his head in a way to indicate that he had left somewhere for good. "Son," Mr. Shiftlet said, "I see you want a ride."

The boy didn't say he did or he didn't but he opened the door of the car and got in, and Mr. Shiftlet started driving again. The child held the suitcase on his lap and folded his arms on top of it. He turned his head and looked out the window away from Mr. Shiftlet. Mr. Shiftlet felt oppressed. "Son," he said after a minute, "I got the best old mother in the world so I reckon you only got the second best."

The boy gave him a quick dark glance and then turned his face back out the window.

"It's nothing so sweet," Mr. Shiftlet continued, "as a boy's mother. She taught him his first prayers at her knee, she give him love when no other would, she told him what was right and what wasn't, and she seen that he done the right thing. Son," he said, "I never rued a day in my life like the one I rued when I left that old mother of mine."

The boy shifted in his seat but he didn't look at Mr. Shiftlet. He unfolded his arms and put one hand on the door handle.

"My mother was a angel of Gawd," Mr. Shiftlet said in a very strained voice. "He took her from heaven and giver to me and I left her." His eyes were instantly clouded over with a mist of tears. The car was barely moving.

The boy turned angrily in the seat. "You go to the devil!" he cried. "My old woman is a flea bag and yours is a stinking pole cat!" and with that he flung the door open and jumped out with his suitcase into the ditch.

Mr. Shiftlet was so shocked that for about a hundred feet he drove along slowly with the door still open. A cloud, the exact color of the boy's hat and shaped like a turnip, had descended over the sun, and another, worse looking, crouched behind the car. Mr. Shiftlet felt that the rottenness of the world was about to engulf him. He raised his arm and let it fall again to his breast. "Oh Lord!" he prayed. "Break forth and wash the slime from this earth!"

The turnip continued slowly to descend. After a few minutes there was a guffawing peal of thunder from behind and fantastic raindrops, like tin-can tops, crashed over the rear of Mr. Shiftlet's car. Very quickly he stepped on the gas and with his stump sticking out the window he raced the galloping shower into Mobile.

Study Questions

1. Describe Mrs. Crater's attitude toward her deaf-mute daughter.

2. What makes Mrs. Crater trust Mr. Shiftlet? Which of his remarks to her does she ignore?

3. What things make Mr. Shiftlet happy? Find examples of his pleasure.

4. After abandoning Lucynell in the eating place, Shiftlet passes a road sign warning: "Drive carefully. The life you save may be your own." How do the sign and the story's title apply to Shiftlet?

5. Explain the episode with the hitchhiker. Why does Shiftlet call the boy "son" and try to persuade him not to run away from his mother? How does the last scene relate to the title?

6. What evidence can you cite that Shiftlet represents an evil force?

Ralph Ellison 1914—

As a child Ralph Ellison said that he and his friends "discussed mastering ourselves and everything in sight as though no such thing as racial discrimination existed." Ellison went on to master the art of creative writing. He is also an accomplished musician. Both his love of writing and love of music are evident in the astounding novel, *Invisible Man* (1952). One of the important influences on Ellison, the writer, was Richard Wright (see page 469). After they met in New York City in 1937, they became close personal and literary friends. Under Wright's tutelage, Ellison began to study the craft of writing. Ellison also began contributing to various periodicals and edited *The Negro Quarterly* for a time.

Invisible Man, which won a National Book Award, and *Shadow and Act,* a collection of essays, are Ellison's only books. Yet, he is considered a major American writer because *Invisible Man* has been acclaimed by some as the best American novel of the twentieth century. He continues to write short stories and reviews, and to teach. Presently he is Albert Schweitzer Professor in Humanities at New York University.

The story included here is one of his earlier efforts. The characters also appear in his novel.

Did You Ever Dream Lucky?

RALPH ELLISON

AFTER THE HURRIED good-bys the door had closed and they sat at the table with the tragic wreck of the Thanksgiving turkey before them, their heads turned regretfully toward the young folks' laughter in the hall. Then they could hear the elevator open and shut and the gay voices sinking swiftly beneath the floor and they were left facing one another in a room suddenly quiet with disappointment. Each of them, Mary, Mrs. Garfield, and Portwood, missed the young roomers, but in his disappointment Portwood had said something about young folks being green and now Mary was challenging him.

"Green," she said, "shucks, you don't know nothing about green!"

"Just wait a minute now," Portwood said, pushing back from the table, "Who don't? Who you talking about?"

"I'm talking about you," Mary said. "Them chillun is gone off to the dance, so *I must* be talking 'bout you. And like I *shoulda* said, you don't even know green when you see it."

"Let me get on out of here," Portwood said, getting up. "Mrs. Garfield, she's just tuning up to lie. I can't understand why we live here with an ole lying woman like her anyway. And contentious with it too. Talking 'bout *I* don't know nothing 'bout green. Why, I been meeting green folks right at the dam' station for over twenty-five years. . . ."

"Sit down, man. Just sit on back down," said Mary, placing her hand upon the heavy cut-glass decanter. "You got nowhere in this whole wide world to go—probably cause you make so much noise with your mouth. . . ."

Mrs. Garfield smiled with gentle amusement. She'd been through it all before. A retired cook whose husband was dead, she had roomed with Mary almost as long as Portwood and knew that just as this was his way of provoking Mary into telling a story, it was Mary's way of introducing the story she would tell. She watched Mary cut her eyes from Portwood's frowning face to look through the window to where, far beyond the roofs of Harlem, mist-shrouded buildings pierced the sky. It was raining.

"It's gon' be cold out there on the streets this winter," Mary said. "I guess you know all about that."

"Don't be signifying[1] at me," Portwood said. "You must aim to *lie* me into the streets. Well, I ain't even thinking about moving."

"You'll move," Mary said. "You'll be glad to move. And you still won't know nothing 'bout green."

"Then you tell us, Miss Mary," Mrs. Garfield said. "Don't pay Portwood any mind."

Portwood sat down, shaking his head hopelessly. "Now she's bound to lie. Mrs. Garfield, you done *guaranteed* she go' lie. And just look at her," he said, his voice rising indignantly, "sitting there looking like a lady preacher or something!"

"Portwood, I done tole you 'bout your way of talking," Mary began, but suddenly the stern façade of her face collapsed and they were all laughing.

"Hush, y'all," Mary said, her eyes gleaming. "Hush!"

"Don't try to laugh out of it," Portwood said, "I maintain these youngsters nowadays is green. They black and trying to git to heaven in a Cadillac. They think their education proves that we old southern folks is fools who don't know nothing 'bout life or loving or nothing 'bout living in the world. They green, I tell you! How we done come this far and lived this long if we didn't learn nothing 'bout life? Answer me that!"

"Now, Portwood," Mrs. Garfield said gently, "They're not that bad, the world just looks different to their eyes."

"Don't tell me, I see 'em when they get off the trains. Long as I been a Red Cap[2] I've seen thousands of 'em, and dam' nigh everyone of 'em is green. And just cause these here is rooming with you, Moms, don't make 'em no different. Here you done fixed this fine Thanksgiving dinner and they caint hardly finish it for rushing off somewhere. Too green to be polite. Don't even know there ain't no other ole fool woman like you renting rooms in Harlem who'll treat 'em like kinfolks. Don't tell me 'bout. . . ."

"Shh," Mrs. Garfield said, as the sound of voices leaving the elevator came to them, "they might be coming back."

They listened. The voices grew gaily up the hall, then, blending with a remote peel of chimes, faded beyond a further wall. Mrs. Garfield sighed as they looked at one another guiltily.

"Shucks," Portwood said, "by now they just about beating the door down, trying to get into that dance. Like I was telling y'all . . ."

"Hush, Portwood!" Mary said. "What *green?*" She said, singing full-throatedly now,

---

1 **signifying:** making an indirect negative comment about a person.

2 **Red Cap:** person who helps train passengers with their luggage. Uniform includes a red cap.

her voice suddenly folk-toned and deep with echoes of sermons and blue trombones,[3] "Lawd, *I* was green. That's what I'm trying to tell you. Y'all hear me? *I, Me, Mary Raaaambo,* was green."

"You telling me?" Portwood laughed. "Is you telling *me?*" Nevertheless he leaned forward with Mrs. Garfield now, surrendering once more to Mary's once-upon-a-time antiphonal[4] spell, waiting to respond to her stated theme: green.

"Here y'all," she said, beckoning for their glasses with one hand and lifting the decanter with the other. "Git some wine in y'all's stomachs so's it can warm y'alls' old-time blood."

They drank ceremoniously with lowered eyes, waiting for Mary's old contralto to resume its flight, its tragic-comic ascendence.

"Sho, I was green," she continued. "Green as anybody what ever left the farm and come to town. Shucks, here you criticizing those youngsters for rushing to the dance 'cause they hope to win that auto—that ain't nothing, not to what I done. Cause like them chillun and everybody else, I was after money. And I was full grown, too. Times was hard. My husband had done died and I couldn't get nothing but part-time work and didn't nobody have enough to eat. My daughter Lucy and me couldn't even afford a ten cents movies so we could go forget about it. So Lawd, this evening we're sitting in the window watching the doings down in the streets. Y'all know how it gits round here in the summertime, after it has been hot all day and has cooled off a bit: Folks out strolling or hanging on the stoops and hollering out the windows, chillun yelling and ripping and romping and begging for pennies to buy that there shaved ice with the red sirup poured over it. Dogs barking—y'all know how it is round here in the summertime. All

that talk and noise and Negroes laughing loud and juke boxes blaring and like-a-that. Well, it's 'bout that time on one of them kinda days, and one of them store-front churches[5] is just beginning to jump. You can hear them clapping their hands and shouting and the tambourines is a-shaking and a-beating, and that ole levee camp trombone they has is going *Wah-wah, Wah-wah, Wah-wah-wah!* Y'all know, just like it really has something to do with the good Lawd's business—when all of a sudden two autos decides to see which is the toughest."

"A wreck?" Portwood said. "What the newspapers call a *collision?*"

"That's it," Mary said, sipping her wine, "one of the biggest smashups you ever seen. Here we is up in the window on the fourth floor and it's happening right down below us. Why, it's like two big bulls has done charged and run headon. I tell you, Mrs. Garfield, it was something! Here they is," she said, shifting two knives upon the cloth, "one's coming thisa way, and the other's coming thata way, and when they gits right here, WHAM! They done come together and something flies out of there like a cannon ball. Then for a second it gets real quiet. It's like everybody done stopped to take a breath at the same time—all except those clapping hands and tambourines and that ole nasty-mouthed trombone (that fool was sounding like he done took over and started preaching the gospel by now). Then, Lawd," she said, rocking forward for emphasis, "*glass* is falling, *dust* is rising, *women* is screaming—Oh, such a commotion. Then all of a sudden all you can hear is Negroes' feet slapping the sidewalks . . ."

"Never mind them feet," Portwood said, "what was it that flew out of there?"

"I'm fixing to tell you now, fool. When the cars come together me and Lucy sees that thing bust outa there like a comet and fly off to one

---

3 **sermons . . . trombones:** reference to Afro-American preaching style and music, the Blues.
4 **antiphonal** (an tif'ə nəl): reference to call and response pattern of Afro-American folk culture.

5 **store-front churches:** religious services held in commercial buildings, often former grocery stores.

side somewhere. Lucy said, 'Mama, did you see what I seen?' 'Come on, chile,' I says, 'Let's us get ourselfs on down there!' And good people, that's when we started to move! Lawd, we flew down them stairs. I didn't even take time to pull off my apron or my house shoes. Just come a-jumping. Oh, it was a sight, I tell you. Everybody and his brother standing round trying to see if anybody was killed and measuring the skid marks and waiting for the ambulance to come—the man coulda died before that ambulance got there——"

"Well, how about it, Moms, was anybody hurt?"

"Yes, they was, but I ain't your mama, an ole rusty Negro like you! Sho' they was hurt. One man was all cut up and bleeding and the other knocked cold as a big deep freeze. They thought he was dead.

"But me and Lucy don't waste no time with none of that. We gets busy looking for what we seen shoot out of them cars. I whispers, 'Chile, where did it hit?' And she points over near the curb. And sho 'nough, when I starts slow-dragging my leg along the gutter my foot hits against something heavy, and when I hears it clink together my heart almost flies out of my mouth . . ."

"My Lord, Miss Mary! What was it?" Mrs. Garfield said, her eyes intense. "You don't mean to tell me it was——"

Mary gave her a flat look. "I'm goin' to tell you," she said, taking a taste of wine. "I give y'all my word I'm gon' tell you—I calls to Lucy, 'Gal, come over here a minute,' justa looking 'round to see if anybody'd seen me. And she come and I whispers to her, 'Now don't let on we found anything, just get on the other side of me and make like you trying to kick me on the foot. Go on, gal,' I says, 'Don't argue with me—And watch out for my bunion!' And Lawd, she kicks that bag and this time I'm sho, 'cause I hear that sweet metal-like sound. 'What you think it is' I says and she leans close to me, eyes done got round as silver dollars, says, 'Mother' (always called me

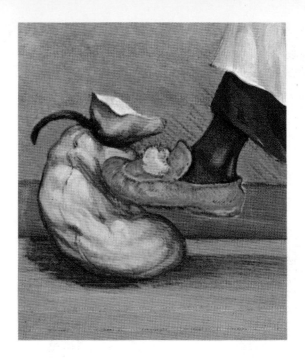

mother steada 'mama,' when she was excited or trying to be proper or something) says, 'Mother, that's money!' 'Shhh, fool,' I tole her, 'you don't have to tell eve'ybody.'

"'But, Mother, what are we going to do?'

"'Just stand still a secon', I says. 'Just quiet down. Don't move. Take it easy! Make out like you watching what they doing over yonder with those cars. Gimme time to figure this thing out . . .'"

She laughed. "Lawd, I was sweating by the gallon. Here I am standing in the street with my foot on a bag full of somebody's money! I don't know what to do. By now the police is all around us and I don't know when whichever one of them men who was hurt is gonna rise up and start yelling for it. I tell you, I musta lost five pounds in five minutes, trying to figure out the deal."

"Miss Mary, I wish I could have seen you," Mrs. Garfield said.

"Well, I'm glad you didn't; I was having trouble enough. Oh it was agonizing. Everytime somebody walks toward us I almost faint.

And Lucy, she's turning this-away and that-away, real fast, like she's trying to invent a new dance. 'Do something, Mother,' she says. 'Please hurry up and do something!' Till finally I caint stand it and just flops down on the curbstone and kicks the bag kinda up under my skirts. Lawd, today!" she sang, then halted to inspect Portwood, who, with his head on his arms, laughed in silent glee. "What's the matter with you, fool?"

"Go on, tell the lie," Portwood said. "Don't mind poor me. You really had larceny in your heart that day."

"Well," Mary grinned, " 'bout this time old Miz Brazelton, a meddlesome ole lady who lived across the hall from me, she comes up talking 'bout, 'Why, Miss Mary, don't you know a woman of your standing in the community oughtn't to be sitting on the curb like some ole common nobody?' Like all Mary Rambo's got to do is worry 'bout what somebody might think about her—I looks and I knows the only way to git rid of the fool is to bawl her out. 'Look here, Miz Brazelton,' I says, 'this here's my own ole rusty tub I'm sitting on and long as I can haul it 'round without your help I guess I can put it down wherever I please . . . .' "

"You a rough woman, Moms," Portwood said with deep resonance, his face a judicial frown. "Rough!"

"I done tole you 'bout calling me Moms!" Mary warned.

"Just tell the lie," Portwood said. "Then what happen?"

"I know that type," Mrs. Garfield said. "With them you do sometimes have to be radical."

"You know it too?" Mary said. "Radical sho is the word. You shoulda seen her face. I really didn't want to hurt that ole woman's feelings, but right then I had to git shed of the fool.

"Well, she leaves and I'm still sitting there fighting with myself over what I oughta do. Should I report what we'd found, or just take it on upstairs? Not that I meant to be dishonest, you know, but like everybody else in New York if something-for-nothing comes along, I wanted to be the one to git it. Besides, anybody fool enough to have that much money riding around with him in a car *deserves* to lose it."

"He sho dam' do," Portwood said. "He *dam'* sho do!"

"Well, all at once Lucy shakes me and here comes the ambulance, justa screaming.

" 'Mother, we better go,' Lucy says. And me I don't know *what* to do. By now the cops is pushing folks around and I knows soon as they see me they bound to find out what kinda egg this is I'm nesting on. Then all of a sudden it comes over me that I'm still wearing my apron! Lawd, I reaches down and touches that bag and my heart starts to going ninety miles a minute. It feels like a heapa money! And when I touches that thick cloth bag you can hear it clinking together. 'Lucy, chile,' I whispers, 'stand right in front of me while the ole lady rolls this heavy stuff up in her apron . . .' "

"Oh, Miss Mary," Mrs. Garfield said, shaking her head, "You'd given in to the devil."

"I'm in his arms, girl, in his hairy arms! And Lucy in on the deal. She's hurrying me up and I picks up that bag and no sooner'n I do, here comes a cop!"

"Oh my, Miss Mary!" cried Mrs. Garfield.

"Woman," said Mary, "you don't know; you have no *idea*. He's one of these tough-looking young cops, too. One of them that thinks he has to beat you up just to prove he's in command of things. Here he comes, swinging up to Lucy like a red sledge hammer, telling folks to move along—Ain't seen *me,* cause I'm still sitting down. And when he comes up to Lucy I starts to moaning like I'm sick: 'Please, mister officer,' I says, kinda hiding my face, 'we just fixin' to leave.' Well, suh, his head shoots round Lucy like a turkey gobbler's and he sees me. Says, 'What's the matter, madam, wuz you in this wreck?'—and in a real nice voice too. Then Lucy—Lawd, that

Lucy was smart; up to that time I didn't know my chile could lie. But Lucy looks the cop dead in the eye and says, 'Officer, we be going in a minute. My mother here is kinda nauchus from looking at all that blood.'"

"Oh, Miss Mary, she didn't say that!"

"She sho did, and it worked! Why the cop bends down and tries to help me to my feet and I says, 'Thank you, officer, just let me rest here a second and I be all right.' Well, suh, he leaves us and goes on off. But by now I got the bag in my apron and gets up moaning and groaning and starts out across the street, kinda bent over like, you know, with Lucy helping me along. Lawd, that bag feels like a thousand pounds. And everytime I takes a step it gets heavier. And on top of that, looks like we never going to cross the street, cause everybody in the block is stopping us to ask what's wrong: 'You sick Miss Mary?'; 'Lucy, what done happen to your mother?'; 'Do she want a doctor?'; 'Po' thing, she done got herself overexcited'—and all likea that. Shucks! I'm overexcited, all right, that bag's 'bout to give me a nervous breakdown!"

"When we finally make it up to the apartment, I'm so beat that I just flops into a chair and sits there panting. Don't even take the bag outa my apron, and Lucy, she's having a fit. 'Open it up, Mother, let's see what's in it,' she says. But I figures we better wait, cause after all, they might miss the money and come searching for it. You see, after I done worked so hard gitting it up there, I had decided to keep it sho 'nough . . ."

"You had given in to the devil," Mrs. Garfield said.

"Who?" said Mary, reaching for the wine, "I'm way, *way* past the giving-in stage."

"This world is surely a trial," Mrs. Garfield mused. "It truly is."

"And you can say that again," said Mary, "cause it's the agonizing truth."

"What did you do then, Miss Mary?"

"Pass me your glass, Portwood," Mary said, reaching for the decanter.

"Never mind the wine," said Portwood, covering his glass with his hand. "Get back to what *happened!*"

"Well, we goes to the bathroom—wait, don't say it!" she warned, giving Portwood a frown. "We goes to the bathroom and I gits up on a chair and drops that bag dead into the flush box."

"Now Miss Mary, really!"

"Girl, yes! I knowed wouldn't nobody think to look for it up there. It coulda been hid up in heaven somewhere. Sho! I dropped it in there, then I sent Lucy on back downstairs to see if anybody'd missed it. She musta hung 'round there for over an hour. Police and the newspaper people come and made pictures and asked a heapa questions and everything, but nothing 'bout the bag. Even after the wreckers come and dragged that pile of brand new junk away—still nothing 'bout the bag."

"Everything going in y'all's favor," Portwood said.

"Uhhuh, everything going our way."

"Y'all had it made, Moms," Portwood said, "Why you never tole this lie before?"

"The devil is truly powerful," Mrs. Garfield said, "Almost as powerful as the Lord. Even so, it's strange nobody missed *that* much money!"

"Now that's what me and Lucy thought . . ."

Portwood struck the table, "What I want to know is how much money was in the bag?"

"I'm coming to that in a second," Mary said.

"Yeah, but why you taking so long?"

"Who's telling this lie, Portwood, me or you?" said Mary.

"You was 'til you got off the track."

"Don't forget your manners, Portwood," Mrs. Garfield said.

"I'm not, but looks like to me y'all think money ought to be as hard to get in a lie somebody's telling as it is to get carrying folks' bags."

"Or as 'tis to git you to hush your mouth," said Mary. "Anyway, we didn't count it right then. We was scaird. I knowed I was doing wrong, holding on to something wasn't really mine. But that wasn't stopping me."

"Y'all was playing a little finders-keepers," Portwood said, resting back.

"Yeah, and concentrating on the keeping part."

"But why didn't you just *look* at the money, Miss Mary?"

"Cause we mighta been tempted to spend some of it, girl."

"Yeah, and y'all mighta give yourself away," Portwood said.

"Ain't it the truth! And that bag was powerful enough as it was. It was really working on us. Me and Lucy just sitting 'round like two ole hens on a nest, trying to guess how much is in it. Then we tries to figure whether it was dollars or fifty-centies. Finally we decides that it caint be less'n five or ten dollar gold pieces to weigh so much."

"But how on earth could you resist looking at it?" Mrs. Garfield said.

"Scaird, chile; scaird. We was like a couple

kids who somebody's done give a present and tole 'em it would disappear if they opened it before Christmas. And know something else, neither one of us ever had to go to the bathroom so much as when us had that bag up there in that flush box. I got to flushing it just to hear it give out that fine clinking sound."

Portwood groaned, "I know you was gon' lie," he said. "*I knowed* it."

"Hush, man, hush!" Mary laughed. "I know our neighbors musta got sick and tired of hearing us flush that thing. But I tell you, everytime I pulled the chain it was like ringing up money in the cash register! I tell you, it was disintegrating! Whew! I'd go in there and stay a while and come out. Next thing I know there'd be Lucy going in. Then we got shamed and started slipping past one another. She'd try to keep hid from me, and me from her. I tell you, that stuff was working on us like a dose of salts! Why, after a few days I got so I couldn't work, just sat 'round thinking 'bout that doggone bag. And naturally, I done most of my thinking up there on the throne."

"Didn't I tell you she was tuning up to lie," Portwood laughed. "If she don't stop I'm dead gon' call the police."

"This here's the agonizing truth I'm telling y'all," said Mary.

"I wouldn't have been able to stand it, Miss Mary. I would have had to get it over with."

"They shoulda been looking for it by now," Portwood said, "all that money."

"That's what us thought," said Mary. "And we got to figuring why they didn't. First we figgers maybe it was because the man who was hurt so bad had died. But then we seen in the papers that he got well . . . ."

"Maybe they was gangsters," Portwood said.

"Yeah, we thought of that too; gangsters or bootleggers."

"Yeah, yeah, either one of them coulda been carrying all that money—or gamblers even."

"Sho they could. Me and Lucy figgered that maybe they thought the cops had took the money or that they was trying to find it theyselves on the q.t.,[6] y'know."

"Miss Mary, you were either very brave or very reckless."

"Neither one, girl," Mary said, "just broke and hongry. And don't talk about brave, shucks, we was scaird to answer the doorbell at night. Let me tell you, we was doing some tall figuring. Finally I got so I couldn't eat and Lucy couldn't sleep. We was evil as a coupla lady bears at cubbing time."

"You just couldn't stand all that prosperity, huh, Moms?"

"It was a burden, all right. And everytime we pulled the chain it got a few dollars more so."

Mrs. Garfield smiled. "Mr. Garfield often said that the possession of great wealth brought with it the slings and arrows of outrageous responsibility."

"Mrs. Garfield," Mary mused, "you know you had you a right smart man in him? You really did. And looks like when you got stuff saved up like that you got the responsibility of keeping some of it circulating. Even without looking at it we got to figuring how to spend it. Lucy, she wants to go into business. Why she *almost* persuaded me to see about buying a building and opening a restaurant! And as if *that* wasn't enough trouble to git into, she decides she's goin' take the third floor and open her a beauty shop. Oh, we had it all planned!" She shook her head.

"And y'all still ain't looked at it," Portwood said.

"Still ain't seen a thing."

"Dam!"

"You had marvelous self-control," Mrs. Garfield said.

"Yeah, I did," Mary said, "until that day Lucy went to the dentist. Seems I just couldn't hold out no longer. Seems like I got to thinking 'bout that bag and couldn't stop. I looked at the newspaper and all those ads. Reminded

---

6 q.t.: quietly, secretly.

me of things I wanted to buy; looked out the window and saw autos; I tried to read the Bible and as luck would have it I opened it to where it says something 'bout 'Store ye up riches in heaven,' or 'Cast your bread upon the waters.' It really had me on a merry-go-round. I just had to take a peep! So I went and pulled down all the shades and started the water running in the tub like I was taking me a bath—turned on every faucet in the house—then I climbed up there with a pair of scissors and reached in and raised that bag up and just looked at it awhile.

"It had done got *cooold!* It come up *cooold,* with the water dripping off it like some old bucket been deep down in a well. Done turned green with canker, y'all! I just couldn't resist it no longer. I really couldn't, I took them scissors and snipped me a piece outa that bag and took me a good, *looong* look. And let me tell you, dear people, after I looked I was so excited I had to get down from there and put myself to bed. My nerves just couldn't take it . . ."

"It surely must have been an experience, Miss Mary."

"Woman, you don't know. You really don't know. You hear me? *I had to go to bed!*"

"Heck, with that much money you could afford to go to bed," said Portwood.

"Wait, le'me tell you. I'm laying up there moaning and groaning when here come Lucy and she's in one of her talking moods. Soon as I seen her I knowed pretty soon she was going to want to talk 'bout that bag and I truly

dreaded telling her that I'd done looked into it without her. I says, 'Baby, I don't feel so good. You talk to me later' . . . But y'all think that stopped her? Shucks, all she does is to go get me a bottle of cold beer she done brought me and start to running her mouth again. And, just like I knowed she was gon' do, she finally got round to talking 'bout that bag. What ought we to buy *first,* she wants to know. Lawd, that pore chile, whenever she got her mind set on a thing! Well suh, I took me a big swoller of beer and just lay there like I was thinking awhile."

"You were really good companions," Mrs. Garfield said. "There is nothing like young people to make life rich and promising. Especially if they're your own children. If only Mr. Garfield and I . . ."

"Mrs. Garfield, let her finish this lie," Portwood said, "*then* we can talk about you and Mr. Garfield."

"Oh, of course," Mrs. Garfield said, "I'm sorry, Miss Mary, you know I didn't really mean to interrupt."

"Pay that pore fool no min'," Mary said. "I wish I had Lucy with me right this minit!"

"Is this lie about money or chillun," Portwood said. "Y'all here 'bout to go serious. I want to know what you tole Lucy *then.* What did y'all start out to buy?"

"If you hadn't started monkeying with Mrs. Garfield you'da learned by now," Mary said. "Well, after I lay there and thought awhile I tole her, 'Well, baby, if you want to know the truth 'bout what I think, *I* think we oughta buy us an auto.'

"Well suh, you coulda knocked her over with a feather. 'A car!' she says, 'why Mother, I didn't know you was interested in a car. We don't want to be like these ole ignorant Negroes who buy cars and don't have anything to go with it and no place to keep it,' she says. Says, 'I'm certainly surprised at you, Mother. I never would've dreamed you wanted a *car,* not the very first thing.'

"Oh, she was running off a mile a minute.

And looking at me like she done caught me kissing the preacher or the iceman or somebody! 'We want to be practical,' she says, 'We don't want to throw our money away . . .'

"Well, it almost killed me. 'Lucy, honey,' I says, 'that's just what your mama's trying to do, be practical. That's why I say let's git us an auto.'

"'But, Mama,' she says, 'a car isn't practical at all.'

"'Oh yes it is,' I says, 'Cause how else is we gon' use two sets of auto chains?'——

"And do y'all know," said Mary, sitting up suddenly and balancing the tips of her fingers on her knees, her face a mask of incredulity, "I had to hop outa bed and catch that chile before she swayed dead away in a faint!"

"Yeah," Portwood laughed, falling back in his chair, "and you better hop up from there and catch me."

Mrs. Garfield's voice rose up girlishly, "Oh Miss Mary," she laughed, "you're just fooling."

Mary's bosom heaved, "I wish I was, girl," she said, "I sho wish I was."

"How 'bout that? Tire chains," Portwood said. "All that larceny for some dam' tire chain!"

"Fool," said Mary, "didn't I tell you you didn't know nothing 'bout green? There I was thinking I done found me a bird nest on the ground. C'mon now," she said chuckling at the gullibility of all mankind, "let's us finish the wine."

Portwood winked at Mrs. Garfield. "Hey, Moms, tell us something . . ."

"I ain't go' tell you again that I ain't yo' mama," said Mary.

"I just want you to tell us one last thing . . ."

Mary looked at him warily, "What is it? I got no more time for your foolishness now, I got to git up from here and fix for them chillun."

"Never mind them youngsters," said Portwood, "just tell us if you ever dreamed lucky?"

Mary grinned, "Ain't I just done tole you?" she said. "Sho I did, but I woke up cold in hand. Just the same though," she added thoughtfully, "I still hope them youngsters win that there auto."

"Yes," Mrs. Garfield said, "And wouldn't it be a comfort, Miss Mary? Just to know that they *can* win one, I mean . . .?"

Mary said that it certainly would be.

Study Questions

1. What does Mary mean when she says to Portwood, "You don't know nothing about green!"? What leads her to make this remark? What does she know about "green"?

2. What is the relationship between Portwood, Mary, and Mrs. Garfield? How does the reader learn what their relationship is?

3. What are the different ways in which suspense is used in this story?

4. What is the meaning of the "one last thing" Portwood wants to know? What is the meaning of Mrs. Garfield's concluding question?

5. In what ways can you compare this story with Langston Hughes's poem, "Lenox Avenue Mural" (p. 89)? How are they similar? How do they differ?

Norman Mailer   1923 —

Norman Mailer was graduated from Harvard in 1943, where he won a number of literary prizes. He then served in the South Pacific during World War II. On his return he achieved instant fame with his powerful novel of jungle warfare, *The Naked and the Dead* (1945). Although he has written other novels, Mailer has not been content with the career of a conventional novelist. Increasingly he has experimented with narrative forms mixing fiction, journalism, social commentary, and autobiography. *The Armies of the Night* (1968) dealt with the Vietnam protest movement. *Of a Fire on the Moon* (1970) was an excursion into the realm of spaceflight. He has produced a brilliant study of capital punishment in *The Executioner's Song* (1979) and published his twenty-first book, *Pieces and Pontifications* in 1982.

SPRAY PAINTED ROBE *Jim Dine* 1977

The Notebook

NORMAN MAILER

THE WRITER was having a fight with his young lady. They were walking toward her home, and as the argument continued, they walked with their bodies farther and farther apart.

The young lady was obviously providing the energy for the quarrel. Her voice would rise a little bit, her head and shoulders would move toward him as though to add weight to her words, and then she would turn away in disgust, her heels tapping the pavement in an even precise rhythm which was quite furious.

The writer was suffering with some dignity. He placed one leg in front of the other, he looked straight ahead, his face was sad, he would smile sadly from time to time and nod his head to every word she uttered.

"I'm sick and tired of you," the young lady exclaimed. "I'm sick and tired of your being so superior. What do you have to be superior about?"

"Nothing," the writer said in so quiet a

voice, so gentle a tone that his answer might as well have been, "I have my saintliness to be superior about."

"Do you ever give me anything?" the young lady asked, and provided the response herself. "You don't even give me the time of day. You're the coldest man I've ever known."

"Oh, that's not true," the writer suggested softly.

"Isn't it? Everybody thinks you're so nice and friendly, everybody except anybody who knows you at all. Anybody who knows you, knows better."

The writer was actually not unmoved. He liked this young lady very much, and he did not want to see her unhappy. If with another part of his mind he was noticing the way she constructed her sentences, the last word of one phrase seeming to provide the impetus for the next, he was nonetheless paying attention to everything she said.

"Are you being completely fair?" he asked.

"I've finally come to understand you," she said angrily. "You don't want to be in love. You just want to say the things you're supposed to say and watch the things you're supposed to feel."

"I love you. I know you don't believe me," the writer said.

"You're a mummy. You're nothing but a . . . an Egyptian mummy."

The writer was thinking that when the young lady became angry, her imagery was at best somewhat uninspired. "All right, I'm a mummy," he said softly.

They waited for a traffic light to change. He stood at the curb, smiling sadly, and the sadness on his face was so complete, so patient and so perfect, that the young lady with a little cry darted out into the street and trotted across on her high heels. The writer was obliged to run a step or two to catch up with her.

"Your attitude is different now," she continued. "You don't care about me. Maybe you used to, but you don't care any more. When you look at me, you're not really looking at all. I don't exist for you."

"You know you do."

"You wish you were somewhere else right now. You don't like me when I'm nasty. You think I'm vulgar. Very well, then, I'm vulgar. I'm too vulgar for your refined senses. Isn't that a pity? Do you think the world begins and ends with you?"

"No."

"No, what?" she cried.

"Why are you angry? Is it because you feel I didn't pay enough attention to you tonight? I'm sorry if I didn't. I didn't realize I didn't. I do love you."

"Oh, you love me; oh, you certainly do," the young lady said in a voice so heavy with sarcasm that she was almost weeping. "Perhaps I'd like to think so, but I know better." Her figure leaned toward his as they walked. "There's one thing I will tell you," she went on bitterly. "You hurt people more than the cruelest person in the world could. And why? I'll tell you why. It's because you never feel anything and you make believe that you do." She could see he was not listening, and she asked in exasperation, "What are you thinking about now?"

"Nothing. I'm listening to you, and I wish you weren't so upset."

Actually the writer had become quite uneasy. He had just thought of an idea to put into his notebook, and it made him anxious to think that if he did not remove his notebook from his vest pocket and jot down the thought, he was likely to forget it. He tried repeating the idea to himself several times to fix it in his memory, but this procedure was never certain.

"I'm upset," the young lady said. "Of course, I'm upset. Only a mummy isn't upset, only a mummy can always be reasonable and polite because they don't feel anything." If they had not been walking so quickly she would have stamped her foot. "What are you thinking about?"

"It's not important," he said. He was thinking that if he removed the notebook from his pocket, and held it in the palm of his hand, he might be able to scribble in it while they walked. Perhaps she would not notice.

It turned out to be too difficult. He was obliged to come to a halt beneath a street light. His pencil worked rapidly in nervous elliptic script while he felt beside him the pressure of her presence. *Emotional situation deepened by notebook,* he wrote. *Young writer, girl friend. Writer accused of being observer, not participant in life by girl. Gets idea he must put in notebook. Does so, and brings the quarrel to a head. Girl breaks relationship over this.*

"You have an idea now," the young lady murmured.

"Mmm," he answered.

"That notebook. I knew you'd pull out that notebook." She began to cry. "Why, you're nothing but a notebook," she shrieked, and ran away from him down the street, her high heels mocking her misery in their bright tattoo upon the sidewalk.

"No, wait," he called after her. "Wait, I'll explain."

It occurred to the writer that if he were to do such a vignette,[1] the nuances could be altered. Perhaps the point of the piece should be that the young man takes out his notebook because he senses that this would be the best way to destroy what was left of the relationship. It was a nice idea.

Abruptly, it also occurred to him that maybe this was what he had done. Had he wished to end his own relationship with his own young lady? He considered this, priding himself on the fact that he would conceal no motive from himself, no matter how unpleasant.

Somehow, this did not seem to be true. He did like the young lady, he liked her very much, and he did not wish the relationship to end yet. With some surprise, he realized that she was almost a block away. Therefore, he began to run after her. "No, wait," he called out. "I'll explain it to you, I promise I will." And as he ran the notebook jiggled warmly against his side, a puppy of a playmate, always faithful, always affectionate.

---

1 **vignette** (vin yet'): a short verbal description.

Study Questions

1. What is happening in this story?
2. How do you know what the "young lady's" viewpoint is? What is the writer's viewpoint? With whom do you sympathize? Why?
3. How does James Baldwin's statement (page 66) that the artist "must actively cultivate that state which most men, necessarily, must avoid: the state of being alone" apply to this story?

Composition

1. "The Notebook" is quite a *short* story, but very provocative. Write an essay in which you tell whether or not you agree with the writer's attitude. Be sure to include your opinion on whether or not the writer is deliberately trying to break off the relationship. Conclude with a statement on which you think is more important—developing your talent, or developing a relationship.
2. Write this same story the way the girl would repeat what happened to a friend. Include all the incidents from her point of view.

Jessamyn West   1907 —

Jessamyn West was born in Indiana. Her parents and grandparents were Quakers. Her first book, *The Friendly Persuasion,* was a collection of stories about Quaker life in Indiana and was highly acclaimed for its warm and sensitive realism. West has also published several other collections of short stories (*Except for Me and Thee; Love, Death, and the Ladies' Drill Team; Cress Delahanty*). In addi-tion she has written novels (*The Witch Diggers, The Massacre at Fall Creek*), autobiographical accounts (*Hide and Seek: A Continuing Journey; To See the Dream*), and a play (*A Mirror for the Sky*). In the following story, West explores the delicate relationship between love and pride and between the writer as an observer and a participant of life.

Breach of Promise

JESSAMYN WEST

EVERY AFTERNOON between two and four, depending upon the amount of business or conversation he had encountered on his route, the mail carrier came by in his ramshackle, mud-spattered car. He didn't drive up the lane to the house, a lane a quarter of a mile long and crossing at one point a brook, which after heavy rains was more than a brook, but put the mail in the wobbly tin box, set the flag, honked three times, and drove on.

Ordinarily I waited for these three honks before I walked down to the box. But now and then, because I was at that time so eagerly hoping for a certain letter, I would convince myself, in spite of the fact that I had been listening intently, that the mail carrier had passed without my hearing him. Invariably, after I had walked to the box on these occasions to find I had been mistaken, the mail carrier would be unusually late. Then, because my work had already been interrupted and because my eagerness for the letter I awaited always made me hopeful that the mail carrier would be along in another minute or two, I didn't return to the house. Instead, I paced up and down the lane, stopping usually at the brook to examine the veining in some curious pebble or to watch an island of foam, seemingly as imperishable as the pebble, float by.

At the time, I would be scarcely aware, however, of the objects I scanned. All of my consciousness would be focused in a fury of attention on the wished for letter: imagining its size, shape, color to the eye, weight to the hand, the heavy down strokes of the writing, even the post mark, Yorba Linda, California.

The letter, not the one which I wanted but the one of which I am writing, came on a day when I was in this manner examining pebbles at the brookside. The mail carrier saw me and honked three times but, nervous and irritated after what had seemed my long wait, I continued obstinately to bend over my pebble. He honked again, I picked up the pebble I had been admiring and with it in my hand walked down to the mailbox.

"You got another letter here addressed to that other name," he told me.

He held this letter close to his chest, as if it were a winning card in a crucial game. The mail carrier had never been reconciled to the fact that I received letters addressed in two ways: to my "own" name, and to what he called "that other name," the name I used in my writing. The letter I had hoped for would not be addressed "to that other name," so I didn't care how long he held his square white envelope to his chest.

"It's addressed care of the Seulkes," he said (the Seulkes were the people with whom I was boarding, the house at the end of the lane), "so I reckon it's for you."

He ended on a rising note and looked at me, through spectacles as blurred and spattered as some old windowpane. "It's from Persis Hughes," he said. "You know her?"

"No," I told him, though I knew that a Mr. Hughes owned a large farm, down the road a mile or so and that he had a grown daughter.

"Funny thing," he said. "Persis writing you when she didn't know you."

There was no use telling him that writers get letters from people they don't know, so I agreed with him. "Yes," I said, "it's a funny thing."

"You'd think she'd just walk up the pike if she had anything to say to us and save her three cents."

"Yes," I said again.

He finally handed me the letter from Persis Hughes, but he hadn't finished with talking yet.

"I notice it takes four days for a letter from California to reach you," he said.

"If they don't air-mail it," I agreed.

"You get homesick, back here by yourself?" he asked.

"I'm pretty busy working," I told him and he didn't notice that I hadn't answered his question.

"Working?" he asked, and I could see that he thought I had found myself a job of some kind in town.

"Writing," I said, and from the way he repeated, "Oh, writing," it was plain writing wasn't his idea of work. But he drove on without any more questions, leaving me standing by the mailbox, Persis Hughes' letter in one hand, my prettily veined pebble in the other. On a sudden impulse I opened the box, placed the smooth little stone in its tin emptiness and tightly closed the lid. I did this without thinking, but I suppose that bitterly, subconsciously, I was thinking, I asked for bread and you gave me a stone, and that I felt some relief in thus being able to objectify my emotions, to symbolize my self-pity.

I didn't open my letter from Persis Hughes until I reached my room. Though if the letter I wanted had come I would have read it six times over before I reached the house. My room at the Seulkes' was a perfect place for reading unwanted mail. It was sad, sad. Strange, unpleasant colors, peculiar furniture, odd smells, and a most distressing, a really horrifying picture.

This picture was of the Seulkes' only son Albert, aged twelve, taken three days before he died of lockjaw. After Albert's death Mrs. Seulke had had his picture enlarged, covered with convex glass, and framed. And now Albert, looking, it seemed, already swollen, feverish, and in pain watched me the whole time I was in the room.

A marble-topped "center table," a wicker rocker with crocheted back and arm tidies, a wooden chair, one of the dinette set which the Seulkes used in their kitchen, these together with a large brass bed, made up the furnishings of my room.

I lived on that bed like a castaway on a desert island, like a lone survivor on a raft. It was my desk, chair, filing cabinet, table, sofa, home, world. Neither of the chairs was fit to sit on and the marble-topped table was too encumbered with decorative feet, claws, and legs to permit any one with feet and legs of his own to get near it. It was on this bed, under Albert's picture, that I read Persis Hughes' letter.

Dear Miss or Madam [the letter began]: I have heard that you are married but since I do not know for sure about this and do not want to call you Madam if you are really Miss, I address you thus.

I know you are a writer. I have read several of your stories in magazines. Some of them were interesting to me, and I suppose all must have been interesting to somebody because I do not think editors pay money for stories unless they are pretty sure about this.

This is not a "fan" letter though, to say I like your stories, for frankly some of them I do not because they do not seem to me to be about real life, but about some idea you have which you think is "real life." Or maybe you know it isn't, but write about it because you think it is better than real life. Or maybe more interesting.

What I want to ask you is this, wouldn't you like to *do* some *good* by your writing? That is not just *write about* goodness. You usually do write about good people, etc., but I don't think this does any real good in the world and it may do harm. People may read about all these good characters of yours and say to themselves, "Well, if the world is such a good place a little badness from me won't do any particular harm."

"And wouldn't you like to find out more about real life, too? Not just your own ideas about life which you think will make a good story, but *real* life, the way a woman suffers it?

I know a writer writes for money. So what I have to ask you is this, not only wouldn't you like to do some good with your writing and find out more about how things really are than you seem to know, (judging by your stories) but also make some money?

I could have invited you for a social call, to have supper with me, then have asked you these things. But I think that would have been sailing under false colors, which I do not care to do. Now that you

know my purpose is mainly not social would you care to have supper with me on Tuesday of next week at six o'clock? I will be honored by your presence. Please reply.

Sincerely,
Persis Hughes.

When I finished Persis Hughes' letter it was dark. I had read it a line or two at a time, not caring about it, thinking only of my own letter, the one which had not arrived. I remembered all those letters in stories and novels which never arrive or rather which are ironically, delayed or lost until their arrival means nothing. I had almost convinced myself that my own letter had been held up in a like way, that all I needed to do was to send a telegram saying, "Your letter was delayed, wire contents," to have by bedtime an answering wire and the words I had awaited the past weeks.

Almost, but not quite. By the time Persis Hughes' letter was read I had given up this silly dream. Would I like to know life, "the way a woman suffers it"? This made me smile. Persis Hughes was not much over twenty, if what I had heard was true. Still, I knew I would go to see her. For the mail carrier had been right. I was lonely here, heartsick.

Mr. Seulke drove me down the pike toward the Hughes' on Tuesday evening. I didn't tell him where I was going. Persis Hughes' father was a widower and I did not care to be twitted about him, as I would have been had Mr. Seulke known my destination, for nothing so interested him as what he called "he-ing and she-ing."

Mr. Seulke was very imaginative about such things. The first time I had hired him to drive me I asked him to take me to a small stream for the afternoon and pick me up later. With a sudden downward look Mr. Seulke had asked me, "Who you meeting, sis?"

At first I didn't understand his meaning and answered quite literally that I was going only to walk along the stream because it was beautiful and to note the kinds of trees and bushes which grew by it.

"That's your story, sis," he had said. "You stick to it."

I asked Mr. Seulke to let me out a short distance from the Hughes' farm. "You needn't come after me," I told him. "I have a way home." Persis Hughes, when I accepted her invitation, had told me she and her father would drive me back to the Seulkes'.

I can't write what Mr. Seulke said then, though to him it was no more than a half-humorous gallantry and nothing that any woman in that neighborhood would have taken amiss.

The Hughes' house was a nice place to be walking toward in the dusk. Chrysanthemums, bronze and gold, though grayish in the dark, were staked up along the path which led to the front door, and light, soft and yellow from kerosene lamps, shone out through the windows. Persis Hughes herself answered my knock and asked me in. She seemed neither nervous nor emotional, the two things I had feared. A gusty fall wind was blowing and she shut the door quickly behind me.

"Father's old-fashioned," she said. "He likes supper early, and he eats it early, so there'll be only the two of us to eat now."

She put away my coat and purse and let me into the dining room. It was a real dining room, a room planned only for eating and there was nothing in it which did not have to do with eating or one's comfort while eating or afterward: a big, fumed-oak sideboard, six fumed-oak chairs, a china closet through whose curving glass sides cut glass sparkled. Under each of the two windows was a Boston fern in a wicker fern stand and between these was a narrow couch upholstered in red rep on which one might rest or nap after eating. The table itself was round, covered with a white cloth whose corners touched the floor and lighted by a hanging kerosene lamp. In one corner of the room the isinglass eye of a small

wood stove glowed rosily and its fire made an occasional dry tick, tick.

Persis Hughes seated me opposite her at the table. Between us was a very fine meal: an old hen, baked with dressing, glazed parsnips, baked squash, gravy, a casserole of tomatoes, slaw, a sponge cake covered with boiled custard, and besides these a number of jams and relishes.

"Did you cook all this?" I asked Persis.

"Oh, yes," she said. "Who else? There'd be only my father to cook if I didn't."

"Do you like cooking?" I asked.

"Not particularly," she said, "but it had to be done and I like good things to eat. So I cook as quickly and well as I can."

She carved the hen deftly, filling my plate with dark meat, white meat, dressing, gravy. I watched her as she did this. Afterward, but not then, I tried to see Persis Hughes through a man's eyes, which is a mistake, a thing a woman can never do. A woman, summoning all the latent masculinity she possesses, focusing it like a spyglass to peer through, remembering every item of female appearance ever lovingly described by man, will still see awry, unlike a man.

No, this particular spyglass is useless, and at that time it did not occur to me to look through it at Persis Hughes, anyway. I thought only, as I watched her carve, that she was very pretty. Persis Hughes was plumper, perhaps, than she should have been. She was hazel-eyed and had wavy sorrel-colored hair which was piled high on her head in a loose knot.

It was I, who for a time, in spite of what she had said in her letter, tried to keep the evening "social." "How long have you lived here?" "All my life." "Where did you go to school?" "Local high school and the Cincinnati Conservatory." "Oh, you play?" "Yes." "What instrument?" "Piano, that is I did." "Why did you give it up?" "I can't write music and I don't want to go through life going do-do-do to another man's tune." I suppose I showed my surprise at this.

"Would you want to spend the rest of your life reading aloud what other people wrote?" she asked.

"I don't know," I replied. "Perhaps if I were good at it. One likes to really succeed at something."

She refilled our plates and as she did so she asked, "Did you ever see yourself unexpectedly in a mirror and not know yourself?"

I had of course, and I said, "Yes. It's an awful experience, isn't it?"

"Did anyone," she asked, "ever see herself in a mirror, not recognize herself, but think, what a beautiful, stylish woman that is coming down the street?"

This was something I had never thought of. "I suppose not. We're only surprised at our ugliness not at our good looks."

"Then," said Persis, "we all actually look far worse than we have any idea we do."

"I'm afraid so."

"Writing is a kind of mirror, isn't it?" she asked.

"A mirror?" I repeated, seeing how this was at once true and not true.

"I mean," she said, "a man might see himself truly for the first time in his life in a story, mightn't he? See how he really was, wicked and ugly perhaps, instead of handsome and good."

"He might, but he'd probably not recognize himself. Just as we'd never recognize ourselves in the mirror on the street except that the awful woman approaching us is wearing our hat, walking in our shoes, carrying our purse."

"That's just it," said Persis eagerly. "*He'd* recognize himself in the same way. He'd read the story and think to himself, why that's what I said, that's what I wore that day, that's where we went and what we ate. He'd have to recognize himself by these things. Then, seeing himself as someone else saw him he'd see how bad, how foolish he'd been. And he would be filled with remorse."

I began to understand Persis Hughes' letter—a little. "If he *did* recognize himself," I asked, "and he *was* filled with remorse, what would he do then?"

"Change," she said promptly. "Mend his ways. Do what he promised."

She left the table to get more custard for our cake and poured us both coffee. She took no more than two bites of her own dessert, then carried her coffee over to the sofa and sat there bolt upright sipping it. "Please go ahead and eat," she said. "I'm not hungry."

I did eat. The cake and custard were very good.

"I thought perhaps you would write this story," she said.

"What story?" I asked.

"Dallas'," she said. "Dallas' and mine."

"Who is Dallas?" I asked.

"A man," she said. "The man who promised to marry me."

"I don't know him. I don't know your story."

"You could meet him," she said. "He doesn't live far from here. And I'd tell you everything about us. I've thought over everything so much these past weeks I could talk to you all night and not a word would be untrue. I see and hear it all of the time. But you wouldn't know that is, probably."

Not know that long, never dissolving panorama of memory? That sound track which runs on and on repeating the very words which are most painful to hear? That film which replays, even against the closed eyes, particularly against the closed eyes, the very scenes one longs to forget?

"What good would it do if I were to write this story? How would it help you or anyone else?"

"Dallas would read it. He reads a great deal. And if he didn't happen to have the magazine it was in, I'd see he got it. Then it wouldn't be like the mirror. He would say to himself, 'If that is how I really am, God help me, I will change.'"

"Why do you want him to change?" I asked.

"I want him to do what he promised. I want him to marry me." She saw that my coffee cup was empty and refilled it from the pot she had left to keep warm on the stove.

There were so many objections to her scheme that I didn't know which to point out first. "Even if I wrote it," I said, "this story, you couldn't be sure a magazine would print it."

She wouldn't believe this. "It would be so real, so true," she said, "they would have to. They could see it was nothing anyone had imagined. That it was what a real person had suffered."

"Do you like to read about suffering?" I asked her.

"Yes," she said, "I do. I don't feel so alone then."

"Editors don't think that," I told her. "They think people want to read about happiness."

"Editors!" she said scornfully. "What do they know about people? Happiness, happiness, happiness! It breaks my heart to read about happiness."

"It breaks my heart to write about it sometimes, too," I said.

"Then why do it? I didn't intend to say this, but all those happy stories of yours! They sound silly to me. Besides," she said changing her tack very swiftly, "this might have a happy ending."

"Even so," I told her, "written in the best way I know, no one might want to print it."

She had a new idea. "It might be even better to have it printed in the *Republican*. That way Dallas would be sure to see it."

The *Republican* was Lane County's weekly paper. "I didn't know the *Republican* ever printed stories," I said.

"It doesn't. But it would if I paid them. Oh, I have the money to do it all right," she said, as if I had questioned her. "My mother left me," she stopped, as if her native hill-country suspicion and shrewdness had just reminded her that she was talking, after all, to a stranger with whom reticence about money matters was advisable, "a considerable sum," she finished. "I will also pay *you*," she said, "in that case, whatever a magazine would. And this way you'd have a sure thing. Not have to take a chance on an editor's liking it."

She put her coffee cup down on the floor with a gesture of finality, as if everything had been settled.

I said there had to be more in a piece of writing than promise of pay, otherwise writers wouldn't be writing at all but doing something that paid regularly the first of every month.

"You could do good, too," she reminded "by writing this story. Doesn't that interest you?"

"How?" I asked.

"You will help a man keep his word. And you will help save him from being ruined. For if he doesn't marry me, I will sue him for breach of promise. And if I do I will take from him everything he has. I can do it," she assured me. "I have his letters."

She picked up her cup again trying to find a few more drops in it. I refilled both our cups. Coffee keeps me awake, but I didn't expect to sleep anyway that night.

"I know exactly what the story should be called," she said.

"What?" I asked.

"'Breach of Promise'."

"That isn't a very interesting title," I said, "not very pleasant or inviting."

"What do I care about that? Interesting! Pleasant! That title will catch Dallas Hindshaw's eye, because he knows very well what I will do if he doesn't marry me. 'Breach of promise'," she repeated. "Yes, that's it."

I said nothing. What is there to say to the naïveté which outlines and names a piece of writing for you as specifically as if the work involved were of the same order as that needed for spading a garden plot or scrubbing a piece of linoleum? Perhaps Persis Hughes saw some of this in my mind. Anyway she said rather sadly, "Doesn't our story interest you?"

I couldn't help smiling. "I don't know your

story," I told her, "the story of Persis Hughes and Dallas Hindshaw."

"What do you want me to tell you about Dallas and me?" she asked.

"Whatever you like." I put my empty coffee cup on the table, pushed the table nearer the wall, turned down the wick in the lamp, pulled up a second chair for a footrest, and prepared to listen. "Tell me whatever you like."

Persis lay back against the red sofa's bulging, built-in hump. The wind had died down, but not enough to stop the rustling of some vine against the wall of the house or to end the slight movement of the overhead lamp.

"I remember it all so well—the train we met on—his first words, everything. The only trouble is that our story is so strange, so unusual, it's hard to tell you. It isn't as if it were everyone's story."

But that was exactly what it was, everyone's story—my story. "Dallas was already on the Seymour train when I got on."—Does it make any difference whether the train runs between Cincinnati and Seymour or San Francisco and Salinas, if *he* is on it?—"It was snowing—that made it seem so much more close, private, shut away from everyone else."—What difference does the weather make? In rain, in a wind storm, in a time of quiet, not a leaf stirring, if *he* is there everyone else is shut away.—"Dallas had such a nice way of eating. I've never enjoyed seeing other people eat, but Dallas' hands went flying around the table, helping me, helping himself, and when he chewed there was no sign of it except a kind of shadow on his cheek. It was a pleasure to watch Dallas eat."—Whatever *he* does is a pleasure to watch: things unbearable in anyone else, how pretty they are in him; flip, flip, two aspirin on the back of the tongue, a gulp of water washing them down, and the smooth Adam's apple momentarily jutting out under the skin, the only grace in that, is *his* grace.—Ted's grace. "Dallas loved my faults, freckles, stubby eye-

lashes, anger, he didn't exclude them." *He* loves the whole person, always, unites what is severed and makes what was fractional complete.—"Dallas says there is no one else, so why doesn't he marry me? When he wanted to so much? All I need do is wake him up, show him himself in the mirror. Wake him up from this crazy dream he's in."

This crazy dream—this crazy dream—I put in more wood in the stove. They were burning apple wood. The wind came up again and the lamp's arc widened. Back in the house a clock kept striking, quarters, halves, and wholes. After the hour struck there was always a little quaver, a kind of audible tremor as if the effort of the transition had almost overwhelmed the clock's mechanism.

Persis Hughes took down her hair, wound it up again in a tighter knot, took it down and braided it. Her father came to the door with so big a yawn I could scarcely make out his face.

"Good night, girls," he said. "I'll lay down with my clothes on for a little snooze, call me when you want me." I stopped listening to Persis Hughes and thought my own thoughts and listened again and couldn't tell where my thoughts left off and her words began, so moved back and forth between the two and mixed them up thoroughly.

"That is Dallas' and my story," she concluded, unbraided her hair, sat up, leaned forward so that her face parted her long wavy hair the way a rock parts a waterfall. "Now you know it well enough to write it."

"Too well," I told her, "to write it."

"How can you know it too well?" she asked.

I couldn't say I had lived it.

"It's like the multiplication table. I know it by heart. I wouldn't write that."

"Do it for me," she urged.

"I can't. You can only write about what you don't know, and find out about it in the writing."

"You won't do it then?"

"I can't."

"You won't!"

"Very well, I won't. Besides, it wouldn't help you any."

"All right, then, I will sue him. You like to write about good people but you won't be troubled to do good. I will sue Dallas Hindshaw, and everything he has I will take away from him."

If she could not understand writing, I could not understand suing. We were at a standstill. "Do you love Dallas Hindshaw?"

"Were you asleep?" she asked.

"Then why do you want to ruin him, make public everything that is private and sacred?"

"I am honor bound to do so," she said. "It is a terrible thing to do but I am honor bound to try everything to bring him back."

"Bring him back!" I said. "You will make him hate you."

"If he won't marry me, I hope he will hate me enough to want to kill me. I hope every morning he will wake up thinking how he could kill me, put his hands around my throat and strangle me, or open up my dress and plunge a knife in my heart."

"You are crazy," I said. But I knew she wasn't crazy. She was speaking the truth.

"All right, I am crazy. If Dallas Hindshaw doesn't love me he must hate me. He must *do* something about me."

"You will be suing him for money. It will look to him and everyone else that you care for his money. That you can be paid with money for not having his love."

"Dallas' money is part of him. He worked for it, he invented this machine, peddled it about from house to house. If I have his money I have part of him. But I do not want a part of him. I want Dallas. Write our story."

"No," I said.

"Will you go to see him then? You might change your mind."

"I won't change my mind. And how could I go see him? What excuse have I for calling on a man I've never seen?"

"Women go to see him all the time to buy this machine. It shreds up vegetables, makes them come out finer than shavings. You could go to his house to buy one."

She was suddenly exhausted and sleepy. She fell down onto the sofa as if she were boneless, her head resting on the deepest swelling of the hump so that her hair flowed backward over it, touching the floor.

"Shall I tell him you sent me?" I asked angrily. Had I moved away from the painful emotions of my own life to be caught up in a pain that wasn't even my own? Was I to become that absurd creature, a woman without a husband who knows how husbands should be handled? The childless woman, full of advice to mothers?

"Whatever you want," she said, closed her eyes, and slept. It was three. I put another stick in the fire, blew out the lamp, and settled onto my two hard chairs. In California it was one, the October air warm; those who slept were quiet in their beds and those who were wakeful had company to solace their wakefulness. Had *he* company?

Toward morning Persis Hughes turned on her side and I saw that she was no longer sleeping. I asked her the queston which had been in my mind.

"What happened?"

"What happened?" she repeated drowsily.

"Between you and Dallas? Why does he no longer love you?"

Then she was wide awake and furious. "I tell you he does love me."

"But he won't marry you. What happened?"

"Nothing happened," she said, "nothing, nothing, nothing. Don't ask me that again."

I didn't, but I knew better. Something has always happened when we deny it so strenuously. Something we cannot bear to face.

At daybreak I walked home to the Seulkes', undressed, slept till noon under Albert's accusing picture, awakened, ate a package of dried figs, spent the afternoon writing a long letter, put the California address on it, and at dusk destroyed it. Then I washed, dressed, and went downstairs to supper.

When supper was over I said, "Will you drive me over to Dallas Hindshaw's, Mr. Seulke?"

"You planning to spend the night out again, sis?"

"No," I said, "tonight I plan to spend in my own comfortable bed."

Usually I try to keep Mr. Seulke's conversation in channels of seemliness. But as we drove along that evening I thought, you're sixty years old, Mr. Seulke, and these are matters you've had on your mind since the age of ten, or younger. If you've learned anything, Mr. Seulke, if you've got any knowledge in fifty years of thinking, speak up. If experience is a lamp, turn up the wick, Mr. Seulke, light the way for stumbling feet. Shine your light on Persis and Dallas and Ted and me. Shine it on hate and love and deceit. Shine it on hope deferred, Mr. Seulke, that maketh the heart to sicken. Shine it on a wife away from home, Mr. Seulke, lost and waiting and full of pride.

But Mr. Seulke, the minute he saw nonresistance in me, was interested in nothing but the weather, spoke of nothing but the weather. It was a mild evening, the sky curded with clouds. Occasional long drops of rain like warm fingers (there was no glass on the right-hand side of Mr. Seulke's Tudor) touched our faces.

Mr. Seulke wiped the drops from his brown face. "But it won't rain," he said. "My mother could foretell the weather and I've heired enough of her gift to prophesy wet from dry." Sniffing the air and prophesying, mild as the evening itself, Mr. Seulke drove the Tudor skillfully along the narrow graveled roads toward Dallas Hindshaw's. He pointed out Hindshaw's house from a distance. As we came nearer I saw it was small, a cabin really with an open porch extending across its front.

"Hindshaw," said Mr. Seulke, "is an interesting fellow and of an inventive turn of mind. He's made considerable, I understand, with this vegetable reamer of his. A pity he's humpbacked."

Rousing from the lull of the weather talk, I said, "Humpbacked? That must be another Hindshaw. The Hindshaw I know isn't humpbacked."

"Know?" asked Mr. Seulke. "My understanding was you'd never seen him."

"I haven't," I said, thinking of the six hours talk in which he had seemed to be present, "but I've heard him spoken of considerably."

"Persis Hughes?"

"Yes," I said.

"Hindshaw jilted her," said Mr. Seulke, "and you can take for sour grapes anything she has to say about him."

But this fox had said the grapes he couldn't get were sweet, not sour; that had been the whole burden of Persis' story!

"See for yourself," said Mr. Seulke, pointing, "he's humpbacked," and I saw on the porch steps a figure, even in the growing darkness, plainly misformed.

"I'll wait for you, sis," said Mr. Seulke, and there was nothing for it but to walk up that long, shell-lined path toward the man who sat motionless, watching me approach.

"Mr. Hindshaw?" I asked.

The man on the porch step was smoking a pipe. One hand was buried in the long black and white hair of a small dog which lay beside him, the other was lifted above his head clasping the post he leaned against. He was gazing out across the countryside which his cabin, situated on a little rise, overlooked. He shifted his eyes from the landscape to me but didn't get up.

"I've come to ask," I said diffidently, "if I could buy one of your vegetable reamers."

Mr. Hindshaw then got to his feet. Except for his deformity he would have been a very tall man. As it was, he was taller than I, dark, withdrawn, much thickened and broken about the neck and shoulders.

"I'm sorry," he said. "I don't sell them here any more—only in stores."

That seemed to end the visit. Mr. Hindshaw stood, obviously willing for me to leave; the dog got up, ready to walk to the gate with me; a lean, big-faced gray cat at the other end of the porch folded her feet beneath her in anticipation of the return of solitude. Still I stood there thinking, why won't you marry her? She'd rescue you from all of this, she'd have lights in the house at this hour, a white cloth on the table, the table set, and two bowls on the back porch, one for the cat, one for the dog. She'd be willing to play a note or two for you on the piano, after you'd eaten, and lie, without talking, her hair hanging over the edge of the sofa while you smoked your pipe. She's ten years younger than you; if she's naïve, you could teach her whatever it is you think she'd be better for knowing. It isn't everyone in the world who'll love you, Mr. Hindshaw, and Persis loves you, desperately. So much, to judge by her talk, she doesn't even know your back isn't straight. You loved her once, promised to marry her, and she hasn't changed. What's come over you, Mr. Hindshaw, why have *you* changed?

With all the craft and skill of a person whose own plans miscarry, I stood there making plans for Mr. Hindshaw, even thinking that he might say, "It was all a mistake," and that I might carry this word to Persis. But Mr. Hindshaw said nothing. His live pipe dying unsmoked in his hand, Mr. Hindshaw waited for me to leave.

"Persis Hughes told me about the reamer."

Mr. Hindshaw turned, knocked out his pipe on the post behind him. "That was kind of her," he said, and once more waited.

"She's very beautiful," I said.

"Yes, she is," agreed Dallas Hindshaw.

"She will sue you," I said, "for breach of promise if you don't marry her." I felt be-witched saying these things, as if I had not the power to choose what I would say, as if I were Persis Hughes herself.

"So Persis tells me," said Mr. Hindshaw.

I hoped he would sick his dog on me, throw his pipe at my head, get rid of me. I could not mention his back, say, Persis loves you, hunchback and all, where will you find another like that? I did say, "Persis loves you just as you are."

Then I ran down the steps and down the path toward Mr. Seulke's car but I heard Dallas Hindshaw say, "I'm afraid you're mistaken."

Mr. Seulke said, "You left in kind of a hurry, sis."

"Yes," I said, "I did."

"Get your reamer?"

"He doesn't sell them at his house any more."

"I could have told you that," said Mr. Seulke, "but I figured you wanted an excuse to talk to the fellow." He turned into the home driveway. "Well," he asked, "what do you make of our jilter?"

I didn't know what to make of the jilter or of Persis, or of Albert with his unanswered question, or of the empty mailbox, or of Mr. Seulke, purely a weather man nowadays. I lived on my hard bed, did the writing and note-taking I had come to do and was glad, as winter drew on and the trial of Hughes *versus* Hindshaw for Breach of Promise was announced, that I was called away. The books I had asked for were available at the State Library; they didn't circulate, I should have to come up to the capital to use them. I'll go tomorrow, I thought, and not come back until the trial is over. The thought of the trial had been a horror to me, like the wreck along the highway, which the eye, knowing it will be sickened, still seeks out. I'll go tomorrow, not come back until the trial is over. And not have any mail forwarded, I thought. Since reason had not worked, I would try magic. If I made the gestures of not caring about my letter, went off without leaving a forwarding address, no longer listened impatiently for the mailman, perhaps it would come.

I lived in a hotel room near the State Library, a room very high and lodged between two jutting wings of the hotel like a matchbox in a crevice of the Apennines. It was a great pleasure to be free of hoping for the letter I had no right to hope for, free of the temptation to attend the trial, and able to work on the old books. I went to the library early and stayed late, writing down much that I needed to know and much that was useless but which I could not resist. My notebooks were filled with long lists, I was happy, almost drugged, as a child becomes repeating a series of words until finally they are without meaning, nothing but a loop of sound binding him to mystery.

The wonderful names in the old newspapers; the names a writer can never achieve, names which only a loving mother can imagine: Alert Miller, Talkington Trueblood, Cashie Wade, Leadona Leahigh, Else Grin, Omer Bland.

The names of fish: Bass, salmon, pike, buffalo, red horse.

Of apples: Imperial Winesap, Baldwin, Romanite, Russert, Northern Spy, all these ripening in October.

The useless facts: A good deer skin fetched 50 cents, raccoons $37\frac{1}{2}$ cents, muskrat 25 cents.

Then, coming in after lunch one day, another list, in a folded newspaper left on my table, caught my eye: "Dearest, dear heart, sweet sorrel, Puss-Precious, my burning bush, long-loved, long-loving. These," the article continued "are but a few of the terms of endearment culled from the love letters of Dallas Hindshaw and addressed by him to Persis Hughes. These letters have formed the high light of the Breach of Promise suit in which Miss Hughes, daughter of Clayton M. Hughes, prominent Lane County farmer, is attempting to obtain $10,000.00 of Mr. Hindshaw in lieu of marriage, which she says he promised her."

My eyes went from one list to the other, from my list, got out of the books in the State Library, to this other list, the words written first in the letters of Dallas Hindshaw, and copied now in a city newspaper. They went from, "muskrats, Northern Spies" to "dear heart, dear Tawny, long-loved, long-loving." Was Persis right? Walled up in a crack in the Apennines, did I avoid what she called "life, as a woman suffers it"? Should I stop reading about the past, go back to the Seulkes', go to the trial, go down to the mailbox? Was there a letter waiting for me there? And if there wasn't, write myself? Say, "Dear husband, having no word from you these past three weeks I hasten to assure you that I regret my hasty leave-taking, my long silence. It is enough that you love me. You need not also—"

But perhaps there *was* a letter waiting. Was it this, instead of the trial which took me back to the Seulkes'? I don't know. There was no letter, anyway, and the trial had ended the day before I got back. Persis, who had asked for ten thousand dollars, had been given five.

"That poor fool, Hindshaw," said Mr. Seulke, on the evening I returned, "he asked to have his money taken away from him." But I was too tired, after my trip and after searching through my mail for the letter which had not arrived, to listen to him, and I went upstairs to my hard bed and wrote nothing myself—letter *or* list—but relived old scenes.

Next afternoon the mailman honked three times and I flew downstairs, but Mr. Seulke was waiting to tell me about the trial.

"That poor fool, Hindshaw!" he began again. "Wouldn't have a lawyer, and set on representing himself! And for all the good he done himself he'd better've given the girl the money in the first place and spared making himself the laughing stock of the country with all those letters of his read out loud."

"Did he say he hadn't promised to marry her?"

"In a way he did," said Mr. Seulke, "but small good it done him, letter after letter saying, 'My sweet pigeon, I can hardly wait till we are married.' Sweet pigeon!" said Mr. Seulke laughing. "Sweet vulture is what he thinks now, I reckon."

"What defense *did* he have?" I asked.

"None," said Mr. Seulke flatly. "He had no defense, only a quirk in his mind. He wouldn't marry Persis Hughes he said because she was changed. She wasn't the girl he had asked to marry him in the first place because that girl accepted he was humpbacked, and this girl, the one he was refusing to marry, did not accept it. He called up two dozen witnesses to testify that she never would mention his hump, talked about him as if it didn't exist, and tried to make out, in her own mind, and to others, he was straight-backed. I've got a hump, he said, and the person who don't accept my hump don't accept me."

"Why didn't she?" I asked. Why didn't I? *He* was made that way when I married *him.*

"Why didn't she what?" said Mr. Seulke.

"Accept his hump? Accept the fact his back was crooked?"

"I don't know *why* she didn't," said Mr. Seulke, "but I know when it started. And I know it was the cause of Dallas Hindshaw's refusing to marry her. I was there and I saw it happen."

I remembered my question that night at Persis Hughes' and her, "Nothing, nothing nothing! Nothing happened."

"What was it?" I asked.

"It was a dance at Zenith and I was as close to them as I am to you. Dallas was a good dancer and a young fellow passing by clapped Dallas on the back and said, 'This frog sure can hop.' He meant it a compliment or at most a joke and Dallas took it so. But Persis slapped the boy not once but a half-dozen times and screamed, "It's not, it's straight." Hindshaw grabbed her, 'My back's crooked but my mind's straight,' he said, and that was the beginning. That's what broke them up."

"Did Hindshaw tell this at the trial?"

"Not in so many words, but he said—'I do not intend to be half-wed to somebody who sorts me out and marries what suits her, only. I could sue Persis Hughes,' he said, 'with as much justice as she sues me, for she has not kept her promise to my hump. And as I was made shorter than most men,' he says, 'by reason of a horse stepping on me when I was a boy now I will not be still further whittled down by a woman's marrying part of me only and maiming me beyond the first damage.'

"So it went," said Mr. Seulke. "But Hindshaw had no real defense and nobody thought the girl didn't have a legal right to the money. But nobody would've wanted to stand in her shoes to get it."

Mr. Seulke followed me out onto the porch, sniffed a few times, and said, "It's going to snow."

It was already snowing, a first, soft, downward feathering.

"What do you make of it?" asked Mr. Seulke. "You seen and talked to them both."

"I don't know, Mr. Seulke, I don't know what to make of it." I didn't want to make anything of it, its meaning was striking too close.

I stood there on the porch, the big flakes blowing against my face like cold cobwebs. Mr. Seulke stood there, too, not speaking, so presently I went down the lane toward the mailbox. I remembered saying to Persis Hughes, "I understand it all too well, it's like the multiplication table," and remembered Dallas' words, "She didn't keep her promise to my hump." Do you understand that? I asked myself.

I jumped across the brook, cold now as it ran across its pretty stones and specked with falling snow. I hesitated, as I always did, to open the box, then did so quickly. The only letter in the box was one from Persis. In my disappointment I couldn't pick it up for awhile, but stood looking at it, and the orange-veined pebble beside it. Finally, I took it out and opened it.

Dear Miss Marsden [it began]: Though I know

now that this is only your writing name, not your real name, it seems more natural to me because I used it first, so I keep on doing so. I understand that you have left the Seulkes' but trust that this will be forwarded to you.

I am sorry you did not come to the trial and still sorrier you would not write the story. But it was too late to worry about this now. I did as I said I would and as I think I was duty bound to do, that is, show Dallas Hindshaw that I was willing to do anything to get him to marry me, even sue him.

I don't regret having done this but I find I don't want his money now and I want you to know it. So will you seal up and mail this envelope which I have enclosed and addressed, after you have read what is in it? You will see I am not keeping the money.

Since you live quite a ways off I don't expect we'll see each other again and I want to wish you the best of luck in everything, and hope you understand I did what I was honor bound to do.

> Sincerely and with good wishes,
> Persis Hughes

I read the letter Persis Hughes had enclosed as I had been told to do, replaced it, and sealed the envelope. It was addressed to Dallas Hindshaw. All this trouble, all this sorrow, and who had moved a step forward? I, I told myself, I have moved a step forward. It was the truth. When I put the letter back in the mailbox I took the stone out and at the brook I stooped down and laid it once more beside its brothers at the water's edge, then I walked on up to the house. "Sort him out," and make him pay for refusing the sorting—and give the money back. It made no sense.

Mr. Seulke still stood on the porch, arms folded, watching the weaving patterns of the falling snow. "Well, did you get your letter, sis?" he asked.

I had never spoken to Mr. Seulke of my letter, nor of any letter for that matter, but I felt neither evasive nor glib now.

"No," I said, "it didn't come."

"What do you figure on doing now?" he asked.

"I'm going home," I said.

"Home? I didn't know you had a home, sis."

"I have."

"Home and husband?"

"Home and husband."

"That's more like it, sis."

"It is," I said.

I went upstairs to write and stop my waiting.

Study Questions

1. "Breach of Promise" is actually two stories: that of the writer and that of the central characters involved in the "breach." Briefly retell the events in the "breach" story, the events related to the Persis Hughes/Dallas Hindshaw relationship.

2. Do you think that Persis really loved Dallas? Why or why not? Do you think Dallas was correct in refusing to marry Persis? Why or why not?

3. The second story concerns the writer and her own personal life. Where is she when the story begins? What is she doing there? What letter is she waiting for?

4. At the end of the story, the writer says, "All this trouble, all this sorrow, and who had moved a step forward? I, I told myself, I have moved a step forward. It was the truth." What does she mean? How has she "moved a step forward"?

Perhaps Tillie Olsen's writing is best characterized as revealing a remarkable attention to detail and a passionate economy of language. For the most part, her characters are ordinary working people who somehow find themselves embattled by the business of living. Born in Omaha, Nebraska, she has also worked as a typist-transcriber. Her stories have appeared in *Best American Short Stories*

of 1951 and 1961. In 1961 she received the O. Henry Award for the best story of the year. Olsen has also published *Yonnondio* (1974), the odyssey of a poor Midwestern family.

"I Stand Here Ironing" is from her prize-winning collection, *Tell Me a Riddle.* In it she explores a mother-daughter relationship in a contemporary setting.

I Stand Here Ironing

TILLIE OLSEN

I STAND HERE IRONING, and what you asked me moves tormented back and forth with the iron.

"I wish you would manage the time to come in and talk with me about your daughter. I'm sure you can help me understand her. She's a youngster who needs help and whom I'm deeply interested in helping."

"Who needs help." Even if I came, what good would it do? You think because I am her mother I have a key, or that in some way you could use me as a key? She has lived for nineteen years. There is all that life that has happened outside of me, beyond me.

And when is there time to remember, to sift, to weigh, to estimate, to total? I will start and there will be an interruption and I will have to gather it all together again. Or I will become engulfed with all I did or did not do, with what should have been and what cannot be helped.

She was a beautiful baby. The first and only one of our five that was beautiful at birth. You do not guess how new and uneasy her tenancy in her now-loveliness. You did not know her all those years she was thought homely, or see her poring over her baby pictures, making me tell her over and over how beautiful she had been—and would be, I would tell her—and was now, to the seeing eye. But the seeing eyes were few or nonexistent. Including mine.

I nursed her. They feel that's important nowadays. I nursed all the children, but with her, with all the fierce rigidity of first motherhood, I did like the books then said. Though her cries battered me to trembling and my breasts ached with swollenness, I waited till the clock decreed.

Why do I put that first? I do not even know if it matters, or if it explains anything.

She was a beautiful baby. She blew shining bubbles of sound. She loved motion, loved

light, loved color and music and textures. She would lie on the floor in her blue overalls patting the surface so hard in ecstasy her hands and feet would blur. She was a miracle to me, but when she was eight months old I had to leave her daytimes with the woman downstairs to whom she was no miracle at all, for I worked or looked for work and for Emily's father, who "could no longer endure" (he wrote in his good-by note) "sharing want with us."

I was nineteen. It was the pre-relief, pre-WPA world of the depression. I would start running as soon as I got off the streetcar, running up the stairs, the place smelling sour, and awake or asleep to startle awake, when she saw me she would break into a clogged weeping that could not be comforted, a weeping I can yet hear.

After a while I found a job hashing at night so I could be with her days, and it was better. But it came to where I had to bring her to his family and leave her.

It took a long time to raise the money for her fare back. Then she got chicken pox and I had to wait longer. When she finally came, I hardly knew her, walking quick and nervous like her father, looking like her father, thin, and dressed in a shoddy red that yellowed her skin and glared at the pock marks. All the baby loveliness gone.

She was two. Old enough for nursery school they said, and I did not know then what I know now—the fatigue of the long day, and the lacerations of group life in the nurseries that are only parking places for children.

Except that it would have made no difference if I had known. It was the only place there was. It was the only way we could be together, the only way I could hold a job.

And even without knowing, I knew. I knew the teacher that was evil because all these years it had curdled into my memory, the little boy hunched in the corner, her rasp, "Why aren't you outside, because Alvin hits you? that's no reason, go out, scaredy." I knew Emily hated it even if she did not clutch and implore "Don't go, Mommy" like the other children, mornings.

She always had a reason why we should stay home. Momma, you look sick, Momma. I feel sick. Momma, the teachers aren't there today, they're sick. Momma, there was a fire there last night. Momma, it's a holiday today, no school, they told me.

But never a direct protest, never rebellion. I think of our others in their three-, four-year-oldness—the explosions, the tempers, the denunciations, the demands—and I feel suddenly ill. I put the iron down. What in me demanded that goodness in her? And what was the cost, the cost to her of such goodness?

The old man living in the back once said in his gentle way: "You should smile at Emily more when you look at her." What *was* in my face when I looked at her? I loved her. There were all the acts of love.

It was only with the others I remembered what he said, and it was the face of joy, and not of care or tightness or worry I turned to them—too late for Emily. She does not smile easily, let alone almost always as her brothers and sisters do. Her face is closed and somber, but when she wants, how fluid. You must have seen it in her pantomimes; you spoke of her rare gift for comedy on the stage that rouses a laughter out of the audience so dear they applaud and applaud and do not want to let her go.

Where does it come from, that comedy? There was none of it in her when she came back to me that second time, after I had had to send her away again. She had a new daddy now to learn to love, and I think perhaps it was a better time. Except when we left her alone nights, telling ourselves she was old enough.

"Can't you go some other time, Mommy, like tomorrow?" she would ask. "Will it be just a little while you'll be gone? Do you promise?"

The time we came back, the front door open, the clock on the floor in the hall. She rigid awake. "It wasn't just a little while. I didn't cry. Three times I called you, just three times, and then I ran downstairs to open the door so you could come faster. The clock talked loud. I threw it away, it scared me when it talked."

She said the clock talked loud again that night I went to the hospital to have Susan. She was delirious with the fever that comes before red measles, but she was fully conscious all the week I was gone and the week after we were home when she could not come near the new baby or me.

She did not get well. She stayed skeleton thin, not wanting to eat, and night after night she had nightmares. She would call for me, and I would rouse from exhaustion to sleepily call back, "You're all right, darling—go to sleep—it's just a dream," and if she still called, in a sterner voice, "now go to sleep Emily, there's nothing to hurt you." Twice, only twice, when I had to get up for Susan anyhow, I went in to sit with her.

Now when it is too late (as if she would let me hold and comfort her like I do the others) I get up and go to her at once at her moan or restless stirring. "Are you awake, Emily? Can I get you something, dear?" And the answer is always the same: "No, I'm all right, go back to sleep, Mother."

They persuaded me at the clinic to send her away to a convalescent home in the country where "she can have the kind of food and care you can't manage for her, and you'll be free to concentrate on the new baby." They still send children to that place. I see pictures on the society page of sleek young women planning affairs to raise money for it, or dancing at the affairs, or decorating Easter eggs or filling Christmas stockings for the children.

They never have a picture of the children, so I do not know if the girls still wear those gigantic red bows and the ravaged looks on the every other Sunday when parents can come to visit "unless otherwise notified"—as we were notified the first six weeks.

Oh it is a handsome place, green lawns and tall trees and fluted flower beds. High up on the balconies of each cottage the children stand, the girls in their red bows and white dresses, the boys in white suits and giant red ties. The parents stand below shrieking up to be heard and the children shriek down to be heard, and between them the invisible wall "Not To Be Contaminated by Parental Germs or Physical Affection."

There was a tiny girl who always stood hand in hand with Emily. Her parents never came. One visit she was gone. "They moved her to Rose Cottage," Emily shouted in explanation. "They don't like you to love anybody here."

She wrote once a week, the labored writing of a seven-year-old. "I am fine. How is the baby. If I write my leter nicly I will have a star. Love." There never was a star. We wrote every other day, letters she could never hold or keep but only hear read—once. "We simply do not have room for children to keep any personal possessions," they patiently explained when we pieced one Sunday's shrieking together to plead how much it would mean to Emily, who loved so to keep things, to be allowed to keep her letters and cards.

Each visit she looked frailer. "She isn't eating," they told us. (They had runny eggs for breakfast or mush with lumps, Emily said later, I'd hold it in my mouth and not swallow. Nothing ever tasted good, just when they had chicken.)

It took us eight months to get her released home, and only the fact that she gained back so little of her seven lost pounds convinced the social worker.

I used to try to hold and love her after she came back, but her body would stay stiff, and after a while she'd push away. She ate little. Food sickened her, and I think much of life too. Oh she had physical lightness and brightness, twinkling by on skates, bouncing like a ball up and down, up and down, over the jump rope, skimming over the hill; but these were momentary.

She fretted about her appearance, thin and dark and foreign-looking at a time when every little girl was supposed to look or thought she should look a chubby blonde replica of Shirley Temple. The doorbell sometimes rang for her, but no one seemed to come and play in the house or be a best friend. Maybe because we moved so much.

There was a boy she loved painfully through two school semesters. Months later she told me how she had taken pennies from my purse to buy him candy. "Licorice was his favorite and I brought him some every day, but he still liked Jennifer better'n me. Why, Mommy?" A question I could never answer.

School was a worry to her. She was not glib or quick in a world where glibness and quickness were easily confused with ability to learn. To her overworked and exasperated teachers she was an over-conscientious "slow learner" who kept trying to catch up and was absent entirely too often.

I let her be absent, though sometimes the illness was imaginary. How different from my now-strictness about attendance with the others. I wasn't working. We had a new baby, I was home anyhow. Sometimes, after Susan grew old enough, I would keep her home from school, too, to have them all together.

Mostly Emily had asthma, and her breathing, harsh and labored, would fill the house with a curiously tranquil sound. I would bring the two old dresser mirrors and her boxes of collections to her bed. She would select beads and single earrings, bottle tops and shells, dried flowers and pebbles, old postcards and scraps, all sorts of oddments; then she and Susan would play Kingdom, setting up landscapes and furniture, peopling them with action.

Those were the only times of peaceful companionship between her and Susan. I have edged away from it, that poisonous feeling between them, that terrible balancing of hurts and needs I had to do between the two, and did so badly, those earlier years.

Oh there are conflicts between the others too, each one human, needing, demanding, hurting, taking—but only between Emily and Susan, no, Emily toward Susan, that corroding resentment. It seems so obvious on the surface, yet it is not obvious. Susan, the second child, Susan, golden- and curly-haired and chubby, quick and articulate and assured, everything in appearance and manner Emily was not. Susan, not able to resist Emily's precious things, losing or sometimes clumsily breaking them; Susan telling jokes and riddles to company for applause, while Emily sat silent (to say to me later: that was *my* riddle, Mother, I told it to Susan); Susan, who for all the five years' difference in age was just a year behind Emily in developing physically.

I am glad for that slow physical development that widened the difference between her and her contemporaries, though she suffered over it. She was too vulnerable for that terrible world of youthful competition, of preening and parading, of constant measuring of yourself against every other, of envy, "If I had that copper hair," "If I had that skin. . . ." She tormented herself enough about not looking like the others, there was enough of the unsureness, the having to be conscious of words before you speak, the constant caring—what are they thinking of me?—without having it all magnified by the merciless physical drives.

Ronnie is calling. He is wet and I change him. It is rare there is such a cry now. That time of motherhood is almost behind me when the ear is not one's own but must always be racked and listening for the child cry, the child call. We sit for a while and I hold him, looking out over the city spread in charcoal with its soft aisles of light. *"Shoogily,"* he breathes and curls closer. I carry him back to bed, asleep. *Shoogily.* A funny word, a family word, inherited from Emily, invented by her to say: *comfort.*

In this and other ways she leaves her seal, I say aloud. And startle at my saying it. What do I mean? What did I start to gather together, to try and make coherent? I was at the terrible, growing years. War years. I do not remember them well. I was working, there were four smaller ones now, there was not time for her. She had to help be a mother, and housekeeper, and shopper. She had to set her seal. Mornings of crisis and near hysteria trying to get lunches packed, hair combed, coats and shoes found, everyone to school or Child Care on time, the baby ready for transportation. And always the paper scribbled on by a smaller one, the book looked at by Susan then mislaid, the homework not done. Running out to that huge school where she was one, she was lost, she was a drop; suffering over the unpreparedness, stammering and unsure in her classes.

There was so little time left at night after the kids were bedded down. She would struggle over books, always eating (it was in those years she developed her enormous appetite that is legendary in our family) and I would be ironing, or preparing food for the next day, or writing V-mail to Bill, or tending the baby. Sometimes, to make me laugh, or out of her despair, she would imitate happenings or types at school.

I think I said once: "Why don't you do something like that in the school amateur shows?" One morning she phoned me at work, hardly understandable through the weeping: "Mother, I did it. I won, I won; they gave me first prize; they clapped and clapped and wouldn't let me go."

Now suddenly she was Somebody, and as imprisoned in her difference as she had been in anonymity.

She began to be asked to perform at other high schools, even in colleges, then at city and state-wide affairs. The first one we went to, I only recognized her that first moment when thin, shy, she almost drowned herself into the curtains. Then: Was this Emily? the control, the command, the convulsing and deadly clowning, the spell, then the roaring, stamping audience, unwilling to let this rare and precious laughter out of their lives.

Afterwards: You ought to do something about her with a gift like that—but without money or knowing how, what does one do? We have left it all to her, and the gift has as often eddied inside, clogged and clotted, as been used and growing.

She is coming. She runs up the stairs two at a time with her light graceful step, and I know she is happy tonight. Whatever it was that occasioned your call did not happen today.

"Aren't you ever going to finish the ironing, Mother? Whistler painted his mother in a rocker. I'd have to paint mine standing over an ironing board." This is one of her communicative nights and she tells me everything and nothing as she fixes herself a plate of food out of the icebox.

She is so lovely. Why did you want me to come in at all? Why were you concerned? She will find her way.

She starts up the stairs to bed. "Don't get me up with the rest in the morning." "But I thought you were having midterms." "Oh, those," she comes back in, kisses me, and says quite lightly, "in a couple of years when we'll all be atom-dead they won't matter a bit."

She has said it before. She *believes* it. But because I have been dredging the past, and all that compounds a human being is so heavy and meaningful in me, I cannot endure it tonight.

I will never total it all. I will never come in to say: She was a child seldom smiled at. Her father left me before she was a year old. I worked her first six years when there was work, or I sent her home and to his relatives. There were years she had care she hated. She was dark and thin and foreign-looking in a world where the prestige went to blondness and curly hair and dimples; she was slow where glibness was prized. She was a child of anxious, not proud, love. We were poor and could not afford for her the soil of easy growth. I was a young mother, I was a distracted mother. There were the other children pushing up, demanding. Her younger sister was all that she was not. There were years she did not let me touch her. She kept too much in herself, her life was such she had to keep too much in herself. My wisdom came too late. She has much to her and probably little will come of it. She is a child of her age, of depression, of war, of fear.

Let her be. So all that is in her will not bloom—but in how many does it? There is still enough left to live by. Only help her to know—help make it so there is cause for her to know—that she is more than this dress on the ironing-board, helpless before the iron.

Study Questions

1. "Only help her to know—help make it so there is cause for her to know—that she is more than this dress on the ironing board, helpless before the iron." Judging by these last lines of the story, what do you think the mother wants her daughter to know?

2. In reading this story do you learn more about the mother or about the daughter? What details and characteristics are you given about each character?

3. The school counselor describes Emily as "a youngster who needs help." What help do you think Emily needs? To what extent has she found satisfaction with her life-style?

4. At the end of the story why does her mother find Emily's attitude difficult to "endure"?

5. What is the point of view from which this story is written? How does the point of view affect your understanding of the story?

Raymond Barrio   1921 —

Raymond Barrio, artist, art teacher, and writer, was born in West Orange, New Jersey. Initially, he was unable to find a publisher for his novel. So he established his own printing press in his garage and published *The Plum Plum Pickers* himself in 1969. The following excerpt is taken from that book. Barrio's work is now available from commercial publishers. A much wider audience is able to share the moving experience of migrant farm workers like Manuel Gutierrez.

from The Plum Plum Pickers

RAYMOND BARRIO

DAWN.
Outside, the coolest night.
Outside, the soft, plush, lingering sheen of nightlight.

Within his breezy airconditioned shack Manuel lay half asleep in the middle of the biggest apricot orchard in the world, nothing but apricot trees all around, in one of a long double row of splintered boards nailed together and called a shack. A migrant's shack. He struggled to come awake. Everything seemed to be plugged up. A distant roar closed in steadily. He awoke in a cold sweat. He sat up abruptly in the cold darkness.

The roar grew louder and louder. He leaned forward, hunched in his worn, torn covers, and peered through the grimy window. A huge black monster was butting through trees, moving and pitching about, its headlights piercing the armor of night, then swinging away again as the roaring lessened. Manuel smiled. The roar of a tractor. He rubbed the sleep from his eyes. He stretched his aching arms and shoulders. He thought of Lupe and the kids back in Drawbridge.

On the very brink of the full onslaught of summer's punishing heat, with the plums and pears and apricots fattening madly on every vine, branch, bush and limb in every section of every county in the country, pickers were needed right now immediately on every farm and orchard everywhere and all at once. The frantic demand for pickers increased rapidly as

the hot days mounted. That sure looked good out there. What a cool job that was. Driving a tractor at night. Maybe he could get Ramiro to teach him to drive one.

Manuel well knew what his physical energy was.

His physical energy was his total worldly wealth.

No matter how anxious he was to work, he did have his limit. He had to rest his body. The finger joint he'd injured still hurt. He missed Lupe's chatter. He'd signed up with that shrewd contractor, Roberto Morales, that shrewd, fat, energetic contratista, manipulator of migrating farm workers, that smiling middleman who promised to deliver so many hands to the moon at such and such a time at such and such an orchard at such and such a price, for such a small commission. A tiny percentage. Such a little slice. Silvery slavery—modernized.

Roberto Morales, an organization man, was a built-in toll gate. A parasite. A collector of drops of human sweat. An efficiency expert. Had he not been Mexican, he would have made a fantastic capitalist, like Turner. He was Turner upside down. Sucking blood from his own people. With the help and convenient connivance of Turner's insatiable greed.

The agricultural combine's imperative need to have its capital personally plucked when ripe so as to materialize its honest return on its critical investment in order to keep its executives relaxed in blue splendor in far-off desert pools, was coupled to the migrant workers' inexorable and uncompromising need to earn pennies to fend off stark starvation.

Good money.
Good dough.
Good hard work.
Pick fast.
Penny a bucket.
Check off.
Get the count right.
Cotsplumsprunespeachesbeanspeas.

Pods.
The seed of life.
And:—don't complain. . . .

Manuel lay back in the blackness. As the darkness receded and the light of day started creeping imperiously across its own land, he thought that these powerful orchard land owners were awfully generous to give him such a beautiful hostel to stop in overnight. The skylight hotel. There the land stood. A heaving, sleeping mother earth. A marvelous land. Ripening her fruit once again. Once more. Ripening it fatly and pregnantly for the thousandth time. It must be plucked said the wise man. For it cannot hang around on limbs a minute extra. At no man's convenience. As soon as the baby's ready. Lush and full of plump juices. Hugging its new seed around its own ripeness. The plum and the cot and the peach and the pear must plummet again to earth. Carrying the seed of its own delicate rebirth and redestruction back home to earth again. A clever mother earth who in her all-but-unbelievable generosity was capable of giving man fivefold, tenfold the quantity of fruit he could himself eat, five times fifty, and yet the pickers were never paid enough to satisfy their hunger beyond their actual working hours. And yet it was called a moral world. An ethical world. A good world. A happy world. A world full of golden opportunities. Manuel simply couldn't figure it out.

What was wrong with the figures?

Why was mother earth so generous? And men so greedy?

You got twenty-five cents a basket for tomatoes. A dollar a crate for some fruit. You had to work fast. That was the whole thing. A frantic lunatic to make your barely living wage. If you had no rent to pay, it was OK. You were ahead, amigo. Pay rent, however, stay in one place, and you couldn't migrate after other easy pickings. The joy of working was looking over your dreams locked to hunger.

Manuel studied the whorls in the woodwork whirling slowly, revealed in the faint crepuscular[1] light penetrating his shack. His cot was a slab of half-inch plywood board twenty-two inches wide and eight feet long, the width of the shack, supported by two two-by-four beams butted up against the wall at both ends beneath the side window. The shack itself was eight by twelve by seven feet high. Its roof had a slight pitch. The rain stains in the ceiling planks revealed the ease with which the rain penetrated. Except for two small panes of glass exposed near the top, most of the window at the opposite end was boarded up. A single, old, paint-encrusted door was the only entry. No curtains. No interior paneling. Just a shack. A shack of misery. He found he was able to admire and appreciate the simplicity and the strength of the construction. He counted the upright studs, level, two feet apart, the double joists across the top supporting the roof. Cracks and knotholes aplenty, in the wall siding, let in bright chinks of light during the day and welcome wisps of clear fresh air at night. The rough planking of the siding was stained dark. The floor was only partly covered with odd sections of plywood. Some of the rough planking below was exposed, revealing cracks leading down to the cool black earth beneath. A small thick table was firmly studded to a portion of the wall opposite the door. A few small pieces of clear lumber stood bunched together unsung, unused, unhurried, in the far corner. An overhead shelf, supported from the ceiling by a small extending perpendicular arm, containing some boxes of left-over chemicals and fertilizers, completed the furnishings in his temporary abode.

It was habitable.

He could raise his family in it.

If they were rabbits.

The first rays of a brute new day clinked in through the small rectangle of panes. The ray hovered, then peaked, then rested on the covers pushed up by his knees. He recalled his mountain trips with his uncle to the great forbidding barrancas[2] near Durango in Central Mexico, and stopping to rest in the middle of the wild woods, and coming unexpectedly upon a crumbling, splintered hulk of a shack that was all falling apart. It barely gave them shelter from the sudden pelting storm they were trying to escape, he as a young frightened boy, but shelter it was—and how beautiful that experience was, then, for they were free, daring, adventurers, out there in that wilderness, alone and daring, with nothing between them and God's own overpowering nature, alone. They belonged to nothing. To no one. But themselves. They were dignity purified. No one forced them to go or stay there. They were delighted and grateful to the shack. For the protection it afforded them. Though it was hardly more than a ratty pile of splinters. Far worse than this one he was now occupying . . . but also somehow far more beautiful in his memory.

And now. Here he was. Shut up in this miserable shack. So sturdily built. Thinking how it sickened him inside because it was more a jail cell than a shelter. He didn't care how comfortable and convenient the growers made the shacks for him. They were huts of slavery. What he wanted was an outlet for his pride. A sudden fierce wave of anger made him want to cross the shack with his fists. There had to be some way to cross the ungulfable bridge. Why was necessity always the bride of hunger? To be free . . . ah, and also to be able to eat all one wanted. My heart, mi corazón, why did work always have to blend with such misery? The welcome warmth of the sun's early rays, penetrating more, warmed his frame. But it was a false, false hope. He knew it. The work that lay ahead of him that day would drain and

---

1 **crepuscular** (kri pus′ kyə lər): resembling twilight.

2 **barrancas** (bə-räng′ kəs): a deep ravine or gorge.

stupify and fatigue him once again to the point of senseless torpor, ready to fall over long before the work day was done. And that fatigue wasn't nearly so bad to bear as the deadly repetitous monotony of never changing, never resting, doing the same plucking over and over and over again. But he had to do it. He had no choice. It was all he could do. It had to be done if he wanted the money. And he had to have the money, if he wanted to feed his family. The brain in his arms was his only capital. Not very much, true, but it was the only sacrifice he could offer the money gods, the only heart he could offer on the pyramid of gold.

His life. La gran vida.

Wide awake now, fully refreshed, his whole body lithe and toned, Manuel was ashamed to find himself eager to start in work, knowing that he would do well, but ashamed because he could think of nothing he would rather do more. The final step.

The final the final the final the final the final step.

To want to work oneself to death. A la muerte. It wasn't the work itself that bothered him. It was the total immersion, the endless, ceaseless, total use of all his energies and spirit and mind and being that tore him apart within. He didn't know what else he was good for or could do with his life. But there had to be something else. He had to be something more than a miserable plucking animal. Pluck pluck pluck. Feed feed feed. Glug glug glug. Dressing quickly, rolling up his blanket roll and stuffing it into a corner to use again that night, Manuel stepped coolly out into the morning sweetness and breathed the honey-scented humidity rinsing air rising from the honied soil, and joined the thickening throng of his fellow pluckers milling about the large open barn serving as a cookout. Feeding all the pickers was another of the fat man's unholy prerogatives, for he cheated and overpriced on meals too. Roberto Morales, the fat man, the shrewd contratista, was a bully man, busily darting his blob about, exhorting his priceless pickers to hurry, answering questions, giving advice, in the cool half-light, impatiently, pushing, giving orders. Manuel, in order to avoid having to greet him, scowled at his toes when Roberto came trouncing by, saying, "Apúrense, compañeros, hurry, hurry, hurry, amigos." Sure. Amigos. Sí. Sí. Frens. They all gulped their food down hurriedly, standing. Just like home. Paper plates, plastic cups. Wooden spoons. And bits of garbage flying into large canisters. Then in the still cool nightlike morning air, like a flood of disturbed birds, they all picked up their pails and filed into the orchard.

The apricots were plump.

Smooth.

A golden syrupy orange.

Manuel popped two into his mouth, enjoying their cool natural sweetness after the bitter coffee. He knew he could not eat too many. His stomach muscles would cramp. Other pickers started pulling rapidly away from him. Let them. Calmly he calculated the struggle. Start the press sure, slow, and keep it going steady. Piecework. Fill the bucket, fill another, and still another. The competition was among a set of savages, as savage for money as himself, savages with machetes, hacking their way through the thickets of modern civilization back to the good old Aztec days, waiting to see who'd be first in line to wrench his heart out. Savage beasts, eager to fill as many buckets as possible in as short a time as possible, cleaning out an entire orchard, picking everything in sight clean, tons of fruit, delivering every bit of ripe fruit to the accountants in their cool air conditioned orifices.

The competition was not between pickers and growers.

It was between pickers—Jorge and Guillermo.

Between the poor and the hungry, the desperate, and the hunted, the slave and the slave, slob against slob, the depraved and himself.

You were your own terrible boss. That was the cleverest part of the whole thing. The picker his own bone picker, his own willing built-in slave driver. God, that was good! That was where they . . . drained your brain and directed your sinews and nerves and muscles with invisible fingers. To fatten their coffers. And drive you to your coffin. That sure was smart. Meant to be smart. Bookkeepers aren't dumb. You worked hard because you wanted to do that hard work above everything else. Pick fast pick hard pick furious pick pick pick. They didn't need straw bosses studying your neck to see if you kept bobbing up and down to keep your picking pace up. Like the barn-stupid chicken, you drove yourself to do it. You were your own money monkey foreman, monkey on top of your own back.

You over-charged yourself.

With your own frenzy.

Neat.

You pushed your gut and your tired aching arms and your twitching legs pumping adrenalin until your tongue tasted like coarse sand-paper.

You didn't even stop to take a drink for fear you'd get fined, fired, or bawled out.

And then, after all that effort, you got your miserable pay.

Would the bobbing boss's sons stoop to that?

His fingers were loose and dexterous now. The plump orange balls plopped pitter patter like heavy drops of golden rain into his swaying, sweaty canvas bucket. His earnings depended entirely on how quickly he worked and how well he kept the pressure up. The morning sun was high. The sweet shade was fragrant and refreshing and comfortable under the leafy branches. The soil too was still cool and humid. It was going to be another hot one.

There.

Another row ended.

He swung around the end of the row and for a moment he was all alone, all by himself. He looked out far across the neighboring alfalfa field, dark green and rich and ripe. Then he looked at the long low Diablo Range close by, rising up into the misty pale blue air kept cool by the unseen bay nearby. This was all his. For a flowing, deceptive minute, all this rich, enormous terrain was all his. All this warm balmy baby air. All this healthful sunny breeze. All those hills, this rich fertile valley, these orchards, these tiled huertas, these magnificent farms all, all his . . . for his eyes to feast upon. It was a moment he wished he could capture forever and etch permanently on his memory, making it a part of living life for his heart to feast joyously on, forever. Why couldn't he stop? Why? Why couldn't he just put the bucket down and open his arms and walk into the hills and merge himself with the hills and just wander invisibly in the blue?

What Manuel couldn't really know was that he was completing yet another arc in the unending circle that had been started by one of his Mexican forebears exactly two hundred years before—for even the memory of history was also robbed from him—when Gaspar de Portola, hugging the coastline, nearing present-day San Francisco, climbed what is now Sweeney Ridge, and looked down upon San Francisco's magnificent landlocked Bay, overlooking what is now the International Airport.

Both don Gaspar and don Manuel were landlords and landless at precisely the same instant of viewing all this heady beauty. And both were equally dispossessed. Both were also possessed of a keen sense of pride and natural absorption with the ritual and mystery of all life. The living that looked mighty good in a flash to Manuel lasted a good deal longer for don Gaspar whose stumbling accident swept him into honored and indelible pages of glorious history.

Manuel was now a mere straw among the enormous sludge of humanity flowing past, a creature of limb and his own driving appetites, a creature of heed and need. Swinging around another end run he placed his ladder on the next heavy limb of the next pregnant tree. He reached up. He plucked bunches of small golden fruit with both hands. He worked like a frenzied windmill in slow motion. He cleared away an arc as far as the circumference of his plucking fingers permitted. A living model for da Vinci's outstretched man. Adam heeding God's moving finger. He moved higher. He repeated another circle. Then down and around again to another side of the tree, until he cleared it, cleared it of all visible, viable, delectable, succulent fruit. It was sweet work. The biggest difference between him and the honey-gathering ant was that the ant had a home.

Several pickers were halfway down the next row, well in advance of him. He was satisfied he was pacing himself well. Most of the band was still behind him. The moving sun, vaulting the sky dome's crackling earth parting with its bronzing rays, pounded its fierce heat into every dead and living crevice. Perspiration poured down his sideburns, down his forehead, down his cheek, down his neck, into his ears, off his chin. He tasted its saltiness with the tip of his dry tongue. He wished he'd brought some salt tablets. Roberto Morales wasn't about to worry about the pickers, and Manuel wasn't worried either. Despite the heat, he felt some protection from the ocean and bay. It had been much, much worse in Texas, and much hotter in Delano in the San Joaquin valley and worst of all in Satan's own land, the Imperial Valley.

No matter which way he turned, he was trapped in an endless maze of apricot trees, as though forever, neat rows of them, neatly planted, row after row, just like the blackest bars on the jails of hell. There had to be an end. There had to be. There—trapped. There had to be a way out. Locked. There had to be a respite. Animal. The buckets and the crates kept piling up higher. Brute. He felt alone. Though surrounded by other pickers. Beast. Though he was perspiring heavily, his shirt was powder dry. Savage. The hot dry air sucking every drop of living moisture from his brute body. Wreck. He stopped and walked to

the farthest end of the first row for some water, raised the dented dipper from the brute tank, drank the holy water in great brute gulps so he wouldn't have to savor its tastelessness, letting it spill down his torn shirt to cool his exhausted body, to replenish his brute cells and animals pores and stinking follicles and pig gristle, a truly refined wreck of an animal, pleased to meetcha. Predator.

LUNCH.

Almost too exhausted to eat, he munched his cheese with tortillas, smoked on ashes, then lay back on the cool ground for half an hour. That short rest in the hot shade replenished some of his humor and resolve. He felt his spirit swell out again like a thirsty sponge in water. Then up.again. The trees. The branches again. The briarly branches. The scratching leaves. The twigs tearing at his shirt sleeves. The ladder. The rough bark. The endlessly unending piling up of bucket upon box upon crate upon stack upon rack upon mound upon mountain. He picked a mountain of cots automatically. An automator. A beast. A ray of enemy sun penetrated the tree that was hiding him and split his forehead open. His mind whirred. He blacked out. Luckily he'd been leaning against a heavy branch. His feet hooked to the ladder's rung. His half-filled bucket slipped from his grasp and fell in slow motion, splattering the fruit he'd so laboriously picked. To the ground. Roberto happened by and shook his head. "Whatsamatter, can't you see straight, pendejo." Manuel was too tired even to curse. He should have had some salt pills.

MIDAFTERNOON.

The summer's fierce zenith passed overhead. It passed. Then dropped. It started to light the ocean behind him, back of the hills. Sandy dreams. Cool nights. Cold drinks. Soft guitar music with Lupe sitting beside him. All wafting through his feverish moments. Tiredness drained his spirit of will. Exhaustion drained his mind. His fingers burned. His arms flailed the innocent trees. He was slowing down. He could hardly fill his last bucket. Suddenly the whistle blew. The day's work at last ended.

Ended!

The contratista Roberto Morales stood there.

His feet straddled. Mexican style. A real robber. A Mexican general. A gentlemanly, friendly, polite, grinning, vicious, thieving brute. The worst kind. To his own people. Despite his being a fellow Mexican, despite his torn old clothing, everyone knew what kind of clever criminal he was. Despite his crude, ignorant manner, showing that he was one of them, that he'd started with them, that he grew up with them, that he'd suffered all the sordid deprivations with them, he was actually the shrewdest, smartest, richest cannibal in forty counties around. They sure couldn't blame the gueros[3] for this miscarriage. He was a crew chief. How could anyone know what he did to his own people? And what did the gueros care? So the anglo growers and guero executives, smiling in their cool filtered offices, puffing their elegant thin cigars, washed their clean blond bloodless dirtless hands of the whole matter. All they did was hire Roberto Morales. Firm, fair and square. For an agreed-upon price. Good. How he got his people down to the pickings was no concern of theirs. They were honest, those gueros. They could sleep at night. They fulfilled their end of the bargain, and cheated no one. Their only crime; their only soul grime indeed was that they just didn't care how that migratory scum lived. It was no concern of theirs. Their religion said it was no concern of theirs. Their wives said it was no concern of theirs. Their aldermen said it was no concern of theirs. Their—

Whenever Roberto Morales spoke, Manuel had to force himself not to answer. He had to keep his temper from flaring.

"Now," announced Morales at last, in his friendliest tone. "Now, I must take two cents from every bucket. I am sorry. There was a miscalculation. Everybody understands. Everybody?" He slid his eyes around, smiling, palms up.

The tired, exhausted pickers gasped as one.

Yes. Everyone understood. Freezing in place. After all that hard work.

"Any questions, men?"

Still grinning, knowing, everyone realizing that he had the upper hand, that that would mean a loss of two or three dollars out of each picker's pay that day, a huge windfall for Morales.

"You promised to take nothing!" Manuel heard himself saying. Everyone turned in astonishment to stare at Manuel.

"I said two cents, hombre. You got a problem or what?"

"You promised."

The two men, centered in a huge ring of red-ringed eyes, glared at each other. Reaching for each other's jugular. The other exhausted animals studied the tableau through widening eyes. It was so unequal. Morales remained calm, confident, studying Manuel. As though memorizing his features. He had the whole advantage. Then, with his last remaining energy, Manuel lifted his foot and clumsily tipped over his own last bucket of cots. They rolled away in all directions around everyone's feet.

Roberto Morales' eyes blazed. His fists clenched. "You pick them up, Gutierrez."

So. He knew his name. After all. For answer, Manuel kicked over another bucket, and again the fruit rolled away in all directions.

Then an astonishing thing happened.

All the other pickers moved toward their

---

3 **gueros:** fair skinned people; the growers.

own buckets still standing beside them on the ground awaiting the truck gatherer, and took an ominous position over them, straddling their feet over them. Without looking around, without taking his eyes off Manuel, Roberto Morales said sharply, "All right. All right, men. I shall take nothing this time."

Manuel felt a thrill of power course through his nerves.

He had never won anything before. He would have to pay for this, for his defiance, somehow, again, later. But he had shown defiance. He had salvaged his money savagely and he had earned respect from his fellow slaves. The gringo[s] . . . would never know of this little incident, and would probably be surprised, and perhaps even a little mortified, for a few minutes. But they wouldn't care a bit. It was bread, pan y tortillas out of his children's mouths. But they still wouldn't give it a thought. Manuel had wrenched Morales' greedy fingers away and removed a fat slug of a purse from his sticky grasp. And in his slow way, in his stupid, accidental, dangerous way, Manuel had made an extravagant discovery, as don Gaspar had also made two centuries before, in almost exactly the same spot. And that was—that a man counted for something. For men, Manuel dimly suspected, are built for something more important and less trifling than the mere gathering of prunes and apricots, hour upon hour, decade upon decade, insensibly, mechanically, antlike. Men are built to experience a certain sense of honor and pride.

Or else they are dead before they die.

Study Questions

1. What situation causes Manuel to ask the questions, "Why was mother earth so generous? And men so greedy?"

2. Why do you think the author gives such a detailed description of the inside of Manuel's shack?

3. Explain the statement: "The brain in his arms was his only capital."

4. How does the author communicate Manuel's utter frustration after the lunch break? How does this foreshadow his later behavior?

5. Why do you think Manuel is able to endure everything except Roberto's extortion? Why do the other workers join him?

6. What is the effect of the series of short statements made in describing Manuel's work? How do they contrast with the descriptions of the land and nature?

Vocabulary

The surname of Raymond Barrio, author of *The Plum Plum Pickers,* has made a place for itself in the vocabularies of many non-Spanish-speaking people. Along with *machismo,* "an exaggerated sense of manliness," *barrio* is one of the most recent additions to English from the Spanish language.

"American (though not British) English has possibly borrowed more terms from Spanish than from any other language."[1] All but a few of these words have been borrowed since 1800. Prior to that time, words borrowed by English speakers from Spanish were limited chiefly to those which Spanish explorers had learned from the Indians of the New World: *chocolate, cocoa,* and *tomato* from Mexico; *canoe,*[2] *cannibal, hammock, hurricane,* and *potato* from the Caribbean.

"Direct loans of words from Spanish, in Texas and farther west, first appeared in large numbers between 1800 and 1850."[3] During that period, American pioneers made contact with Spanish-speaking peoples who already lived there. Typical borrowings of this time interval, along with dates of their first recorded use in English, include the following: *bonanza,* 1844; *bronco,* 1850; *canyon,* 1834; *corral,* 1829; *fiesta,* 1844; *lasso,* 1831; *patio,* 1827; *peon,* 1826; *plaza,* 1836; *ranch,* l808; *rodeo,* 1844; and *sombrero,* 1823.

Since 1850, there has been a fairly steady stream of further word-borrowings from the Spanish language, including such terms as *alfalfa, cafeteria, chili con carne, filibuster, huarache, incommunicado, junta, machete, marijuana, politico, poncho, siesta, stevedore, taco, tamale, tequila, tornado.*

Besides all these words, our borrowings include: names of several states such as Colorado, Montana, and Nevada; names of many cities and towns, like El Paso, Las Cruces, Los Alamos, Pueblo, Sacramento, Toledo; and communities named after saints, such as San Antonio and Santa Barbara.

The following list of names for various members of the animal kingdom have all entered English from the Spanish language:

alligator	bonito	jaguar	mosquito	palomino
armadillo	coyote	llama	mustang	pinto

In a standard collegiate dictionary, find the entry for each of these names. On a separate sheet of paper, explain the etymology, or word history, of each name. Some of these etymologies refer to languages of Indians of the Western Hemisphere (e.g., *Nahuatl, Quechua, Tupi-Guarani*). When such is the case, look up the separate dictionary entry on the name of the Indian language and find out where it was, or is, spoken. Include such information found as you interpret each etymology.

---

1 H.L. Mencken, *The American Language* (4th ed., New York: Alfred A. Knopf, 1963), p. 191.
2 *Canoe* was first recorded in a ship's log kept by Christopher Columbus.
3 Mencken, *loc. cit.*

John Updike   1932—

Preeminent among contemporary writers, John Updike has excelled in three forms: the novel, short story, and light verse. He has produced twenty books in twenty years. Updike grew up in a small Pennsylvania town. Part of his adult life has been spent in New York City on the staff of *The New Yorker* magazine. Among his books are *Poorhouse Fair* (1959), *The Centaur* (1963), *Rabbit Run* (1972), and *Bech's Back* (1982). His novel, *Rabbit is Rich* (1981) won a Pulitzer Prize, an American Book Award, and an award from the National Book Critics' Circle. Most of Updike's fiction concerns familial experiences in suburban America. He often shows the failure of parents and children to communicate. In the story below, taken from *Museums and Women and Other Stories* (1972), he captures a father's dawning awareness of his daughter.

Man and Daughter in the Cold

JOHN UPDIKE

"LOOK AT THAT GIRL SKI!" The exclamation arose at Ethan's side as if, in the disconnecting cold, a rib of his had cried out; but it was his friend, friend and fellow-teacher, an inferior teacher but superior skier, Matt Langley, admiring Becky, Ethan's own daughter. It took an effort, in this air like slices of transparent metal interposed everywhere, to make these connections and to relate the young girl, her round face red with windburn as she skimmed down the run-out slope, to himself. She was his daughter, age thirteen. Ethan had twin sons, two years younger, and

his attention had always been focussed on their skiing, on the irksome comedy of their double needs—the four boots to lace, the four mittens to find—and then their cute yet grim competition as now one and now the other gained the edge in the expertise of geländesprungs[1] and slalom[2] form. On their trips north into the mountains, Becky had come along for the ride. "Look how solid she is," Matt went on. "She

---

1 **geländesprungs** (gə len də shprô ng´): jumps made from a crouching position using both poles.
2 **slalom**: a zigzag race downhill.

doesn't cheat on it like your boys—those feet are absolutely together." The girl, grinning as if she could hear herself praised, wiggle-waggled to a flashy stop that sprayed snow over the men's ski tips.

"Where's Mommy?" she asked.

Ethan answered, "She went with the boys into the lodge. They couldn't take it." Their sinewy little male bodies had no insulation; weeping and shivering, they had begged to go in after a single T-bar run.

"What sissies," Becky said.

Matt said, "This wind is wicked. And it's picking up. You should have been here at nine; Lord, it was lovely. All that fresh powder, and not a stir of wind."

Becky told him, "Dumb Tommy couldn't find his mittens, we spent an *hour* looking, and then Daddy got the Jeep stuck." Ethan, alerted now for signs of the wonderful in his daughter, was struck by the strange fact that she was making conversation. Unafraid, she was talking to Matt without her father's intercession.

"Mr. Langley was saying how nicely you were skiing."

"You're Olympic material, Becky."

The girl perhaps blushed; but her cheeks could get no redder. Her eyes, which, were she a child, she would have instantly averted, remained a second on Matt's face, as if to estimate how much he meant it. "It's easy down here," Becky said. "It's babyish."

Ethan asked, "Do you want to go up to the top?" He was freezing standing still, and the gondola would be sheltered from the wind.

Her eyes shifted to his, with another unconsciously thoughtful hesitation. "Sure. If you want to."

"Come along, Matt?"

"Thanks, no. It's too rough for me; I've had enough runs. This is the trouble with January—once it stops snowing, the wind comes up. I'll keep Elaine company in the lodge." Matt himself had no wife, no children. At thirty-eight, he was as free as his students, as light on his skis and as full of brave know-how. "In case of frostbite," he shouted after them, "rub snow on it."

Becky effortlessly skated ahead to the lift shed. The encumbered motion of walking on skis, not natural to him, made Ethan feel asthmatic: a fish out of water. He touched his parka pocket, to check that the inhalator was there. As a child he had imagined death as something attacking from outside, but now he saw that it was carried within; we nurse it for years, and it grows. The clock on the lodge wall said a quarter to noon. The giant thermometer read two degrees above zero. The racks outside were dense as hedges with idle skis. Crowds, any sensation of crowding or delay, quickened his asthma; as therapy he imagined the emptiness, the blue freedom, at the top of the mountain. The clatter of machinery inside the shed was comforting, and enough teen-age boys were boarding gondolas to make the ascent seem normal and safe. Ethan's breathing eased. Becky proficiently handed her poles to the loader points up; her father was always caught by surprise, and often as not fumbled the little maneuver of letting his skis be taken from him. Until, five years ago, he had become an assistant professor at a New Hampshire college an hour to the south, he had never skied; he had lived in those Middle Atlantic cities where snow, its moment of virgin beauty by, is only an encumbering nuisance, a threat of suffocation. Whereas his children had grown up on skis.

Alone with his daughter in the rumbling isolation of the gondola, he wanted to explore her, and found her strange—strange in her uninquisitive child's silence, her accustomed poise in this ascending egg of metal. A dark figure with spreading legs veered out of control beneath them, fell forward, and vanished. Ethan cried out, astonished, scandalized; he imagined the man had buried himself alive. Becky was barely amused, and looked away before the dark spots struggling in the drift were lost from sight. As if she might know, Ethan asked, "Who was that?"

"Some kid." Kids, her tone suggested, were in plentiful supply; one could be spared.

He offered to dramatize the adventure ahead of them: "Do you think we'll freeze at the top?"

"Not exactly."

"What do you think it'll be like?"

"Miserable."

"Why are we doing this, do you think?"

"Because we paid the money for the all-day lift ticket."

"Becky, you think you're pretty smart, don't you?"

"Not really."

The gondola rumbled and lurched into the shed at the top; an attendant opened the door, and there was a howling mixture of wind and of boys whooping to keep warm. He was roughly handed two pairs of skis, and the handler, muffled to the eyes with a scarf, stared as if amazed that Ethan was so old. All the others struggling into skis in the lee of the shed were adolescent boys. Students: after fifteen years of teaching, Ethan tended to flinch from youth—its harsh noises, its cheerful rapacity, its cruel onward flow as one class replaced another, ate a year of his life, and was replaced by another.

Away from the shelter of the shed, the wind was a high monotonous pitch of pain. His cheeks instantly ached, and the hinges linking the elements of his face seemed exposed. His septum[3] tingled like glass—the rim of a glass being rubbed by a moist finger to produce a note. Drifts ribbed the trail, obscuring Becky's ski tracks seconds after she made them, and at each push through the heaped snow his scope of breathing narrowed. By the time he reached the first steep section, the left half of his back hurt as it did only in the panic of a full asth-

matic attack, and his skis, ignored, too heavy to manage, spread and swept him toward a snowbank at the side of the trail. He was bent far forward but kept his balance; the snow kissed his face lightly, instantly, all over; he straightened up, refreshed by the shock, thankful not to have lost a ski. Down the slope Becky had halted and was staring upward at him, worried. A huge blowing feather, a partition of snow, came between them. The cold, unprecedented in his experience, shone through his clothes like furious light, and as he rummaged through his parka for the inhalator he seemed to be searching glass shelves backed by a black wall. He found it, its icy plastic the touch of life, a clumsy key to his insides. Gasping, he exhaled, put it into his mouth, and inhaled; the isoproterenol spray, chilled into drops, opened his lungs enough for him to call to his daughter, "Keep moving! I'll catch up!"

Solid on her skis, she swung down among the moguls and wind-bared ice, and became small, and again waited. The moderate slope seemed a cliff; if he fell and sprained anything, he would freeze. His entire body would become locked tight against air and light and thought. His legs trembled; his breath moved in and out of a narrow slot beneath the pain in his back. The cold and blowing snow all around him constituted an immense crowding, but there was no way out of this white cave but to slide downward toward the dark spot that was his daughter. He had forgotten all his lessons. Leaning backward in an infant's tense snowplow, he floundered through alternating powder and ice.

"You O.K., Daddy?" Her stare was wide, its fright underlined by a pale patch on her cheek.

He used the inhalator again and gave himself breath to tell her, "I'm fine. Let's get down."

In this way, in steps of her leading and waiting, they worked down the mountain, out of the worst wind, into the lower trail that ran between birches and hemlocks. The cold had

---

3 **septum:** bone and cartilage between the nostrils.

the quality not of absence but of force: an inverted burning. The last time Becky stopped and waited, the colorless crescent on her scarlet cheek disturbed him, reminded him of some injunction, but he could find in his brain, whittled to a dim determination to persist, only the advice to keep going, toward shelter and warmth. She told him, at a division of trails, "This is the easier way."

"Let's go the quicker way," he said, and in this last descent recovered the rhythm—knees together, shoulders facing the valley, weight forward as if in the moment of release from a diving board—not a resistance but a joyous acceptance of falling. They reached the base lodge, and with unfeeling hands removed their skis. Pushing into the cafeteria, Ethan saw in the momentary mirror of the door window that his face was a spectre's; chin, nose, and eyebrows had retained the snow from that near-fall near the top. "Becky, look," he said, turning in the crowded warmth and clatter inside the door. "I'm a monster."

"I know, your face was absolutely white, I didn't know whether to tell you or not. I thought it might scare you."

He touched the pale patch on her cheek. "Feel anything?"

"No."

"Damn. I should have rubbed snow on it."

Matt and Elaine and the twins, flushed and stripped of their parkas, had eaten lunch; shouting and laughing with a strange guilty shrillness, they said that there had been repeated loudspeaker announcements not to go up to the top without face masks, because of frostbite. They had expected Ethan and Becky to come back down on the gondola, as others had, after tasting the top. "It never occurred to us," Ethan said. He took the blame upon himself by adding, "I wanted to see the girl ski."

Their common adventure, and the guilt of his having given her frostbite, bound Becky and Ethan together in complicity for the rest

of the day. They arrived home as sun was leaving even the tips of the hills; Elaine had invited Matt to supper, and while the windows of the house burned golden Ethan shovelled out the Jeep. The house was a typical New Hampshire farmhouse, less than two miles from the college, on the side of a hill, overlooking what had been a pasture, with the usual capacious porch running around three sides, cluttered with cordwood and last summer's lawn furniture. The woodsy sheltered scent of these porches, the sense of rural waste space, never failed to please Ethan, who had been raised in a Newark half-house, then a West Side apartment, and just before college a row house in Baltimore, with his grandparents. The wind had been left behind in the mountains. The air was as still as the stars. Shovelling the light dry snow became a lazy dance. But when he bent suddenly, his knees creaked, and his breathing shortened so that he paused. A sudden rectangle of light was flung from the shadows of the porch. Becky came out into the cold with him. She was carrying a lawn rake.

He asked her, "Should you be out again? How's your frostbite?" Though she was a distance away, there was no need, in the immaculate air, to raise his voice.

"It's O.K. It kind of tingles. And under my chin. Mommy made me put on a scarf."

"What's the lawn rake for?"

"It's a way you can make a path. It really works."

"O.K., you make a path to the garage and after I get my breath I'll see if I can get the Jeep back in."

"Are you having asthma?"

"A little."

"We were reading about it in biology. Dad, see, it's kind of a tree inside you, and every branch has a little ring of muscle around it, and they tighten." From her gestures in the dark she was demonstrating, with mittens on.

What she described, of course, was classic unalloyed asthma, whereas his was shading into emphysema, which could only worsen.

But he liked being lectured to—preferred it, indeed, to lecturing—and as the minutes of companionable silence with his daughter passed he took inward notes on the bright quick impressions flowing over him like a continuous voice. The silent cold. The stars. Orion[4] behind an elm. Minute scintillae in the snow at his feet. His daughter's strange black bulk against the white; the solid grace that had stolen upon her. The conspiracy of love. His father and he shovelling the car free from a sudden unwelcome storm in Newark, instantly gray with soot, the undercurrent of desperation, his father a salesman and must get to Camden. Got to get to Camden, boy, get to Camden or bust. Dead of a heart attack at forty-seven. Ethan tossed a shovelful into the air so the scintillae flashed in the steady golden chord from the house windows. Elaine and Matt sitting flushed at the lodge table, parkas off, in deshabille, as if sitting up in bed. Matt's way of turning a half circle on the top of a mogul, light as a diver. The cancerous unwieldiness of Ethan's own skis. His jealousy of his students, the many-headed immortality of their annual renewal. The flawless tall cruelty of the stars. Orion intertwined with the silhouetted elm. A black tree inside him. His daughter, busily sweeping with the rake, childish yet lithe, so curiously demonstrating this preference for his company. Feminine of

---

4 **Orion**: a constellation of stars.

her to forgive him her frostbite. Perhaps, flattered on skis, felt the cold her element. Her womanhood soon enough to be smothered in warmth. A plow a mile away painstakingly scraped. He was missing the point of the lecture. The point was unstated: an absence. He was looking upon his daughter as a woman but without lust. The music around him was being produced, in the zero air, like a finger on crystal, by this hollowness, this generosity of negation. Without lust, without jealousy. Space seemed love, bestowed to be free in, and coldness the price. He felt joined to the great dead whose words it was his duty to teach.

The Jeep came up unprotestingly from the fluffy snow. It looked happy to be penned in the garage with Elaine's station wagon, and the skis, and the oiled chain saw, and the power mower dreamlessly waiting for spring. Ethan was happy, precariously so, so that rather than break he uttered a sound: "Becky?"

"Yeah?"

"You want to know what else Mr. Langley said?"

"What?" They trudged toward the porch, up the path the gentle rake had cleared.

"He said you ski better than the boys."

"I bet," she said, and raced to the porch, and in the precipitate way, evasive and female and pleased, that she flung herself to the top step he glimpsed something generic and joyous, a pageant that would leave him behind.

Study Questions

1. Why does Ethan suggest that he and his daughter go to the top of the ski slope? What warnings does Ethan receive about the dangers of skiing down the slope?

2. How is Becky responsible for guiding her father back to the lodge?

3. How has common adventure brought Becky and Ethan together? What new awareness does the father have about Becky at the end of the story?

4. Explain how the setting, January weather, description of the terrain, and ski jargon contribute to the effectiveness of the story.

5. Imagine this story told from the point of view of the daughter rather than the father. What perceptions might Becky have had as a result of the adventure with her father?

Vocabulary

Each item below begins with one *italicized* word followed by three other words. On a separate sheet of paper, write both the *italicized* word and the one **antonym** following it which has the most nearly opposite meaning. Do not use a dictionary.

1. *avert:*	quit	intend	promote
2. *dishabille:*	uniform	relax	bruise
3. *encumbered:*	cleaned	borrowed	aided
4. *generic:*	voluntary	fatal	unique
5. *precipitate:*	wordless	careful	wonderful
6. *proficient:*	incompetent	entire	unexpected
7. *rapacity:*	loyalty	danger	selflessness
8. *scintilla:*	unity	liability	immensity
9. *unprecedented:*	current	footloose	customary
10. *veering:*	unsnarling	unswerving	uninviting

Check your answers in a dictionary and correct any errors. At the same time, find and write a definition for each *italicized* word.

Toni Morrison   1931 —

Before she begun her writing career, Toni Morrison taught literature at Texas Southern University and briefly at her alma mater, Howard University. She has also taught at Yale and Barnard. Since 1966 she has been an editor at Random House Publishers. Morrison's first two novels, *The Bluest Eye* (1970) and *Sula* (1974), are both set in a small midwestern town similar to Morrison's birthplace, Lorain, Ohio. Her novel, *Song of Solomon* (1977), won the

National Book Critics' Circle Award. It was also a Book-of-the-Month Club selection, the first book by an Afro-American author so designated since Richard Wright's *Native Son* in 1940. Her most recent novel, *Tar Baby* (1981), also received wide acclaim.

Morrison's specialty is examining the manifestations of tormented, frustrated lives. In the excerpt from *The Bluest Eye* included here, we see an early expression of that frustration.

from The Bluest Eye

TONI MORRISON

MY DADDY'S FACE is a study. Winter moves into it and presides there. His eyes become a cliff of snow threatening to avalanche; his eyebrows bend like black limbs of leafless trees. His skin takes on the pale, cheerless yellow of winter sun; for a jaw he has the edges of a snowbound field dotted with stubble; his high forehead is the frozen sweep of the Erie, hiding currents of gelid thoughts that eddy in darkness. Wolf killer turned hawk fighter, he worked night and day to keep one from the door and the other from under the windowsills. A Vulcan guarding the flames, he gives us instructions about which doors to keep closed or opened for proper distribution of heat, lays kindling by, discusses qualities of coal, and teaches us how to rake, feed, and bank the fire. And he will not unrazor his lips until spring.

Winter tightened our heads with a band of cold and melted our eyes. We put pepper in the feet of our stockings, Vaseline on our faces, and stared through dark icebox mornings at four stewed prunes, slippery lumps of oatmeal, and cocoa with a roof of skin.

But mostly we waited for spring, when there could be gardens.

By the time this winter had stiffened itself into a hateful knot that nothing could loosen, something did loosen it, or rather someone. A someone who splintered the knot into silver threads that tangled us, netted us, made us long for the dull chafe of the previous boredom.

This disrupter of seasons was a new girl in school named Maureen Peal. A high-yellow dream child with long brown hair braided into two lynch ropes that hung down her back. She was rich, at least by our standards, as

BLUE INTERIOR MORNING   *Romare Beardon*

rich as the richest of the white girls, swaddled in comfort and care. The quality of her clothes threatened to derange Frieda and me. Patent-leather shoes with buckles, a cheaper version of which we got only at Easter and which had disintegrated by the end of May. Fluffy sweaters the color of lemon drops tucked into skirts with pleats so orderly they astounded us. Brightly colored knee socks with white borders, a brown velvet coat trimmed in white rabbit fur, and a matching muff. There was a hint of spring in her sloe green eyes, something summery in her complexion, and a rich autumn ripeness in her walk.

She enchanted the entire school. When teachers called on her, they smiled encouragingly. Black boys didn't trip her in the halls; white boys didn't stone her, white girls didn't suck their teeth when she was assigned to be their work partners; black girls stepped aside when she wanted to use the sink in the girls' toilet, and their eyes genuflected under sliding lids. She never had to search for anybody to eat with in the cafeteria—they flocked to the table of her choice, where she opened fastidious lunches, shaming our jelly-stained bread with egg-salad sandwiches cut into four dainty squares, pink-frosted cupcakes, stocks of celery and carrots, proud, dark apples. She even bought and liked white milk.

Frieda and I were bemused, irritated, and fascinated by her. We looked hard for flaws to restore our equilibrium, but had to be content at first with uglying up her name, changing Maureen Peal to Meringue Pie. Later a minor epiphany was ours when we discovered that she had a dog tooth—a charming one to be sure—but a dog tooth nonetheless. And when we found out that she had been born with six fingers on each hand and that there was a little bump where each extra one had been removed, we smiled. They were small triumphs, but we took what we could get—snickering behind her back and calling her Six-finger-dog-tooth-meringue-pie. But, we had to do it alone, for none of the other girls would cooperate with our hostility. They adored her.

When she was assigned a locker next to mine, I could indulge my jealousy four times a day. My sister and I both suspected that we were secretly prepared to be her friend, if she would let us, but I knew it would be a dangerous friendship, for when my eye traced the white border patterns of those Kelly-green knee socks, and felt the pull and slack of my brown stockings, I wanted to kick her. And when I thought of the unearned haughtiness in her eyes, I plotted accidental slammings of locker doors on her hand.

As locker friends, however, we got to know each other a little, and I was even able to hold a sensible conversation with her without visualizing her fall off a cliff, or giggling my way into what I thought was a clever insult.

One day, while I waited at the locker for Frieda, she joined me.

"Hi."

"Hi."

"Waiting for your sister?"

"Uh-huh."

"Which way do you go home?"

"Down Twenty-first Street to Broadway."

"Why don't you go down Twenty-second Street?"

"'Cause I live on Twenty-first Street."

"Oh. I can walk that way, I guess. Partly, anyway."

"Free country."

Frieda came toward us, her brown stockings straining at the knees because she had tucked the toe under to hide a hole in the foot.

"Maureen's gonna walk part way with us."

Frieda and I exchanged glances, her eyes begging my restraint, mine promising nothing.

It was a false spring day, which, like Maureen, had pierced the shell of a deadening winter. There were puddles, mud, and an inviting warmth that deluded us. The kind of day on which we draped our coats over our heads, left our galoshes in school, and came down with croup the following day. We always responded to the slightest change in weather, the most minute shifts in time of day. Long before seeds were stirring, Frieda and I were scruffing and poking at the earth, swallowing air, drinking rain. . . .

As we emerged from the school with Maureen, we began to moult immediately. We put our head scarves in our coat pockets, and our coats on our heads. I was wondering how to maneuver Maureen's fur muff into a gutter when a commotion in the playground distracted us. A group of boys was circling and holding at bay a victim, Pecola Breedlove.

Bay Boy, Woodrow Cain, Buddy Wilson, Junie Bug—like a necklace of semiprecious stones they surrounded her. Heady with the smell of their own musk, thrilled by the easy power of a majority, they gaily harassed her.

"Black e mo. Black e mo. Yadaddsleepsnekked. Black e mo black e mo ya dadd sleeps nekked. Black e mo . . ."

They had extemporized a verse made up of two insults about matters over which the victim had no control: the color of her skin and speculations on the sleeping habits of an adult, wildly fitting in its incoherence. That they themselves were black, or that their own father had similarly relaxed habits was irrelevant. It was their contempt for their own blackness that gave the first insult its teeth. They seemed to have taken all of their smoothly cultivated ignorance, their exquisitely learned self-hatred, their elaborately designed hopelessness and sucked it all up into a fiery cone of scorn that had burned for ages in the hollows of their minds—cooled—and spilled over lips of outrage, consuming whatever was in its path. They danced a macabre ballet around the victim, whom, for their own sake, they were prepared to sacrifice to the flaming pit.

Black e mo Black e mo Ya daddy sleeps nekked.
Stch ta ta stch ta ta
stach ta ta ta ta ta

Pecola edged around the circle crying. She had dropped her notebook, and covered her eyes with her hands.

We watched, afraid they might notice us and turn their energies our way. Then Frieda, with set lips and Mama's eyes, snatched her coat from her head and threw it on the ground. She ran toward them and brought her books down on Woodrow Cain's head. The circle broke. Woodrow Cain grabbed his head.

"Hey, girl!"

"You cut that out, you hear?" I had never heard Frieda's voice so loud and clear.

Maybe because Frieda was taller than he was, maybe because he saw her eyes, maybe because he had lost interest in the game, or maybe because he had a crush on Frieda, in any case Woodrow looked frightened just long enough to give her more courage.

"Leave her 'lone, or I'm gone tell everybody what you did!"

Woodrow did not answer; he just walled his eyes.

Bay Boy piped up, "Go on, gal! Ain't nobody bothering you."

"You shut up, Bullet Head." I had found my tongue.

"Who you calling Bullet Head?"

"I'm calling you Bullet Head, Bullet Head."

Frieda took Pecola's hand. "Come on."

"You want a fat lip?" Bay Boy drew back his fist at me:

"Yeah. Gimme one of yours."

"You gone get one."

Maureen appeared at my elbow, and the boys seemed reluctant to continue under her springtime eyes so wide with interest. They buckled in confusion, not willing to beat up three girls under her watchful gaze. So they listened to a budding male instinct that told them to pretend we were unworthy of their attention.

"Come on, man."

"Yeah. Come on. We ain't got time to fool with them."

Grumbling a few disinterested epithets, they moved away.

I picked up Pecola's notebook and Frieda's coat, and the four of us left the playground.

"Old Bullet Head, he's always picking on girls."

Frieda agreed with me. "Miss Forrester said he was incorrigival."

"Really?" I didn't know what that meant, but it had enough of a doom sound in it to be true of Bay Boy.

While Frieda and I clucked on about the near fight, Maureen, suddenly animated, put her velvet-sleeved arm through Pecola's and began to behave as though they were the closest of friends.

"I just moved here. My name is Maureen Peal. What's yours?"

"Pecola."

"Pecola? Wasn't that the name of the girl in *Imitation of Life?*"

"I don't know. What is that?"

"The picture show, you know. Where this mulatto girl hates her mother 'cause she is black and ugly but then cries at the funeral. It was real sad. Everybody cries in it. Claudette Colbert too."

"Oh." Pecola's voice was no more than a sigh.

"Anyway, her name was Pecola too. She

was so pretty. When it comes back, I'm going to see it again. My mother has seen it four times."

Frieda and I walked behind them, surprised at Maureen's friendliness to Pecola, but pleased. Maybe she wasn't so bad, after all. Frieda had put her coat back on her head, and the two of us, so draped, trotted along enjoying the warm breeze and Frieda's heroics.

"You're in my gym class, aren't you?" Maureen asked Pecola.

"Yes."

"Miss Erkmeister's legs sure are bow. I bet she thinks they're cute. How come she gets to wear real shorts, and we have to wear those old bloomers? I want to die every time I put them on."

Pecola smiled but did not look at Maureen.

"Hey." Maureen stopped short. "There's an Isaley's. Want some ice cream? I have money."

She unzipped a hidden pocket in her muff and pulled out a multifolded dollar bill. I forgave her those knee socks.

"My uncle sued Isaley's," Maureen said to the three of us. "He sued the Isaley's in Akron. They said he was disorderly and that that was why they wouldn't serve him, but a friend of his, a policeman, came in and beared the witness, so the suit went through."

"What's a suit?"

"It's when you can beat them up if you want to and won't anybody do nothing. Our family does it all the time. We believe in suits."

At the entrance to Isaley's Maureen turned to Frieda and me, asking, "You all going to buy some ice cream?"

We looked at each other. "No," Frieda said.

Maureen disappeared into the store with Pecola.

Study Questions

1. How does the opening description of the father relate to what follows? What do you learn about the father?

2. What event at school breaks up the girls' winter monotony?

3. What examples does the narrator give of ways in which she and her sister are "bemused, irritated, and fascinated" by Maureen Peal?

4. Why do the girls defend Pecola Breedlove? What part does Maureen play in the rescue?

5. Do you think the two sisters learned anything from this experience? Why will their attitude toward Maureen change? not change?

6. In what ways does this story illustrate the theme of The Individual in society?

Composition

1. *The Bluest Eye* includes a number of metaphors and similes. For example the father is described: "Wolf killer turned hawk fighter, he worked night and day to keep one from the door and the other from under the windowsills." Select two other metaphors or two similes from the story. Write an explanation of what this one and the two you select mean. Con-

clude by telling why they are either effective or ineffective.

2. Write this same story from Maureen's point of view. Tell how she feels as the new student in school. Present her response to the attention she receives. Also give her opinion of the other girls.

Vocabulary

A. In each of the following sentences based upon the selection from *The Bluest Eye,* a blank indicates where a word has been omitted. From among the five words listed beneath each sentence, choose the one that fits the **sentence context** most logically and meaningfully. On a separate sheet of paper number 1–10. Write each answer. Do not use a dictionary.

1. Daddy's forehead is like the frozen surface of the Erie, under which hidden thoughts bubble, swirl, and ＿＿ in the cold darkness.

   chafe　　eddy　　deplore　　hornswoggle　　induce

2. Frieda and I became almost ＿＿ with jealous self-pity when we compared the quality and beauty of Maureen's clothes with the cheap ugliness of our own.

   deranged　　flawless　　haughty　　jubilant　　moderate

3. Instead of choking down jelly-stained bread for lunch, as we did, Maureen nibbled at tiny, ＿＿ prepared egg salad sandwiches and dainty pink-frosted cupcakes.

   anemically　　buxomly　　congruently
   fastidiously　　horrendously

4. The information that Maureen had a dog tooth came as a minor, but joyous ＿＿ to Frieda and me.

   brocade　　dogma　　epiphany　　falange　　inertia

5. A group of boys circled a female victim, taunting her about her skin color and ＿＿ aloud about her father's sleeping habits.

   leavening　　negotiating　　pending
   reinstating　　speculating

6. The boys had combined smoothly cultivated ignorance, elaborately designed hopelessness, and ＿＿ learned self-hatred into a fiery cone of scorn.

   beneficently　　connubially　　exquisitely
   florally　　gutturally

7. The boys were dancing a ＿＿ ballet around their victim, whom, for their own sake, they would gladly have sacrificed to the flaming pit.

   chronological　　fragile　　gullible　　judicious　　macabre

8. Instinct told the boys to pretend we girls were unworthy of their attention; and so, grumbling a few harsh ＿＿ , they moved away.

   epithets　　gussets　　ingenues　　liturgies　　nonentities

9. Our teacher, Miss Forrester, had said that Old Bullet Head's habit of picking on girls was ＿＿＿ , a practice she had repeatedly failed to break him of.

euphonious   gravid   hypochondriac
incorrigible   liquescent

10. Suddenly acting very ＿＿＿ , Maureen smiled and introduced herself, put her arm through Pecola's, and began walking the girl toward the ice cream parlor.

animated   bilious   claustrophobic   dank   ephemeral

B. Now, with the help of both the story text and a dictionary, verify each answer you have given in the above exercise. Correct any errors.

C. There are two or more meanings, either slightly or greatly different, for each word that serves as a correct answer in the above exercise. Regardless of the order in which these meanings are presented in a dictionary, copy all of them as follows: (1) the definition of the word as used in the exercise; and then (2) the remaining definition(s).

Saul Bellow   1915——

Saul Bellow is regarded by many readers and literary critics as one of the most important novelists in contemporary America. Among his nine widely respected publications since the 1940s are *Dangling Man, Henderson the Rain King, Herzog, Humboldt's Gift,* and the latest, *The Dean's December* (1982). In 1976 Bellow received the Nobel Prize for Literature, perhaps the ultimate recognition of a writer's contribution to literature. In his acceptance speech, Bellow compared the novel to a "lean-to" or "hovel" in which "the spirit takes shelter." He regards the novel as the medium through which meaning and existence can be made visible and appreciated: "it [the novel] promises us meaning, harmony, and even justice . . ."

In the following story, "A Father-to-Be," Bellow explores the existence of one "modern" man, his fears, and his attempts to come to terms with a sense of meaning.

A Father-to-Be

SAUL BELLOW

THE STRANGEST NOTIONS had a way of forcing themselves into Rogin's mind. Just thirty-one and passable-looking, with short black hair, small eyes, but a high, open forehead, he was a research chemist, and his mind was generally serious and dependable. But on a snowy Sunday evening while this stocky man, buttoned to the chin in a Burberry coat and walking in his preposterous gait—feet turned outward—was going toward the subway, he fell into a peculiar state.

He was on his way to have supper with his fiancée. She had phoned him a short while ago and said, "You'd better pick up a few things on the way."

"What do we need?"

"Some roast beef, for one thing. I bought a quarter of a pound coming home from my aunt's."

"Why a quarter of a pound, Joan?" said Rogin, deeply annoyed. "That's just about enough for one good sandwich."

"So you have to stop at a delicatessen. I had no more money."

He was about to ask, "What happened to the thirty dollars I gave you on Wednesday?" but he knew that would not be right.

"I had to give Phyllis money for the cleaning woman," said Joan.

Phyllis, Joan's cousin, was a young divorcee, extremely wealthy. The two women shared an apartment.

"Roast beef," he said, "and what else?"

"Some shampoo, sweetheart. We've used up all the shampoo. And hurry, darling, I've missed you all day."

"And I've missed you," said Rogin, but to tell the truth he had been worrying most of the time. He had a younger brother whom he was putting through college. And his mother, whose annuity wasn't quite enough in these days of inflation and high taxes, needed money too. Joan had debts he was helping her to pay, for she wasn't working. She was looking for something suitable to do. Beautiful, well educated, aristocratic in her attitude, she couldn't clerk in a dime store; she couldn't model clothes (Rogin thought this made girls vain and stiff, and he didn't want her to); she couldn't be a waitress or a cashier. What could she be? Well, something would turn up and meantime Rogin hesitated to complain. He paid her bills—the dentist, the department store, the osteopath, the doctor, the psychiatrist. At Christmas, Rogin almost went mad. Joan bought him a velvet smoking jacket with frog fasteners, a beautiful pipe, and a pouch. She bought Phyllis a garnet brooch, an Italian silk umbrella, and a gold cigarette holder. For other friends, she bought Dutch pewter and Swedish glassware. Before she was through, she had spent five hundred dollars of Rogin's money. He loved her too much to show his suffering. He believed she had a far better nature than his. She didn't worry about money. She had a marvelous character, always cheerful, and she really didn't need a psychiatrist at all. She went to one because Phyllis did and it made her curious. She tried too much to keep up with her cousin, whose father had made millions in the rug business.

While the woman in the drugstore was wrapping the shampoo bottle, a clear idea suddenly arose in Rogin's thoughts: Money surrounds you in life as the earth does in death. Superimposition is the universal law. Who is free? No one is free. Who has no burdens? Everyone is under pressure. The very rocks, the waters of the earth, beasts, men, children—everyone has some weight to carry. This idea was extremely clear to him at first. Soon it became rather vague, but it had a great effect nevertheless, as if someone had given him a valuable gift. (Not like the velvet smoking jacket he couldn't bring himself to wear, or the pipe it choked him to smoke.) The notion that

all were under pressure and affliction, instead of saddening him, had the opposite influence. It put him in a wonderful mood. It was extraordinary how happy he became and, in addition, clear-sighted. His eyes all at once were opened to what was around him. He saw with delight how the druggist and the woman who wrapped the shampoo bottle were smiling and flirting, how the lines of worry in her face went over into lines of cheer and the druggist's receding gums did not hinder his kidding and friendliness. And in the delicatessen, also, it was amazing how much Rogin noted and what happiness it gave him simply to be there.

Delicatessens on Sunday night, when all other stores are shut, will overcharge you ferociously, and Rogin would normally have been on guard, but he was not tonight, or scarcely so. Smells of pickle, sausage, mustard, and smoked fish overjoyed him. He pitied the people who would buy the chicken salad and chopped herring; they could do it only because their sight was too dim to see what they were getting—the fat flakes of pepper on the chicken, the soppy herring, mostly vinegar-soaked stale bread. Who would buy them? Late risers, people living alone, waking up in the darkness of the afternoon, finding their refrigerators empty, or people whose gaze was turned inward. The roast beef looked not bad, and Rogin ordered a pound.

While the storekeeper was slicing the meat, he yelled at a Puerto Rican kid who was reaching for a bag of chocolate cookies, "Hey, you want to pull me down the whole display on yourself? You, *chico,* wait a half a minute." This storekeeper, though he looked like one of Pancho Villa's bandits, the kind that smeared their enemies with syrup and staked them down on anthills, a man with toadlike eyes and stout hands made to clasp pistols hung around his belly, was not so bad. He was a New York man, thought Rogin—who was from Albany himself—a New York man toughened by every abuse of the city, trained to suspect everyone. But in his own realm, on the board behind the counter, there was justice. Even clemency.

The Puerto Rican kid wore a complete cowboy outfit—a green hat with white braid, guns, chaps, spurs, boots, and gauntlets—but he couldn't speak any English. Rogin unhooked the cellophane bag of hard circular cookies and gave it to him. The boy tore the cellophane with his teeth and began to chew one of those dry chocolate disks. Rogin recognized his state—the energetic dream of childhood. Once, he too, had found these dry biscuits delicious. It would have bored him now to eat one.

What else would Joan like? Rogin thought fondly. Some strawberries? "Give me some frozen strawberries. No, raspberries, she likes those better. And heavy cream. And some rolls, cream cheese, and some of those rubber-looking gherkins."

"What rubber?"

"Those, deep green, with eyes. Some ice cream might be in order, too."

He tried to think of a compliment, a good comparison, an endearment, for Joan when she'd open the door. What about her complexion? There was really nothing to compare her sweet, small, daring, shapely, timid, defiant, loving face to. How difficult she was, and how beautiful!

As Rogin went down into the stony, odorous, metallic, captive air of the subway, he was diverted by an unusual confession made by a man to his friend. These were two very tall men, shapeless in their winter clothes, as if their coats concealed suits of chain mail.

"So, how long have you known me?" said one.

"Twelve years."

"Well, I have an admission to make," he said. "I've decided that I might as well. For years I've been a heavy drinker. You didn't know. Practically an alcoholic."

But his friend was not surprised, and he answered immediately, "Yes, I did know."

"You knew? Impossible! How could you?"

Why, thought Rogin, as if it could be a secret! Look at that long, austere, alcohol-washed face, that drink-ruined nose, the skin by his ears like turkey wattles, and those whisky-saddened eyes.

"Well, I did know, though."

"You couldn't have. I can't believe it." He was upset, and his friend didn't seem to want to soothe him. "But it's all right now," he said. "I've been going to a doctor and taking pills, a new revolutionary Danish discovery. It's a miracle. I'm beginning to believe they can cure you of anything and everything. You can't beat the Danes in science. They do everything. They turned a man into a woman."

"That isn't how they stop you from drinking, is it?"

"No, I hope not. This is only like aspirin. It's superaspirin. They called it the aspirin of the future. But if you use it, you have to stop drinking."

Rogin's illuminated mind asked of itself while the human tides of the subway swayed back and forth, and cars linked and transparent like fish bladders raced under the streets: How come he thought nobody would know what everybody couldn't help knowing? And, as a chemist, he asked himself what kind of compound this new Danish drug might be, and started thinking about various inventions of his own, synthetic albumen, a cigarette that lit itself, a cheaper motor fuel. Ye gods, but he needed money! As never before. What was to be done? His mother was growing more and more difficult. On Friday night, she had neglected to cut up his meat for him, and he was hurt. She had sat at the table motionless, with her long-suffering face, severe, and let him cut his own meat, a thing she almost never did. She had always spoiled him and made his brother envy him. But what she expected now! Oh, Lord, how he had to pay, and it had never even occurred to him formerly that these things might have a price.

Seated, one of the passengers, Rogin recovered his calm, happy, even clairvoyant state of mind. To think of money was to think as the world wanted you to think; then you'd never be your own master. When people said they wouldn't do something for love or money, they meant that love and money were opposite passions and one the enemy of the other. He went on to reflect how little people knew about this, how they slept through life, how small a light the light of consciousness was. Rogin's clean, snub-nosed face shone while his heart was torn with joy at these deeper thoughts of our ignorance. You might take this drunkard as an example, who for long years thought his closest friends never suspected he drank. Rogin looked up and down the aisle for this remarkable knightly symbol, but he was gone.

However, there was no lack of things to see. There was a small girl with a new white muff; into the muff a doll's head was sewn, and the child was happy and affectionately vain of it, while her old man, stout and grim, with a huge scowling nose, kept picking her up and resettling her in the seat, as if he were trying to change her into something else. Then another child, led by her mother, boarded the car, and this other child carried the very same doll-faced muff, and this greatly annoyed both parents. The woman, who looked like a difficult, contentious woman, took her daughter away. It seemed to Rogin that each child was in love with its own muff and didn't even see the other, but it was one of his foibles to think he understood the hearts of little children.

A foreign family next engaged his attention. They looked like Central Americans to him. On one side the mother, quite old, dark-faced, white-haired, and worn out; on the other a son with the whitened, porous hands of a dish-washer. But what was the dwarf who sat between them—a son or a daughter? The hair was long and wavy and the cheeks smooth, but the shirt and tie were masculine. The overcoat was feminine, but the shoes—the shoes were a puzzle. A pair of brown oxfords with an outer seam like a man's, but Baby Louis heels like a woman's—a plain toe like a man's, but a strap across the instep like a woman's. No stockings. That didn't help much. The dwarf's fingers were beringed, but without a wedding band. There were small grim dents in the cheeks. The eyes were puffy and concealed, but Rogin did not doubt that they could reveal strange things if they chose and that this was a creature of remarkable understanding. He had for many years owned de la Mare's *Memoirs of a Midget*. Now he took a resolve; he would read it. As soon as he had decided, he was free from his consuming curiosity as to the dwarf's sex and was able to look at the person who sat beside him.

Thoughts very often grow fertile in the subway, because of the motion, the great company, the subtlety of the rider's state as he rattles under streets and rivers, under the foundations of great buildings, and Rogin's mind had already been strangely stimulated. Clasping the bag of groceries from which there rose odors of bread and pickle spice, he was following a train of reflections, first about the chemistry of sex determination, the X and Y chromosomes, hereditary linkages, the uterus, afterward about his brother as a tax exemption. He recalled two dreams of the night before. In one, an undertaker had offered to cut his hair, and he had refused. In another, he had been carrying a woman on his head. Sad dreams, both! Very sad! Which was the woman—Joan or Mother? And the undertaker—his lawyer? He gave a deep sigh, and by force of habit began to put together his synthetic albumen that was to revolutionize the entire egg industry.

Meanwhile, he had not interrupted his examination of the passengers and had fallen into a study of the man next to him. This was a man whom he had never in his life seen before but with whom he now suddenly felt linked through all existence. He was middle-aged, sturdy, with clear skin and blue eyes. His hands were clean, well formed, but Rogin did not approve of them. The coat he wore was a fairly expensive blue check such as Rogin would never have chosen for himself. He would not have worn blue suède shoes, either, or such a faultless hat, a cumbersome felt animal of a hat encircled by a high, fat ribbon. There are all kinds of dandies, not all of them are of the flaunting kind; some are dandies of respectability, and Rogin's fellow passenger was one of these. His straight-nosed profile was handsome, yet he had betrayed his gift, for he was flat-looking. But in his flat way he seemed to warn people that he wanted no difficulties with them, he wanted nothing to do with them. Wearing such blue suède shoes, he could not afford to have people treading on his feet, and he seemed to draw about himself a circle of privilege, notifying all others to mind their own business and let him read his paper. He was holding a *Tribune,* and perhaps it would be overstatement to say that he was reading. He was holding it.

His clear skin and blue eyes, his straight and purely Roman nose—even the way he sat—all strongly suggested one person to Rogin: Joan. He tried to escape the comparison, but it couldn't be helped. This man not only looked like Joan's father, whom Rogin detested; he looked like Joan herself. Forty years hence, a son of hers, provided she had one, might be like this. A son of hers? Of such a son, he himself, Rogin, would be the father. Lacking in dominant traits as compared with Joan, his heritage would not appear. Probably the children would resemble her. Yes, think forty years ahead, and a man like this, who sat by him knee to knee in the hurtling car among their fellow creatures, unconscious participants in a sort of great carnival of transit—such a man would carry forward what had been Rogin.

This was why he felt bound to him through all existence. What were forty years reckoned against eternity! Forty years were gone, and he was gazing at his own son. Here he was. Rogin was frightened and moved. "My son! My son!" he said to himself, and the pity of it almost made him burst into tears. The holy

and frightful work of the masters of life and death brought this about. We were their instruments. We worked toward ends we thought were our own. But no! The whole thing was so unjust. To suffer, to labor, to toil and force your way though the spikes of life, to crawl through its darkest carverns, to push through the worst, to struggle under the weight of economy, to make money—only to become the father of a fourth-rate man of the world like this, so flat-looking with his ordinary, clean, rosy, uninteresting, self-satisfied, fundamentally bourgeois face. What a curse to have a dull son! A son like this, who could never understand his father. They had absolutely nothing, but nothing in common, he and this neat, chubby, blue-eyed man. He was so pleased, thought Rogin, with all he owned and all he did and all he was that he could hardly unfasten his lip. Look at that lip, sticking up at the tip like a little thorn or egg tooth. He wouldn't give anyone the time of day. Would this perhaps be general forty years from now? Would personalities be chillier as the world aged and grew colder? The inhumanity of the next generation incensed Rogin. Father and son had no sign to make to each other. Terrible! Inhuman! What a vision of existence it gave him. Man's personal aims were nothing, illusion. The life force occupied each of us in turn in its progress toward its own fulfillment, trampling on our individual humanity, using us for its own ends like mere dinosaurs or bees, exploiting love heartlessly, making us engage in the social process, labor, struggle for money, and submit to the law of pressure, the universal law of layers, superimposition!

What the blazes am I getting into? Rogin thought. To be the father of a throwback to *her* father. The image of this white-haired, gross, peevish, old man with his ugly selfish blue eyes revolted Rogin. This was how his grandson would look. Joan, with whom Rogin was now more and more displeased, could not help that. For her, it was inevitable. But did it have to be

inevitable for him? Well, then, Rogin, you fool, don't be a damned instrument. Get out of the way!

But it was too late for this, because he had already experienced the sensation of sitting next to his own son, his son and Joan's. He kept staring at him, waiting for him to say something, but the presumptive son remained coldly silent though he must have been aware of Rogin's scrutiny. They even got out at the same stop—Sheridan Square. When they stepped to the platform, the man, without even looking at Rogin, went away in a different direction in his detestable blue-checked coat, with his rosy, nasty face.

The whole thing upset Rogin very badly. When he approached Joan's door and heard Phyllis's little dog Henri barking even before he could knock, his face was very tense. I won't be used, he declared to himself. I have my own right to exist. Joan had better watch out. She had a light way of by-passing grave questions he had given earnest thought to. She always assumed no really disturbing thing would happen. He could not afford the luxury of such a carefree, debonair attitude himself, because he had to work hard and earn money so that disturbing things would *not* happen. Well, at the moment this situation could not be helped, and he really did not mind the money if he could feel that she was not necessarily the mother of such a son as his subway son or entirely the daughter of that awful, obscene father of hers. After all, Rogin was not himself so much like either of his parents, and quite different from his brother.

Joan came to the door, wearing one of Phyllis's expensive housecoats. It suited her very well. At first sight of her happy face, Rogin was brushed by the shadow of resemblance; the touch of it was extremely light, almost figmentary, but it made his flesh tremble.

She began to kiss him, saying, "Oh, my baby. You're covered with snow. Why didn't you wear your hat? It's all over its little head"—her favorite third-person endearment.

"Well, let me put down this bag of stuff. Let me take off my coat," grumbled Rogin, and escaped from her embrace. Why couldn't she wait making up to him? "It's so hot in here. My face is burning. Why do you keep the place at this temperature? And that damned dog keeps barking. If you didn't keep it cooped up, it wouldn't be so spoiled and noisy. Why doesn't anybody ever walk him?"

"Oh, it's not really so hot here! You've just come in from the cold. Don't you think this housecoat fits me better than Phyllis? Especially across the hips. She thinks so, too. She may sell it to me."

"I hope not," Rogin almost exclaimed.

She brought a towel to dry the melting snow from his short black hair. The flurry of rubbing excited Henri intolerably, and Joan locked him up in the bedroom, where he jumped persistently against the door with a rhythmic sound of claws on the wood.

Joan said, "Did you bring the shampoo?"

"Here it is."

"Then I'll wash your hair before dinner. Come."

"I don't want it washed."

"Oh, come on," she said, laughing.

Her lack of consciousness of guilt amazed him. He did not see how it could be. And the carpeted, furnished, lamplit, curtained room seemed to stand against his vision. So that he felt accusing and angry, his spirit sore and bitter, but it did not seem fitting to say why. Indeed, he began to worry lest the reason for it all slip away from him.

They took off his coat and his shirt in the bathroom, and she filled the sink. Rogin was full of his troubled emotions; now that his chest was bare he could feel them even more and he said to himself, I'll have a thing or two to tell her pretty soon. I'm not letting them get away with it. "Do you think," he was going to tell her, "that I alone was made to carry the burden of the whole world on me? Do you think I was born to be taken advantage of and sacrificed? Do you think I'm just a natural resource, like a coal mine, or oil well, or fishery, or the like? Remember, that I'm a man is no reason why I should be loaded down. I have a soul in me no bigger or stronger than yours.

"Take away the externals, like the muscles, deeper voice, and so forth, and what remains? A pair of spirits, practically alike. So why shouldn't there also be equality? I can't always be the strong one."

"Sit here," said Joan, bringing up a kitchen stool to the sink. "Your hair's gotten all matted."

He sat with this breast against the cool enamel, his chin on the edge of the basin, the green, hot, radiant water reflecting the glass and the tile, and the sweet, cool, fragrant juice of the shampoo poured on his head. She began to wash him.

"You have the healthiest-looking scalp," she said. "It's all pink."

He answered, "Well, it should be white. There must be something wrong with me."

"But there's absolutely nothing wrong with you," she said, and pressed against him from behind, surrounding him, pouring the water gently over him until it seemed to him that the water came from within him, it was the warm fluid of his own secret loving spirit overflowing into the sink, green and foaming, and the words he had rehearsed he forgot, and his anger at his son-to-be disappeared altogether, and he sighed, and said to her from the water-filled hollow of the sink, "You always have such wonderful ideas, Joan. You know? You have a kind of instinct, a regular gift."

Study Questions

1. As Rogin "was going toward the subway, he fell into a peculiar state." What is Rogin's "peculiar state"? What does he begin to reminisce about? What revelation does he have early in the story?

2. What type of a person is Joan? Is she dependent or independent? self-indulgent or giving? Give examples from the story to support your evaluation.

3. What type of a person is Rogin? Is he dependent or independent? an observer of life or a participant? cold or loving? Tell how you know.

4. What does Rogin fear? why? What does he do about his fears?

5. Early in the story Rogin comes to the realization that "superimposition is the universal law." What does this mean, personally, to him? What is his "burden"?

6. Do you think Rogin will ever become a father? Why or why not?

7. In the final scene has Rogin clearly voiced his concerns and needs to others, or has he simply given in? What is your final opinion of Rogin?

Annie Dillard   1945 —

Annie Dillard once wrote, "I live by a creek, Tinker's Creek, in a valley in Virginia's Blue Ridge . . . It's a good place to live; there's a lot to think about. The creeks—Tinker and Carvins—are an active mystery, fresh every minute. Theirs is the mystery of continuous creation." Annie Dillard moved to the Roanoke Valley of Virginia in 1965. There she began the observations and writing which became her first prose book, *Pilgrim at Tinker Creek.* The book was enthusiastically received and won a Pulitzer Prize in 1974.

Born in Pittsburgh, Pennsylvania, Dillard now lives in Washington where she has taken up residence "on an island in Puget Sound, in a wooden room furnished by one enormous window, one cat, one spider, and one person." In 1974 she published her first volume of poems, *Tickets for a Prayer Wheel. Holy the Firm,* a book of religious observation, appeared in 1977. *Living By Fiction* and *Teaching a Stone to Talk: Expeditions and Encounters* were published in 1982.

Dillard is not interested in cold observation, but in observation and wonder. The selection here from *Pilgrim at Tinker's Creek* is an excellent example of her ability to observe and to marvel, and to catch that sensation in words.

Seeing

ANNIE DILLARD

WHEN I WAS SIX or seven years old, growing up in Pittsburgh, I used to take a precious penny of my own and hide it for someone else to find. It was a curious compulsion; sadly, I've never been seized by it since. For some reason I always "hid" the penny along the same stretch of sidewalk up the street. I would cradle it at the roots of a sycamore, say, or in a hole left by a chipped-off piece of sidewalk. Then I would take a piece of chalk, and, starting at either end of the block, draw huge arrows leading up to the penny from both directions. After I learned to write I labeled the arrows: SUR-PRISE AHEAD or MONEY THIS WAY. I was greatly excited, during all this arrow-drawing, at the thought of the first lucky passer-by who would receive in this way, regardless of merit, a free gift from the universe. But I never lurked about. I would go straight home and not give the matter another thought, until, some months later, I would be gripped again by the impulse to hide another penny.

It is still the first week in January, and I've got great plans. I've been thinking about seeing. There are lots of things to see, unwrapped gifts and free surprises. The world is fairly studded and strewn with pennies cast broadside from a generous hand. But—and this is the point—who gets excited by a mere penny? If you follow one arrow, if you crouch motionless on a bank to watch a tremulous ripple thrill on the water and are rewarded by the sight of a muskrat kit paddling from its den, will you count that sight a chip of copper only, and go your rueful way? It is dire poverty indeed when a man is so malnourished and fatigued that he won't stoop to pick up a penny. But if you cultivate a healthy poverty and simplicity, so that finding a penny will literally make your day, then, since the world is in fact planted in pennies, you have with your poverty bought a lifetime of days. It is that simple. What you see is what you get.

I used to be able to see flying insects in the air. I'd look ahead and see, not the row of hemlocks across the road, but the air in front of it. My eyes would focus along that column of air, picking out flying insects. But I lost interest, I guess, for I dropped the habit. Now I can see birds. Probably some people can look at the grass at their feet and discover all the crawling creatures. I would like to know grasses and sedges—and care. Then my least journey into the world would be a field trip, a series of happy recognitions. Thoreau, in an expansive mood, exulted, "What a rich book might be made about buds, including, perhaps, sprouts!" It would be nice to think so. I cherish mental images I have of three perfectly happy people. One collects stones. Another—an Englishman, say—watches clouds. The third lives on a coast and collects drops of seawater which he examines microscopically and mounts. But I don't see what the specialist sees, and so I cut myself off, not only from the total picture, but from the various forms of happiness.

Unfortunately, nature is very much a now-you-see-it, now-you-don't affair. A fish flashes, then dissolves in the water before my eyes like so much salt. Deer apparently ascend bodily into heaven; the brightest oriole fades into leaves. These disappearances stun me into stillness and concentration; they say of nature that it conceals with a grand nonchalance, and they say of vision that it is a deliberate gift, the revelation of a dancer who for my eyes only flings away her seven veils. For nature does reveal as well as conceal: now-you-don't-see-it, now-you-do. For a week last September migrating red-winged blackbirds were feeding heavily down by the creek at the back of the house. One day I went out to investigate the racket; I walked up to a tree, an Osage orange, and a hundred birds flew away. They simply materialized out of the tree. I saw a tree, then a whisk of color, then a tree again. I walked closer and another hundred blackbirds took flight. Not a branch, not a twig budged: the birds were apparently weightless as well as invisible. Or, it was as if the leaves of the Osage orange had been freed from a spell in the form of red-winged blackbirds; they flew from the tree, caught my eye in the sky, and vanished. When I looked again at the tree the leaves had reassembled as if nothing had happened. Finally I walked directly to the trunk of the tree and a final hundred, the real diehards, appeared, spread, and vanished. How could so many hide in the tree without my seeing them? The Osage orange, unruffled, looked just as it had looked from the house, when three hundred red-winged blackbirds cried from its crown. I looked downstream where they flew, and they were gone. Searching, I couldn't spot one. I wandered downstream to force them to play their hand, but they'd crossed the creek and scattered. One show to a customer. These appearances catch at my throat; they are the free gifts, the bright coppers at the roots of trees. . . .

But the artificial obvious is hard to see. My eyes account for less than one percent of the weight of my head; I'm bony and dense; I see what I expect. I once spent a full three minutes looking at a bullfrog that was so unexpectedly large I couldn't see it even though a dozen enthusiastic campers were shouting directions. Finally I asked, "What color am I looking for?" and a fellow said, "Green." When at last I picked out the frog, I saw what painters are up against: the thing wasn't green at all, but the color of wet hickory bark.

The lover can see, and the knowledgeable. I visited an aunt and uncle at a quarter-horse ranch in Cody, Wyoming. I couldn't do much of anything useful, but I could, I thought, draw. So, as we all sat around the kitchen table after supper, I produced a sheet of paper and drew a horse. "That's one lame horse," my aunt volunteered. The rest of the family joined in: "Only place to saddle that one is his neck"; "Looks like we better shoot the poor thing, on account of those terrible growths." Meekly, I slid the pencil and paper down the table. Everyone in that family, including my three young cousins, could draw a horse. Beautifully. When the paper came back it looked as though five shining, real quarter horses had been corraled by mistake with a papier-mâché moose; the real horses seemed to gaze at the monster with a steady, puzzled air. I stay away from horses now, but I can do a creditable goldfish. The point is that I just don't know what the lover knows; I just can't see the artificial obvious that those in the know construct. The herpetologist[1] asks the native, "Are there snakes in that ravine?" "Nosir." And the herpetologist comes home with, yessir, three bags full. Are there butterflies on that mountain? Are the bluets in bloom, are there arrowheads here, or fossil shells in the shale? . . .

"Still," wrote van Gogh[2] in a letter, "a great deal of light falls on everything." If we are blinded by darkness, we are also blinded by light. When too much light falls on everything, a special terror results. Peter Freuchen describes the notorious kayak sickness to which Greenland Eskimos are prone. "The Greenland fjords are peculiar for the spells of completely quiet weather, when there is not enough wind to blow out a match and the water is like a sheet of glass. The kayak hunter must sit in his boat without stirring a finger so as not to scare the shy seals away. . . . The sun, low in the sky, sends a glare into his eyes, and the landscape around moves into the realm of the unreal. The reflex from the mirror-like water hypnotizes him, he seems to be unable to move, and all of a sudden it is as if he were floating in a bottomless void, sinking, sinking, and sinking. . . . Horror-stricken, he tries to stir, to cry out, but he cannot, he is completely paralyzed, he just falls and falls." Some hunters are especially cursed with this panic, and bring ruin and sometimes starvation to their families.

Sometimes here in Virginia at sunset low clouds on the southern or northern horizon are completely invisible in the lighted sky. I only know one is there because I can see its reflection in still water. The first time I discovered this mystery I looked from cloud to no-cloud in bewilderment, checking my bearings over and over, thinking maybe the ark of the covenant was just passing by south of Dead Man Mountain. Only much later did I read the explanation: polarized light from the sky is very much weakened by reflection, but the light in clouds isn't polarized. So invisible clouds pass among visible clouds, till all slide over the mountains; so a greater light extinguishes a lesser as though it didn't exist.

In the great meteor shower of August, the Perseid, I wail all day for the shooting stars I miss. They're out there showering down, committing hara-kiri[3] in a flame of fatal attraction, and hissing perhaps at last into the ocean. But at dawn what looks like a blue dome clamps down over me like a lid on a pot. The stars and planets could smash and I'd never know. Only a piece of ashen moon occasionally climbs up or down the inside of the dome, and our local star[4] without surcease explodes on our heads. We have really only that one

---

1 **herpetologist:** an expert in a branch of zoology which deals with reptiles and amphibians.
2 **van Gogh:** Dutch painter.

3 **hara-kiri:** suicide.
4 **local star:** the sun.

light, one source for all power, and yet we must turn away from it by universal decree. Nobody here on the planet seems aware of this strange, powerful taboo, that we all walk about carefully averting our faces, this way and that, lest our eyes be blasted forever.

Darkness appalls and light dazzles; the scrap of visible light that doesn't hurt my eyes hurts my brain. What I see sets me swaying. Size and distance and the sudden swelling of meanings confuse me, bowl me over. I straddle the sycamore log bridge over Tinker Creek in the summer. I look at the lighted creek bottom: snail tracks tunnel the mud in quavering curves. A crayfish jerks, but by the time I absorb what has happened, he's gone in a billowing smokescreen of silt. I look at the water: minnows and shiners. If I'm thinking minnows, a carp will fill my brain till I scream. I look at the water's surface: skaters, bubbles, and leaves sliding down. Suddenly, my own face, reflected, startles me witless. Those snails have been tracking my face! Finally, with a shuddering wrench of the will, I see clouds, cirrus clouds. I'm dizzy, I fall in. This looking business is risky.

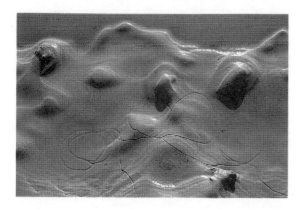

Once I stood on a humped rock on nearby Purgatory Mountain, watching through binoculars the great autumn hawk migration below, until I discovered that I was in danger of joining the hawks on a vertical migration of my own. I was used to binoculars, but not, apparently, to balancing on humped rocks while looking through them. I staggered. Everything advanced and receded by turns; the world was full of unexplained foreshortenings and depths. A distant huge tan object, a hawk the size of an elephant, turned out to be the browned bough of a nearby loblolly pine. I followed a sharp-shinned hawk against a featureless sky, rotating my head unawares as it flew, and when I lowered the glass a glimpse of my own looming shoulder sent me staggering. What prevents the men on Palomar[5] from falling, voiceless and blinded, from their tiny, vaulted chairs? . . .

I chanced on a wonderful book by Marius von Senden, called *Space and Sight*. When Western surgeons discovered how to perform safe cataract operations, they ranged across Europe and America operating on dozens of men and women of all ages who had been blinded by cataracts since birth. Von Senden collected accounts of such cases; the histories are fascinating. Many doctors had tested their patients' sense perceptions and ideas of space both before and after the operations. The vast majority of patients, of both sexes and all ages, had, in von Senden's opinion, no idea of space whatsoever. Form, distance, and size were so many meaningless syllables. A patient "had no idea of depth, confusing it with roundness." Before the operation a doctor would give a blind patient a cube and a sphere; the patient would tongue it or feel it with his hands, and name it correctly. After the operation the doctor would show the same objects to the patient without letting him touch them; now he had no clue whatsoever what he was seeing. One patient called lemonade "square" because it pricked on his tongue as a square shape pricked on the touch of his hands. Of another postoperative patient, the doctor writes, "I have found in her no notion of size, for example,

5 **Palomar:** Mount Palomar in southern California, site of an observatory.

not even within the narrow limits which she might have encompassed with the aid of touch. Thus when I asked her to show me how big her mother was, she did not stretch out her hands, but set her two index-fingers a few inches apart." Other doctors reported their patients' own statements to similar effect. "The room he was in . . . he knew to be but part of the house, yet he could not conceive that the whole house could look bigger"; "Those who are blind from birth . . . have no real conception of height or distance. A house that is a mile away is thought of as nearby, but requiring the taking of a lot of steps. . . . The elevator that whizzes him up and down gives no more sense of vertical distance than does the train of horizontal."

For the newly sighted, vision is pure sensation unencumbered by meaning: "The girl went through the experience that we all go through and forget, the moment we are born. She saw, but it did not mean anything but a lot of different kinds of brightness." Again, "I asked the patient what he could see; he answered that he saw an extensive field of light, in which everything appeared dull, confused, and in motion. He could not distinguish objects." Another patient saw "nothing but a confusion of forms and colours." When a newly sighted girl saw photographs and paintings, she asked, " 'Why do they put those dark marks all over them?' 'Those aren't dark marks,' her mother explained, 'those are shadows. That is one of the ways the eye knows that things have shape. If it were not for shadows many things would look flat.' 'Well, that's how things do look,' Joan answered. 'Everything looks flat with dark patches.' "

But it is the patients' concepts of space that are most revealing. One patient, according to his doctor, "practiced his vision in a strange fashion; thus he takes off one of his boots, throws it some way off in front of him, and then attempts to gauge the distance at which it lies; he takes a few steps towards the boot and tries to grasp it; on failing to reach it, he moves on a step or two and gropes for the boot until he finally gets hold of it." "But even at this stage, after three weeks' experience of seeing," von Senden goes on, " 'space,' as he conceives it, ends with visual space, i.e., with colour-patches that happen to bound his view. He does not yet have the notion that a larger object (a chair) can mask a smaller one (a dog), or that the latter can still be present even though it is not directly seen."

In general the newly sighted see the world as a dazzle of color-patches. They are pleased by the sensation of color, and learn quickly to name the colors, but the rest of seeing is tormentingly difficult. Soon after his operation a patient "generally bumps into one of these colour-patches and observes them to be substantial, since they resist him as tactual objects do. In walking about it also strikes him—or can if he pays attention—that he is continually passing in between the colours he sees, that he can go past a visual object, that a part of it then steadily disappears from view; and that in spite of this, however he twists and turns—whether entering the room from the door, for example, or returning back to it—he always has a visual space in front of him. Thus he gradually comes to realize that there is also a space behind him, which he does not see."

The mental effort involved in these reasonings proves overwhelming for many patients. It oppresses them to realize, if they ever do at all, the tremendous size of the world, which they had previously conceived of as something touchingly manageable. It oppresses them to realize that they have been visible to people all along, perhaps unattractively so, without their knowledge or consent. A disheartening number of them refuse to use their new vision, continuing to go over objects with their tongues, and lapsing into apathy and despair. "The child can see, but will not make use of his sight. Only when pressed can he with difficulty be brought to look at objects in his neighbourhood; but more than a foot away it is impossible to bestir him to the necessary ef-

fort." Of a twenty-one-year-old girl, the doctor relates, "Her unfortunate father, who had hoped for so much from this operation, wrote that his daughter carefully shuts her eyes whenever she wishes to go about the house, especially when she comes to a staircase, and that she is never happier or more at ease than when, by closing her eyelids, she relapses into her former state of total blindness." A fifteen-year-old boy, who was also in love with a girl at the asylum for the blind, finally blurted out, "No, really, I can't stand it any more; I want to be sent back to the asylum again. If things aren't altered, I'll tear my eyes out."

Some do learn to see, especially the young ones. But it changes their lives. One doctor comments on "the rapid and complete loss of that striking and wonderful serenity which is characteristic only of those who have never yet seen." A blind man who learns to see is

ashamed of his old habits. He dresses up, grooms himself, and tries to make a good impression. While he was blind he was indifferent to objects unless they were edible; now, "a sifting of values sets in . . . his thoughts and wishes are mightily stirred and some few of the patients are thereby led into dissimulation, envy, theft and fraud."

On the other hand, many newly sighted people speak well of the world, and teach us how dull is our own vision. To one patient, a human hand, unrecognized, is "something bright and then holes." Shown a bunch of grapes, a boy calls out, "It is dark, blue and shiny. . . . It isn't smooth, it has bumps and hollows." A little girl visits a garden. "She is greatly astonished, and can scarcely be persuaded to answer, stands speechless in front of the tree, which she only names on taking hold of it, and then as 'the tree with the lights in

it.' " Some delight in their sight and give themselves over to the visual world. Of a patient just after her bandages were removed, her doctor writes, "The first things to attract her attention were her own hands; she looked at them very closely, moved them repeatedly to and fro, bent and stretched the fingers, and seemed greatly astonished at the sight." One girl was eager to tell her blind friend that "men do not really look like trees at all," and astounded to discover that her every visitor had an utterly different face. Finally, a twenty-two-year-old girl was dazzled by the world's brightness and kept her eyes shut for two weeks. When at the end of that time she opened her eyes again, she did not recognize any objects, but, "the more she now directed her gaze upon everything about her, the more it could be seen how an expression of gratification and astonishment overspread her features; she repeatedly exclaimed: 'Oh God! How beautiful!'" . . .

Seeing is of course very much a matter of verbalization. Unless I call my attention to what passes before my eyes, I simply won't see it. It is, as Ruskin says, "not merely unnoticed, but in the full, clear sense of the word, un-seen." My eyes alone can't solve analogy tests using figures, the ones which show, with in-creasing elaborations, a big square, then a small square in a big square, then a big tri-angle, and expect me to find a small triangle in a big triangle. I have to say the words, describe what I'm seeing. If Tinker Mountain erupted, I'd be likely to notice. But if I want to notice the lesser cataclysms of valley life, I have to maintain in my head a running description of the present. It's not that I'm observant; it's just that I talk too much. Otherwise, especially in a strange place, I'll never know what's happen-ing. Like a blind man at the ball game, I need a radio.

When I see this way I analyze and pry. I hurl over logs and roll away stones; I study the bank a square foot at a time, probing and tilt-ing my head. Some days when a mist covers the mountains, when the muskrats won't show and the microscope's mirror shatters, I want to climb up the blank blue dome as a man would storm the inside of a circus tent, wildly, dan-gling, and with a steel knife claw a rent in the top, peep, and, if I must, fall.

But there is another kind of seeing that in-volves a letting go. When I see this way I sway transfixed and emptied. The difference be-tween the two ways of seeing is the difference between walking with and without a camera. When I walk with a camera, I walk from shot to shot, reading the light on a calibrated meter. When I walk without a camera, my own shut-ter opens, and the moment's light prints on my own silver gut. When I see this second way I am above all an unscrupulous observer. . . .

Study Questions

1. As the title indicates, this selection is about different levels of seeing. What are the levels described?

2. How does Dillard's use of her childhood habit of hiding pennies relate to her discussion of seeing?

3. After describing several cases in which light can be frightening, Dillard says, "This looking business is risky." What do you think she means?

4. According to this essay, why do some previously blind people have dif-ficulty in accepting sight? How is this problem related to Dillard's obser-vation that seeing can be risky?

5. At the end of the selection Dillard describes two ways of using one's sight as "walking with and without a camera." What is the distinction? What does it mean to be an "unscrupulous observer"?

6. Find examples of descriptions which helped you to "see" the thing be-ing described.

John Crowe Ransom   1888-1974

A Methodist minister's son, John Crowe
Ransom spent his boyhood in small towns
in Tennessee. He entered Vanderbilt University at the age of fifteen and later became a
Rhodes scholar at Oxford University in
England. After his return to the United
States, he taught English at Vanderbilt for
nearly twenty-five years. During this period
he published much of his poetry in a little
magazine called *The Fugitive.* Then in 1937
he moved to Kenyon College in Ohio,
where he founded and edited for twenty
years the *Kenyon Review,* one of the nation's
most influential literary quarterlies. In 1941
he published a book called *The New Criticism,* which set forth a theory of reading
literary texts closely without reference to
information outside the work.

Dead Boy

JOHN CROWE RANSOM

The little cousin is dead, by foul subtraction,
A green bough from Virginia's aged tree,
And none of the county kin like the transaction,
Nor some of the world of outer dark, like me.

A boy not beautiful, nor good, nor clever,   5
A black cloud full of storms too hot for keeping,
A sword beneath his mother's heart—yet never
Woman bewept her babe as this is weeping.

A pig with a pasty face, so I had said,
Squealing for cookies, kinned by poor pretense   10
With a noble house. But the little man quite dead,
I see the forbears' antique lineaments.

The elder men have strode by the box of death
To the wide flag porch, and muttering low send round
The bruit[1] of the day. O friendly waste of breath!   15
Their hearts are hurt with a deep dynastic wound.

He was pale and little, the foolish neighbors say;
The first-fruits, saith the Preacher, the Lord hath taken;
But this was the old tree's late branch wrenched away,
Grieving the sapless limbs, the shorn and shaken.   20

---

1 **bruit** (brüt): *Archaic.* din or noise.

Study Questions

1. How has the poet employed unusual diction and unflattering details to keep the poem from becoming merely another sentimental comment on death?

2. In which lines does the narrator's reaction appear? How does his reaction differ from that of the boy's family?

3. Contrast the feelings of the neighbors, the preacher, and the relatives in the last stanza.

4. Where does the tree image appear in the poem? What does "tree" refer to in the second line? What do "sapless limbs" in the last line refer to?

Wallace Stevens 1879-1955

For over forty years Wallace Stevens was both a full-time poet and a full-time insurance company executive in Hartford, Connecticut. He was successful in both roles. Stevens was born in Pennsylvania and educated at Harvard College and New York University Law School. He was practicing law in New York City when his first poems were published in *Poetry* magazine in 1914. Eventually his volumes of poetry were brought together in *The Collected Poems of*

Wallace Stevens, which received the National Book Award and a Pulitzer Prize in 1955.

The reader who is puzzled by "Thirteen Ways of Looking at a Blackbird" should be consoled by the fact that professional critics have widely disagreed in their interpretations. The poem probably does not have a single identifiable meaning. Instead it is an effort to tease the reader's imagination through "looking" (seeing, musing, perceiving, imagining).

Thirteen Ways of Looking at a Blackbird

WALLACE STEVENS

I

Among twenty snowy mountains,
The only moving thing
Was the eye of the blackbird.

II

I was of three minds,
Like a tree
In which there are three blackbirds.

III

The blackbird whirled in the autumn winds.
It was a small part of the pantomime.

IV

A man and a woman
Are one.
A man and a woman and a blackbird
Are one.

V

I do not know which to prefer,
The beauty of inflections
Or the beauty of innuendoes,
The blackbird whistling
Or just after.

VI

Icicles filled the long window
With barbaric glass.
The shadow of the blackbird
Crossed it, to and fro.
The mood
Traced in the shadow
An indecipherable cause.

LUCIFER *Jackson Pollack* 1947

VII

O thin men of Haddam,[1]
Why do you imagine golden birds?
Do you not see how the blackbird
Walks around the feet
Of the women about you?

VIII

I know noble accents
And lucid, inescapable rhythms;
But I know, too,
That the blackbird is involved
In what I know.

---

1 **Haddam**: a town in Connecticut.

IX

When the blackbird flew out of sight,
It marked the edge
Of one of many circles.

X

At the sight of blackbirds
Flying in a green light,
Even the bawds of euphony
Would cry out sharply.

XI

He rode over Connecticut
In a glass coach.
Once, a fear pierced him,
In that he mistook
The shadow of his equipage[2]
For blackbirds.

---

2 **equipage**: carriage outfitted with horses and servants.

XII

The river is moving.
The blackbird must be flying.

XIII

It was evening all afternoon.
It was snowing
And it was going to snow.
The blackbird sat
In the cedar-limbs.

Study Questions

1. Each of the thirteen stanzas may be read as a little poem in itself, a little picture designed to stimulate the reader's imagination. For example, stanza I establishes the blackbird in its natural setting and suggests at least four contrasts between the bird and the mountains. Which can you identify?

2. How does stanza II bring a human element into the scene? In what way do stanzas III and IV expand the idea of relationships in nature?

3. Stanza V introduces an aesthetic response to nature. What is the distinction made between "inflections" and "innuendoes"? Where else does the poem deal with questions of beauty?

4. Stanza VI raises the question of appearance vs. reality by referring to the "shadow" of the blackbird. What other references in this stanza are there to appearances or to impermanence? Variations on the theme of perception are also evident in stanzas VII and XI. Can you find them?

5. Other thematic concerns in the poem are the passage of time and seasonal change. Find examples of both of these.

6. This poem has a structural development. It is not just thirteen random thoughts on blackbirds. Discuss the ways in which the poet has arranged his ideas.

Richard Eberhart   1904—

Richard Eberhart was born in Minnesota
and educated at Dartmouth College in New
Hampshire. Some of his earliest work appeared while he was a student at Cambridge
University in England in an anthology, *New
Signatures*. The poets included there had in
common a desire to enrich the language and
style of poetry for the new age. This was in
1932; however, Eberhart continues to enrich
the language. Among his numerous publications are: *A Bravery of Earth* (1930), *Reading
the Spirit* (1936), *The Visionary Farms* (a
drama) 1952, and *Collected Poems 1930–1960*.
He has also been awarded the Bollingen
Prize in 1962 and the Pulitzer Prize in
1966.

"The Horse Chestnut Tree" is characteristic of Eberhart's ability to perceive "sermons
in stones"—or, in this case, trees.

The Horse Chestnut Tree

RICHARD EBERHART

Boys in sporadic but tenacious droves
Come with sticks, as certainly as Autumn,
To assault the great horse chestnut tree.

There is a law governs their lawlessness.
Desire is in them for a shining amulet   5
And the best are those that are highest up.

They will not pick them easily from the ground.
With shrill arms they fling to the higher branches,
To hurry the work of nature for their pleasure.

I have seen them trooping down the street   10
Their pockets stuffed with chestnuts shucked, unshucked.
It is only evening keeps them from their wish.

Sometimes I run out in a kind of rage
To chase the boys away: I catch an arm,
Maybe, and laugh to think of being the lawgiver.   15

I was once such a young sprout myself
And fingered in my pocket the prize and trophy.
But still I moralize upon the day

And see that we, outlaws on God's property,
Fling out imagination beyond the skies,   20
Wishing a tangible good from the unknown.

And likewise death will drive us from the scene
With the great flowering world unbroken yet,
Which we held in idea, a little handful.

Study Questions

1. Describe what is happening in "The Horse Chestnut Tree." What words and phrases indicate that this is a regular occurrence?

2. The speaker says of the boys who assault his tree, "There is a law that governs their lawlessness." What is that law?

3. Why does the speaker laugh at "being the lawgiver"? How does that fit with his showing "a kind of rage"?

4. After describing what happens, the speaker begins to think about the event, beginning with line 16. What are the speaker's ideas about the event? How does the speaker relate this event to larger, more profound ideas?

5. Eberhart employs some unusual word combinations which result in an efficiency of expression. For example, in line 1, he refers to "tenacious droves" of boys. What does this combination of words mean to you? Other unusual combinations are:

   line 8—shrill arms   line 23—flowering world
   line 21—tangible good   line 24—held in idea, a little handful

   What do these mean to you? Can you find other similar phrases in the poem?

Theodore Roethke   1908-1963

Theodore Roethke (ret' kē) was one of the many contemporary American poets who chose academic life along with the profession of a poet. He was, for several years before his death, Professor of English at the University of Washington. Among the several collections of his poetry are *The Lost Son* (1948) and *The Waking* (1953), for which he won a Pulitzer Prize.

The countryside in his native state of Michigan and the greenhouse owned by his father play a dominant role in his poetry. They provided him with a feeling for the miracle of nature. They also encouraged an awareness of the roots of things that seem to terrify yet discipline the spirit.

The Waking

THEODORE ROETHKE

I wake to sleep, and take my waking slow.
I feel my fate in what I cannot fear.
I learn by going where I have to go.

We think by feeling. What is there to know?
I hear my being dance from ear to ear.   5
I wake to sleep, and take my waking slow.

Of those so close beside me, which are you?
God bless the Ground! I shall walk softly there,
And learn by going where I have to go.

Light takes the Tree; but who can tell us how?   10
The lowly worm climbs up a winding stair;
I wake to sleep, and take my waking slow.

Great Nature has another thing to do
To you and me; so take the lively air,
And, lovely, learn by going where to go.   15

This shaking keeps me steady. I should know.
What falls away is always. And is near.
I wake to sleep, and take my waking slow.
I learn by going where I have to go.

Study Questions

1. If the reader paraphrases the opening four words of the poem as "I am born to die," what would the following words in stanza 1 mean: "waking," "fate," "going where I have to go"?

2. The speaker seems certain of the relationship between life and death but is still puzzled. What do you think "What is there to know?" in line 4 means? In line 7 and line 10 there are also questions. What do they indicate?

3. The images in stanza 4 show the speaker's awareness of the interrelationship among three levels of life: vegetation, lower organic life, and higher organic life. What images represent each of these levels? How are all three going through the same life-to-death process?

4. Although the speaker accepts the inevitability of death, another feeling grows out of the acceptance. Stanza 5 states that Nature has "another thing" (other than death) to do for us. What is that other thing?

5. The speaker emphasizes his affirmative approach to life by repetition. Point out the two lines which express this affirmation and trace them through the poem.

A. R. Ammons   1926—

More than any other living modern poet,
A.R. ("Archie") Ammons succeeds in relating the intricacies of science to the mystery
of human nature in casual language.
Ammons, born in Whiteville, North Carolina, is now Professor of English at Cornell
University, Ithaca, New York. Among his
prolific output are *Sphere* (1974), *Diversifica-
tions* (1975), *The Snow Poems* (1978), and
Collected Poems, for which he won the National Book Award for Poetry in 1973. His
most recent book, *A Coast of Trees* (1981)
was given a National Book Critics' Circle
Award.

SHINING BACK *Sam Francis* 1958

Involved

A.R. AMMONS

They say last night radiation
storms spilled down the meridians,
cool green tongues of solar
flares, non-human & not
to be humanized, licking at   5
human life: an arctic
air mass shielded us: had I been
out I'd have said,
knowing them masked, burn me: or
thanks for the show: 10
my spine would have flared
sympathetic colors:
as it is I slept through,
burning from a distant source.

Study Questions

1. What is the frightening event described in the first seven lines of this
   poem?

2. In lines 7–12 what does the speaker say his reaction to the event would
   have been?

3. In the final two lines what actually was his reaction?

Gwendolyn Brooks   1917 —

It has been said that Gwendolyn Brooks has "provided a new kind of poetic statement and started a trend that moved poetry from the realm of the academic gown to the realm of the big town."[1] This statement sums up Brooks's unquestioned craftsmanship which she has applied to describing the poor and desperate of Chicago, her home. She also applies her poetic talent to racial discrimination and the rigors of urban life.

In addition to being an accomplished, honored poet, Brooks is also revered for the assistance she has provided to younger poets. Brooks has published several volumes of poetry including *A Street in Bronzeville* (1945), *The Bean Eaters* (1961), *Riot* (1969), *Family Pictures* (1970) and *To Disembark* (1981).

The two poems included here are from her Pulitzer Prize winning book, *Annie Allen* (1950). Although it is not immediately apparent, both of them deal with concepts which are a part of the long tradition of her poetry.

---

1 *Black Writers of America*, New York, The Macmillan Company, 1972, p. 713.

truth

GWENDOLYN BROOKS

And if sun comes
How shall we greet him?
Shall we not dread him,
Shall we not fear him
After so lengthy a   5
Session with shade?

Though we have wept for him,
Though we have prayed
All through the night-years—
What if we wake one shimmering morning to   10
Hear the fierce hammering
Of his firm knuckles
Hard on the door?

Shall we not shudder?—
Shall we not flee   15
Into the shelter, the dear thick shelter
Of the familiar
Propitious haze?

Sweet is it, sweet is it
To sleep in the coolness   20
Of snug unawareness.

The dark hangs heavily
Over the eyes.

"Life for my child is simple, and is good"

GWENDOLYN BROOKS

Life for my child is simple, and is good.
He knows his wish. Yes, but that is not all.
Because I know mine too.
And we both want joy of undeep and unabiding things,
Like kicking over a chair or throwing blocks out of a window   5
Or tipping over an ice box pan
Or snatching down curtains or fingering an electric outlet
Or a journey or a friend or an illegal kiss.
No. There is more to it than that.
It is that he has never been afraid.   10
Rather, he reaches out and lo the chair falls with a beautiful crash,
And the blocks fall, down on the people's heads,
And the water comes slooshing sloppily out across the floor.
And so forth.
Not that success, for him, is sure, infallible.   15
But never has he been afraid to reach.
His lesions are legion.
But reaching is his rule.

Study Questions

1. Truth is often symbolized by illumination and ignorance by darkness. How does the speaker in "truth" use this tradition as an extended metaphor? Find examples.

2. What are the implications of truth's having to *hammer* fiercely with *firm* knuckles *hard* on the door (Lines 11–13)?

3. In line 18 of "truth," why is the haze "propitious"? Why do you think "sleep" is referred to as "sweet" in lines 19–20?

4. In "Life for my child is simple" what is it that both the speaker and the child want?

5. In line 10 of "Life for my child is simple," a basic difference between the two of them is expressed. What is this difference? Why is it important?

6. What do lines 15–18 in "Life for my child is simple" mean to you? Do you think the speaker approves of the child's lack of fear? disapproves? Why?

7. Find examples in both poems of alliteration and of onomatopoeia.

Composition

1. In both poems Brooks uses simple, straightforward language to communicate profound ideas. Find five examples of simple statements which imply something more in the context of the poem. In an essay, repeat each statement, then explain its meaning to you. For example: ". . . never has he been afraid to reach." This means that the child is always eager to try new things.

2. Following Brooks's examples, write a short poem of your own. Decide on the idea you want to use. Think of simple examples which express that idea. Write them down. Try to word them so that your lines form a rhythmical pattern.

Richard Wilbur   1921 —

Richard Wilbur has received practically every major honor available to an American writer, including a Pulitzer Prize in 1957. He has been writing poems since he was eight. As a student he edited his high school newspaper in Montclair, New Jersey, and the college paper at Amherst College. His books of poems include *The Beautiful Changes* (1947), *Ceremony* (1950), *Things of This World* (1956), *Advice to a Prophet* (1961), *Walking to Sleep* (1969), and *The Mind Reader* (1977). He has also translated French poems and plays, Russian and Spanish poems, and provided the lyrics for the Lillian Hellman-Leonard Bernstein comic opera version of *Candide*. Wilbur's idea is that a poem is not addressed to anyone in particular, but has its own life and its own identity. "The Beautiful Changes" is an example of this.

The Beautiful Changes

RICHARD WILBUR

One wading a Fall meadow finds on all sides
The Queen Anne's Lace lying like lilies
On water; it glides
So from the walker, it turns
Dry grass to a lake, as the slightest shade of you   5
Valleys my mind in fabulous blue Lucernes.[1]

The beautiful changes as a forest is changed
By a chameleon's tuning his skin to it;

---

1. **Lucerne:** scenic lake in central Switzerland.

As a mantis, arranged
On a green leaf, grows   10
Into it, makes the leaf leafier, and proves
Any greenness is deeper than anyone knows.

Your hands hold roses always in a way that says
They are not only yours; the beautiful changes
In such kind ways,   15
Wishing ever to sunder
Things and things' selves for a second finding, to lose
For a moment all that it touches back to wonder.

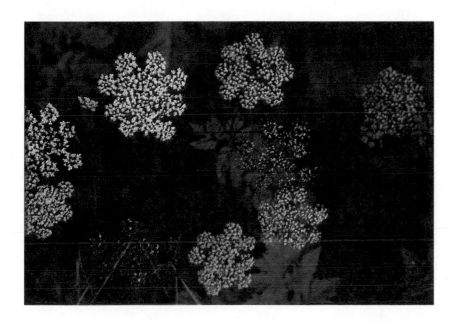

Study Questions

1. What are three examples used to demonstrate how the beautiful in nature changes and increases?

2. The speaker says the person to whom the poem is addressed (lines 5, 13–14) also causes beauty to take on additional meaning. How does the speaker say this happens?

3. What is the metaphor in stanza one? How does it help the reader to "see" the meadow?

4. Find other examples of imagery which help depict the scene.

Robert Hayden   1913-1980

A teacher, scholar, and dramatic critic as well as poet, Robert Hayden brought to his craft a deep sense of history. Hayden's poetry earned him several fellowships and awards, including election to the American Academy of Poets in 1975 and appointment as the Library of Congress's consultant for poetry in 1976. Born in Detroit, he received degrees from Wayne State University and the University of Michigan. He taught at Fisk University and at the University of Michigan. Among Hayden's many publications are *Heart Shape in the Dust* (1940), *A Ballad of Remembrance* (1962), *Words in the Mourning Time* (1970), and an anthology of the poetry of Afro-Americans, *Kaliedoscope* (1967).

Some of Hayden's best work were his Afro-American history poems which he researched carefully. One of them on Frederick Douglass is included here along with a much later poem on a contemporary topic.

Frederick Douglass

ROBERT HAYDEN

When it is finally ours, this freedom, this liberty, this beautiful
and terrible thing, needful to man as air,
usable as the earth; when it belongs at last to our children,
when it is truly instinct, brainmatter, diastole, systole,[1]
reflex action; when it is finally won; when it is more   5
than the gaudy mumbo jumbo of politicians:
this man, this Douglass, this former slave, this Negro
beaten to his knees, exiled, visioning a world
where none is lonely, none hunted, alien,
this man, superb in love and logic, this man   10
shall be remembered. Oh, not with statues' rhetoric,
not with legends and poems and wreaths of bronze alone,
but with the lives grown out of his life, the lives
fleshing his dream of the needful beautiful thing.

---

1 **diastole, systole** (dī as′ tlē, sis′ tlē): normal rhythmical
dilation and contraction of the heart

Study Questions

1. What is the meaning of lines 1–6?

2. How is Douglass described in lines 7–11? How does this characterization correspond to Douglass's autobiography (page 289)?

3. What are the ways (lines 11–12) in which the speaker says Douglass might be remembered? How does the speaker say Douglass will be chiefly remembered?

4. Paraphrase the last two lines. How is the word "needful" used earlier in the poem?

5. What is the form in which this poem is written?

Astronauts

ROBERT HAYDEN

Armored in oxygen,
    faceless in visors—
mirrormasks reflecting
    the mineral glare and
shadow of moonscape—   5
· they walk slowmotion
floating
    the lifeless
dust of Taurus
    Littrow. And Wow, they   10
exclaim, oh boy, this is it.

    And sing, exulting
(though trained to be wary
    of "emotion and
philosophy"), breaking   15
    the calcined stillness
of once Absolute Otherwhere.

Risking edges, earthlings
    to whom only

their machines are friendly   20
    (and God's radar-
watching eye?), they
    labor at gathering
proof of hypothesis;
    in snowshine of sunlight   25
dangerous as radium
    probe detritus[1] for clues.

    What is it we wish them
to find for us, as
    we watch them on our   30
screens? They loom there
    heroic antiheroes,
smaller than myth and
    poignantly human.
Why are we troubled?   35
    What do we want of these men?
What do we want of ourselves?

1 **detritus** (di tri' təs): debris, loose particles
formed by the disintegration of rocks.

Study Questions

1. How are the astronauts described? How is their reaction to the moon landing described?

2. What words and phrases are used to recreate the atmosphere of the moon-walk? How are they effective? ineffective?

3. What is the tone of the poem: serious? humorous? puzzled? How does the rhythmic pattern contribute to the tone?

4. Why do you think the four questions of the last stanza are left unanswered? What answers can you supply?

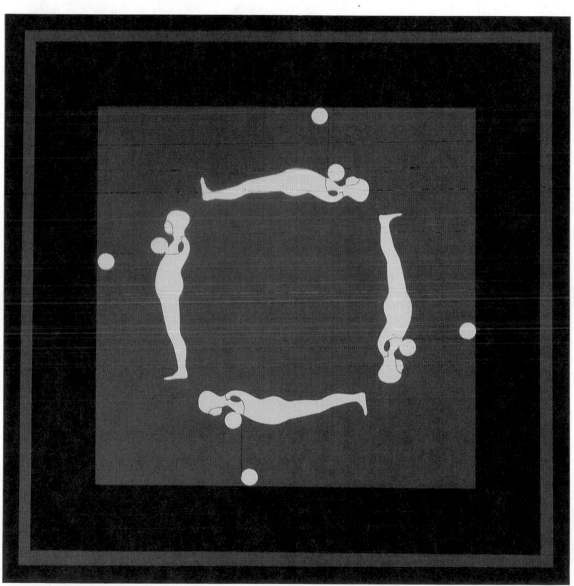

FALLING MAN SERIES:
FOUR FIGURES ON AN ORANGE SQUARE
Ernest Trova 1965

Kuangchi C. Chang 1920 —

Kuangchi C. Chang studied Chinese art and literature in his native Shanghai before coming to the United States. In 1945 he became a graduate student in architecture at Columbia University. After a brief visit to China he returned to the United States in 1949 and has remained here since then. Chang has worked as an architect in New York City and taught oriental art at the University of Oklahoma. His poetry has appeared in a variety of American periodicals. The following poem concerns the experiences of a refugee from Communism.

Garden of My Childhood

KUANGCHI C. CHANG

"Run, run, run,"
Whispered the vine,
"A horde is on the march no Great Wall[1] can halt."
But in the garden of my childhood
The old maple was painting a sunset   5
And the crickets were singing a carol;
No, I had no wish to run.

"Run, run, run,"
Gasped the wind,
"The horde has entered the Wall."   10

---

1 **Great Wall:** 1500 mile wall between China and Mongolia.

Down the scorched plain rode the juggernaut
And crossed the Yangtse[2] as if it were a ditch;
The proverbial rats had abandoned the ship
But I had no intention of abandoning
The garden of my childhood.   15

"Run, run, run,"
Roared the sea,
"Run before the bridge is drawn."
In the engulfed calm after the storm
The relentless tom-tom of the rice-sprout song   20
Finally ripped my armor,
And so I ran.

I ran past the old maple by the terraced hall
And the singing crickets under the latticed wall,
And I kept on running down the walk   25
Paved with pebbles of memory big and small
Without turning to look until I was out of the gate
Through which there be no return at all.

Now, eons later and worlds away,
The running is all done   30
For I am at my destination: Another garden,
Where the unpebbled walk awaits tomorrow's footprints.
Where my old maple will come with the sunset's glow
And my crickets will sing under the wakeful pillow.

---

2 **Yangtse** (yang' tsē): river in China.

Study Questions

1. What are the speaker's reasons for not leaving at the first warning?
2. In stanza three, what force finally persuades the speaker to escape?
3. How does the choice of words contribute to the rapid movement in stanza three?
4. Explain how the central metaphor of the garden relates to both the childhood past and the adult present.
5. How is the last stanza another statement of the American Dream?
6. Contrast this poet's use of the garden image with that of Amy Lowell in "Patterns" (page 490).

Adrienne Rich   1929——

A native of Baltimore, Maryland, Adrienne Rich published her first book of poems, *A Change of World* (1951), during her senior year at Radcliffe College. Other books include *The Diamond Cutters* (1955), *Snapshots of a Daughter-in-Law* (1967), *Diving into the Wreck* (1973), which won the National Book Award, and *Poems 1974–1977*. Her latest work is entitled *A Wild Patience Has Taken Me This Far: Poems 1978–1981*. She learned Dutch in Holland and translated modern Dutch poetry. She has also taught at City College in New York. The subject matter of her poems ranges from intensely personal experiences to radical political and social themes.

Ghost of a Chance

ADRIENNE RICH

You see a man
trying to think.

You want to say
to everything:
Keep off! Give him room!   5
But you only watch,
terrified
the old consolations
will get him at last
like a fish   10
half-dead from flopping
and almost crawling
across the shingle,
almost breathing
the raw, agonizing   15
air
till a wave
pulls it back blind into the triumphant
sea.

IBERIA #2 *Robert Motherwell* 1958

Study Questions

1. A man "trying to think" is compared to a struggling fish. Explain the simile.
2. What could be the "old consolations" which may keep the man from thinking?
3. Why is thinking so difficult?

Composition

1. In a brief essay, explain how "Ghost of a Chance" represents the theme of The Individual. Use examples from the poem to support your statement.
2. Write a description of a situation where other influences interfered with your ability to think. Describe the situation. Tell what interfered and how you were able to cope with it.

Amiri Baraka   1934—

Amiri Baraka was educated at Howard University in Washington, D.C., and Columbia University in New York City. As LeRoi Jones, living in Greenwich Village, he published two volumes of poetry, *Preface to a Twenty Volume Suicide Note* (1961) and *The Dead Lecturer* (1964). He also wrote a book of essays examining a variety of topics having to do with the experiences of African-Americans entitled *Home* (1966). *Blues People* (1963) and *Black Music* (1967) examined the music of African-Americans. Baraka has also written two plays, *Dutchman* and *The Slave* (both 1964). Baraka has been politically active in his home, Newark, New Jersey, in recent years and continues to write. *Selected Poetry of Amiri Baraka/LeRoi Jones* was published in 1979. The poem included here is from his earlier work, and though completely different in tone and subject matter from his recent work, it is an excellent example of his ability to use ordinary words in new ways.

Preface to a Twenty Volume Suicide Note

(for Kellie Jones, born 16 May 1959)

AMIRI BARAKA

Lately, I've become accustomed to the way
The ground opens up and envelops me
Each time I go out to walk the dog.
Or the broad-edged silly music the wind
Makes when I run for a bus . . .   5

Things have come to that.

And now, each night I count the stars,
And each night I get the same number.
And when they will not come to be counted,
I count the holes they leave.   10

Nobody sings anymore.

And then last night, I tiptoed up
To my daughter's room and heard her
Talking to someone, and when I opened
The door, there was no one there . . .   15
Only she on her knees, peeking into

Her own clasped hands.

Study Questions

1. Each of the three stanzas of this poem offers a description of some aspect of the speaker's experience and concludes with a single line of interpretation. In the first stanza, when the poet says, "Things have come to that," what do you think he means?

2. What kind of activity does the speaker describe in the second stanza? How is that description related to "Nobody sings anymore"?

3. The tone of the third stanza is different. How does the speaker signal the change? What is the nature of the change?

Isabella Stewart Gardner   1915—

Isabella Gardner, born in suburban Boston,
was formerly an actress. She starred in such
plays as Noel Coward's *Blithe Spirit* with
Dennis King. She was also associate editor
of *Poetry* magazine. Her books of poetry are
Birthdays from the Ocean (1955), *The Looking
Glass* (1961), and *West of Childhood* (1965).

Summer Remembered

ISABELLA STEWART GARDNER

Sounds sum and summon the remembering of summers.
The humming of the sun
The mumbling in the honey-suckle vine
The whirring in the clovered grass
The pizzicato plinkle of ice in an auburn   5
uncle's amber glass.
The whing of father's racquet and the whack
of brother's bat on cousin's ball
and calling voices call-
ing voices spilling voices . . .   10

The munching of saltwater at the splintered dock
The slap and slop of waves on little sloops
The quarreling of oarlocks hours across the bay
The canvas sails that bleat as they
are blown. The heaving buoy bell-   15
ing HERE I am
HERE you are HEAR HEAR

listen listen listen
The gramophone is wound
the music goes round and around   20
BYE BYE BLUES LINDY'S COMING

TEN FOOT FLOWERS *Andy Warhol*

voices calling calling calling
"Children! Children! Time's Up
Time's Up"

Merrily sturdily wantonly the familial voices   25
cheerily chidingly call to the children TIME'S UP
and the mute children's unvoiced clamor sacks the summer air
crying Mother Mother are you there?

Study Questions

1. The first line sets forth the purpose of the poem. What types of sounds does the speaker remember?
2. How does the poet vary the diction in the list of sounds to avoid monotony? Find examples of alliteration and internal rhyme. What other rhythmical patterns are used?
3. Why would the catalog of memories here be suitable for one of the main characters in Wilder's *Our Town* (see page 533)?

Mari Evans

Mari Evans writes not only poetry, but also lyrics and music. Her short stories and articles have appeared in *Black Books Bulletin, First World* and numerous other journals. In addition to lecturing throughout the United States, she has also taught at Indiana, Northwestern, Purdue, and Cornell universities. Evans was born in Toledo, Ohio, but has spent most of her adult life in Indianapolis, Indiana. Evans has been a John Hay Whitney Fellow and received a Woodrow Wilson Foundation grant. She also has served as a consultant for the Discovery Grant Program of the National Endowment for the Arts. Though continuing to write poetry, Evans is also engaged in an ongoing effort to produce positive Black literature for children. Among her growing list of children's books are *Singing Black, I Look at Me, JD,* and most recently, *Jim Flying High.*

"I Am A Black Woman" is the title poem of her second volume of poetry, which received the First Annual Poetry Award of the Black Academy of Arts and Letters. Her most recent book of poetry is *Nightstar* (1981).

I Am A Black Woman

MARI EVANS

I am a black woman
the music of my song
some sweet arpeggio of tears
is written in a minor key
and I   5
can be heard humming in the night
Can be heard
   humming
in the night

I saw my mate leap screaming to the sea   10
and I/with these hands/cupped the lifebreath
from my issue in the canebrake
I lost Nat's[1] swinging body in a rain of tears

---

1 **Nat:** Nat Turner, hanged for leading a slave rebellion in 1831.

and heard my son scream all the way from Anzio[2]
for Peace he never knew. . . . I   15
learned Da Nang and Pork Chop Hill[3]
in anguish
Now my nostrils know the gas
and these trigger tire/d fingers
seek the softness in my warrior's beard   20

I
am a black woman
tall as a cypress
strong
beyond all definition still   25
defying place
and time
and circumstance
  assailed
    impervious   30
      indestructible
Look
  on me and be
renewed

---

2 **Anzio:** in Italy, site of a battle in World War II.
3 **Da Nang . . . Pork Chop Hill:** site of U. S. military
base in Viet Nam; battle site in Korea.

Study Questions

1. How does the speaker describe her music? What does the humming represent?

2. In the second stanza the speaker lists the trials she has seen by alluding to certain historical events. What are these allusions?

3. In lines 18–20, there is a change in tone. What does the change signal? How does the language of the poem change?

4. What is the response to the generations of suffering? What is the tone of the last stanza?

5. Do you think the events named in stanza two justify the speaker's description in lines 28–30?

6. Compare and contrast the rhythmical patterns of the three stanzas. How does the rhythm reinforce the language?

Robert Lowell   1917 - 1977

Robert Lowell continued the family tradition of writing poetry. Other poets in his Boston family were Amy Lowell (see page 490) and James Russell Lowell. Robert Lowell became one of America's most honored poets. He won two Pulitzer Prizes for his poetry—the first for *Lord Weary's Castle* (1947) and the second for *The Dolphin* (1974). His last book was *Day by Day*, published the week of his death.

Water

ROBERT LOWELL

It was a Maine lobster town—
each morning boatloads of hands
pushed off for granite
quarries on the islands,

and left dozens of bleak   5
white frame houses stuck
like oyster shells
on a hill of rock,

and below us, the sea lapped
the raw little match-stick   10
mazes of a weir,
where the fish for bait were trapped.

Remember? We sat on a slab of rock.
From this distance in time,
it seems the color   15
of iris, rotting and turning purpler,

but it was only
the usual gray rock
turning the usual green
when drenched by the sea.   20

The sea drenched the rock
at our feet all day,
and kept tearing away
flake after flake.

One night you dreamed   25
you were a mermaid clinging to a wharf-pile,
and trying to pull
off the barnacles with your hands.

We wished our two souls
might return like gulls   30
to the rock. In the end,
the water was too cold for us.

Study Questions

1. Where are the two people sitting to observe the Maine lobster town?
2. What words contribute to the atmosphere of gloom in the poem?
3. What does the sea symbolize here?
4. What are the wharf-pile and mermaid images used to describe?
5. What is the theme of the poem?

Sylvia Plath   1932 - 1963

Sylvia Plath has been noted as the writer who renewed for poets the gothic tradition. After being graduated *summa cum laude* from Smith College, Sylvia Plath went to Cambridge University on a Fulbright grant. In England she married the English poet, Ted Hughes, and became a celebrated literary figure. Plath was not comfortable with the attention which she received and questioned her own worth. Plath's poetry is frequently bizarre and she was perpetually concerned with her own death. She published *The Colossus* (1960) and *Ariel* (1963), both books of poems. *The Bell Jar,* an autobiographical novel, was published in 1963. In that same year she committed suicide. Many of her best poems have been published posthumously by her husband in *Sylvia Plath: The Collected Poems* (1982).

Mushrooms

SYLVIA PLATH

Overnight, very
Whitely, discreetly,
Very quietly

Our toes, our noses
Take hold on the loam,   5
Acquire the air.

Nobody sees us,
Stops us, betrays us;
The small grains make room.

Soft fists insist on   10
Heaving the needles,
The leafy bedding,

Even the paving.
Our hammers, our rams,
Earless and eyeless,   15

Perfectly voiceless,
Widen the crannies,
Shoulder through holes. We

Diet on water,
On crumbs of shadow,   20
Bland-mannered, asking

Little or nothing.
So many of us!
So many of us!

We are shelves, we are   25
Tables, we are meek,
We are edible,

Nudgers and shovers
In spite of ourselves.
Our kind multiplies: 30

We shall by morning
Inherit the earth.
Our foot's in the door.

Study Questions

1. Who is speaking in this poem? What is the effect of this point of view on the tone of the poem?
2. How is the subject of the poem reflected in its rhythm and sound?
3. Point out examples of language which are especially vivid in portraying the mushrooms.
4. Discuss the meaning and force of the final stanza.

Robert Penn Warren 1905—

Robert Penn Warren is a Kentuckian who went to Vanderbilt University in Tennessee. He then studied at Oxford University in England as a Rhodes scholar. He has distinguished himself as teacher, critic, poet, and novelist. His best-known work is probably *All the King's Men,* a novel inspired by the career of the Louisiana politician Huey Long. The novel won him a Pulitzer Prize in 1947. In 1958 he won another Pulitzer for *Promises,* the volume from which "Gold Glade" is taken. He has taught at Louisiana State University, the University of Minnesota, and Yale University. As a critic, he has been one of the most influential literary figures in this century.

Gold Glade

ROBERT PENN WARREN

Wandering, in autumn, the woods of boyhood,
Where cedar, black, thick, rode the ridge,
Heart aimless as rifle, boy-blankness of mood,
I came where ridge broke, and the great ledge,
Limestone, set the toe high as treetop by dark edge   5

Of a gorge, and water hid, grudging and grumbling,
And I saw, in mind's eye, foam white on
Wet stone, stone wet-black, white water tumbling,
And so went down, and with some fright on
Slick boulders, crossed over. The gorge-depth drew night on,   10

But high over high rock and leaf-lacing, sky
Showed yet bright, and declivity wooed
My foot by the quietening stream, and so I
Went on, in quiet, through the beech wood:
There, in gold light, where the glade gave, it stood.   15

The glade was geometric, circular, gold,
No brush or weed breaking that bright gold of leaf-fall.
In the center it stood, absolute and bold
Beyond any heart-hurt, or eye's grief-fall.
Gold-massy in air, it stood in gold light-fall,   20

No breathing of air, no leaf now gold-falling,
No tooth-stitch of squirrel, or any far fox bark,
No woodpecker coding, or late jay calling.
Silence: gray-shagged, the great shagbark
Gave forth gold light. There could be no dark.   25

But of course dark came, and I can't recall
What county it was, for the life of me.
Montgomery, Todd, Christian—I know them all.
Was it even Kentucky or Tennessee?
Perhaps just an image that keeps haunting me.   30

No, no! in no mansion under earth,
Nor imagination's domain of bright air,
But solid in soil that gave it its birth,
It stands, wherever it is, but somewhere.
I shall set my foot, and go there.   35

Study Questions

1. What experience is the poet describing?

2. Explain the following phrases: "boy-blankness of mood," "set the toe high as treetop," "The gorge-depth drew night on," "declivity wooed/My foot . . ."

3. How does the poet use alliteration to emphasize his discovery?

4. Why is the tree "Beyond any heart-hurt, or eye's grief-fall"?

5. What is the significance of the silence in stanza five? Discuss Warren's technique in describing the silence.

6. The gold glade, with its central tree, seems to have a special meaning for the poet, to symbolize something. What? What is his conclusion about the glade?

Composition

1. The poems by Ransom, Eberhart, and Warren all talk about little boys, but in different ways and for different reasons. Write a comparison of these three poems. Tell what the topic of each poem is and what theme each treats. Also compare the tone used in each poem. End by telling which poem you preferred and why.

2. Write a description of a little boy whom you know. Tell which poem would be most like him. Be sure to include personal characteristics as well as a physical description. Tell what is unique or ordinary about the boy.

Victor Hernandez Cruz   1949—

Victor Hernandez Cruz moved with his family from a small village in Puerto Rico to New York City when he was four years old. His collected poems include: *Snaps* (1969), *Mainland* (1973), and *Tropicalization* (1976). Cruz writes: "My family life was full of music, guitars and conga drums, maracas and songs. Even when it was five below zero in New York my mother sang warm tropical ballads."

Alone/December/Night

VICTOR HERNANDEZ CRUZ

it's been so long
speaking to people
who think it all
too complex
stupidity in their eyes   5
&
it's been so long
so far from the truth
so far from a roof
to talk to   10
or a hand to touch
or anything to really
love

it's been so long
talking to myself   15
alone
in the night
listening to a music
that is me.

Study Questions

1. In the first section (lines 1–5), what is the speaker's frustration?
2. What does the speaker long for?
3. What is the consequence of the speaker's loneliness?

Vocabulary

In each **verbal analogy** problem below, you will see two *italicized* words. First, establish a relationship between these words. Then, from the five word-pairs which follow, choose the one pair whose relationship is most nearly the same as that of the *italicized* word-pair. Copy all your answers on a separate sheet of paper.

1. *munch* : *chew* ::
   rage : anger   kneel : pray   sure : uncertain   uproot : drag
   eons : worlds

2. *bird* : *sparrow* ::
   grass : clover   anguish : consolation   reach : grasp
   splinter : wood   insect : cricket

3. *electricity* : *shock* ::
   purple : iris   snowshine : sunlight   sea : wave
   near : distant   tears : weep

4. *meek* : *proud* ::
   oyster : shell   add : subtract   legend : myth
   June : winter   mumbo jumbo : puzzle

5. *glass* : *window* ::
   valley : hill   sunder : parts   clamor : stillness   canvas : sail
   forebear : ancestor

6. *farming* : *tractor* ::
   tennis : racquet   knuckles : fist   key : music
   walking : footprint   color : chameleon

7. *simple* : *complex* ::
   to : fro   oxygen : suffocate   mermaid : meadow
   crumbs : bread   branch : forest

8. *Yangtse* : *river* ::
   United States : Maine   Seminole : Native American
   flower : Queen Anne's Lace   sun : Florida   lake : Lucerne

9. *sympathize* : *sympathetic* ::
   humane : humanity   radium : radiant   hypotheses : hypothetical
   civilize : civilization   inflect : inflectional

10. *word* : *sentence* ::
    sleep : wake   lemonade : warm   destination : swim
    rest : shade   city : state

Anne Sexton   1928-1975

Anne Sexton was born in Newton, Massachusetts. She developed her poetic talent during the 1950s while attending seminars given by Robert Lowell (see page 698). Subsequently she published *To Bedlam and Part Way Back* (1960) and *All My Pretty Ones* (1962). The turbulence in her life which led eventually to suicide is reflected in the titles of some of her work *Live or Die* (1966) and *The Awful Rowing Toward God* (1975). Sexton's *Complete Poems* (1981) contains a foreword by the distinguished poet, Maxine Kumin.

Courage

ANNE SEXTON

It is in the small things we see it.
The child's first step,
as awesome as an earthquake.
The first time you rode a bike,
wallowing up the sidewalk.   5
The first spanking when your heart
went on a journey all alone.
When they called you crybaby
or poor or fatty or crazy
and made you into an alien,   10
you drank their acid
and concealed it.

Later,
if you faced the death of bombs and bullets
you did not do it with a banner,   15
you did it with only a hat to
cover your heart.
You did not fondle the weakness inside you

though it was there.
Your courage was a small coal   20
that you kept swallowing.
If your buddy saved you
and died himself in so doing,
then his courage was not courage,
it was love; love as simple as shaving soap.   25

Later,
if you have endured a great despair,
then you did it alone,
getting a transfusion from the fire,
picking the scabs off your heart,   30
then wringing it out like a sock.
Next, my kinsman, you powdered your sorrow,
you gave it a back rub
and then you covered it with a blanket
and after it had slept a while   35
it woke to the wings of the roses
and was transformed.

Later,
when you face old age and its natural conclusion
your courage will still be shown in the little ways,   40
each spring will be a sword you'll sharpen,
those you love will live in a fever of love,
and you'll bargain with the calendar
and at the last moment
when death opens the back door   45
you'll put on your carpet slippers
and stride out.

Study Questions

1. What is the poem about? In what order are the divisions of the subject presented? How are the divisions indicated?

2. What contrasts and comparisons do you see between the incidents in the first section and those in the second?

3. In the third section, what is the meaning of the phrase "my kinsman"?

4. How is the tone similar in the second and third stanzas?

5. How does the last section combine the tone of parts two and three with that of part one? What does the poem finally show us?

Alice Walker   1944—

Born in Eatonton, Georgia, Alice Walker was the eighth child in a family of sharecroppers. She was graduated from Sarah Lawrence College then worked in the Civil Rights Movement in Mississippi. After a period as a magazine editor in New York City, she taught at Wellesley College and at the University of Massachusetts. Walker's poetry includes *Once* (1968), *Revolutionary Petunias* (1973), *Good Night Willie Lee I'll See You in the Morning* (1979). Her novels are *The Third Life of Grange Copeland* (1970), *Meridian* (1976), and *The Color Purple* (1982), which received both the Pulitzer Prize and the American Book Award. She has also written two books of short stories, *In Love and Trouble* and *You Can't Keep a Good Woman Down*.

New Face

ALICE WALKER

I have learned not to worry about love;
but to honor its coming
with all my heart.
To examine the dark mysteries
of the blood   5
with headless heed and
swirl,
to know the rush of feelings
swift and flowing
as water.   10
The source appears to be
some inexhaustible
spring
within our twin and triple
selves;   15
the new face I turn up
to you
no one else on earth
has ever
seen.   20

Study Questions

1. "Love" is an abstract word. What other abstract words does the poet use to describe her feeling about love?
2. What metaphor does she use to make the description concrete?
3. How do the last five lines relate to the first line and to the title? How do these lines provide unity for the poem?

Joyce Carol Oates 1938—

One of the most prolific writers to emerge in the 1960s is Joyce Carol Oates. Although she is primarily a novelist (*Them, Wonderland, Bellefleur, A Bloodsmoor Romance*), she has also written numerous short stories and a collection of poems. Her work is strongly modern and realistic in its concentration on the American scene, the human condition, and the positive and negative aspects of human relationships. In the following poem she gives us a startling view of America and explores a theme common to much modern literature—a sense of loss.

Dreaming America

JOYCE CAROL OATES

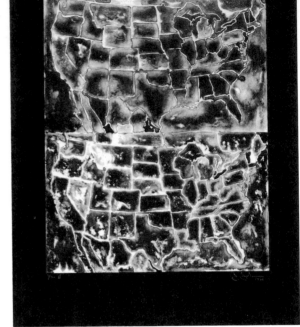

TWO MAPS II *Jasper Johns* 1966

When the two-lane highway was widened
the animals retreated.
Skunks, raccoons, rabbits—even their small corpses
disappeared from the road—transformed into rags
then into designs   5
then into stains
then nothing.

When the highway was linked to another
then to another
six lanes then nine then twelve rose   10
sweeping to the horizon
along measured white lines.
The polled Herefords were sold.
When the cornfields were bulldozed
the farmhouses at their edges turned into shanties;   15
the outbuildings fell.

When the fields were paved over
Frisch's Big Boy rose seventy-five feet in the air.
The *Sunoco* and *Texaco* and *Gulf* signs competed
on hundred-foot stilts   20
like eyeballs on stalks
white optic-nerves
miraculous.
Illuminated at night.

Where the useless stretch of trees lay   25
an orange sphere like a golf ball
announces the Shopping Mall, open
for Thursday evening shopping.
There, tonight, droves of teenagers hunt
one another, alert on the memorized pavement.   30

Where did the country go?—cry the travelers, soaring
past. *Where did the country go?*—ask the strangers.
The teenagers never ask.

Where horses grazed in a dream that had no history,
tonight a thirteen-year-old girl stands dreaming   35
into the window of Levitz's Record Shop.
We drive past, in a hurry. We disappear.
We return.

Study Questions

1. The opening stanza of "Dreaming America" is a strong, emerging image of the disappearance of wildlife in America. What, according to Oates, is the reason for its disappearance?

2. How is the disappearance image extended in the next three stanzas? What has disappeared? What is the replacement?

3. Oates is not simply writing about the growth of shopping malls and the paving of America. She hints at larger issues related to the American character and the American dream. What has happened to each?

4. Why is the poem's title, "Dreaming America," appropriate to her subject?

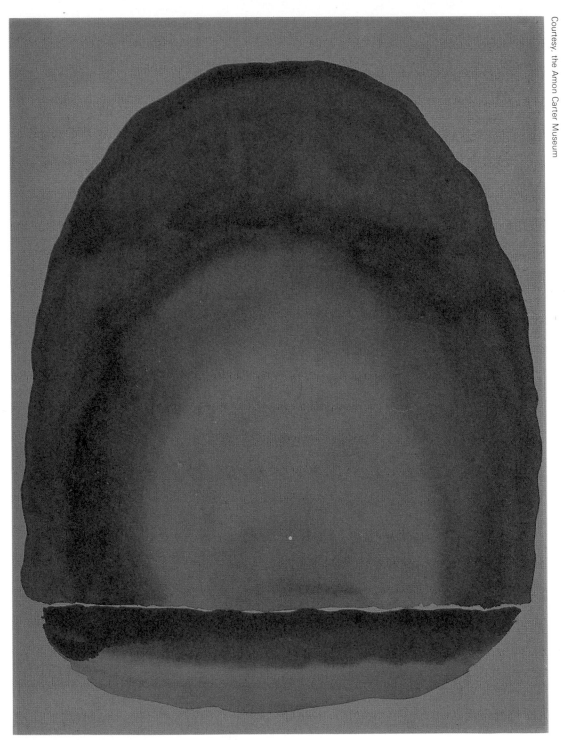

LIGHT COMING ON THE PLAINS II   *Georgia O'Keeffe*

Roberta Hill   1947 —

Roberta Hill, an Oneida Indian, was born
in Wisconsin and graduated from the state
university there. She majored in psychology
before taking a master's degree in fine arts
at the University of Montana. In addition to
writing poetry she teaches creative writing
at Sinte Gleska College in South Dakota.

Dream of Rebirth

ROBERTA HILL

We stand on the edge of wounds, hugging canned meat,
waiting for owls to come grind
nightsmell in our ears. Over fields,
darkness has been rumbling. Crows gather.
Our luxuries are hatred. Grief. Worn-out hands   5
carry the pale remains of forgotten murders.
If I could only lull or change this slow hunger,
this midnight swollen four hundred years.

Groping within us are cries yet unheard.
We are born with cobwebs in our mouths   10
bleeding with prophecies.
Yet within this interior, a spirit kindles
moonlight glittering deep into the sea.
These seeds take root in the hush
of dusk. Songs, a thin echo, heal the salted marsh,   15
and yield visions untrembling in our grip.

I dreamed an absolute silence birds had fled.
The sun, a meagre hope, again was sacred.
We need to be purified by fury.
Once more eagles will restore our prayers.   20
We'll forget the strangeness of your pity.
Some will anoint the graves with pollen.
Some of us may wake unashamed.
Some will rise that clear morning like the swallows.

Study Questions

1. In the first seven lines, how do the images create a picture of despair and hunger?

2. Line 8 signals a historical explanation for the present condition. How do lines 9–11 contribute to this historical image?

3. Hope is introduced beginning with line twelve. What are the images used to describe the coming of hope?

4. Lines 17–20 reinforce the hope with a dream. What is this dream? How is this a part of the American Dream?

8 REVIEW

Study Questions

1. Alexis de Tocqueville (page 46) says, "Thus not only does democracy make every man forget his ancestors, but it hides his descendants and separates his contemporaries from him; it throws him back forever upon himself alone and threatens in the end to confine him entirely within the solitude of his own heart." Find examples of writers in this unit who affirm or deny this assertion. How do they affirm it? deny it?

2. A distinguished historian has said, "The American character, whatever its shortcomings, abounds in courage, creative energy and resourcefulness, and is bottomed upon the profound conviction that nothing in the world is beyond its power to accomplish." Identify selections in this unit which tend to support or refute this statement and discuss how they support or refute it.

3. Compare and contrast the parent/daughter relationships in the Olsen and Updike stories. What point of view does each author use? How are the relationships similar? How do they differ?

4. Compare the poems by Plath, Lowell, and Wilbur. How does each use nature as a metaphor for some other idea?

5. Both the Evans poem and the Sexton poem discuss courage, but in different ways. What are the two ways?

Composition

1. Many selections in this unit are about childhood—some remembered with happiness, some with sadness, some with humor, some with pain. Write a review of the following writers and their memories of childhood: "Garden of My Childhood" by Chang (page 688), "Summer Remembered" by Gardner (page 694), "Alone/December/Night" by Cruz (page 704), and "The Bluest Eye" by Morrison (page 645). Tell how their ideas, images, or feelings are similar. Draw conclusions about the common concerns of remembered childhood.

2. Select one of the three major themes—The Sense of Place, The Individual, The American Dream—and write an essay on how you interpret the theme. Begin by saying what the theme means to you. Then tell why you feel that way. Conclude with how the material in this book has or has not influenced your attitude about that theme.

The Writing Process

We write for a number of different reasons and for a number of different purposes. In all cases our writing is an effort to convey our thoughts on paper. Regardless of the kind of writing, we follow a writing process, which can be broken into stages. These stages are commonly called prewriting, writing, and revision and proofreading. What each of these stages requires of the writer makes up the subject of the Writer's Handbook.

Prewriting

Getting Off to a Good Start

Prewriting is the preparation stage of writing. It consists of the activities you do to get started and take control of the writing situation. Prewriting activities include focusing your topic, generating ideas for your paper, and organizing your ideas.

What Is the Topic? If you have a topic assigned to you, ask, "What is my purpose in writing this composition? How can I best achieve this purpose?" Though these decisions may change as you develop your composition, having these objectives in mind will serve you in getting off to a good start.

If you have a choice of topics, choose one that interests you and that you know some-

thing about. Not only will you transmit this knowledge more effectively to your reader, but you will save yourself time, as you will not need to do as much research.

Should You Limit the Topic? Sometimes an assignment calls for you to write about a general topic. When a topic is general, you must limit it, or focus it, in order to reduce it to a manageable size. For example, you have been assigned the reading of "The Secret Life of Walter Mitty" by James Thurber (page 431). Your written assignment is to describe the conflict between men and women as developed in the story. You would first decide what aspect of this conflict you would focus on. One example would be how the conflict between men and women leads one man to take refuge in daydreams. By limiting your paper to this one aspect of the conflict, you are also limiting what you have to present to explain your viewpoint adequately.

If an assignment requires that you discuss a poem that expresses love, you might choose one that appeals to you as, for example, "Song" by H. D. (page 519). Once you focus on a particular aspect of the love expressed in the poem, such as the beauty of the beloved or the joy of loving, you have only a particular and limited point to develop.

Who Is the Audience? Your **audience** is the group of people to whom or for whom you are writing. You might write a note to a friend, or a letter to a company, or a composition for your class, or a report for the teacher, or a poem to a loved one. Almost all of the writing you do will be to or for someone else—your audience. Try to imagine an audience that is appropriate for your topic. Keeping this audience in mind, you can write to their needs and interests.

Two important questions to ask yourself about your audience are "What do they know?" and "What do I have to write in order to convey my message?" The point is to know your audience and to present enough information to make your point a convincing one. Your responsibility, therefore, is to include all the details necessary and available to support your point.

In writing a report about "Bartleby the Scrivener" (page 299), for example, you can assume that your audience is familiar with the story. But you cannot assume they have reached your conclusions about the story. Therefore, you must use details of the story to support your particular judgments.

What Is the Purpose of the Assignment? Every writing assignment has a purpose, whether it is to demonstrate or show, to inform, to persuade, to entertain or amuse, to discuss, to explain, to describe, to analyze, or to evaluate. Sometimes, the assignment may contain one of the following words to help you determine your specific purpose:

analyze	define	identify
cite	describe	interpret
compare	evaluate	paraphrase
contrast	explicate	summarize

What Form Should the Assignment Take? Writing can take a variety of forms, dependent upon the specific assignment. Make sure you understand what form is required before you begin your assignment. The following are some typical writing forms:

character sketch	essay
directions	journal entry
editorial	paragraph

play	report
poem	short story

What Length Should the Assignment Be? Make sure you understand how long the assignment should be. Some assignments require you to write a paragraph. Some ask for a prescribed number of words or pages. The length of other assignments is left to your good judgment. In such cases you have only to consider what you have to say. Focus the topic in such a way that you can develop it fully in what seems to you a reasonable length. Once written to your satisfaction, conclude the assignment.

What Type of Language Should You Use? Most of the writing you do in school is to demonstrate your knowledge of a certain subject or field. For this purpose, your language should be formal. **Formal English** is the standard English used for serious occasions. It contains good grammar, correct usage, and proper spelling and punctuation. It should also be impersonal, without references such as *I think*, *I believe*, *I know*, and *I see*.

Creative writing allows for more variety in language. You may use **informal English** if it is appropriate for the assignment. For example, you might use dialect to capture the way a character speaks or thinks, as Ralph Ellison does in his story "Did You Ever Dream Lucky?" (page 596) or as Thornton Wilder does in his play *Our Town* (page 533).

EXERCISE 1 Prewriting

Read the assignment directions below. Then answer the questions that follow the directions.

Two documents that shaped the development of the United States are The Mayflower Compact (page 83) and The Declaration of Independence (page 85).

Write a three-paragraph essay on these documents. In your first paragraph, summarize the main points made in The Mayflower Compact. In your second paragraph, summarize the main points made in The Declaration of Independence. In your last paragraph, compare and contrast these two documents.

a. What is the topic of this writing assignment?
b. Since no specific audience is mentioned, what assumption should you make?
c. Which words in the directions explain the purpose of the assignment?
d. What form should the assignment take?
e. What length should the assignment be?

EXERCISE 2 Prewriting

Read the assignment directions below. Then answer the questions that follow the directions.

The Gettysburg Address (page 331) is one of the most memorable presidential speeches in our history. After reading the Gettysburg Address, listen to a current presidential address or press conference. Then write an article for your school newspaper analyzing this speech.

a. What is the topic of this writing assignment?
b. For this assignment, who is your audience?
c. What word in the assignment directions explains your purpose for writing?
d. What form should your writing take?

Generating Ideas

Once you have identified or chosen your topic for writing, you need to generate ideas about it. The ideas that you generate will help you to focus your topic and to develop supporting details. Two questions to ask yourself are "What do I already know about the topic?" and "What do I need to find out?" Two techniques can help you to generate ideas: brainstorming and the journalistic formula. Brainstorming can help you draw out thoughts and information you already have. The journalistic formula can help you discover what you know and what you still need to find out.

Brainstorming. **Brainstorming** is a technique for developing ideas through free association. The purpose is to list as many details and ideas as you can about your topic. When brainstorming, you list whatever ideas come to mind about your topic. You can brainstorm by yourself, although sometimes this technique is more productive when done with a group. For example, imagine your topic is Granny in "The Jilting of Granny Weatherall" (page 473). Part of your brainstorming can be to list all of the characteristics you've learned about Granny. Your list might look like this:

- dying
- nearly eighty years old
- fiercely independent
- crotchety
- lives with her daughter Cornelia
- tries to be practical and sensible
- likes to take control of situations
- once fenced in a hundred acres
- had been jilted in her youth
- was married to John
- had five children
- prefers Hapsy
- Catholic
- not religious in an orthodox way

With this information, you have the details needed, for example, to develop a character study of Granny.

The Journalistic Formula. The **journalistic formula** uses questions beginning with the words *who, what, when, where, why,* and *how* to gather information about the topic. Imagine your topic is the settlement of Plymouth

Plantation (page 132). Here are some questions you might ask and find answers to in order to gather information:

- Who was William Bradford?
- Who were some of the other settlers at Plymouth Plantation?
- What problems did the settlers face at Plymouth Plantation?
- What special characteristics helped the settlers to survive?
- When did the settlers establish Plymouth Plantation?
- Where was Plymouth Plantation?
- Where did the settlers come from?
- Why did the settlers leave their native land?
- How did the Indians help the settlers?

The answers to these questions will give you some of the details you need to write about the settlement of Plymouth Plantation.

EXERCISE 3   Generating Ideas

Imagine you have been assigned to write a five-paragraph essay about the function of dreams in each of the following selections: "Did You Ever Dream Lucky?" by Ralph Ellison (page 596), "The Secret Life of Walter Mitty" by James Thurber (page 431), "I Have a Dream" by Martin Luther King, Jr. (page 115), and "Winter Dreams" by F. Scott Fitzgerald (page 92). Use brainstorming to generate ideas about this topic.

EXERCISE 4   Generating Ideas

Imagine that after reading "The Sale of Hessians" by Benjamin Franklin (page 169), you are assigned to write a five-paragraph essay about the role of Hessian soldiers in the American Revolution. Use the journalistic formula to develop ideas about this topic. Then select from the ideas you have developed to limit your topic.

Organizing Your Ideas

Once you have gathered the ideas and the details that you will use to write your paper, you will need to organize them. Having your ideas and details organized will help you in writing your draft. A decision that you must make is how to organize your ideas logically. You will find that one of the following common patterns of organization may apply to your ideas at different times.

Time order is an organization pattern in which you relate events according to the order in which they happened.

Spatial order is a pattern in which you present items according to their position in space.

Order of importance is a pattern in which you present ideas starting with the least important and building up to the most important, or starting with the most important and ending with the least important.

Comparison and contrast is a pattern in which you show the similarities and the differences between items.

Cause and effect is a pattern in which you give reasons for a certain result.

Presenting your ideas in a logical pattern will help give coherence to your writing.

Outlining. Preparing an outline will help you to arrange your ideas in the organizational pattern that you have chosen. Your outline helps you to clarify your main points and related ideas. In your outline you list in order the main points, supporting points, and additional details.

Here is a typical outline form. The Roman numerals introduce the main points, the capital letters supporting points, and the Arabic numerals additional details.

I. _____

  A. _____

    1. _____

    2. _____

B. _____
  1. _____
  2. _____
  3. _____
II. _____
  A. _____
  B. _____
    1. _____
    2. _____
  C. _____

A topic outline lists the main topics and supporting topics as phrases:

I. The Novels of Herman Melville
  A. *Typee*
  B. *Omoo*
  C. *Mardi*
  D. *Redburn*
  E. *White-Jacket*
  F. *Moby-Dick*
  G. *Pierre*
  H. *The Confidence Man*

A sentence outline lists the main and supporting topics as sentences:

I. Not counting his short novel *Billy Budd,* Herman Melville wrote eight novels.
  A. *Typee,* published in 1846, was a popular success.
  B. *Omoo,* published in 1847, was also successful.
  C. *Mardi,* published in 1849, was not as successful.
  D. *Redburn,* published in 1849, was received favorably.
  E. *White-Jacket,* published in 1850, was received favorably.
  F. *Moby-Dick,* published in 1851, was not well received.
  G. *Pierre,* published in 1852, was unpopular.
  H. *The Confidence Man,* published in 1857, was also unpopular.

A scratch outline is simply a rough or preliminary form of your outline. Ideas are listed in order, but informally, without Roman numerals, capital letters, or Arabic numerals.

EXERCISE 5 Outlining

Look again at the assignment in Exercise 3, Generating Ideas (page 720). Make a topic outline for this assignment, arranging your ideas in a logical order.

EXERCISE 6 Outlining

Look again at the assignment in Exercise 4, Generating Ideas (page 720). Make a sentence outline for this assignment, arranging your ideas in a logical order.

Writing

Writing a composition is putting your ideas on paper in sentences and paragraphs. You will find your writing comes more easily if you keep your audience and your purpose in mind and if you follow your outline, in which you arranged your prewriting notes according to a logical organizational pattern.

The First Draft

In your first draft, you give structure to the ideas that you developed during prewriting. Write the draft as well as you can, but do not dwell on any point or worry about correct usage. After you have completed your draft, you will have an opportunity to revise and proofread it.

In writing your first draft, be guided by your outline. There, you have worked out the organization and the relationship between ideas. Now you can develop these ideas into sentences and paragraphs, developing the main points of the outline into topic sentences and the supporting points into your supporting ideas.

Topic Sentence. You use the main points of your outline to write your topic sentences. The **topic sentence** of a paragraph states the main idea, or point, to be developed. The topic sentence may be placed at the beginning of the paragraph, near the middle, or at the end, although often it is placed at the beginning. For example, in the following paragraph from "Rip Van Winkle" by Washington Irving (page 209), the first sentence is the topic sentence. It tells you the topic—the great error in Rip's composition, or make up—and the main idea about this topic—Rip did not like to do any kind of profitable labor.

The great error in Rip's composition was an insuperable aversion to all kinds of profitable labor. It could not be from the want of assiduity or perseverance; for he would sit on a wet rock, with a rod as long and heavy as a Tartar's lance, and fish all day without a murmur, even though he should not be encouraged by a single nibble. He would carry a fowling piece on his shoulder for hours together, trudging through woods and swamps, and up hill and down dale, to shoot a few squirrels or wild pigeons. He would never refuse to assist a neighbor even in the roughest toil, and was a foremost man at all country frolics for husking Indian corn, or building stone fences; the women of the village, too, used to employ him to run their errands, and to do such little odd jobs as their less obliging husbands would not do for them. In a word Rip was ready to attend to anybody's business but his own; but as to doing family duty, and keeping his farm in order, he found it impossible.

A good topic sentence unites the other ideas in the paragraph. It makes clear to the reader the point of the paragraph.

When a topic sentence serves to guide the entire composition, it is called a **thesis statement**. This statement of intent usually is placed at the end of the introductory paragraph.

Support. The rest of the sentences in the paragraph must **support,** or develop, the idea expressed in the topic sentence. Supporting details may take several forms. Facts, reasons, incidents, and examples are among the common kinds of supporting details. In the paragraph you read from "Rip Van Winkle," Irving gives examples of Rip's unprofitable activities.

Concluding Sentence: Some writers choose to use a **concluding sentence** that sums up the supporting details and either restates the main idea or makes a final comment on the topic. In the paragraph from "Rip Van Winkle," Irving uses the last sentence to summarize the series of examples that develop the topic.

EXERCISE 7 Draft

Choose the assignment in Exercise 3 or 4 (page 720). Using your outline and your notes, write a first draft of your essay. Present your main points in topic sentences, and develop the paragraphs with your supporting details.

Revision and Proofreading

Revision

Revision is the stage of writing during which you reconsider your writing and make changes to improve it. When you revise, you keep in mind the overall intent of the writing, its organization, its content, and its language. Ask yourself the following questions and let your answers guide your revising:

Intent

1. Does the writing achieve its purpose?
2. Is the writing appropriate for its audience?

3. Is the writing in the proper form?
4. Is it the correct length?

Organization

1. Are the ideas presented in a clear organizational pattern?
2. Does the writing give proper emphasis to important ideas?

Content

1. Are the main points clearly stated in the topic sentences?
2. Is there adequate support for each point?
3. Is the language appropriate?
4. Are the words the most effective ones to convey the meaning?

Proofreading

Once you have revised your paper, you need to proofread it. **Proofreading** is reading to find and correct errors in spelling, capitalization, punctuation, and usage.

Below is the revised first draft of a paragraph explaining the significance of the title of "The Jilting of Granny Weatherall" (page 473).

To understand ~~the~~ Katherine Anne Porter's story, you must first understand the significance of ~~the~~ its title—"The Jilting of Granny Weatherall." To be jilted is to be rejected or cast aside, and Granny ~~was~~ had been jilted twice in her life. The first time, she had waited in her house for her bridegroom—the priest had waited too—but her bridegroom never came. The bottom seems~~ed~~ to drop out of her world, but she weathers~~ed~~ the pain, just as she has weath-

ered all other situations. Although she later married, she lived her life with an emptiness, knowing ~~She knew~~ "there was something else besides the house and the man and the children," something "not given back." The second time, she waits~~ed~~ on her deathbed for a sign from God—again, the priest ~~waits~~ was there, too, but the sign never ~~comes~~ came. Again she ~~is~~ was rejected ~~There is~~ and left with only darkness.

EXERCISE 8   Revision

Revise and proofread the first draft of your essay.

_____

Your assignments may call for you to write description, exposition, persuasion, interpretation, or critical analysis. While you would follow the steps of the writing process in preparing any kind of writing, you would concentrate on the specific elements that make each type of writing effective. The sections that follow give specific suggestions for each type of writing.

Descriptive Writing

The purpose of **descriptive writing** is to create a clear picture. Good description, however, does more than this. It also leaves the reader with an outstanding impression of the subject described. For example, in the following paragraph from *A Walker in the City* by Alfred Kazin (page 33), the outstanding or major impression of the scene is one of energy and excitement.

> Rush hour above, on every side, below: the iron wheels of the El trains shooting blue-white sparks against the black, black tracks sweeping in from Chinatown and Oliver Street under the black tar roofs and fire escapes and empty window boxes along the grimy black tenements on whose sides I could see the streaky whitewashed letters CHILDREN CRY FOR IT FLETCHER'S CASTORIA CHARLES S. FLETCHER; trolley cars bounding up into the air on each side of me, their bells clanging, clanging; cars sweeping off the bridge and onto the bridge in the narrow last roadways before me.

Good descriptive writing depends on keen observation. In presenting their observations, writers use one or more of the following devices to make their descriptions effective: specific details, vivid words, and figurative language.

Specific Details

Specific details help readers experience the subject described. These details appeal to one or more of the five senses: sight, hearing, taste, touch, and smell. For example, look again at the paragraph from *A Walker in the City*. Notice all the specific details that help you feel you are observing the scene yourself. Although these details appeal primarily to your sense of sight, some also appeal to your sense of touch and of hearing. For example, the tar roofs and the grimy black tenements appeal to your sense of touch, while the iron wheels and the bells clanging appeal to your sense of hearing.

Vivid Words

Vivid words are words that create a precise, or exact, picture. They turn a fuzzy picture into one in sharp focus. For example, in-stead of writing that the trains were coming in, Kazin describes them as sweeping in. Instead of writing that the trolley cars were coming up into the air, Kazin tells exactly how they were coming up—the trolley cars were bounding up into the air.

Figurative Language

Figurative language consists of words and phrases that are not meant to be taken literally, but that have a special, or imaginative, meaning all their own. Three types of figurative language are simile, metaphor, and personification.

Simile. A simile is a comparison between two basically unlike things. A simile uses the word *like* or *as* to make this comparison. For example, in *Of Time and the River*, Thomas Wolfe uses a simile to describe his father walking in the kitchen below Thomas' room (page 28):

> Oh, to hear him prowling like a wakened lion below, the stertorous hoarse frenzy of his furious breath. . . .

Metaphor. A **metaphor** is an implied comparison between two basically unlike things. It does not use the word *like* or *as*. For example, in *Of Time and the River*, Wolfe uses a metaphor to describe the train's twisting and turning (page 26):

> . . . and all the time the great train toils slowly down from the mountain summits with the sinuous turnings of an enormous snake.

Personification. Personification means giving human traits and characteristics to non-human things. For example, in *Of Time and the River*, Wolfe uses personification to describe fury (page 28):

> Who has seen fury riding in the mountains? Who has known fury striding in the storm?

Organization

Typically, description is organized according to spatial order. In **spatial order,** details are presented according to their position in space. For example, something may be described from top to bottom, from right to left, or from inside to outside. In addition, something may be described from a fixed focal point or from a moving focal point. In the paragraph you read from *A Walker in the City*, the scene is described from a fixed focal point. You see the scene through the eyes of the young Kazin, who stands on the staircase leading up to the bridge and looks about him.

In the next passage from *Of Time and the River* (page 26), the scene is described from a moving focal point. You see things through the eyes of of the young man as he looks through the window of a train traveling to New York City.

> The train toils slowly round the mountain grades, the short and powerful blasts of its squat funnel sound harsh and metallic against the sides of rocky cuts. One looks out the window and sees cut, bank, and gorge slide slowly past, the old rock wet and gleaming with the water of some buried mountain spring. The train goes slowly over the perilous and dizzy height of a wooden trestle; far below, the traveller can see and hear the clean foaming clamors of rock-bright mountain water. . . .

EXERCISE Writing a Description

1. Prewriting Choose a topic for a description. For example, you might wish to describe a beach at sunset, a bridge, or a street in your town. Then write the five senses across the top of a sheet of paper. Under each sense, list as many specific details as you can that describe this place.

2. Writing Write a one-paragraph description of the place you have chosen. Begin your description with a topic sentence telling the impression this place creates. In the next five or six sentences, write a detailed description of the place.

3. Revising Read through your paragraph again. Have you included enough specific details? Have you used vivid words? Can you improve the paragraph by using figurative language? Make any necessary changes. Then correct any errors in spelling, punctuation, and capitalization.

Expository Writing

The purpose of **expository writing** is to inform your audience or to explain something to them. The subject of exposition is any kind of explanation, for example, the reasons for the existence of a certain condition, the procedures necessary to accomplish a task, or an analysis of a situation. Therefore, expository writing should be simple and clear, as it is in this example from "The Creative Dilemma" by James Baldwin (page 67).

> The artist is distinguished from all other responsible actors in society—the politicians, legislators, educators, and scientists by the fact that he is his own test tube, his own laboratory, working according to very rigorous rules, however unstated these may be, and cannot allow any consideration to supersede his responsibility to reveal all that he can possibly discover concerning the mystery of the human being. Society must accept some things as real; but he must always know that visible reality hides a deeper one, and that all our action and achievement rests on things unseen. A society must assume that it is stable, but the artist must know, and he must let us know, that there is nothing stable under heaven. One cannot possibly build a

school, teach a child, or drive a car without taking some things for granted. The artist cannot and must not take anything for granted, but must drive to the heart of every answer and expose the question the answer hides.

Organization

Four typical ways of organizing exposition are cause and effect, time order, order of importance, and comparison and contrast. Let us look particularly at comparison and contrast and cause and effect.

Comparison and Contrast. A **comparison and contrast** pattern shows the similarities and the differences between two subjects. For example, in the paragraph you just read from "The Creative Dilemma," Baldwin compares and contrasts the artist with all other members of society.

Cause and Effect. A **cause and effect** pattern starts with the effect or result and then gives the causes or reasons for this effect. For example, the paragraph below from "On Being a Granddaughter" by Margaret Mead (page 75) is organized according to cause and effect. The effect is that Margaret Mead feels comfortable being a woman. The causes for this situation are given in the support sentences of the paragraph.

I think it was my grandmother who gave me my ease in being a woman. She was unquestionably feminine—small and dainty and pretty and wholly without masculine protest or feminine aggrievement. She had gone to college when this was a very unusual thing for a girl to do, she had a firm grasp of anything she paid attention to, she had married and had a child, and she had a career of her own. All this was true of my mother, as well. But my mother was filled with passionate resentment about the condition of women, as perhaps my grandmother might have been had my grandfather lived and had

she borne five children and had little opportunity to use her special gifts and training. As it was, the two women I knew best were mothers and had professional training. So I had no reason to doubt that brains were suitable for a woman. And as I had my father's kind of mind—which was also his mother's—I learned that the mind is not sex-typed.

EXERCISE Writing Exposition

1. Prewriting Choose an area in which you have some special interest, such as camping, ice skating, reading, skiing, singing, or acting. To focus on a topic, consider a particular aspect of this field you wish to explain, such as what something is, how something works, how you perform a certain procedure, or why something is as it is. Use brainstorming to generate ideas about your topic. In an outline, organize your ideas in a pattern that is appropriate for your topic.

2. Writing Write an expository paragraph about your topic. Begin your paragraph with a topic sentence. Write five or six sentences providing supporting details for your main idea. End with a concluding sentence restating your main idea.

3. Revising Read through your paragraph. Is it well organized? Does it have a clear and effective topic sentence? Does every sentence support the idea expressed in the topic sentence? Does your last sentence bring your paragraph to a logical conclusion? Then correct any errors in spelling, punctuation, and capitalization.

Persuasive Writing

The purpose of **persuasive writing** is to get someone to agree with you or to take some action. Persuasive writing attempts to affect or change the reader's views or beliefs. For example, consider the following paragraph from "I Have a Dream" by Martin Luther King, Jr. (page 116). In it, King hopes to persuade American society to replace racial injustice with brotherhood.

> It is obvious today that America has defaulted on this promissory note insofar as her citizens of color are concerned. Instead of honoring this sacred obligation, America has given the Negro people a bad check; a check which has come back marked "insufficient funds." But we refuse to believe that the bank of justice is bankrupt. We refuse to believe that there are insufficient funds in the great vaults of opportunity of this nation. So we have come to cash this check—a check that will give us upon demand the riches of freedom and the security of justice. We have also come to this hallowed spot to remind America of the fierce urgency of now. This is no time to engage in the luxury of cooling off or to take the tranquilizing drug of gradualism. Now is the time to make real the promises of Democracy. Now is the time to rise from the dark and desolate valley of segregation to the sunlit path of racial justice. Now is the time to open the doors of opportunity to all of God's children. Now is the time to lift our nation from the quicksands of racial injustice to the solid rock of brotherhood.

You can achieve effective persuasive writing by following these guidelines: (1) Establish a shared purpose. (2) Show respect. (3) Provide solid evidence. (4) Pay attention to the connotations of words.

Establish a Shared Purpose

When you establish a shared purpose, you provide a reason for the reader to listen to your argument or opinion. Notice that King does not separate himself from America or from its responsibility. He refers to the United States as "our country" and establishes a goal that he and all his fellow Americans can share: "to lift our nation from the quicksands of racial injustice to the solid rock of brotherhood."

In order to establish a shared purpose, you must know your audience. For example, imagine you want to convince a group of business people to provide summer jobs for youths. First, you would have to identify the needs and interests of your audience. What are your readers like? What are their beliefs? What are their goals? Once you have successfully answered these questions, you could show the members of this group how they would be accomplishing their own goals by helping you achieve your goal. For example, you might write that by providing summer jobs for youths they would be training youths for entry level positions and so would have a better qualified pool of people to draw upon when they filled these positions.

Show Respect

The quickest way to alienate an audience is to insult them. An effective way to get them to listen to you is to show that you understand and respect them and their viewpoints. When our views and opinions are attacked, we become defensive. When they are treated with respect, we become more willing to listen. In the paragraph from "I Have a Dream," King treats with respect his fellow Americans. He does not agree with what white America has done to black America, but he refuses to believe that, when presented with the Negro "check," white America will not pay its debt. He does not talk down or call anyone names. He simply wants to remind America of what it already knows, of its own principles.

Provide Solid Evidence

Know why you take the stand you do. Have solid evidence to support your opinions. Most likely, you will not alter anyone's views by simply backing up your opinion with more opinions. However, you do stand a chance of affecting someone's beliefs if you are able to support your opinions with examples, facts, and statistics.

Be careful not to distort your facts in order to accomplish your purpose. Do not try to trick your audience into believing as you do. Trust is an essential ingredient in persuasion. Nothing can be more harmful to your case than for a member of your audience to find out you were dishonest.

Pay Attention To Connotation

Connotation is the emotional impact of words. In presenting your case, use words that have the appropriate connotation, the emotional impact that will help you achieve your purpose. For example, in the paragraph from "I Have a Dream," King wishes to arouse negative feelings about racial injustice. Therefore, he refers to it as "quicksand." He wishes to arouse positive feelings about racial equality; therefore, he calls it "the solid rock of brotherhood." He wishes to arouse negative feelings about gradualism. Therefore, he refers to it as a "tranquilizing drug." To arouse negative feeling, he refers to "the dark and desolate valley of segregation," while to arouse positive feelings, he refers to "the sunlit path of racial justice."

Suppose you wanted to open a store to sell old clothing to middle-class teenagers. You might have more success if you called your store an antique clothing boutique than if you called it a used clothing store.

EXERCISE Writing Persuasion

1. Prewriting Choose a topic about which you feel strongly. Now decide what you want to happen as a result of your writing. Next, identify your audience. Establish a shared goal, a reason they should listen to your opinions or take some action. Use the journalistic formula to generate information about your topic.

2. Writing Write a persuasive essay about your topic. In the introductory paragraph, establish a shared goal and explain your purpose for writing. In the next one or two paragraphs, present the evidence supporting your position. Present your evidence in order of importance. In the concluding paragraph, summarize the information you have presented and again state what you expect your audience to do or to believe.

3. Revising Reread your essay. Will your essay bring about the desired change? Have you established a shared goal? Have you maintained a respectful tone? Have you provided solid evidence? Have you presented your position accurately and fairly? Does your language carry the appropriate connotation? Correct any errors in spelling, punctuation, and capitalization.

Interpretive Writing

The purpose of **interpretive writing** is to show your understanding of what an author is saying and of what a work of literature means. When you write interpretively, you uncover the significance of the work for your readers and reveal its hidden meaning. For example, consider the following paragraph from "Seeing" by Annie Dillard (page 660).

When I was six or seven years old, growing up in Pittsburgh, I used to take a precious penny of my own and hide it for someone else to find. It was a curious compulsion; sadly, I've never been seized by it since. For some reason I always "hid" the penny along the same stretch of sidewalk up the street. I would cradle it at the roots of a sycamore, say, or in a hole left by a chipped-off piece of sidewalk. Then I would take a piece of chalk, and, starting at either end of the block, draw huge arrows leading up to the penny from both directions. After I learned to write I labeled the arrows: SURPRISE AHEAD or MONEY THIS WAY. I was greatly excited, during all this arrow-drawing, at the thought of the first lucky passer-by who would receive in this way, regardless of merit, a free gift from the universe. But I never lurked about. I would go straight home and not give the matter another thought, until, some months later, I would be gripped again by the impulse to hide another penny.

On the surface, the paragraph above is about a child hiding pennies. However, the paragraph has a deeper meaning. What is its hidden meaning? Since the paragraph is from an essay called "Seeing," we should first look at how this paragraph relates to the idea of seeing. We know that only those who see—who look and follow the signs—will find the penny. Next we should see if the penny has a symbolic meaning. What does the penny mean to the child who hides it? To the child, the penny represents a treasure. Now, by adding together these details, we can interpret the paragraph: For those who see, or who are willing to look, the universe holds treasures.

The following steps will help you write effective interpretations.

Reread the Work

One reading is rarely sufficient to grasp the underlying meaning of a work. Reread the work until you can see beyond its surface meaning to its significance. Do not rush. Give yourself time to think about the work, to mull over its import.

Write a Thesis Statement

A **thesis statement** expresses your theme idea. It tells what you think the work means. After you have reread the work, write a thesis statement expressing your ideas about the work. This statement will guide your note taking.

Take Notes

As you read the work again, take notes that develop and support your thesis statement. Note any key words. Jot down any statements characters make that seem significant. Note any significant actions. Note any important passages, passages that give you insight into the meaning of the work. Record any symbols and your interpretation of these symbols.

When you take notes, make sure to record the page on which you found the material. If you are interpreting poetry, record the line or lines. When you use quotations from a work in your essay, you must cite the page or the line number. Double check the accuracy of your notes. Have you noted the exact wording of quotations? If you have recorded a line of poetry, have you punctuated it correctly?

Clarify Details

An interpretation is not merely a listing of details from the work. It is a synthesis, a combining of the separate elements to reveal what may not be apparent to the casual reader. In your interpretation, make clear the meaning of each detail you present and show how it supports your thesis.

EXERCISE 1   Writing an Interpretation

Assignment   On the surface, Paul Laurence Dunbar's "Sympathy" (page 398) expresses the poet's sympathy for and understanding of the caged bird. However, the caged bird has a symbolic meaning, a meaning in which it stands for something more than itself. Uncovering this meaning can help you uncover the deeper meaning of the poem. Write a five-paragraph essay interpreting the poem.

1. Prewriting   Assume your audience consists of your classmates. Read the poem as many times as necessary to grasp its deeper meaning. Write a thesis statement expressing this meaning. Then read the poem again, this time taking detailed notes. For each note, indicate which line or lines the information is from. Use brainstorming and the journalistic formula to generate ideas. Finally, organize your notes and make an outline. Consider using the following main points: Summary, What the Caged Bird Feels, Why the Caged Bird Beats Its Wings, Why the Caged Bird Sings, and Conclusion.

2. Writing   Write a five-paragraph essay interpreting the poem. Begin with a meaningful title, one suggesting your point of view. Be sure to name the work in the title. In the first paragraph, briefly summarize the poem and state your thesis. In the next three paragraphs, develop the points on your outline to support your thesis. Quote specific lines from the poem to support your points. Put the line numbers in parentheses after each quotation. In the last paragraph, summarize your points and reach a conclusion.

3. Revising   Read through your essay. Is your interpretation sound? Have you clearly stated your thesis? Have you provided details that support your thesis? Have you clarified these details? Have you quoted accurately? Correct any errors in spelling, capitalization, and punctuation.

EXERCISE 2   Writing an Interpretation

Assignment   "Big Two-Hearted River: Part II" by Ernest Hemingway (page 452) relates the story of what at first appears to be a simple fishing trip. However, this story has a deeper significance. Think about Nick's interactions with nature. Then write a five-paragraph essay revealing the story's deeper meaning.

1. Prewriting   Assume your audience consists of your classmates. Read the story as many times as necessary to grasp its deeper meaning. Write a thesis statement expressing this meaning. Then read quickly through the story again, this time taking notes. Record any significant statements or actions. For each note, record the page on which you found the information. Use brainstorming and the journalistic formula to generate ideas. Finally, make an outline in which you indicate the main points you will make in your essay.

2. Writing   Write a five-paragraph essay interpreting the story. Begin with an attractive title, one including the name of the work. In the first paragraph, briefly summarize the story and state your thesis. In your next three paragraphs, develop the points that support your thesis. In the last paragraph, summarize your points and reach a conclusion.

3. Revising   Read your essay. Is your interpretation sound? Have you clearly stated your thesis? In your development paragraphs, have you presented the points that support your thesis? Have you clarified these details? Have you quoted accurately? Correct any errors in spelling, capitalization, and punctuation.

Critical Writing

The purpose of **critical writing** is to make a judgment or to evaluate a work. In a critical analysis, you take apart a literary work and examine its essential elements in order to make a judgment. Among these elements are the plot, the characters, the point of view, the setting, the mood, the theme, and the style. By analyzing these elements, you determine what works, what doesn't work, what is interesting, and what is dull. Of course, you support your evaluation with evidence.

Evidence

Evidence in a critical analysis takes the form of details from the work itself. For example, if you find the use of symbols effective, provide examples of these symbols. If you find the characters interesting and well developed, cite the details that make them this way. If you find the solution to the story's problem effective, tell the details of the plot that make the solution believable.

As you can see, note taking is an essential ingredient in writing critically. In your notes, cite specific details that back up your judgments.

You will find the following guidelines helpful for writing your own critical analysis.

Background Information

Background information is information about the author and the author's other works. This information helps to put the work being discussed in perspective and to shed light on it. For example, in discussing a story by Hemingway, it might be helpful to mention his careful control of sentence structure in the body of his work. In dis-

cussing a poem by e. e. cummings, it might be helpful to mention his unorthodox treatment of punctuation and capitalization in the body of his poetry.

Providing background information means doing research. Use reference books, including biographies, bibliographies, and encyclopedias, to find out about the author. In your analysis discuss how the background information you have found relates to the work you are critiquing.

Summary

Provide a brief summary of the work you are discussing. Include enough information to familiarize your readers with the work, to establish a common ground.

Analysis

Analyze the work. Explain what you think the intent of the writer is. Examine both the content of the work and its structure.

Of course, you may be analyzing only one element of the work. If, for example, you are analyzing the plot, look at the series of actions that make up the story. If you are analyzing characterization, examine the method by which the writer reveals the character's personality. If you are analyzing point of view, focus on the method by which the story is told. If you are analyzing setting, discuss how effectively time and place are used in the work. If you are analyzing mood, discuss the atmosphere or feeling of the work. If you are analyzing language, concentrate on the use of imagery and figurative devices. If you are analyzing the use of irony, focus on the difference between the expected outcome and the way things actually turn out.

Criticism

Criticize the work. Pull together all your information and reach a judgment about the work. What are its good points? What are its weaknesses? Is it effective? Does the work achieve the writer's purpose? Did it keep you interested? Did it bore you? Support your judgments with details from the work.

Title

Write an attractive title for your critical analysis. Your title should suggest the content of your critical analysis and include the title of the work being discussed.

EXERCISE 1 Analyzing the Selection

Wry humor is a characteristic of all of the stories of Flannery O'Connor, and nowhere is it more evident than in her method of characterization. Read "The Life You Save May Be Your Own" by Flannery O'Connor (page 588), and think about the characters. Then answer the following questions.

1. How is Mr. Shiftlet flawed? How does the daughter react when she sees him?
2. How is the daughter flawed? How does Mr. Shiftlet react when he sees her?
3. Whose reaction is more honest? What other evidence can you find of a deceitful nature?
4. Mr. Shiftlet poses two questions. The first is, "What is a man?" On the basis of Mr. Shiftlet's actions, how do you think the author would have us answer this question?
5. The second question is, "What is man for?" On the basis of the title of the story and Mr. Shiflet's behavior with the hitchhiker, how do you think the author would have us answer this question? How would she have us feel about the workings of grace and salvation?

EXERCISE 2 Writing a Critical Analysis

Like many other O'Connor stories, wry wit is evident in the author's development of characters in "The Life You Save May Be Your Own" (page 588). Analyze the author's method of characterization. Then evaluate the story.

1. Prewriting Assume that your audience is your teacher and your classmates. Read the story through again, this time taking notes on characterization. Then form a thesis statement evaluating the story. Do research to find background information on O'Connor's other works. Perhaps read two or three of these stories for yourself. Use brainstorming and the journalistic formula to generate ideas. Then make an outline using the following main points: Background, Summary, Characterization, Evaluation, and Conclusion.

2. Writing Write a five-paragraph critical analysis, developing each point on your outline into a paragraph. Include your thesis statement in your first paragraph. In the last paragraph, summarize your points and reach a conclusion. Write a title that tells your readers what your critical analysis is about.

3. Revising Read over your critical analysis. Have you provided adequate background information? Does this information shed light on the story you are analyzing? Have you included enough information in your summary to create a common ground? Have you focused your analysis on the method of characterization? Is your analysis sound? Is your criticism fair? Is it well supported? Does your concluding paragraph sum up your main points? Have you mentioned the title and the author of the work in your critical analysis? Have you quoted accurately? Correct any errors in spelling, capitalization, and punctuation.

Literary Terms Handbook

abstract word: a word representing an idea or generality, rather than a concrete thing that can be perceived directly with the senses. *Love, loyalty, obedience, hatred, disgust,* and *joy* are all abstract words. Generally, concrete words are more powerful and effective than abstract ones. Thus when poets express an abstract idea, they often do so by comparing it to something concrete. In "Lenox Avenue Mural" (page 89), Langston Hughes compares a deferred dream to "a raisin in the sun" that has withered and dried up. A deferred dream is an abstract concept; by comparing it to a withered raisin, the poet has made it seem more concrete.

allegory: a narrative in which the characters and the setting stand for abstract qualities and ideas. The writer of an allegory is not primarily trying to make the characters and their actions realistic, but to make them representative of ideas or truths. Allegory is related to symbolism, but allegory usually makes a one-to-one equation between things; a symbol, on the other hand, usually has a number of possible meanings. "Young Goodman Brown" (page 235) is an allegory. (See also **symbol.**)

alliteration: the repetition of initial consonant sounds of two or more words that are close together. Alliteration can give a poem a musical quality, and it can also emphasize the words having the same sound. The alliteration of the *b* and *t* sounds in these lines from "At the Fishhouses" (page 523) emphasizes the words *bitter, bring,* and *burn,* as well as *tasted, taste,* and *tongue:*

> If you tasted it, it would first taste bitter,
> then briny, then surely burn your tongue.

allusion: a reference to a person or an event from history or literature. Thoreau makes several allusions in "Where I Lived and What I Lived For" (page 278); one of which is to Aurora, the goddess of dawn in ancient Roman and Greek mythology: "I have been as sincere a worshipper of Aurora as the Greeks."

ambiguity: the existence of a character, situation, or event in a work of literature that may be interpreted in more than one way. Ambiguity is present when there are no clear answers to the problems that have been raised. It also exists when a character or a deed appears good in some ways, but bad in others. Ambiguity is an important factor in "Young Goodman Brown" (page 235). Goodman Brown's wife and his acquaintances seem ambiguous to him: He has believed them to be good, decent people, but he sees them participating in an evil meeting in the forest. The satanic retreat is itself ambiguous: Did it really happen, or did Goodman Brown dream it? The theme of "Young Goodman Brown" is that human nature, itself, is ambiguous, containing both good and evil, and that those who cannot accept this, like Goodman Brown, are condemned to lives of despair.

anachronism: anything in a work of literature that did not exist at the time of the work's setting.

analogy: the comparison of the likeness of one thing to another; similarity. An analogy is usually made to make something unknown clear by likening it to something familiar. An analogy may also be used in argument to show that a certain thing which is true of one case will also be true of a similar second case. In an analogy in "Sinners in the Hands of an Angry God" (page 160), God's ability to send human souls to hell is compared to a person holding a spider over a fire: "The God that holds you over the pit of hell, much as one holds a spider, or some loathsome insect over the fire, . . . is dreadfully provoked. . . . And there is no other reason to be given why you have not dropped into hell since you arose this morning, but that God's hand has held you up."

antagonist: a character whom the protagonist of a story or play struggles against. Scratchy Wilson tries to start a gunfight with Jack Potter in "The Bride Comes to Yellow Sky" (page 52). Potter is the protagonist, and Wilson is his antagonist. While all stories have a protagonist, many stories do not have an antagonist. "Man and Daughter in the Cold" (page 639), for example, has a protagonist, Ethan, but no antagonist.

aphorism: a brief statement expressing some general truth. Emerson's statement in "Self-Reliance" (page 225) that "a foolish consistency is the hobgoblin of little minds" is an aphorism.

aside: in drama, a character's private thoughts that are spoken while others are present on the stage, but which supposedly are not overheard by other characters. During Emily's burial in *Our Town* (page 533), for example, the dead people talk to each other, but their conversation is not overheard by the mourners.

assonance: a form of rhyme in which the vowel sounds of two or more words are alike, but the consonants are different; for example, *late* and *raid*, *hold* and *foam*. Poets occasionally use assonance at the end of lines in place of the usual perfect rhymes. More frequently, assonance is used within lines simply for the musical effect of a repeated sound. "The people will live on" (page 495) contains this line, "This old anvil laughs at many a broken hammer." The repetition of the *a* sounds in *anvil*, *laughs*, and *hammer* is an example of assonance.

atmosphere: the dominant mood, feeling, or emotion created by the author in a work of literature. Descriptive details about the setting and characters help create an atmosphere. For example, "I Hear America Singing" (page 42) contains the descriptive words *blithe*, *strong*, *delicious*, *robust*, and *melodious*. These help to create an atmosphere of exhilaration and confidence.

autobiography: a person's written account of his or her own life. Autobiographers usually write about the most important things that have happened to them—the highlights of their careers, for example. In the excerpt from his autobiography (page 289), Frederick Douglass explains how the cruel treatment he received from a slave owner made him determined to be free.

ballad: a narrative poem written in highly rhythmic stanzas and concerned with adventure and deep emotion. The ballad is a very old form of poetry. Ballads were originally sung, and only later were they written down. A ballad that has been written down as it was created, as opposed to one that has been passed down orally and only written down later, is called a **literary ballad.**

Ballads are usually written in **ballad stanzas.** Each stanza has four lines; the fourth line rhymes with the second. In typical **ballad rhythm,** the second and fourth lines of each stanza have three accented syllables each. In the first and third lines of the stanza, there are four accented syllables.

biography: a person's life story written by another person. Biographers must find as much information as possible about the life of the person they are writing about. Then they must decide which facts to include and which to leave out.

blank verse: See **iambic meter.**

cacophony: the use of words with harsh and grating sounds, or words that are hard to pronounce. Poets usually use cacophony to create unpleasant or disturbing images, as in this passage from "The Bride Comes to Yellow Sky" (page 52): "Presently they heard from the distance the sound of a shot, followed by three wild yowls . . . There was a shuffling of feet." Cacophony is produced by the words *wild yowls,* and *shuffling*; the image of the gunshot heard in the reader's imagination, contributes an additional unpleasant sound.

central character: See **character.**

character: a person (or, occasionally, an animal) in a work of literature. While all the characters are important, the reader is most interested in the thoughts and deeds of the **central character.** Hetty Fifield is the central character in "A Church Mouse" (page 386), and it is with her experiences and feelings that the reader is most concerned.

characterization: the method by which a writer shows a character's personality. Writers characterize people by the way in which they describe them. For example, in the excerpt from *The Plum Plum Pickers* (page 629), Manuel is described as "having a keen sense of pride." A character's actions, thoughts, and words also reveal something about his or her personality. Mary's story in "Did You Ever Dream Lucky?" (page 596) reveals her sense of humor, especially her ability to laugh at herself. In addition, a writer may characterize a person by showing how others feel about him or her. The minister's wife in "Four Meetings" (page 364), for example, speaks sarcastically of the Countess, referring to her "with the most scathing accent."

climax: the turning point in a story or play; the point at which the reader learns how things will turn out. The reader's interest and suspense are highest at this point. The climax of "The Life You Save May Be Your Own" (page 588) occurs when Mr. Shiftlet, after marrying Lucynell, leaves her in the restaurant and takes the car.

comedy: a play that is humorous and usually has a happy ending. A comedy may be funny because of the humorous situations it presents. Also, the characters themselves may be funny because of their personality traits. Most comedies use both humorous situations and amusing characters.

complication: the introduction into the plot of problems that the main character must solve. These problems develop as a result of the story's basic conflict. Complication begins in "Bartleby the Scrivener" (page 299) when Bartleby first refuses to do a task given to him by the story's narrator. When this happens, the narrator tries to get Bartleby to accept the conditions of his job. The narrator's attempt to make Bartleby function in the real world constitutes the story's conflict.

concrete word: a word representing something that can be perceived directly by the senses. *Shoe, girl, hamburger, smack, cry,* and *damp* are all concrete words. Writers strive for concrete language because it is generally more powerful and specific than abstract language. (Also see **abstract word.**)

conflict: the struggle between opposing forces around which the action of a work of literature revolves. The central character may struggle against another character or characters, as Hetty struggles against Caleb Gale and the other selectmen in "A Church Mouse" (page 386). However, in "The Bear" (page 440) the struggle takes place between people and some aspect of nature. The opposing forces may even be within a character's mind. In the selection from *The Storm and Other Stories* (page 409), Mildred's conflict concerns her feelings for the hired hand, Fred Evelyn.

connotation: the suggested or implied meaning of a word; the feelings that a word may produce that go beyond the word's dictionary meaning, or denotation. *Munch* and *chew* mean basically the same thing, but *munch* has a livelier, more carefree connotation. If the poet had used *chewing* instead of *munching* in this line from "Summer Remembered" (page 694), the connotation would be considerably different: "The munching of salt water at the splintered dock." (See also **denotation.**)

consonance: the repetition of the consonant sounds in two or more words having different vowel sounds and located close together in a poem. *Sun-soon* and *pitter-patter* are word pairs having consonance. The words *soil* and *soul* in these lines from "Song of the Son" (page 514), are an example of consonance:

> Though late, O soil, it is not too late yet
> To catch thy plaintive soul, leaving, soon gone.

Another example is *silvery slavery*, the term used to describe the exploitation of migrant farm workers in *The Plum Plum Pickers* (page 629).

contrast: the technique of showing the differences between two things, such as characters, setting, or ideas. The selection from *The Plum Plum Pickers* (page 629) contrasts the luxurious and extravagant lives of agricultural executives with the hardship suffered by the farm workers they employ: Executives "relaxed in blue splendor in far-off desert pools," while migrant workers "earn pennies to fend off stark starvation."

couplet: two consecutive lines of poetry that rhyme and have the same metrical length. A couplet often expresses a complete thought. "Departmental" (page 499) is written in couplets, as is shown by these lines:

> No one stands round to stare
> It is nobody else's affair.
> It couldn't be called ungentle.
> But how thoroughly departmental.

denotation: the exact dictionary meaning of a word. (See also **connotation.**)

descriptive essay: See **essay.**

descriptive poem: a short poem about a person, scene, situation, or occasion which reveals the poet's feelings about what is being described. "Astronauts" (page 686) is a descriptive poem that conveys Robert Hayden's reaction to a moon landing.

dialogue: the words spoken by the characters in a play or story.

drama: a work of literature designed to be performed by actors and actresses in front of an audience; a play. The term *drama* may also refer more generally to the entire literary heritage of plays. The appeal of drama lies in its ability to stir strong emotions in people. Drama has many of the same elements as fiction: plot, conflict, characters, setting, mood, theme. But the action of a drama, unlike that of most fiction, is told through the characters' dialogue. A discussion of Modern American Drama is on p. 530.

empathy: sharing the feelings of a character or characters in a work of literature. When readers or playgoers experience empathy, they feel, in their imaginations, the same emotions and even physical sensations that a character experiences. The vivid descriptions in "The Pit and the Pendulum" (page 260), for example, help the reader feel the terror, despair, and revulsion that the narrator experiences in his struggle to escape the tortures of the Inquisition.

episode: an incident in a story or play. The plot is usually made up of a series of episodes that are closely related to each other. In a play, one episode often ends and another begins each time a major character enters or leaves the stage. In *Our Town* (page 533), for example, one episode begins when Mrs. Gibbs, Mrs. Soames, and Mrs. Webb come on the stage. During this episode, they discuss Simon Stimson's drinking. The episode ends when Mrs. Webb and Mrs. Soames leave the stage.

essay: a short work that explores a particular topic. Essays may be humorous, but more commonly they are serious. A **formal essay** presents a serious, logically organized discussion of a topic that is important to the writer. Its purpose is to inform or persuade the reader, or to analyze a topic. *The Declaration of Independence* (page 85) is a formal essay in which Thomas Jefferson analyzes the reasons why the thirteen American colonies were breaking away from England. This is also a **persuasive essay**—an essay in which a writer tries to convince the reader that a particular opinion is correct. Jefferson argues that the American colonists had no choice but to declare their independence.

In an **informal essay,** the author adopts a more personal, casual approach, writing almost as if he or she were talking to the reader. Unlike a formal essay, an informal essay does not need to be about a serious topic. The writing style the author uses is often as important, or even more important, than the content of an informal essay. N. Scott Momaday's style (page 119), which is conversational, effectively communicates his reverence for nature.

Essays can be written about almost anything. In a **descriptive essay,** the writer recreates and shares impressions of persons, places, objects, and experiences by giving concrete details. In the excerpt from *A Walker in the City* (page 31), Alfred Kazin describes the section of New York city in which he lived as a child, and in doing so conveys what it was like to live there at that time.

On the other hand, a **narrative essay** tells a story to make a point. The events narrated in the essay may be real or imaginary. In the excerpt from "I Know Why the Caged Bird Sings" (page 110), Maya Angelou tells the true story of how she got a job as a conductor on a San Francisco streetcar. This narrative relates her struggle to secure a job previously denied to Afro-Americans.

An Essay in which a writer attempts to explain a topic or a subject is called an **expository essay.** In "Of Individualism in Democratic Countries" (page 45), Alexis de Tocqueville explains how the spirit of individualism in a democracy may operate to isolate people from each other.

euphony: the use of a pleasant, harmonious-sounding combination of words, generally in poetry. The alliteration of the *w* sound in the fourth line of this stanza from "To Helen" (page 272) helps produce euphony:

> Helen, thy beauty is to me
> Like those Nicéan barks of yore,
> That gently, o'er a perfumed sea,
> The weary, wayworn wanderer bore
> To his own native shore.

exaggeration: See **hyperbole.**

exposition: an introductory section in a play or story that presents the characters, setting, and mood and gives the reader or audience any information necessary for understanding what is happening. In the exposition of "A Delicate Balance" (page 48), for example, the reader learns that Romero Estrada sweeps sidewalks for local shop owners, who in turn do small favors for Romero. The exposition also introduces the other major characters: Barelas, the barber, and his son Seferino.

expository essay: See **essay.**

extended metaphor: See **metaphor.**

falling action: the part of a play or story following the climax, during which the conflict is resolved and there is decreasing tension and suspense. In "The Chrysanthemums" (page 461), the falling action consists of Elisa's behavior after she sees the discarded flowers.

fiction: a work of literature that has imaginary characters, events, or settings. A fictional story may sometimes contain real people or events, and it may have a setting that actually exists or existed. But fiction is not an account of things as they actually happened. The writer changes things in some way. "Did You Ever Dream Lucky?" (page 596), for example, is set in Harlem, a real place, but the story is fiction because the characters and events are products of the author's imagination.

figurative language (also called **figures of speech**): a word or expression not meant literally, but intended to be understood imaginatively. For example, mushrooms do not literally have "pale fists," nor are they "bland mannered," as the poet portrays them in "Mushrooms" (page 700). But these examples of figurative language convey a certain quality of mushrooms: their pale and dull appearance. **Similes, metaphors, personification,** and **hyperbole** are all types of figurative language.

first-person point of view: See **point of view.**

flashback: a sudden shift backward in time. In a flashback, the writer interrupts the present action to insert an episode that took place at an earlier time. Usually this is done by having a character think back to something that happened some time before. A flashback usually gives the reader information that makes the present situation more understandable, or accounts for a character's motivation. While Ethan and his daughter are shoveling snow in "Man and Daughter in the Cold" (page 639), for example, Ethan remembers a similar occasion when he helped his own father shovel snow. He also recalls how his father died of a heart attack at age forty-seven. Ethan's recollection of a shared moment with his father, now dead, helps the reader understand why Ethan cherishes his own daughter's companionship.

foot: each unit of the metrical pattern of accented syllables within a line of verse. A foot usually contains one accented syllable and one or two unaccented syllables. "Thanatopsis" (page 221) has five feet in each of its lines. Usually, each foot has an unaccented syllable followed by an accented one. This type of foot is an iambic foot.

> Tŏ hím/who ín/the lóve/ŏf Ná/tŭre hólds/
> Cŏmmú/niŏn with/her ví/sĭble fórms,/shĕ spéaks . . .

Note that the fourth foot in the second line has two unaccented syllables followed by an accented one.

foreshadowing: a clue or hint in a story or play that gives the reader some indication of what will eventually happen. Very early in "The Life You Save May Be Your Own" (page 588), the main character expresses an interest in the old woman's car. He introduces himself as Tom Shiftlet, but says that he might just as easily be Aaron Sparks or George Speeds. All three of these last names—Shiftlet, Sparks, and Speeds—have something to do with cars. These details all foreshadow Shiftlet's taking the car.

formal essay: See **essay.**

free verse: poetry that has no regular sequence or pattern of rhythm. There is no **meter** in free verse, only the rhythm of language as it is spoken. The lines are usually not all the same length. "Thirteen Ways of Looking at a Blackbird" (page 670) is written in free verse, as shown by these lines:

> When the blackbird flew out of sight,
> It marked the edge
> Of one of many circles.

hero/heroine: a character in a story who shows exceptional physical or moral courage. **Hero** refers to a male character; **heroine** to a female.

hyperbole: an obvious and extravagant exaggeration not meant to be taken literally. An example is found in "Concord Hymn" (page 231), when the poet says that the American colonial soldiers fired "the shot heard round the world." The farmers' gunfire was clearly not heard all around the world. However, this hyperbole conveys the far-reaching effects of the American Revolution.

iambic meter: the meter in which each **foot** consists of an unaccented syllable followed by an accented one. In poetry written in English, iambic meter is used more than any other meter.

If the lines in a poem each have five iambic feet, the poem is written in **iambic pentameter.** Shakespeare's plays are written mainly in iambic pentameter. Unrhymed iambic pentameter is called **blank verse.** Sonnets are also written in iambic pentameter as shown by these lines from Edgar Allan Poe's "Sonnet—To Science" (page 273):

> Hŏw shoúld/hĕ lóve/thĕe? oŕ/hŏw deém/thee wíse,
> Who woúldst/nŏt leáve/hĭm ín/hĭs wán/dĕríng/

image: a mental picture or impression that appeals to one of the senses. An image can involve sight, hearing, touch, taste, or smell. Consider these lines from "I Am A Black Woman" (page 696):

> I am a black woman
> the music of my song
> some sweet arpeggio of tears
> is written in a minor key . . .

The words *black woman* and *tears* produce visual images. *Music, song, sweet arpeggio,* and *minor key* are all perceived in the imagination by the sense of hearing. The images in the lines from "I Am A Black Woman" convey both the beauty and the distress of a black woman's experience.

While images are important in all types of literature, they are especially important in poetry. Through **imagery,** all the separate images taken together, poets are able to convey many impressions with few words. The imagery of a work of literature often reveals the writer's tone or meaning.

inciting moment: a point following the opening, or exposition, of a story or play at which an event occurs that stirs up the central conflict, and thus sets the plot in motion. The inciting moment presents the major character with a situation he or she must deal with in some way. The inciting moment in the selection from *The Storm and Other Stories* (page 409) happens when Mildred drops her book and the young farmhand picks it up for her. This moment marks the beginning of Mildred's interest in the farmhand.

incongruity: the quality or state of incompatibility, unconformity, or lack of harmony. Writers often use incongruity in the language they select. They might use language which does not match the subject being described, or they might use words that do not seem appropriate to the topic they are writing about. The author, for example, might describe something unimportant or humble as though it were very important and gravely serious. Incongruous language often has a humorous effect, as when Rip Van Winkle is said to belong to "a kind of perpetual club of the sages, philosophers, and other idle personages of the village" (page 208).

informal essay: See **essay.**

internal rhyme: See **rhyme.**

irony: a contrast between the way things seem to be and the way they actually are; contrast between the expected outcome and the way things actually turn out. Irony may sometimes have a humorous effect. Irony is the source of the humor in "The Invalid's Story" (page 351), for example, the awful odor comes from limburger cheese and not the corpse, as the characters believe. Irony may also be sad or even tragic. In "Four Meetings" (page 364), Caroline Spencer eagerly looks forward to visiting many places in Europe. When she finally goes to Europe, however, she spends only one day there, because she is persuaded to give her money to her cousin.

levels of meaning: the progression of themes in a work of literature, moving from the specific concern for the fate of the central character to a more general concern for broader issues. The first level of meaning is always concerned specifically with what happens to the central character. Other levels of meaning may come from the reader's application of the main character's problem to a group to which the character belongs. Still another level may come from the relevance of the main character's conflict to society as a whole.

The first level of meaning in "The Chrysanthemums" (page 461) relates simply to Elisa Allen and her chrysanthemums. The flowers provide the beauty and emotional outlet that her life otherwise lacks, and the wandering repairman hurts her by throwing them away. The second level of meaning extends this specific situation to apply to people in general. It concerns the need for beauty and passion in people's lives, and the unhappiness that results when this need is denied.

Many stories, especially humorous ones, have only one level of meaning. This is the case with "The Invalid's Story" (page 351).

light verse: a form of verse designed specifically to be amusing. Although it may be about subjects normally treated seriously, light verse is always meant to be humorous.

literary ballad: See **ballad.**

local color: the term used to designate a work of fiction, usually a short story, whose primary purpose is to reveal the characteristics of a region and the people who live there. Many works of fiction do this to some extent, but in a local-color story, the setting is all-important. "A Wagner Matinée" (page 420) is an example of a story that could not take place in any other setting.

lyric poetry: poetry that expresses the poet's feelings. Lyric poems are usually fairly short and are often written in reaction to an experience. In "Stopping by Woods on a Snowy Evening" (page 503), Robert Frost reveals his response to a drive through the woods on a snowy winter evening. Unlike narrative poems, lyric poems do not tell stories. A lyric poem may describe an event, as does "Stopping by Woods on a Snowy Evening," but its primary purpose is to relate the poet's feelings about the event.

metaphor: a suggested or implied comparison

between two things. This kind of comparison, unlike a simile, does not use the word *like* or *as*. Rather, a metaphor suggests that something *is* something else. When, in "Where I Lived and What I Lived For" (page 278), Thoreau says that "there was pasture enough for my imagination," he is using a metaphor to compare his imagination to an animal that grazes for food.

When a metaphor extends throughout an entire poem, it is called an **extended metaphor.** "Garden of My Childhood" (page 688) is an example of an extended metaphor. In the central metaphor, childhood is likened to a protected, quiet garden that the child must eventually leave.

meter: the regular pattern in which accented and unaccented syllables alternate in the lines of a poem. (See also **foot** and **iambic meter.**)

motivation: the reasons why a character acts as he or she does. Tommy Castelli, in "The Prison" (page 580), wants to help the girl he sees stealing candy. His motivation is the wish to keep her from making the same mistake he made when he was young.

narrative essay: See **essay.**

narrative poem: a poem that tells a story. "The Tide Rises, the Tide Falls" (page 251) is the story of a traveler who gets carried out to sea by the rising tide.

narrator: the person who tells a story or poem. The narrator may be the author or a character in the story. (See also **point of view.**)

nonfiction narrative: a true story; a narrative about real events and people. The excerpt from *The History of Plymouth Plantation* (page 132) is a true account of the Pilgrim colonists' search for a suitable place to settle. As with all nonfiction, the events in the story happen just as the writer describes them. Unlike fiction, a nonfiction narrative is not the creation of the author's imagination.

nonsense verse: a form of **light verse** in which the humor results from unusual rhythm, play on words, or absurd ideas. Nonsense verse often uses exaggerated rhymes schemes and sometimes contains words that do not really exist.

novel: a narrative written in prose about fictional characters and events. A **novella** is a short novel—shorter than a full-length novel, but longer than a short story. A novel, like a short story, has a plot, characters, conflict, and setting. But all of these are generally much more complex than in a short story.

omniscient point of view: See **point of view.**

onomatopoeia: the use of words that imitate or suggest the sound of the thing to which they refer. Some examples of onomatopoeia in "Summer Remembered" (page 694) are the words *whirring, plinkle,* and *mumbling.*

pace: the rate at which a story moves; its beat or rhythm. When there is much action, a story has a fast pace. A lot of description and dialogue usually produce a slow pace. Different parts of the same story may have different paces. "The Secret Life of Walter Mitty" (page 431) is an example of this. Mitty's fantasies are exciting and fast paced; however, during the intervals in the story when Mitty's real life intrudes into his fantasy world, the pace of the story is much slower.

parable: a story that illustrates a moral lesson, religious principle, or general truth. In one parable in the *Bible,* the word of God is compared to seeds that a farmer plants. Some seeds sprout and grow because they fall in fertile soil. Other seeds, however, fall on rocks and among thorns, and do not grow. Similarly, according to the parable, some people learn from the teachings of God, but others ignore God's word.

paradox: a statement containing two ideas that seem to contradict each other, but which actually expresses a truth. In "I Have a Dream" (page 115), Martin Luther King, Jr., says that "the Negro . . . finds himself an exile in his own land." By this paradox, King means that Black Americans cannot participate fully in many aspects of American society.

personification: giving human characteristics to something that is not human. In "The Author to Her Book" (page 148), Anne Bradstreet personifies her book of poems as a rebellious child whom she loves in spite of its imperfections:

> At thy return my blushing was not small,
> my rambling brat (in print) should mother call . . .

persuasive essay: See **essay.**

play: the acting out of a narrative or story by a person or persons who move and speak in front of an audience or camera. A **playwright** is a person who writes a play.

plot: the series of actions which make up a work of fiction. In a well-constructed plot, these actions are usually linked to one another through cause-and-effect in a way that brings out the author's meaning. A typical plot (which an author may vary in one way or another) will: (1) open with a scene of exposition, (2) introduce the conflict (inciting moment) either during or immediately after the exposition, (3) present the rising action by developing the major conflict, and perhaps adding less important ones, (4) reach the crisis or climax, a decisive scene after which the conflict should logically turn out one way or the other, (5) show the falling action (which may be very little or quite lengthy) and the final resolution of the conflict.

point of view: person through whose eyes a reader sees what happens in a story; in other words, the voice through which a writer tells the story. The writer, of course, is really the person telling the story, but sometimes an author will make one of the characters in the story narrate the events that happen. Such a story has a **first-person point of view.** The term "first person" refers to the pronouns "I" and "we"; the narrator is the "I" of a story with a first-person point of view. Herman Melville is the author of "Bartleby the Scrivener" (page 299), but the lawyer who employs Bartleby narrates the story of Bartleby's strange behavior. The narrator does not have to be the central character or even a major character; for example, Caroline Spencer, rather than the narrator, is the central character of "Four Meetings" (page 364).

Often, rather than having a character tell the story, the author will act as narrator. When the narrator knows everything that goes on and sees into the minds of all the characters, the story has an **omniscient point of view.** Omniscient means "knowing everything." "The Bride Comes to Yellow Sky" (page 52), is written from the omniscient point of view. The author directly reveals the thoughts of several characters —Jack Potter, his bride, Wilson, and the porters on the train, for example. The reader's perspective is not confined only to one character.

When the reader sees into the mind of only one character, even though no character in the story acts as narrator, the point of view is **third-person limited.** As in the first-person point of view, the writer reveals the thoughts of only one character, and the reader knows only what this character knows. But unlike first-person point of view, no "I" character narrates the story. "Winter Dreams" (page 92) is written from the third-person limited point of view. The reader knows only what Dexter Green is thinking. The thoughts and feelings of other characters, such as Judy Jones, must be inferred from what they say and what Dexter thinks about them.

prologue: an opening section or scene that serves as an introduction to a work of literature or a play.

protagonist: the central character in a play or work of fiction; the character about whom the reader or audience is most concerned. Tommy Castelli is the protagonist of "The Prison" (page 580). (See also **antagonist.**)

pun: a play on words involving two words that sound alike or a word that has two different meanings. In "The Life You Save May Be Your Own" (page 588), Mr. Shiftlet's assertion that he was once in the "Arm Service" is an example of a pun. He means, of course, Armed Service—the army. Since Mr. Shiftlet has lost half of one arm, the author is making a pun on "armed" and "arm"—i.e., forelimb.

quatrain: a stanza of four lines. This is the most common stanza form in poetry written in English. Usually quatrains within the same poem all have the same rhyme scheme. The quatrains in "Brahma" (page 232) each have the rhyme scheme *abab*.

refrain: a line or phrase repeated at regular points in a poem, usually at the end of each stanza. A refrain can also be an entire stanza repeated at certain points in a poem. The refrain in "My Lost Youth" (page 247) is this:

> *A boy's will is the wind's will,*
> *And the thoughts of youth are long, long thoughts.*

resolution: the portion of a story or play that follows the climax, and in which the conflict is brought to an end in some way. Up to the climax, the suspense continues to mount; the resolution is a time of decreasing tension. The climax of "A Church Mouse" (page 386) occurs when Caleb Gale and the other selectmen agree to let Hetty Fifield live in the church. During the resolution of the story, Hetty delights in her newly won security, joyfully ringing the church bell on Christmas morning.

Some stories end at the climax and have no resolution. "The Pit and the Pendulum" (page 260), for example, ends when the narrator's life is saved by General Lasalle. This is the story's climax.

rhyme: the repetition of words or syllables with similar sounds. This repetition occurs at specific places in a poem, usually at the ends of lines. **Internal rhyme** is present when words rhyme within the same line of a poem.

A poem's **rhyme scheme,** or pattern of rhyme, is indicated by letters. The small letter *a* is used for the first rhyming sound, *b* for the second, and so forth. Each stanza of "Song of the Son" (page 514) has the rhyme scheme *abbaa*.

rhythm: the pattern in which accented and unaccented syllables are repeated in each line of a poem; the beat of a poem. Each line of "Brahma" (page 232) has four accented syllables alternating with four unaccented ones. Each line begins with an unaccented syllable. (See also **meter.**)

rising action: the part of a play, story, or novel in which complications develop. The rising action is a time of heightening suspense and tension. It continues until the climax. The rising action in "The Bear" (page 440) begins when, at age ten, the boy accompanies the adult hunters on their annual expedition into the forest, and encounters the bear for the first time. The rising action ends at the story's climax, when the boy gets close enough to the bear to shoot it, but refuses to do so.

satire: a work of literature that ridicules something that is wrong with some aspect of human behavior or with society in general. A satirist will often exaggerate faults in order to show how absurd they are. While satire is often humorous, the satirist's main purpose is to criticize rather than entertain. "The Sale of the Hessians" (page 169), for example, criticizes the use of German mercenary soldiers by the British during the Revolutionary War. It does so by making the ruler of Hesse seem interested not in the well-being or courage of the soldiers he has sent to help the British, but only in the money the British will pay him.

scene: a division of a play in which there is a change in time or place. Often plays are divided into acts, and the acts further subdivided into scenes. When one scene ends and another begins, the curtain is usually drawn or the stage darkened.

The script of a play may indicate scene divisions by numbers. On the other hand, scenes may be designated simply by stage directions specifying that the time or location changes. In *Our Town* (page 533), the Stage Manager usually informs the audience when a scene changes. When the scene shifts from Mr. Morgan's soda fountain to George and Emily's wedding, for example, the Stage Manager says: "Well, . . . now we're ready to get on with the wedding."

script: the written version of a play, movie, or television program. It usually includes a list of characters, as well as the dialogue and the stage directions. The script of *Our Town* begins on page 533.

selection of detail: the choice a writer makes regarding which details to include about aspects of the story such as setting, characters, and action. An author cannot include every detail about a character's appearance, for example, so a choice must be made. The reader often gets clues about the meaning of a story from the author's selection of detail. Near the beginning of "The Secret Life of Walter Mitty" (page 431), for instance, an argument occurs between Walter and his wife about whether he needs to wear boots and gloves. The details of this argument show that Mrs. Mitty treats Walter as if he couldn't take care of himself. The use of these details helps to account for Walter Mitty's fantasy life.

setting: the time and place in which a work of literature takes place. "Captivity Narrative" (page 150) is set in Massachusetts during the year 1675.

short story: a short work of fiction that usually can be read in one sitting. Short stories generally have only a few characters and events, with the conflict centering on one main character. The conflict in "The Jilting of Granny Weatherall" (page 473), for example, involves the inability of the central character—the dying Granny—to come to terms with certain things in her past, particularly the jilting she experienced.

simile: a comparison using the word *like* or *as*. In this simile from "What Are Years?" (page 521), Marianne Moore compares a person who accepts mortality, and gains vigor and endurance from this acceptance, to the sea surging within a chasm:

> . . . *He*
> *sees deep and is glad, who*
>   *accedes to mortality*
> *and in his imprisonment, rises*
> **upon himself as**
> *the sea in a chasm, struggling to be*
> *free and unable to be,*
>   *in its surrendering*
>   *finds its continuing.*

sonnet: a fourteen-line poem written in iambic pentameter and expessing a single complete idea. There are two traditional types of sonnet. In the Italian sonnet (so named because the form originated in Italy), the first eight lines rhyme in the scheme *abba, abba*; the last six rhyme *cdc, cdc*. "From the Dark Tower" (page 526) is a variation of the Italian sonnet form; the last six lines rhyme *ccddee*. The Shakespearean sonnet, sometimes called the English sonnet, consists of three quatrains and a couplet. The first quatrain has the rhyme scheme *abab*, the second *cdcd*, and the third *efef*. The couplet rhymes *gg*. "Pity me not because the light of day" (page 507) is a Shakespearean sonnet.

stage convention: a practice in the writing or performance of a play sometimes unrealistic, but that an audience is accustomed to accept. For example, the Gibbs' house in *Our Town* (page 533) is indicated merely by a table and chairs on the right side of the stage.

stage directions: the playwright's instructions to the director and actors within the script of a play, indicating how something should be done. Stage directions may indicate what the stage or set should look like, how an actor or actress should say a certain line, or what actions characters should perform. Stage directions in Act I of *Our Town* (pages 534–35) specify the following: Mrs. Gibbs, *a plump, pleasant woman in the middle thirties, comes "downstairs" right. She pulls up an imaginary window shade in her kitchen and starts to make a fire in her stove.*

stanza: a division in a poem consisting of a group of related lines. Every stanza in a poem usually has the same number of lines, as well as the same pattern of rhyme and rhythm. The stanzas of "Gold Glade" (page 702) have five lines each. The rhyme scheme in each stanza is *ababb*.

stream of consciousness: a method of telling a story in which a writer lets the reader know every thought that enters a character's mind. This method tries to imitate the way in which people actually think. Therefore, the character's thoughts are presented in the order in which they occur, and this order is not necessarily logical. When the stream-of-consciousness technique is used, the story is always written from the first-person point of view.

subplot: a minor conflict in a play or story, less important than the main plot, and sometimes involving secondary characters. The subplot is always related to the main plot in some way. Simon Stimson's drinking problem and eventual suicide forms the one subplot in *Our Town* (page 533). This subplot exists to show that small-town life has its unpleasant and even tragic aspects.

surprise ending: an unexpected conclusion to a work of literature. The surprise in "Did You Ever Dream Lucky?" (page 596) comes when Mary discovers that the bag she found at the scene of the car accident contains not coins but chains.

symbol: an object or event that represents something else in addition to its literal meaning. Music in "A Wagner Matinée" (page 420) is, on the literal level, something that Aunt Georgiana once enjoyed very much. However, in her life as a Nebraska farm wife, she had had to abandon music almost entirely. In addition to this literal meaning, music is also a symbol of the cultural beauty and refinement that are lacking in Aunt Georgiana's life on the prairie. Similarly, the narrator's stiff gown in "Patterns" (page 490) becomes a symbol of the rigidity and conformity she rebels against in her mind. (See also **allegory.**)

technique: the manner and method by which an author writes a work of literature. Writers of fiction, for example, must choose how to develop characters, conflict, and plot. Writers also need to decide the point of view from which a story will be told, how to build suspense, and what atmosphere to create. Still other decisions involve whether to use devices such as foreshadowing or flashbacks. A playwright must further decide

what stage directions are necessary and how to divide a play into acts and scenes. A poet must choose such things as verse form, rhyme scheme, and imagery. All these choices, taken together, make up the writer's technique.

theme: the main idea of a work of literature; the message the writer conveys. Except in unusual cases, such as fables, the theme is rarely expressed directly; rather, it is implied. The theme of "Richard Cory" (page 488) might be stated this way: Appearances are sometimes deceiving; people who seem to be prosperous and fortunate may actually be very desperate.

third person-limited point of view: See **point of view.**

tone: the implied attitude of a writer toward the subject he or she is writing about. Like atmosphere, tone is communicated by the details and descriptive words an author chooses, but tone is not the same as atmosphere. Atmosphere is the general mood or feeling created within a work of literature. Tone refers specifically to the author's own attitude toward the characters and events in the story, poem, or play. The mood of "Young Goodman Brown" (page 235), for instance, is gloomy, doubtful, and despairing, and is communicated by descriptive details such as *dreary road, uncertain light, black mass of cloud,* and *frenzied gestures.* Hawthorne's tone toward Young Goodman Brown is reproachful and pitying. Hawthorne's reproach is conveyed through Goodman Brown's own words as he leaves his wife, Faith: "What a wretch I am to leave her on such an errand!" Hawthorne's pity is evident in this passage, which describes Brown after his experience in the forest: "A stern, a sad, a darkly meditative, a distrustful, if not a desperate man did he become from the night of the fearful dream."

tragedy: a play having a serious mood and ending in death or disaster for the protagonist. A tragedy is usually about a hero who is good, even noble, in most ways, but who has some flaw or makes some mistake that brings about the final disaster.

unity: the effect achieved when all parts of a literary work contribute to one main impression or goal. This goal may be the development of a theme, the creation of a mood, or the revelation of a character. In a unified work of literature, the writer selects only those details of plot, character, or image that contribute to the major idea or mood. Nothing distracts the reader. The action in *Our Town* (page 533) covers several years, yet unity is achieved both by the comments of the Stage Manager and the reappearance of all the major characters at intervals throughout the play. The unchanging setting—the town of Grover's Corners—also contributes to the play's unity.

willing suspension of disbelief: the reader's willingness to accept a make-believe world created in a fantasy or other unrealistic types of literature. Writers of unrealistic literature usually include many realistic, believable details in their works. This partial realism helps the readers accept the fantastic elements—to suspend their disbelief. Most of the details of everyday life in "Rip Van Winkle" (page 208), for example, accurately reflect life in the Catskill Mountains during the last half of the eighteenth century. Rip, himself, is a familiar type of person, as are all the other characters in the story. These realistic details help the reader accept Rip's encounter with Hendrik Hudson and his subsequent twenty-year nap.

Glossary

The glossary includes unfamiliar words used in this anthology. In most cases words that are footnotes in the text are not included here. The order and kinds of information given in an entry are shown below:

1. The defined word is divided into syllables. For example: **con·den·sa·tion**.

2. Pronunciation. The pronunciation of each defined word is given. For example: **syn·chro·nize** (sing′krə nīz).

3. Accents. The mark ′ is placed after a syllable with primary or heavy accent, and the mark ′ after a syllable shows a secondary or lighter accent, as in **in·com·pre·hen·si·ble** (in′kom pri hen′sə bəl).

4. The part of speech and, when useful, information about the singular or plural form.

5. Definition. The words are always defined according to their use in the book; in addition, other commonly used meanings are frequently given.

6. Alternate spellings. For example: **di·shev·eled** . . . —Also, **dishevelled**.

7. Derivative parts of speech. Other commonly used parts of speech derived from an entry are frequently given. For example: **pred·a·tor** . . . —**predatory**, *adj.*

    The following abbreviations are used:

adj.	adjective
adv.	adverb
n.	noun
pl.	plural
v.	verb

Pronunciation Key

a, hat, cap; **ā**, age, face; **ä**, father, far; **b**, bad, rob; **ch**, child, much; **d**, did, red; **e**, let, best; **ē**, equal, be; **ėr**, term, learn; **f**, fat, if; **g**, go, bag; **h**, he, how; **i**, it, pin; **ī**, ice, five; **j**, jam, enjoy; **k**, kind, seek; **l**, land, coal; **m**, me, am; **n**, no, in; **ng**, long, bring; **o**, hot, rock; **ō**, open, go; **ô**, order, all; **oi**, oil, voice; **ou**, house, out; **p**, paper, cup; **r**, run, try; **s**, say, yes; **sh**, she, rush; **t**, tell, it; **th**, thin, both; **ŦH**, then, smooth; **u**, cup, butter; **u̇**, full, put; **ü**, rule, move; **v**, very, save; **w**, will, woman; **y**, young, yet; **z**, zero, breeze; **zh**, measure, seizure; **ə** represents: a in about, e in taken, i in pencil, o in lemon, u in circus.

Y as in Fr. *du;* **à** as in Fr. *ami;* **œ** as in Fr. *peu;* **N** as in Fr. *bon;* **H** as in Ger. *ach.*

a·base (ə bās′), v. to make lower in rank, condition, or character; degrade.

a·bate (ə bat′), v. **1.** lessen in force or intensity; reduce or decrease. **2.** put an end to; stop.

ab·er·ra·tion (ab′ə rā′shən), n. **1.** a temporary mental disorder. **2.** a deviating from the right path or usual course of action.

ab·hor·rence (ab hôr′əns), n. **1.** a feeling of very great hatred. **2.** something detested.

ab·ject (ab′jekt), adj. **1.** so low or degraded as to be hopeless; wretched; miserable. **2.** deserving contempt; despicable. **3.** slavish.

a·bridge (ə brij′), v. **1.** make shorter by using fewer words but retaining the sense and substance; condense. **2.** make less; diminish; curtail.

ab·ro·gate (ab′rə gāt), v. **1.** abolish or annul by an authoritative act; repeal; cancel. **2.** do away with.

a·brupt (ə brupt′), adj. **1.** characterized by a sudden change; unexpected. **2.** short or sudden in speech or manner; blunt.

ab·solve (ab solv′), v. **1.** to pronounce or set (a person) free from sin, guilt, blame, or their penalties or consequences. **2.** set free (from a promise, obligation, or duty); release.

ab·sorp·tion (ab sôrp′shən), n. great interest (in something).

ab·stain (ab stān′), v. hold oneself back voluntarily, especially because of one's principles; refrain.

ac·co·lade (ak′ə lād), n. recognition of merit; praise in recognition of an accomplishment; award.

ac·qui·esce (ak′wē es′), v. give consent by keeping silent or by not making objections; accept (the conclusions or arrangements of others); accede. —**acquiescence,** n.

Pronunciation Key, respellings, and definitions in the Glossary are from SCOTT, FORESMAN ADVANCED DICTIONARY by E. L. Thorndike and Clarence L. Barnhart. Copyright © 1979 by Scott, Foresman and Company. Reprinted by permission.

---

hat, āge, fär; let, ēqual, tėrm;
it, īce; hot, ōpen, ôrder;
oil, out; cup, pùt, rüle;
ch, child; ng, long; sh, she;
th, thin; ŦH, then; zh, measure;

ə represents *a* in about, *e* in taken,
i in pencil, *o* in lemon, *u* in circus.

ad·her·ent (ad hir′ənt), n. a faithful supporter or follower.

ad·mon·ish (ad mon′ish), v. **1.** advise against something; warn. **2.** scold gently; reprove. **3.** urge strongly; advise earnestly. —**admonition,** n.

ad·ren·al·ine (ə dren′l ən), n. hormone secreted by the medulla of the adrenal glands, which speeds up the heartbeat and thereby increases bodily energy and resistance to fatigue.

aes·thet·ic (es thet′ik), adj. **1.** based on or determined by beauty rather than by practically useful, scientific, or moral considerations. **2.** having or showing an appreciation of beauty in nature or art.

af·fec·ta·tion (af′ek tā′shən), n. **1.** behavior that is not natural, but assumed to impress others. **2.** mannerism or choice of language that indicates a tendency toward this.

af·firm (ə ferm′), v. declare positively to be true; maintain firmly; assert.

a·lac·ri·ty (ə lak′rə tē), n. **1.** brisk and eager action; liveliness. **2.** cheerful willingness.

al·ien (ā′lyən), n., adj. —n. **1.** person who is not a citizen of the country in which he lives. **2.** person belonging to a different ethnic or social group; stranger; foreigner. —adj. **1.** of or by another country; foreign. **2.** entirely different from one's own; strange.

alms·house (ämz′hous′), n. home for very poor persons supported at public expense or, in Great Britain, by private charity.

al·ter·ca·tion (ôl′tər kā′shən), n. an angry dispute; noisy quarrel; wrangle.

am·big·u·ous (am big′yü əs), adj. **1.** of doubtful position or classification. **2.** having or permitting more than one interpretation or explanation. **3.** not clearly defined; doubtful; uncertain.

a·mi·a·ble (ā′mē ə bəl), adj. having a good-natured and friendly disposition; pleasant and agreeable.

am·u·let (am′yə lit), n. locket, carved image, or some other small object worn as a magic charm against evil or disease.

a·nach·ro·nism (ə nak′rə niz′əm), n. **1.** error in fixing a date or dates; erroneous reference of an event, circumstance, or custom to a wrong, especially an earlier date. **2.** anything out of keeping with a specified time, especially something proper to a former age but not to the present.

an·ni·hi·late (ə nī′ə lāt), v. destroy completely; wipe out of existence.

an·ti·phon (an′tə fon), *n.* psalm, hymn, or prayer sung or chanted in alternate parts. **—antiphonal,** *adj.*

a·pos·tro·phe (ə pos′trə fē), *n.* words addressed to an absent person as if he were present or to a thing or idea as if it could hear or reply.

a·poth·e·o·sis (ə poth′ē ō′sis), *n.* **1.** a glorified ideal. **2.** the raising of a human being to the rank of a god; deification.

ap·pa·ri·tion (ap′ə rish′ən), *n.* **1.** a supernatural sight or thing; ghost or phantom. **2.** the appearance of something strange, remarkable, or unexpected.

ap·pre·hen·sion (ap′ri hen′shən), *n.* **1.** expectation of misfortune; dread of impending danger; fear. **2.** arrest.

ap·pro·ba·tion (ap′rə bā′shən), *n.* **1.** favorable opinion; approval. **2.** act of formally and authoritatively approving; sanction.

ar·du·ous (är′jü əs), *adj.* **1.** hard to do; requiring much effort; difficult. **2.** using up much energy; strenuous.

ar·peg·gi·o (är pej′ē ō), *n.* in music: **1.** the sounding of the notes of a chord in rapid succession instead of simultaneously. **2.** chord played in this way.

ar·tic·u·late (är tik′yə lit), *adj.* able to put one's thoughts into words easily and clearly.

ar·ti·fact (är′tə fakt), *n.* anything made by human skill or work, especially a tool or weapon.

as·sail (ə sāl′), *v.* **1.** attack repeatedly with violent blows. **2.** attack with hostile words, arguments, or abuse.

as·sid·u·ous (ə sij′ü əs), *adj.* careful and attentive; diligent.

aug·ment (ôg ment′), *v.* make or become greater in size, number, amount, or degree; increase or enlarge.

aus·tere (ô stir′), *adj.* **1.** stern in manner or appearance; harsh. **2.** severe in self-discipline; strict in morals. **3.** severely simple. **4.** grave; somber; serious. **—austerity,** *n.*

a·verse (ə vèrs′), *adj.* having a strong or fixed dislike; opposed or unwilling. **—aversion,** *n.*

ba·nal (bā′nl), *adj.* not new or interesting; commonplace; trite.

be·guile (bi gīl′), *v.* **1.** trick or mislead (a person); deceive; delude. **2.** win the attention of; entertain; amuse.

be·mused (bi myüzd′), *adj.* **1.** confused; bewildered; stupefied. **2.** absorbed in thought.

be·nev·o·lent (bə nev′ə lənt), *adj.* wishing or intended to promote the happiness of others; kindly; charitable.

be·rate (bi rāt′), *v.* scold sharply; upbraid.

bland (bland), *adj.* **1.** smoothly agreeable and polite. **2.** soothing to the palate or digestive tract. **3.** gentle or soothing

blas·phe·my (blas′fə mē), *n.* abuse or contempt for God or sacred things.

buoy (boi), *n.* a floating object anchored on the water to warn against hidden rocks or shallows or to indicate the safe part of a channel.

cal·cine (kal′sīn), *v.* burn (something) to ashes or powder.

ca·pa·cious (kə pā′shəs), *adj.* able to hold much; large and roomy; spacious.

ca·pit·u·late (kə pich′ə lāt), *v.* surrender on certain terms or conditions.

cat·a·clysm (kat′ə kliz′əm), *n.* **1.** a great flood, earthquake, or any sudden, violent change in the earth. **2.** any violent change or upheaval.

cha·me·le·on (kə mē′lē ən), *n.* **1.** a small lizard that can change the color of its skin to blend with its surroundings. **2.** a changeable or fickle person.

chide (chīd), *v.* find fault; speak in rebuke. **—chidingly,** *adv.*

co·a·lesce (kō′ə les′), *v.* **1.** grow together. **2.** unite into one body. **3.** mass party; combine.

co·her·ent (kō hir′ənt), *adj.* **1.** logically connected; consistent. **2.** sticking together; holding together. **—incoherence,** *n.* lack of logical connection.

com·mis·e·rate (kə miz′ə rāt′), *v.* feel or express sorrow for another's suffering or trouble; sympathize with; pity.

com·pe·tent (kom′pə tənt), *adj.* **1.** properly qualified; able; fit. **2.** legally qualified. **—incompetent,** *adj.* lacking ability.

com·pli·ance (kəm plī′əns), *n.* **1.** a doing as another wishes; yielding to a request or command. **2.** tendency to yield to others.

com·pul·sion (kəm pul′shən), *n.* **1.** impulse that is hard to resist. **2.** use of force; force; coercion.

con·den·sa·tion (kon′den sā′shən), *n.* a changing of a gas or vapor to a liquid.

con·jec·ture (kən jek′chər), *v.* to form an opinion admittedly without sufficient evidence for proof; guessing. **—conjecture,** *n.*

con·niv·ance (kə nī′vəns), *n.* pretended ignorance or secret encouragement of wrongdoing.

con·nu·bi·al (kə nü′bē əl), *adj.* of or having to do with marriage.

con·sci·en·tious (kon′shē en′shəs), *adj.* **1.** careful to do what one knows is right; controlled by conscience. **2.** done with care to make it right; painstaking.

con·spic·u·ous (kən spik′yü əs), *adj.* **1.** easily seen; clearly visible. **2.** worthy of notice; remarkable.

con·ster·na·tion (kon′stər nā′shən), *n.* great dismay; paralyzing terror.

con·strict (kən strikt′), *v.* draw together; contract; compress.

con·strue (kən strü′), *v.* show the meaning of; explain; interpret.

con·sum·mate (kon′sə māt), *v.* bring to completion; realize; fulfill.

con·tem·po·ra·ne·ous (kən tem′pə rā′nē əs), *adj.* **1.** belonging to or living in the same period of time. **2.** of the same age or date. **3.** of or having to do with the present time; modern. **—contemporaneousness,** *n.*

con·ten·tious (kən ten′shəs), *adj.* fond of arguing; given to disputing; quarrelsome.

con·vo·lu·tion (kon′və lü′shən), *n.* **1.** a coiling, winding, or twisting together. **2.** an irregular fold or ridge on the surface of the brain.

cor·rode (kə rōd′), *v.* eat away gradually, especially by or as if by chemical action.

coun·te·nance (koun′tə nəns), *n.* **1.** expression of the face. **2.** face; features.

cov·e·nant (kuv′ə nənt), *n.* **1.** a solemn agreement between two or more persons or groups to do or not to do a certain thing; compact. **2.** a formal agreement that is legal. **—covenant,** *v.*

cred·it·a·ble (kred′ə tə bəl), *adj.* bringing credit or honor.

cryp·tic (krip′tik), *adj.* having a hidden meaning; secret; mysterious.

dec·a·dent (dek′ə dənt), *adj.* falling off; growing worse; declining; decaying.

---

hat, āge, fär; let, ēqual, tėrm;
it, īce; hot, ōpen, ôrder;
oil, out; cup, pût, rüle;
ch, child; ng, long; sh, she;
th, thin; ŦH, then; zh, measure;

ə represents *a* in about, *e* in taken,
i in pencil, *o* in lemon, *u* in circus.

de·cliv·i·ty (di kliv′ə tē), *n.* a downward slope.

dec·or·ous (dek′ər əs), *adj.* acting properly; in good taste; well-behaved; dignified. **—decorum,** *n.*

def·er·ence (def′ər əns), *n.* **1.** a yielding to the judgment, opinion, wishes of another. **2.** great respect. **3.** in deference to, out of respect for the wishes or authority of. **—deferential,** *adj.* **—deferentially,** *adv.*

de·gen·e·rate (*v.* di jen′ə rāt′; *adj., n.* di jen′ər it), *v.* grow worse; decline in physical, mental, or moral qualities. **—degenerate,** *adj., n.*

de·lec·ta·ble (di lek′tə bəl), *adj.* very pleasant; delightful.

del·e·ter·i·ous (del′ə tir′e əs), *adj.* causing harm; injurious.

del·uge (del′yüj), *n.* **1.** a great flood. **2.** a heavy fall of rain. **3.** any overwhelming rush. **—deluge,** *v.*

de·mean·or (di mē′nər), *n.* way a person looks and acts; behavior; manner.

de·nun·ci·a·tion (di nun′sē ā′shən), *n.* expression of strong disapproval; public condemnation; denouncing.

de·range (di rānj′), *v.* **1.** disturb the order or arrangement of; throw into confusion. **2.** make insane.

de·ri·sive (di rī′siv), *adj.* that ridicules; mocking.

des·ha·bille (dez′ə bēl′), *n.* see dishabille.

de·sist (di zist′), *v.* stop doing something; cease.

des·pot·ism (des′pə tis′əm), *n.* **1.** government by an absolute ruler. **2.** tyranny or oppression. **—despot,** *n.*

des·ul·to·ry (des′əl tôr′ē), *adj.* jumping from one thing to another; without aim or method; unconnected.

de·vi·ate (dē′vē āt), *v., n., —v.* **1.** turn aside (from a way, course, rule, truth); diverge. **2.** cause to turn aside; deflect. **—n.** an individual who shows a marked difference from the norm. **—deviate,** *adj.*

dex·ter·ous (dek′stər əs), *adj.* skillful in using the hands or body. Also, **dextrous.**

di·min·u·tive (də min′yə tiv), *adj., n. —adj.* **1.** very small; tiny; minute. **2.** (in grammar) expressing smallness. **—n.** **1.** a small person or thing. **2.** word or part of a word expressing smallness. The suffixes *-kin, -let,* and *-ling* are diminutives.

dis·cern (də zėrn′), *v.* see clearly; perceive the difference between (two or more things); distinguish or recognize.

dis·dain (dis dān′), *v., n. —v.* think unworthy of oneself or one's notice; regard or treat with contempt; scorn. **—n.** a disdaining; feeling of scorn.

dis·ha·bille (dis′ə bēl′), *n.* **1.** informal, careless dress. **2.** condition of being partly undressed. Also, **des·habille.**

di·shev·eled (də shev′əld), *adj.* **1.** not neat; rumpled; mussed; untidy. **2.** hanging loosely or in disorder. —Also, **dishevelled.**

dis·pu·ta·tious (dis′pyə tā′shəs), *adj.* fond of disputing; inclined to argue; contentious.

dis·sim·u·late (di sim′yə lāt), *v.* disguise or hide under a pretense. —**dissimulation,** *n.*

dis·so·lu·tion (dis′ə lü′shən), *n.* **1.** a breaking up or ending of an association of any kind. **2.** the breaking up of an assembly by ending its session. **3.** ruin. **4.** death.

dys·pep·si·a (dis pep′sē ə), *n.* indigestion.

ef·fi·ca·cy (ef′ə kə sē), *n.* power to produce the effect wanted; effectiveness.

ef·flu·vi·um (i flü′vē əm), *n., pl.* **-vi·a** (vē ə), **-vi·ums.** vapor or odor, usually unpleasant.

ef·fron·ter·y (ə frun′tər ē), *n.* shameless boldness; impudence.

e·lic·it (i lis′it), *v.* draw forth; bring out.

el·lip·sis (i lip′sis), *n.* **1.** omission of a word or words needed to complete the grammatical construction, but not the meaning, of a sentence. **2.** marks (. . . or * * *) used to show an omission in writing or printing. —**elliptic,** *adj.*

e·lon·gate (i lông′gāt), *v.* make or become longer; lengthen; extend; stretch.

e·lude (i lüd′), *v.* **1.** avoid or escape by cleverness; slip away from; evade. **2.** baffle. —**elusive,** *adj.*

em·i·nent (em′ə nənt), *adj.* **1.** above all or most others; outstanding; distinguished. **2.** high; lofty.

e·mit (i mit′), *v.* **1.** give off; send out; discharge. **2.** utter; express.

en·cum·brance (en kum′brəns), *n.* something useless or in the way; hindrance; burden.

en·ig·mat·ic (en′ig mat′ik), *adj.* like a riddle; baffling; puzzling.

e·on (ē′ən), *n.* a very long period of time; many thousands of years.

e·piph·a·ny (i pif′ə nē), *n.* **1.** a sudden manifestation or perception of essential nature or meaning of something as in a sudden flash of recognition. **2.** an intuitive grasp of reality through something (an event) simple and striking.

ep·i·thet (ep′ə thet), *n.* an insulting or contemptuous word or phrase used in place of a person's name.

e·pit·o·me (i pit′ə mē), *n.* person or thing that is typical or representative of something.

ep·och (ep′ək), *n.* **1.** period of time; era; age. **2.** period of time in which striking things happened.

e·qua·nim·i·ty (ē′kwə nim′ə tē), *n.* evenness of mind or temper; calmness; composure.

e·qui·lib·ri·um (ē′kwə lib′rē əm), *n.* **1.** state of balance; condition in which opposing forces exactly balance or equal each other. **2.** mental poise.

e·ther·e·al (i thir′ē əl), *adj.* **1.** light; airy; delicate. **2.** not of the earth; heavenly.

eu·pho·ny (yü′fə nē), *n.* pleasing effect to the ear; agreeable sound; agreeableness of speech sounds as uttered or combined in utterance.

ev·a·nes·cence (ev′ə nes′ns), *n.* a fading away; vanishing.

e·vince (i vins′), *v.* **1.** show clearly; manifest. **2.** show that one has (a certain quality, trait).

ex·cru·ci·at·ing (ek skrü′shē ā′ting), *adj.* **1.** causing great suffering; very painful; torturing. **2.** excessively elaborate; extreme.

ex·e·cra·ble (ek′sə krə bəl), *adj.* abominable; detestable.

ex·em·plar·y (eg zem′plər ē), *adj.* **1.** worth imitating; serving as a model or pattern. **2.** serving as a warning to others.

ex·tem·po·rize (ek stem′pə rīz′), *v.* **1.** speak, play, sing, or dance, composing as one goes along; improvise. **2.** prepare offhand; make for the occasion.

ex·tort (ek stôrt′), *v.* obtain (money, a promise) by threats, force, fraud, or illegal use of authority.

fa·cade or **fa·çade** (fə säd′), *n.* **1.** outward appearance **2.** the front part of a building.

fas·cism (fash′iz′əm), *n.* **1.** the principles or methods of a government or a political party favoring rule by dictator, with strong control of industry and labor by the central government, great restrictions upon the freedom of individuals, and extreme nationalism and militarism. **2.** any movement favoring such a system of government.

fas·tid·i·ous (fa stid′ē əs), *adj.* hard to please; dainty in taste; easily disgusted.

fat·u·ous (fach′ü əs), *adj.* stupid but self-satisfied; foolish; silly.

fer·vid (fėr′vid), *adj.* **1.** full of strong feeling; intensely emotional; ardent; spirited. **2.** intensely hot.

fran·chise (fran′chīz), *n.* **1.** privilege or right granted by a government to an individual or individuals. **2.** right to vote. —**franchise,** *v.*

ga·ble (gā′bəl), *n.* **1.** end of a ridged roof, with the three-cornered piece of wall that it covers. **2.** an end wall with a gable.

gar·goyle (gär′goil), *n.* spout for carrying off rain water, ending in a grotesque figure of a head that projects from the gutter of a building.

ge·ner·ic (jə ner′ik), *adj.* **1.** characteristic of a genus, kind, or class. **2.** having to do with a class or group of similar things; not specific or special.

gen·u·flect (jen′yə flekt), *v.* bend the knee as an act of reverence or worship.

glean (glēn), *v.* **1.** gather (grain) left on a field by reapers. **2.** gather little by little.

gul·li·bil·i·ty (gul′ə bil′ə tē), *n.* tendency to be easily deceived or cheated. —**gullible,** *adj.*

hei·nous (hā′nəs), *adj.* very wicked; extremely offensive; hateful.

hy·poth·e·sis (hī poth′ə sis), *n.* something assumed because it seems likely to be a true explanation.

ig·no·ble (ig nō′bəl), *adj.* **1.** without honor; disgraceful; base. **2.** not of noble birth or position; humble.

ig·no·min·i·ous (ig′nə min′ē əs), *adj.* **1.** shameful; disgraceful; dishonorable. **2.** contemptible. **3.** lowering one's dignity; humiliating.

im·merse (i mėrs′), *v.* **1.** dip or lower into a liquid until covered by it. **2.** involve deeply; absorb. —**immersion,** *n.*

im·pen·e·tra·ble (im pen′ə trə bəl), *adj.* that cannot be penetrated, pierced, or passed.

im·per·i·ous (im pir′ē əs), *adj.* **1.** haughty or arrogant; domineering; overbearing. **2.** not to be avoided; necessary; urgent. —**imperiously,** *adv.*

im·per·ti·nent (im pėrt′n ənt), *adj.* **1.** rudely bold; impudent. **2.** not pertinent; not to the point; out of place. —**impertinence,** *n.*

im·per·turb·a·ble (im′pər tėr′bə bəl), *adj.* not easily excited or disturbed; calm.

im·per·vi·ous (im pėr′vē əs), *adj.* **1.** allowing no passage; impermeable. **2.** not open to argument or suggestions.

im·preg·na·ble (im preg′nə bəl), *adj.* able to resist attack; not yielding to force or persuasion.

im·pu·ni·ty (im pyü′nə tē), *n.* freedom from punishment, injury or other bad consequences.

in·al·ien·a·ble (in ā′lyə nə bəl), *adj.* that cannot be given or taken away; that cannot be transferred to another.

in·cen·tive (in sen′tiv), *n.* thing that urges a person on; cause of action or effort; motive; stimulus.

in·com·pre·hen·si·ble (in′kom pri hen′sə bəl), *adj.* impossible to understand.

in·con·ti·nent (in kon′tə nənt), *adj.* without self-control.

in·cor·ri·gi·ble (in kôr′ə jə bəl), *adj., n.* —*adj.* too firmly fixed in bad ways or an annoying habit to be reformed or changed.

in·cred·u·lous (in krej′ə ləs), *adj.* **1.** not ready to believe; doubting; skeptical. **2.** showing a lack of belief. —**incredulity,** *n.*

in·cre·ment (in′krə mənt), *n.* **1.** an increasing or becoming greater; increase; growth. **2.** amount or portion added to a thing so as to increase it; addition.

in·de·ci·pher·a·ble (in′di sī′fər ə bəl), *adj.* incapable of being interpreted, read, or understood; illegible.

in·del·i·ble (in del′ə bəl), *adj.* that cannot be erased or removed; permanent.

in·dig·na·tion (in′dig nā′shən), *n.* anger at something unworthy, unjust, unfair, or mean; anger mixed with scorn; righteous anger.

in·dom·i·ta·ble (in dom′ə tə bəl), *adj.* that cannot be conquered; unyielding.

in·ex·or·a·ble (in ek′sər ə bəl), *adj.* not influenced by pleading or entreaties; relentless; unyielding.

in·ex·plic·a·ble (in′ik splik′ə bəl), *adj.* that cannot be explained, understood, or accounted for; mysterious.

in·fal·li·ble (in fal′ə bəl), *adj.* **1.** free from error; that cannot be mistaken. **2.** absolutely reliable; sure.

in·flec·tion (in flek′shən), *n.* a change in the tone or pitch of the voice.

in·im·i·ta·ble (in im′ə tə bəl), *adj.* impossible to imitate or copy; matchless.

in·nu·en·do (in′yü en′dō), *n.* **1.** an indirect hint or reference; insinuation. **2.** an indirect suggestion meant to discredit a person.

hat, āge, fär; let, ēqual, term;
it, īce; hot, ōpen, ôrder;
oil, out; cup, pùt, rüle;
ch, child; ng, long; sh, she;
th, thin; ŦH, then; zh, measure;

ə represents *a* in about, *e* in taken,
i in pencil, *o* in lemon, *u* in circus.

in·or·di·nate (in ôrd′n it), *adj.* much too great; not kept within proper limits; excessive. **—inordinately,** *adv.*

in·sa·tia·ble (in sā′shə bəl), *adj.* that cannot be satisfied; extremely greedy. **—insatiate** (in sā′shē it), *adj.*

in·scru·ta·ble in skrü′tə bəl), *adj.* that cannot be understood; so mysterious or obscure that one cannot make out its meaning.

in·so·lent (in′sə lənt), *adj.* boldly rude; intentionally disregarding the feelings of others; insulting.

in·su·per·a·ble (in sü′pər ə bəl), *adj.* that cannot be passed over or overcome; insurmountable.

in·ter·mi·na·ble (in tėr′mə nə bəl), *adj.* **1.** never stopping; unceasing; endless. **2.** so long as to seem endless.

in·ter·mit·tent (in′tər mit′nt), *adj.* stopping for a time and beginning again; pausing at intervals.

in·ti·ma·tion (in′tə mā′shən), *n.* **1.** an indirect suggestion, hint. **2.** announcement; notice.

in·to·na·tion (in′tō nā′shən), *n.* the rise and fall in the pitch of the voice during speech.

in·vet·er·ate (in vet′ər it), *adj.* **1.** confirmed in a habit, practice, feeling; habitual. **2.** long and firmly established; deeply rooted.

in·vin·ci·ble (in vin′sə bəl), *adj.* unable to be conquered; impossible to overcome; unconquerable.

in·vi·o·la·ble (in vī′ə lə bəl), *adj.* **1.** that must not be violated or injured; sacred. **2.** that cannot be violated or injured.

ir·i·des·cent (ir′ə des′nt), *adj.* displaying changing colors; changing color when moved or turned.

is·sue (ish′ü), *n.* child or children; offspring.

ju·di·cious (jü dish′əs), *adj.* having, using, or showing good judgment; wise; sensible.

jug·ger·naut (jug′ər nôt), *n.* **1.** something to which people blindly devote themselves or are cruelly sacrificed. **2.** a frightening, invisible machine or force that destroys anything in its path.

jux·ta·pose (juk′stə pōz′), *v.* put close together; place side by side.

lan·guid (lang′gwid), *adj.* **1.** without energy; drooping; weak; weary. **2.** without interest or enthusiasm; indifferent; listless. **3.** not brisk or lively; sluggish; dull.

le·sion (lē′shən), *n.* **1.** an injury; hurt. **2.** an abnormal change in the structure of an organ or body tissue, caused by disease or injury.

le·thar·gic (lə thär′jik), *adj.* **1.** unnaturally drowsy; sluggish; dull. **2.** producing drowsiness or sluggishness.

lin·e·a·ment (lin′ē ə mənt), *n.* part or feature, especially a part or feature of a face with attention to its outline.

lo·qua·cious (lō kwā′shəs), *adj.* talking much; fond of talking.

lu·cid (lü′sid), *adj.* **1.** marked by clearness of reasoning, expression, or arrangement; easy to follow or understand. **2.** clear in intellect; rational; sane. **3.** translucent; clear. **4.** shining; bright; luminous.

lu·gu·bri·ous (lü gü′brē əs), *adj.* too sad; overly mournful.

ma·ca·bre (mə kä′brə), *adj.* causing horror; gruesome; horrible; ghastly.

mal·ice (mal′is), *n.* active ill will; wish to hurt or make suffer; rancor.

mal·le·a·ble (mal′ē ə bəl), *adj.* **1.** adaptable; yielding. **2.** that can be hammered, rolled, or extended into various shapes without being broken.

ma·nip·u·late (mə nip′yə lāt), *v.* **1.** handle or treat, especially skillfully. **2.** manage cleverly, sometimes using personal influence, especially unfair influence. **3.** change for one's own purpose or advantage.

mel·an·chol·y (mel′ən kol′ē), *adj.* **1.** depressed in spirits; sad; gloomy. **2.** causing sadness; depressing. **—melancholy,** *n.*

me·rid·i·an (mə rid′ē ən), *n.* **1.** an imaginary great circle passing through any place on the earth's surface and through the North and South Poles. **2.** the half of such a circle from pole to pole. All the places on the same meridian have the same longitude.

met·a·mor·phose (met′ə môr′fōz), *v.* change in form, structure, or substance by or as if by witchcraft; transform.

mis·cal·cu·late (mis kal′kyə lāt), *v.* calculate wrongly or incorrectly. **—miscalculation,** *n.*

molt (mōlt), *v.* shed the feathers, skin, hair, shell, antlers, before a new growth. Also, **moult.**

mon·o·lith (mon′l ith), *n.* **1.** a single large block of stone. **2.** monument, column, statue formed of a single large block of stone. **3.** nation or political party that in its rigid and unyielding attitudes and policies suggests a massive block of stone.

mo·rose (mə rōs′), *adj.* gloomy; sullen; ill-humored.

moult (mōlt), *v.* see molt.

myr·i·ad (mir′ē əd), *adj.* **1.** ten thousand. **2.** countless; innumerable. **—myriad,** *n.*

ne·ga·tion (ni gā′shən), *n.* **1.** a denying; denial. **2.** absence or opposite of some positive thing or quality.

nim·bus (nim′bəs), *n.* **1.** halo. **2.** a bright red cloud surrounding a god, person, or thing.

nu·ance (nü äns′), *n.* a shade of expression, feeling, meaning.

o·blique (ə blēk′), *adj.* **1.** neither perpendicular to nor parallel with a given line or surface; not straight up and down or straight across; slanting. **2.** not straightforward; indirect.

o·blit·e·rate (ə blit′ə rāt′), *v.* **1.** remove all traces of; blot out; efface. **2.** blot out so as to leave no distinct traces; make unrecognizable.

ob·scur·i·ty (əb skúr′ə tē), *n.* **1.** lack of clearness; difficulty in being understood. **2.** something obscure; thing hard to understand; point or passage not clearly expressed; doubtful or vague meaning. **3.** condition of being unknown. **4.** lack of light; dimness.

ob·se·qui·ous (əb sē′kwē əs), *adj.* polite or obedient from hope of gain or from fear; servile; fawning.

ob·strep·er·ous (əb strep′ər əs), *adj.* **1.** loud or noisy; boisterous; clamorous. **2.** unruly; disorderly.

om·i·nous (om′ə nəs), *adj.* of bad omen; unfavorable; threatening.

o·paque (ō pāk′), *adj.* **1.** not letting light through; not transparent or translucent. **2.** not shining; dark; dull.

pall (pôl), *n.* **1.** a dark, gloomy covering. **2.** a heavy, dark cloth, often made of velvet, spread over a coffin, a hearse, or a tomb.

par·a·dox (par′ə doks), *n.* **1.** statement that may be true but seems to say two opposite things. EXAMPLES. "More haste, less speed." "The child is father to the man." **2.** statement that is false because it says two opposite things.

pa·tron·ize (pā′trə nīz), *v.* **1.** to be a regular cus-

---

hat, āge, fär; let, ēqual, tėrm;
it, īce; hot, ōpen, ôrder;
oil, out; cup, pút, rüle;
ch, child; ng, long; sh, she;
th, thin; out; cup, pút, rüle;
ch, child; ng, long; sh, she;
th, thin; ₮H, then; zh, measure;

ə represents *a* in about, *e* in taken,
i in pencil, *o* in lemon, *u* in circus.

---

tomer of; give regular business to. **2.** to support or protect. **3.** treat in a haughty, condescending way.

pen·i·tent (pen′ə tənt), *adj.* sorry for sinning or doing wrong; repenting; repentant. —**penitent,** *n.*

pe·remp·to·ry (pə remp′tər ē), *adj.* **1.** leaving no choice; decisive; final; absolute. **2.** allowing no denial or refusal **3.** imperious; dictatorial.

per·ni·cious (pər nish′əs), *adj.* **1.** that will destroy or ruin; causing great harm or damage; very injurious. **2.** fatal; deadly.

per·pet·u·al (pər pech′ü əl), *adj.* **1.** lasting forever; eternal. **2.** never ceasing; continuous; constant.

per·se·vere (per′sə vir′), *v.* continue steadily in doing something hard; persist.

per·ti·nence (pert′n əns), *n.* a being to the point; fitness; relevance.

phlegm (flem), *n.* **1.** coolness; calmness. **2.** sluggish disposition or temperament; indifference.

pique (pēk), *v.* **1.** cause a feeling of anger in; wound the pride of. **2.** arouse; stir up.

piz·zi·ca·to (pit′sə kä′tō), *adj.* in music, played by plucking the strings of a musical instrument with the finger instead of using the bow.

plac·id (plas′id), *adj.* pleasantly calm or peaceful; quiet.

plain·tive (plān′tiv), *adj.* expressive of sorrow; mournful; sad.

poign·ant (poi′nyənt), *adj.* **1.** very painful; piercing. **2.** stimulating to the mind, feelings, or passions; keen; intense.

po·lar·i·za·tion (pō′lər ə zā′shən), *n.* (in optics) a state, or the production of a state, in which rays of light exhibit different properties in different directions. —**polarize,** *v.*

prec·i·pice (pres′ə pis), *n.* **1.** a very steep or almost vertical face of a rock; cliff, crag, or steep mountainside. **2.** situation of great peril; critical position.

pre·cip·i·ta·tion (pri sip′ə tā′shən), *n.* **1.** a hastening or hurrying. **2.** unwise or rash rapidity.

pre·ci·sion (pri sizh′ən), *n.* fact or condition of being exact; accuracy. —**precise,** *adj.*

pred·a·tor (pred′ə tər), *n.* animal or person that lives by killing other animals for its food. —**predatory,** *adj.*

pred·e·ces·sor (pred′ə ses′ər), *n.* **1.** a person holding a position or office before another. **2.** thing that came before another.

pre·rog·a·tive (pri rog′ə tiv), *n.* right or privilege that nobody else has.

pre·sump·tion (pri zump′shən), *n.* **1.** unpleasant

boldness. **2.** thing taken for granted; assumption; supposition.

pre·ten·tious (pri ten′shəs), *adj.* **1.** making claims to excellence or importance. **2.** doing things for show or to make a fine appearance; showy.

pro·gen·i·tor (prō jen′ə tər), *n.* ancestor in the direct line; forefather.

pro·pi·tious (prə pish′əs), *adj.* **1.** holding well; favorable. **2.** favorably inclined; gracious.

pro·pri·e·ty (prə prī′ə tē), *n.* **1.** quality or condition of being proper; fitness. **2.** proper behavior.

pro·sa·ic (prō zā′ik), *adj.* like prose; matter-of-fact; ordinary; not exciting.

pro·ver·bi·al (prə vėr′bē əl), *adj.* **1.** of proverbs; expressed in a proverb. **2.** well-known.

prov·i·dence (prov′ə dəns), *n.* God's care and help.

prov·o·ca·tion (prov′ə ka′shən), *n.* an act or thing that stirs up, induces, starts into action.

pru·dent (prüd′nt), *adj.* **1.** planning carefully ahead of time; sensible; discreet. **2.** characterized by good judgment or good management.

pu·gi·lis·tic (pyü′jə lis′tik), *adj.* of or having to do with boxing.

qui·es·cent (kwī es′nt), *adj.* quiet and motionless; inactive; still.

rav·en·ous (rav′ə nəs), *adj.* **1.** greedy. **2.** very hungry.

re·cip·ro·cate (ri sip′rə kāt), *v.* **1.** give, do, feel, or show in return. **2.** cause to move with an alternating backward and forward motion.

rec·om·pense (rek′əm pens), *v.* **1.** pay (a person); pay back; reward. **2.** make a fair return for (an action, anything lost, damage, done, or hurt received). **—recompense,** *n.*

rec·ti·tude (rek′tə tud), *n.* **1.** upright conduct or character; honesty; righteousness. **2.** direction in a straight line; straightness.

re·it·e·rate (rē it′ərāt′), *v.* say or do several times; repeat (an action or demand) again and again.

re·lin·quish (ri ling′kwish), *v.* **1.** give up; let go; release. **2.** abandon. **3.** renounce; resign.

re·mu·ne·ra·tive (ri myü′nə rā′tiv), *adj.* that brings reward; paying; profitable.

ren·e·gade (ren′ə gād), *n.* deserter from a religious faith, a political party; traitor.

rep·li·ca (rep′lə kə), *n.* a copy or close reproduction.

ret·ri·bu·tion (ret′rə byü′shən), *n.* a deserved punishment; return for evil done.

ret·ro·spect (ret′rə spekt), *n.* **1.** survey of past time or events; thinking about the past. **2.** in retrospect, when looking back.

rev·er·ie (rev′ər ē), *n.* **1.** dreamy thoughts; dreamy thinking of pleasant things. **2.** condition of being lost in dreamy thoughts.

re·vert (re vėrt′), *v.* **1.** go back; return. **2.** go back to a former possessor or to his heirs.

rhet·or·ic (ret′ər ik), *n.* **1.** art of using words effectively in speaking or writing. **2.** mere display in language.

ru·di·men·tar·y (rü′də men′tər ē), *adj.* **1.** to be learned or studied first; elementary. **2.** in an early stage of development; undeveloped.

ru·mi·nate (rü′mə nāt), *v.* think or ponder; meditate; reflect.

sac·ri·lege (sak′rə lij), *n.* an intentional injury to anything sacred; disrespectful treatment of anyone or anything sacred.

sa·ga·cious (sə gā′shəs), *adj.* **1.** wise in a keen, practical way; shrewd. **2.** intelligent.

sar·don·ic (sär don′ik), *adj.* bitterly sarcastic, scornful, or mocking.

score (skôr), *v.* cut, scratch, mark, line. **—scored,** *adj.*

sec·u·lar (sek′yə lər), *adj., n.* **—adj. 1.** not religious or sacred; worldly. **2.** living in the world; not belonging to a religious order. **3.** occurring once in an age or century. **—n.** layman.

se·date (si dāt′), *adj.* quiet; calm; serious.

se·ren·i·ty (sə ren′ə tē), *n.* **1.** peace and quiet; calmness. **2.** clearness; brightness.

sin·gu·lar (sing′gyə lər), *adj.* **1.** extraordinary; unusual. **2.** strange; odd; peculiar. **3.** being the only one of its kind.

spec·tral (speak′trəl), *adj.* **1.** of or like a specter; ghostly. **2.** of or produced by a spectrum.

spo·rad·ic (spə rad′ik), *adj.* appearing or happening at intervals in time; occasional.

sto·i·cal (stō′ə kəl), *adj.* like a stoic; indifferent to pleasure and pain; self-controlled.

stric·ture (strik′chər), *n.* **1.** an unfavorable criticism; critical remark. **2.** binding restriction.

sub·lime (sə blīm′), *adj.* lofty or elevated in thought, feeling, language; noble; grand; exalted.

suc·cu·lent (suk′yə lənt), *adj.* full of juice; juicy.

sun·der (sun′dər), *v.* put asunder; separate; part; split.

sun·dry (sun′drē), *adj.* several, various.

su·per·cil·i·ous (sü′pər sil′ē əs), *adj.* haughty, proud, and contemptuous; disdainful; showing scorn or indifference because of a feeling of superiority.

su·per·flu·ous (sü pèr′flü əs), *adj.* **1.** more than is needed. **2.** needless; unnecessary.

sur·cease (sər sēs′), *n.* end; cessation.

sur·mise (sər mīz′), *n.* formation of an idea with little or no evidence; a guessing. —**surmise,** *v.*

syn·chro·nize (sing′krə nīz), *v.* **1.** make agree in time. **2.** occur at the same time. **3.** move or take place at the same rate and exactly together.

tan·gi·ble (tan′jə bəl), *adj.* **1.** that can be touched or felt by touch. **2.** real; actual; definite. —*n.* something tangible.

te·di·ous (tē′dē əs), *adj.* long and tiring; boring; wearisome.

tem·pest (tem′pist), *n.* **1.** a violent windstorm, usually accompanied by rain, hail, or snow. **2.** a violent disturbance.

te·nac·i·ty (ti nas′ə tē), *n.* **1.** firmness in holding fast. **2.** stubbornness; persistence. **3.** firmness in holding together; toughness. —**tenacious,** *adj.*

ten·ta·tive (ten′tə tiv), *adj.* **1.** done as a trial or experiment; experimental. **2.** hesitating.

ten·ure (ten′yər), *n.* **1.** a holding or possessing. **2.** length of time of holding or possessing. **3.** conditions or terms on which anything is held or occupied.

ter·res·tri·al (tə res′trē əl), *adj.* **1.** of the earth; not of the heavens. **2.** of land, not water. **3.** living on the ground, not in the air or water or in trees. **4.** growing on land.

tor·por (tôr′pər), *n.* torpid condition or quality; apathy; lethargy.

tran·sient (tran′shənt), *adj.* **1.** passing soon; fleeting; not lasting. **2.** passing through and not staying long. —**transient,** *n.*

trans·lu·cent (tran slü′snt), *adj.* letting light through without being transparent. —**translucence,** *n.*

trans·mu·ta·tion (tran′smyə tā′shən), *n.* a change from one nature, substance, or form into another.

trem·u·lous (trem′yə ləs), *adj.* **1.** quivering. **2.** timid; fearful. **3.** that wavers; shaky.

trep·i·da·tion (trep′ə dā′shən), *n.* **1.** nervous dread; fear; fright. **2.** a trembling.

trib·u·la·tion (trib′yə lā′shən), *n.* great trouble; severe trial; affliction.

un·prec·e·dent·ed (un pres′ə den′tid), *adj.* never done before; never known before.

un·scru·pu·lous (un skrü′pyə ləs), *adj.* not careful about right or wrong; without principles or conscience.

u·surp (yü zėrp′), *v.* seize and hold (power, position, authority) by force or without right. —**usurpation,** *n.*

va·gar·y (və gėr′ē), *n.* **1.** an odd fancy; extravagant notion. **2.** odd action; freak.

ve·he·ment (vē′ə mənt), *adj.* **1.** having or showing strong feeling; caused by strong feeling; eager; passionate. **2.** forceful; violent.

ver·dure (vėr′jər), *n.* **1.** fresh greenness. **2.** a fresh growth of green grass, plants, or leaves.

vi·gnette (vi nyet′), *n.* a literary sketch; short verbal description.

vi·ra·go (və rā′gō), *n.* a violent, bad-tempered, or scolding woman.

vir·u·lent (vir′yə lənt), *adj.* **1.** very poisonous or harmful; deadly. **2.** (of disease) characterized by a rapid and severe malignant or infectious condition. **3.** intensely bitter or spiteful; violently hostile.

vis·age (viz′ij), *n.* **1.** face. **2.** appearance or aspect.

vi·vac·i·ty (vī vas′ə tē), *n.* liveliness; sprightliness; animation; gaiety.

vo·rac·i·ty (və ras′ə tē), *n.* a being greedy in eating; a being very eager.

vul·ner·a·ble (vul′nər ə bəl), *adj.* **1.** that can be wounded or injured; open to attack. **2.** sensitive to criticism, temptations, influences.

wan·ton (won′tən), *adj.* frolicsome; playful. —**wantonly,** *adv.*

ze·nith (zē′nith), *n.* **1.** the point in the heavens directly overhead; point opposite nadir. **2.** the highest point; apex.

Index by Types of Literature

Index of Vocabulary Skills

Index of Authors and Titles

Acknowledgments *continued from page iv.*

Mifflin Company. Copyright 1955 by Houghton Mifflin Company. Reprinted by permission. Also for the poem "Courage" from *The Awful Rowing toward God* by Anne Sexton published by Houghton Mifflin Company. Copyright © 1975 by Loring Conant, Jr. Reprinted by permission.

Little, Brown and Company for "After great pain, a formal feeling comes-" from *The Complete Poems of Emily Dickinson* edited by Thomas H. Johnson. Copyright 1929 by Martha Dickinson Bianchi; renewed 1957 by Mary L. Hampson. By permission of Little, Brown and Company. Also for the poem "Southbound on the Freeway" from *New & Selected Things Taking Place* by May Swenson. Copyright © 1963 by May Swenson. By permission of Little, Brown and Company in association with the Atlantic Monthly Press.

Liveright Publishing Corporation for the poem "Astronauts," which is reprinted from *American Journal* by Robert Hayden, by permission of Liveright Publishing Corporation: Copyright © 1980 by Irma Hayden. Copyright © 1978 by Robert Hayden. Also for "Frederick Douglass," which is reprinted from *Angle of Ascent,* New and Selected Poems, by Robert Hayden, with the permission of Liveright Publishing Corporation. Copyright © 1975, 1972, 1970, 1966 by Robert Hayden. Also for the poem "Song of the Son," which is reprinted from *Cane* by Jean Toomer, by permission of Liveright Publishing Corporation. Copyright 1923 by Boni & Liveright. Copyright renewed 1951 by Jean Toomer.

Macmillan Publishing Company for "Silence" by Marianne Moore. Reprinted with permission of Macmillan Publishing Company from *Collected Poems* by Marianne Moore. Copyright 1935 by Marianne Moore, renewed 1963 by Marianne Moore and T. S. Eliot. Also for "What Are Years?" by Marianne Moore. Reprinted with permission of Macmillan Publishing Company from *Collected Poems* by Marianne Moore. Copyright 1941 by Marianne Moore, renewed 1969 by Marianne Moore.

New Directions Publishing Corporation for "Song" by Hilda Doolittle, from *Collected Poems* of H. D. Copyright ©1925, 1953 by Norman Holmes Pearson. Reprinted by permission of New Directions. Also for "Spring and All" from *Collected Earlier Poems* of William Carlos Williams. Copyright 1938 by New Directions Publishing Corporation. Reprinted by permission of New Directions.

W. W. Norton & Company, Inc., for "Involved," which is reprinted from *The Selected Poems,* 1951–1977, by A. R. Ammons, with the permission of W. W. Norton & Company, Inc. Copyright © 1977, 1975, 1974, 1972, 1971, 1970, 1966, 1965, 1964, 1955 by A. R. Ammons. Also for "Ghost of a Chance," which is reprinted from *Snapshots of a Daughter-in-Law,* Poems, 1954–1962, by Adrienne Rich, by permission of W. W. Norton & Company, Inc. Copyright © 1956, 1957, 1958, 1959, 1960, 1961, 1962, 1963, 1967 by Adrienne Rich Conrad.

Harold Ober Associates, Incorporated, for the poem "A Black Man Talks of Reaping" from *Personals* by Arna Bontemps. Copyright © 1963 by Arna Bontemps. Also for the poem "Lenox Avenue Mural" from *Montage of a Dream Deferred* by Langston Hughes. Copyright © 1951 by Langston Hughes. Both reprinted by permission of Harold Ober Associates.

Oxford University Press, New York, for "The Horse Chestnut Tree" from *Collected Poems 1930–1976* by Richard Eberhart. Copyright © 1960, 1976 by Richard Eberhart. Reprinted by permission of Oxford University Press, Inc. Also for "This Is an Amer-ican" by Hector St. John de Crevecoeur from *The Oxford Anthology of American Literature,* edited by William Rose Benét and Norman Pearson.

Princeton University Press for "Huswifery" and "Meditation Six," in *The Poetical Works of Edward Taylor,* ed. with an Introduction and Notes by Thomas H. Johnson. Copyright 1939 by Rockland, 1943 by Princeton University Press. Reprinted by permission of Princeton University Press.

G. P. Putnam's Sons for "The Notebook" by Norman Mailer. Reprinted by permission of G. P. Putnam's Sons from *Advertisements for Myself* by Norman Mailer. Copyright © 1959 by Norman Mailer.

Random House, Inc., for the excerpt from *I Know Why the Caged Bird Sings,* by Maya Angelou. Copyright © 1969 by Maya Angelou. Reprinted by permission of Random House, Inc. Also for "The Bear" by William Faulkner. Copyright 1942 and renewed 1970 by Estelle Faulkner and Jill Faulkner Summers. Reprinted by permission of Random House, Inc. An expanded version of this story appears in *Go Down Moses* by William Faulkner. Also for "Man and Daughter in the Cold" by John Updike. Copyright © 1968 by John Updike. Reprinted from *Museums and Women and Other Stories,* by John Updike, by permission of Alfred A. Knopf, Inc. Also for the poem "Alone/December/Night" by Victor Hernandez Cruz. Copyright © 1969 by Victor Hernandez Cruz. Reprinted from *Snaps,* by Victor Hernandez Cruz, by permission of Random House, Inc. Also for "Mushrooms" by Sylvia Plath. Copyright © 1960 by Sylvia Plath. Reprinted from *The Colossus and Other Poems,* by Sylvia Plath, by permission of Alfred A. Knopf, Inc. Also for "Dead Boy" by John Crowe Ransom. Copyright 1927 by Alfred A. Knopf, Inc., and renewed 1955 by John Crowe Ransom. Reprinted from *Selected Poems, A Revised and Enlarged Edition,* by John Crowe Ransom, by permission of Alfred A. Knopf, Inc. Also for "Manhole Covers" by Karl Shapiro. Copyright © 1962 by Karl Shapiro. Reprinted from *Collected Poems 1940–1978,* by Karl Shapiro, by permission of Random House, Inc. Also for "Thirteen Ways of Looking at a Blackbird" by Wallace Stevens. Copyright 1923, 1951 by Wallace Stevens. Reprinted from *The Collected Poems of Wallace Stevens,* by Wallace Stevens, by permission of Alfred A. Knopf, Inc. Also for "Gold Glade" by Robert Penn Warren. Copyright © 1957 by Robert Penn Warren. Reprinted from *Promises: Poems 1954–1956,* by Robert Penn Warren, by permission of Random House, Inc. Also for the excerpts from "The History of Plymouth Plantation" by William Bradford and for "The Mayflower Compact" by William Bradford, both in *Of Plymouth Plantation,* edited by Samuel Eliot Morison. Published 1952 by Alfred A. Knopf, Inc. Also for "The Bride Comes to Yellow Sky" by Stephen Crane, from *The Collected Works of Stephen Crane,* published by Alfred A. Knopf, Inc. Also for "Of Individualism in Democratic Countries" from *Democracy in America,* Volumes I and II, by Alexis de Tocqueville, translated by Henry Reeve. Copyright, 1945 by Alfred A. Knopf, Inc.

Charles Scribner's Sons for "Winter Dreams" by F. Scott Fitzgerald from *All the Sad Young Men,* which is reprinted by permission of Charles Scribner's Sons. Copyright 1922 Frances Scott Fitzgerald Lanahan; renewal copyright 1950. Also for "Big, Two-Hearted River: Part II" by Ernest Hemingway from *In Our Time,* which is reprinted by permission of Charles Scribner's Sons. Copyright 1925 Charles Scribner's Sons; renewal copyright 1953 Ernest Hemingway. Also for the excerpt from *Of Time and the River* by Thomas Wolfe. Copyright 1935 Charles Scribner's Sons; renewal copyright © 1963 Paul Gitlin, Administrator CTA. Used by permission of Charles Scribner's Sons. Also for the Poem "Richard Cory" from *The Children of Night* by Edwin Arlington Robinson (1897). Reprinted by permission of Charles Scribner's Sons.

Mrs. James Thurber for "The Secret Life of Walter Mitty" by James Thurber. Copr. © 1942 James Thurber. Copr. © 1970 Helen Thurber. From *My World and Welcome To It*, published by Harcourt Brace Jovanovich. Originally printed in *The New Yorker*. Used by permission of Mrs. James Thurber.

The University of Chicago Press for the poem "Summer Remembered" by Isabella Gardner. Reprinted from *The Looking Glass* by Isabella Gardner by permission of The University of Chicago Press. © 1961 by The University of Chicago.

Viking Penguin Inc. for "A Father-to-Be" from *Mosby's Memoirs and Other Stories* by Saul Bellow. Copyright © 1955, 1968 by Saul Bellow. Reprinted by permission of Viking Penguin Inc. This story appeared originally in *The New Yorker*. Also for "The Chrysanthemums" from *The Long Valley* by John Steinbeck. Copyright 1937 by John Steinbeck. Copyright renewed © 1965 by John Steinbeck. Reprinted by permission of Viking Penguin Inc.

Edward J. Acton, Inc., for "The Creative Dilemma" from *Creative America* by James Baldwin. Appeared originally in *Saturday Review*, February 8, 1964, under subtitle "The war of an artist." Reprinted by arrangement with the author's agent, Edward J. Acton, Inc.

Margaret Walker Alexander for the poem "Iowa Farmer" by Margaret Walker from her book *For My People*. Copyright 1942 by Yale University Press. Reprinted by permission of the author.

The American Scholar for the poem "Garden of My Childhood" by Kuangchi C. Chang. Reprinted from *The American Scholar*, Volume 26, Number 3, Summer, 1957. Copyright © 1957 by the United Chapters of Phi Beta Kappa. By permission of the publishers.

José Armas for his story "A Delicate Balance" as included in *Nuestro*, May 1978. Reprinted by permission of the author.

Raymond Barrio for the excerpt from pages 53–62 of his book *The Plum Plum Pickers*. © Copyright 1969 by Raymond Barrio. Reprinted by permission of the author.

Chatto and Windus Ltd, London, for "The Horse Chestnut Tree" from *Collected Poems* by Richard Eberhart. Reprinted by permission of the British publishers.

Joan Daves for "I Have a Dream" by Martin Luther King, Jr., from *The New York Times*, August 29, 1963. Copyright © 1963 by Martin Luther King, Jr. Reprinted by permission of Joan Daves.

Dodd, Mead & Company, Inc., for "Sympathy" by Paul Laurence Dunbar. Reprinted by permission of Dodd, Mead & Company, Inc. from *The Complete Poems of Paul Laurence Dunbar*.

Norma Millay Ellis for "Pity me not because the light of day" by Edna St. Vincent Millay. From *Collected Poems*, Harper & Row. Copyright 1923, 1951 by Edna St. Vincent Millay and Norma Millay Ellis. Reprinted by permission.

Mari Evans for her poem "I Am a Black Woman." From *I Am A Black Woman* by Mari Evans, published by Wm. Morrow & Company, 1970, by permission of the author.

Harvard University Press for "Letter to Her Husband" by Abigail Adams (May 7, 1776), slightly adapted from *The Book of Abigail and John—Selected Letters of the Adams Family 1762–1784*, edited and with an introduction by S. H. Butterfield, Marc Friedlaender, and Mary-Jo Kline. Copyright 1975 by the Massachusetts Historical Society. Used by permission of Harvard University Press. Also for the poems "After great pain," "Because I could not stop for Death," "The Soul selects her own Society," and "Success is counted sweetest" by Emily Dickinson. Reprinted by permission of the publishers and the Trustees of Amherst College from *The Poems of Emily Dickinson*, edited by Thomas H. Johnson, Cambridge, Massachusetts: The Belknap Press of Harvard University Press, Copyright © 1951, 1955, 1979, 1983, by the President and Fellows of Har-

vard College.

Hawaii Review for the poem "Lost Sister" by Cathy Song. Reprinted by permission of *Hawaii Review*, University of Hawaii at Manoa.

Roberta Hill for her poem "Dream of Rebirth," from *American Poetry Review*, Vol. 2, No. 6. Reprinted by permission of the author.

Olwyn Hughes, England, for the poem "Mushrooms" by Sylvia Plath from her book *The Colossus*, published by Faber and Faber, London. Copyright Ted Hughes 1967. Reprinted by permission.

Alexander R. James, Ireland, for "Four Meetings" from *The Complete Tales of Henry James 1876–1882*, published by J. B. Lippincott, 1962. Reprinted by permission.

Louisiana State University Press for the excerpt from *The Storm and Other Stories* by Kate Chopin, from *The Complete Works of Kate Chopin*, edited by Per Seyerstad, 1969. Also for the poem "Dreaming America" by Joyce Carol Oates. Reprinted by permission of Louisiana State University Press from *The Fabulous Beasts* by Joyce Carol Oates, copyright © 1975.

Mohawk Nation for the abridged excerpt from *The Great Law of Peace of the Longhouse People*, Iroquois Confederacy. Published by Akwesasne Notes, the Mohawk Nation at Akwesasne, N.Y. Used by permission.

N. Scott Momaday for the excerpt from his article "A Vision Beyond Time and Place," from *Life* Magazine, July 2, 1971. © 1971 Time Inc. Used by permission of the author.

William Morris Agency, Inc., for "Did You Ever Dream Lucky?" by Ralph Ellison. Copyright © 1954 Ralph Ellison. Reprinted by permission of William Morris Agency, Inc., on behalf of the Author.

William Morrow & Company, Inc., for "On Being a Granddaughter" from *Blackberry Winter* by Margaret Mead. Copyright © 1972 by Margaret Mead. By permission of William Morrow & Company. Also for "Preface to a Twenty Volume Suicide Note (For Kellie Jones, born May 1959)" from *Selected Poetry of Amiri Baraka/LeRoi Jones* (1979). Copyright © 1961 by LeRoi Jones. By permission of William Morrow & Company.

Tillie Olsen for "I Stand Here Ironing" from her book *Tell Me a Riddle*. Copyright © 1961 by Tillie Olsen. A Delacorte Press/Seymour Lawrence Book. Used by permission of the author.

Russell & Volkening, Inc., for "Breach of Promise" by Jessamyn West. Appeared originally in *Harper's* Magazine, 1953. Copyright © 1953 by Harper & Brothers. Reprinted by permission of Russell & Volkening, as agents for the author.

Ricardo Sanchez for his poem "i yearn." Copyright © 1975 by Ricardo Sanchez. Reprinted by permission of the author.

Leslie M. Silko for her poem "Where Mountain Lion Lay Down With Deer" from *Voices of the Rainbow*, edited by Kenneth Rosen. Reprinted by permission of Leslie M. Silko.

Twayne Publishers for "America" by Claude McKay from *Selected Poems of Claude McKay*. Copyright 1953 by Twayne Publishers, Inc. Reprinted with the permission of Twayne Publishers, A Division of G. K. Hall & Co., Boston.

Louis B. Wright and Marion Tinling for the excerpt from *History of the Dividing Line Run* in *The London Diary 1717–1721 and Other Writings* by William Byrd, edited by Louis B. Wright and Marion Tinling. Used by permission of the editors.

Footnote respellings and definitions are from *Scott, Foresman Advanced Dictionary* by E. L. Thorndike and Clarence L. Barnhart. Copyright © 1979 by Scott, Foresman and Company. Reprinted by permission of the publishers.

Credits

Design and Photograph Research

DESIGN OFFICE / San Francisco

Cover

JOHN MARTUCCI STUDIO / Boston

Illustration

DICK COLE / A Father-To-Be
KINUKO CRAFT / A Church Mouse
DAVID GROVE / Our Town
KEN HAMILTON / The Prison
HEATHER PRESTON / Bartleby the Scrivener; Did You Ever Dream Lucky?

Photographs, Paintings, Prints, Drawings, Sculpture

Page
2   "Untitled" Saul Steinberg/Kortebein Collection
3   "Colonial Cubism," Stuart Davis/Walker Art Center, gift of the T.B. Walker Foundation
4   TOP LEFT "Map," Jasper Johns/Leo Castelli, collection of The Museum of Modern Art, New York, gift of Mr. and Mrs. Robert Scull
4   TOP RIGHT Owen Franken/Stock, Boston
4   BOTTOM "Washington Crossing the Delaware," Emanuel Gottlieb Leutze/Metropolitan Museum of Art, gift of John Stewart Kennedy, 1897
5   TOP "Trout Fishing, Lake St. John," Winslow Homer/Museum of Fine Arts, Boston, William Wilkus Warren Fund
5   BOTTOM © Burk Uzzle/Magnum
6 - 7 © Charles Steinhacker/Black Star
7   TOP LEFT © Paul Dix
7   TOP RIGHT © Roger Malloch/Magnum
9   "Indian Ovens, New Mexico 1923," Laura Gilpin/Laura Gilpin Collection, Amon Carter Museum, Fort Worth, Texas
12 Detail of a woodcut in Bernhard von Breydenbach, *Peregrinationes In Terram Sanctam*, Mainz, 1486
17 © Morton Beebe/Image Bank
20 TOP LEFT © David Cavagnaro
20 CENTER LEFT © Tom Tracy
20 BOTTOM LEFT © David Cavagnaro
20 TOP RIGHT © Morton Beebe/Image Bank
22 © Eric Simmons/Stock, Boston
27 "Moon and Wall Encrustations," Minor White/Minor White Archive © The Trustees of Princeton University
33 "Under the El," Bernice Abbott/Lunn Gallery
36 "Highway, 1977," James Rosenquist/Leo Castelli
38 "Coiffure," Manuel Alvarez Bravo, 1937-1939, 7⁷⁄₁₆ x 9³⁄₈"/ Museum of Modern Art, gift of Edgar J. Kaufman, Jr.
39 © Jeffrey Fox/Woodfin Camp
41 "The Letterack," Peto/Metropolitan Museum of Art
43 "Colonial Cubism," Stuart Davis/Walker Art Center, gift of the T. B. Walker Foundation
44 "Untitled," Saul Steinberg/Kortebein Collection
47 "Chambered Nautilus," Edward Weston/International Museum of Photography at George Eastman House
49 © Bruce J. Kortebein

451 © John Bryson
453 George Silk © Time Inc.
457 © Burton McNeely/Image Bank
465 "Chrysanthemums," William Merritt Chase/National Gallery of Art,
Washington, D.C., gift of Chester Dale
469 © Dan Guravich
476 "James," Olivia Parker
477 "Eliza," Olivia Parker
480 © R. Walker/Bruce Coleman
483 "Soldier, Sailor and Policeman," Charles Demuth/Hirshhorn Museum and
Sculpture Garden, Smithsonian Institution/Scala/EPA
489 "Flesh Striped Tie," Jim Dine/Hirshhorn Museum and Sculpture Garden,
Smithsonian Institution, photo Lee Stalsworth
490 "The Jacket," Bernard Perlin, 1951, casein tempera on cardboard/
Whitney Museum of American Art, photo by Roy Elkind
497 "Woman's Work," John Sloan/Cleveland Museum of Art, gift of Amelia Elizabeth White
499 "Arundel Castle," Frank Stella/Hirshhorn Museum and Sculpture Garden,
Smithsonian Institution
503 © Nicholas Foster/Image Bank
505 © Tom Stack
507 © David W. Hamilton/Image Bank
508 "The Beach," William Baziotes, 1955, oil on canvas, 36 x 48"/
Whitney Museum of American Art, purchase
510 "Orion," Victor Vasarely/Hirshhorn Museum and Sculpture Garden,
Smithsonian Institution
512 **"Broken Window," Brett Weston, 1937, 7½ x 9⅝"/ Museum of Modern Art,
New York, gift of Albert M. Bender**
517 "Still Music" *(detail),* Ben Shahn/Phillips Collection
520 "Mist," Adolph Gottleib/Solomon R. Guggenheim Museum
523 TOP © Paul Fusco/Magnum
523 BOTTOM Roy King
528 Ibid
529 "West Chester Court House," Horace Pippin/Pennsylvania Academy of the Fine Arts,
Bequest of David J. Grossman in honor of Mr. and Mrs. Charles S. Grossman
and Mr. and Mrs. Meyer Speiser
578 "Chief," Franz Kline, oil on canvas, 58⅜" x 6'½"/Museum of Modern Art, New York,
gift of Mr. and Mrs. David M. Solinger
579 © Erich Hartmann/Magnum
606 "Spray-Painted Robe," Jim Dine, 1977, hand colored etching and lithograph,
41½ x 29⁷/₁₆"/Museum of Modern Art, New York, gift of the artist
615 **"The Letter," Mary Cassatt, 1891, etching and aquatint/The Metropolitan Museum of
Art, gift of Paul J. Sachs, 1916**
624 "Circumnavigation of the Blood," Fredrich Sommer/Light Gallery, New York
630 © Peter Southwick/Stock, Boston
639 "Frosted Window No. II," Paul Caponigro/Center for Creative Photography
646 "Blue Interior Morning," Romare Bearden/from the collection of
The Chase Manhattan Bank
663 © David Cavagnaro
665 © Charles Harbutt/Magnum
666 © John Brook
669 "Qui Riposano," George Krause/Phototopia Gallery, Philadelphia, Pennsylvania
671 "Lucifer," Jackson Pollock/Mr. and Mrs. Harry W. Anderson Collection
673 Teledyne Geotronics
677 "Shining Back," Sam Francis, 1958/Solomon R. Guggenheim Museum
679 "Chicago 25," Aaron Siskind/Light Gallery, New York
680 © Jeffrey Fox/Woodfin Camp
683 © Ernst Haas
685 © Jill Freedman/Magnum
687 "Falling Man Series: Four Figures on an Orange Square," Ernest Trova, 1965, serigraph,
printed in color, 25¹/₁₆" x 25¹/₁₆"/Museum of Modern Art, New York, John B. Turner Fund
688 "Empress," Olivia Parker
691 "Iberia No. 2," Robert Motherwell/courtesy of the artist

695 "10 Foot Flowers," Andy Warhol/Sotheby Parke-Bernet/EPA
699 "Guardian," Morris Graves/Krannert Art Museum, University of Illinois
701 "Toadstool and Grasses," Paul Strand/© 1971 by the Estate of Paul Strand
703 © Nicholas Devore III/Bruce Coleman
704 "White World," Mark Toby/Hirshhorn Museum and Sculpture Garden,
Smithsonian Institution
706 © Henri Cartier-Bresson/Magnum
709 © Dewitt Jones/Woodfin Camp
710 "Two Maps II," Jasper Johns, 1966, lithograph printed in black, 25$^9/_{16}$ x 25$^1/_{16}$"/
Museum of Modern Art, New York, gift of the Celeste and Armand Bartos Foundation
712 "Light Coming On the Plains II," Georgia O'Keeffe/Amon Carter Museum, Forth Worth

ABCDEFGHIJ0898765
Printed in the United States of America